VIII

Essays Religious and Mixed

MATTHEW ARNOLD

ESSAYS RELIGIOUS AND MIXED

Edited by R. H. Super

ANN ARBOR   THE UNIVERSITY OF MICHIGAN PRESS

Editor's Preface

As the title is intended to suggest, the present volume is made up principally of two of Arnold's books, *Last Essays on Church and Religion* (1877) and *Mixed Essays* (1879), both of them collections of separate essays previously published in the magazines and reviews. To these have been added the Preface to his edition of six of Johnson's *Lives of the Poets*, his anonymous review of *German Letters on English Education* (discovered by Professor Fraser Neiman and published in his *Essays, Letters, and Reviews by Matthew Arnold*), the anonymous review of Charles P. O'Conor's *Songs of a Life*, entitled "A Deptford Poet" (discovered by Dean Roger L. Brooks), and the very brief prefatory note on Edoardo Fusco from *Macmillan's Magazine*. The last two have not previously been reprinted. One anonymous review, *The Autobiography of Mrs. Fletcher*, printed as Arnold's by Professor Neiman, was not his and is not reprinted here. The Appendixes give what reports are available of three of Arnold's after-dinner speeches of 1873–77 and a sampling of his notes to the school text edition of Johnson's *Lives*. It can safely be said that no other volume in this edition will show within a single pair of covers so wide a range of Arnold's interests, illustrated by such first-rate essays as "A French Critic on Milton" and "A French Critic on Goethe," "Equality," "The Church of England," and that comprehensive summary of his theology, "A Psychological Parallel."

This volume follows the pattern of its predecessors. The Critical and Explanatory Notes aim at showing the circumstances under which the essays were conceived and written, at explaining what a twentieth-century reader of them might need explanation of, and at indicating the sources of Arnold's quotations and allusions. An occasional stroke of good luck has enabled the editor to turn up some sources he might hardly have expected to find; on the other hand he has failed to identify some allusions the reader has every right to expect him to be helpful with. It is perhaps better to keep the successive volumes of the edition coming out than to aim at an illusory perfection in infinite time.

The Textual Notes, as usual in the present edition, indicate the variants between the latest texts published in Arnold's lifetime (which form the basis of the present text) and the earlier forms of the essays. Changes in punctuation and insignificant alterations in conventions of spelling have usually not been indicated, but every change in paragraphing and every shift from a semicolon to a full stop or the reverse is recorded. For a man who quoted so frequently and from such a wide range of sources, Arnold is remarkably accurate; nevertheless there are errors, and the larger of them are indicated in the Critical and Explanatory Notes, the more minute are remedied in the text and indicated in the Textual Notes; these last are mainly of the sort that escape a proof-reader's eye because they have a superficial plausibility, but still mar the sense of the passage. Arnold's revisions of his work in this volume occasionally correct factual errors that must have been called to his attention, but for the most part are stylistic. The meticulousness with which he went over some of the *Last Essays* suggests both the difficulty he found in expressing himself gracefully and accurately upon his subject and the importance he attached to those essays.

For valuable spade-work in annotating individual essays I am indebted to my former students Mrs. Dorothy Klein Barber, David C. Cylkowski, Ralph S. Eberly, James P. Lucier, Mrs. Dona Barcy Lurie, Robert E. Rhodes, Richard E. Ruland, Jerold J. Savory, and Mrs. Jean Coffman Waldman. I am also most grateful for the various assistance of Mr. Frank Durham, editor of the *Kentish Mercury*, Professors J. D. Jump, R. H. Robbins, J. M. Robson, W. H. Stone, and my colleague J. P. Kent. The volume, and others to follow, were largely prepared during a year of study provided by the generous support of the John Simon Guggenheim Memorial Foundation and the Horace H. Rackham Fund of the University of Michigan.

Contents

A Deptford Poet*

The right function of poetry is to animate, to console, to rejoice
—in one word, to *strengthen*. This function modern poetry
seldom fulfils. It has thought, fancy, ingenuity; it often makes
us admire its author's powers, sometimes interests us, sometimes
instructs us, occasionally puzzles us; but it in general leaves our   5
poor humanity as rueful and broken-backed, to say the very
least, as it found it. Mr. O'Conor's poetry has many deficiencies;
he is, we believe, an Irish working man settled at Deptford.
Many a pupil-teacher might correct his grammar for him,
might perhaps even correct his spelling. But his volume—which   10
we opened, we confess, with the sense of dejected weariness
with which after long experience one opens new volumes of
verse—his volume has gaiety, tune, pathos; it invigorates. We
will try to give a specimen or two which may make the readers
of the *Pall Mall Gazette* share our feelings.   15
    We are told that Mr. O'Conor's songs are sung by Irish work-
men, and we are not surprised at it. He is best when his themes
are Irish, drawn from his native country and his intimate experience. He is weakest when he is most general. Yet even in his
treatment of general and hackneyed topics there frequently   20
breaks out a spirit and a vigorous freshness. Song has often been
addressed as *The Poet's Love;* but this title to a poem does not
lead us to expect a strain so enlivening as what follows:—

> 'Tis often and often I wonder
> Why Song came my poor lot to share.   25
> 'Tis said, ere her harp she here carried

* "Songs of a Life," &c. By Charles P. O'Conor. (Printed at the *Kentish Mercury* office, Blackheath-road, Greenwich. 1875.)

I

She could have been much better married.
Ah! I and my attic are bare.

Save a Christ and a small bust of Dante,
A Sèvres vase full of dead flowers,
5   A couch with a many-patch'd quilt on,
A Bible, a Shakspeare, a Milton—
With these I pass many sweet hours.

And then there's the lord of the attic;
Ne'er mind what the exquisite say!
10   The time was, a stranger was sadness—
The time was, the morn brought him gladness—
The time was, his heart was more gay!

The "Sèvres vase" would probably make but a poor figure at
the sale of Mr. Gladstone's collection, yet it has a worth of its
15   own notwithstanding.

Ireland, however, "Ireland of the streams," is the inspirer of
what is best in Mr. O'Conor's volume. Ireland, Australia, America—the cabin at home and the emigrant's encampment across
the sea—what a world of passion and sentiment for Irish hearts
20   is in those words and images? Mr. O'Conor gives a voice finely
to it in his Backwoods Song:—

We camp beneath the tall pines,
We're trappers true and tried;
From early dawn till shadows fall,
25   O'er hills and dales we ride.
At evening in the clearing
Dear Ireland's hills we see,
Where freedom fell through striking well
For God and Country.

30   The shades of night are falling.
Light or shade fail to bind
The broken-hearted exile
From the land he left behind.
But a truce to grief! Let's pledge
35   *Every home and altar free!*

And be our boast, our backwoods toast:
For God and Country!

For God and Country!
For God and Country!
Boys, be our toast and proudest boast,   5
For God and Country!

Sometimes the emigrant's strain is milder and more pensive:—

Here, while the waves around us play,
On memory's wings we'll hie away
To her encircled in the fold   10
Of ocean—home of hearts still bold!

      *   *   *   *   *

Yon upland heights, now saffron-hued,
Have seen my youthful idol wooed.
That elm-tree huge, which time made less,
Has heard the fondly whisper'd *yes*.   15
Glint still the shadows where, at rest,
Cairn Mor shows golden-topp'd his crest?
Is Galtee Dhu as bleak and bare,
Old time, as when we wander'd there?

'Tis morning. O'er sweet Funcheon, hark,   20
On freshen'd pinion soars the lark!
By Leabeac Callagh, weird and lone,
The mavis too with merry tone
Flies sunward till in heaven's blue
Mavis and lark are lost to view.   25
I stand by Glentworth's abbey hoar
And long for wings like them to soar.

Humour is mixed with tenderness in these recollections of home
and kindred. The *Vanithee*, or good old housewife, of his native
Ireland evokes from the unforgetting exile the following pleas-   30
ant strain in her honour:—

Let some go praise our maidens fair—
To me a jewel rich and rare,

A gem, a priceless gem to me,
Is Ireland's pride, the Vanithee.

When winter nights were cold and long,
Who cheer'd our hearts with jest and song
Till laughter shook the old roof tree?
Oh, who but Ireland's Vanithee!

Who oft on feast of Hallowe'en
Made glad the heart of each colleen,
And burn'd the nuts? *He'll cross the sea,*
And *She'll get wed*, said Vanithee.

'Twas sad from Erin's hills to part;
But oh, what mostly broke my heart
And made it grieve to exiled be
Was parting with the Vanithee.

She's dear to me, and, by the day!
You may believe the words I say:—
Were I a king, a queen should be
My dear old, brave old Vanithee.

Come, fill we to the brim each cup,
And froth it up, boys, froth it up!
Here's Ireland, o'er the deep blue sea!
Here's Ireland's pride, the Vanithee!

So sings the emigrant with his eyes cast back towards his home;
and the old people at home, in their turn, look sadly over
towards America and Australia, which have taken from them
so much that they love:—

Mavrone! there's nought of joy for me,
With care I'm growing old.
To me 'tis winter since the day,
Bound for the North Americay,
My Johnny cross'd the big salt sea
To win both fame and gold.
Oh, he was plazing to the sight!
His arm was strong! his eye was bright!
Ullulu! ulla ullala!
My heart's broke since Johnny went away.

More cheerily and firmly, as befits his sex, speaks the emigrant's
father:—

> What though the memory brings us pain?
> John's letters I will read again.
> The boy is well! thank God for that! 5
> And "Mary has grown strong and fat
> Since coming to Australia;"
> And "Little Bob"—our John's first son—
> "Can ride a horse and fire a gun
> Here in this great Australia." 10
> But what gets over me, old dame,
> John's staying there I hold to blame—
> It must be an un-English clime,
> Else why do they in summer time
> Have winter in Australia? 15
>
> Give me the holly on the wall,
> The mistletoe hung in the hall,
> The snow four feet upon the moor,
> The welcome greeting at the door—
> A fig for all Australia! 20
> With pipe and ale at ingle-side,
> Give me our homes at Christmas-tide,
> England and not Australia!
> Give me the land our fathers trod,
> The land that's bless'd by freedom's God, 25
> The home no tyrant can enslave,
> The soil that's bred the true and brave,
> Whose sons have made Australia!

After all, truth and nature here get the better of our poet's
Hibernian animosities. The land "whose sons have made Aus- 30
tralia" is and can be no other than the whole United Kingdom,
the common birthplace of this one great nation. In some mournful lines at the end of his book Mr. O'Conor lets us see that the
course of his patriotism in the narrower sense, his exclusively
Irish patriotism, has by no means run smooth:— 35

> I sang the yearnings of the soul the soulless among,
> Who, when wassail made them frantic, made the night air ring
> With the thrilling songs and ballads 'twas my gift to sing.

Ah, they wore their fetters gaily, those centuried slaves,
Though vowing to their tyrant-lords woe and bloody graves,
When inspired by song and tabor they would shout *To arms!*
And make the night air hideous with their bootless alarms!

5   The vulgar Irish insurrectionist could hardly be better hit off.
But we prefer to dwell, not on the "bootless alarms" of Irish
nationalism, "inspired by song and tabor," but on that which in
the Irish race for ever charms and interests us. What treasures
of passion and tenderness are in this people; what natural music,
10 what lyrical force, what gaiety! Young, rich, fortunate, riding
in the park, dining at Maidenhead, finishing the day with three
balls, a human being has no great merit, one would think, in
being happy; and yet how many of us with these advantages
only succeed in boring and being bored, and in feeling "the
15 mortal coldness of the soul like death itself come down!" But
here is a poor Irishman with a soul for refinement and delight,
whose lot is to work with his hands down at Deptford, with
frail health, work uncertain, and a wife and children to maintain; yet he manages to feel and to illustrate the truth of
20 Schiller's excellent saying that "all art is dedicated to *joy!*" We
understand that Mr. O'Conor is candidate for a humble place as
school-board visitor in his neighbourhood. We wish him success, and perhaps the London School Board might act wisely in
occasionally setting at their Mrs. Markses a sympathetic poet
25 instead of a Cerberus. However, in affording places for its
writers of song, the world is not often happy, and we are not
sanguine about placing Mr. O'Conor; but the readers of the
Pall Mall Gazette will, we hope, not a few of them, give five
shillings for his book.

Edoardo Fusco

In this country there are some who still remember Edoardo Fusco, who between the years 1854 and 1859 taught Italian and modern Greek in London and at Eton. He inspired interest even on a first acquaintance; and the interest could not but grow, as one came to know him better, into singular confidence and esteem. He was born at Trani, in Apulia, in the year 1824. He took an ardent part in the revolutionary movement which in 1848 broke out in the kingdom of Naples; when it failed he took refuge at Corfu, and after passing four or five years at Corfu, Athens, and Constantinople, acquainting himself thoroughly with the state of Turkey, and making himself known by several publications, he came to London in 1854, when the Crimean war broke out, and remained in this country until the war of Italian Independence in 1859. Then he returned to Italy, and from the time that peace was established, laboured unceasingly in the cause of what he thought the great want for Italy—education. He became inspector-in-chief of the schools, both primary and secondary, in all the provinces of the old kingdom of Naples; he was charged with the delicate and difficult task of re-organizing the clerical schools when they were opened anew after having been closed by the Government; he edited the *Progresso Educativo*, and at the time of his death, in December, 1873, he had the chair of Anthropology and Pedagogy in the university of Naples. I saw much of him while I was visiting Italian schools for the Schools Inquiry Commission in 1865. He had a strong liking for England and English life, a strong sense of what was faulty in Italian life and habits. There was much in his work at Naples to harass and try him, much elsewhere to invite and tempt him away. But in that southern Italy, such a

7

fairy-land to the foreign idler, so full of harsh cares and toils to the serious patriot, was his post; and there he laboured, and died there.

The following lecture is the first of a short course given by him in English, at Queen's College, in London. The course is interesting by its subject. The human spirit finds animation and enlargement in having these *weltgeschichtliche Massen,* as Goethe calls them, presented to it—these broad masses of the world's main history. Fusco's treatment of his great subject is clear and instructive, although his point of view is, naturally, too Italian. An Italian is always apt to count literary and artistic achievement as all in all in a nation's life; to concentrate his thoughts upon this, which has been Italy's glory, and to forget what has been her curse—a relaxed moral fibre. To Dante's definition of civilization—*civilization is the development of the human faculties*—we may oppose Goethe's: *civilization is a higher conception of political and military relations, with skill to bear oneself in the world, and to strike in when necessary.* Neither definition quite satisfies; but Goethe's is at least as true as Dante's. Perhaps a man of the north would do well to keep before his mind Dante's, and an Italian Goethe's. Fusco, however, if in writing the history of European development he took too little note of Italy's deficiencies in the *virtus verusque labor* of practical life, was in his own practical life nobly free from those deficiencies, and indeed made it the work of that life to cure them in his nation.

Last Essays
on
Church and Religion

Qu'on fonde la foi profonde!

Bishop Butler and the Zeit-Geist[1]

In Scotland, I imagine, you have in your philosophical studies small experience of the reverent devotion formerly, at any rate, paid at Oxford to text-books in philosophy, such as the *Sermons* of Bishop Butler, or the *Ethics* of Aristotle. Your students in philosophy have always read pretty widely, and have not concentrated themselves, as we at Oxford used to concentrate ourselves, upon one or two great books. However, in your study of the Bible you got abundant experience of our attitude of mind towards our two philosophers. Your text-book was right; there were no mistakes *there*. If there was anything obscure, anything hard to be comprehended, it was your ignorance which was in fault, your failure of comprehension. Just such was our mode of dealing with Butler's *Sermons* and Aristotle's *Ethics*. Whatever was hard, whatever was obscure, the text-book was all right, and our understandings were to conform themselves to it. What agonies of puzzle has Butler's account of self-love, or Aristotle's of the intellectual virtues, caused to clever undergraduates and to clever tutors; and by what feats of astonishing explanation, astonishingly acquiesced in, were those agonies calmed! Yet the true solution of the difficulty was in some cases, undoubtedly, that our author, as he stood, was not right, not satisfactory. As to secular authors, at any rate, it is indisputable that their works are to be regarded as contributions to human knowledge, and not more. It is only experience which assures us that even the poetry and artistic form of certain epochs has not,

---

1 The two following discourses were delivered as lectures at the Edinburgh Philosophical Institution. They had the form, therefore, of an address to hearers, not readers; and they are printed in that form in which they were delivered.

in fact, been improved upon, and is, therefore, classical. But the
same experience assures us that in all matters of knowledge
properly so called,—above all, of such difficult knowledge as are
questions of mind and of moral philosophy,—any writer in past
5   times must be on many points capable of correction, much of
what he says must be capable of being put more truly, put
clearer. Yet we at Oxford used to read our Aristotle or our
Butler with the same absolute faith in the classicality of their
matter as in the classicality of Homer's form.

10   The time inevitably arrives, to people who think at all seriously, when, as their experience widens, they ask themselves
what they are really to conclude about the masters and the
works thus authoritatively imposed upon them in their youth.
Above all, of a man like Butler one is sure to ask oneself this,—
15   an Englishman, a Christian, a modern, whose circumstances and
point of view we can come pretty well to know and to understand, and whose works we can be sure of possessing just as he
published them and meant them to stand before us. And Butler
deserves that one should regard him very attentively, both on
20   his own account, and also because of the immense and confident
laudation bestowed upon his writings. Whether he completely
satisfies us or no, a man so profoundly convinced that "virtue,—
the law of virtue written on our hearts,—is the law we are born
under;" a man so staunch in his respectful allegiance to reason, a
25   man who says: "I express myself with caution, lest I should be
mistaken to vilify reason, which is indeed the only faculty we
have wherewith to judge concerning anything, even revelation
itself;" a man, finally, so deeply and evidently in earnest, filled
with so awful a sense of the reality of things and of the madness
30   of self-deception: "Things and actions are what they are, and
the consequences of them will be what they will be; why then
should we desire to be deceived?"—such a man, even if he was
somewhat despotically imposed upon our youth, may yet well
challenge the most grave consideration from our mature man-
35   hood. And even did we fail to give it willingly, the strong consenting eulogy upon his achievements would extort it from us.
It is asserted that his three Sermons on Human Nature are, in the
department of moral philosophy, "perhaps the three most valu-

able essays that were ever published." They are this, because they contain his famous doctrine of conscience,—a doctrine which, being in those sermons "explained according to the strict truth of our mental constitution, is irresistible." Butler is therefore said, in the words of another of his admirers, "by pursuing precisely the same mode of reasoning in the science of morals as his great predecessor Newton had done in the system of nature, to have formed and concluded a happy alliance between faith and philosophy." And again: "Metaphysic, which till then had nothing to support it but mere abstraction or shadowy speculation, Butler placed on the firm basis of observation and experiment." And Sir James Mackintosh says of the *Sermons* in general: "In these sermons Butler has taught truths more capable of being exactly distinguished from the doctrines of his predecessors, more satisfactorily established by him, more comprehensively applied to particulars, more rationally connected with each other, and therefore more worthy of the name of *discovery*, than any with which we are acquainted, if we ought not, with some hesitation, to except the first steps of the Grecian philosophers towards a theory of morals." The *Analogy* Mackintosh calls "the most original and profound work extant in any language on the philosophy of religion." Such are Butler's claims upon our attention.

It is true, there are moments when the philosophy of religion and the theory of morals are not popular subjects, when men seem disposed to put them out of their minds, to shelve them as sterile, to try whether they cannot get on without them. Mr. John Morley, in that interesting series of articles on Diderot which he has lately published in the *Fortnightly Review*, points out how characteristic and popular in the French Encyclopædia was its authors' "earnest enthusiasm for all the purposes, interests, and details of productive industry, for physical science and the practical arts;" how this was felt to be a welcome relief to people tired of metaphysical and religious discussions. "Intellectually," says he, "it was the substitution of interest in things for interest in words." And undoubtedly there are times when a reaction of this sort sets in, when an interest in the processes of productive industry, in physical science and the practical arts, is

called *an interest in things*, and an interest in morals and religion is called *an interest in words*. People really do seem to imagine that in seeing and learning how buttons are made, or *papier mâché*, they shall find some new and untried vital resource; that
5 our prospects from this sort of study have something peculiarly hopeful and animating about them, and that the positive and practical thing to do is to give up religion and turn to them. However, as Butler says in his sermon on Self-Deceit: "Religion is true, or it is not. If it be not, there is no reason for any concern
10 about it." If, however, it be true, it is important, and then it requires attention; as in the same sermon Butler says, in his serious way: "We cannot be acquainted with, nor in any propriety of speech be said to know, anything but what we attend to." And he speaks of the disregard of men for what he calls
15 "the reproofs and instructions" that they meet with in religion and morals, as a disregard of what is "exactly suitable to the state of their own mind and the course of their behaviour;"—more suitable, he would certainly have thought, than being instructed how buttons are made, or *papier mâché*. I am entirely of Butler's
20 opinion. And though the posture of mind of a good many clever persons at the present day is that of the French Encyclopædists, yet here in the capital of Scotland, of that country which has been such a stronghold of what I call "Hebraism," of deep and ardent occupation with righteousness and religion, you will
25 not complain of my taking for my subject so eminent a doctor in the science of these matters as Butler, and one who is said to have established his doctrine so firmly and impregnably. I can conceive no claim more great to advance on a man's behalf, and none which it more behoves us to test accurately. Let us
30 attempt to satisfy ourselves how far, in Butler's case, the claim is solid.

2.

But first we should have before our minds a notion of the life and circumstances of the man with whose works we are going to deal. Joseph Butler was born on the 18th of May 1692,
35 at Wantage in Berkshire. His father was a retired tradesman, a Dissenter, and the son was sent to a Dissenting school. Even

before he left school, he had his first correspondence with Dr. Samuel Clarke on certain points in Clarke's *Demonstration of the Being and Attributes of God*, and he wrote to a friend that he "designed to make truth the business of his life." Dissent did not satisfy him. He left the Presbyterian body, to which his father belonged, and was entered, in 1714, at Oxford, at Oriel College. There he formed a friendship with Edward Talbot, a Fellow of Oriel, son of Bishop Talbot, and brother to the future Lord Chancellor Talbot; and this friendship determined the outward course of Butler's life. It led to his being appointed preacher at the Rolls Chapel in 1719, the year after his ordination as priest, and when he was only twenty-six years old. There the famous Sermons were preached, between 1719 and 1726. Bishop Talbot appointed him, in 1722, to the living of Haughton, in the diocese of Durham; and, in 1725, transferred him to the rich living of Stanhope, in the same diocese. After obtaining Stanhope, Butler resigned, in 1726, his preachership at the Rolls, and published his Fifteen Sermons. They made no noise. It was four years before a second edition of them was required. Butler, however, had friends who knew his worth, and in 1733 he was made chaplain to Lord Chancellor Talbot, in 1736 Clerk of the Closet to Queen Caroline, the wife of George the Second. In this year he published the *Analogy*. Queen Caroline died the year afterwards, and Butler returned to Stanhope. But Queen Caroline had, before her death, strongly recommended him to her husband; and George the Second, in 1738, made him Bishop of Bristol, then the poorest of sees, with an income of but some £400 a year. About eighteen months afterwards, Butler was appointed to the deanery of St. Paul's, when he resigned Stanhope and passed his time between Bristol and London, acquiring a house at Hampstead. He attended the House of Lords regularly, but took no part, so far as is known, in the debates. In 1746 he was made Clerk of the Closet to the King, and in 1750 he was translated to the great and rich see of Durham. Butler's health had by this time given way. In 1751 he delivered his first and only charge to the clergy of Durham, the famous charge upon the *Use and Importance of External Religion*. But in June 1752 he was taken in a state of extreme weak-

ness to Bath, died there on the 16th of June, and was buried in
his old cathedral of Bristol. When he died, he was just sixty
years of age. He was never married.

Such are, in outline, the external facts of Butler's life and history. To fill up the outline for us there remain a very few
anecdotes, and one or two letters. Bishop Philpotts, of Exeter,
who afterwards followed Butler in the living of Stanhope,
sought eagerly at Stanhope for some traditions of his great
predecessor. All he could gather was, that Butler had been much
beloved, that he rode about on a black pony and rode very fast,
and that he was greatly pestered by beggars because of his
known easiness. But there has been preserved Butler's letter to
Sir Robert Walpole on accepting the see of Bristol, and a passage
in this letter is curious, as coming from such a man. He expresses
his gratitude to the King, and then proceeds thus:—

"I know no greater obligation than to find the Queen's conde-
scending goodness and kind intentions towards me transferred to
his Majesty. Nor is it possible, while I live, to be without the most
grateful sense of his favour to me, whether the effects of it be
greater or less; for this must, in some measure, depend upon acci-
dents. Indeed, the bishopric of Bristol is not very suitable either to
the condition of my fortune or the circumstances of my preferment,
nor, as I should have thought, answerable to the recommendation
with which I was honoured. But you will excuse me, sir, if I think of
this last with greater sensibility than the conduct of affairs will admit of. But without entering further into detail, I desire, sir, you
will please to let his Majesty know that I humbly accept this instance of his favour with the utmost possible gratitude."

As one reads that passage, it is impossible not to have the
feeling that we are in the somewhat arid air of the eighteenth
century. Ken or Leighton, in the seventeenth century, could
not have written it; and in Butler's own century that survivor of
the saints, Wilson of Sodor and Man, could not have written it.
And indeed the peculiar delicacy and loveliness which attaches
to our idea of a saint does not belong to Butler. Nobly severe
with himself he was, his eye was single. Austerely just, he follows with awe-filled observance the way of duty;—this is his
stamp of character. And his liberality and his treatment of

patronage, even though we may not find in him the delicacy of the saint, are yet thorough and admirable because they are determined by this character. He said to his secretary: "I should be ashamed of myself if I could leave ten thousand pounds behind me." There is a story of a man coming to him at Durham with a project for some good work. The plan struck Butler's mind; he sent for his house-steward, and asked him how much money there was in his hands. The steward answered that he had five hundred pounds. "Five hundred pounds!" said Butler, "what a shame for a bishop to have so much money! Give it away, give it all to this gentleman for his charitable plan!" Open house and plain living were Butler's rule at Durham. He had long been disgusted, he said, with the fashionable expense of time and money in entertainments, and was determined it should receive no countenance from his example. He writes to one who congratulated him on his translation to Durham:—

"If one is enabled to do a little good, and to prefer worthy men, this indeed is a valuable of life, and will afford satisfaction at the close of it; but the change of station in itself will in no wise answer the trouble of it, and of getting into new forms of living; I mean in respect to the peace and happiness of one's own mind, for in fortune to be sure it will."

Again one has a sense, from something in the phraseology and mode of expression, that one is in the eighteenth century; but at the same time what a perfect impression of integrity and simplicity do Butler's words leave! To another congratulator he writes:—

"I thank you for your kind congratulations, though I am not without my doubts and fears how far the occasion of them is a real subject of congratulation to me. Increase of fortune is insignificant to one who thought he had enough before; and I foresee many difficulties in the station I am coming into, and no advantage worth thinking of, except some greater power of being serviceable to others; and whether this be an advantage depends entirely on the use one shall make of it; I pray God it may be a good one. It would be a melancholy thing, in the close of life, to have no reflections to entertain oneself with but that one had spent the revenues of the bishopric of Durham in a sumptuous course of living, and enriched one's

friends with the promotions of it, instead of having really set one-self to do good, and promote worthy men; yet this right use of for-tune and power is more difficult than the generality of even good people think, and requires both a guard upon oneself, and a strength
5 of mind to withstand solicitations, greater (I wish I may not find it) than I am master of."

There are not half a dozen of Butler's private letters pre-served. It was worth while, therefore, to quote his letter to Walpole; and it was but just, after quoting that letter, to quote
10 these to his congratulators.

Like Bishop Philpotts, one may well be tantalised at not knowing more of a man so full of purpose, and who has made his mark so deeply. Butler himself, however, helped to baffle us. The codicil to his will, made in 1752, not two months before his
15 death, concludes thus:—"It is my positive and express will, that all my sermons, letters, and papers whatever, which are in a deal box, locked, directed to Dr. Forster, and now standing in the little room within my library at Hampstead, be burnt without being read by any one, as soon as may be after my decease."
20 His silent, inward, concentrated nature pondered well and de-cided what it meant to give to the world;—gave it, and would give no more. A characteristic habit is mentioned of him, that he loved to walk alone, and to walk at night. He was an im-mense reader. It is said of him that he read every book he could
25 lay his hands upon; but it was all digested silently, not exhib-ited in the way of extract and citation. Unlike the seventeenth century divines, he hardly ever quotes. As to his tastes and habits, we are informed, further, that he was fond of religious music, and took for his under-secretary an ex-chorister of St.
30 Paul's, that he might play to him upon the organ. He liked building and planting, and one of his few letters preserved bears witness to these tastes, and is altogether so character-istic, and, in the paucity of records concerning Butler, so val-uable, that I will quote it. It is to the Duchess of Somerset,
35 and written in 1751, just after he had taken possession of the see of Durham:—

"I had a mind to see Auckland before I wrote to your Grace; and as you take so kind a part in everything which contributes to my

satisfaction, I am sure you will be pleased to hear that the place is a
very agreeable one, and fully answering expectations, except that
one of the chief prospects, which is very pretty (the river Wear,
with hills much diversified rising above it), is too bare of wood; the
park, not much amiss as to that, but I am obliged to pale it anew all   5
round, the old pale being quite decayed. This will give an opportunity, with which I am much pleased, to take in forty or fifty acres
competently wooded, though with that enlargement it will scarce be
sufficient for the hospitality of the country. These, with some little
improvements and very great repairs, take up my leisure time.   10

"Thus, madam, I seem to have laid out a very long life for myself;
yet, in reality, everything I see puts me in mind of the shortness and
uncertainty of it: the arms and inscriptions of my predecessors,
what they did and what they neglected, and (from accidental circumstances) the very place itself, and the rooms I walk through and   15
sit in. And when I consider, in one view, the many things of the
kind I have just mentioned which I have upon my hands, I feel the
burlesque of being employed in this manner at my time of life. But
in another view, and taking in all circumstances, these things, as
trifling as they may appear, no less than things of greater impor-   20
tance, seem to be put upon me to do, or at least to begin; whether I
am to live to complete any or all of them, is not my concern."

With Butler's taste for building and improving is connected a
notable incident. While at Bristol he restored the episcopal
palace and chapel, and in the chapel he put up an altar-piece,   25
which is described as "of black marble, inlaid with a milk-white
cross of white marble, which is plain, and has a good effect." For
those bare Hanoverian times this was a reredos case. Butler's
cross excited astonishment and gave offence, and Lord Chancellor Hardwicke begged a subsequent Bishop of Bristol, Dr.   30
Young, to have it taken down. Young made the excellent answer,
that it should never be said that Bishop Young had pulled down
what Bishop Butler had set up; and the cross remained until the
palace was burnt and the marble altar-piece destroyed in the
Bristol riots in 1831. But the erection of this cross was connected   35
with his remarks, in his Durham Charge, on the *Use and Importance of External Religion*, and caused it to be reported that
Butler had died in the communion of the Church of Rome.
Pamphleteers and newspaper-writers handled the topic in the

style which we know so well. Archbishop Secker thought it
necessary to write in denial of his friend's perversion, owning,
as he did so, that for himself he wished the cross had not been
put up. And Butler's accuser replied, as "Phileleutheros," to
Secker, that "such anecdote had been given him, and that he
was yet of opinion there is not anything improbable in it, when
it is considered that the same prelate put up the Popish insignia
of the cross in his chapel, when at Bristol; and in his last episcopal charge has squinted very much towards that superstition."
Another writer not only maintained that the cross and the
Durham charge together "amounted to full proof of a strong
attachment to the idolatrous communion of the Church of
Rome," but volunteered to account for Butler's "tendency this
way," as he called it. This he did "from the natural melancholy
and gloominess of Dr. Butler's disposition, from his great fond-
ness for the lives of Romish saints, and their books of mystic
piety; from his drawing his notions of teaching men religion,
not from the New Testament, but from philosophical and political opinions of his own; and, above all, from his transition
from a strict Dissenter amongst the Presbyterians to a rigid
Churchman, and his sudden and unexpected elevation to great
wealth and dignity in the Church." It was impossible that Butler
should be understood by the ordinary religious world of his
own day. But no intelligent man can now read the Durham
Charge without feeling that its utterer lives in a higher world
than that in which disputes between Catholicism and Protestantism, and questions of going over to Rome, or at any rate
"squinting very much towards that superstition," have their
being. Butler speaks as a man with an awful sense of religion,
yet plainly seeing, as he says, "the deplorable distinction" of his
own age to be "an avowed scorn of religion in some, and a
growing disregard to it in the generality." He speaks, with "the
immoral thoughtlessness," as he called it, of the bulk of mankind
astounding and grieving his soul, and with the single desire "to
beget a practical sense of religion upon their hearts." "The form
of religion," he says, with his invincible sense for reality, "may
indeed be where there is little of the thing itself; but the thing
itself cannot be preserved amongst mankind without the form."

And the form he exhorts to is no more than what nowadays all religious people would think matter of course to be practised, and where not practised, to be enjoined: family prayer, grace at meals, that the clergy should visit their parishioners and should lay hold of natural opportunities, such as confirmation or sickness, for serious conversation with them and for turning their thoughts towards religion.

Butler met John Wesley, and one would like to have a full record of what passed at such a meeting. But all that we know is this: that when Butler was at Bristol, Wesley, who admired the *Analogy*, and who was then preaching to the Kingswood miners, had an interview with him; and that Butler "expressed his pleasure at the seriousness which Wesley's preaching awakened, but blamed him for sanctioning that violent physical excitement which was considered almost a necessary part of the so-called new birth."

I have kept for the last the description we have from Surtees, the historian of Durham, of Butler's person and manners:—

"During the short time that he held the see," says Surtees, "he conciliated all hearts. In advanced years and on the episcopal throne, he retained the same genuine modesty and native sweetness of disposition which had distinguished him in youth and in retirement. During the ministerial performance of the sacred office, a divine animation seemed to pervade his whole manner, and lighted up his pale, wan countenance, already marked with the progress of disease."

From another source we hear:—

"He was of a most reverend aspect;—his face thin and pale, but there was a divine placidness in his countenance, which inspired veneration and expressed the most benevolent mind. His white hair hung gracefully on his shoulders, and his whole figure was patriarchal."

This description would not ill suit Wesley himself, and it may be thought, perhaps, that here at any rate, if not in the letter to Sir Robert Walpole, we find the saint. And, doubtless, where the eye is so single and the thoughts are so chastened as they were with Butler, the saintly character will never be far off. But still the total impression left by Butler is not exactly, I repeat, that of a saint.

Butler stood alone in his time and amongst his generation. Yet the most cursory reader can perceive that, in his writings, there is constant reference to the controversies of his time, and to the men of his generation. He himself has pointed this out as a possible cause of obscurity. In the preface to the second edition of his *Sermons* he says:—

"A subject may be treated in a manner which all along supposes the reader acquainted with what has been said upon it both by ancient and modern writers, and with what is the present state of opinion in the world concerning such subject. This will create a difficulty of a very peculiar kind, and even throw an obscurity over the whole before those who are not thus informed; but those who are, will be disposed to excuse such a manner, and other things of the like kind, as a saving of their patience."

This reference to contemporary opinion, if it sometimes occasions difficulty in following Butler, makes his treatment of his subject more real and earnest. Nearly always he has in mind something with which he has actually come in conflict. When he recurs so persistently to self-love, he is thinking of the "strange affectation in many people of explaining away all particular affections, and representing the whole of life as nothing but one continual exercise of self-love," by which he had so often been made impatient. One of the signal merits of Mr. Pattison's admirable sketch, in *Essays and Reviews*, of the course of religious ideas in England from the Revolution to the middle of the eighteenth century, is that it so clearly marks this correspondence, at the time when Butler wrote, between what English society argued and what English theology answered. Society was full of discussions about religion, of objections to eternal punishment as inconsistent with the Divine goodness, and to a system of future rewards as subversive of a disinterested love of virtue:—

"The deistical writers," says Mr. Pattison, "formed the atmosphere which educated people breathed. The objections the *Analogy* meets are not new and unseasoned objections, but such as had worn well, and had borne the rub of controversy, because they were genuine. It was in society, and not in his study, that Butler had learned the weight of the deistical arguments."

And in a further sentence Mr. Pattison, in my opinion, has almost certainly put his finger on the very determining cause of the *Analogy's* existence:—

"At the Queen's philosophical parties, where these topics (the deistical objections) were canvassed with earnestness and freedom, Butler must often have felt the impotence of reply in detail, and seen, as he says, 'how impossible it must be, in a cursory conversation, to unite all this into one argument, and represent it as it ought.'"

This connecting of the *Analogy* with the Queen's philosophical parties seems to me an idea inspired by true critical genius. The parties given by Queen Caroline,—a clever and strong-minded woman,—the recluse and grave Butler had, as her Clerk of the Closet, to attend regularly. Discussion was free at them, and there Butler no doubt heard in abundance the talk of what is well described as the "loose kind of deism which was the then tone of fashionable circles." The *Analogy*, with its peculiar strain and temper, is the result. "Cavilling and objecting upon any subject is much easier than clearing up difficulties; and this last part will always be put upon the defenders of religion." Surely that must be a reminiscence of the "loose kind of deism" and of its maintainers! And then comes the very sentence which Mr. Pattison has in part quoted, and which is worth quoting entire:—

"Then, again, the general evidence of religion is complex and various. It consists of a long series of things, one preparatory to and confirming another, from the very beginning of the world to the present time. And 'tis easy to see how impossible it must be, in a cursory conversation, to unite all this into one argument and represent it as it ought; and, could it be done, how utterly indisposed people would be to attend to it. I say in a cursory conversation, whereas unconnected objections are thrown out in a few words and are easily apprehended, without more attention than is usual in common talk. So that notwithstanding we have the best cause in the world, and though a man were very capable of defending it, yet I know not why he should be forward to undertake it upon so great a disadvantage and to so little good effect, as it must be done amidst the gaiety and carelessness of common conversation."

In those remarks to the Durham clergy, Butler, I say again, was surely thinking of difficulties with which he had himself wrestled, and of which the remembrance made the strenuous tone of his *Analogy*, as he laboured at it, yet more strenuous. What a *sæva indignatio* burns in the following passage from the conclusion to that work:—

"Let us suppose that the evidence of religion in general, and of Christianity, has been seriously inquired into by all reasonable men among us. Yet we find many professedly to rejéct both, upon speculative principles of infidelity. And all of them do not content themselves with a bare neglect of religion, and enjoying their imaginary freedom from its restraints. Some go much beyond this. They deride God's moral government over the world. They renounce his protection and defy his justice. They ridicule and vilify Christianity, and blaspheme the Author of it; and take all occasions to manifest a scorn and contempt of revelation. This amounts to an active setting themselves against religion, to what may be considered as a positive principle of irreligion, which they cultivate within themselves, and whether they intend this effect or not, render habitual, as a good man does the contrary principle. And others, who are not chargeable with all this profligateness, yet are in avowed opposition to religion, as if discovered to be groundless."

And with the same penetrating tone of one who has seen with his own eyes that of which he complains, has heard it with his own ears, suffered from it in his own person, Butler, in 1740, talks of "the dark prospect before us from that profligateness of manners and scorn of religion which so generally abound;" and, in 1751, speaking in the last year but one of his life, he thus begins his charge to the clergy of Durham:—

"It is impossible for me, my brethren, upon our first meeting of this kind, to forbear lamenting with you the general decay of religion in this nation, which is now observed by every one, and has been for some time the complaint of all serious persons. The influence of it is more and more wearing out of the minds of men, even of those who do not pretend to enter into speculations upon the subject. But the number of those who do, and who profess themselves unbelievers, increases, and with their numbers their zeal."

One cannot but ask oneself, when one considers the steadiness of our country through the French Revolution, when one considers the power and prevalence of religion, even after every deduction has been made for what impairs its strength,—the power and prevalence, I say, of religion in our country at this hour,—one cannot but ask oneself whether Butler was not overdesponding, whether he saw the whole real state of things, whether he did not attach over-importance to certain workings which he did see. Granted that he himself did something to cure the evil which he describes; granted that others did something. Yet, had the evil existed fully as he describes it, I doubt whether he, and Wesley, and all the other physicians, could have cured it. I doubt, even, whether their effort would itself have been possible. Look at a contemporary of Butler in France,—a man who, more than any one else, reminds me of Butler,—the great French statesman, the greatest, in my opinion, that France has ever had; look at Turgot. Turgot was like Butler in his mental energy, in his deep moral and intellectual ardour, his strenuousness. "Every science, every language, every literature, every business," says Michelet, "interested Turgot." But that in which Turgot most resembled Butler was what Michelet calls his *férocité*,—what I should rather call his *sæva indignatio*. Like Butler, Turgot was filled with an astonished, awful, oppressive sense of "the immoral thoughtlessness" of men; of the heedless, hazardous way in which they deal with things of the greatest moment to them; of the immense, incalculable misery which is due to this cause. "The greatest evils in life," Turgot held, just as Butler did, "have had their rise from somewhat which was thought of too little importance to be attended to." And for these serious natures religion, one would think, is the line of labour which would naturally first suggest itself. And Turgot was destined for the Church; he prepared to take orders, like Butler. But in 1752, when Butler lay dying at Bath, Turgot,— the true spiritual yoke-fellow of Butler, with Butler's sacred horror at men's frivolity, with Butler's sacred ardour for rescu-

ing them from the consequences of it,—Turgot, at the age of
twenty-five, could stand religion, as in France religion then
presented itself to him, no longer. "*Il jeta ce masque*," says
Michelet, adopting an expression of Turgot's own; "he flung
5 away that mask." He took to the work of civil government; in
what spirit we many of us know, and whoever of us does not
know should make it his business to learn. Nine years afterwards
began his glorious administration as Intendant of the Limousin,
in which for thirteen years he showed what manner of spirit he
10 was of. When, in 1774, he became Minister and Controller-
General, he showed the same thing on a more conspicuous stage.
"Whatsoever things are true, whatsoever things are nobly serious, whatsoever things are just, whatsoever things are pure,
whatsoever things are of good report,"—that is the history of
15 Turgot's administration! He was a Joseph Butler in government.
True, his work, though done as secular administration, has in
fact and reality a religious character; all work like his has a
religious character. But the point to seize is here: that in our
country, in the middle of the eighteenth century, a man like
20 Butler is still possible in religion; in France he is only possible
in civil government. And that is what I call a true "decay of
religion, the influence of it more and more wearing out of the
minds of men." The very existence and work of Butler proves,
in spite of his own desponding words, that matters had not in
25 his time gone so far as this in England.

But indeed Mr. Pattison, in the admirable essay which I have
mentioned, supplies us with almost positive evidence that it had
not. Amongst a number of instructive quotations to show the
state of religion in England between 1700 and 1750, Mr. Pattison
30 gives an extract from a violent newspaper, *The Independent
Whig*, which had been attacking the clergy for their many and
great offences, and counselling them to mend their ways. And
then the article goes on:—

"The High Church Popish clergy will laugh in their sleeves at
35 this advice, and think there is folly enough yet left among the laity
to support their authority; and will hug themselves, and rejoice over
the ignorance of the Universities, the stupidity of the drunken

squires, the panic of the tender sex, *and the never-to-be-shaken constancy of the multitude.*"

The date of that extract is 1720. The language is the well-known language of Liberal friends of progress, when they speak of persons and institutions which are inconvenient to them. But it proves, to my mind,—and there is plenty of other evidence to prove the same thing,—it proves that religion, whatever may have been the deficiencies of itself and of its friends, was nevertheless, in 1720, still a very great and serious power in this country. And certainly it did not suddenly cease to be so between 1720 and 1750.

No, Butler's mournful language has in it, one may be almost certain, something of exaggeration. To a man of Butler's seriousness the world will always afford plenty of matter for apprehension and sorrow. And to add to this were certain special circumstances of his time, peculiarly trying to an earnest dealer, such as he was, with great thoughts and great interests. There was his bitter personal experience of "the loose kind of deism which was the tone of fashionable circles." There was his impatience,—half contemptuous, half indignant,—of a state of things where, as Mr. Pattison says, "the religious writer had now to appear at the bar of criticism," but of *such* criticism! For, "if ever there was a time," says Mr. Pattison, again, "when abstract speculation was brought down from inaccessible heights and compelled to be intelligible, it was the period from the Revolution to 1750." This in itself was all very good, and Butler would have been the last man to wish it otherwise. But to whom was abstract speculation required thus to make itself intelligible? To the "fashionable circles," to the whole multitude of loose thinkers and loose livers, who might choose to lend half an ear for half an hour to the great argument. "It must gain," we are told, "the wits and the town." Hence the *sæva indignatio.*

And therefore Butler, when he gets into the pulpit, or when he sits down at his writing-table, will have the thing out with his adversaries. He will "unite it all into one argument and represent it as it ought," and he will fairly argue his objectors down. He will place himself on their own ground, take their

own admissions, and will prove to them, in a manner irresistible to any fair thinker, that they are wrong, and that they
are bound to make their life and practice, what it is not, religious.

5   There is a word which I have often used, and with my use of
which some of those who hear me may possibly be familiar: the
Greek word *epieikes* or *epieikeia*, meaning that which is at once
reasonable and prepossessing, or "sweet reasonableness." The
original meaning of the word *epieikes* is, that which has an air of
10 consummate truth and likelihood, and which, by virtue of having this air, is prepossessing. And *epieikeia* is well rendered by
"sweet reasonableness," because that which above all things has
an air of truth and likelihood, that which, therefore, above all
things, is prepossessing, is whatever is sweetly reasonable. You
15 know what a power was this quality in the talkings and dealings
of Jesus Christ. *Epieikeia* is the very word to characterise true
Christianity. And true Christianity wins, not by an argumentative victory, not by going through a long debate with a person,
examining the arguments for his case from beginning to end,
20 and making him confess that, whether he feels disposed to yield
or no, yet in fair logic and fair reason he ought to yield. No, but
it puts something which tends to transform him and his practice,
it puts this particular thing in such a way before a man that he
feels disposed and eager to lay hold of it. And he does, there-
25 fore, lay hold of it, though without at all perceiving, very often,
the whole scheme to which it belongs; and thus his practice gets
changed. This, I think, every one will admit to be Christianity's
most true and characteristic way of getting people to embrace
religion. Now, it is to be observed how totally unlike a way
30 it is to Butler's, although Butler's object is the same as Christianity's: to get people to embrace religion. And the object being
the same, it must strike every one that the way followed by
Christianity has the advantage of a far greater effectualness than
Butler's way; since people are much more easily attracted into
35 making a change than argued into it. However, Butler seems to
think that enough has been done if it has been proved to people,
in such a way as to silence their arguments on the other side, that
they *ought* to make a change. For he says expressly:—

"There being, as I have shown, such evidence for religion as is sufficient in reason to influence men to embrace it, to object that it is not to be imagined mankind *will* be influenced by such evidence is nothing to the purpose of the foregoing treatise (his *Analogy*). For the purpose of it is not to inquire what sort of creatures mankind are, but what the light and knowledge which is afforded them requires they should be; to show how in reason they ought to behave, not how in fact they will behave. This depends upon themselves and is their own concern—the personal concern of each man in particular. And how little regard the generality have to it, experience, indeed, does too fully show. But religion, considered as a probation, has had its end upon all persons to whom it has been proposed with evidence sufficient in reason to influence their practice; for by this means they have been put into a state of probation, let them behave as they will in it."

So that, in short, Butler's notion of converting the loose deists of fashionable circles comes to this: by being plied with evidence sufficient *in reason* to influence their practice, they are to be put into a state of probation; let them behave as they will in it. Probably no one can hear such language without a secret dissatisfaction. For, after all, the object of religion is conversion, and to change people's behaviour. But where, then, is the use of saying that you will inquire not what people *are*, but how in reason they ought to behave? Why, it is what they *are* which determines their sense of how they ought to behave. Make them, therefore, so to feel what they are, as to get a fruitful sense of how they ought to behave. The Founder of Christianity did so; and whatever success Christianity has had, has been gained by this method.

However, Butler's line is what it is. We are concerned with what we can use of it. With his argumentative triumph over the loose thinkers and talkers of his day, so far as it is a triumph won by taking their own data and using their own admissions, we are not concerned unless their admissions and their data are ours too. And they are not. But it is affirmed, not only that the loose deists of fashionable circles could not answer the *Analogy;* it is affirmed, farther, that the *Analogy* is unanswerable. It is asserted, not only that Hobbes or Shaftesbury delivered an unsatisfactory theory of morals, and that Butler in

his *Sermons* disputed their reasonings with success; but it is asserted, farther, that Butler, on his side, "pursued precisely the
same mode of reasoning in the science of morals as his great
predecessor, Newton, had done in the system of nature," and
that by so doing Butler has "formed and concluded a happy
alliance between faith and philosophy." Achievement of this
kind is what the "Time-Spirit," or *Zeit-Geist*, which sweeps
away so much that is local and personal, will certainly respect.
Achievement of this sort deeply concerns us. An unanswerable
work on the evidence of religion, a science of human nature
and of morals reached by a method as sure as Newton's, a happy
alliance between faith and philosophy,—what can concern us
more deeply? If Butler accomplished all this, he does indeed give
us what we can use; he is indeed great. But supposing he should
turn out not to have accomplished all this, what then? Does he
vanish away? Does he give us nothing which we can use? And
if he does give us something which we can use, what is it? and
if he remains a great man to us still, why does he?

3.

Let us begin with the *Sermons at the Rolls*, Butler's first publication. You have heard, for I have quoted it, the unbounded
praise which has been given to the three sermons *On Human
Nature*. And they do indeed lay the foundation for the whole
doctrine of the *Sermons at the Rolls*, of the body of sermons
wherein is given Butler's system of moral philosophy. Their
argument is familiar, probably, to many of us. Let me recite it
briefly by abridging the best of all possible accounts of it,—
Butler's own account in his preface:—

"Mankind has various instincts and principles of action. The generality of mankind obey their instincts and principles, all of them,
those propensions we call good as well as the bad, according to the
constitution of their body and the external circumstances which
they are in. They are not wholly governed by self-love, the love of
power, and sensual appetites; they are frequently influenced by
friendship, compassion, gratitude; and even a general abhorrence of
what is base, and liking of what is fair and just, take their turn

amongst the other motives of action. This is the partial inadequate notion of human nature treated of in the first discourse, and it is by this nature, if one may speak so, that the world is in fact influenced and kept in that tolerable order in which it is.

"Mankind in thus acting would act suitably to their whole nature, if no more were to be said of man's nature than what has been now said. But that is not a complete account of man's nature. Somewhat further must be brought in to give us an adequate notion of it—namely, that one of those principles of action—*conscience* or *reflection*—compared with the rest as they all stand together in the nature of man, plainly bears upon it marks of authority over all the rest, and claims the absolute direction of them all, to allow or forbid their gratification; a disapprobation of reflection being in itself a principle manifestly superior to a mere propension. And the conclusion is, that to allow no more to this superior principle or part of our nature than to other parts, to let it govern and guide only occasionally in common with the rest, as its turn happens to come, from the temper and circumstances one happens to be in—this is not to act conformably to the constitution of man, neither can any human creature be said to act conformably to his constitution and nature, unless he allows to that superior principle the absolute authority which is due to it. And this conclusion is abundantly confirmed from hence—that one may determine what course of action the economy of man's nature requires, without so much as knowing in what degrees of *strength* the several principles prevail, or which of them have *actually* the greatest influence."

And the whole scope and object of the three sermons *On Human Nature*, Butler describes thus:—

"They were intended to explain what is meant by the nature of man, when it is said that virtue consists in following, and vice in deviating from it; and by explaining to show that the assertion is true."

Now, it may be at once allowed that Butler's notion of human nature as consisting of a number of instincts and principles of action, with conscience as a superior principle presiding over them, corresponds in a general way with facts of which we are all conscious, and if practically acted upon would be found to work satisfactorily. When Butler says: "Let any plain honest man before he engages in any course of action, ask himself,

'Is this I am going about right, or is it wrong? Is it good or is it evil?' and I do not in the least doubt but that this question would be answered agreeably to truth and virtue by almost any fair man in almost any circumstance;"—when Butler says this, he is on solid ground, and his whole scheme has its rise, indeed, in the sense that this ground *is* solid. When he calls our nature "the voice of God within us;" or when he suggests that there may be "distinct from the reflection of reason, a mutual *sympathy* between each particular of the species, a *fellow-feeling* common to mankind;" or when he finely says of conscience, "Had it strength as it has right, had it power as it has manifest authority, it would absolutely govern the world;"—in all this, Butler is in contact with the most precious truth and reality, and so far as this truth and reality inform the scheme which he has drawn out for human nature, his scheme has life in it.

Equally may it be allowed, that the errors, which his scheme is designed to correct, are errors indeed. If the Epicureans, or Hobbes, or any one else, "explain the desire of praise and of being beloved, as no other than desire of safety; regard to our country, even in the most virtuous character, as nothing but regard to ourselves; curiosity as proceeding from interest or pride; as if there were no such passions in mankind as desire of esteem, or of being beloved, or of knowledge;"—if these delineators of human nature represent it thus, they represent it fantastically. If Shaftesbury, laying it down that virtue is the happiness of man, and encountered by the objection that one may be not convinced of this happy tendency of virtue or may be of a contrary opinion, meets the objection by determining that the case is without remedy, then this noble moralist moralises ill. If Butler found some persons (probably the loose deists of fashionable circles) "who, upon principle, set up for suppressing the affection of compassion as a weakness, so that there is I know not what of fashion on this side, and by some means or other the whole world, almost, is run into the extremes of insensibility towards the distresses of their fellow-creatures;" —if this was so, then the fashionable theory of human nature was vicious and false, and Butler, in seeking to substitute a better for it, was quite right.

But Butler himself brings in somebody as asking: "Allowing that mankind hath the rule of right within itself, what obligations are we under to attend to and follow it?" And he answers this question quite fairly: "Your obligation to obey this law, is its being the law of your nature." But let us vary the question a little, and let us ask Butler: "Suppose your scheme of human nature to correspond in a general way, but no more, with facts of which we are conscious, and to promise to work practically well enough, what obligations are we under to attend to and follow it?" Butler cannot now answer us: "Your obligation to obey this law, is its being the law of your nature." For this is just what is not yet made out. All that we suppose to be yet made out about Butler's scheme of human nature,—its array of instincts and principles with the superior principle of conscience presiding,—is, that the scheme has a general correspondence with facts of human nature whereof we are conscious. But the time comes,—sooner or later the time comes,—to individuals and even to societies, when the foundations of the great deep are broken up, and everything is in question, and people want surer holding-ground than a sense of general correspondence, in any scheme and rule of human nature proposed to them, with facts whereof they are conscious. They ask themselves what this sense of general correspondence is really worth. They sift the facts of which they are conscious, and their consciousness of which seemed to lend a credibility to the scheme proposed. They insist on strict verification of whatever is to be admitted; and the authority of the scheme with them stands or falls according as it does or does not come out undamaged, after all this process has been gone through. If Butler's scheme of human nature comes out undamaged after being submitted to a process of this kind, then it is indeed, as its admirers call it, a Newtonian work. It is a work "placed on the firm basis of observation and experiment;" it is a true work of *discovery*. His doctrine may, with justice, be then called "an irresistible doctrine made out according to the strict truth of our mental constitution."

Let us take Butler's natural history of what he calls "our instincts and principles of action." It is this:—They have been implanted in us; put into us ready-made, to serve certain ends

intended by the Author of our nature. When we see what each
of them "is in itself, as placed in our nature by its Author, it will
plainly appear for what ends it was placed there." "Perfect
goodness in the Deity," says Butler, "is the principle from
whence the universe was brought into being, and by which it is
preserved; and general benevolence is the great law of the whole
moral creation." But some of our passions and propensions seem
to go against goodness and benevolence. However, we could
not do without our stock of passions and propensions of all
sorts, because "that would leave us without a sufficient principle of action." "Reason alone," argues Butler—

"Reason alone, whatever any one may wish, is not in reality a sufficient motive of virtue in such a creature as man; but this reason,
joined with those affections which God has impressed upon his
heart; and when these are allowed scope to exercise themselves, but
under strict government and direction of reason, then it is we act
suitably to our nature, and to the circumstances God has placed us
in."

And even those affections, which seem to create difficulties for
us, are purposely given, Butler says—

"Some of them as a guard against the violent assaults of others,
and in our own defence; some in behalf of others; and all of them
to put us upon, and help to carry us through, a course of behaviour
suitable to our condition."

For

"As God Almighty foresaw the irregularities and disorders, both
natural and moral, which would happen in this state of things, he
hath graciously made some provision against them, by giving us
several passions and affections, which arise from, or whose objects
are, those disorders. Of this sort are fear, resentment, compassion,
and others, of which there could be no occasion or use in a perfect
state, but in the present we should be exposed to greater inconveniences without them, though there are very considerable ones
which they themselves are the occasions of."

This is Butler's natural history of the origin of our principles
of action. I take leave to say that it is *not* based on observation

and experiment. It is not physiology, but fanciful hypothesis. Therefore it is not Newtonian, for Newton said: *Hypotheses non fingo*. And suppose a man, in a time of great doubt and unsettlement, finding many things fail him which have been confidently pressed on his acceptance, and looking earnestly for   5
something which he feels he can really go upon and which will prove to him a sure stay;—suppose such a man coming to Butler, because he hears that in the ethical discussions of his sermons Butler supplies, as Mackintosh says, "truths more satisfactorily established by him, and more worthy of the name of *discovery*,   10
than perhaps any with which we are acquainted." Well, such a man, I think, when he finds that Butler's ethics involve an immense hypothesis to start with, as to the origin and final causes of all our passions and affections, cannot but feel disconcerted and impatient.   15

And disconcerted and impatient, I am afraid, we must for the present leave him.

II

Butler designs to found a sure system of morals, and, in order to found it, he, as we have seen, tells us how we originally came by our instincts and affections. They were, he tells us, "placed   20
in us by God, to put us upon and help to carry us through a course of behaviour suitable to our condition." Here, as every one will admit, we cannot directly verify the truth of what our author says. But he also examines such and such of our affections in themselves, to make good his theory of their origin and final   25
causes. And here we can verify the degree in which his report of facts, and the construction he puts upon them, carries us along with it, inspires us with confidence in his scheme of human nature.

Butler notices, that compassion for the distresses of others is   30
felt much more generally than delight in their prosperity. And he says:—

"The reason and account of which matter is this: when a man has obtained any particular advantage or felicity, his end is gained, and he does not, in that particular, want the assistance of another; there   35

was therefore no need of a distinct affection towards that felicity of
another already obtained, neither would such affection directly
carry him on to do good to that person; whereas men in distress
want assistance, and compassion leads us directly to assist them. The
5   object of the former is the present felicity of another; the object of
the latter is the present misery of another. It is easy to see that the
latter *wants* a particular affection for its relief, and that the former
does not want one, because it does not want assistance."

Such an explanation, why compassion at another's distress is
10 stronger than satisfaction at another's prosperity, was well
suited, no doubt, to Butler's theory of the origin and final
causes of all our affections. But will any one say that it carries a
real student of nature along with it and inspires him with confidence, any more than Hobbes's resolution of all benevolence
15 into a mere love of power?—that it is not just as fantastic?

Again, take Butler's account of the passion of anger and resentment. There is sudden anger, he says, and there is deliberate
anger:—

"The reason and end for which man was made liable to the pas-
20 sion of sudden anger is, that he might be better qualified to prevent,
and likewise (or perhaps chiefly) to resist and defeat, sudden force,
violence, and opposition, considered merely as such. It stands in our
nature for self-defence, and not for the administration of justice.
Deliberate anger, on the other hand, is given us to further the ends
25 of justice; not natural but moral evil, not suffering but injury, raises
that anger; it is resentment against vice and wickedness."

And—

"The natural object of settled resentment, then, being injury, as
distinct from pain or loss, it is easy to see that to prevent and to
30 remedy such injury, and the miseries arising from it, is the end for
which this passion was implanted in man."

But anger has evident dangers and abuses. True. But—

"Since it is necessary, for the very subsistence of the world, that
injury, injustice, and cruelty should be punished; and since compas-
35 sion, which is so natural to mankind, would render that execution
of justice exceedingly difficult and uneasy, indignation against vice
and wickedness is a balance to that weakness of pity, and also to

anything else which would prevent the necessary methods of severity."

And it is the business of the faculty of conscience, or reflection, to tell us how anger may be innocently and rightly employed, so as to serve the end for which God placed it in our nature.

In times when everything is conventional, when no one looks very closely into himself or into what is told him about his moral nature, this sort of natural history may, perhaps, look likely enough, and may even pass for Newtonian. But let a time come when, as I say, the foundations of the great deep are broken up, when a man searches with passionate earnestness for something certain, and can and will henceforth build upon facts only; then the arbitrary assertions of such a psychology as this of Butler's will be felt to be perfectly fantastic and unavailing.

And even when the arbitrary and fantastic character of his psychology is not so apparent, Butler will be felt constantly to puzzle and perplex, rather than to satisfy us. He will be felt not to carry us along with him, not to be convincing. He has his theory that our appetites and affections are all placed in our nature by God, that they are all equally natural, that they all have a useful end to serve and have respect to that end solely; that the principle of conscience is implanted in us for the sake of arbitrating between them, of assigning to certain among them a natural superiority, of using each in its right measure and of guiding it to its right end; and that the degree of strength, in which any one of our affections exists, affords no reason at all for following it. And Butler's theory requires, moreover, that self-love shall be but one out of our many affections, that it shall have a strictly defined end of its own, and be as distinct from those affections which seem most akin to it, and which are therefore often confounded with it, as it is from those,—such as benevolence, we will say,—which nobody is tempted to confound with it. Such is Butler's theory, and such are its requirements. And with this theory, we find him declaring that compassion is a primitive affection implanted in us from the first by the Author of Nature to lead us to public spirit, just as hunger was implanted in us from the first to lead us to our own personal good, and from the same cause: namely, that reason and cool self-love would not by themselves have been sufficient to lead us to the end in view, without the appetite and the affection.

5   "The private interest of the individual would not be sufficiently provided for by reasonable and cool self-love alone; *therefore* the appetites and passions *are placed* within as a guard and further security, without which it would not be taken due care of. It is manifest, our life would be neglected were it not for the calls of hunger
10   and thirst and weariness, notwithstanding that without them reason would assure us, that the recruits of food and sleep are the necessary means of our preservation. It is therefore absurd to imagine that, without affection (the affection of compassion), the same reason alone would be more effectual to engage us to perform the du-
15   ties we owe to our fellow-creatures."

The argument may be ingenious, but can anything be more unsatisfactory? And is it not, to use Butler's words, "absurd to imagine" that in this manner, and by this parallel plan, and thus to supplement one another, hunger and reasonable self-love,
20   compassion and "a settled reasonable principle of benevolence to mankind," did really have their rise in us?

Presently we find Butler marvelling that persons of superior capacity should dispute the obligation of compassion and public spirit, and asking if it could ever occur to a man of plain
25   understanding to think "that there was absolutely no such thing in mankind as affection to the good of others,—*suppose of parents to their children.*" As if the affection of parents to their children was an affection to the good of others of just the same natural history as public spirit!—as if the two were alike in their
30   primariness, alike in their date of obligation, alike in their kind of evidence! One is an affection of rudimentary human nature, the other is a slow conquest from rudimentary human nature. And once more:—

"To endeavour to get rid of the sorrow of compassion, by turning
35   from the wretched, is as unnatural," says Butler, "as to endeavour to get rid of the pain of hunger, by keeping from the sight of food."

Now, we are to consider this as a practical argument by which to bring a man, all unsettled about the rule of his conduct, to

cultivate in himself compassion. Surely such an argument would
astonish rather than convince him! He would say: "Can it be so,
since we see that men continually do the one, never the other?"
But Butler insists, and says:—

"That we can do one with greater success than we can the other,   5
is no proof that one is less a violation of nature than the other. Compassion is a call, a demand of nature, to relieve the unhappy, as hunger is a natural call for food."

Surely, *nature, natural,* must be used here in a somewhat artificial manner, in order to get this argument out of them! Yet   10
Butler professes to stick to plain facts, not to sophisticate, not to
refine.

"Let me take notice," he says, "of the danger of going beside or
beyond the plain, obvious, first appearances of things, upon the subject of morals and religion."   15

But is it in accordance with the plain, obvious, first appearances
of things, to pronounce compassion to be a call, a demand of
nature to relieve the unhappy, precisely in the same manner as
hunger is a natural call for food; and to say that to neglect one
call is just as much a violation of nature as the other? Surely   20
Butler could not talk in this way, unless he had first laid it down
that all our affections are in themselves equally natural, and that
no degree of greater strength and frequency can make one affection more natural than the other. They are all, according to
him, voices of God. But the principle of reflection or con-   25
science,—a higher voice of God,—decides how and when each
is to be followed. And when Butler has laid this down, he has no
difficulty in affirming that it is as unnatural not to relieve the
distressed as not to eat when one is hungry. Only one feels, not
convinced and satisfied, but in doubt whether he *ought* to have   30
laid it down, when one sees that it conducts him to such an
affirmation.

Yet once more. The affection of compassion not only proves
that it is as unnatural to turn away from distress as to turn from
food when one is hungry. It proves, also, that this world was   35
intended neither to be a mere scene of unhappiness and sorrow,
nor to be a state of any great satisfaction or high enjoyment.
And it suggests the following lesson for us:—

"There being that distinct affection implanted in the nature of man tending to lessen the miseries of life, that particular provision made for abating its sorrows more than for increasing its positive happiness, this may suggest to us what should be our general aim
5   respecting ourselves in our passage through this world, namely, to endeavour chiefly to escape misery, keep free from uneasiness, pain, and sorrow, or to get relief and mitigation of them; to propose to ourselves peace and tranquillity of mind rather than pursue after high enjoyments."

10 And Butler goes on to enumerate several so-called high enjoyments, such as "to make pleasure and mirth and jollity our business, and be constantly hurrying about after some gay amusement, some new gratification of sense or appetite." And he points out, what no wise man will dispute, that these do not
15 confer happiness, and that we do wrong to make them our end in life. No doubt; yet meanwhile, in his main assertion that man's proper aim is escape from misery rather than positive happiness, Butler goes clean counter to the most intimate, the most sure, the most irresistible instinct of human nature. As a little known
20 but profound French moralist, Senancour, has said admirably: "The aim for man is to augment the feeling of joy, to make our expansive energy bear fruit, and to combat, in all thinking beings, the principle of degradation and misery." But Butler goes counter, also, to the clear voice of our religion. "Rejoice
25 and give thanks!" exhorts the Old Testament; "Rejoice evermore!" exhorts the New. This, and not mere escape from misery, getting freedom from uneasiness, pain, and sorrow, or getting mitigation of them, is what (to turn Butler's words against himself) "the constitution of nature marks out as the
30 course we should follow and the end we should aim at." And a scheme of human nature, meant to serve as a rule for human conduct, cannot, however ingenious, be said to explain things irresistibly according to the strict truth of our mental constitution, when we find it strongly at variance with the facts of that
35 constitution on a point of capital importance.

Even at past fifty years of age I approach the subject, so terrible to undergraduates, of Butler's account of self-love, with a shiver of uneasiness. Yet I will point out how Butler's own arbi-

trary definition of self-love, a definition which the cast of his
scheme of human nature renders necessary, creates the difficulties of his assiduous, laboured, and unsatisfying attempt to
reconcile self-love with benevolence. He describes self-love,
occasionally, as "a general desire of our own happiness." And he   5
knew well enough, that the pursuit of our own interest and
happiness, rightly understood, and the obedience to God's com-
mands, "must be in every case one and the same thing." Nevertheless, Butler's constant notion of the pursuit of our interest is,
that it is the pursuit of our *temporal* good, as he calls it; the cool   10
consideration of our own temporal advantage. And he expressly
defines his self-love, which he names "a private contracted affection," as "a regard to our private good, our private interest."
Private interest is the favourite expression: "a cool pursuit of
our private interest." Now to say, that there is no opposition   15
between a general desire for our own happiness, and a love of
our neighbour, has nothing puzzling in it. But to define self-
love as a private contracted affection, consisting in a cool deliberate pursuit of our private interest, and then to say, as
Butler does, that from self-love, thus defined, love of our   20
neighbour is no more distant than hatred of our neighbour, is to
sophisticate things. Butler may make it out by stipulating that
self-love shall merely mean pursuing our private interest, and
not pursuing it in any particular manner, just as he makes out
that not to relieve the distressed is as unnatural to a man as not   25
to eat when he is hungry, by stipulating that all our affections
shall be considered equally natural. But he does not convince a
serious student by these refinements, does not carry such a student with him, does not help such a student, therefore, a step
nearer towards practice. And a moralist's business is to help   30
towards practice.

The truth is, all this elaborate psychology of Butler's, which
satisfies us so little,—so little, to use Coleridge's excellent expression, *finds* us,—is unsatisfying because of its radical defective-
ness as natural history. What he calls our instincts and prin-   35
ciples of action, which are in truth the most obscure, changing,
interdependent of phenomena, Butler takes as if they were
things as separate, fixed, and palpable as the bodily organs which

the dissector has on his table before him. He takes them as if, just as he now finds them, there they had always been, and there they must always be; as if benevolence had always gone on secreting love of our neighbour, and compassion a desire to
5 relieve misery, and conscience right verdicts, just as the liver secretes bile. Butler's error is that of the early chemists, who imagined things to be elements which were not, but were capable of being resolved and decomposed much farther. And a man who is thrown fairly upon himself, and will have the naked
10 truth, must feel that it is with Butler's principles and affections as it was with the elements of the early chemists; they are capable of being resolved and decomposed much farther, and solid ground is not reached until they are thus decomposed. "There is this principle of reflection or conscience in mankind."
15 —"True," the student may answer; "but what and whence is it? It had a genesis of some kind, and your account of its genesis is fantastic. What is its natural genesis, and what the natural genesis of your benevolence, compassion, resentment, and all the rest of them? Till I know this, I do not know where I am in
20 talking about them."—But into this vast, dimly lighted, primordial region of the natural genesis of man's affections and principles, Butler never enters.

Yet in this laboratory arose those wonderful compounds with which Butler deals, and the source of his ruling faculty of con-
25 science is to be traced back thither. There, out of the simple primary instinct, which we may call the instinct or effort *to live,* grew our affections; and out of the experience of those affections, in their result upon the instinctive effort to live, grew reflection, practical reason, conscience. And the all-ruling effort
30 to live is, in other words, *the desire for happiness;* that desire which Butler,—because he identifies it with self-love, and defines self-love as the cool pursuit of our private interest, of our temporal good,—is so anxious to treat as only one motive out of many, and not authoritative. And this instinct rules because
35 it is *strongest;* although Butler is so anxious that no instinct shall rule because it is strongest. And our affections of all kinds, too, according as they serve this deep instinct or thwart it, are superior in *strength,*—not in present strength, but in permanent

strength; and have degrees of *worth* according to that superiority. And benevolence, or a regard to the good of others, *does*
often conflict with the private contracted affection of self-love,
or a regard to our private interest, with which Butler denies that
it conflicts at all. But it has the call to contend with it, and the
right to get the better of it, because of its own superiority in
permanent strength. And this superiority it derives from the
experience, painfully and slowly acquired, that it serves our
instinct to live, our desire for happiness, better than the private
contracted affection does; that the private contracted affection,
if we follow it, thwarts this instinct. For men are solidary, or
co-partners; and not isolated. And conscience, in a question of
conflict between a regard to the good of others and a regard to
our private good, is the sense of experience having proved and
established, that, from this reason of men's being really solidary,
our private good ought in a conflict of such kind to give way;
and that our nature is violated,—that is, our instinct to live is
thwarted,—if it does not. That this sense finds in us a pre-adaptation to it, and a presentiment of its truth, may be inferred from
its being a sense of facts which are a real condition of human
progress. But whatever may be the case as to our pre-adaptation
to it and presentiment of it, the great matter in favour of the
sense is, that the experience reported by it is *true;* that the thing
is so. People may say, they have not got this sense that their
instinct to live is served by loving their neighbour;—they may
say that they have, in other words, a dull and uninformed conscience. But that does not make the experience the less a true
thing, the real experience of the race. Neither does it make the
sense of this experience to be, any the less, genuine conscience.
And it is genuine conscience, because it apprehends what does
really serve our instinct to live, our desire for happiness. And
when Shaftesbury supposes the case of a man thinking vice and
selfishness to be truly as much for his advantage as virtue and
benevolence, and concludes that such a case is without remedy, the answer is: Not at all; let such a man get conscience,
get right experience. And if the man does not, the result is not
that he goes on just as well without it; the result is, that he is
lost.

Butler, indeed, was evidently afraid of making the desire of happiness to be that which we must set out with in explaining human nature. And he was afraid of it for this reason: because he was apprehensive of the contracted self-love, and of the con-
5 tracted judgments, of the individual. But if we say *the instinct to live* instead of *the desire of happiness*,—and the two mean the same thing, and *life* is a better and more exact word to use than *happiness*, and it is, moreover, the Bible-word,—then the difficulty vanishes. For, as man advances in his development, he be-
10 comes aware of two lives, one permanent and impersonal, the other transient and bound to our contracted self; he becomes aware of two selves, one higher and real, the other inferior and apparent; and that the instinct in him truly to live, the desire for happiness, is served by following the first self and not the
15 second. It is not the case that the two selves do not conflict; they do conflict. It is not true that the affections and impulses of both alike are, as Butler says, the voice of God; the self-love of Butler, the "cool study of our private interest," is not the voice of God. It is a hasty, erroneous interpretation by us, in our long, ten-
20 tative, up-struggling development, of the instinct to live, the desire for happiness, which *is* the voice of our authentic nature, the voice of God. And it has to be corrected by experience. Love of our neighbour, Butler's *benevolence*, is the affection by which experience bids us correct it. Many a hard lesson does the
25 experience involve, many a heavy blow. But the satisfaction of our instinct to live, of our desire for happiness, depends on our making and using the experience.

And so true is this history of the two lives in man, the two selves,—both arising out of the instinct to live in us, out of the
30 feeling after happiness, but one correcting and at last dominating the other,—that the psychology of Jesus Christ, which without the least apparatus of system is yet incomparably exacter than Butler's, as well as incomparably more illuminative and fruitful,—this psychology, I say, carries every one with it
35 when it treats these two lives in man, these two selves, as an evident, capital fact of human nature. Jesus Christ said: "Renounce *thyself!*" and yet he also said: "What is a man profited, if he gain the whole world, and yet lose *himself*, be mulcted of

himself?" He said: "I am come that men might have *life*, and might have it more abundantly; and ye will not come to me that ye may have *life!*" And yet he also said: "Whosoever will save his *life*, shall lose it." So certain is it that we have two lives, two selves; and that there is no danger in making the instinct to live, the desire of happiness, to be, as it really is, that which we must set out with in explaining human nature, if we add that only in the impersonal life, and with the higher self, is the instinct truly served and the desire truly satisfied; that experience is the long, painful, irresistible, glorious establishment of this fact, and that conscience is the recognition of that experience.

Now, as Butler fears to set out, in explaining human nature, with the desire for happiness, because he imagines each man cutting and carving arbitrarily for his own private interest in pursuit of happiness, so he apprehends a man's cutting and carving arbitrarily, and with mistaken judgment, for the happiness of others. He supposes a man fancying that an overbalance of happiness to mankind may be produced by committing some great injustice, and says very truly that a man is not on that account to commit it. And he concludes that "we are constituted so as to condemn injustice abstracted from all consideration what conduct is likeliest to produce an overbalance of happiness or misery." And he thinks that his theory of our affections being all implanted separately in us, ready-made and full-grown, by a Divine Author of Nature, his theory of the dignified independence, on the part of virtue and conscience, of all aim at happiness, is thereby proved. So far from it, that man did not even propose to himself the worthier aim, as it now is seen by us to be, of the production of *general* happiness, in feeling his way to the laws of virtue. He proposed to himself the production simply of his own happiness. But experience of what made for *this*, such experience slowly led him to the laws of virtue;— laws abridging in a hundred ways what at first seemed his own happiness, and implying the solidarity of himself and his happiness with the race and theirs. This is what experience brought him to, and what conscience is concerned with: a number of laws determining our conduct in many ways, and implying our solidarity with others. But experience did not bring him to the

rule of every man just aiming, "according to the best of his judgment," at what might "have the appearance of being likely to
produce an overbalance of happiness to mankind in their present
state." It did not conduct him to this, or establish for him any
such rule of action as this. This is not his *experience*, and conscience turns on experience. It is not in the form of carving for
men's apparent happiness in defiance of the common rules of
justice and virtue, that the duty of caring for other men's happiness makes itself felt to us, but in the form of an obedience to
the common rules themselves of justice and of virtue. Those
rules, however, had indubitably in great part their rise in the
experience, that, by seeking solely his own private happiness, a
man made shipwreck of life.

In morals, we must not rely just on what may "have the appearance" to the individual, but on the experience of the race
as to happiness. To that experience, the individual, as one of the
race, is profoundly and intimately adapted. He may much more
safely conform himself to such experience than to his own crude
judgments upon "appearances;" nay, such experience has, if he
deals with himself fairly, a much stronger hold upon his conviction. Butler confuses the foreseen overbalance of happiness or
misery, which, as the result of experience in the race, has silently
and slowly determined our calling actions virtuous or vicious,
with that overbalance which each transient individual may
think he can foresee. The transient individual must not cut and
carve in the results of human experience, according to his crude
notions of what may constitute human happiness. His thought
of the obligation laid upon him by those rules of justice and
virtue, wherein the moral experience of our race has been
summed up, must rather be: "The will of mortal man did not
beget it, neither shall oblivion ever put it to sleep." But the rules
had their origin in man's desire for happiness notwithstanding.

2.

Impressive, then, as the *Sermons at the Rolls* are, and much as
they contain which is precious, I do not think that these sermons, setting forth Butler's theory of the foundation of morals,

will satisfy any one who in disquietude, and seeking earnestly
for a sure stay, comes for help to them. But the *Sermons at the
Rolls* were published in 1726, when Butler was but thirty-four
years old. They were all preached in the eight years between
1718 and 1726,—between the twenty-sixth year of Butler's life   5
and the thirty-fourth. The date is important. At that age a man
is, I think, more likely to attempt a highly systematic, intricate
theory of human nature and morals, than he is afterwards. And
if he does attempt it, it cannot well be satisfactory. The man is
hardly ripe for it, he has not had enough experience. So at least   10
one is disposed to say, as one regards the thing from the point of
view of a more mature age oneself. The *Analogy* did not come
till ten years after the Sermons. The *Analogy* appeared in 1736,
when Butler was forty-four. It is a riper work than the *Sermons
at the Rolls*. Perhaps it will seem in me the very height of over-   15
partiality to the merits of old age, of that unpopular condition
which I am myself approaching, if I say, that I would rather
have had the *opus magnum* of such a man as Butler, and on such
a subject as the philosophy of religion, ten years later from him
still. I would rather have had it from him at fifty-four than at   20
forty-four. To me, the most entirely satisfactory productions
of Butler are the *Six Sermons on Public Occasions*, all of them
later than the *Analogy;* the *Charge to the Clergy of Durham*,
delivered the year before his death; and a few fragments, also
dating from the close of his life.   25

But let us be thankful for what we have. The *Analogy* is a
work of great power; to read it, is a very valuable mental exercise. Not only does it contain, like the Sermons, many trains of
thought and many single observations which are profound and
precious, but the intellectual conduct of the work, so to speak,   30
seems to me to be more that of a master, to be much firmer
and clearer, more free from embarrassment and confusion, than
that of the Sermons. Of course the form of the work gave
Butler advantages which with the form of a sermon he could
not have. But the mental grasp, too, is, I think, visibly stronger 35
in the *Analogy*.

I have drawn your attention to the terms of unbounded
praise in which the *Analogy* is extolled. It is called "unanswer-

able." It is said to be "the most original and profound work extant in any language on the philosophy of religion." It is asserted, that, by his *Analogy*, Butler "placed metaphysic, which till then had nothing to support it but mere abstraction or
5   shadowy speculation, on the firm basis of observation and experiment."

I have also told you what is to my mind the one sole point of interest for us now, in a work like the *Analogy*. To those who search earnestly,—amid that break-up of traditional and con-
10 ventional notions respecting our life, its conduct, and its sanctions, which is undeniably befalling our age,—for some clear light and some sure stay, does the *Analogy* afford it to them? A religious work cannot touch us very deeply as a mere intellectual feat. Whether the *Analogy* was or was not calculated to
15 make the loose Deists of fashionable circles, in the year of grace 1736, feel uncomfortable, we do not, as I said the other night, care two straws, unless we hold the argumentative positions of those Deists; and we do not. What has the *Analogy* got to enlighten and help *us?* is the one important question.
20   Its object is to make men embrace religion. And that is just what we all ought most to desire: to make men embrace religion, which we may see to be full of what is salutary for them. Yet how many of them will not embrace it! Now, to every one with whom the impediment to its reception is not simply moral,
25 —culpable levity, or else a secret leaning to vice,—Butler professes to make out clearly in his *Analogy* that they *ought* to embrace it, and to embrace it, moreover, in the form of what is called orthodox Christianity, with its theosophy and miracles. And he professes to establish this by the analogy of religion,—
30 first of natural religion, then of revealed religion,—to the constitution and laws of nature.

Elsewhere I have remarked what advantage Butler had against the Deists of his own time, in the line of argument which he chose. But how does his argument in itself stand the scrutiny
35 of one who has no counter-thesis, such as that of the Deists, to make good against Butler? How does it affect one who has no wish at all to doubt or cavil, like the loose wits of fashionable society who angered Butler, still less any wish to mock; but

who comes to the *Analogy* with an honest desire to receive from it anything which he finds he can use?

Now, I do not remember to have anywhere seen pointed out the precise break-down, which such an inquirer must, it seems to me, be conscious of in Butler's argument from analogy. The argument is of this kind:—The reality of the laws of moral government of *this* world, says Butler, implies, by analogy, a like reality of laws of moral government in the second world, where we shall be hereafter.—The analogy is, in truth, used to prove not only the probable continuance of the laws of moral government, but also the probable existence of that future world in which they will be manifested. It *does* only prove the probable continuance of the laws of moral government in the future world, *supposing* that second world to exist. But for that existence it supplies no probability whatever. For it is not the laws of moral government which give us proof of this present world in which they are manifested; it is the experience that this present world actually exists, and is a place in which these laws are manifested. Show us, we may say to Butler, that a like place presents itself over again after we are dead, and we will allow that by analogy the same moral laws will probably continue to govern it. But this is all which analogy can prove in the matter. The positive existence of the world to come must be proved, like the positive existence of the present world, by *experience*. And of this experience Butler's argument furnishes, and can furnish, not one tittle.

There may be other reasons for believing in a second life beyond the grave. Christians in general consider that they get such grounds from revelation. And people who come to Butler with the belief already established, are not likely to ask themselves very closely what Butler's analogical reasoning on its behalf is good for. The reasoning is exercised in support of a thesis which does not require to be made out for them. But whoever comes to Butler in a state of genuine uncertainty, and has to lean with his whole weight on Butler's reasonings for support, will soon discover their fundamental weakness. The weakness goes through the *Analogy* from beginning to end. For example:—

"The states of life in which we ourselves existed formerly, in the womb and in our infancy, are almost as different from our present in mature age as it is possible to conceive any two states or degrees of life can be. Therefore, that we are to exist hereafter in a state as different (suppose) from our present as this is from the former, is but according to the analogy of nature."

There it is in the first chapter! But we have *experience* of the several different states succeeding one another in man's present life; that is what makes us believe in their succeeding one another here. We have no experience of a further different state beyond the limits of this life. If we had, we might freely admit that analogy renders it probable that that state may be as unlike to our actual state, as our actual state is to our state in the womb or in infancy. But that there *is* the further different state must first, for the argument from analogy to take effect, be proved from experience.

Again:—

"Sleep, or, however, a swoon, shows us," says Butler, "that our living powers exist when they are not exercised, and when there is no present capacity of exercising them. Therefore, there can no probability be collected from the reason of the thing that death will be their destruction."

But "the reason of the thing," in this matter, is simply experience; and we have experience of the living powers existing on through a swoon, we have none of their existing on through death.

Or, again, the form of the argument being altered, but its vice being still of just the same character:—"All presumption of death's being the destruction of living beings must go upon supposition that they are compounded and so discerptible." So says Butler, and then off he goes upon a metaphysical argument about consciousness being a single and indivisible power. But a doubter, who is dealing quite simply with himself, will stop Butler before ever his metaphysical argument begins, and say: "Not at all; the presumption of death's being the destruction of living beings does not go upon the supposition that they are compounded and so discerptible; it goes upon the unbroken experience that the living powers then cease."

Once more. "We see by experience," says Butler, "that men may lose their limbs, their organs of sense, and even the greatest part of these bodies, and yet remain the same living agents." Yes, we do. But that conscious life is possible with *some* of our bodily organs gone, does not prove that it is possible without *any*. We admit the first because it is shown to us by experience; we have no experience of the second.

I say, a man who is looking seriously for firm ground, cannot but soon come to perceive what Butler's argument in the *Analogy* really amounts to, and that there is no help to be got from it. "There is no shadow of anything unreasonable," begins Butler always, "in conceiving so-and-so,—in the conception of natural religion, in the conception of revealed religion." The answer of any earnest man must be in some words of Butler's own: "Suppositions are not to be looked on as true, because not incredible." "But," says Butler, "it is a fact that this life exists, and there are analogies in this life to the supposed system of natural and revealed religion. The existence of that system, therefore, is a fact also." "Nay," is the answer, "but we affirm the fact of this life, not because 'there is no shadow of anything unreasonable in conceiving it,' but because we experience it." As to the *fact*, experience is the touchstone.

"There is nothing incredible," argues Butler again, "that God, the moral and intelligent Author of all things, will reward and punish men for their actions hereafter, for the whole course of nature is a present instance of his exercising that government over us which implies in it rewarding and punishing." But how far does our positive experience go in this matter? What is fact of positive experience is, that inward satisfaction (let us fully concede this to Butler) follows one sort of actions, and inward dissatisfaction another; and, moreover, that also outward rewards and punishments do very generally follow certain actions. In this sense we *are* punished and rewarded; that is certain. And one must add, surely, that our not being punished and rewarded more completely and regularly might quite well, one would think, have been what suggested to mankind the notion of a second life, with a restitution of all things. But, be that as it may, we have no *experience*,—I say what is the mere undoubted fact,—we have no *experience* that it is a quasi-human agent, whom Butler calls the Author of Nature, a Being moral and intelligent, who thus rewards and punishes us.

But Butler alleges, that we have, not indeed experience of this, but demonstration. For he says that a uniform course of operation, this world as we see it, *nature*, necessarily implies an operating agent. It necessarily implies an intelligent designer with a will and a character, a ruler all-wise and all-powerful. And this quasi-human agent, this intelligent designer with a will and a character, since he is all-wise and all-powerful, and since he governs the world, and evidently, by what we see of natural rewards and punishments, exercises moral government over us here, but admittedly not more than in *some degree*, not yet *the perfection* of moral government,—this Governor must be reserving the complete consummation of his moral government for a second world hereafter. And the strength of Butler's argument against the Deists lay here: that they held, as he did, that a quasi-human agent, an intelligent designer with a will and a character, was demonstrably the author and governor of nature.

But in this supposed demonstrably true starting-point, common both to Butler and to the Deists, we are in full metaphysics. We are in that world of "mere abstraction or shadowy speculation," from which Butler was said to have rescued us and placed us on the firm basis of observation and experiment. The proposition that this world, as we see it, necessarily implies an intelligent designer with a will and a character, a quasi-human agent and governor, cannot, I think, but be felt, by any one who is brought fairly face to face with it and has to rest everything upon it, not to be self-demonstrating, nay, to be utterly impalpable. Evidently it is not of the same experimental character as the proposition that we *are* rewarded and punished according to our actions; or that, as St. Augustine says, *Sibi pœna est omnis inordinatus animus*. The proposition of St. Augustine produces, when it is urged, a sense of satisfying conviction, and we can go on to build upon it. But will any one say that the proposition, that the course of nature implies an operating agent with a will and a character, produces or can produce a like sense of satisfying conviction, and can in like manner be built upon? It cannot.

It does not appeal, like the other, to what is solid. It appeals, really, to the deep anthropomorphic tendency in man; and this tendency, when we examine the thing coolly, we feel that we cannot trust.

However, the proposition is thought to have scientific support in arguments drawn from *being, essence.* But even thus supported it never, I think, can produce in any one a sense of satisfying conviction; it produces, at most, a sense of puzzled submission. To build religion, or anything else which is to stand firm, upon such a sense as this, is vain. Religion must be built on ideas about which there is no puzzle. Therefore, in order to get rid of this foundation of puzzle for religion, and with a view to substituting a surer foundation, I have elsewhere tried to show in what confusion the metaphysical arguments drawn from *being, essence,* for an intelligent author of nature with a will and a character, have their rise. The assertion of such an author is then left with our anthropomorphic instinct as its sole warrant, and is seen not to be a safe foundation whereon to build all our certainties in religion. It is not axiomatic, it is not experimental. It deals with what is, in my judgment, altogether beyond our experience; it is purely abstract and speculative. A plain man, when he is asked how he can affirm that a house is made by an intelligent designer with a will and a character, and yet doubt whether a tree is made by an intelligent designer with a will and a character, must surely answer that he affirms a house to have been made by such a designer because he has experience of the fact, but that of the fact of a tree being made by such a designer he has none. And if pressed, how then can the tree possibly be there? surely the answer: "Perhaps from the tendency to grow!" is not so very unreasonable.

Butler admits that the assertion of his all-foreseeing, all-powerful designer, with a will and a character, involves grave difficulties. "Why anything of hazard and danger should be put upon such frail creatures as we are, may well be thought a difficulty in speculation." But he appeals, and no man ever appealed more impressively than he, to the sense we must have of our ignorance. Difficulties of this kind, he says, "are so apparently and wholly founded in our ignorance, that it is wonderful

they should be insisted upon by any but such as are weak
enough to think they are acquainted with the whole system of
things." And he speaks of "that infinitely absurd supposition
that we know the whole of the case." But does not the common
account of God by theologians, does not Butler's own assertion of the all-foreseeing, quasi-human designer, with a will and
a character, go upon the supposition that we know, at any rate,
a very great deal, and more than we actually do know, of the
case? And are not the difficulties alleged created by that supposition? And is not the appeal to our ignorance in fact an appeal to us, having taken a great deal for granted, to take something more for granted:—namely, that what we at first took for
granted has a satisfactory solution somewhere beyond the reach
of our knowledge?

Then, however, the argument from analogy is again used to
solve our difficulties. It is hard to understand how an almighty
moral Creator and Governor, designing the world as a place of
moral discipline for man, should have so contrived things that
the moral discipline altogether fails, in a vast number of cases, to
take effect. Butler, however, urges, that the world may have
been intended by its infinite almighty Author and Governor for
moral discipline, although, even, "the generality of men do not
improve or grow better in it;" because we see that "of the seeds
of vegetables, and bodies of animals, far the greatest part decay
before they are improved to maturity, and appear to be utterly
destroyed." But surely the natural answer is, that there is no
difficulty about millions of seeds missing their perfection, because we do not suppose nature an Infinite Almighty and Moral
Being; but that the difficulty in the other case is because we do
suppose God such a Being.

However, against the Deists who started with assuming a
quasi-human agent, a Being of infinite wisdom and power with a
will and a character, as a necessary conception, Butler's argument is very effective. And he says expressly that in his *Analogy*
the validity of this conception "is a principle gone upon as
proved, and generally known and confessed to be proved." But,
however, Butler in his *Analogy* affirms also (and the thing is important to be noted) "the direct and fundamental proof of Chris-

tianity" to be, just what the mass of its adherents have always supposed it to be:—miracles and the fulfilment of prophecy. And from a man like Butler this dictum will certainly require attention, even on the part of an inquirer who feels that Butler's metaphysics, and his argument from analogy, are unavailing.

But any clear-sighted inquirer will soon perceive that Butler's ability for handling these important matters of miracles and prophecy is not in proportion to his great powers of mind, and to his vigorous and effective use of those powers on other topics. Butler could not well, indeed, have then handled miracles and prophecy satisfactorily; the time was not ripe for it. Men's knowledge increases, their point of view changes, they come to see things differently. That is the reason, without any pretence of intellectual superiority, why men are now able to view miracles and prophecy more justly than Butler did. The insufficiency of his treatment of them is, indeed, manifest. Can anything be more express or determinate, he asks, than the fulfilment of prophecy mentioned in the Epistle to the Hebrews,— the fulfilment of the words, "Sacrifice and offering thou wouldest not, but a *body* hast thou prepared me," by the offering for man's sins of the *body* of Jesus Christ upon the cross? A man like Butler could not nowadays use an argument like that. He could not be unaware that the writer of the Epistle is using the false rendering of the Greek Bible, *a body hast thou prepared me*, instead of the true rendering of the original, *mine ears hast thou opened*, and gets his fulfilment of prophecy out of that false rendering;—a fulfilment, therefore, which is none at all.

Neither could Butler now speak of the Bible-history being all of it equally "authentic genuine history," or argue in behalf of this thesis as he does. It must evidently all stand or fall together, he argues; now, "there are characters in the Bible with all the internal marks imaginable of their being real." Most true, is the answer; there is plenty of fact in the Bible, there is also plenty of legend. John the Baptist and Simon Peter have all the internal marks imaginable of their being real characters; granted. But one Gospel makes Jesus disappear into Egypt directly after his birth, another makes him stay quietly on in Palestine. That John the Baptist and Simon Peter are real characters does not make this consistent history. As well say that because Mirabeau and Danton are real characters, an addition to Louis the Sixteenth's history which made him to be spirited away from Varennes into Germany, and then to come back after some time and resume his career in France, would not jar. No. "Things are what they are, and the consequences of them will be what they will be." And the accounts in the Gospels of the Holy Child's incarnation and infancy, and very many things in the Bible besides, are legends.

Again. "The belief of miracles by the Apostles and their contemporaries must be a proof of those facts, for they were such as came under the observation of their senses." The simple answer is: "But we know what the observation of men's senses, under certain circumstances, is worth." Yet further: "Though it is not of equal weight, yet it is of weight, that the martyrs of the next age, notwithstanding they were not eye-witnesses of those facts, as were the Apostles and their contemporaries, had however full opportunity to inform themselves whether they were true or not, and gave equal proof of their believing them to be true." The simple answer again is: "The martyrs never dreamed of informing themselves about the miracles in the manner supposed; for they never dreamed of doubting them, and could not have dreamed of it." If Butler cannot prove religion and Christianity by his reasonings from metaphysics and from analogy, most certainly he will not prove them by these reasonings on Bible-history.

But the wonderful thing about the *Analogy* is the poor insignificant result, even in Butler's own judgment,—the puny total outcome,—of all this accumulated evidence from analogy, metaphysics, and Bible-history. It is, after all, only "evidence which keeps the mind in doubt, perhaps in perplexity." The utmost it is calculated to beget is, "a serious doubting apprehension that it *may* be true." However, "in the daily course of life," says Butler, "our nature and condition necessarily require us to act upon evidence much lower than what is commonly called probable." In a matter, then, of such immense practical importance as religion, where the bad consequences of a mistake may be so incalculable, we ought, he says, unhesitatingly to act upon imperfect evidence. "It ought, in all reason, considering its infinite importance, to have nearly the same influence upon practice, as if it were thoroughly believed!" And such is, really, the upshot of the *Analogy*. Such is, when all is done, the "happy alliance" achieved by it "between faith and philosophy."

But we *do* not, in the daily course of life, act upon evidence which *we ourselves conceive* to be much lower than what is commonly called probable. If I am going to take a walk out of Edinburgh, and thought of choosing the Portobello road, and a travelling menagerie is taking the same road, it is certainly possible that a tiger may escape from the menagerie and devour me if I take that road; but the evidence that he will is certainly, also, much lower than what is commonly called probable. Well, I do not, on that low degree of evidence, avoid the Portobello road and take another. But the duty of acting on such a sort of evidence is really made by Butler the motive for a man's following the road of religion,—the way of peace.

How unlike, above all, is this motive to the motive always supposed in the book itself of our religion, in the Bible! After reading the *Analogy* one goes instinctively to bathe one's spirit in the Bible again, to be refreshed by its boundless certitude and exhilaration. "The Eternal is the strength of my life!" "The foundation of God standeth sure!"—that is the constant tone of religion in the Bible. "If I tell you the *truth*, why do ye not believe me?—the *evident* truth, that whoever comes to me has life; and evident, because whoever *does* come, gets it!" That is the evidence to constrain our practice which is offered by Christianity.

3.

Let us, then, confess it to ourselves plainly. The *Analogy*, the great work on which such immense praise has been lavished, is, for all real intents and purposes now, a failure; it does not serve. It seemed once to have a spell and a power; but the *Zeit-Geist* breathes upon it, and we rub our eyes, and it has the spell and the power no longer. It has the effect upon me, as I contemplate it, of a stately and severe fortress, with thick and

high walls, built of old to control the kingdom of evil;—but the
gates are open, and the guards gone.

For to control the kingdom of evil the work was, no doubt,
designed. Whatever may be the proper tendencies of Deism as a
5 speculative opinion, there can be no doubt, I think, that the
loose Deism of fashionable circles, as seen by Butler, had a
tendency to minimize religion and morality, to reduce and im-
pair their authority. Butler's Deists were, in fact, for the most
part free-living people who said, *We are Deists*, as the least they
10 could say; as another mode of saying: "We think little of religion in general, and of Christianity in particular." Butler, who
felt to the bottom of his soul the obligation of religion in general, and of Christianity in particular, set himself to establish the
obligation of them against these lax people, who in fact denied
15 it. And the religion and the Christianity, of which Butler set
himself to establish the obligation, were religion and Christianity in the form then received and current. And in this form
he could establish their obligation as against his Deistical opponents. But he could not establish them so as quite to suit his
20 own mind and soul, so as to satisfy himself fully.

Hence his labour and sorrow, his air of weariness, depression,
and gloom;—the air of a man who cannot get beyond "evidence
which keeps the mind in doubt, perhaps in perplexity." Butler
"most readily acknowledges that the foregoing treatise" (his
25 *Analogy*) "is by no means satisfactory; very far indeed from
it." He quotes the Preacher's account of what he himself had
found in life, as the true account of what man may expect here
below:—"Great ignorance of the works of God and the method
of his providence in the government of the world; great labour
30 and weariness in the search and observation he employs himself
about; and great disappointment, pain, and even vexation of
mind upon that which he remarks of the appearances of things
and of what is going forward upon this earth." "The result of
the Preacher's whole review and inspection is," says Butler,
35 "sorrow, perplexity, a sense of his necessary ignorance." That
is certainly a true description of the impression the Preacher
leaves on us of his own frame of mind; and it is not a bad description of Butler's frame of mind also. But so far is it from

being a true description of the right tone and temper of man according to the Bible-conception of it, that the Book of Ecclesiastes, which seems to recommend that temper, was nearly excluded from the Canon on this very account, and was only saved by its animating return, in its last verses, to the gen- 5 uine tradition of Israel: "Let us hear the conclusion of the whole matter: fear God and keep his commandments, for this is the whole duty of man."

But yet, in spite of his gloom, in spite of the failure of his *Analogy* to serve our needs, Butler remains a personage of real 10 grandeur for us. This pathetic figure, with its earnestness, its strenuous rectitude, its firm faith both in religion and in reason, does in some measure help us, does point the way for us. But-ler's profound sense, that inattention to religion implies "a dis-solute immoral temper of mind," engraves itself upon his read- 15 ers' thoughts also, and comes to govern them. His conviction, that religion and Christianity do somehow "in themselves en-tirely fall in with our natural sense of things," that they are true, and that their truth, moreover, is somehow to be estab-lished and justified on plain grounds of reason,—this wholesome 20 and invaluable conviction, also, gains us as we read him. The ordinary religionists of Butler's day might well be startled, as they were, by this bishop with the strange, novel, and unhal-lowed notion, full of dangerous consequence, of "referring mankind to a law of nature or virtue, written on their hearts." 25 The pamphleteer, who accused Butler of dying a Papist, de-clares plainly that he for his part "has no better opinion of the certainty, clearness, uniformity, universality, etc., of this law, than he has of the importance of external religion." But Butler *did* believe in the certainty of this law. It was the real founda- 30 tion of things for him. With awful reverence, he saluted, and he set himself to study and to follow, this "course of life marked out for man by nature, whatever that nature be." And he was for perfect fairness of mind in considering the evidence for this law, or for anything else. "It is fit things be stated and consid- 35 ered as they really are." "Things are what they are, and the consequences of them will be what they will be; why, then, should we desire to be deceived?" And he believed in reason.

"I express myself with caution, lest I should be mistaken to vilify reason, which is indeed the only faculty we have wherewith to judge concerning anything, even revelation itself." Such was Butler's fidelity to that sacred light to which religion
5 makes too many people false,—reason.

It always seems to me, that with Butler's deep sense that "the government of the world is carried on by general laws;" with his deep sense, too, of our ignorance,—nay, that "it is indeed, in general, no more than effects that the most knowing are ac-
10 quainted with, for as to *causes*, they are as entirely in the dark as the most ignorant,"—he would have found no insuperable difficulty in bringing himself to regard the power of "the law of virtue we are born under," as an idea equivalent to the religious idea of the power of God, without determining, or think-
15 ing that he had the means to determine, whether this power was a quasi-human agent or not. But a second world under a righteous judge, who should redress the imperfect balance of things as they are in this world, seemed to Butler indispensable. Yet no one has spoken more truly and nobly than he, of the natural
20 victoriousness of virtue, even in this world. He finds a tendency of virtue to prevail, which he can only describe as "somewhat moral in the essential constitution of things;" as "a declaration from the Author of Nature, determinate and not to be evaded, in favour of virtue and against vice." True, virtue is often over-
25 borne. But this is plainly a perversion. "Our finding virtue to be hindered from procuring to itself its due superiority and advantages, is no objection against its having, in the essential nature of the thing, a tendency to procure them." And he can see, he says, "in the nature of things, a tendency in virtue and vice to
30 produce the good and bad effects now mentioned, in a greater degree than they do in fact produce them." Length of time, however, is required for working this fully out; whereas "men are impatient and for precipitating things." "There must be sufficient length of time; for the complete success of virtue, as of
35 reason, cannot, from the nature of the thing, be otherwise than gradual." "Still, the constitution of our nature is as it is; our happiness and misery *are* trusted to our conduct, and made to depend upon it." And our comfort of hope is, that "though the

higher degree of distributive justice, which nature points out
and leads towards, is prevented for a time from taking place, it
is by obstacles which the state of this world unhappily throws in
its way, and which therefore are in their nature temporary."
And Butler supposes and describes an ideal society upon earth,   5
where "this happy tendency of virtue," as he calls it, should at
last come to prevail, in a way which brings straight to our
thoughts and to our lips the Bible-expression: *the kingdom of
God*. However, Butler decides that good men cannot now unite
sufficiently to bring this better society about; that it cannot,   10
therefore, be brought about in the present known course of
nature, and that it must be meant to come to pass in another
world beyond the grave.

Now, the very expression which I have just used, *the kingdom of God*, does certainly, however little it may at present be   15
usual with religious people to think so, it does certainly suggest
a different conclusion from Butler's. It does point to a transformation of this present world through the victory of what
Butler calls virtue, and what the Bible calls righteousness, and
what in general religious people call goodness; it does suggest   20
such transformation as possible. This transformation is the great
original idea of the Christian Gospel; nay, it is properly the
Gospel or *good news* itself. "The kingdom of God is at hand,"
said Jesus Christ, when he first came preaching; "repent, and
believe the good news." Jesus "talked" to the people "about the   25
kingdom of God." He told the young man, whom he called to
follow him, to "go and spread the news of the kingdom of God."
In the Acts, we find the disciples "preaching the kingdom of
God," "testifying concerning the kingdom of God," still in their
Master's manner and words. And it is undeniable that whoever   30
thinks that virtue and goodness will finally come to prevail in
this present world so as to transform it, who believes that they
are even now surely though slowly prevailing, and himself
does all he can to help the work forward,—as he acquires in
this way an experimental sense of the truth of Christianity   35
which is of the strongest possible kind, so he is, also, entirely in
the tradition and ideas of the Founder of Christianity. In like
manner, whoever places immortal life in coming to live, even

here in this present world, with that higher and impersonal life
on which, in speaking of self-love, we insisted,—and in thus no
longer living to himself but *living*, as St. Paul says, *to God*,—
does entirely conform himself to the doctrine and example of
5 the Saviour of mankind, Jesus Christ, who "annulled death, and
brought life and immortality to light through the Gospel." And
could Butler, whose work has many precious and instructive
pointings this way, have boldly entered the way and steadily
pursued it, his work would not, I think, have borne the em-
10 barrassed, inconclusive, and even mournful character, which is
apparent in it now.

Let us not, however, overrate the mournfulness of this great
man, or underrate his consolations. The power of religion which
actuated him was, as is the case with so many of us, better, pro-
15 founder, and happier, than the scheme of religion which he
could draw out in his books. Nowhere does this power show itself more touchingly than in a fragment or two,—memoranda
for his own use,—which are among the last things that his pen
wrote before death brushed it from his hand for ever. "Hunger
20 and thirst after righteousness," he writes, "till filled with it by
being made partaker of the divine nature!" And again he writes,
using and underscoring words of the Latin Vulgate which are
more earnest and expressive than the words of our English
version in that place: "*Sicut oculi servorum* intenti sunt *ad
25 manum dominorum suorum, sicut oculi ancillæ ad manum
dominæ suæ, ita oculi nostri ad Deum nostrum, donec miserea-
tur nostri;*—As the eyes of servants *are bent* towards the hand
of their masters, and the eyes of a maiden towards the hand of
her mistress, even so are our eyes towards our God, until he have
30 mercy upon us."

Let us leave Butler, after all our long scrutiny of him, with
these for his last words!

The Church of England[1]

I have heard it confidently asserted, that the Church of England is an institution so thoroughly artificial, and of which the justification, if any justification for it can be found, must be sought in reasons so extremely far-fetched, that only highly trained and educated people can be made to see that it has a possible defence at all, and that to undertake its defence before a plain audience of working men would be hopeless. It would be very interesting to try the experiment; and I had long had a half-formed design of endeavouring to show to an audience of working men the case, as I for my part conceived it, on behalf of the Church of England. But meanwhile there comes to me my friend, your President, and reminds me of an old request of his that I should some day speak in this hall, and presses me to comply with it this very season. And if I am to speak at Sion College, and to the London clergy, and at this juncture, how can I help remembering my old design of speaking about the Church of England;—remembering it, and being tempted, though before a very different audience, to take that subject?

Jeremy Taylor says: "Every minister ought to concern himself in the faults of them that are present, but not of the absent." "Every minister," he says again, "ought to preach to his hearers and urge *their* duty; St. John the Baptist told the soldiers what the soldiers should do, but troubled not their heads with what was the duty of the Scribes and Pharisees." And certainly one should not defend the Church of England to an audience of clergy and to an audience of artisans in quite the same way. But perhaps one ought not to care to put at all before the

[1] The following discourse was delivered as an address to the London clergy at Sion College.

63

clergy the case for the Church of England, but rather one
should bring before them the case against it. For the case of the
Church of England is supposed to be their own case, and they
are the parties interested; and to commend their own case to the
5 parties interested is useless, but what may do them most good is
rather to show them its defects. And in this view, the profitable
thing for the London clergy at Sion College to hear, would be,
perhaps, a lecture on disestablishment, an exhortation to "happy
despatch."

10 Yet this is not so, for the simple reason that the Church of
England is not a private sect but a national institution. There
can be no greater mistake than to regard the cause of the Church
of England as the cause of the clergy, and the clergy as the
parties concerned for the maintenance of the Church of En-
15 gland. The clergy are a very small minority of the nation. As
the Church of England will not be abolished to gratify the
jealousy of this and that private sect, also a small minority of the
nation, so neither will it be maintained to gratify the interest of
the clergy. Public institutions must have public reasons for
20 existing; and if at any time there arise circumstances and dangers which induce a return to those reasons, so as to set them in
a clear light to oneself again and to make sure of them, the
clergy may with just as much propriety do this, or assist at its
being done,—nay, they are as much bound to do it,—as any
25 other members of the community.

But some one will perhaps be disposed to say, that though
there is no impropriety in your hearing the Church of England
defended, yet there is an impropriety in my defending it to you.
A man who has published a good deal which is at variance with
30 the body of theological doctrine commonly received in the
Church of England and commonly preached by its ministers,
cannot well, it may be thought, stand up before the clergy as a
friend to their cause and to that of the Church. Professed ardent
enemies of the Church have assured me that I am really, in their
35 opinion, one of the worst enemies that the Church has,—a much
worse enemy than themselves. Perhaps that opinion is shared by
some of those who now hear me. I make bold to say that it is
totally erroneous. It is founded in an entire misconception of the

character and scope of what I have written concerning religion. I regard the Church of England as, in fact, a great national society for the promotion of what is commonly called *goodness*, and for promoting it through the most effectual means possible, the only means which are really and truly effectual for the object: through the means of the Christian religion and of the Bible. This plain practical object is undeniably the object of the Church of England and of the clergy. "Our province," says Butler, whose sayings come the more readily to my mind because I have been very busy with him lately, "our province is virtue and religion, life and manners, the science of improving the temper and making the heart better. This is the field assigned us to cultivate; how much it has lain neglected is indeed astonishing. He who should find out one rule to assist us in this work would deserve infinitely better of mankind than all the improvers of other knowledge put together." This is indeed true religion, true Christianity. *Illi sunt veri fideles Tui*, says the "Imitation," *qui totam vitam suam ad emendationem disponunt.* Undoubtedly this is so; and the more we come to see and feel it to be so, the more shall we get a happy sense of clearness and certainty in religion.

Now, to put a new construction upon many things that are said in the Bible, to point out errors in the Bible, errors in the dealings of theologians with it, is exactly the sort of "other knowledge" which Butler disparages by comparison with a knowledge more important. Perhaps he goes too far when he disparages it so absolutely as in another place he does, where he makes Moses conclude, and appears to agree with Moses in concluding, that "*the only knowledge*, which is of any avail to us, is that which teaches us our duty, or assists us in the discharge of it." "If," says he, "the discoveries of men of deep research and curious inquiry serve the cause of virtue and religion, in the way of proof, motive to practice, or assistance in it; or if they tend to render life less unhappy and promote its satisfactions, then they are most usefully employed; but bringing things to light, alone and of itself, is of no manner of use any otherwise than as an entertainment or diversion." "Bringing things to light" is not properly to be spoken of, I think, quite in this fashion. Still, with the low *comparative* rank which Butler assigns to it we will not quarrel. And when Butler urges that "knowledge is not our proper happiness," and that "men of research and curious inquiry should just be put in mind not to mistake what they are doing," we may all of us readily admit that his admonitions are wise and salutary.

And therefore the object of the Church, which is in large the promotion of goodness, and the business of the clergy, which is to teach men their duty and to assist them in the discharge of it, do really and truly interest me more, and do appear in my eyes as things more valuable and important, than the object and business pursued in those writings of mine which are in question,—writings which seek to put a new construction on much in the Bible, to alter the current criticism of it, to invalidate the conclusions of theologians from it. If the two are to conflict, I had rather that it should be the object and business of those writings which should have to give way. Most certainly the establishment of an improved biblical criticism, or the demolition of the systems of theologians, will never in itself avail to teach men their duty or to assist them in the discharge of it. Perhaps, even, no one can very much give himself to such objects without running some risk of over-valuing their importance and of being diverted by them from practice.

But there are times when practice itself, when the very object of the Church and of the clergy,—the promotion of goodness through the instrumentality of the Christian religion and of the Bible,—is endangered, with many persons, from the predominance of the systems of theologians, and from the want of a new and better construction than theirs to put upon the Bible. And ours is a time of this kind; such, at least, is my conviction. Nor are persons free to say that we had better all of us stick to practice, and resolve not to trouble ourselves with speculative questions of biblical and theological criticism. No; such questions catch men in a season and manner which does not depend on their own will, and often their whole spirit is bewildered by them and their former hold on practice seems threatened. Well then, at this point and for those persons, the criticism which I have attempted is designed to come in; when, for want of some such new criticism, their practical hold on the Bible and on the Christian religion seems to be threatened. The criticism is not presented as something universally salutary and indispensable, far less as any substitute for a practical hold upon Christianity and the Bible, or of at all comparable value with it. The user may even, if he likes, having in view the risks which beset practice from the misemployment of such criticism, say while he uses it that he is but making himself friends through the mammon of unrighteousness.

It is evident that the author of such criticism, holding this to be its relation to the object of the Church of England and to the business of the clergy, and holding it so cheap by comparison with that object and that business, is by no means constituted, through the fact of his having published it, an enemy of the Church and clergy, or precluded from feeling and expressing a hearty desire for their preservation.

II

I have called the Church of England,—to give the plainest and most direct idea I could of its real reason for existing,—*a great national society for the promotion of goodness*. Nothing interests people, after all, so much as goodness;[1] and it is in human nature that what interests men very much they should not leave to private and chance handling, but should give to it a public institution. There may be very important things to which public institution is not given; but it will generally turn out, we shall find, that they are things of which the whole community does not strongly feel the importance. Art and literature are very important things, and art and literature, it is often urged, are not matters of public institution in England; why, then, should religion be? The answer is, that so far as art and literature are not matters of public institution like religion, this is because the whole community has not felt them to be of vital interest and importance to it, as it feels religion to be. In only one fa-

[1] "We have no clear conception of any positive moral attribute in the Supreme Being, but what may be resolved up into goodness."—Butler, in Sermon *Upon the Love of Our Neighbour*.

mous community, perhaps, has the people at large felt art and
literature to be necessaries of life, as with us the people at large
has felt religion to be. That community was ancient Athens.
And in ancient Athens art and literature were matters of pub-
5   lic and national institution, like religion. In the Christian nations
of modern Europe we find religion, alone of spiritual concerns,
to have had a regular public organisation given to it, because
alone of spiritual concerns religion was felt by every one to interest the nation profoundly, just like social order and security.
10   It is true, we see a great community across the Atlantic, the
United States of America, where it cannot be said that religion
does not interest people, and where, notwithstanding, there is
no public institution and organisation of religion. But that is
because the United States were colonised by people who, from
15 special circumstances, had in this country been led to adopt the
theory and the habit, then novel, of separatism; and who carried
the already formed theory and habit into America, and there
gave effect to it. The same is to be said of some of our chief
colonial dependencies. Their communities are made up, in a
20 remarkably large proportion, out of that sort and class of English people in whom the theory and habit of separatism exist
formed, owing to certain old religious conflicts in this country,
already. The theory and the habit of separatism soon make a
common form of religion seem a thing both impossible and un-
25 desirable; and without a common form of religion there cannot well be a public institution of it. Still, all this does not make
the public institution of a thing so important as religion to be
any the less the evident natural instinct of mankind, their plain
first impulse in the matter; neither does it make that first impulse
30 to be any the less in itself a just one.
    For a just one it is in itself, surely. All that is said to make it
out to be so, said by Butler for instance,—whom I have already
quoted, and whose practical view of things is almost always so
sound and weighty,—seems to me of an evidence and solidity
35 quite indisputable. The public institution of religion, he again
and again insists, is "a standing publication of the Gospel," "a
serious call upon men to attend to it," and therefore of an
"effect very important and valuable." A visible Church, with a

publicly instituted form of religion, is, he says, "like a city upon a hill,—a standing memorial to the world of the duty which we owe our Maker; to call men continually, both by example and instruction, to attend to it, and, by the form of religion ever before their eyes, remind them of the reality; to be the reposi- 5 tory of the oracles of God; to hold up the light of revelation in aid to that of nature, and propagate it throughout all generations to the end of the world." "That which men have accounted religion," he says again, in his charge to the clergy of Durham, "has had, generally speaking, a great and conspicuous 10 part in all public appearances, and the face of it has been kept up with great reverence throughout all ranks from the highest to the lowest; and without somewhat of this nature, piety will grow languid even among the better sort of men, and the worst will go on quietly in an abandoned course, with fewer interrup- 15 tions from within than they would have, were religious reflections forced oftener upon their minds, and, consequently, with less probability of their amendment." Here, I say, is surely abundant reason suggested, if the thing were not already clear enough of itself, why a society for the promotion of good- 20 ness, such as the Church of England in its fundamental design is, should at the same time be a national society, a society with a public character and a publicly instituted form of proceeding.

And yet with what enemies and dangers is this reasonable and 25 natural arrangement now encompassed here! I open the *Fortnightly Review* for the beginning of the present year,[1] in order to read the political summary, sure to be written with ability and vigour, and to find there what lines of agitation are in prospect for us. Well, I am told in the political summary that the 30 disestablishment of the Church of England is "a question which the very Spirit of Time has borne on into the first place." The Spirit of Time is a personage for whose operations I have myself the greatest respect; whatever he does, is, in my opinion, of the gravest effect. And he has borne, we are told, the question of the 35 disestablishment of the Church of England into the very first rank of questions in agitation. "The agitation," continues the

[1] 1876.

summarist, "is the least factitious of any political movement that
has taken place in our time. It is the one subject on which you
are most certain of having a crowded meeting in any large town
in England. It is the one bond of union between the most important groups of Liberals. Even the Tapers and Tadpoles of
politics must admit that this party is rapidly becoming really
formidable."

Then our writer proceeds to enumerate the forces of his
party. It comprises practically, he says, the whole body of the
Protestant Nonconformists; this is, indeed, a thing of course.
But the Wesleyans, too, he adds, are almost certainly about to
join it; while of the Catholics it is calculated that two-thirds
would vote for "the policy of taking away artificial advantages
from a rival hierarchy."

"From within the Church itself," he goes on, "there are gradually
coming allies of each of the three colours: Sacramentalists, weary
of the Erastian bonds of Parliament and the Privy Council; Evan-
gelicals, exasperated by State connivance with a Romanising reaction; Broad Churchmen, who are beginning to see, first, that the laity
in a Free Church would hold the keys of the treasury, and would
therefore be better able than they are now to secure liberality of
doctrine in their clergy; and, secondly, are beginning to see that the
straining to make the old bottles of rite and formulary hold the wine
of new thought withers up intellectual manliness, straightforward-
ness, and vigorous health of conscience, both in those who practise
these economies and in those whom their moderation fascinates."

The thing could not well be more forcibly stated, and the
prospect for the Established Church does indeed, as thus presented, seem black enough. But we have still to hear of the
disposition of the great body of the flock, of the working multitudes. "As for the working classes," the writer says, "the religious portion would follow the policy of the sect to which
the individual happened to belong; while that portion which is
not attached either to church or chapel, apart from personal or
local considerations of accidental force, would certainly go for
disestablishment. Not a single leader of the industrial class,
with any pretence to a representative character, but is already
strongly and distinctly pledged." And the conclusion is, that

"the cause of disestablishment, so far from being the forlorn crusade of a handful of fanatics, is in fact a cause to which a greater number of Radicals of all kinds may be expected to rally than to any other cause whatever." And therefore this cause should be made by all Liberals, the writer argues, the real object, and other things should be treated as secondary and contributory to it. "Let us reform our electoral machinery," says he, "by all means, but let us understand, and make others understand, that we only seek this because we seek something else: the disestablishment of the Episcopal Church in England." Such is the programme of what calls itself "scientific liberalism."

By far the most formidable force in the array of dangers which this critic has mustered to threaten the Church of England, is the estrangement of the working classes,—of that part of them, too, which has no attachment to Dissent, but which is simply zealous about social and political questions. This part may not be overwhelming in numbers, but it is the living and leading part of the whole to which it belongs. Its sentiment tends to become, with time, the sentiment of the whole. If its sentiment is unalterably hostile to the Church of England, if the character of the Church is such that this must needs be so and remain so, then the question of disestablishment is, I think, settled. The Church of England cannot, in the long run, stand.

The ideal of the working classes is a future,—a future on earth, not up in the sky,—which shall profoundly change and ameliorate things for them; an immense social progress, nay, a social transformation; in short, as their song goes, "a good time coming." And the Church is supposed to be an appendage to the Barbarians, as I have somewhere, in joke, called it; an institution devoted above all to the landed gentry, but also to the propertied and satisfied classes generally; favouring immobility, preaching submission, and reserving transformation in general for the other side of the grave.

Such a Church, I admit, cannot possibly nowadays attach the working classes, or be viewed with anything but disfavour by them. But certainly the superstitious worship of existing social facts, a devoted obsequiousness to the landed and propertied and satisfied classes, does not inhere in the Christian religion.

The Church does not get it from the Bible. Exception is taken
to its being said that there is communism in the Bible, because
we see that communists are fierce, violent, insurrectionary people, with temper and actions abhorrent to the spirit of the Bible.
5 But if we say, on the one hand, that the Bible utterly condemns
all violence, revolt, fierceness, and self-assertion, then we may
safely say, on the other hand, that there is certainly communism
in the Bible. The truth is, the Bible enjoins endless self-sacrifice
all round; and to any one who has grasped this idea, the super-
10 stitious worship of property, the reverent devotedness to the
propertied and satisfied classes, is impossible. And the Christian
Church has, I boldly say, been the fruitful parent of men who,
having grasped this idea, have been exempt from this superstu-
tion. Institutions are to be judged by their great men; in the end,
15 they take their line from their great men. The Christian Church,
and the line which is natural to it and which will one day prevail in it, is to be judged from the saints and the tone of the
saints. Now really, if there have been any people in the world
free from illusions about the divine origin and divine sanctions
20 of social facts just as they stand,—open, therefore, to the popular hopes of a profound renovation and a happier future,—it has
been those inspired idiots, the poets and the saints. Nobody
nowadays attends much to what the poets say, so I leave them
on one side. But listen to a saint on the origin of property;
25 listen to Pascal. " 'This dog belongs to *me*,' said these poor
children; 'that place in the sun is *mine!*' Behold the beginning
and the image of all usurpation upon earth!" Listen to him in-
structing the young Duke of Roannez as to the source and
sacredness of his rank and his estates. First as to his estates:—

30 "Do you imagine," he says, "that it is by some way of nature that
your property has passed from your ancestors to you? Such is not
the case. This order is but founded on the simple will and pleasure
of legislators, who may have had good reasons for what they did,
but not one of their reasons was taken from any natural right of
35 yours over these possessions. If they had chosen to ordain that this
property, after having been held by your father during his lifetime,
should revert to the commonwealth after his death, you would have
had no ground for complaint. Thus your whole title to your prop-

erty is not a title from nature, but a title of human creation. A different turn of imagination in the law-makers would have left you poor; and it is only that combination of the chance which produced your birth with the turn of fancy producing laws advantageous to you, which makes you the master of all these possessions." 5

And then, the property having been dealt with, comes the turn of the rank:—

"There are two sorts of grandeurs in the world; grandeurs which men have set up, and natural grandeurs. The grandeurs which men have set up depend on the will and pleasure of men. Dignities and 10 nobility are grandeurs of this kind. In one country they honour nobles, in another commoners; here the eldest son, there the youngest son. Why? because such has been men's will and pleasure."

There, certainly, speaks a great voice of religion without any superstitious awe of rank and of property! The treasures of 15 Pascal's scorn are boundless, and they are magnificent. They are poured out in full flood on the superstitious awe in question. The only doubt may be, perhaps, whether they are not poured out on it too cruelly, too overwhelmingly. But in what secular writer shall we find anything to match them? 20

Ay, or in what saint or doctor, some one will say, of the Church of England? If there is a stronghold of stolid deference to the illusions of the aristocratic and propertied classes, the Church of England, many people will maintain, is that stronghold. It is the most formidable complaint against the Church, 25 the complaint which creates its most serious danger. There is nothing like having the very words of the complainants themselves in a case of this sort. "I wish," says Mr. Goldwin Smith, "I wish the clergy would consider whether something of the decline of Christianity may not be due to the fact that for ages 30 Christianity has been accepted by the clergy of the Established Church as the ally of political and social injustice." "The Church of England," says Mr. John Morley, "is the ally of tyranny, the organ of social oppression, the champion of intellectual bondage." There are the leaders!—and the *Beehive* shall 35 give us the opinion of the rank and file. "The clergy could not take money from the employing classes and put it into the pockets of the employed; but they might have insisted on such a humane consideration and Christian regard for human welfare, as would have so influenced men's dealings in regard to each other as to prevent our present misery and suffering."

5   You will observe, by the way, and it is a touching thing to witness, that the complaint of the real sufferers, as they think themselves, is in a strain comparatively calm and mild; how much milder than the invective of their literary leaders! Still, the upshot of the complaint is the same with both. The Church

10   shares and serves the prejudices of rank and property, instead of contending with them.

Now, I say once more that every Church is to be judged by its great men. Theirs are the authoritative utterances. They survive. They lay hold, sooner or later, and in proportion to their

15   impressiveness and truth, on the minds of Churchmen to whom they come down. They strike the note to be finally taken in the Church. Listen, then, to this on "the seemingly enormous discrimination," as the speaker calls it, "among men":—

"That distinction which thou standest upon, and which seemeth

20   so vast, between thy poor neighbour and thee, what is it? whence did it come? whither tends it? It is not anywise natural, or according to primitive design. Inequality and private interest in things (together with sicknesses and pains, together with all other infelicities and inconveniences) were the by-blows of our guilt; sin introduced

25   these degrees and distances; it devised the names of rich and poor; it begot these ingrossings and inclosures of things; it forged those two small pestilent words, *meum* and *tuum*, which have engendered so much strife among men, and created so much mischief in the world; these preternatural distinctions were, I say, brooded by our fault,

30   and are in great part fostered and maintained thereby; for were we generally so good, so just, so charitable as we should be, they could hardly subsist, especially in that measure they do. God, indeed (for promoting some good ends and for prevention of some mischiefs apt to spring from our ill-nature in this our lapsed state, particularly

35   to prevent the strife and disorder which scrambling would cause among men, presuming on equal right and parity of force), doth suffer them in some manner to continue; but we mistake if we think that natural equality and community are in effect quite taken away;

or that all the world is so cantonised among a few that the rest have no share therein."

Who is it who says that? It is one of the eminently representative men of the English Church, its best and soundest moralist; a man sober-minded, weighty, esteemed;—it is Barrow. And it is Barrow in the full blaze of the Restoration, in his Hospital Sermon of 1671.

Well, then, a fascinated awe of class-privileges, station, and property, a belief in the divine appointment, perfectness, and perpetuity of existing social arrangements, is not the authentic tradition of the Church of England. It is important to insist upon this, important for the Church to feel and avow it, because no institution with these prejudices could possibly carry the working classes with it. And it is necessary for the Church, if it is to live, that it should carry the working classes with it. Suffer me, after quoting to you Jeremy Taylor and Butler and Pascal and Barrow, to quote to you a much less orthodox personage: M. Renan. But what I am going to quote from him is profoundly true. He has been observing that Christianity, at its outset, had an immense attraction for the popular classes, as he calls them; "the popular classes whom the State and religion neglected equally." And he proceeds: "Here is the great lesson of this history for our own age; the times correspond to one another; the future will belong to that party which can get hold of the popular classes and elevate them." "But in our days," M. Renan adds, "the difficulty is far greater than it ever was." And this is true; the difficulty is great, very great. But the thing has to be done, and the Church is the right power to do it.

Now, the Church tends, people say, at present to become more mixed and popular than it used to be in the composition of its clergy. They are recruited from a wider field. Sometimes one hears this lamented, and its disadvantages insisted upon. But, in view of a power of comprehending popular ideals and sympathising with them, it has, I think, its advantage. No one can overlook or deny the immense labours and sacrifices of the clergy for the improvement of the condition of the popular, the working classes;—for their schools, for instance, and for their

physical well-being in countless ways. But this is not enough
without a positive sympathy with popular ideals. And the great
popular ideal is, as I have said, an immense renovation and
transformation of things, a far better and happier society in the
5   future than ours is now. Mixed with all manner of alloy and
false notions this ideal often is, yet in itself it is precious, it is
true. And let me observe, it is also the ideal of our religion. It is
the business of our religion to make us believe in this very ideal;
it is the business of the clergy to profess and to preach it. In
10 this view it is really well to consider, how entirely our religious
teaching and preaching, and our creeds, and what passes with us
for "the gospel," turn on quite other matters from the fundamental matter of the primitive gospel, or good news, of our
Saviour himself. This gospel was the ideal of popular hope and
15 longing, an immense renovation and transformation of things:
the kingdom of God. "Jesus came into Galilee proclaiming the
good news of God and saying: The time is fulfilled and the
kingdom of God is at hand; repent and believe the good news."
Jesus went about the cities and villages "proclaiming the good
20 news of the kingdom." The multitudes followed him, and he
"took them and talked to them about the kingdom of God." He
told his disciples to preach this. "Go thou, and spread the news
of the kingdom of God." "Into whatever city ye enter, say to
them: The kingdom of God has come nigh unto you." He told
25 his disciples to pray for it,—to pray: "Thy kingdom come!" He
told them to seek and study it before all things. "Seek first God's
righteousness and kingdom." He said that the news of it should
be published throughout the world. "This good news of the
kingdom shall be proclaimed in the whole world, for a witness
30 to all nations." And it was a kingdom here on earth, not in some
other world unseen. It was "God's will done, as in heaven, so on
earth."

And in this line the preaching went on for some time after
our Saviour's death. Philip, in Samaria, "delivers the good news
35 concerning the kingdom of God." Paul, at Ephesus, "discusses
and persuades concerning the kingdom of God." At Rome,
he "testifies to the kingdom of God," "proclaims the kingdom
of God." He tells the Corinthians that Christ sent him "not to

baptize but to deliver the good news,"—the good news of the kingdom of God. True, additions soon appear to the original gospel, which explain how preaching came to diverge from it. The additions were inevitable. The kingdom of God was realisable only through Jesus,—was impossible without Jesus. And therefore the preaching concerning Jesus had necessarily to be added to the preaching concerning the kingdom. Accordingly, we find Philip "delivering the good news concerning the kingdom of God, *and the name of Jesus Christ.*" We find him "delivering (to the eunuch) the good news of *Jesus.*" We find Paul "proclaiming *Jesus, that he is the Son of God,*" "proving *that he is the Christ,*" putting, as the foremost matter of the "good news," Christ's death and resurrection.

"The kingdom" was to be won through faith in Christ; in Christ crucified and risen, and crucified and risen, I freely admit, in the plain material sense of those words. And, moreover, "the kingdom" was conceived by the apostles as the triumphant return of Christ, in the lifetime of the very generation then living, to judge the world and to reign in glory with his saints. The disciples conceived "the kingdom," therefore, amiss; it was hardly possible for them not to do so. But we can readily understand how thus, as time went on, Christian preaching came more and more to drop, or to leave in the background, its one primitive gospel, *the good news of the kingdom,* and to settle on other points. Yet whoever reverts to it, reverts, I say, to the primitive *gospel;* which is the good news of an immense renovation and transformation of this world, by the establishment of what the Sermon on the Mount calls (in the most authentic reading of the passage) "God's righteousness and kingdom." This was the ideal of Jesus:—the establishment on earth of God's kingdom, of felicity, not by the violent processes of our Fifth Monarchy men, or of the German Anabaptists, or of the French Communists, but by the establishment on earth of God's righteousness.

But it is a contracted and insufficient conception of the gospel which takes into view only the establishment of *righteousness,* and does not also take into view the establishment of *the kingdom.* And the establishment of the kingdom does imply an

immense renovation and transformation of our actual state of
things;—that is certain. This, then, which is the ideal of the
popular classes, of the multitude everywhere, is a legitimate
ideal. And a Church of England, devoted to the service and
5　ideals of any limited class,—however distinguished, wealthy, or
powerful,—which is perfectly satisfied with things as they are,
is not only out of sympathy with the ideal of the popular classes;
it is also out of sympathy with the gospel, of which the ideal
does, in the main, coincide with theirs. True, the most clear
10　voice one could even desire in favour of such an ideal is found
to come, as we have seen, from the Church of England, from a
representative man among the clergy of that Church. But it is
important that the clergy, as a body, should sympathise heartily
with that ideal. And this they can best bring themselves to do,
15　any of them who may require such bringing, by accustoming
themselves to see that the ideal is the true original ideal of their
religion and of its Founder.

　　I have dwelt a long while upon this head, because of its extreme importance. If the Church of England is right here, it has,
20　I am persuaded, nothing to fear either from Rome, or from the
Protestant Dissenters, or from the secularists. It cannot, I think,
stand secure unless it has the sympathy of the popular classes.
And it cannot have the sympathy of the popular classes unless
it is right on this head. But, if it is right on this head, it may, I
25　feel convinced, flourish and be strong with their sympathy,
and with that of the nation in general. For it has natural allies in
what Burke, that gifted Irishman, so finely calls "the ancient
and inbred integrity, piety, good nature, and good humour of
the English people." It has an ally in the English people's piety.
30　If the matter were not so serious, one could hardly help smiling
at the chagrin and manifest perplexity of such of one's friends
as happen to be philosophical radicals and secularists, at having
to reckon with religion again when they thought its day was
quite gone by, and that they need not study it any more or take
35　account of it any more, but it was passing out, and a kind of new
gospel, half Bentham, half Cobden, in which they were themselves particularly strong, was coming in. And perhaps there is
no one who more deserves to be compassionated than an elderly

or middle-aged man of this kind, such as several of their Parliamentary spokesmen and representatives are. For perhaps the younger men of the party may take heart of grace, and acquaint themselves a little with religion, now that they see its day is by no means over. But, for the older ones, their mental habits are formed, and it is almost too late for them to begin such new studies. However, a wave of religious reaction *is* evidently passing over Europe; due very much to our revolutionary and philosophical friends having insisted upon it that religion was gone by and unnecessary, when it was neither the one nor the other. And what one sees in France, and elsewhere, really makes some words of Butler (if you are not yet tired of Butler) read like a prophecy:—

"Indeed," he says, "amongst creatures naturally formed for religion, yet so much under the powers of imagination, so apt to deceive themselves, as men are, superstition is an evil which can never be out of sight. But even against this, true religion is a great security; and the only one. True religion takes up that place in the mind which superstition would usurp, and so leaves little room for it; and likewise lays us under the strongest obligations to oppose it. On the contrary, the danger of superstition cannot but be increased by the prevalence of irreligion; and by its general prevalence the evil will be unavoidable. For the common people, wanting a religion, will of course take up with almost any superstition which is thrown in their way; and in process of time, amidst the infinite vicissitudes of the political world, the leaders of parties will certainly be able to serve themselves of that superstition, whatever it be, which is getting ground; and will not fail to carry it on to the utmost length their occasions require."

And does not one see at the present day, in the very places where irreligion had prevailed most, superstition laying hold of those who seemed the last people likely to be laid hold of by it, and politicians making their game out of this state of things? Yet that there should spring up in Paris, for instance, a Catholic Working Men's Union, and that it should prosper, will surprise no one who considers how strong is the need in human nature for a moral rule and bridle, such as religion, even a superstitious one, affords; and how entirely the Paris workman was without

anything of the kind. La Rochefoucauld, who is here a witness
whom no one will challenge, says most truly: "It is harder to
keep oneself from being governed than to govern others."
Obedience, strange as it may sound, is a real need of human
nature;—above all, moral and religious obedience. And it is less
hard to a Paris workman to swallow beliefs which one would
have thought impossible for him, than to go on in life and conduct in unchartered freedom, like a wave of the sea, driven with
the wind and tossed. Undoubtedly, then, there are in the popular classes of every country forces of piety and religion capable
of being brought into an alliance with the Church, the national
society for the promotion of goodness, in that country. And of
no people may this be more certainly said than of ours.

Still, there is in this English people an *integrity*, as Burke calls
it,—a native fund of downrightness, plain honesty, integrity,—
which makes our popular classes very unapt to cheat themselves in religion, and to swallow things down wholesale out of
sentiment, or even out of weariness of moral disorder and from
need of a moral rule. And therefore I said that Rome was not a
real danger for us, and that in the integrity of the English people
the Church of England had a natural ally. I say this in view of
the popular classes. Higher up, with individuals, and even with
small classes, sentiment and fantasy, and morbid restlessness and
weariness, may come in. But with the popular classes and with
the English people as a whole, it is in favour of the Church that
it is what Butler called it, and what it is sometimes reproached
for being: a *reasonable* Establishment. And it *is* a reasonable
Establishment, and in the good sense. I know of no other Establishment so reasonable. Churches are characterised, I have said,
by their great men. Show me any other great Church of which a
chief doctor and luminary has a sentence like this sentence,
splendide verax, of Butler's: "Things are what they are, and
the consequences of them will be what they will be; why, then,
should we desire to be deceived?" To take in and to digest such
a sentence as that, is an education in moral and intellectual
veracity. And after all, intensely Butlerian as the sentence is, yet
Butler came to it because he is *English;* because at the bottom
of his nature lay such a fund of integrity.

Show me another great Church, again, in which a theologian, arguing that a religious doctrine of the truth of which a man is not sure,—the doctrine, let us suppose, of a future state of rewards and punishments,—may yet properly be made to sway his conduct and practice (a recommendation which seems to me, I must confess, impossible to be carried into effect); but show me in another Church a theologian arguing thus, yet careful at the same time to warn us, that we have no business to tamper with our sense of evidence, by *believing* the doctrine any the more on the ground of its practical importance to us. For this is what Butler says:—"To be influenced," he says, "by this consideration in our *judgment*, to believe or disbelieve upon it, is indeed as much prejudice as anything whatever." The force of integrity, I say, can no farther go.

And, distracted as is the state of religious opinion amongst us at this moment, in no other great Church is there, I believe, so much sincere desire as there is in the Church of England,—in clergy as well as in laity,—to get at the real truth. In no other great Church is there so little false pretence of assured knowledge and certainty on points where there can be none; so much disposition to see and to admit with Butler, in regard to such points and to the root of the whole matter in religion, that "mankind are for placing the stress of their religion anywhere rather than upon virtue," and that mankind are wrong in so doing. To this absence of charlatanism, to this largeness of view, to this pressing to the genuine root of the matter, all the constituents assigned to the English people's nature by Burke,—our people's piety, their integrity, their good nature, their good humour, but above all, their *integrity*,—contribute to incline them. That the Church should show a like inclination, is in its favour as a National Church.

Equally are these constituents of the English character, and the way of thinking which naturally springs from them, in favour of the Church as regards the attacks of the political Dissenters. Plain directness of thinking, a largeness and good-naturedness of mind, are not favourable judges, I think, for the Dissenters at the present moment,—for their grievances and for their operations. A sense of piety and religion in the nation is to

be supposed to start with. And I suppose it to be clear that the
contention no longer is, even on the part of the Dissenters themselves, that a certain Church-order is alone scriptural and is
therefore necessary, and that it is that of the Dissenters, not of
the Church; or that the *Gospel* consists in one or two famous
propositions of speculative doctrine, and that the Dissenters
make it so to consist, while the Church does not. At any rate,
the nation in general will no longer regard *this* contention as
serious, even if some Dissenters do. The serious contention is,
that there ought to be perfect religious equality, as it is called;
and that the State ought not to adopt, and by adopting to favour
and elevate above the rest, one form of religion out of the many
forms that are current.

But surely, the moment we consider religion and Christianity
in a large way as goodness, and a Church as a society for the
promotion of goodness, all that is said about having such a society before men's eyes as a city set upon a hill, all that is said
about making the Gospel more and more a witness to mankind,
applies in favour of the State adopting some form of religion or
other,—that which seems best suited to the majority,—even
though it may not be perfect; and putting that forward as the
national form of religion. "A reasonable establishment *has*,"
surely, as Butler says, "a tendency to keep up a sense of real religion and real Christianity in a nation." That seems to me to be
no more than the plain language of common sense. And I think
what follows is true also:—"And it is moreover necessary for
the encouragement of learning, some parts of which the Scrip-
ture-revelation absolutely requires should be cultivated."

But what seems to me quite certain is, that, if goodness is the
end, and "all good men are," as Butler says, "equally concerned
in promoting that end," then, as he goes on to conclude, "to
do it more effectually they ought to unite in promoting it;
which yet is scarce practicable upon any new models, and
quite impossible upon such as every one would think unexceptionable." And as for such, he says, as "think ours liable to objections, it is possible they themselves may be mistaken, and
whether they are or no, the very nature of society requires some
compliance with others. Upon the whole, therefore, these per-

sons would do well to consider how far they can with reason satisfy themselves in neglecting what is certainly right on account of what is doubtful whether it be wrong; and when the right is of so much greater consequence one way than the supposed wrong can be the other." Here Butler seems to me to be on impregnable ground, and it is the ground which the largest and surest spirits amongst us have always pitched upon. Sir Matthew Hale, the most moderate of men and the most disposed to comprehension, said: "Those of the separation were good men, but they had narrow souls, who would break the peace of the Church about such inconsiderable matters as the points in difference were." Henry More, that beautiful spirit, is exactly to the same effect. "A little religion may make a man schismatical, but a great deal will surely make a man decline division where things are tolerable, which is the case of our English Church." And the more a large way of thinking comes to spread in this nation, which by its good nature and good humour has a natural turn for it, the more will this view come to prevail. It will be acknowledged that the Church is a society for the promotion of goodness; that such a society is the stronger for being national, and ought to be national; that to make its operations, therefore, more effectual, all good men ought to unite in it, and that the objections of the Protestant Dissenters to uniting in it are trivial.

At least, their *religious* objections to uniting in it are trivial. Their objections from the annoyance and mortification at having, after they have once separated and set up forms of their own, to give in and to accept the established form, and their allegations of their natural jealousy at having to see, if they do not accept it, the clergy preferred before them by being invested with the status of national ministers of religion—these objections are much more worthy of note. But, in the first place, whatever preference is given, is given for the sake of the whole community, not of those preferred. And many preferences, for its own sake and for what it judges to be the public good, the whole community may and must establish. But that which, as men's minds grow larger, will above all prevent the objections and complaints of the Dissenters from winning sympathy and

from attaining effect, is that, in the second place, it will be more
and more distinctly perceived that their objections and complaints are, to speak truly, *irreligious* objections and complaints,
and yet urged in the sphere of religion.

5   To philosophical Radicals in or out of Parliament, who think
that religion is all a chimæra, and that in a matter so little important the fancies of the Dissenters, whose political aid is valuable, may well be studied and followed, this will seem nothing.
But the more the sense of religion grows, and of religion in a
10   large way,—the sense of the beauty and rest of religion, the
sense that its charm lies in its grace and peace,—the more will
the present attitude, objections, and complaints of the Dissenters indispose men's minds to them. They will, I firmly believe, lose ground; they will not keep hold of the new genera-
15   tions. In most of the mature Dissenters the spirit of scruple, ob-
jection-taking, and division, is, I fear, so ingrained, that in any
proffered terms of union they are more likely to seize occasion
for fresh cavil than occasion for peace. But the new generations
will be otherwise minded. As to the Church's want of grace
20   and peace in disputing the ground with Dissent, the justice of
what Barrow says will be more and more felt:— "He that being
assaulted is constrained to stand on his defence, may not be said
to be in peace; yet his not being so (involuntarily) is not to be
imputed to him." But the Dissenters have not this, the Church's
25   excuse, for being men of war in a sphere of grace and peace.
And they turn themselves into men of war more and more.

Look at one of the ablest of them, who is much before the
public, and whose abilities I unfeignedly admire: Mr. Dale.
Mr. Dale is really a pugilist, a brilliant pugilist. He has his arena
30   down at Birmingham, where he does his practice with Mr.
Chamberlain, and Mr. Jesse Collings, and the rest of his band;
and then from time to time he comes up to the metropolis, to
London, and gives a public exhibition here of his skill. And a
very powerful performance it often is. And the *Times* observes,
35   that the chief Dissenting ministers are becoming quite the intellectual equals of the ablest of the clergy. Very likely; this sort
of practice is just the right thing for bracing a man's intellectual
muscles. I have no fears concerning Mr. Dale's intellectual mus-

cles; what I am a little uneasy about is his religious temper. The essence of religion is grace and peace. And though, no doubt, Mr. Dale cultivates grace and peace at other times, when he is not busy with his anti-Church practice, yet his cultivation of grace and peace can be none the better, and must naturally be something the worse, for the time and energy given to his pugilistic interludes. And the more that mankind, instead of placing their religion in all manner of things where it is not, come to place it in sheer goodness, and in grace and peace,—and this is the tendency, I think, with the English people,—the less favourable will public opinion be to the proceedings of the political Dissenters, and the less has the Church to fear from their pugnacious self-assertion.

Indeed, to eschew self-assertion, to be,—instead of always thinking about one's freedom, and one's rights, and one's equality,—to be, as Butler says, "as much afraid of subjection to mere arbitrary will and pleasure in ourselves as to the arbitrary will of others," is the very temper of religion. What the clergy have to desire,—and the clergy of London may well bear to hear this, who have, as a body, been so honourably distinguished for their moderation and their intelligence,—what the clergy have to aim at, is the character of simple instruments for the public good. What they have to shun, is their action having at all the appearance of mere arbitrary will and pleasure of the individual. One can hardly speak about the Church at this moment without touching on the Burials Bill. Give me leave to say, that the dangerous thing to the Church, as regards this vexed question of burials, has been the opening afforded, in the exclusion of unbaptized persons, to the exercise of what might always seem, and often was, the exercise of mere arbitrary will and pleasure in the individual clergyman. This, it seems to me, ought certainly to be abandoned; and here, surely, is an occasion for remembering St. Paul's dictum, that "Christ sent him not to baptize, but to preach the good news." If this exclusion were wholly abandoned, if the option of silent funerals, and of funerals with a shortened service, were also given, I think as much would have been done as it is for the public advantage (I put the advantage of the clergy out of question altogether,—they have none but

that of the community), in the special circumstances of this country, to do. I do not believe it would be necessary to do more, in order to remove all real sense of grievance, and to end, for sensible people, the need for further occupying themselves
5   with this whole barren and retarding question of *Church and Dissent.*

And I, for my part, now leave this question, I hope, for ever. I became engaged in it against my will, from being led by particular circumstances to remark the deteriorating effect of the
10 temper and strifes of Dissent upon good men, the lamentable waste of power and usefulness which was thereby caused; and from being convinced that the right settlement was to be reached in one way only: not by disestablishment, but by comprehension and union. However, as one grows old, one feels
15 that it is not one's business to go on for ever expostulating with other people upon their waste of life, but to make progress in grace and peace oneself. And this is the real business of the Church, too: to make progress in grace and peace. Force the Church of England has certainly some; perhaps a good deal. But
20 its true strength is in relying, not on its powers of force, but on its powers of attractiveness. And by opening itself to the glow of the old and true ideal of the Christian Gospel, by fidelity to reason, by placing the stress of its religion on goodness, by cultivating grace and peace, it will inspire attachment, to which
25 the attachment which it inspires now, deep though that is, will be as nothing; it will last, be sure, as long as this nation.

A Last Word on the Burials Bill

In my address at Sion College I touched for a moment on the now much-discussed question of the Burials Bill. I observed, that whatever resembled an arbitrary assertion of his own private will and pleasure should be shunned by a clergyman; that the exercise of his right of refusing burial to unbaptized persons often resembled, and not unfrequently was, such an assertion; and that it would be for the advantage of the Church to abandon this right. I added that if this were done, and if the option of a silent service, or of a shortened service, in place of the present Burial Service, were also given, as much would have been conceded to the Dissenters, in the matter of burials, as justice requires, as much as it is for the public interest to concede, and as much as it will finally, I think, be found necessary to concede.

But much more than this is claimed for the Dissenters. Mr. Osborne Morgan's Bill lays down, that "it is just and right to permit the performance in parish churchyards of other burials than those of the Church of England, and by other persons than the ministers of that Church." And the *Times* says in recommendation of Mr. Osborne Morgan's Bill:—

"A just legislature has to put the business on the basis of justice and truth. It will consider what a Dissenter or his friends desire, and what, being in accordance with his or their wishes, will be no injustice or untruth. It does really seem late in the day to have to prove that the imposition of a service at variance with the whole course of a man's life, opinions, and practice, is an injustice and an untruth. An Englishman has a right to worship in the style he thinks truest and best, just as he has a right to dress as he likes, to select his own acquaintances, or to choose his own pursuits. Let the Dissenting

minister then," concludes the *Times*, "enter the churchyard, and
have his own say over his own spiritual son or daughter; and let the
incumbent cease to intrench himself in the vain illusion of an inviolable churchyard in a parish which has long ceased to be his ex-
5 clusive domain."

Lord Selborne, too, in the debate on Lord Granville's resolution upon the subject of burials, treated it as a matter quite
clear and self-evident, that to deny this right to Dissenters was
a violation of the established English principle of religious lib-
10 erty:—

"Is there any conceivable logical answer," he asked, "to the observation, that in these cases you deny after death that religious liberty which in every other respect is given to the deceased during
the whole of their lives? You deny this liberty in the present state
15 of things in two ways: by refusing to them the liberty of being religious in their own way, and by imposing upon them the necessity
of being religious in your way." "The feelings of the great majority
of the laity," Lord Selborne adds, "when it is brought home to them
that there is this violation of the established principle of religious
20 liberty in dealing with interments, will go more and more with those
who complain of this grievance."

A number of clergymen, many of them bearing names well
known and respected, have proposed, as "a reasonable concession to the feelings of Nonconformists," to "grant permission
25 to a recognised minister or representative of any religious body
to perform in the churchyard a funeral service consisting of
passages of Holy Scripture, prayers, and hymns." But absolute
liberty is the right claimed, and these limitations are evidently
inconsistent with it. "We are afraid," says the *Times* of the
30 clergymen's proposal, "that even with the most liberal interpretation, this restriction leaves out of account some communities
for whose rights the supporters of the Bill would contend as
strenuously as for those of others. *But it is a misapprehension,
it is to be apprehended, of the essential nature of a Noncon-
35 formist, to suppose that he would ever pledge himself to conform to anything.* The essence of his demand is to claim free
access to sacred places, which the necessity of nature compels
him to use, with such observances as the principles of his com-

munion may prescribe." Yes, "necessity of nature." For, it is argued, "while every other public incident of a man's life may be optional, he must be buried." And therefore, contends the *Times* to exactly the same effect as Lord Selborne, "let the natural necessity of burial be once admitted, and the necessity of according religious freedom in the satisfaction of it must inevitably be allowed."

Finally, it is said that in all other Christian countries, except Spain, the right of burying their dead in the parish churchyard, with their own services and their own ministers, is conceded to Dissenters. And here again, then, is a reason why in England too the clergyman should, as the *Times* says, "cease to intrench himself in the vain illusion of an inviolable churchyard in a parish which has long ceased to be his exclusive domain;" should "let the Dissenting minister enter the ground, and have his own say over his own spiritual son or daughter."

I have been asked, how the concession which I spoke of at Sion College can be thought sufficient, when it is so much less than what the Dissenters themselves and their friends demand, than what some of the best of the clergy offer to concede, than what natural justice and the recognised English principle of religious liberty require, and than what is almost universally conceded in the rest of Christendom? And I am asked this by those who approach the question, just as I approach it myself, in a spirit perfectly disinterested. They, like myself, have no political object to serve by answering it in a way favourable to the Dissenters, they do not care whether or not it is the liberal-looking, popular, taking thing so to answer it. And, on the other hand, they have no need to bid for the support of the clergy; they are, moreover, without the least touch of ecclesiastical bias. They simply want to get the question answered in a way to satisfy their own minds and consciences, want to find out what is really the right and reasonable course to pursue. And for their satisfaction, and also for my own, I return for a moment to this matter of burials, before finally leaving the whole question of Church and Dissent; that I may not seem to be leaving it with a curt and inconsiderate judgment on a matter where the feelings of the Dissenters are strongly interested.

II

What is the intention of all forms of public ceremonial and ministration? It is, that what is done and said in a public place, and bears with it a public character, should be done and said worthily. The public is responsible for it. The public gets credit
5 and advantage from it if it is done worthily, is compromised and harmed by it if it is done unworthily. The mode, therefore, of performing public functions in places invested with a public character is not left to the will and pleasure of chance individuals. It is expressly designed to rise above the level which would
10 be thence given. If there is a sort of ignobleness and vulgarity *(was uns alle bändigt, das Gemeine)* which comes out in the crude performance of the mass of mankind left to themselves, public forms, in a higher strain and of recognised worth, are designed to take the place of such crude performance. They are a
15 kind of schooling, which may educate gradually such performance into something better, and meanwhile may prevent it from standing forth, to its own discredit and to that of all of us, as public and representative. This, I say, is evidently the design of all forms for public use on serious and solemn occasions. No
20 one will say that the common Englishman glides off-hand and by nature into a strain pure, noble, and elevated. On the contrary, he falls with great ease into vulgarity. But no people has shown more attachment than the English to old and dignified forms calculated to save us from it.
25 Such is the origin and such is the defence of the use of a set form of burial-service in our public churchyards. It stands on the same ground as the use of all appointed forms whatever, in public places and on serious occasions. It is designed to save public places and occasions, and to save our character as a commu-
30 nity, from being discredited through what the caprice and vulgarity of individuals might prompt them to. The moment a place has a public and national character, there emerges the requirement of a public form for use there. And therefore it is really quite marvellous to find a man of Lord Selborne's acute-
35 ness maintaining, that to withhold from the Dissenting minister

the right, as the *Times* says, "to enter the churchyard and have his own say over his own spiritual son or daughter," is to "deny after death that religious liberty, which in every other respect is given to the deceased during the whole of their lives." To be sure, Lord Selborne was speaking in a parliamentary debate, where perhaps it is lawful to employ any fallacy which your adversaries cannot at the moment expose. But is it possible that Lord Selborne can himself have been deceived by the argument, that to refuse to Dissenters the liberty to have what services they please performed over them in the parish churchyard, is to "deny after death that religious liberty, which in every other respect is given to the deceased during the whole of their lives?" True, the deceased have had religious liberty during their lives, have been free to choose what religious services they pleased. But where? In private places. They have no more been free, during their lifetime, to have what proceedings they liked in the parish church and in the parish churchyard, than to have what proceedings they liked in the House of Lords or in the Court of Chancery. And for the same reason in each case: that these places are public places, and that to safeguard the worthy use of public places we have public forms.

That liberty, then, in his choice of religious proceedings, which the deceased Dissenter enjoyed during his lifetime, or which any Englishman enjoys, is a liberty exercisable only in private places. The Dissenter, like other people, enjoys just the same liberty after his death. To refuse to any and every individual the liberty to dictate after his death what shall be done and said in a place set apart for national use, and belonging to the public, is just the same abridgment of his religious liberty,—as much and as little an abridgment of it,—as he has been subjected to during the whole course of his life. He has never during his whole life been free to have, in such a place, whomsoever he likes "enter the ground and have his own say." He is not free to have it after his death.

It is impossible to establish a distinction between a man's rights in regard to his burial, and his rights in regard to other public incidents, as they are called, of his life. They are optional, it is sometimes said; burial is necessary. Even were this true, it

would prove nothing as to a need for exemption in burial, rather
than in other matters, from the requirement of public forms in
public places. Burial is necessary, but not burial in public places.
But the proposition is practically not true. For practical purposes, and in regard to mankind in general, it is not true that
marriage is optional. It is not even true that religious worship is
optional. Human nature being what it is, and society being what
it is, religious worship and marriage may both of them, like burial, be called necessary. They come in the regular course of
things and engage men's sentiments widely and deeply. And
everything that can be said about the naturalness of a man's
wishing to be buried in the parish churchyard by a minister of
his own persuasion and with a service to his own liking, may be
said about the naturalness of his wishing to be married in the
parish church in like fashion. And the same of worshipping in
the parish church. It is natural that a man should wish to enjoy,
in his own parish church, worship of his own choice, conducted
by a minister of his own selecting. And the hearty believers in
a man's natural right to have in the parish churchyard a burial
to his own liking, do not conceal that they believe also in a man's
natural right to have in the parish church a worship to his own
liking. "Let me be honest about it," said Sir Wilfrid Lawson at
Carlisle; "if you let the Nonconformist into the churchyard,
that is only a step towards letting him into the church." The
two rights do, in fact, stand on precisely the same footing. If the
naturalness of a man's wishing for a thing creates for him a right
to do it, then a Dissenter can urge his right to have his own minister say his say over him in the parish churchyard. Equally can
he urge his right to have his own minister say his say to him in
the parish church.

What bars the right is in both cases just the same thing: the
higher right of the community. For the credit and welfare of
the community, public forms are appointed to be observed in
public places. The will and pleasure of individuals is not to have
sway there. This is what bars the Nonconformist's right to have
in his lifetime what minister and service he likes in the parish
church. It is also what bars his right to have after his death what
minister and service he likes in the parish churchyard.

Certain clergymen have been arbitrary, insolent, and vexatious, in exercising the power given to them by that rubric which excludes unbaptized persons from a legal claim to the burial-service of the Church of England. I can understand people being provoked into a desire to "give a lesson," as Lord Coleridge said, to such clergymen, by admitting Dissenting ministers to perform burial-services in the churchyard. I can understand the better spirits among the clergy being disposed, out of shame and regret at the doings of some of their brethren, to concede to Dissenters what they desire in the matter of burials. I can understand their being disposed to concede it, too, out of love of peace, and from the wish to end disputes and to conciliate adversaries by abandoning a privilege. But the requirement of a fixed burial-service in the parish churchyard is not made for the benefit of the clergy, or in order to confer upon the clergy a privilege. It is made for the benefit of the community. It is not to be abandoned out of resentment against those who abuse it, or out of generosity on the part of the more liberal clergy. They are generous with what is really, however it may appear to them, not a privilege of theirs, but a safeguard of ours. If it is for the advantage of the community that in public places some public form should be followed, if the community runs risk of discredit from suffering individuals to say and do what they like in such places, and if the burial-service of the Church of England is enjoined on this principle, then it is not to be given up in order to punish the folly of some of the clergy or to gratify the generosity of others. If the principle on which it has been enjoined is sound, the service is to be retained for the sake of this principle.

And so evidently sound is the principle, that the politicians who take the Dissenters' cause in hand cannot help feeling its force. Mr. Osborne Morgan proposes, while allowing the Dissenters to have their own services in the parish churchyard, to "make proper provision for order and decency." Lord Granville stipulates that the services shall be conducted "in an orderly and Christian manner." But unless these are mere words, meant to save appearances but not to have any real operation, we are thus brought back to the use of some public and recognised form for

burials in the parish churchyard. And the burial-service of the
Church of England was meant for a public and recognised form
of this kind, which people at large could accept, and which en-
sured an "orderly and Christian" character to proceedings in the
5 parish churchyard. Proceedings dependent solely on the will
and pleasure of chance individuals, and liable to bear the marks
of their "natural taste for the bathos," as Swift calls it, cannot
ensure this character. But proceedings in a public place ought
to have it. And that they ought, the very politicians who advo-
10 cate the Dissenters' cause admit.

So it is a case for revision of the public form of burial at present imposed. The burial-service of the Prayer Book was meant
to be used in the parish churchyard over all Christians,—meant
to suit all. It does not suit all. Some people object to things in
15 the service itself. More object to being strictly confined to that
service only. More still object to being deprived, in their burial,
of the offices of a minister of their own persuasion. On the other
hand, a self-willed clergyman is enabled by a rubric of the burial-service to withhold its use in some cases where its use is de-
20 sired, and where to withhold it is both foolish and cruel. Such
is the present state of things. And it has to be dealt with by
means of some change or other, which shall remove causes for
just discontent, without abandoning the principle of requiring
proper and worthy forms to be observed at proceedings in the
25 parish churchyard.

III

There is division among Christians, and in no country are
they found all agreeing to adopt the same forms and ministers of
religion. Different bodies of Christians have their own forms
and ministers. And except in England these different bodies
30 have, it is said, the churchyard in common. In Ireland it is so. In
Scotland there is, as in England, an Established Church; yet in
Scotland the forms and ministers of other religious bodies are
admitted to the use of the parish churchyard. In France the
Catholics are in an enormous majority, yet Protestants can be
35 buried with their own forms in the graveyards of Catholic

churches. In Germany, where both Catholics and Protestants are found in great numbers, and much intermixed, the church-yards of the one confession are open to the burial-rites of the other.

Now, in comparing the Church of England with other Churches, it is right to remember one character which distinguishes it from all of them. The Church of England was meant, in the intention of those who settled it at the Reformation, to satisfy the whole English people and to be accepted by them. It was meant to include both Catholics and Protestants in a compromise between old and new, rejecting Romish corruptions and errors, but retaining from Catholicism all that was sound and truly attaching, and thus to provide a revised form of religion, adapted to the nation at large as things then stood, and receivable by it. No other Church has been settled with the like design. And therefore no other Church stands precisely on the like ground in offering its formularies to people. For whereas other Churches, in offering their formularies to people, offer them with the recommendation that here is truth and everywhere else is error, the Church of England, in offering its formularies to Englishmen, offers them with the recommendation that here is truth presented expressly so as to suit and unite the English nation. And therefore to no Church can dissent be so mortifying as to the Church of England; because dissent is the denial, not only of her profession of the truth, but also of her success in her direct design. However, this cannot make things otherwise than they are. The Church of England, whatever may have been its design, does not manage to satisfy every one any more than the Churches in other countries. And whatever special mortification she may have cause for, in seeing, around her, forms and ministers of religion other than her own, that is no reason why she should be less liberal in her dealings with them than the Churches in other countries. Either she must manage to suit them herself, or she must be liberal to them.

Reciprocity, at any rate, is but fair. If the burial-rites of the Church of England are admitted to Presbyterian churchyards in Scotland, and to Catholic churchyards in Ireland, the burial-rites of Scotch Presbyterians and of Irish Catholics ought surely

to be admitted to Anglican churchyards. There can be no fear
that the burial-rite of either should do discredit to the churchyard. The funerals of Scotch Presbyterians are conducted, I believe, in silence. In a silent interment there can be nothing of-
5 fensive. The Catholic offices for the dead are the source from
whence our own are taken. In either case we have the security
for decency which the deliberate public consent of large and
well-known bodies of our fellow Christians affords on behalf of
the burial-rites in use with them. Great bodies, like these, are
10 not likely to have given their sanction to a form of burial-service discreditable to a public churchyard and inadmissible there.
And if we had only to deal with the Presbyterians and the Catholics, the burials question would present itself under conditions
very different from those which now do actually attend it. Nay,
15 if the English Dissenters were reducible, even, to a few great
divisions,—suppose to the well-known three denominations,—
and either there were a common form of burial-service among
these denominations, or each denomination had its own; and if
the Dissenters were content to be thus classed, and to adhere
20 either to a single form of Dissenters' burial-service, or to one
out of two or three; then, also, the case would be different.

But these are not the conditions under which we are dealing
with the burials question. The dissidence of Dissent and the
Protestantism of the Protestant religion have brought the Dis-
25 senters in England to classify themselves, not in two or three
divisions, but in, I believe, one hundred and thirty-eight. And
their contention is, that no matter how they may split themselves up, they have still their right to the churchyard,—new
sects as much as old, small sects as much as great, obscure sects
30 as much as famous; Ranters, Recreative Religionists, and Peculiar People, as much as Presbyterians and Baptists. And no man
is entitled to tell them that they must manage to agree among
themselves upon one admissible form of burial-service or upon
one or two admissible forms. That would be restricting their
35 religious liberty. "It is a misapprehension," the *Times*, their advocate, tells us, "of the essential nature of a Nonconformist, to
suppose that he could ever pledge himself to conform to anything. The essence of his demand is to claim free access to sa-

cred places, which the necessity of nature compels him to use, with such observances as the principles of his communion may prescribe." Whether the observances are seemly, and such as to befit a public and venerable place, we are not to ask. Probably the Dissenters themselves think that a man's conscience recommending them to him makes them so. And what Lord Granville and Mr. Osborne Morgan and the political friends of the Dissenters think on this matter, and how they propose to ensure the decent and Christian order for which they stipulate, and at the same time not to violate that essential principle of a Nonconformist's nature which forbids him in religion "ever to pledge himself to conform to anything," does not quite appear. Perhaps they have not looked into the thing much. Or they may think that it does not matter much, and that the observances of one body of religionists are likely to be about as good as those of another.

Yet surely there is likely to be a wide difference between the observances of a great body like the Presbyterians, counting its adherents by hundreds of thousands, having existed for a long time, and possessing a well-known reason for existence,—counting, also, amongst its adherents, a great mass of educated people, —there is likely to be a wide difference between the observances of a body like this, and the observances of such a body, say, as the Peculiar People. Both are Dissenters in England. But one affords the same sort of security, that its proceedings in a parish churchyard will be decorous, which Anglicanism itself affords. The other affords no such security at all. And it is precisely in the country churchyards, if accessible to them, that the observances of ignorant and fanatical little sects would parade themselves; for these sects are found above all in country places, where there are no cemeteries, and not in great towns, where there are. And we are not to take security against such a violation of the parish churchyard, by requiring the hundred and thirty-eight Dissenting sects to agree to one or more authorisable forms of burial-service for themselves, if they object to the burial-service of the Church of England, because, where religious observances are concerned, "it is the essential nature of a Nonconformist not to pledge himself to conform to any-

thing!" But the Nonconformist's pretension, to be dispensed
from pledging himself thus, can only be allowed so long as he
is content to forego, in exercising it, the use of places with a
public and national character. To admit such a pretension in
those using, for any purpose, a place with a public and national
character, is a mere plunge into barbarism.

The example of foreign countries is quoted, and of the foreign countries most like our own, France and Germany. In
France there are many churchyards with a separate portion for
Protestants, and in this separate portion Protestants are buried
with their own rites and by their own ministers. This, as has
been pointed out, is not what our Dissenters wish for or would
accept. In Germany there is no such separation, and Protestants
are buried in Catholic churchyards by their own ministers, with
their own rites. But, in either case, *what* Protestants? In France,
Protestants belonging to the Reformed, or Calvinistic, Church;
a Church with a great history, a Church well known, with a
well-known rite, and paid and recognised by the State equally
with the Catholic Church. In Germany, Protestants belonging
to the Lutheran Church, to the Calvinistic Church, and to the
Church formed by the union of the two. Like the Reformed
Church in France, these are all of them public bodies, with a
public status, a recognised rite, and offering sound security for
their proper use of a public place like the churchyard. Do English people imagine that in France or Germany, whose liberality is vaunted at the expense of ours, Ranters or Recreative Religionists or Peculiar People are all of them free to "have their
say" in the parish churchyards? Do they imagine that in the
use, such as it is, of Catholic churchyards by Protestants in
France and Germany, the "essential principle" of our English
Nonconformist, "not to pledge himself to conform to anything," is allowed to have sway? If they do, they are very much
mistaken.

Nothing, therefore, in the example of France and Germany
condemns the taking a security from those who are admitted
to use their burial-rites in the parish churchyard. If Catholics
and the three Dissenting denominations were admitted, each
with a recognised burial-service, to our churchyards, that would

be, in a general way, a following of the precedent set by France and Germany;—at any rate, of the precedent set by Germany. But to this the Nonconformists themselves will never consent, therefore it is idle to propose it. And there are other reasons, too, for not proposing such an arrangement in this country. In the first place, it is not required in order to ensure religious burial for Christians of all kinds. The Church of England, as has been already said, was expressly meant to serve the needs of the whole community. And speaking broadly and generally, one may say that the whole Christian community has at present a legal right to her burial-offices, and does obtain them. The Catholic Church does not bury Protestants, but the Church of England buries Protestants and Catholics alike. Then, too, the mass of the Protestant Dissenters use the burial-service of the Church of England without objection. And the country is accustomed from of old to see used in the parish churchyards this burial-service only, and to see it performed by the clergyman only. Public feeling would certainly be displeased by a startling innovation in such a matter, without urgent need. And there is no urgent need. Again, there is certainly a danger that Catholics, their position towards the Church of England being what it is, might be disposed, if they were admitted with their ceremonies to the parish churchyards, to make capital, as the phrase is, out of that event, to render it subservient to farther ends of their own. And this danger does not exist on the Continent, for there the Catholics stand towards no Protestant Church in the position which here they hold towards the Church of England. It does not exist in Scotland, where the Established Church is not (I may say it, I hope, as I mean it, without offence) a sufficiently great affair to tempt Catholics to make capital out of the admission of their rites to the parish churchyards. All this would incline one to keep the practice as to burials in the main as it is now, in the English churchyards, unless there is some clear hardship in it.

Such a hardship is found by some people in the mere fact of not being free to choose one's own rite and one's own minister. As to the free choice of rite in a public place, enough has been said; and it is admitted that in itself the burial-rite of the Church

of England is not generally unacceptable. There remains the
hardship of not being able to have one's own minister to bury
one. The language used by Lord Granville on this topic was
surprising. No doubt, the feelings may be soothed and pleased
by the thought that the service over one's remains will be performed by a friend and acquaintance, not by a stranger. But to
say that the sentiment demanding this satisfaction is so deep and
natural that its demands must without fail be obeyed, and that
much ought to be sacrificed in order to enable us to obey them,
is really ridiculous. From the nature of things, such a sentiment
cannot generally be indulged. Life and its chances being what
they are, to expect that the minister, whose services we require
to bury us, shall be at the same time a friend or acquaintance,
shall be at any rate a man of our own choosing, is extravagant.
That the form fixed for him to follow in ministering over us
shall in itself be proper and acceptable, is the great matter. This
being once secured, the more we forget the functionary in the
service, the better. The Anglican burial-service has a person
appointed to read it: the parish clergyman. In itself, the Anglican burial-service is considered, by the great majority of Protestant Dissenters, fit and acceptable. And it is taken, almost
every word of it, from the Catholic offices of religion, the old
common form of worship for Christendom. For a national
Christian burial-service this is surely enough. The service is both
approved and approvable. But Lord Granville's sentiment, it
seems, is wounded, unless he may also approve the minister who
is to read it over him. I should never have credited him with so
much scrupulosity.

A parishioner's right to be buried in the parish churchyard,
with this approved and approvable burial-service, is what we
really have to guard. The real grievance is when this right is
infringed. It is occasionally infringed, and infringed very im-
properly and vexatiously. The means for infringing it are afforded by the rubric prefixed to the burial-service, a rubric
directing that "the office ensuing is not to be used for any that
die unbaptized, or excommunicate, or have laid violent hands
upon themselves." Excommunication is no longer practised. To
refuse the burial-office to suicides is a penal measure, in the ab-

stract perhaps consonant with public opinion, practically, however, in all but extreme cases, evaded by treating the suicide as of unsound mind. In the denial of the burial-office to "any that die unbaptized" lies the true source of grievance.

The office is meant for Christians, and this was what the rubric intended, no doubt, to mark; baptism being taken as the stamp common to all Christians. But a large and well-known sect of Christians, the Baptists, defer baptism until the recipient is of adult age, and their children, therefore, if they die, die unbaptized. To inquire whether a child presented for burial is a Baptist's child or not, is an inquiry which no judicious and humane clergyman would make. The office was meant for Christians, and Baptists are Christians, for surely they do not cease to be so because of their tenet of adult baptism. Adult baptism was undoubtedly the primitive usage, although the change of usage adopted by the Church was natural and legitimate, and the sticklers (as may so often be said of the sticklers in these questions) would have been wiser had they acquiesced in it. But the rubric dresses the clergyman in an authority for investigating and excluding, which enables a violent and unwise man to play tricks that might, indeed, make the angels weep. Where he has the law on his side, he can refuse the burial-service outright to innocent infants and children the most piously brought up; he can, under pretence of doubt and inquiry, adjourn, and often withhold it, where he has not.

Such a man does harm to the Church; but it is not likely that he will have the sense to see this, when he has not eyes to see what harm he does to himself. There may not be many of such men, but a few make a great noise, and do a great deal of mischief. There is no stronger proof of the immense power of inspiring attachment which the Church of England possesses, and of the lovable and admirable qualities shown by many of the clergy, than that the Church should still have so strong a hold upon the affections of the country, in spite of such mischief-makers. If the Church ever loses it and is broken up, it will be by their fault. It was the view of this sort of people with their want of temper and want of judgment, the view of their mischievous action, exerting itself with all the pugnacity and te-

nacity of the British character, and of their fatal prominence,
which moved Clarendon, a sincere friend of the Church of
England, to that terrible sentence of his: "Clergymen, who understand the least, and take the worst measure of human affairs,
5   of all mankind that can write and read!"

The truly desirable, the indispensable change in the regulation of burials, is to remove the power of doing mischief which
such persons now enjoy. And the best way to remove it, is to
strike out the first rubric to the burial-service altogether. Ex-
10 communicated persons there are none to exclude. What is
gained by insisting on the exclusion of suicides? In nine cases
out of ten, the plea of unsound mind is at present used to prevent their exclusion, from the natural feeling that to exclude
them is really to visit their offence, not upon them, but upon
15 their relations and friends,—to punish the living for the fault of
the dead. Where ought the widest latitude of merciful construction to be more permitted, where ought rigidity in sen-
tencing, condemning, and excluding to be more discouraged,
than in giving or withholding Christian burial? Of the test of
20 baptism we have just now spoken. It was meant as a test of the
Christian profession of those buried in a Christian churchyard.
The test excludes many whose Christian profession is undoubted. But with regard to this profession, again, where is the
virtue of being jealously critical after a man's death and when
25 he is brought for burial? What good end can be served by severity here, what harm prevented? Those who were avowedly
and notoriously not Christians, will, it may be supposed, have
forbidden their friends to bring them for Christian burial. If
their friends do bring them, that is in fact to recant on behalf of
30 the dead his errors, and to make him profess Christianity. Surely
the Church can be satisfied with that, so far, at least, as not to
refuse him burial! But, in fact, the great majority of those who
reject Christianity, and who openly say so, have nevertheless
been baptized, and cannot be excluded from Christian burial.
35 Can it be imagined, that the mere rite of baptism is a rite the
non-performance of which on a man during his lifetime makes
the Christian burial of him, after his death, a vain and impious
mockery? Yes, clergymen can be found who imagine even this.

Clergymen write and print that their conscience will not suffer them to pronounce words of hope over an unbaptized person, because Jesus Christ said: "Except a man be born of water and of the Spirit, he cannot enter into the kingdom of God." Perhaps no vagaries in the way of misinterpretation of Scripture-texts ought to cause surprise, the thing is so common. But this misinterpretation of Jesus Christ's words is peculiarly perverse, because it makes him say just the very opposite of what he meant to say. "Except a man *be cleansed and receive a new influence,*" Jesus meant to say, "he cannot enter into the kingdom of God." And St. Peter explains what this *being cleansed* is: "The answer of a good conscience towards God,"—of which baptism is merely the figure. Reliance on miracles, reliance on supposed privileges, reliance on external rites of any kind, are exactly what our Saviour meant, in the words given in the Fourth Gospel, to condemn;—reliance on anything, except an interior change.

The rubric in question, therefore, might with advantage be expunged altogether. If clergymen complain that they shall then be compelled to pronounce words of hope and assurance in cases where it is shocking, and a mere mockery, to use them, it is to be said that this they are just as much compelled to do now. But no doubt such a necessity ought not to be imposed upon the clergy. And in some cases, so long as the service stands as it does now, it *is* imposed upon them, and this equally whether the rubric is struck out or not. The words expressing good hope concerning the particular person buried impose it. But perhaps what has been said of the unadvisableness of using the occasion of burial for passing sentence of condemnation or pronouncing an opinion *against* the particular person dead, is true also, though certainly in a much less degree, of using it for pronouncing an opinion in his favour. We are intruding into things too much beyond our ken. At any rate, even though the bystanders, who know the history of the departed, may well in their hearts apply specially to him the hopes and promises for the righteous, the general burial-service has another function. It moves in a higher region than this region of personal application. Its grandeur lies in its being a service over *man* buried. "We commit his body

to the ground in the sure and certain hope of the resurrection
to eternal life," is exactly right. *The* resurrection, not this or
that individual's resurrection. We affirm our sure and certain
hope, that for *man* a resurrection to eternal life there is. To add
anything like a pronouncement concerning this or that man's
special share in it, is not the province of a general service. The
words, "as our hope is this our brother doth," would really be
better away. For the sake of the service itself, its truth, solemnity, and impressiveness, they would be better away. And if
they were away, there would be removed with them a source
of shock and distress to the conscience of the officiating clergyman, which exists now, and which, he might say, would exist
even more were the introductory rubric expunged.

The requirement of a fixed and noble form, consecrated by
use and sentiment, as the national burial-service in our parish
churchyards, is a thing of the highest importance and value.
Speech-making and prayer-making, substitutions or additions
of individual invention, hazarded *ex tempore*, seem to me unsuitable and undesirable for such a place and such an occasion.
In general, what it is sought to give utterance to by them can
find its proper expression in the funeral-sermon at another time.
With hymns the case is different. They are not inventions made
off-hand by individuals round the grave. We at least know what
they will be, and we are safe in them from the incalculable sur-
prises and shocks of a speech or an outpouring. Hymns, such as
we know them, are a sort of composition which I do not at all
admire. I freely say so now, as I have often said it before. I regret their prevalence and popularity amongst us. Taking man in
his totality and in the long run, bad music and bad poetry, to
whatever good and useful purposes a man may often manage
to turn them, are in themselves mischievous and deteriorating
to him. Somewhere and somehow, and at some time or other, he
has to pay a penalty and to suffer a loss for taking delight in
them. It is bad for people to hear such words and such a tune as
the words or tune of, *O happy place! when shall I be, my God,
with thee, to see thy face?*—worse for them to take pleasure in
it. And the time will come, I hope, when we shall feel the un-

satisfactoriness of our present hymns, and they will disappear
from our religious services. But that time has not come yet, and
will not be brought about soon or suddenly. We must deal with
circumstances as they exist for us. Hymns are extremely popular both with Church-people and with Dissenters. Church and
Dissent meet here on a common ground; and both of them admit, in hymns, an element a good deal less worthy, certainly,
than the regular liturgy, but also a good deal less fixed. In the
use of hymns we have not, then, as in the use of speeches and
extemporaneous prayings, a source of risk to our public religious services from which they are at present free; for they allow of hymns already. Here are means for offering, without
public detriment, a concession to Dissenters, and for gratifying
their wishes. Many of them would like, in burying their friends,
to sing a hymn at the grave. Let them. Some concession has
been already proposed in the way of allowing a hymn to be
sung as the funeral enters the churchyard. Let the concession be
made more free and ample; let a hymn or hymns be admitted as
a part of the regular service at the grave. The mourners should
have to give notice beforehand to the clergyman of their wish
for the hymn, and it ought to be taken from one of the collections in general use.

This hymnody would lengthen the burial-service. In view of
this, I should like to suggest one alteration in that beautiful and
noble service; an alteration by which time might be got for the
hymn when desired, and which would moreover in itself be,
I cannot but think, an improvement. The burial-service has
but one lesson, taken out of the fifteenth chapter of the First
Epistle to the Corinthians. The passage taken is very long, and,
eloquent and interesting as it is, yet it is also, as a whole, very
difficult to understand. I should say that it is difficult as a whole
because as a whole it is embarrassed, were it not that many people cannot conceive of an inspired writer as ever embarrassed. I
will not raise questions of this kind now. But difficult the lesson
certainly is; difficult, and also very long. Yet it has parts which
are most grand and most edifying; and which also, taken by
themselves, are quite clear. And a lesson of Scripture should

make, as far as possible, a broad, deep, simple, single impression; and it should bring out that impression quite clear. Above all, a lesson used at the burial of the dead, and with the hearers' minds affected as they then are, should do this. It should be a real *lesson*, not merely a *lection;* which,—from our habit of taking for this purpose long readings, hardly ever less than an entire chapter, and in which many matters are treated,—our lessons read in church too often are.

Now the offices in our Prayer Book are, as has been already said, for the most part made up out of the old Catholic offices, the common religious offices of Christendom before it was divided. But whoever looks at a Catholic service-book will find that the lessons there are in general very much shorter than ours. There are more of them and they are much shorter, aiming at being as far as possible, all of them, complete wholes in themselves, and at producing one distinct, powerful, total impression; which is the right aim for lessons to follow. To this end chapters are broken up, and parts of them taken by themselves, and verses left out, and things which are naturally related brought together. And this not in the least with a controversial design, or to favour what are called Romish doctrines, but simply to produce a clearer and stronger impression. The unknown arranger of these old lessons has simply followed the instinct of a true critic, the promptings of a sound natural love for what is clear and impressive. And in following this, he gives an instance of the truth of what I have somewhere said, that practically, in many cases, Catholics are less superstitious in their way of dealing with the Bible than Protestants.

The fifteenth chapter of the first Epistle to the Corinthians appears in the Catholic offices for the dead, but in detached portions; each portion thus becoming more intelligible, and producing a greater effect. Thus the seven verses from the beginning of the 20th verse *(Now is Christ risen from the dead)*, to the end of the 26th *(The last enemy that shall be destroyed is death)*, form one lesson, and a most impressive one. Another admirable and homogeneous lesson is given by taking the verses from the 41st *(There is one glory of the sun)*, to the end of the

50th *(Neither doth corruption inherit incorruption)*, then passing from thence to the beginning of the 53rd *(For this corruptible must put on incorruption)*, and continuing down to the end of the next verse *(Death is swallowed up in victory)*. Here we have two separate lessons, much shorter, even both of them together, than the present lesson, and (I think it will be found) more impressive by being detached from it.

But a lesson from the Old Testament is surely to be desired also. Who would not love to hear, in such a service, that magnificent prophecy on the breathing of life into the dry bones, the first ten verses of the thirty-seventh chapter of Ezekiel? This also is to be found as one of the lessons in the Catholic offices for the dead. In the same offices is another lesson, even more desirable, it seems to me, to have in our burial-service;— a lesson, the most explicit we have, a lesson from our Saviour himself on the resurrection of the dead. Simply that short passage of the fifth chapter of St. John, from the 24th verse to the end of the 29th;—the passage containing the verse: *The hour is coming, and now is, when the dead shall hear the voice of the Son of God, and they that hear shall live.*

Thus we have, instead of one long and difficult lesson, four short, clear, and most powerfully impressive ones. Let the rubric before the existing lesson be changed to run as follows:— "Then shall be read one or more of these lessons following;" and we shall have the means of making time for the hymn, if hymns are desired, without unduly lengthening the service; and if hymns are not desired, we shall be richer in our lessons than we are now.

But the hymn at the grave is not the only concession which we can without public detriment make in this matter to the Dissenters. Many Dissenters prefer to bury their dead in silence. Silent funerals are the practice in the Church of Scotland, and, I believe, with Presbyterians generally. To silent funerals in the parish churchyard there can manifestly be, on the score of order, propriety, and dignity, no objection. A clergyman cannot feel himself aggrieved at having to perform them. The public cannot feel aggrieved by their being performed in a place of

solemn and public character. Whenever, therefore, it is desired
that burial in the parish churchyard should take place in silence,
the clergyman should be authorised and directed to comply
with this desire.

IV

5   Thus I have sought to make clear and to justify what I meant
by that short sentence about burials which occurred in what I
said at Sion College, and at which a certain dissatisfaction was
expressed by some whom I am loth to dissatisfy. The precise
amount of change recommended, and the reasons for making it,
10   and for not making it greater, have now been fully stated. To
sum up the changes recommended, they are as follows:—The
first rubric to be expunged; four lessons to be substituted for
the present single lesson, and the rubric preceding it to run:—
"Then shall be read one or more of these lessons following;" the
15   words, *as our hope is this our* brother *doth,* to be left out; a
hymn or hymns, from one of the collections in general use, to
be sung at the grave if the friends of the deceased wish it, and
if they notify their desire to the clergyman beforehand; silent
burial to be performed on the like conditions.
20   The Dissenters, some of them, demand a great deal more than
this, and their political friends try to get a great deal more for
them. What I have endeavoured is to find out what to a fair
and sensible man, without any political and partisan bias whatever, honestly taking the circumstances of our country into ac-
25   count and the best way of settling this vexed question of burials,
—to find out what to such a man would seem to be reasonable
and expedient. Nor are the concessions and changes proposed
so insignificant. I believe the majority of the Dissenters themselves would be satisfied with them. Certainly this would be the
30   case if we count the Methodists with the Dissenters, and do not
mean by Dissenters, as people sometimes mean, the political Dissenters only. And those who are incensed with the folly of some
of the clergy in this matter, and desire to punish them, would
probably find that they could inflict upon these men of arbi-
35   trary temper no severer punishment, than by simply taking

away from them, where burials are concerned, the scope for
exercising it. However, my object in what I have proposed is
not to punish certain of the clergy, any more than to mortify
certain of the Dissenters, but simply to arrive at what is most
for the good and for the dignity of the whole community. Certainly it is postulated that to accept some public form shall be
the condition for using public and venerable places. But really
this must be clear, one would think, to any one but a partisan,
if he at all knows what "things lovely and of good report" are,
and the value of them. It must be clear to many of the warmest
adversaries of the Church. It is not hidden, I am sure, from Mr.
John Morley himself, who is a lover of culture, and of elevation,
and of beauty, and of human dignity. I am sure he feels, that
what is here proposed is more reasonable and desirable than
what his Dissenting friends demand. *Scio, rex Agrippa, quia
credis.* He is keeping company with his Festus Chamberlain,
and his Drusilla Collings, and cannot openly avow the truth;
but in his heart he consents to it.

And now I do really take leave of the question of Church and
Dissent, as I promised. Whether the Dissenters will believe it or
not, my wish to reconcile them with the Church is from no desire to give their adversaries a victory and them a defeat, but
from the conviction that they are on a false line; from sorrow
at seeing their fine qualities and energies thrown away, from
hope of signal good to this whole nation if they can be turned
to better account. "The dissidence of Dissent, and the Protestantism of the Protestant religion," have some of mankind's
deepest and truest instincts against them, and cannot finally prevail. If they prevail for a time, that is only a temporary stage in
man's history; they will fail in the end, and will have to confess
it.

It is said, and on what seems good authority, that already in
America, that Paradise of the sects, there are signs of reaction,
and that the multitude of sects there begin to tend to agglom-
erate themselves into two or three great bodies. It is said, too,
that whereas the Church of Rome, in the first year of the present century, had but one in two hundred of the population of
the United States, it has now one in six or seven. This at any rate

is certain, that the great and sure gainer by the dissidence of Dissent and the Protestantism of the Protestant religion is the Church of Rome. Unity and continuity in public religious worship are a need of human nature, an eternal aspiration of Christendom; but unity and continuity in religious worship joined with perfect mental sanity and freedom. A Catholic Church transformed is, I believe, the Church of the future. But what the Dissenters, by their false aims and misused powers, at present effect, is to extend and prolong the reign of a Catholic Church *un*transformed, with all its conflicts, impossibilities, miseries. That, however, is what the Dissenters, in their present state, cannot and will not see. For the growth of insight to recognise it, one must rely, both among the Dissenters themselves and in the nation which has to judge their aims and proceedings, on the help of time and progress;—time and progress, in alliance with *the ancient and inbred integrity, piety, good nature, and good humour of the English people.*

A Psychological Parallel

Whoever has to impugn the soundness of popular theology will most certainly find parts in his task which are unwelcome and painful. Other parts in it, however, are full of reward. And none more so than those, in which the work to be done is positive, not negative, and uniting, not dividing; in which what survives in Christianity is dwelt upon, not what perishes; and what offers us points of contact with the religion of the community, rather than motives for breaking with it. Popular religion is too forward to employ arguments which may well be called arguments of despair. "Take me in the lump," it cries, "or give up Christianity altogether. Construe the Bible as I do, or renounce my public worship and solemnities; renounce all communion with me, as an imposture and falsehood on your part. Quit, as weak-minded, deluded blunderers, all those doctors and lights of the Church who have long served you, aided you, been dear to you. Those teachers set forth what are, in your opinion, errors, and go on grounds which you believe to be hollow. Whoever thinks as you do, ought, if he is courageous and consistent, to trust such blind guides no more, but to remain staunch by his new lights and himself."

It happens, I suppose, to most people who treat an interesting subject, and it happens to me, to receive from those whom the subject interests, and who may have in general followed one's treatment of it with sympathy, avowals of difficulty upon certain points, requests for explanation. But the discussion of a subject, more especially of a religious subject, may easily be pursued longer than is advisable. On the immense difference which there seems to me to be between the popular conception of Christianity and the true conception of it, I have said what I

wished to say. I wished to say it, partly in order to aid those
whom the popular conception embarrassed; partly because, having frequently occasion to assert the truth and importance of
Christianity against those who disparaged them, I was bound in
honesty to make clear what sort of Christianity I meant. But
having said, however imperfectly, what I wished, I leave, and
am glad to leave, a discussion where the hope to do good must
always be mixed with an apprehension of doing harm. Only, in
leaving it, I will conclude with what cannot, one may hope, do
harm: an endeavour to dispel some difficulties raised by the
arguments of despair, as I have called them, of popular religion.

I have formerly spoken at much length of the writings of St.
Paul, pointing out what a clue he gives us to the right understanding of the word *resurrection*, the great word of Christianity; and how he deserves, on this account, our special interest
and study. It is the *spiritual* resurrection of which he is thus the
instructive expounder to us. But undoubtedly he believed also
in the miracle of the physical resurrection, both of Jesus himself and for mankind at large. This belief those who do not admit the miraculous will not share with him. And one who does
not admit the miraculous, but who yet had continued to think
St. Paul worthy of all honour and his teaching full of instruction, brings forward to me a sentence from an eloquent and
most popular author, wherein it is said that "St. Paul—surely no
imbecile or credulous enthusiast—vouches for the reality of the
(physical) resurrection, of the appearances of Jesus after it, and
of his own vision." Must then St. Paul, he asks, if he was mistaken in thus vouching,—which whoever does not admit the
miraculous cannot but suppose,—of necessity be an "imbecile
and credulous enthusiast," and his words and character of no
more value to us than those of that slight sort of people? And
again, my questioner finds the same author saying, that to suppose St. Paul and the Evangelists mistaken about the miracles
which they allege, is to "insinuate that the faith of Christendom
was founded on most facile and reprehensible credulity, and
this in men who have taught the spirit of truthfulness as a primary duty of the religion which they preached." And he in-
quires whether St. Paul and the Evangelists, in admitting the

miraculous, were really founding the faith of Christendom on most facile and reprehensible credulity, and were false to the spirit of truthfulness taught by themselves as the primary duty of the religion which they preached.

Let me answer by putting a parallel case. The argument is that St. Paul, by believing and asserting the reality of the physical resurrection and subsequent appearances of Jesus, proves himself, supposing those alleged facts not to have happened, an imbecile or credulous enthusiast, and an unprofitable guide. St. Paul's vision we need not take into account, because even those who do not admit the miraculous will readily admit that he had his vision, only they say it is to be explained naturally. But they do not admit the reality of the physical resurrection of Jesus and of his appearances afterwards, while yet they must own that St. Paul did. The question is, does either the belief of these things by a man of signal truthfulness, judgment, and mental power in St. Paul's circumstances, prove them to have really happened; or does his believing them, in spite of their not having really happened, prove that he cannot have been a man of great truthfulness, judgment, and mental power?

Undeniably St. Paul was mistaken about the imminence of the end of the world. But this was a matter of expectation, not experience. If he was mistaken about a grave fact alleged to have already positively happened, such as the bodily resurrection of Jesus, he must, it is argued, have been a credulous and imbecile enthusiast.

II

I have already mentioned elsewhere[1] Sir Matthew Hale's belief in the reality of witchcraft. The contemporary records of this belief in our own country and among our own people, in a century of great intellectual force and achievement, and when the printing press fixed and preserved the accounts of public proceedings to which the charge of witchcraft gave rise, are of extraordinary interest. They throw an invaluable light for us on the history of the human spirit. I think it is not an illusion of na-

[1] *God and the Bible,* p. 369.

tional self-esteem to flatter ourselves that something of the English "good nature and good humour" is not absent even from
these repulsive records; that from the traits of infuriated, infernal cruelty which characterise similar records elsewhere, par-
5   ticularly among the Latin nations, they are in a great measure
free. They reveal, too, beginnings of that revolt of good sense,
gleams of that reason, that criticism, which was presently to
disperse the long-prevailing belief in witchcraft. At the beginning of the eighteenth century Addison, though he himself
10   looks with disfavour on a man who wholly disbelieves in ghosts
and apparitions, yet smiles at Sir Roger de Coverley's belief in
witches, as a belief which intelligent men had outgrown, a sur-
vival from times of ignorance. Nevertheless, in 1716, two
women were hanged at Huntingdon for witchcraft. But they
15   were the last victims, and in 1736 the penal statutes against
witchcraft were repealed. And by the end of the eighteenth
century, the majority of rational people had come to disbelieve,
not in witches only, but in ghosts also. Incredulity had become
the rule, credulity the exception.

20   But through the greater part of the seventeenth century
things were just the other way. Credulity about witchcraft was
the rule, incredulity the exception. It is by its all-pervadingness,
its seemingly inevitable and natural character, that this credulity of the seventeenth century is distinguished from modern
25   growths which are sometimes compared with it. In the addic-
tion to what is called spiritualism, there is something factitious
and artificial. It is quite easy to pay no attention to spiritualists
and their exhibitions; and a man of serious temper, a man even
of matured sense, will in general pay none. He will instinctively
30   apply Goethe's excellent caution: that we have all of us a nervous system which can easily be worked upon, that we are most
of us very easily puzzled, and that it is foolish, by idly perplex-
ing our understanding and playing with our nervous system, to
titillate in ourselves the fibre of superstition. Whoever runs after
35   our modern sorcerers may indeed find them. He may make acquaintance with their new spiritual visitants who have succeeded to the old-fashioned imps of the seventeenth century,—

to the Jarmara, Elemauzer, Sack and Sugar, Vinegar Tom, and
Grizzel Greedigut, of our trials for witchcraft. But he may also
pass his life without troubling his head about them and their
masters. In the seventeenth century, on the other hand, the belief in witches and their works met a man at every turn, and
created an atmosphere for his thoughts which they could not
help feeling. A man who scouted the belief, who even disparaged it, was called Sadducee, atheist, and infidel. Relations of
the conviction of witches had their sharp word of "condemnation for the particular opinion of some men who suppose there
be none at all." They had their caution to him "to take heed
how he either despised the power of God in his creatures, or
vilipended the subtlety and fury of the Devil as God's minister
of vengeance." The ministers of religion took a leading part in
the proceedings against witches; the Puritan ministers were here
particularly busy. Scripture had said: *Thou shalt not suffer a
witch to live.* And, strange to say, the poor creatures tried and
executed for witchcraft appear to have usually been themselves
firm believers in their own magic. They confess their compact
with the Devil, and specify the imps, or familiars, whom they
have at their disposal. All this, I say, created for the mind an
atmosphere from which it was hard to escape. Again and again
we hear of the "sufficient justices of the peace and discreet mag-
istrates," of the "persons of great knowledge," who were satisfied with the proofs of witchcraft offered to them. It is abundantly clear that to take as solid and convincing, where a witch
was in question, evidence which would now be accepted by no
reasonable man, was in the seventeenth century quite compati-
ble with truthfulness of disposition, vigour of intelligence, and
penetrating judgment on other matters.

Certainly these three advantages,—truthfulness of disposition,
vigour of intelligence, and penetrating judgment,—were possessed in a signal degree by the famous Chief Justice of Charles
the Second's reign, Sir Matthew Hale. Burnet notices the remarkable mixture in him of sweetness with gravity, so to the
three fore-named advantages we may add gentleness of temper.
There is extant the report of a famous trial for witchcraft be-

fore Sir Matthew Hale.[1] Two widows of Lowestoft in Suffolk, named Rose Cullender and Amy Duny, were tried before him at Bury St. Edmunds, at the Spring Assizes in 1664, as witches. The report was taken in Court during the trial, but was not pub-
5 lished till eighteen years afterwards, in 1682. Every decade, at that time, saw a progressive decline in the belief in witchcraft. The person who published the report was, however, a believer; and he considered, he tells us, that "so exact a relation of this trial would probably give more satisfaction to a great many per-
10 sons, by reason that it is pure matter of fact, and that evidently demonstrated, than the arguments and reasons of other very learned men that probably may not be so intelligible to all read- ers; especially, this being held before a judge whom for his in- tegrity, learning, and law, hardly any age either before or since
15 could parallel; who not only took a great deal of pains and spent much time in this trial himself, but had the assistance and opin- ion of several other very eminent and learned persons." One of these persons was Sir Thomas Browne of Norwich, the author of the *Religio Medici* and of the book on *Vulgar Errors*.
20   The relation of the trial of Rose Cullender and Amy Duny is indeed most interesting and most instructive, because it shows us so clearly how to live in a certain atmosphere of belief will govern men's conclusions from what they see and hear. To us who do not believe in witches, the evidence on which Rose
25 Cullender and Amy Duny were convicted carries its own natu- ral explanation with it, and itself dispels the charge against them. They were accused of having bewitched a number of children, causing them to have fits, and to bring up pins and nails. Several of the witnesses were poor ignorant people. The weighty evi-
30 dence in the case was that of Samuel Pacy, a merchant of Lowes- toft, two of whose children, Elizabeth and Deborah, of the ages of eleven and nine, were said to have been bewitched. The younger child was too ill to be brought to the Assizes, but the elder was produced in Court. Samuel Pacy, their father, is de-
35 scribed as "a man who carried himself with much soberness dur- ing the trial, from whom proceeded no words either of passion

---

[1] Reprinted in *A Collection of Rare and Curious Tracts relating to Witchcraft*. London, 1838.

or malice, though his children were so greatly afflicted." He deposed that his younger daughter, being lame and without power in her limbs, had on a sunshiny day in October "desired to be carried on the east part of the house to be set upon the bank which looketh upon the sea." While she sat there, Amy Duny, who as well as the other prisoner is shown by the evidence to have been by her neighbours commonly reputed a witch, came to the house to get some herrings. She was refused, and went away grumbling. At the same moment the child was seized with violent fits. The doctor who attended her could not explain them. So ten days afterwards her father, according to his own deposition, "by reason of the circumstances aforesaid, and in regard Amy Duny is a woman of an ill fame and commonly reported to be a witch and a sorceress, and for that the said child in her fits would cry out of Amy Duny as the cause of her malady, and that she did affright her with apparitions of her person, as the child in the intervals of her fits related, did suspect the said Amy Duny for a witch, and charged her with the injury and wrong to his child, and caused her to be set in the stocks." While she was there, two women asked her the reason of the illness of Mr. Pacy's child. She answered: "Mr. Pacy keeps a great stir about his child, but let him stay until he hath done as much by his children as I have done by mine." Being asked what she had done to hers, she replied that "she had been fain to open her child's mouth with a tap to give it victuals." Two days afterwards Pacy's elder daughter, Elizabeth, was seized with fits like her sister's; "insomuch that they could not open her mouth to preserve her life without the help of a tap which they were obliged to use." The children in their fits would cry out: "There stands Amy Duny" or "Rose Cullender" (another reputed witch of Lowestoft); and, when the fits were over, would relate how they had seen Amy Duny and Rose Cullender shaking their fists at them and threatening them. They said that bees or flies carried into their mouths the pins and nails which they brought up in their fits. During their illness their father sometimes made them read aloud from the New Testament. He "observed that they would read till they came to the name of *Lord*, or *Jesus*, or *Christ*, and then before they could pronounce either

of the said words they would suddenly fall into their fits. But
when they came to the name of *Satan* or *Devil* they would clap
their fingers upon the book, crying out: 'This bites, but makes
me speak right well.' " And when their father asked them why
they could not pronounce the words *Lord*, or *Jesus*, or *Christ*,
they answered: "Amy Duny saith, I must not use that name."

It seems almost an impertinence nowadays to suppose, that
any one can require telling how self-explanatory all this is, without recourse to witchcraft and magic. These poor rickety children, full of disease and with morbid tricks, have their imagination possessed by the two famed and dreaded witches of their
native place, of whose prowess they have heard tale after tale,
whom they have often seen with their own eyes, whose presence has startled one of them in her hour of suffering, and round
whom all those ideas of diabolical agency, in which they have
been nursed, converge and cluster. The speech of the accused
witch in the stocks is the most natural speech possible, and the
fulfilment which her words received in the course of Elizabeth
Pacy's fits is perfectly natural also. However, Sir Thomas
Browne (who appears in the report of the trial as "Dr. Brown,
of Norwich, a person of great knowledge"), being desired to
give his opinion on Elizabeth Pacy's case and that of two other
children who on similar evidence were said to have been bewitched by the accused,—Sir Thomas Browne

"was clearly of opinion that the persons were bewitched; and said
that in Denmark there had been lately a great discovery of witches,
who used the very same way of afflicting persons by conveying pins
into them, and crooked, as these pins were, with needles and nails.
And his opinion was that the Devil in such cases did work upon the
bodies of men and women upon a natural foundation, . . . for he conceived that these swooning fits were natural, and nothing else but
what they call *the mother*, but only heightened to a great excess by
the subtlety of the Devil, co-operating with the malice of these
which we term witches, at whose instance he doth these villainies."

That was all the light to be got from the celebrated writer on
Vulgar Errors. Yet reason, in this trial, was not left quite without witness:—

"At the hearing the evidence, there were divers known persons, as Mr. Serjeant Keeling, Mr. Serjeant Earl, and Mr. Serjeant Bernard, present. Mr. Serjeant Keeling seemed much unsatisfied with it, and thought it not sufficient to convict the prisoners; for admitting that the children were in truth bewitched, yet, said he, it can   5 never be applied to the prisoners upon the imagination only of the parties afflicted. For if that might be allowed, no person whatsoever can be in safety; for perhaps they might fancy another person, who might altogether be innocent in such matters."

In order, therefore, the better to establish the guilt of the   10 prisoners, they were made to touch the children whom they were said to have bewitched. The children screamed out at their touch. The children were "blinded with their own aprons," and in this condition were again touched by Rose Cullender; and again they screamed out. It was objected, not that the children's   15 heads were full of Rose Cullender and Amy Duny and of their infernal dealings with them, but that the children might be counterfeiting their malady and pretending to start at the witch's touch though it had no real power on them:—

"Wherefore, to avoid this scruple, it was privately desired by the   20 judge, that the Lord Cornwallis, Sir Edward Bacon, Mr. Serjeant Keeling, and some other gentlemen then in Court, would attend one of the distempered persons in the further part of the hall, whilst she was in her fits, and then to send for one of the witches to try what would then happen, which they did accordingly. And Amy Duny   25 was conveyed from the bar and brought to the maid; they put an apron before her eyes, and then one other person touched her hand, which produced the same effect as the touch of the witch did in the Court. Whereupon the gentlemen returned, openly protesting that they did believe the whole transaction of this business was a mere   30 imposture."

This, we are told, "put the Court and all persons into a stand. But at length Mr. Pacy did declare that possibly the maid might be deceived by a suspicion that the witch touched her when she did not." And nothing more likely; but what does this prove?   35 That the child's terrors were sincere; not that the so-called witch had done the acts alleged against her. However, Mr. Pacy's solution of the difficulty was readily accepted. If the children were not shamming out of malice or from a love of imposture, then "it is very evident that the parties were bewitched, and that when they apprehend that the persons who have done them this wrong are near, or touch them, then, their spirits being more than ordinarily moved with rage and anger, they do use more violent gestures of their bodies."

Such was the evidence. The accused did not confess themselves guilty. When asked what they had to say for themselves, they replied, as well they might: "Nothing material to anything that had been proved." Hale then charged the jury. He did not even go over the evidence to them:—

"Only this he acquainted them: that they had two things to inquire after. First, whether or no these children were bewitched; secondly, whether the prisoners at the bar were guilty of it. That there were such creatures as witches he made no doubt at all. For, first, the Scriptures had affirmed so much; secondly, the wisdom of all nations had provided laws against such persons, which is an argument of their confidence of such a crime. And such hath been the judgment of this kingdom, as appears by that Act of Parliament which hath provided punishments proportionable to the quality of the offence. And he desired them strictly to observe their evidence, and desired the great God of Heaven to direct their hearts in this weighty thing they had in hand. For to condemn the innocent, and to let the guilty go free, were both an abomination to the Lord."

The jury retired. In half an hour they came back with a verdict of *guilty* against both prisoners. Next morning the children who had been produced in court were brought to Hale's lodgings, perfectly restored:—

"Mr. Pacy did affirm, that within less than half an hour after the witches were convicted, they were all of them restored, and slept well that night; only Susan Chandler felt a pain like pricking of pins in her stomach."

And this seems to have removed all shadow of doubt or misgiving:—

"In conclusion, the judge and all the court were fully satisfied with the verdict, and thereupon gave judgment against the witches that they should be hanged. They were much urged to confess, but would not. That morning we departed for Cambridge; but no re-prieve was granted, and they were executed on Monday, the 17th of March (1664) following, but they confessed nothing."

Now, the inference to be drawn from this trial is not by any means that Hale was "an imbecile or credulous enthusiast." The whole history of his life and doings disproves it. But the belief in witchcraft was in the very atmosphere which Hale breathed, as the belief in miracle was in the very atmosphere which St. Paul breathed. What the trial shows us is, that a man of veracity, judgment, and mental power, may have his mind thoroughly governed, on certain subjects, by a foregone conclusion as to what is likely and credible. But I will not further enlarge on the illustration which Hale furnishes to us of this truth. An illustra-tion of it, with a yet closer applicability to St. Paul, is supplied by another worthy of the seventeenth century.

III

The worthy in question is very little known, and I rejoice to have an opportunity of mentioning him. *John Smith!*—the name does not sound promising. He died at the age of thirty-four, having risen to no higher post in the world than a college fel-lowship. "He proceeded leisurely by orderly steps," says Simon Patrick, afterwards Bishop of Ely, who preached his funeral-sermon, "not to what he could get, but to what he was fit to undertake." John Smith, born in 1618 near Oundle in North-amptonshire, was admitted a scholar of Emanuel College at Cambridge in 1636, a fellow of Queen's College in 1644. He be-came a tutor and preacher in his college; died there, "after a tedious sickness," on the 7th of August 1652, and was buried in his college-chapel. He was one of that band of Cambridge Pla-tonists, or *latitude men*, as in their own day they were called, whom Burnet has well described as those "who, at Cambridge, studied to propagate better thoughts, to take men off from be-ing in parties, or from narrow notions, from superstitious con-ceits and fierceness about opinions." Principal Tulloch has done an excellent work in seeking to reawaken our interest in this

noble but neglected group. His book[1] is delightful, and it has, at the same time, the most serious value. But in his account of his worthies, Principal Tulloch has given, I cannot but think, somewhat too much space to their Platonic philosophy, to their
5 disquisitions on spirit and incorporeal essence. It is not by these that they merited to live, or that, having passed away from men's minds, they will be brought back to them. It is by their extraordinarily simple, profound, and just conception of religion. Placed between the sacerdotal religion of the Laudian clergy on
10 the one side, and the notional religion of the Puritans on the other, they saw the sterility, the certain doom of both;—saw that stand permanently such developments of religion could not, inasmuch as Christianity was not what either of them supposed, but was a *temper*, a *behaviour*.
15   Their immediate recompense was a religious isolation of two centuries. The religious world was not then ripe for more than the High Church conception of Christianity on the one hand, or the Puritan conception on the other. The Cambridge band ceased to acquire recruits, and disappeared with the century.
20 Individuals knew and used their writings; Bishop Wilson of Sodor and Man, in particular, had profited by them. But they made no broad and clear mark. And this was in part for the reason already assigned, in part because what passed for their great work was that revival of a spiritualist and Platonic philosophy,
25 to which Principal Tulloch, as I have said, seems to me to have given too much prominence. By this attempted revival they could not and cannot live. The theology and writings of Owen are not more extinct than the *Intellectual System* of Cudworth. But in a history of the Cambridge Platonists, works of the
30 magnitude of Cudworth's *Intellectual System of the Universe* must necessarily, perhaps, fill a large space. Therefore it is not so much a history of this group which is wanted, as a republication of such of their utterances as show us their real spirit and power. Their spiritual brother, "the ever memorable Mr.
35 John Hales," must certainly, notwithstanding that he was at Oxford, not Cambridge, be classed along with them. The re-

[1] *Rational Theology and Christian Philosophy in England in the Seventeenth Century;* 2d edition, Edinburgh and London, 1874.

mains of Hales of Eton, the sermons and aphorisms of Whichcote, the sermon preached by Cudworth before the House of
Commons with the second sermon printed as a companion to
it, single sayings and maxims of Henry More, and the *Select
Discourses* of John Smith,—there are our documents! In them
lies enshrined what the *latitude men* have of value for us. It were
well if Principal Tulloch would lay us under fresh obligations
by himself extracting this and giving it to us; but given some
day, and by some hand, it will surely be.

For Hales and the Cambridge Platonists here offer, formulated with sufficient distinctness, a conception of religion true,
long obscured, and for which the hour of light has at last come.
Their productions will not, indeed, take rank as great works of
literature and style. It is not to the history of literature that
Whichcote and Smith belong, but to the history of religion.
Their contemporaries were Bossuet, Pascal, Taylor, Barrow. It
is in the history of literature that these men are mainly eminent,
although they may also be classed, of course, among religious
writers. What counts highest in the history of religion as such,
is, however, to give what at critical moments the religious life
of mankind needs and can use. And it will be found that the
Cambridge Platonists, although neither epoch-making philosophers nor epoch-making men of letters, have in their conception
of religion a boon for the religious wants of our own time, such
as we shall demand in vain from the soul and poetry of Taylor,
from the sense and vigour of Barrow, from the superb exercita-
tions of Bossuet, or the passion-filled reasoning and rhetoric of
Pascal.

The *Select Discourses* of John Smith, collected and published
from his papers after his death, are, in my opinion, by much the
most considerable work left to us by this Cambridge school.
They have a right to a place in English literary history. Yet the
main value of the *Select Discourses* is, I repeat, religious, not
literary. Their grand merit is that they insist on the profound
natural truth of Christianity, and thus base it upon a ground
which will not crumble under our feet. Signal and rare indeed
is the merit, in a theological instructor, of presenting Christianity to us in this fashion. Christianity is true; but in general the

whole plan for grounding and buttressing it chosen by our theological instructors is false, and, since it is false, it must fail us
sooner or later. I have often thought that if candidates for orders were simply, in preparing for their examination, to read
and digest Smith's great discourse, *On the Excellency and No-*
bleness of True Religion, together with M. Reuss's *History of*
Christian Theology at the time of the Apostles, and nothing
further except the Bible itself, we might have, perhaps, a hope
of at last getting, as our national guides in religion, a clergy
which could tell its bearings and steer its way, instead of being, as we now see it, too often conspicuously at a loss to do
either.

Singularly enough, about fifteen years before the trial at Bury
St. Edmunds of the Lowestoft witches, John Smith, the author
of the *Select Discourses,* had in those very eastern counties to
deliver his mind on the matter of witchcraft. On Lady-day
every year, a Fellow of Queen's College, Cambridge, was required to preach at Huntingdon a sermon against witchcraft
and diabolical contracts. Smith, as one of the Fellows of
Queen's, had to preach this sermon. It is printed tenth and last
of his *Select Discourses,* with the title: *A Christian's Conflicts*
and Conquests; or, a Discourse concerning the Devil's Active
Enmity and Continual Hostility against Man, the Warfare of a
Christian Life, the Certainty of Success and Victory in this
Spiritual Warfare, the Evil and Horridness of Magical Arts and
Rites, Diabolical Contracts, &c. The discourse has for its text
the words: "Resist the devil, and he will flee from you."

The preacher sets out with the traditional account of "the
prince of darkness, who, having once stained the original beauty
and glory of the divine workmanship, is continually striving to
mould and shape it more and more into his own likeness." He
says:—

"It were perhaps a vain curiosity to inquire whether the number
of evil spirits exceeds the number of men; but this is too, too certain,
that we never want the secret and latent attendance of them. . . .
Those evil spirits are not yet cast out of the world into outer darkness, though it be prepared for them; the bottomless pit hath not yet
shut its mouth upon them."

And he concludes his sermon with a reflection and a caution, called for, he says, by the particular occasion. The reflection is that—

"Did we not live in a world of professed wickedness, wherein so many men's sins go in open view before them to judgment, it might be thought needless to persuade men to resist the devil when he appears in his own colours to make merchandise of them, and comes in a formal way to bargain with them for their souls; that which human nature, however enthralled to sin and Satan in a more mysterious way, abhors, and none admit but those who are quite degenerated from human kind."

And he adds the caution, that—

"The use of any arts, rites or ceremonies not understood, of which we can give no rational or divine account, this indeed is nothing else but a kind of magic which the devil himself owns and gives life to, though he may not be corporeally present, or require presently any further covenant from the users of them. The devil, no question, is present to all his own rites and ceremonies, though men discern him not, and may upon the use of them secretly produce those effects which may gain credit to them. Among these rites we may reckon insignificant forms of words, with their several modes and manners of pronunciation, astrological arts, and whatsoever else pretends to any strange effects which we cannot with good reason either ascribe to God or nature. As God will only be conversed withal in a way of light and understanding, so the devil loves to be conversed with in a way of darkness and obscurity."

But between his exordium and his conclusion the real man appears. Like Hale, Smith seems to have accepted the belief in witchcraft and in diabolical contracts which was regnant in his day. But when he came to deal with the belief as an idea influencing thought and conduct, he could not take it as the people around him took it. It was his nature to seek a firm ground for the ideas admitted by him; above all, when these ideas had bearings upon religion. And for witchcraft and diabolical operation, in the common conception of them as external things, he could find no solid ground, for there was none; and therefore he could not so use them. See, therefore, how profoundly they are transformed by him! After his exordium he makes an entirely fresh

departure:—"When we say the devil is continually busy with us, I mean not only some apostate spirit as one particular being, but that spirit of apostasy which is lodged in all men's natures." Here, in this *spirit of apostasy which is lodged in all men's na-*
5 *tures,* Smith had what was at bottom experimental and real. And the whole effort of the sermon is to substitute this for what men call the devil, hell, fiends, and witches, as an object for their serious thought and strenuous resistance:—

"As the kingdom of heaven is not so much without men as within,
10 as our Saviour tells us; so the tyranny of the devil and hell is not so much in some external things as in the qualities and dispositions of men's minds. And as the enjoying of God, and conversing with him, consists not so much in a change of place as in the participation of the divine nature and in our assimilation unto God; so our convers-
15 ing with the devil is not so much by a mutual local presence as by an imitation of a wicked and sinful nature derived upon men's own souls. . . . He that allows himself in any sin, or useth an unnatural dalliance with any vice, does nothing else in reality than entertain an *incubus demon.*"

20 This, however, was by no means a view of diabolical posses-sion acceptable to the religious world and to its Puritan min-isters:—

"I know these expressions will seem to some very harsh and unwel-come; but I would beseech them to consider what they will call that
25 spirit of malice and envy, that spirit of pride, ambition, vain-glory, covetousness, injustice, uncleanness, etc., that commonly reigns so much and acts so violently in the minds and lives of men. Let us speak the truth, and call things by their own names; so much as there is of sin in any man, so much there is of the diabolical nature. Why do we
30 defy the devil so much with our tongues, while we entertain him in our hearts? As men's love to God is ordinarily nothing else but the mere tendency of their natures to something that hath the name of God put upon it, without any clear or distinct apprehension of him, so their hatred of the devil is commonly nothing else but an inward
35 displacency of nature against something entitled by the devil's name. And as they commonly make a God like to themselves, such a one as they can best comply with and love, so they make a devil most unlike to themselves, which may be anything but what they them-selves are, that so they may most freely spend their anger and hatred

upon him; just as they say of some of the Ethiopians who used to paint the devil white because they themselves are black. This is a strange, merry kind of madness, whereby men sportingly bereave themselves of the supremest good, and insure themselves, as much as may be, to hell and misery; they may thus cheat themselves for a while, but the eternal foundation of the Divine Being is immutable and unchangeable. And where we find wisdom, justice, loveliness, goodness, love, and glory in their highest elevations and most unbounded dimensions, that is He; and where we find any true participations of these, there is a true communication of God; and a defection from these is the essence of sin and the foundation of hell."

Finally (and I quote the more freely because the author whom I quote is so little known),—finally our preacher goes on to even confute his own exordium:—

"It was the fond error of the Manichees that there was some solid *principium mali*, which, having an eternal existence of its own, had also a mighty and uncontrollable power from within itself whereby it could forcibly enter into the souls of men, and, seating itself there, by some hidden influences irresistibly incline and inforce them to evil. But we ourselves uphold that kingdom of darkness, which else would tumble down and slide into that nothing from whence it came. *All sin and vice is our own creature;* we only give life to them which indeed are our death, and would soon wither and fade away did we substract our concurrence from them."

O fortunate Huntingdon Church, which admitted for even one day such a counterblast to the doctrines then sounding from every pulpit, and still enjoined by Sir Robert Phillimore!

That a man shares an error of the minds around him and of the times in which he lives, proves nothing against his being a man of veracity, judgment, and mental power. This we saw by the case of Hale. But here, in our Cambridge Platonist, we have a man who accepts the erroneous belief in witchcraft, professes it publicly, preaches on it; and yet is not only a man of veracity and intelligence, but actually manages to give to the error adopted by him a turn, an aspect, which indicates its erroneousness. Not only is he of help to us generally, in spite of his error; he is of help to us in respect of that very error itself.

Now, herein is really a most striking analogy between our little-known divine of the seventeenth century and the great

Apostle of the Gentiles. St. Paul's writings are in every one's hands. I have myself discussed his doctrine at length. And for our present purpose there is no need of elaborate exposition and quotation. Every one knows how St. Paul declares his belief that "Christ rose again the third day, and was seen of Cephas, then of the twelve; after that, he was seen of above five hundred brethren at once."[1] Those who do not admit the miraculous can yet well conceive how such a belief arose, and was entertained by St. Paul. *The resurrection of the just* was at that time a ruling idea of a Jew's mind. Herod at once, and without difficulty, supposed that John the Baptist was *risen from the dead*. The Jewish people without difficulty supposed that Jesus might be one of the old prophets, *risen from the dead*. In telling the story of the crucifixion men added, quite naturally, that when it was consummated, "many bodies of the saints which slept *arose and appeared unto many*." Jesus himself, moreover, had in his lifetime spoken frequently of his own coming resurrection. Such beliefs as the belief in bodily resurrection were thus a part of the mental atmosphere in which the first Christians lived. It was inevitable that they should believe their Master to have risen again in the body, and that St. Paul, in becoming a Christian, should receive the belief and build upon it.

But Paul, like our Cambridge Platonist, instinctively sought in an idea used for religion a side by which the idea could enter into his religious experience and become real to him. No such side could be afforded by the mere external fact and miracle of Christ's bodily resurrection. Paul, therefore, as is well known, by a prodigy of religious insight seized another aspect for the resurrection than the aspect of physical miracle. He presented resurrection as a spiritual rising which could be appropriated and enacted in our own living experience. "If One died in the name of all, then all died; and he died in the name of all, that they who live should no more live unto themselves, but unto him who died and rose again in their name."[2] Dying became thus no longer a bodily dying, but a dying to sin; rising to life no longer a bodily resurrection, but a living to God. St.

[1] 1 Cor. xv. 4, 5, 6.   [2] 2 Cor. v. 14, 15.

Paul here comes, therefore, upon that very idea of death and resurrection which was the central idea of Jesus himself. At the very same moment that he shares and professes the popular belief in Christ's miraculous bodily resurrection,—the idea by which our Saviour's own idea of resurrection has been 5 overlaid and effaced,—St. Paul seizes also this other truer idea or is seized by it, and bears unconscious witness to its unique legitimacy.

Where, then, is the force of that *argument of despair*, as we called it, that if St. Paul vouches for the bodily resurrection of 10 Jesus and for his appearance after it, and is mistaken in so vouching, then he must be "an imbecile and credulous enthusiast," untruthful, unprofitable? We see that for a man to believe in preternatural incidents, of a kind admitted by the common belief of his time, proves nothing at all against his general truthfulness 15 and sagacity. Nay, we see that even while affirming such preternatural incidents, he may with profound insight seize the true and natural aspect of them, the aspect which will survive and profit when the miraculous aspect has faded. He may give us, in the very same work, current error and also fruitful and pro- 20 found new truth, the error's future corrective.

IV

But I am treating of these matters for the last time. And those who no longer admit, in religion, the old basis of the preternatural, I see them encountered by scruples of their own, as well as by scruples raised by their opponents. Their opponents, the par- 25 tisans of miracle, require them if they refuse to admit miracle to throw aside as imbecile or untruthful all their instructors and inspirers who have ever admitted it. But they themselves, too, are sometimes afraid, not only of being called inconsistent and insincere, but of really meriting to be called so, if they do not 30 break decidedly with the religion in which they have been brought up, if they at all try still to conform to it and to use it. I have now before me a remarkable letter, in which the writer says:—

"There is nothing I and many others should like better than to take service as ministers in the Church as *a national society for the promotion of goodness;* but how can we do so, when we have first to declare our belief in a quantity of things which every intelligent
5   man rejects?"

Now, as I have examined the question whether a man who rejects miracles must break with St. Paul because Paul asserted them, so let me, before I end, examine the question whether such a man must break with the Church of his country and
10 childhood.

Certainly it is a strong thing to suppose, as the writer of the above-quoted letter supposes, a man taking orders in the Church of England who accepts, say, the view of Christianity offered in *Literature and Dogma.* For the Church of England presents as
15 science, and as necessary to salvation, what it is the very object of that book to show to be *not* science and *not* necessary to salvation. And at his ordination a man is required to declare that he, too, accepts this for science, as the Church does. Formerly a deacon subscribed to the Thirty-nine Articles, and to a decla-
20 ration that he acknowledged "all and every the articles therein contained to be agreeable to the word of God." A clerk, admitted to a benefice with cure, declared "his unfeigned assent and consent to all the matters contained in the Articles." At present, I think, all that is required is a general consent to what-
25 ever is contained in the Book of Common Prayer. But the Book of Common Prayer contains the Thirty-nine Articles. And the Eighth Article declares the Three Creeds to be science, science "thoroughly to be received and believed." Now, whether one professes an "unfeigned assent and consent" to this Article, as
30 contained among the Thirty-nine Articles, or merely "a general consent" to it, as contained in the Prayer Book, one certainly, by consenting to it at all, professes to receive the Three Creeds as science, and as true science. And this is the very point where it is important to be explicit and firm. Whatever else the
35 Three Creeds may be, they are not science, truly formulating the Christian religion. And no one who feels convinced that they are not, can sincerely say that he gives even a general consent to whatever is contained in the Prayer Book, or can at pres-

ent, therefore, be ordained a minister of the Church of England.

The obstacle, it will be observed, is in a test which lies outside of the Ordination Service itself. The test is a remnant of the system of subscriptions and tests formerly employed so vigorously. It was meant as a reduction and alleviation of that old yoke. To obtain such a reduction seemed once to generous and ardent minds, and indeed once was, a very considerable conquest. But the times move rapidly, and even the reduced test has now a great power of exclusion. If it were possible for Liberal politicians ever to deal seriously with religion, they would turn their minds to the removal of a test of this sort, instead of playing with political dissent or marriage with a deceased wife's sister. The Ordination Service itself, on a man's entrance into orders, and the use of the Church services afterwards, are a sufficient engagement. Things were put into the Ordination Service which one might have wished otherwise. Some of them are gone. The introduction of the Oath of Supremacy was a part, no doubt, of all that *lion and unicorn* business which is too plentiful in our Prayer Book, on which Dr. Newman has showered such exquisite raillery, and of which only the Philistine element in our race prevents our seeing the ridiculousness. But the Oath of Supremacy has now no longer a place in the Ordination Service. Apart, however, from such mere matters of taste, there was and still is the requirement, in the Ordering of Deacons, of a declaration of unfeigned belief in all the canonical Scriptures of the Old and New Testament. Perhaps this declaration can have a construction put upon it which makes it admissible. But by its form of expression it recalls, and appears to adopt, the narrow and letter-bound views of Biblical inspiration formerly prevalent,—prevalent with the Fathers as well as with the Reformers,—but which are now, I suppose, generally abandoned. I imagine the clergy themselves would be glad to substitute for this declaration the words in the Ordering of Priests, where the candidate declares himself "persuaded that the Holy Scriptures contain sufficiently all doctrine required for eternal salvation through faith in Jesus Christ." These words present no difficulty, nor is there any other serious difficulty, that I can see, raised by the Ordination Service for either priests or deacons. The declaration of a general consent to the Articles is another matter; although perhaps, in the present temper of men's minds, it could not easily be got rid of.

The last of Butler's jottings in his memorandum-book is a
5   prayer to be delivered "from *offendiculum* of scrupulousness." He was quite right. Religion is a matter where scrupulousness has been far too active, producing most serious mischief; and where it is singularly out of place. I am the very last person to wish to deny it. Those, therefore, who declared their consent to
10 the Articles long ago, and who are usefully engaged in the ministry of the Church, would in my opinion do exceedingly ill to disquiet themselves about having given a consent to the Articles formerly, when things had not moved to the point where they are now, and did not appear to men's minds as they now appear.
15 "Forgetting those things which are behind and reaching forth unto those things which are before," should in these cases be a man's motto. The Church is properly a national society for the promotion of goodness. For him it is such; he ministers in it as such. He has never to use the Articles, never to rehearse them.
20 He has to rehearse the prayers and services of the Church. Much of these he may rehearse as the literal, beautiful rendering of what he himself feels and believes. The rest he may rehearse as an approximative rendering of it;—as language *thrown out* by other men, in other times, at immense objects which deeply en-
25 gaged their affections and awe, and which deeply engage his also; objects concerning which, moreover, adequate statement is impossible. To him, therefore, this approximative part of the prayers and services which he rehearses will be poetry. It is a great error to think that whatever is thus perceived to be poetry
30 ceases to be available in religion. The noblest races are those which know how to make the most serious use of poetry.

But the Articles are plain prose. They aim at the exactitude of a legal document. They are a precise profession of belief, formulated by men of our own nation three hundred years ago,
35 in regard, amongst other things, to parts of those services of the Church of which we have been speaking. At all points the Articles are, and must be, inadequate; but into the question of their general inadequacy we need not now enter. One point is suffi-

cient. They present the Creeds as science, exact science; and this, at the present time of day, very many a man cannot accept. He cannot rightly, then, profess in any way to accept it; cannot, in consequence, take orders.

But it is easy for such a man to exaggerate to himself the barrier between himself and popular religion. The barrier is not so great as he may suppose; and it is expedient for him rather to think it less great than it is, than more great. It will insensibly dwindle, the more that he, and other serious men who think as he does, strive so far as they can to act as if it did not exist. It will stand stiff and bristling the more they act as if it were insurmountable. The Church of our country is to be considered as a national Christian society for the promotion of goodness, to which a man cannot but wish well, and in which he might rejoice to minister. To a right-judging mind, the cardinal points of belief for either the member or the minister of such a society are but two: *Salvation by Righteousness* and *Righteousness by Jesus Christ.* Salvation by Righteousness,—there is the sum of the Old Testament: Righteousness by Jesus Christ,—there is the sum of the New. For popular religion, the cardinal points of belief are of course a good deal more numerous. Not without adding many others could popular religion manage to benefit by the first-named two. But the first-named two have its adherence. It is from the very effort to benefit by them that it has added all the rest. The services of the Church are full of direct recognitions of the two really essential points of Christian belief: *Salvation by Righteousness* and *Righteousness by Jesus Christ.* They are full, too, of what may be called approximate recognitions of them;—efforts of the human mind, in its gradual growth, to develop them, to fix them, to buttress them, to make them clearer to itself, to bring them nearer, by the addition of miracle and metaphysic. This is poetry. The Articles say that this poetry is exact prose. But the Articles are no more a real element of the Prayer Book than Brady and Tate's metrical version of the Psalms, which has now happily been expelled. And even while the Articles continue to stand in the Prayer Book, yet a layman can use the Prayer Book as if they and their definitions did not exist. To be ordained, however, one must adhere

to their definitions. But, putting the Articles aside, will a layman, since he is free, would a clergyman, if he were free, desire
to abandon the use of all those parts of the Prayer Book which
are to be regarded as merely approximative recognitions of its
5 two central truths, and as poetry? Must all such parts one day,
as our experience widens and this view of their character comes
to prevail, be eliminated from our public worship? The question is a most important one.

For although the Comtists, by the mouth of their most elo-
10 quent spokesman, tell us that " 'tis the pedantry of sect alone
which can dare to monopolise to a special creed those precious
heirlooms of a common race," the ideas and power of religion,
and propose to remake religion for us with new and improved
personages, and rites, and words; yet it is certain that here as
15 elsewhere the wonderful force of habit tells, and that the power
of religious ideas over us does not spring up at call, but is intimately dependent upon particular names and practices and
forms of expression which have gone along with it ever since we
can remember, and which have created special sentiments in us.
20 I believe, indeed, that the eloquent spokesman of the Comtists
errs at the very outset. I believe that the power of religion does
of nature belong, in a unique way, to the Bible and to Christianity, and that it is no pedantry of sect which affirms this, but experience. Yet even were it as he supposes, and Christianity were
25 not the one proper bringer-in of righteousness and of the reign
of the Spirit and of eternal life, and these were to be got as well
elsewhere, but still we ourselves had learnt all we know about
them from Christianity,—then for us to be taught them in some
other guise, by some other instructor, would be almost impos-
30 sible. Habits and associations are not formed in a day. Even if
the very young have time enough before them to learn to asso-
ciate religion with new personages and precepts, the middle-
aged and the old have not, and must shrink from such an endeavour. *Mane nobiscum, Domine, nam advesperascit.*

35 Nay, but so prodigious a revolution does the changing the
whole form and feature of religion turn out to be, that it even
unsettles all other things too, and brings back chaos. When it
happens, the civilisation and the society to which it happens are

disintegrated, and men have to begin again. This is what took place when Christianity superseded the old religion of the Pagan world. People may say that there is a fund of ideas common to all religions, at least to all religions of superior and civilised races; and that the personages and precepts, the form and feature, of one such religion may be exchanged for those of another, or for those of some new religion devised by an enlightened eclecticism, and the world may go on all the while without much disturbance. There were philosophers who thought so when Paganism was going out and Christianity coming in. But they were mistaken. The whole civilisation of the Roman world was disintegrated by the change, and men had, I say, to begin again. So immense is the sentiment created by the things to which we have been used in religion, so profound is the wrench at parting with them, so incalculable is the trouble and distraction caused by it. Now, we can hardly conceive modern civilisation breaking up as the Roman did, and men beginning again as they did in the fifth century. But the improbability of this implies the improbability, too, of our seeing all the form and feature of Christianity disappear,—of the religion of Christendom. For so vast a revolution would this be, that it would involve the other.

These considerations are of force, I think, in regard to all radical change in the language of the Prayer Book. It has created sentiments deeper than we can see or measure. Our feeling does not connect itself with *any* language about righteousness and religion, but with *that* language. Very much of it we can all use in its literal acceptation. But the question is as to those parts which we cannot. Of course, those who can take them literally will still continue to use them. But for us also, who can no longer put the literal meaning on them which others do, and which we ourselves once did, they retain a power, and something in us vibrates to them. And not unjustly. For these old forms of expression were men's sincere attempt to set forth with due honour what we honour also; and the sense of the attempt gives a beauty and an emotion to the words, and makes them poetry. The Creeds are in this way an attempt to exalt to the utmost, by assigning to him all the characters which to mankind

seemed to confer exaltation, Jesus Christ. I have elsewhere called
the Apostles' Creed the popular science of Christianity, and the
Nicene Creed its learned science; and in one view of them they
are so. But in another and a better view of them, they are, the
one its popular poetry, the other its learned or,—to borrow the
word which Schopenhauer applied to Hegel's philosophy,—its
scholastic poetry. The one Creed exalts Jesus by concrete images, the other by an imaginative play of abstract ideas. These
two Creeds are the august amplifications, or the high elucida-
tions, which came naturally to the human spirit working in love
and awe upon that inexhaustible theme of profound truth: *Sal-*
vation through Jesus Christ. As such, they are poetry for us;
and poetry consecrated, moreover, by having been on the
tongue of all our forefathers for two thousand years, and on
our own tongue ever since we were born. As such, then, we can
feel them, even when we no longer take them literally; while, as
approximations to a profound truth, we can *use* them. We cannot call them science, as the Articles would have us; but we can
still feel them and still use them. And if we can do this with the
Creeds, still more can we do it with the rest of the services in
the Prayer Book.

As to the very and true foundations, therefore, of the Christian religion,—the belief that salvation is by righteousness, and
that righteousness is by Jesus Christ,—we are, in fact, at one
with the religious world in general. As to the true object of the
Church, that it is the promotion of goodness, we are at one with
them also. And as to the form and wording of religion,—a form
and wording consecrated by so many years and memories,—
even as to this we need not break with them either. They and
we can remain in sympathy. Some changes will no doubt befall
the Prayer Book as time goes on. Certain things will drop away
from its services, other things will replace them. But such
change will happen, not in a sweeping way;—it will come very
gradually, and by the general wish. It will be brought about,
not by a spirit of scrupulosity, innovation, and negation, but by
a prevalent impulse to express in our church-services somewhat
which is felt to need expression, and to be not sufficiently expressed there already.

After all, the great confirmation to a man in believing that the cardinal points of our religion are far fewer and simpler than is commonly supposed, is that such was surely the belief of Jesus himself. And in like manner, the great reason for continuing to use the familiar language of the religion around us as approximative language, and as poetry, although we cannot take it literally, is that such was also the practice of Jesus. For evidently it was so. And evidently, again, the immense misapprehension of Jesus and of his meaning, by popular religion, comes in part from such having been his practice. But if Jesus used this way of speaking in spite of its plainly leading to such misapprehension, it must have been because it was the best way and the only one. For it was not by introducing a brand-new religious language, and by parting with all the old and cherished images, that popular religion could be transformed; but by keeping the old language and images, and as far as possible conveying into them the soul of the new Christian ideal.

When Jesus talked of the Son of Man coming in his glory with the holy angels, setting the good on his right hand and the bad on his left, and sending away the bad into everlasting fire prepared for the devil and his angels, was he speaking literally? Did Jesus mean that all this would actually happen? Popular religion supposes so. Yet very many religious people, even now, suppose that Jesus was but using the figures of Messianic judgment familiar to his hearers, in order to impress upon them his main point:—what sort of spirit and of practice did really tend to salvation, and what did not. And surely almost every one must perceive, that when Jesus spoke to his disciples of their sitting on thrones judging the twelve tribes of Israel, or of their drinking new wine with him in the kingdom of God, he was adopting their material images and beliefs, and was not speaking literally. Yet their Master's thus adopting their material images and beliefs could not but confirm the disciples in them. And so it did, and Christendom, too, after them; yet in this way, apparently, Jesus chose to proceed. But some one may say, that Jesus used this language because he himself shared the materialistic notions of his disciples about the kingdom of God, and thought that coming upon the clouds, and sitting upon thrones, and drinking wine, would really occur in it, and was mistaken in thinking so. And yet there are plain signs that this cannot be the right account of the matter, and that Jesus did not really share the beliefs of his disciples or conceive the kingdom of God as they did. For they manifestly thought,—even the wisest of them, and after their Master's death as well as before it,—that this kingdom was to be a sudden, miraculous, outward transformation of things, which was to come about very soon and in their own lifetime. Nevertheless they themselves report Jesus saying what is in direct contradiction to all this. They report him describing the kingdom of God as an inward change requiring to be spread over an immense time, and coming about by natural means and gradual growth, not suddenly, miraculously. Jesus compares the kingdom of God to a grain of mustard seed and to a handful of leaven. He says: "So is the kingdom of God, as a man may cast seed in the ground, and may go to bed and get up night and day, and the seed shoots and extends he knoweth not how."[1] Jesus told his disciples, moreover, that the good news of the kingdom had to be preached *to the whole world.* The whole world must first be evangelised, no work of one generation, but of centuries and centuries; and then, but not till then, should *the end*, the last day, the new world, the grand transformation of which Jewish heads were so full, finally come. True, the disciples also make Jesus speak as if he fancied this end to be as near as they did. But it is quite manifest that Jesus spoke to them, at different times, of two *ends:* one, the end of the Jewish state and nation, which any one who could "discern the signs of that time" might foresee; the other, the end of the world, the instatement of God's kingdom;—and that they confused the two ends together. Undeniably, therefore, Jesus saw things in a way very different from theirs, and much truer. And if he uses their materialising language and imagery, then, it cannot have been because he shared their illusions. Nevertheless, he uses it.

And the more we examine the whole language of the Gospels, the more we shall find it to be not language all of the speaker's own, and invented by him for the first time, but to be full of

---

[1] Mark iv. 26, 27.

reminiscence and quotation. How deeply all the speakers' minds are governed by the contents of one or two chapters in Daniel, everybody knows. It is impossible to understand anything of the New Testament, without bearing in mind that the main pivot, on which all that is said turns, is supplied by half a dozen verses of Daniel. "The God of heaven shall set up a kingdom which shall never be destroyed, and shall stand for ever. There shall be a time of trouble, such as never was since there was a nation even to that same time. I beheld, till the thrones were cast down, and the Ancient of days did sit; and, behold, one like the Son of man came with the clouds of heaven, and came to the Ancient of days; the judgment was set and the books were opened. And many of them that sleep in the dust of the earth shall awake, some to everlasting life, and some to shame and everlasting contempt."[1] The language of this group of texts, I say, governs the whole language of the New Testament speakers. The disciples use it literally, Jesus uses it as poetry. But all use it.

Those texts from Daniel almost every reader of the Bible knows. But unless a man has an exceedingly close acquaintance with the prophets, he can have no notion, I think, how very much in the speeches of Jesus is not original language of his own, but is language of the Old Testament,—the religious language on which both he and his hearers had been nourished,— adopted by Jesus, and with a sense of his own communicated to it. There is hardly a trait in the great apocalyptic speech of the twenty-fourth chapter of St. Matthew, which has not its original in some prophet. Even where the scope of Jesus is most profoundly new and his own, his phrase is still, as far as may be, old. In the institution of the Lord's Supper his *new covenant* is a phrase from the admirable and forward-pointing prophecy in the thirty-first chapter of Jeremiah.[2] The *covenant in my blood* points to Exodus,[3] and probably, also, to an expression in that strange but then popular medley, the book of Zechariah.[4] These phrases, familiar to himself and to his hearers, Jesus willingly adopted.

[1] Dan. ii. 44; xii. 1, 2; vii. 9, 10, 13.   [2] Verses 31–34.
[3] Exod. xxiv. 8.   [4] Zech. ix. 11.

But if we confine to the Old Testament alone our search for parallel passages, we shall have a quite insufficient notion of the extent to which the language of Jesus is not his own original language, but language and images adopted from what was current at the time. It is this which gives such pre-eminent value to the Book of Enoch. That book,—quoted, as every one will remember, in the Epistle of Jude,[1]—explains what would certainly appear, if we had not this explanation, to be an enlargement and heightening by Jesus, in speaking about the end of the world, of the materialistic data furnished by the Old Testament. For if he thus added to them, it may be said, he must surely have taken them literally. But the Book of Enoch exhibits just the farther stage reached by these data, between the earlier decades of the second century before Christ when the Book of Daniel was written, and the later decades to which belongs the Book of Enoch. And just this farther growth of Messianic language and imagery it was, with which the minds of the contemporaries of Jesus were familiar. And in speaking to them Jesus had to deal with this familiarity. Uncanonical, therefore, though the Book of Enoch be,—for it came too late, and perhaps contains things too strange, for admission into the Canon,—it is full of interest, and every one should read it. The Hebrew original and the Greek version, as is well known, are lost; but the book passed into the Æthiopic Bible, and an Æthiopic manuscript of it was brought to this country from Abyssinia by Bruce, the traveller. The first translator and editor of it, Archbishop Laurence, did his work, Orientalists say, imperfectly, and the English version cannot be trusted. There is an excellent German version; but I wish that the Bishop of Gloucester and Bristol, who is, I believe, an Æthiopic scholar, would give us the book correctly in English.

The Book of Enoch has the names and terms which are already familiar to us from the Old Testament: Head or Ancient of days, Son of man, Son of God, Messiah. It has in frequent use a designation for God, *the Lord of Spirits,* and designations for the Messiah, *the Chosen One, the Just One,* which we come

[1] Verse 14.

upon in the New Testament,[1] but which the New Testament did not, apparently, get from the Old. It has the angels accompanying the Son of Man to judgment, and the Son of Man "sitting on the throne of his glory." It has, again and again, the well-known phrase of the New Testament: *the day of judgment;* it has its outer darkness and its hell-fire. It has its beautiful expression, *children of light.* These additions to the Old Testament language had passed, when Jesus Christ came, into the religion of the time. He did not create them, but he found them and used them. He employed, as sanctions of his doctrine, his contemporaries' ready-made notions of hell and judgment, just as Socrates did. He talked of the outer darkness and the unquenchable fire, as Socrates talked of the rivers of Tartarus. And often, when Jesus used phrases which now seem to us to be his own, he was adopting phrases made current by the Book of Enoch. When he said: "It were better for that man he had never been born;" when he said: "Rejoice because your names are written in heaven;" when he said: "Their angels do always behold the face of my Father which is in heaven;" when he said: "The brother shall deliver up the brother to death and the father the child;" when he said: "Then shall the righteous shine forth as the sun in the kingdom of their Father," he was remembering the Book of Enoch. When he said: "Tell it to *the church;*" when he said to Peter: "Thou art Peter, and upon this rock will I build *my church*, and the gates of hell shall not prevail against it,"—expressions which, because of the word *church*, some reject, and others make the foundation for the most illusory pretensions,—Jesus was but recalling the Book of Enoch. For in that book the expression, *the company* or *congregation* (in Greek *ecclesia*) *of the just* or *righteous*,—of the destined rulers of the coming kingdom of the saints,—has become a consecrated phrase. The Messiah, the founder of that kingdom, is the Just One; "the congregation of the just" are those who follow the Just One, the Just One's company or *ecclesia*. When Peter, therefore, made his ardent declaration of faith, Jesus answered:

[1] *The Father of Spirits* in Hebrews xii. 9; *the Chosen One* in Luke xxiii. 35; *the Just One* in Acts xxii. 14.

"Rock is thy name, and on this rock will I build my company, and the power of death shall not prevail against it." Behold at its source the colossal inscription round the dome of St. Peter's: *Tu es Petrus, et super hanc petram ædificabo ecclesiam*
5   *meam!*

The practical lesson to be drawn from all this is, that we should avoid violent revolution in the words and externals of religion. Profound sentiments are connected with them; they are aimed at the highest good, however imperfectly appre-
10 hended. Their form often gives them beauty, the associations which cluster around them give them always pathos and solemnity. They are to be used as poetry; while at the same time to purge and raise our view of that ideal at which they are aimed, should be our incessant endeavour. Else the use of them is mere
15 dilettanteism. We should seek, therefore, to use them as Jesus did. How freely Jesus himself used them, we see. And yet what a difference between the meaning he put upon them and the meaning put upon them by the Jews! In how general a sense alone can it with truth be said, that he and even his disciples had
20 the same aspirations, the same final aim! How imperfectly did his disciples apprehend him; how imperfectly must they have reported him! But the result has justified his way of proceeding. For while he carried with him, so far as was possible, his disciples, and the world after them, and all who even now see him
25 through the eyes of those first generations, he yet also marked his own real meaning so indelibly, that it shows and shines clearly out, to satisfy all whom,—as time goes on, and experience widens, and more things are known,—the old imperfect apprehension dissatisfies. And it is not to be supposed that a re-
30 jection of all the poetry of popular religion is necessary or advisable now, any more than when Jesus came. But it is an aim which may well indeed be pursued with enthusiasm, to make the true meaning of Jesus, in using that poetry, emerge and prevail. For the immense pathos, so perpetually enlarged upon, of his
35 life and death, does really culminate here: that Christians have so profoundly misunderstood him.

And perhaps I may seem to have said in this essay a great deal about what was merely poetry to Jesus, but too little about what

was his real meaning. What this was, however, I have tried to
bring out elsewhere. Yet for fear, from my silence about it here,
this essay should seem to want due balance, let me end with
what a man who writes it down for himself, and meditates on it,
and entitles it *Christ's religion*, will not, perhaps, go far wrong   5
[in]. It is but a series of well-known sayings of Jesus himself, as
the Gospels deliver them to us. But by putting them together in
the following way, and by connecting them, we enable ourselves, I think, to understand better both what Jesus himself
meant, and how his disciples came with ease,—taking the say-   10
ings singly and interpreting them by the light of their preconceptions,—to mistake them. We must begin, surely, with that
wherewith both he and they began;—with that wherewith
Christianity itself begins, and wherein it ends: "the kingdom of
God."   15

The time is fulfilled and the kingdom of God is at hand!
change the inner man and believe the good news!

He that believeth hath eternal life. He that heareth my word,
and believeth him that sent me, hath eternal life, and cometh not
into judgment, but hath passed from death to life. Verily, verily,   20
I say unto you, The hour cometh and now is, when the dead
shall hear the voice of the Son of God, and they that hear shall
live.

I am come forth from God and am here, for I have not come
of myself, but he sent me. No man can come unto me except the   25
Father that sent me draw him; and I will raise him up in the last
day. He that is of God heareth the words of God; my doctrine
is not mine but his that sent me. He that receiveth me receiveth
him that sent me.

And why call ye me Lord, Lord, and do not what I say? If ye   30
know these things, happy are ye if ye do *them. Cleanse that*
which is within; *the evil thoughts from within, from the heart,*
they *defile the man. And why seest thou the mote that is in thy*
brother's eye, but perceivest not the beam that is in thine own
eye? Take heed to yourselves against insincerity; God knoweth   35
your hearts; blessed are the pure in heart, for they shall see God!

Come unto me, all that labour and are heavy-burdened, and

I will give you rest. Take my yoke upon you, and learn of me that I am mild and lowly in heart, and ye shall find rest unto your souls. For my yoke is kindly, and my burden light.

I am the bread of life; he that cometh to me shall never hun-
5 *ger, and he that believeth on me shall never thirst. I am the living bread; as the living Father sent me, and I live by the Father, so he that eateth me, even he shall live by me. It is the spirit that maketh live, the flesh profiteth nothing; the words which I have said unto you, they are spirit and they are life. If a man keep my*
10 *word, he shall never see death. My sheep hear my voice, and I know them, and they follow me, and I give unto them eternal life, and they shall never perish.*

If a man serve me, let him follow *me; and where I am, there shall also my servant be. Whosoever doth not carry his cross*
15 *and come after me, cannot be my disciple. If any man will come after me, let him renounce himself, and take up his cross daily, and follow me. For whosoever will save his life shall lose it; but whosoever shall lose his life for my sake and the sake of the good news, the same shall save it. For what is a man profited, if he*
20 *gain the whole world, but lose* himself, *be mulcted* of himself? *Therefore doth my Father love me, because I lay down my life that I may take it again. A new commandment give I unto you, that ye love one another. The Son of man came not to be served but to serve, and to give his life a ransom for many.*

25 *I am the resurrection and the life; he that believeth on me, though he die, shall live; and he that liveth and believeth on me shall never die. I am come that ye might have life, and that ye might have it more abundantly. I cast out devils and I do cures to-day and to-morrow; and the third day I shall be perfected.*
30 *Yet a little while, and the world seeth me no more; but ye see me, because I live and ye shall live. If ye keep my commandments ye shall abide in my love, like as I have kept my Father's commandments and abide in his love. He that loveth me shall be loved of my Father, and I will love him, and will manifest my-*
35 *self to him. If a man love me, he will keep my word, and my Father will love him, and we will come unto him, and make our abode with him.*

I am the good shepherd; the good shepherd lays down his life for the sheep. And other sheep I have, which are not of this fold; them also must I bring, and they shall be one flock, one shepherd. Fear not, little flock, for it is your Father's good plea-sure to give you the kingdom.

My kingdom is not of this world; the kingdom of God com- 5
eth not with observation; behold, the kingdom of God is within you! Whereunto shall I liken the kingdom of God? It is like a grain of mustard seed, which a man took and cast into his gar-den, and it grew, and waxed a great tree, and the fowls of the air lodged in the branches of it. It is like leaven, which a woman 10
took, and hid in three measures of meal, till the whole was leav-ened. So is the kingdom of God, as a man may cast seed in the ground, and may go to bed and get up night and day, and the seed shoots and extends he knoweth not how.

And this good news of the kingdom shall be preached in the 15
whole world, for a witness to all nations; and then shall the end come.

With such a construction in his thoughts to govern his use of it, Jesus loved and freely adopted the common wording and imagery of the popular Jewish religion. In dealing with the 20 popular religion in which we have been ourselves bred, we may the more readily follow his example, inasmuch as, though all error has its side of moral danger, yet, evidently, the misconception of their religion by Christians has produced no such grave moral perversion as we see to have been produced in the 25 Scribes and Pharisees by their misconception of the religion of the Old Testament. The fault of popular Christianity as an endeavour after *righteousness by Jesus Christ* is not, like the fault of popular Judaism as an endeavour after *salvation by righteousness*, first and foremost a moral fault. It is, much more, an intel- 30 lectual one. But it is not on that account insignificant. Dr. Mozley urges, that "no inquiry is obligatory upon religious minds in matters of the supernatural and miraculous," because, says he, though "the human mind must refuse to submit to anything contrary to moral sense in Scripture," yet, "there is no moral 35 question raised by the fact of a miracle, nor does a supernatural doctrine challenge any moral resistance." As if there were no

possible resistance to religious doctrines, but a resistance on the ground of their immorality! As if intellectual resistance to them counted for nothing! The objections to popular Christianity are not moral objections, but intellectual revolt against its demon-
5 strations by miracle and metaphysics. To be intellectually convinced of a thing's want of conformity to truth and fact is surely an insuperable obstacle to receiving it, even though there be no moral obstacle added. And no moral advantages of a doctrine can avail to save it, in presence of the intellectual conviction of
10 its want of conformity with truth and fact. And if the want of conformity exists, it is sure to be one day found out. "Things are what they are, and the consequences of them will be what they will be;" and one inevitable consequence of a thing's want of conformity with truth and fact is, that sooner or later the
15 human mind perceives it. And whoever thinks that the ground-belief of Christians is true and indispensable, but that in the account they give of it, and of the reasons for holding it, there is a want of conformity with truth and fact, may well desire to find a better account and better reasons, and to prepare the way
20 for their admission and for their acquiring some strength and consistency in men's minds, against the day when the old means of reliance fail.

But, meanwhile, the ground-belief of all Christians, whatever account they may give to themselves of its source and sanctions,
25 is in itself an indestructible basis of fellowship. Whoever believes the final triumph of Christianity, the Christianisation of the world, to have all the necessity and grandeur of a natural law, will never lack a bond of profound sympathy with popular religion. Compared with agreement and difference on this point,
30 agreement and difference on other points seem trifling. To believe that, whoever are ignorant that righteousness is salvation, "the Eternal shall have them in derision;" to believe that, whatever may be the substitute offered for the righteousness of Jesus, a substitute however sparkling, yet "whosoever drinketh of
35 *this* water shall thirst again;" to desire truly "to have strength to escape all the things which shall come to pass and to stand before the Son of Man,"—is the one authentic mark and seal of the household of faith. Those who share in this belief and in this

desire are fellow-citizens of the "city which hath foundations."
Whosoever shares in them not, is, or is in danger of any day becoming, a wanderer, as St. Augustine says, through "the waste
places fertile in sorrow;" a wanderer "seeking rest and finding
none." *In all things I sought rest; then the Creator of all things*   5
gave me commandment and said: Let thy dwelling be in Jacob,
and thine inheritance in Israel! And so was I established in Sion;
likewise in the beloved city he gave me rest, and in Jerusalem
was my power.

Preface
[to *Last Essays*]

The present volume closes the series of my attempts to deal directly with questions concerning religion and the Church. Indirectly such questions must often, in all serious literary work, present themselves; but in this volume I make them my direct
5   object for the last time. Assuredly it was not for my own pleasure that I entered upon them at first, and it is with anything but reluctance that I now part from them. Neither can I be ignorant what offence my handling of them has given to many whose good-will I value, and with what relief they will learn that the
10   handling is now to cease. Personal considerations, however, ought not in a matter like this to bear sway; and they have not, in fact, determined me to bring to an end the work which I had been pursuing. But the thing which I proposed to myself to do has, so far as my powers enabled me to do it, been done. What I
15   wished to say has been said. And in returning to devote to literature, more strictly so-called, what remains to me of life and strength and leisure, I am returning, after all, to a field where work of the most important kind has now to be done, though indirectly, for religion. I am persuaded that the transformation
20   of religion, which is essential for its perpetuance, can be accomplished only by carrying the qualities of flexibility, perceptiveness, and judgment, which are the best fruits of letters, to whole classes of the community which now know next to nothing of them, and by procuring the application of those qualities to mat-
25   ters where they are never applied now.

A survey of the forms and tendencies which religion exhibits at the present day in England has been made lately by a man of genius, energy, and sympathy—Mr. Gladstone. Mr. Gladstone seems disposed to fix as the test of value, for those several forms, their greater or lesser adaptedness to the mind of masses of our people. It may be admitted that religion ought to be capable of reaching the mind of masses of men. It may be admitted that a religion not plain and simple, a religion of abstractions and intellectual refinements, cannot influence masses of men. But it is an error to imagine that the mind of our masses, or even the mind of our religious world, is something which may remain just as it now is, and that religion will have to adapt itself to that mind just as it now is. At least as much change is required, and will have to take place, in that mind as in religion. Gross of perception and materialising that mind is, at present, still disposed to be. Yet at the same time it is undeniable that the old anthropomorphic and miraculous religion, suited in many respects to such a mind, no longer reaches and rules it as it once did. A check and disturbance to religion thence arises. But let us impute the disturbance to the right cause. It is not to be imputed merely to the inadequacy of the old materialising religion, and to be remedied by giving to this religion a form still materialising, but more acceptable. It is to be imputed, in at least an equal degree, to the grossness of perception and materialising habits of the popular mind, which unfit it for any religion not lending itself, like the old popular religion, to those habits; while yet, from other causes, that old religion cannot maintain its sway. And it is to be remedied by a gradual transformation of the popular mind, by slowly curing it of its grossness of perception and of its materialising habits, not by keeping religion materialistic that it may correspond to them.

The conditions of the religious question are, in truth, profoundly misapprehended in this country. In England and in America religion has retained so much hold upon the affections of the community, that the partisans of popular religion are easily led to entertain illusions; to fancy that the difficulties of their case are much less than they are, that they can make terms which they cannot make, and save things which they cannot save. A good medicine for such illusions would be the perusal of the criticisms which *Literature and Dogma* has encountered on the Continent. Here in England that book passes, in general, for a book revolutionary and anti-religious. In foreign critics of

the liberal school it provokes a feeling of mingled astonishment
and impatience; impatience, that religion should be set on new
grounds when they had hoped that religion, the old ground having in the judgment of all rational persons given way, was going
5   to ruin as fast as could fairly be expected; astonishment, that any
man of liberal tendencies should not agree with them.

Particularly striking, in this respect, were the remarks upon
Literature and Dogma of M. Challemel-Lacour, in France, and
of Professor de Gubernatis, in Italy. Professor de Gubernatis is
10 perhaps the most accomplished man in Italy; he is certainly one
of the most intelligent. M. Challemel-Lacour is, or was, one of
the best, gravest, most deeply interesting and instructive, of
French writers. His admirable series of articles on Wilhelm von
Humboldt, which I read a good many years ago in the *Revue*
15 *des Deux Mondes,* still live as fresh in my memory as if I had
read them yesterday. M. Challemel-Lacour has become an ardent politician. It is well known how politics, in France, govern
men's treatment of the religious question. Some little temper and
heat are excusable, undoubtedly, when religion raises in a man's
20 mind simply the image of the clerical party and of his sworn
political foes. Perhaps a man's view of religion, however, must
necessarily in this case be somewhat warped. Professor de Gubernatis is not a politician; he is an independent friend of progress, of high studies, and of intelligence. His remarks on *Lit-*
25 *erature and Dogma,* therefore, and on the attempt made in
that book to give a new life to religion by giving a new sense
to words of the Bible, have even a greater significance than
M. Challemel-Lacour's. For Italy and for Italians, says Professor
de Gubernatis, such an attempt has and can have no interest
30 whatever. "In Italy the Bible is just this:—for priests, a sacred
text; for infidels, a book full of obscenities and contradictions;
for the learned, an historical document to be used with great
caution; for lovers of literature, a collection of very fine specimens of Oriental poetic eloquence. But it never has been, and
35 never will be, a fruitful inspirer of men's daily life." "And how
wonderful," Professor de Gubernatis adds, "that any one should
wish to make it so, and should raise intellectual and literary discussions having this for their object!" "It is strange that the hu-

man genius should take pleasure in combating in such narrow
lists, with such treacherous ground under one's feet, with such
a cloudy sky over one's head;—and all this in the name of freedom of discussion!" "What would the author of *Literature and
Dogma* say," concludes Professor de Gubernatis, "if Plato had   5
based his republic upon a text of Hesiod;—*se Platone avesse
fondata la sua Repubblica sopra un testo d'Esiodo?*" That is to
say, the Bible has no more solidity and value, as a basis for human life, than the *Theogony*.

Here we have, undoubtedly, the genuine opinion of Conti-   10
nental liberalism concerning the religion of the Bible and its future. It is stated with unusual frankness and clearness, but it is
the genuine opinion. It is not an opinion which at present prevails at all widely either in this country or in America. But when
we consider the immense change which, in other matters where   15
tradition and convention were the obstacles to change, has be-
fallen the thought of this country since the Continent was
opened at the end of the great war, we cannot doubt that in
religion, too, the mere barriers of tradition and convention will
finally give way, that a common European level of thought will   20
establish itself, and will spread to America also. Of course there
will be backwaters, more or less strong, of superstition and ob-
scurantism; but I speak of the probable development of opinion
in those classes which are to be called progressive and liberal.
Such classes are undoubtedly the multiplying and prevailing   25
body both here and in America. And I say that, if we judge the
future from the past, these classes, in any matter where it is tradition and convention that at present isolates them from the
common liberal opinion of Europe, will, with time, be drawn
almost inevitably into that opinion.   30

The partisans of traditional religion in this country do not
know, I think, how decisively the whole force of progressive
and liberal opinion on the Continent has pronounced against the
Christian religion. They do not know how surely the whole
force of progressive and liberal opinion in this country tends to   35
follow, so far as traditional religion is concerned, the opinion of
the Continent. They dream of patching up things unmendable,
of retaining what can never be retained, of stopping change at a

point where it can never be stopped. The undoubted tendency
of liberal opinion is to reject the whole anthropomorphic and
miraculous religion of tradition, as unsound and untenable. On
the Continent such opinion has rejected it already. One cannot
5   blame the rejection. "Things are what they are," and the religion of tradition, Catholic or Protestant, *is* unsound and untenable. A greater force of tradition in favour of religion is all
which now prevents the liberal opinion in this country from
following Continental opinion. That force is not of a nature to
10 be permanent, and it will not, in fact, hold out long. But a very
grave question is behind.

    Rejecting, henceforth, all concern with the obsolete religion
of tradition, the liberalism of the Continent rejects also, and on
the like grounds, all concern with the Bible and Christianity. To
15 claim for the Bible the direction, in any way, of modern life, is,
we hear, as if Plato had sought to found his ideal republic "upon
a text of Hesiod." The real question is whether this conclusion,
too, of modern liberalism is to be admitted, like the conclusion
that traditionary religion is unsound and obsolete. And it does
20 not find many gainsayers. Obscurantists are glad to see the question placed on this footing: that the cause of traditionary religion, and the cause of Christianity in general, must stand or fall
together. For they see but very little way into the future; and
in the immediate present this way of putting the question tells,
25 as they clearly perceive, in their favour. In the immediate present many will be tempted to cling to the traditionary religion
with their eyes shut, rather than accept the extinction of Christianity. Other friends of religion are busy with fantastic projects, which can never come to anything, but which prevent
30 their seeing the real character of the situation. So the thesis of
modern liberals on the Continent, that Christianity in general
stands on the same footing as traditionary religion and must
share its fate, meets with little direct discussion or opposition.
And liberal opinion everywhere will at last grow accustomed to
35 finding that thesis put forward as certain, will become familiar-
ised with it, will suppose that no one disputes it. This in itself
will tend to withhold men from any serious return upon their
own minds in the matter. Meanwhile the day will most certainly

arrive, when the great body of liberal opinion in this country will adhere to the first half of the doctrine of Continental liberals;—will admit that traditionary religion is utterly untenable. And the danger is, that from the habits of their minds, and from seeing the thing treated as certain, and from hearing nothing urged against it, our liberals may admit as indisputable the second half of the doctrine too: that Christianity, also, is untenable.

And therefore is it so all-important to insist on what I call the *natural truth* of Christianity, and to bring this out all we can. Liberal opinion tends, as we have seen, to treat traditional religion and Christianity as identical; if one is unsound, so is the other. Especially, however, does liberal opinion show this tendency among the Latin nations, on whom Protestantism did not lay hold; and it shows it most among those Latin nations of whom Protestantism laid hold least, such as Italy and Spain. For Protestantism was undoubtedly, whatever may have been its faults and miscarriages, an assertion of the natural truth of Christianity for the mind and conscience of men. The question is, whether Christianity has this natural truth or not. It is a question of fact. In the end the victory belongs to facts, and he who contradicts them finds that he runs his head against a wall. Our traditional religion turns out not to have, in fact, natural truth, the only truth which can stand. The miracles of our traditional religion, like other miracles, did not happen; its metaphysical proofs of God are mere words. Has or has not Christianity, in fact, the same want of natural truth as our traditional religion? It is a question of immense importance. Of questions about religion, it may be said to be at the present time, for a serious man, the only important one.

Now, whoever seeks to show the natural truth of a thing which professes to be for general use, ought to try to be as simple as possible. He ought not to allow himself to have any recourse either to intellectual refinements or to sentimental rhetoric. And therefore it is well to start, in bringing out the truth of Christianity, with a plain proposition such as everybody, one would think, must admit: the proposition that conduct is a very important matter. I have called conduct three-fourths of life. M. Challemel-Lacour quarrels greatly with the proposition. Cer-

tainly people in general do not behave as if they were convinced
that conduct is three-fourths of life. Butler well says that even
religious people are always for placing the stress of their religion anywhere other than on virtue;—virtue being simply the
good direction of conduct. We know, too, that the Italians at
the Renascence changed the very meaning of the word virtue
altogether, and made their *virtù* mean a love of the fine arts and
of intellectual culture. And we see the fruits of the new definition in the Italy of the seventeenth and eighteenth centuries. We
will not, then, there being all this opposition, offer to settle the
exact proportion of life which conduct may be said to be. But
that conduct is, at any rate, a very considerable part of life, will
generally be admitted.

It will generally be admitted, too, that all experience as to
conduct brings us at last to the fact of two selves, or instincts,
or forces,—name them how we will, and however we may suppose them to have arisen,—contending for the mastery in man:
one, a movement of first impulse and more involuntary, leading
us to gratify any inclination that may solicit us, and called generally a movement of man's ordinary or passing self, of sense,
appetite, desire; the other, a movement of reflection and more
voluntary, leading us to submit inclination to some rule, and
called generally a movement of man's higher or enduring self,
of reason, spirit, will. The thing is described in different words
by different nations and men relating their experience of it, but
as to the thing itself they all, or all the most serious and important among them, agree. This, I think, will be admitted. Nor
will it be denied that they all come to the conclusion that for a
man to obey the higher self, or reason, or whatever it is to be
called, is happiness and life for him; to obey the lower is death
and misery. It will be allowed, again, that whatever men's minds
are to fasten and rest upon, whatever is to hold their attention
and to rule their practice, naturally embodies itself for them in
certain examples, precepts, and sayings, to which they perpetually recur. Without a frame or body of this kind, a set of
thoughts cannot abide with men and sustain them. "If ye abide
in me," says Jesus, "ye shall know the truth, and the truth shall
make you free;"—not if you keep skipping about all over the

world for various renderings of it. "It behoves us to know," says
Epictetus, "that a principle can hardly establish itself with a
man, unless he every day utters the same things, hears the same
things, and applies them withal to his life." And naturally the
body of examples and precepts, which men should use for this   5
purpose, ought to be those which most impressively represent
the principle, or the set of thoughts, commending itself to their
minds for respect and attention. And the more the precepts are
used, the more will men's sentiments cluster around them, and
the more dear and solemn will they be.   10

Now to apply this to Christianity. It is evident that to what
they called *righteousness*,—a name which covers all that we
mean by conduct,—the Jewish nation attached pre-eminent,
unique importance. This impassioned testimony of theirs to the
weight of a thing admittedly of very considerable importance,   15
has its own value of a special kind. But it is well known how
imperfectly and amiss the Jewish nation conceived righteousness. And finally, when their misconceived righteousness failed
them in actual life more and more, they took refuge in imaginings about the future, and filled themselves with hopes of a *king-* 20
dom of God, a *resurrection*, a *judgment*, an *eternal life*, bringing
in and establishing for ever this misconceived righteousness of
theirs. As God's agent in this work of restoring the kingdom to
Israel they promised to themselves an Anointed and Chosen
One, *Christ the son of God*.[1]   25

Jesus Christ found, when he came among his countrymen, all
these phrases and ideas ruling their minds. Conduct or righteousness, a matter admittedly of very considerable importance, and
which the Jews thought of paramount importance, they had
come entirely to misconceive, and had created an immense po-   30
etry of hopes and imaginings in favour of their misconception.
What did Jesus do? From his countrymen's errors about righteousness he reverted to the solid, authentic, universal fact of
experience about it: the fact of the higher and lower self in man,
inheritors the one of them of happiness, the other of misery. He   35
possessed himself of it, he made it the centre of his teaching. He

---

[1] John xx. 31.

made it so in the well-known formula, his *secret:* "He that will
save his life shall lose it; he that do lose his life shall save it." And
by his admirable figure of the *two lives* of man, the real life and
the seeming life, he connected this profound fact of experience
with that attractive poetry of hopes and imaginings which possessed the minds of his countrymen. Eternal life? Yes, the life in
the higher and undying self of man. Judgment? Yes, the trying,
in conscience, of the claims and instigations of the two lives, and
the decision between them. Resurrection? Yes, the rising from
bondage and transience with the lower life to victory and permanence with the higher. The kingdom of God? Yes, the reign
amongst mankind of the higher life. The Christ the son of God?
Yes, the bringer-in and founder of this reign of the higher life,
this true kingdom of God.

But we can go farther. Observers say, with much appearance
of truth, that all our passions may be run up into two elementary instincts: the reproductive instinct and the instinct of self-
preservation. It is evident to what these instincts will in themselves carry the man who follows the lower self of sense, and
appetite, and first impulse. It is evident, also, that they are directly controlled by two forces which Christianity, following
that law of the higher life which St. Paul names indifferently
the *law of God*, the *law of our mind*, the *line of thought of the
spirit*[1]—has set up as its two grand virtues: kindness and pureness, charity and chastity. If any virtues could stand for the
whole of Christianity, these might. Let us have them from the
mouth of Jesus Christ himself. "He that loveth his life shall lose
it; a new commandment give I unto you that ye love *one another*." There is charity. "Blest are the pure in heart, for they
shall see God." There is purity.

We go here simply on experience, having to establish the
natural truth of Christianity. That the "new commandment" of
charity is enjoined by the Bible, gives it therefore, we shall suppose, no force at all, unless it turns out to be enjoined also by
experience. And it is enjoined by experience if experience shows
that it is necessary to human happiness,—that men cannot get

---

[1] φρόνημα τοῦ πνεύματος.

on without it. Now really if there is a lesson which in our day
has come to force itself upon everybody, in all quarters and by
all channels, it is the lesson of the *solidarity*, as it is called by
modern philosophers, of men. If there was ever a notion tempting to common human nature, it was the notion that the rule of   5
"every man for himself" was the rule of happiness. But at last it
turns out as a matter of experience, and so plainly that it is coming to be even generally admitted,—it turns out that the only
real happiness is in a kind of impersonal higher life, where the
happiness of others counts with a man as essential to his own.   10
He that loves his life does really turn out to lose it, and the new
commandment proves its own truth by experience.

And the other great Christian virtue, pureness? Here the case
is somewhat different. One hears doubts raised, nowadays, as to
the natural truth of this virtue. While science has adopted, as a   15
truth confirmed by experience, the Christian idea of charity,
long supposed to conflict with experience, and has decked it
out with the grand title of *human solidarity*, one may hear many
doubts thrown, in the name of science and reason, on the truth
and validity of the Christian idea of pureness. As a mere *com-*   20
mandment this virtue cannot have the authority which it once
had, for the notion of *commandments* in this sense is giving way.
And on its natural truth, when the thing comes to be tested by
experience, doubts are thrown. Well, experience must decide.
It is a question of fact. "There is no honest woman who is not   25
sick of her trade," says La Rochefoucauld. "I pass for having
enjoyed life," said Ninon in old age, "but if any one had told
me beforehand what my life was going to be I would have
hanged myself." Who is right? On which side is *natural truth?*
It will be admitted that there can hardly be a more vital ques-   30
tion for human society. And those who doubt on which side is
natural truth, and who raise the question, will have to learn by
experience. But finely touched souls have a presentiment of a
thing's natural truth even though it be questioned, and long before the palpable proof by experience convinces all the world.   35
They have it quite independently of their attitude towards traditional religion. "May the idea of *pureness*, extending itself to
the very morsel which I take into my mouth, grow ever clearer

in me and clearer!"[1] So prayed Goethe. And all such well-in-
spired souls will perceive the profound natural truth of the idea
of pureness, and will be sure therefore, that the more boldly it
is challenged, the more sharply and signally will experience
5   mark its truth. So that of the two great Christian virtues, charity
and chastity, kindness and pureness, the one has at this moment
the most signal testimony from experience to its intrinsic truth
and weight, and the other is expecting it.

All this may enable us to understand how admirably fitted are
10 Jesus Christ and his precepts to serve as mankind's standing reminder as to conduct,—to serve as men's religion. Jesus Christ
and his precepts are found to hit the moral experience of mankind, to hit it in the critical points, to hit it lastingly; and, when
doubts are thrown upon their really hitting it, then to come out
15 stronger than ever. And we know how Jesus Christ and his precepts won their way from the very first, and soon became the
religion of all that part of the world which most counted, and
are now the religion of all that part of the world which most
counts. This they certainly in great part owed, even from the
20 first, to that instinctive sense of their natural fitness for such a
service, of their natural truth and weight, which amidst all mis-
apprehensions of them they inspired.

Moreover, we must always keep in sight one specially important element in the power exercised by Jesus Christ and his pre-
25 cepts. And that is, the impression left by Jesus of what we call
sweet reason in the highest degree; of consummate justness in
what he said, perfect balance, unerring felicity. For this impression has been a great element of progress. It made half the charm
of the religion of Jesus in the first instance, and it makes it still.
30 But it also serves in an admirable way against the misapprehen-
sions with which men received, as we have said, and could not
but receive, the natural truth he gave them, and which they
made up along with that truth into their religion. For it is felt
that anything exaggerated, distorted, false, cannot be from Je-
35 sus; that it must be human perversion of him. There is always
an appeal open, and a return possible, to the acknowledged

1 "Möge die Idee des *Reinen,* die sich auf den Bissen erstreckt den ich
in den Mund nehme, immer lichter in mir werden!"

sweet reason of Jesus, to his "grace and truth." And thus Christians, instead of sticking for ever because of their religion to errors which they themselves have put into their religion, find in their religion itself a ground for breaking with them. For example: medieval charity and medieval chastity are manifestly 5 misgrowths, however natural,—misgrowths unworkable and dangerous,—of the ideas of kindness and pureness. Then they cannot have come from Jesus; they cannot be what Jesus meant. Such is the inevitable inference; and Christianity here touches a spring for self-correction and self-readjustment which is of 10 the highest value.

And, finally, the figure and sayings of Jesus, embodying and representing men's moral experience to them, serving them as a perpetual reminder of it, by a fixed form of words and observances holding their attention to it, and thus attaching them, have 15 attracted to themselves, by the very force of time, and use, and association, a mass of additional attachment, and a host of sentiments the most tender and profound.

This, then, is what we mean by saying that Christianity has natural truth. By this truth things must stand, not by people's 20 wishes and asseverations about them. *Omnium Deus est, cujus, velimus aut nolimus, omnes sumus,* says Tertullian. "The God of all of us is the God that we all belong to whether we will or no." The Eternal that makes for righteousness is such a God; and he is the God of Christianity. Jesus explains what this God 25 would have of us; and the strength of Jesus is that he explains it right. The natural experimental truth of his explanations is their one claim upon us; but this is claim enough. Does the thing, being admittedly most important, turn out to be as he says? If it does, then we "belong to him whether we will or no." 30

A recent German writer, wishing to exhalt Schopenhauer at the expense of Jesus, says that both Jesus and Schopenhauer taught the true doctrine of self-renouncement, but that Schopenhauer faced the pessimism which is that doctrine's natural accompaniment, whereas Jesus sought to escape from it by the 35 dream of a paradise to come. This critic credits Jesus, as usual, with the very misconceptions against which he strove. It was the effort of Jesus to place the bliss, the eternal life of popular

religion, not where popular religion placed it, in a fantastic paradise to come, but in the joy of self-renouncement. This was the
"eternal life" of Jesus; this was his "joy;"—the joy which he
desired that his disciples, too, might have full and complete,
might have "fulfilled in themselves." His depth, his truth, his
rightness, come out in this very point; that he saw that self-renouncement *is* joy, and that human life, in which it takes place,
is therefore a blessing and a benefit. And just exactly here is his
superiority to Schopenhauer. Jesus hits the plain natural truth
that human life is a blessing and a benefit, while Schopenhauer
misses it. "It is evident, even *a priori*, that the world is doomed
to evil, and that it is the domain of irrationality. In abstinence
from the further propagation of mankind is salvation. This
would gradually bring about the extinction of our species, and,
with our extinction, that of the universe, since the universe requires for its existence the co-operation of human thought."
The fault of this sort of thing is, that it is plainly, somehow or
other, a paradox, and that human thought (I say it with due
deference to the many persons for whom Schopenhauer is just
now in fashion) instinctively feels it to be absurd. The *fact* is
with Jesus. "The Eternal is king, the earth may be *glad* thereof."
Human life is a blessing and a benefit, and constantly improv-
able, because in self-renouncement is a fount of joy, "springing
up unto everlasting life." Not only, "It is more *right* to give
than to receive," more rational, more necessary; but, "It is more
blessed to give than to receive."

The *fact*, I say, the real *fact*, is what it imports us to reach. A
writer of remarkable knowledge, judgment, and impartiality,
M. Maurice Vernes, of the *Revue Scientifique*, objects to the
contrast of an earlier intuition of Israel, *Righteousness tendeth
to life, the righteous is an everlasting foundation,* with a later
"Aberglaube," such as we find in the Book of Daniel, and such
as Jesus had to deal with. He objects to the contrast of the doctrine of Jesus with the metaphysics of the Church. M. Maurice
Vernes is one of those, of whom there are so many, who have a
philosophical system of history,—a history ruled by the law of
progress, of evolution. Between the eighth century before our
era and the second, the law of evolution must have been at
work. Progress must have gone on. Therefore the Messianic

ideas of the Book of Daniel must be a higher stage than the ideas of the great prophets and wise men of the eighth and ninth centuries. Again. The importation of metaphysics into Christianity means the arrival of Greek thought, Western thought,—the enrichment of the early Christian thought with new elements. This is evolution, development. And therefore, apparently, the Athanasian Creed must be a higher stage than the Sermon on the Mount.

Let us salute with respect that imposing generality, the law of evolution. But let us remember that, in each particular case which comes before us, what concerns us is, surely, the *fact* as to that particular case. And surely, as a matter of fact, the ideas of the great prophets and wise men of the eighth or ninth century before Christ are profounder and more true than the ideas of the eschatologist of the Book of Daniel. As a matter of fact, again, the ideas of Jesus in the Sermon on the Mount are surely profounder and more true than the ideas of the theologian of the Athanasian Creed. Ins and outs of this kind may settle their business with the general law of evolution as they can; but our business is with the fact. And the fact, surely, is here as we have stated it.

M. Vernes further objects to our picking and choosing among the records of Jesus, and pronouncing that whatever suits us shall be held to come from Jesus, and whatever does not suit us from his reporters. But here, again, it is a question of fact;—a question, which of two things is, in fact, more likely? Is it, in fact, more likely that Jesus, being what we can see from certain of the data about him that he was, should have been in many points misunderstood and misrepresented by his followers; or that, being what by those data he was, he should also have been at the same time the thaumaturgical personage that his followers imagined? The more reasonable Jesus is likewise, surely, the more real one.

I believe, then, that the real God, the real Jesus, will continue to command allegiance, because we do, in fact, "belong to them." I believe that Christianity will survive because of its natural truth. Those who fancied that they had done with it, those who had thrown it aside because what was presented to them under its name was so unreceivable, will have to return to it

again, and to learn it better. The Latin nations,—even the southern Latin nations,—will have to acquaint themselves with that
fundamental document of Christianity, the Bible, and to discover wherein it differs from "a text of Hesiod." Neither will
5 the old forms of Christian worship be extinguished by the
growth of a truer conception of their essential contents. Those
forms, thrown out at dimly-grasped truth, approximative and
provisional representations of it, and which are now surrounded
with such an atmosphere of tender and profound sentiment,
10 will not disappear. They will survive as poetry. Above all,
among the Catholic nations will this be the case. And, indeed,
one must wonder at the fatuity of the Roman Catholic Church,
that she should not herself see what a future there is for her
here. Will there never arise among Catholics some great soul,
15 to perceive that the eternity and universality, which is vainly
claimed for Catholic dogma and the ultramontane system, might
really be possible for Catholic worship? But to rule over the
moment and the credulous has more attraction than to work for
the future and the sane.

20   Christianity, however, will find the ways for its own future.
What is certain is that it will not disappear. Whatever progress
may be made in science, art, and literary culture,—however
much higher, more general, and more effective than at present
the value for them may become,—Christianity will be still there
25 as what these rest against and imply; as the indispensable background, the *three-fourths of life*. It is true, while the remaining
fourth is ill-cared for, the three-fourths themselves must also
suffer with it. But this does but bring us to the old and true
Socratic thesis of the interdependence of virtue and knowledge.
30 And we cannot, then, do better than conclude with some excellent words of Mr. Jowett, doing homage, in the preface introducing his translation of Plato's Protagoras, to that famous thesis. "This is an aspect of the truth which was lost almost as soon
as it was found; and yet has to be recovered by every one for
35 himself who would pass the limits of proverbial and popular
philosophy. The moral and intellectual are always dividing, yet
they must be reunited, and in the highest conception of them
are inseparable."

MIXED ESSAYS

A French Critic on Milton

Mr. Trevelyan's Life of his uncle must have induced many people to read again Lord Macaulay's *Essay on Milton*. With the *Essay on Milton* began Macaulay's literary career, and, brilliant as the career was, it had few points more brilliant than its beginning. Mr. Trevelyan describes with animation that decisive first success. The essay appeared in the *Edinburgh Review* in 1825. Mr. Trevelyan says, and quite truly:—

"The effect on the author's reputation was instantaneous. Like Lord Byron, he awoke one morning and found himself famous. The beauties of the work were such as all men could recognise, and its very faults pleased. . . . The family breakfast-table in Bloomsbury was covered with cards of invitation to dinner from every quarter of London. . . . A warm admirer of Robert Hall, Macaulay heard with pride how the great preacher, then well-nigh worn out with that long disease, his life, was discovered lying on the floor, employed in learning by aid of grammar and dictionary enough Italian to enable him to verify the parallel between Milton and Dante. But the compliment that, of all others, came most nearly home,—the only commendation of his literary talent which even in the innermost domestic circle he was ever known to repeat,—was the sentence with which Jeffrey acknowledged the receipt of his manuscript: 'The more I think, the less I can conceive where you picked up that style.'"

And already, in the *Essay on Milton*, the style of Macaulay is, indeed, that which we know so well. A style to dazzle, to gain admirers everywhere, to attract imitators in multitude! A style brilliant, metallic, exterior; making strong points, alternating invective with eulogy, wrapping in a robe of rhetoric the thing it represents; not, with the soft play of life, following and rendering the thing's very form and pressure. For, indeed, in rendering things in this fashion, Macaulay's gift did not lie. Mr. Trevelyan reminds us that in the preface to his collected Essays, Lord Macaulay himself "unsparingly condemns the redundance of youthful enthusiasm" of the *Essay on Milton*. But the unsoundness of the essay does not spring from its "redundance of youthful enthusiasm." It springs from this: that the writer has not for his aim to see and to utter the real truth about his object. Whoever comes to the *Essay on Milton* with the desire to get at the real truth about Milton, whether as a man or as a poet, will feel that the essay in nowise helps him. A reader who only wants rhetoric, a reader who wants a panegyric on Milton, a panegyric on the Puritans, will find what he wants. A reader who wants criticism will be disappointed.

This would be palpable to all the world, and every one would feel, not pleased, but disappointed, by the *Essay on Milton*, were it not that the readers who seek for criticism are extremely few; while the readers who seek for rhetoric, or who seek for praise and blame to suit their own already established likes and dislikes, are extremely many. A man who is fond of rhetoric may find pleasure in hearing that in *Paradise Lost* "Milton's conception of love unites all the voluptuousness of the Oriental haram, and all the gallantry of the chivalric tournament, with all the pure and quiet affection of an English fireside." He may glow at being told that "Milton's thoughts resemble those celestial fruits and flowers which the Virgin Martyr of Massinger sent down from the gardens of Paradise to the earth, and which were distinguished from the productions of other soils not only by superior bloom and sweetness, but by miraculous efficacy to invigorate and to heal." He may imagine that he has got something profound when he reads that, if we compare Milton and Dante in their management of the agency of supernatural beings,—"the exact details of Dante with the dim intimations of Milton,"—the right conclusion of the whole matter is this:—

"Milton wrote in an age of philosophers and theologians. It was necessary, therefore, for him to abstain from giving such a shock to their understandings as might break the charm which it was his object to throw over their imaginations. It was impossible for him to

adopt altogether the material or the immaterial system. He therefore took his stand on the debateable ground. He left the whole in
ambiguity. He has doubtless, by so doing, laid himself open to the
charge of inconsistency. But though philosophically in the wrong
he was poetically in the right."   5

Poor Robert Hall, "well-nigh worn out with that long disease, his life," and, in the last precious days of it, "discovered
lying on the floor, employed in learning, by aid of grammar and
dictionary, enough Italian to enable him to verify" this ingenious criticism! Alas! even had his life been prolonged like Hez-   10
ekiah's, he could not have verified it, for it is unverifiable. A
poet who, writing "in an age of philosophers and theologians,"
finds it "impossible for him to adopt altogether the material or
the immaterial system," who, therefore, "takes his stand on the
debateable ground," who "leaves the whole in ambiguity," and   15
who, in doing so, "though philosophically in the wrong, was
poetically in the right!" Substantial meaning such lucubrations
have none. And in like manner, a distinct and substantial meaning can never be got out of the fine phrases about "Milton's
conception of love uniting all the voluptuousness of the Orien-   20
tal haram, and all the gallantry of the chivalric tournament, with
all the pure and quiet affection of an English fireside;" or about
"Milton's thoughts resembling those celestial fruits and flowers
which the Virgin Martyr of Massinger sent down from the gardens of Paradise to the earth;" the phrases are mere rhetoric.   25
Macaulay's writing passes for being admirably clear, and so ex-
ternally it is; but often it is really obscure, if one takes his de-
liverances seriously, and seeks to find in them a definite meaning. However, there is a multitude of readers, doubtless, for
whom it is sufficient to have their ears tickled with fine rhetoric; 30
but the tickling makes a serious reader impatient.

Many readers there are, again, who come to an Essay on Milton with their minds full of zeal for the Puritan cause, and for
Milton as one of the glories of Puritanism. Of such readers the
great desire is to have the cause and the man, who are already   35
established objects of enthusiasm for them, strongly praised.
Certainly Macaulay will satisfy their desire. They will hear that
the Civil War was "the great conflict between Oromasdes and

Arimanes, liberty and despotism, reason and prejudice;" the
Puritans being Oromasdes, and the Royalists Arimanes. They
will be told that the great Puritan poet was worthy of the august cause which he served. "His radiant and beneficent career
5 resembled that of the god of light and fertility." "There are a
few characters which have stood the closest scrutiny and the
severest tests, which have been tried in the furnace and have
proved pure, which have been declared sterling by the general
consent of mankind, and which are visibly stamped with the
10 image and superscription of the Most High. Of these was Milton." To descend a little to particulars. Milton's temper was
especially admirable. "The gloom of Dante's character discol-
ours all the passions of men and all the face of nature, and tinges
with its own livid hue the flowers of Paradise and the glories of
15 the eternal throne." But in our countryman, although "if ever
despondency and asperity could be excused in any man, they
might have been excused in Milton," nothing "had power to
disturb his sedate and majestic patience." All this is just what an
ardent admirer of the Puritan cause and of Milton would most
20 wish to hear, and when he hears it he is in ecstasies.

But a disinterested reader, whose object is not to hear Puritanism and Milton glorified, but to get at the truth about them,
will surely be dissatisfied. With what a heavy brush, he will say
to himself, does this man lay on his colours! The Puritans Oro-
25 masdes, and the Royalists Arimanes? What a different strain
from Chillingworth's, in his sermon at Oxford at the beginning
of the Civil War! "Publicans and sinners on the one side," said
Chillingworth, "Scribes and Pharisees on the other." Not at all a
conflict between Oromasdes and Arimanes, but a good deal of
30 Arimanes on both sides. And as human affairs go, Chillingworth's version of the matter is likely to be nearer the truth
than Macaulay's. Indeed, for any one who reads thoughtfully
and without bias, Macaulay himself, with the inconsistency of
a born rhetorician, presently confutes his own thesis. He says
35 of the Royalists: "They had far more both of profound and of
polite learning than the Puritans. Their manners were more engaging, their tempers more amiable, their tastes more elegant,
and their households more cheerful." Is being more kindly affec-

tioned such an insignificant superiority? The Royalists too, then, in spite of their being insufficiently jealous for civil and ecclesiastical liberty, had in them something of Oromasdes, the principle of light.

And Milton's temper! His "sedate and majestic patience;" his freedom from "asperity!" If there is a defect which, above all others, is signal in Milton, which injures him even intellectually, which limits him as a poet, it is the defect common to him with the whole Puritan party to which he belonged,—the fatal defect of *temper*. He and they may have a thousand merits, but they are *unamiable*. Excuse them how one will, Milton's asperity and acerbity, his want of sweetness of temper, of the Shakspearian largeness and indulgence, are undeniable. Lord Macaulay in his Essay regrets that the prose writings of Milton should not be more read. "They abound," he says in his rhetorical way, "with passages, compared with which the finest declamations of Burke sink into insignificance." At any rate, they enable us to judge of Milton's temper, of his freedom from asperity. Let us open the *Doctrine and Discipline of Divorce* and see how Milton treats an opponent. "How should he, a serving man both by nature and function, an idiot by breeding, and a solicitor by presumption, ever come to know or feel within himself what the meaning is of *gentle?*" What a gracious temper! "At last, and in good hour, we come to his farewell, which is to be a concluding taste of his jabberment in law, the flashiest and the fustiest that ever corrupted in such an unswilled hogshead." How "sedate and majestic!"

Human progress consists in a continual increase in the number of those who, ceasing to live by the animal life alone and to feel the pleasures of sense only, come to participate in the intellectual life also, and to find enjoyment in the things of the mind. The enjoyment is not at first very discriminating. Rhetoric, brilliant writing, gives to such persons pleasure for its own sake; but it gives them pleasure, still more, when it is employed in commendation of a view of life which is on the whole theirs, and of men and causes with which they are naturally in sympathy. The immense popularity of Macaulay is due to his being pre-eminently fitted to give pleasure to all who are beginning

to feel enjoyment in the things of the mind. It is said that the
traveller in Australia, visiting one settler's hut after another,
finds again and again that the settler's third book, after the Bible
and Shakspeare, is some work by Macaulay. Nothing can be
5   more natural. The Bible and Shakspeare may be said to be imposed upon an Englishman as objects of his admiration; but as
soon as the common Englishman, desiring culture, begins to
choose for himself, he chooses Macaulay. Macaulay's view of
things is, on the whole, the view of them which he feels to be
10   his own also; the persons and causes praised are those which he
himself is disposed to admire; the persons and causes blamed are
those with which he himself is out of sympathy; and the rhetoric employed to praise or to blame them is animating and excellent. Macaulay is thus a great civiliser. In hundreds of men
15   he hits their nascent taste for the things of the mind, possesses
himself of it and stimulates it, draws it powerfully forth and
confirms it.

But with the increasing number of those who awake to the
intellectual life, the number of those also increases, who, having
20   awoke to it, go on with it, follow where it leads them. And it
leads them to see that it is their business to learn the real truth
about the important men, and things, and books, which interest
the human mind. For thus is gradually to be acquired a stock of
sound ideas, in which the mind will habitually move, and which
25   alone can give to our judgments security and solidity. To be
satisfied with fine writing about the object of one's study, with
having it praised or blamed in accordance with one's own likes
or dislikes, with any conventional treatment of it whatever, is
at this stage of growth seen to be futile. At this stage, rhetoric,
30   even when it is so good as Macaulay's, dissatisfies. And the number of people who have reached this stage of mental growth is
constantly, as things now are, increasing; increasing by the very
same law of progress which plants the beginnings of mental life
in more and more persons who, until now, have never known
35   mental life at all. So that while the number of those who are delighted with rhetoric such as Macaulay's is always increasing,
the number of those who are dissatisfied with it is always increasing too.

And not only rhetoric dissatisfies people at this stage, but conventionality of any kind. This is the fault of Addison's Miltonic criticism, once so celebrated; it rests almost entirely upon convention. Here is *Paradise Lost*, "a work which does an honour to the English nation," a work claiming to be one of the great 5 poems of the world, to be of the highest moment to us. "The *Paradise Lost*," says Addison, "is looked upon by the best judges as the greatest production, or at least the noblest work of genius, in our language, and therefore deserves to be set before an English reader in its full beauty." The right thing, surely, is for 10 such a work to prove its own virtue by powerfully and delightfully affecting us as we read it, and by remaining a constant source of elevation and happiness to us for ever. But the *Paradise Lost* has not this effect certainly and universally; therefore Addison proposes to "set before an English reader, in its full 15 beauty," the great poem. To this end he has "taken a general view of it under these four heads: the fable, the characters, the sentiments, and the language." He has, moreover,

"endeavoured not only to prove that the poem is beautiful in general, but to point out its particular beauties and to determine wherein 20 they consist. I have endeavoured to show how some passages are beautified by being sublime, others by being soft, others by being natural; which of them are recommended by the passion, which by the moral, which by the sentiment, and which by the expression. I have likewise endeavoured to show how the genius of the poet 25 shines by a happy invention, or distant allusion, or a judicious imitation; how he has copied or improved Homer or Virgil, and raises his own imaginations by the use which he has made of several poetical passages in Scripture. I might have inserted also several passages in Tasso which our author has imitated; but as I do not look upon 30 Tasso to be a sufficient voucher, I would not perplex my reader with such quotations as might do more honour to the Italian than the English poet."

This is the sort of criticism which held our grandfathers and great-grandfathers spell-bound in solemn reverence. But it is all 35 based upon convention, and on the positivism of the modern reader it is thrown away. Does the work which you praise, he asks, affect me with high pleasure and do me good, when I try

it as fairly as I can? The critic who helps such a questioner is one who has sincerely asked himself, also, this same question; who has answered it in a way which agrees, in the main, with what the questioner finds to be his own honest experience in the
5 matter, and who shows the reasons for this common experience. Where is the use of telling a man, who finds himself tired rather than delighted by *Paradise Lost*, that the incidents in that poem "have in them all the beauties of novelty, at the same time that they have all the graces of nature;" that "though they are natu-
10 ral, they are not obvious, which is the true character of all fine writing"? Where is the use of telling him that "Adam and Eve are drawn with such sentiments as do not only interest the reader in their afflictions, but raise in him the most melting passions of humanity and commiseration"? His own experience, on
15 the other hand, is that the incidents in *Paradise Lost* are such as awaken in him but the most languid interest; and that the afflictions and sentiments of Adam and Eve never melt or move him passionately at all. How is he advanced by hearing that "it is not sufficient that the language of an epic poem be perspicuous, un-
20 less it be also sublime;" and that Milton's language is both? What avails it to assure him that "the first thing to be considered in an epic poem is the fable, which is perfect or imperfect, according as the action which it relates is more or less so;" that "this action should have three qualifications, should be but one
25 action, an entire action, and a great action;" and that if we "consider the action of the *Iliad*, *Æneid*, and *Paradise Lost*, in these three several lights," we shall find that Milton's poem does not "fall short in the beauties which are essential to that kind of writing"? The patient whom Addison thus doctors will reply,
30 that he does not care two straws whether the action of *Paradise Lost* satisfies the proposed test or no, if the poem does not give him pleasure. The truth is, Addison's criticism rests on certain conventions: namely, that incidents of a certain class *must* awaken keen interest; that sentiments of a certain kind *must*
35 raise melting passions; that language of a certain strain, and an action with certain qualifications, *must* render a poem attractive and effective. Disregard the convention; ask solely whether the incidents *do* interest, whether the sentiments *do* move, whether

the poem *is* attractive and effective, and Addison's criticism collapses.

Sometimes the convention is one which in theory ought, a man may perhaps admit, to be something more than a convention; but which yet practically is not. Milton's poem is of surpassing interest to us, says Addison, because in it, "the principal actors are not only our progenitors but our representatives. We have an actual interest in everything they do, and no less than our utmost happiness is concerned, and lies at stake, in all their behaviour." Of ten readers who may even admit that in theory this is so, barely one can be found whose practical experience tells him that Adam and Eve do really, as his representatives, excite his interest in this vivid manner. It is by a mere convention, then, that Addison supposes them to do so, and claims an advantage for Milton's poem from the supposition.

The theological speeches in the third book of *Paradise Lost* are not, in themselves, attractive poetry. But, says Addison:—

"The passions which they are designed to raise are a divine love and religious fear. The particular beauty of the speeches in the third book consists in that shortness and perspicuity of style in which the poet has couched the greatest mysteries of Christianity. . . . He has represented all the abstruse doctrines of predestination, free-will, and grace, as also the great points of incarnation and redemption (which naturally grow up in a poem that treats of the fall of man) with great energy of expression, and in a clearer and stronger light than I ever met with in any other writer."

But nine readers out of ten feel that, as a matter of fact, their religious sentiments of "divine love and religious fear" are wholly ineffectual even to reconcile them to the poetical tiresomeness of the speeches in question: far less can they render them interesting. It is by a mere convention, then, that Addison pretends that they do.

The great merit of Johnson's criticism on Milton is that from rhetoric and convention it is free. Mr. Trevelyan says that the enthusiasm of Macaulay's *Essay on Milton* is, at any rate, "a relief from the perverted ability of that elaborate libel on our great epic poet, which goes by the name of Dr. Johnson's *Life of Milton*." This is too much in Lord Macaulay's own style. In

Johnson's *Life of Milton* we have the straightforward remarks, on Milton and his works, of a very acute and robust mind. Often they are thoroughly sound. "What we know of Milton's character in domestic relations is that he was severe and arbitrary. His family consisted of women; and there appears in his books something like a Turkish contempt of females as subordinate and inferior beings." Mr. Trevelyan will forgive our saying that the truth is here much better hit than in Lord Macaulay's sentence telling us how Milton's "conception of love unites all the voluptuousness of the Oriental haram, and all the gallantry of the chivalric tournament, with all the pure and quiet affection of an English fireside." But Johnson's mind, acute and robust as it was, was at many points bounded, at many points warped. He was neither sufficiently disinterested, nor sufficiently flexible, nor sufficiently receptive, to be a satisfying critic of a poet like Milton. "Surely no man could have fancied that he read Lycidas with pleasure had he not known the author!" Terrible sentence for revealing the deficiencies of the critic who utters it.

A completely disinterested judgment about a man like Milton is easier to a foreign critic than to an Englishman. From conventional obligation to admire "our great epic poet" a foreigner is free. Nor has he any bias for or against Milton because he was a Puritan,—in his political and ecclesiastical doctrines to one of our great English parties a delight, to the other a bugbear. But a critic must have the requisite knowledge of the man and the works he is to judge; and from a foreigner—particularly perhaps from a Frenchman—one hardly expects such knowledge. M. Edmond Scherer, however, whose essay on Milton lies before me, is an exceptional Frenchman. He is a senator of France and one of the directors of the *Temps* newspaper. But he was trained at Geneva, that home of large instruction and lucid intelligence. He was in youth the friend and hearer of Alexandre Vinet,—one of the most salutary influences a man in our times can have experienced, whether he continue to think quite with Vinet or not. He knows thoroughly the language and literature of England, Italy, Germany, as well as of France. Well-informed, intelligent, disinterested, open-minded, sympathetic, M. Scherer has much in common with the admirable critic whom France has lost—Sainte-Beuve. What he has not, as a critic, is Sainte-Beuve's elasticity and cheerfulness. He has not that gaiety, that radiancy, as of a man discharging with delight the very office for which he was born, which, in the *Causeries*, make Sainte-Beuve's touch so felicitous, his sentences so crisp, his effect so charming. But M. Scherer has the same open-mindedness as Sainte-Beuve, the same firmness and sureness of judgment; and having a much more solid acquaintance with foreign languages than Sainte-Beuve, he can much better appreciate a work like *Paradise Lost* in the only form in which it can be appreciated properly—in the original.

We will commence, however, by disagreeing with M. Scherer. He sees very clearly how vain is Lord Macaulay's sheer laudation of Milton, or Voltaire's sheer disparagement of him. Such judgments, M. Scherer truly says, are not judgments at all. They merely express a personal sensation of like or dislike. And M. Scherer goes on to recommend, in the place of such "personal sensations," the method of historical criticism—that great and famous power in the present day. He sings the praises of "this method at once more conclusive and more equitable, which sets itself to understand things rather than to class them, to explain rather than to judge them; which seeks to account for a work from the genius of its author, and for the turn which this genius has taken from the circumstances amidst which it was developed;"—the old story of "the man and the *milieu*," in short. "For thus," M. Scherer continues, "out of these two things, the analysis of the writer's character and the study of his age, there spontaneously issues the right understanding of his work. In place of an appreciation thrown off by some chance comer, we have the work passing judgment, so to speak, upon itself, and assuming the rank which belongs to it among the productions of the human mind."

The advice to study the character of an author and the circumstances in which he has lived, in order to account to oneself for his work, is excellent. But it is a perilous doctrine, that from such a study the right understanding of his work will "spontaneously issue." In a mind qualified in a certain manner it will—not in all minds. And it will be that mind's "personal sensation." It cannot be said that Macaulay had not studied the character of Milton, and the history of the times in which he lived. But a right understanding of Milton did not "spontaneously issue" therefrom in the mind of Macaulay, because Macaulay's mind was that of a rhetorician, not of a disinterested critic. Let us not confound the method with the result intended by the method—right judgments. The critic who rightly appreciates a great man or a great work, and who can tell us faithfully—life being short, and art long, and false information very plentiful—what we may expect from their study and what they can do for us; he is the critic we want, by whatever methods, intuitive or historical, he may have managed to get his knowledge.

M. Scherer begins with Milton's prose works, from which he translates many passages. Milton's sentences can hardly know themselves again in clear modern French, and with all their inversions and redundancies gone. M. Scherer does full justice to the glow and mighty eloquence with which Milton's prose, in its good moments, is instinct and alive; to the "magnificences of his style," as he calls them:—

"The expression is not too strong. There are moments when, shaking from him the dust of his arguments, the poet bursts suddenly forth, and bears us away in a torrent of incomparable eloquence. We get, not the phrase of the orator, but the glow of the poet, a flood of images poured around his arid theme, a rushing flight carrying us above his paltry controversies. The polemical writings of Milton are filled with such beauties. The prayer which concludes the treatise on Reformation in England, the praise of zeal in the Apology for Smectymnuus, the portrait of Cromwell in the Second Defence of the English people, and, finally, the whole tract on the Liberty of Unlicensed Printing from beginning to end, are some of the most memorable pages in English literature, and some of the most characteristic products of the genius of Milton."

Macaulay himself could hardly praise the eloquence of Milton's prose writings more warmly. But it is a very inadequate criticism which leaves the reader, as Macaulay's rhetoric would leave him, with the belief that the total impression to be got from Milton's prose writings is one of enjoyment and admiration. It is not; we are misled, and our time is wasted, if we are sent to Milton's prose works in the expectation of finding it so. Grand thoughts and beautiful language do not form the staple of Milton's controversial treatises, though they occur in them not unfrequently. But the total impression from those treatises is rightly given by M. Scherer:—

"In all of them the manner is the same. The author brings into play the treasures of his learning, heaping together testimonies from Scripture, passages from the Fathers, quotations from the poets; laying all antiquity, sacred and profane, under contribution; entering into subtle discussions on the sense of this or that Greek or Hebrew word. But not only by his undigested erudition and by his absorption in religious controversy does Milton belong to his age; he belongs to it, too, by the personal tone of his polemics. Morus and Salmasius had attacked his morals, laughed at his low stature, made unfeeling allusions to his loss of sight: Milton replies by reproaching them with the wages they have taken and with the servant-girls they have debauched. All this mixed with coarse witticisms, with terms of the lowest abuse. Luther and Calvin, those virtuosos of insult, had not gone further."

No doubt there is, as M. Scherer says, "something indescribably heroical and magnificent which overflows from Milton, even when he is engaged in the most miserable discussions." Still, for the mass of his prose treatises "miserable discussions" is the final and right word. Nor, when Milton passed to his great epic, did he altogether leave the old man of these "miserable discussions" behind him.

"In his soul he is a polemist and theologian—a Protestant Schoolman. He takes delight in the favourite dogmas of Puritanism: original sin, predestination, free-will. Not that even here he does not display somewhat of that independence which was in his nature. But his theology is, nevertheless, that of his epoch, tied and bound to the letter of Holy Writ, without grandeur, without horizons, without philosophy. He never frees himself from the bondage of the letter. He settles the most important questions by the authority of an obscure text, or a text isolated from its context. In a word, Milton is a great poet with a Salmasius or a Grotius bound up along with him; a genius nourished on the marrow of lions, of Homer, Isaiah, Virgil,

Dante, but also, like the serpent of Eden, eating dust, the dust of
dismal polemics. He is a doctor, a preacher, a man of didactics; and
when the day shall arrive when he can at last realise the dreams of
his youth and bestow on his country an epic poem, he will compose
5 it of two elements, gold and clay, sublimity and scholasticism, and
will bequeath to us a poem which is at once the most wonderful
and the most insupportable poem in existence."

From the first, two conflicting forces, two sources of inspiration, had contended with one another, says M. Scherer, for the
10 possession of Milton,—the Renascence and Puritanism. Milton
felt the power of both:—

"Elegant poet and passionate disputant, accomplished humanist
and narrow sectary, admirer of Petrarch, of Shakspeare, and hair-
splitting interpreter of Bible-texts, smitten with Pagan antiquity and
15 smitten with the Hebrew genius; and all this at once, without effort,
naturally;—an historical problem, a literary enigma!"

Milton's early poems, such as the *Allegro*, the *Penseroso*, are
poems produced while a sort of equilibrium still prevailed in the
poet's nature; hence their charm, and that of their youthful
20 author:—

"Nothing morose or repellent, purity without excess of rigour,
gravity without fanaticism. Something wholesome and virginal, gracious and yet strong. A son of the North who has passed the way of
Italy; a last fruit of the Renascence, but a fruit filled with a savour
25 new and strange!"

But Milton's days proceeded, and he arrived at the latter years
of his life—a life which, in its outward fortunes, darkened more
and more, *alla s'assombrissant de plus en plus*, towards its close.
He arrived at the time when "his friends had disappeared, his
30 dreams had vanished, his eyesight was quenched, the hand of
old age was upon him." It was then that, "isolated by the very
force of his genius," but full of faith and fervour, he "turned
his eyes towards the celestial light" and produced *Paradise Lost*.
In its form, M. Scherer observes, in its plan and distribution,
35 the poem follows Greek and Roman models, particularly the
Æneid. "All in this respect is regular and classical; in this fidelity
to the established models we recognise the literary superstitions

of the Renascence." So far as its form is concerned, *Paradise Lost* is, says M. Scherer, "the copy of a copy, a tertiary formation. It is to the Latin epics what these are to Homer."

The most important matter, however, is the contents of the poem, not the form. The contents are given by Puritanism. But let M. Scherer speak for himself:— 5

> "*Paradise Lost* is an epic, but a theological epic; and the theology of the poem is made up of the favourite dogmas of the Puritans,—the Fall, justification, God's sovereign decrees. Milton, for that matter, avows openly that he has a thesis to maintain; his object is, he tells us at the outset, to 'assert Eternal Providence and justify the ways of God to man.' *Paradise Lost*, then, is two distinct things in one,—an epic and a theodicy. Unfortunately these two elements, which correspond to the two men of whom Milton was composed, and to the two tendencies which ruled his century, these two elements have not managed to get amalgamated. Far from doing so, they clash with one another, and from their juxtaposition there results a suppressed contradiction which extends to the whole work, impairs its solidity, and compromises its value." 10

15

M. Scherer gives his reasons for thinking that the Christian theology is unmanageable in an epic poem, although the gods may come in very well in the *Iliad* and *Æneid*. Few will differ from him here, so we pass on. A theological poem is a mistake, says M. Scherer; but to call *Paradise Lost* a theological poem is to call it by too large a name. It is really a commentary on a biblical text,—the first two or three chapters of Genesis. Its subject, therefore, is a story, taken literally, which many of even the most religious people nowadays hesitate to take literally; while yet, upon our being able to take it literally, the whole real interest of the poem for us depends. Merely as matter of poetry, the story of the Fall has no special force or effectiveness; its effectiveness for us comes, and can only come, from our taking it all as the literal narrative of what positively happened. 20

25

30

Milton, M. Scherer thinks, was not strong in invention. The famous allegory of Sin and Death may be taken as a specimen of what he could do in this line, and the allegory of Sin and Death is uncouth and unpleasing. But invention is dangerous when one is dealing with a subject so grave, so strictly formu- 35

lated by theology, as the subject of Milton's choice. Our poet
felt this, and allowed little scope to free poetical invention. He
adhered in general to data furnished by Scripture, and supplemented somewhat by Jewish legend. But this judicious self-
5   imitation had, again, its drawbacks:—

"If Milton has avoided factitious inventions, he has done so at the
price of another disadvantage; the bareness of his story, the epic
poverty of his poem. It is not merely that the reader is carried up
into the sphere of religious abstractions, where man loses power to
10 see or breathe. Independently of this, everything is here too simple,
both actors and actions. Strictly speaking, there is but one personage before us, God the Father; inasmuch as God cannot appear
without effacing every one else, nor speak without the accomplishment of his will. The Son is but the Father's double. The angels and
15 archangels are but his messengers, nay, they are less; they are but
his decrees personified, the supernumeraries of a drama which would
be transacted quite as well without them.

"Milton has struggled against these conditions of the subject
which he had chosen. He has tried to escape from them, and has
20 only made the drawback more visible. The long speeches with
which he fills up the gaps of the action are sermons, and serve but to
reveal the absence of action. Then as, after all, some action, some
struggle, was necessary, the poet had recourse to the revolt of the
angels. Unfortunately, such is the fundamental vice of the subject,
25 that the poet's instrument has, one may say, turned against him.
What his action has gained from it in movement it has lost in probability. We see a battle, indeed, but who can take either the combat
or the combatants seriously? Belial shows his sense of this, when in
the infernal council he rejects the idea of engaging in any conflict
30 whatever, open or secret, with Him who is All-seeing and Almighty;
and really one cannot comprehend how his mates should have failed
to acquiesce in a consideration so evident. But, I repeat, the poem
was not possible save at the price of this impossibility. Milton, therefore, has courageously made the best of it. He has gone with it all
35 lengths, he has accepted in all its extreme consequences the most inadmissible of fictions. He has exhibited to us Jehovah apprehensive
for his omnipotence, in fear of seeing his position turned, his residence surprised, his throne usurped. He has drawn the angels hurl-
ing mountains at one another's heads, and firing cannon at one an-
40 other. He has shown us the victory doubtful until the Son appears

armed with lightnings, and standing on a car horsed by four Cherubim."

The fault of Milton's poem is not, says M. Scherer, that, with his Calvinism of the seventeenth century, Milton was a man holding other beliefs than ours. Homer, Dante, held other beliefs than ours:— 5

"But Milton's position is not the same as theirs. Milton has something he wants to prove, he supports a thesis. It was his intention, in his poem, to do duty as theologian as well as poet; at any rate, whether he meant it or not, *Paradise Lost* is a didactic work, and the 10 form of it, therefore, cannot be separated from the substance. Now, it turns out that the idea of the poem will not bear examination; that its solution for the problem of evil is almost burlesque; that the character of its heroes, Jehovah and Satan, has no coherence; that what happens to Adam interests us but little; finally, that the action takes 15 place in regions where the interests and passions of our common humanity can have no scope. I have already insisted on this contradiction in Milton's epic; the story on which it turns can have meaning and value only so long as it preserves its dogmatic weight, and, at the same time, it cannot preserve this without falling into theol- 20 ogy,—that is to say, into a domain foreign to that of art. The subject of the poem is nothing if it is not real, and if it does not touch us as the turning-point of our destinies; and the more the poet seeks to grasp this reality, the more it escapes from him."

In short, the whole poem of *Paradise Lost* is vitiated, says 25 M. Scherer, "by a kind of antinomy, by the conjoint necessity and impossibility of taking its contents literally."

M. Scherer then proceeds to sum up. And in ending, after having once more marked his objections and accentuated them, he at last finds again that note of praise, which the reader will 30 imagine him to have quite lost:—

"To sum up: *Paradise Lost* is a false poem, a grotesque poem, a tiresome poem; there is not one reader out of a hundred who can read the ninth and tenth books without smiling, or the eleventh and twelfth without yawning. The whole thing is without solidity; it is 35 a pyramid resting on its apex, the most solemn of problems resolved by the most puerile of means. And, notwithstanding, *Paradise Lost* is immortal. It lives by a certain number of episodes which are for ever famous. Unlike Dante, who must be read as a whole if we want really to seize his beauties, Milton ought to be read only by passages. But these passages form part of the poetical patrimony of the human race."

5   And not only in things like the address to light, or the speeches of Satan, is Milton admirable, but in single lines and images everywhere:—

"*Paradise Lost* is studded with incomparable lines. Milton's poetry is, as it were, the very essence of poetry. The author seems to
10 think always in images, and these images are grand and proud like his soul, a wonderful mixture of the sublime and the picturesque. For rendering things he has the unique word, the word which is a discovery. Every one knows his *darkness visible*."

M. Scherer cites other famous expressions and lines, so famil-
15 iar that we need not quote them here. Expressions of the kind, he says, not only beautiful, but always, in addition to their beauty, striking one as the absolutely right thing *(toujours justes dans leur beauté)*, are in *Paradise Lost* innumerable. And he concludes:—

20   "Moreover, we have not said all when we have cited particular lines of Milton. He has not only the image and the word, he has the period also, the large musical phrase, somewhat long, somewhat laden with ornaments and intricate with inversions, but bearing all along with it in its superb undulation. Lastly, and above all, he has
25 a something indescribably serene and victorious, an unfailing level of style, power indomitable. He seems to wrap us in a fold of his robe, and to carry us away with him into the eternal regions where is his home."

With this fine image M. Scherer takes leave of Milton. Yet the
30 simple description of the man in Johnson's life of him touches us more than any image; the description of the old poet "seen in a small house, neatly enough dressed in black clothes, sitting in a room hung with rusty green, pale but not cadaverous, with chalk stones in his hands. He said that, if it were not for the gout
35 his blindness would be tolerable."

But in his last sentences M. Scherer comes upon what is undoubtedly Milton's true distinction as a poet, his "unfailing level of style." Milton has always the sure, strong touch of the master. His power both of diction and of rhythm is unsurpassable, and it is characterised by being always present—not depending on an access of emotion, not intermittent, but, like the grace of Raphael, working in its possessor as a constant gift of nature. Milton's style, moreover, has the same propriety and soundness in presenting plain matters, as in the comparatively smooth task for a poet of presenting grand ones. His rhythm is as admirable where, as in the line—

"And Tiresias and Phineus, prophets old—"

it is unusual, as in such lines as—

"With dreadful faces throng'd and fiery arms—"

where it is simplest. And what high praise this is, we may best appreciate by considering the ever-recurring failure, both in rhythm and in diction, which we find in the so-called Miltonic blank verse of Thomson, Cowper, Wordsworth. What leagues of lumbering movement! what desperate endeavours, as in Wordsworth's

"And at the 'Hoop' alighted, famous inn,"

to render a platitude endurable by making it pompous! Shakspeare himself, divine as are his gifts, has not, of the marks of the master, this one: perfect sureness of hand in his style. Alone of English poets, alone in English art, Milton has it; he is our great artist in style, our one first-rate master in the grand style. He is as truly a master in this style as the great Greeks are, or Virgil, or Dante. The number of such masters is so limited that a man acquires a world-rank in poetry and art, instead of a mere local rank, by being counted among them. But Milton's importance to us Englishmen, by virtue of this distinction of his, is incalculable. The charm of a master's unfailing touch in diction and in rhythm, no one, after all, can feel so intimately, so profoundly, as his own countrymen. Invention, plan, wit, pathos, thought, all of them are in great measure capable of being detached from the original work itself, and of being exported for admiration abroad. Diction and rhythm are not. Even when a foreigner can read the work in its own language, they are not, perhaps, easily appreciable by him. It shows M. Scherer's thorough knowledge of English, and his critical sagacity also, that he has felt the force of them in Milton. We natives must naturally feel it yet more powerfully. Be it remembered, too, that English literature, full of vigour and genius as it is, is peculiarly impaired by gropings and inadequacies in form. And the same with English art. Therefore for the English artist in any line, if he is a true artist, the study of Milton may well have an indescribable attraction. It gives him lessons which nowhere else from an Englishman's work can he obtain, and feeds a sense which English work, in general, seems bent on disappointing and baffling. And this sense is yet so deep-seated in human nature,—this sense of style,—that probably not for artists alone, but for all intelligent Englishmen who read him, its gratification by Milton's poetry is a large though often not fully recognised part of his charm, and a very wholesome and fruitful one.

As a man, too, not less than as a poet, Milton has a side of unsurpassable grandeur. A master's touch is the gift of nature. Moral qualities, it is commonly thought, are in our own power. Perhaps the germs of such qualities are in their greater or less strength as much a part of our natural constitution as the sense for style. The range open to our own will and power, however, in developing and establishing them, is evidently much larger. Certain high moral dispositions Milton had from nature, and he sedulously trained and developed them until they became habits of great power.

Some moral qualities seem to be connected in a man with his power of style. Milton's power of style, for instance, has for its great character *elevation;* and Milton's elevation clearly comes, in the main, from a moral quality in him,—his pureness. "By pureness, by kindness!" says St. Paul. These two, pureness and kindness, are, in very truth, the two signal Christian virtues, the two mighty wings of Christianity, with which it winnowed and renewed, and still winnows and renews, the world. In kindness, and in all which that word conveys or suggests, Milton does not shine. He had the temper of his Puritan party. We often hear the boast, on behalf of the Puritans, that they produced "our great epic poet." Alas! one might not unjustly retort that they spoiled him. However, let Milton bear his own burden; in his temper he had natural affinities with the Puritans. He has paid for it by limitations as a poet. But, on the other hand, how high, clear, and splendid is his pureness; and how intimately does its might enter into the voice of his poetry! We have quoted some ill-conditioned passages from his prose, let us quote from it a passage of another stamp:—

"And long it was not after, when I was confirmed in this opinion, that he, who would not be frustrate of his hope to write well hereafter in laudable things, ought himself to be a true poem; that is, a composition and pattern of the best and honourablest things; not presuming to sing high praises of heroic men, or famous cities, unless he have in himself the experience and the practice of all that which is praiseworthy. These reasonings, together with a certain niceness of nature, an honest haughtiness and self-esteem, either of what I was or what I might be (which let envy call pride), and lastly that modesty whereof here I may be excused to make some beseeming profession; all these uniting the supply of their natural aid together kept me still above low descents of mind. Next (for hear me out now, readers), that I may tell ye whither my younger feet wandered; I betook me among those lofty fables and romances which recount in solemn cantos the deeds of knighthood founded by our victorious kings, and from hence had in renown over all Christendom. There I read it in the oath of every knight, that he should defend to the expense of his best blood, or of his life if it so befell him, the honour and chastity of virgin or matron; from whence even then I learnt what a noble virtue chastity sure must be, to the defence of which so many worthies by such a dear adventure of themselves had sworn. Only this my mind gave me, that every free and gentle spirit, without that oath, ought to be born a knight, nor needed to expect the gilt spur, or the laying of a sword upon his shoulder, to stir him up both by his counsel and his arm to secure and protect the weakness of any attempted chastity."

Mere fine professions are in this department of morals more common and more worthless than in any other. What gives to Milton's professions such a stamp of their own is their accent of absolute sincerity. In this elevated strain of moral pureness his life was really pitched; its strong, immortal beauty passed into the diction and rhythm of his poetry.

But I did not propose to write a criticism of my own upon
5 Milton. I proposed to recite and compare the criticisms on him by others. Only one is tempted, after our many extracts from M. Scherer, in whose criticism of Milton the note of blame fills so much more place than the note of praise, to accentuate this note of praise, which M. Scherer touches indeed with justness,
10 but hardly perhaps draws out fully enough or presses firmly enough. As a poet and as a man, Milton has a side of grandeur so high and rare, as to give him rank along with the half-dozen greatest poets who have ever lived, although to their master-pieces his *Paradise Lost* is, in the fulfilment of the complete
15 range of conditions which a great poem ought to satisfy, in-dubitably inferior.

Nothing is gained by huddling on "our great epic poet," in a promiscuous heap, every sort of praise. Sooner or later the question: How does Milton's masterpiece really stand to us
20 moderns, what are we to think of it, what can we get from it? must inevitably be asked and answered. We have marked that side of the answer which is and will always remain favourable to Milton. The unfavourable side of the answer is supplied by M. Scherer. "*Paradise Lost* lives; but none the less is it true that
25 its fundamental conceptions have become foreign to us, and that if the work subsists it is in spite of the subject treated by it."

The verdict seems just, and it is supported by M. Scherer with considerations natural, lucid, and forcible. He, too, has his conventions when he comes to speak of Racine and Lamartine.
30 But his judgments on foreign poets, on Shakspeare, Byron, Goethe, as well as on Milton, seem to me to be singularly unin-fluenced by the conventional estimates of these poets, and sin-gularly rational. Leaning to the side of severity, as is natural when one has been wearied by choruses of ecstatic and exag-
35 gerated praise, he yet well and fairly reports, I think, the real impression made by these great men and their works on a mod-ern mind disinterested, intelligent, and sincere. The English reader, I hope, may have been interested in seeing how Milton

and his *Paradise Lost* stand such a survey. And those who are dissatisfied with what has been thus given them may always revenge themselves by falling back upon their Addison, and by observing sarcastically that "a few general rules extracted out of the French authors, with a certain cant of words, has sometimes set up an illiterate heavy writer for a most judicious and formidable critic."

Falkland

"The English are just, but not amiable." A well-bred French-man, who has recently travelled in India, and who published in the *Revue des Deux Mondes* an interesting account of what he saw and heard there, ends with this criticism. The criticism con-
5 veys, he says, as to the English and their rule, the real mind of the best informed and most intelligent of the natives of India with whom he conversed. They admitted the great superiority of the English rule in India to every other which had preceded it. They admitted the good intentions of the English rule:
10 they admitted its activity, energy, incorruptibility, justice. Still, the final impression was this: something wanting in the English, something which they were not. *Les Anglais sont justes, mais pas bons.* "The English are just, but not kind and good."
15 It is proposed to raise, on the field of Newbury, a monument to a famous Englishman who was amiable. A meeting was held at Newbury to launch the project, and Lord Carnarvon made there an excellent speech. I believe the subscription to the mon-ument does not grow very rapidly. The unamiable ones
20 amongst us, the vast majority, naturally perhaps keep their hands in their pockets. But let us take the opportunity, as oth-ers, too, have taken it, for at least recalling Falkland to memory. Let us give our attention for a moment to this phenomenon of an amiable Englishman.
25 Clarendon says:—

"At the battle of Newbury was slain the Lord Viscount Falkland; a person of such prodigious parts of learning and knowledge, of that inimitable sweetness and delight in conversation, of so flowing and obliging a humanity and goodness to mankind, and of that primitive simplicity and integrity of life, that if there were no other brand upon this odious and accursed Civil War than that single loss, it must be most infamous and execrable to all posterity. *Turpe mori, post te, solo non posse dolore.*"

Clarendon's style is here a little excessive, a little Asiatic. And perhaps a something Asiatic is not wholly absent, either, from that famous passage,—the best known, probably, in all the *History of the Rebellion,*—that famous passage which describes Lord Falkland's longing for peace.

"Sitting among his friends, often, after a deep silence and frequent sighs, he would with a shrill and sad accent ingeminate the word *Peace, Peace;* and would passionately profess that the very agony of the war, and the view of the calamities and desolation the kingdom did and must endure, took his sleep from him, and would shortly break his heart."

Clarendon's touch, where in his memoirs he speaks of Falkland, is simpler than in the *History.* But we will not carp at this great writer and faithful friend. Falkland's life was an uneventful one, and but a few points in it are known to us. To Clarendon he owes it that each of those points is a picture.

In his speech at Newbury Lord Carnarvon said: "When we look back to the history of the Civil War, I can think of no character that stands out in higher, purer relief, than Falkland." "Of all the names," says Lord Carnarvon again, "which have come down to us from the Great Rebellion, none have come invested with higher respect and greater honour than the name of Lord Falkland." One asks oneself how this comes to be so. Falkland wrote both in verse and in prose. Both his verse and his prose have their interest, yet as a writer he scarcely counts. He was a gallant soldier, but gallant soldiers are not uncommon. He was an unsuccessful politician, and was reproached with deserting his party. He was Secretary of State for but two years, and in that office he accomplished, and could then accomplish, nothing remarkable. He was killed in the four-and-thirtieth year of his age. Horace Walpole pronounces him a much overrated man. But let us go through the scanty records of his life a little more deliberately.

Lucius Cary, Lord Falkland, was born in 1610. His father, Sir Henry Cary, the first Lord Falkland, went to Ireland as Lord Deputy in 1622, and remained there until 1629. "The son was bred," says Clarendon, "in the court and in the university,
5 but under the care, vigilance, and direction of such governors and tutors, that he learned all his exercises and languages better than most men do in more celebrated places." In 1629 the father, who appears to have been an able man, but violent and unfortunate, returned with broken fortunes to England. Shortly
10 afterwards the son inherited from his maternal grandfather, the Lord Chief Baron Tanfield, who in his will passed over his daughter and her husband the ex-Lord Deputy, a good estate at Burford and Great Tew, in Oxfordshire. At nineteen, then, the young Lucius Cary came into possession of "all his grandfa-
15 ther's land, with two very good houses very well furnished (worth about £2000 per annum), in a most pleasant country, and the two most pleasant places in that country, with a very plentiful personal estate." But, adds Clarendon:—

"With these advantages he had one great disadvantage (which in
20 the first entrance into the world is attended with too much prejudice) in his person and presence, which was in no degree attractive or promising. His stature was low, and smaller than most men; his motion not graceful, and his aspect so far from inviting, that it had somewhat in it of simplicity; and his voice the worst of the three,
25 and so untuned that instead of reconciling, it offended the ear, so that nobody would have expected music from that tongue; and sure no man was ever less beholden to nature for its recommendation into the world. But then no man sooner or more disappointed this general and customary prejudice. That little person and small stat-
30 ure was quickly found to contain a great heart, a courage so keen, and a nature so fearless, that no composition of the strongest limbs and most harmonious and proportioned presence and strength ever more disposed any man to the greatest enterprise; it being his greatest weakness to be too solicitous for such adventures. And that un-
35 tuned tongue and voice easily discovered itself to be supplied and governed by a mind and understanding so excellent, that the wit and weight of all he said carried another kind of admiration in it, and even another kind of acceptation from the persons present, than any ornament of delivery could reasonably promise itself, or is usu-

ally attended with. And his disposition and nature was so gentle and obliging, so much delighted in courtesy, kindness, and generosity that all mankind could not but admire and love him."

For a year or two Falkland moved in the gay life of London, rich, accomplished, popular, with a passion for soldiering, with a passion for letters. He was of Ben Jonson's society at the "Apollo;" he mixed with Suckling, Carew, Davenant, Waller, Sandys, Sir Kenelm Digby; with Selden and Hobbes; with Hales of Eton and Chillingworth—great spirits in little bodies, these two last, like Falkland himself. He contracted a passionate friendship with a young man as promising and as universally beloved as himself, Sir Henry Morison. Ben Jonson has celebrated it; and it was on Morison's early death that Jonson wrote the beautiful lines which every one knows, beginning—

> "It is not growing like a tree,
> In bulk, doth make men better be."

Falkland married, before he was of age, Morison's sister. The marriage gave mortal offence to his father. His father had projected for the young Lucius, says Clarendon, a marriage which might mend his own broken fortunes and ruined credit at court. The son behaved admirably. He offered to resign his whole estate to his father, and to rely entirely upon his father's pleasure for his own maintenance. He had deeds of conveyance prepared to that effect, and brought them to his father for signature:—

"But his father's passion and indignation so far transported him (though he was a gentleman of excellent parts), that he refused any reconciliation and rejected all the offers that were made him of the estate, so that his son remained still in the possession of his estate against his will, for which he found great reason afterwards to rejoice. But he was for the present so much afflicted with his father's displeasure that he transported himself and his wife into Holland, resolving to buy some military command, and to spend the remainder of his life in that profession. But being disappointed in the treaty he expected, and finding no opportunity to accommodate himself with such a command, he returned again into England; resolving to retire to a country life and to his books, that since he was not like to improve himself in arms he might advance in letters.

So began the *convivium philosophicum*, or *convivium theologicum*, of Falkland's life at Great Tew. With a genuine thoroughness of nature, with the high resolve to make up his mind
about the matters of most vital concernment to man, and to
5 make it up on good grounds, he plunged into study. The controversy with Rome was at that moment keen. Agents of conversion to the Romish Church, *corner-creepers* as they were
called, penetrated everywhere. Two young brothers of Falkland himself were won over by them. More and more, there-
10 fore, his thoughts and his studies took a theological turn. On his
first retirement to the country he had declared, says Clarendon,
that "he would not see London in many years, which was the
place he loved of all the world." But his father's death from the
effects of an accident, soon afterwards, forced him back for a
15 time to London. Then, on his return to Oxfordshire, he surrounded himself with friends from the university, who led with
him the life which Clarendon's description has made memorable:—

"His house where he usually resided (Tew or Burford, in Ox-
20 fordshire), being within ten or twelve miles of the university, looked
like the university itself by the company that was always found
there. There were Dr. Sheldon, Dr. Morley, Dr. Hammond, Dr.
Earles, Mr. Chillingworth, and indeed all men of eminent parts and
faculties in Oxford, besides those who resorted thither from Lon-
25 don; who all found their lodgings there as ready as in the colleges;
nor did the lord of the house know of their coming or going, nor
who were in his house, till he came to dinner or supper where all
still met. Otherwise there was no troublesome ceremony or con-
straint, to forbid men to come to the house, or to make them weary
30 of staying there. So that many came thither to study in a better air,
finding all the books they could desire in his library, and all the persons together whose company they could wish, and not find in any
other society. Here Mr. Chillingworth wrote and formed and mod-
elled his excellent book against the learned Jesuit Mr. Nott (*The
35 Religion of Protestants a Safe Way to Salvation*), after frequent debates upon the most important particulars; in many of which he
suffered himself to be overruled by the judgment of his friends,
though in others he still adhered to his own fancy, which was scep-
tical enough even in the highest points."

From "this happy and delightful conversation and restraint" Falkland was in 1639 called away by "the first alarum from the north," Charles the First's expedition to suppress the disturbances in Scotland. After the return of that expedition Falkland sate in the Short Parliament of 1640, which preceded the Long Parliament. The "Short Parliament" sate but a few weeks. Falkland was born a constitutionalist, a hater of all that is violent and arbitrary. What he saw in the Short Parliament made a favourable and deep impression upon him. "From the debates which were there managed with all imaginable gravity and solemnity, he contracted" (says Clarendon) "such a reverence to Parliaments that he thought it really impossible they could ever produce mischief or inconvenience to the kingdom, or that the kingdom could be tolerably happy in the intermission of them."

In the next Parliament this faith in Parliaments was destined to be roughly shaken. The Long Parliament met at the end of 1640. Falkland had a warm admiration for Hampden, and a strong disapprobation of the violent proceedings of the court. He acted with the popular party. He made a powerful speech against ship-money. He was convinced of Strafford's guilt, and joined in his prosecution. He spoke vigorously for the bill to remove the bishops from the House of Lords. But the reason and moderation of the man showed itself from the first. Alone among his party he raised his voice against pressing forward Strafford's impeachment with unfair and vindictive haste. He refused to consider, like the Puritans, the order of bishops as a thing by God's law either appointed or forbidden. He treated it as a thing expedient or inexpedient. And so foolish had been the conduct of the High Church bishops and clergy, so much and so mischievously had they departed from their true province, that it was expedient at that moment, Falkland thought, to remove the bishops from the House of Lords. "We shall find them," he said of the High Church clergy, "to have tithed mint and anise, and have left undone the weightier works of the law. The most frequent subjects, even in the most sacred auditories, have been the *jus divinum* of bishops and tithes, the sacredness of the clergy, the sacrilege of impropriations, the demolishing of Puritanism." But he was careful to add: "We shall make no little compliment to those to whom this charge belongs, if we shall lay the faults of these men upon the *order* of the bishops." And even against these misdoing men he would join in no injustice. To his clear reason sacerdotalism was repulsive. He disliked Laud, moreover; he had a natural antipathy to his heat, fussiness, and arbitrary temper. But he refused to concur in Laud's impeachment.

The Lords threw out the bill for the expulsion of the bishops. In the same session, a few months later, the bill was reintroduced in the House of Commons. But during this time the attitude of the popular party had been more and more declaring itself. The party had professed at first that the removal of the bishops from Parliament was all they wanted; that they had no designs against episcopacy and the Church of England. The strife deepened, and new and revolutionary designs emerged. When, therefore, the bill against the bishops was reintroduced, Falkland voted against it. Hampden reproached him with inconsistency. Hampden said, that "he was sorry to find a noble lord had changed his opinion since the time the last bill to this purpose had passed the House; for he then thought it a good bill, but now he thought this an ill one." But Falkland answered, that "he had been persuaded at that time by that worthy gentleman to believe many things which he had since found to be untrue, and therefore he had changed his opinion in many particulars as well as to things as persons."

The king's party availed themselves eagerly of this changed disposition in a man so much admired and respected. They pressed Falkland to come to the aid of the Crown, and to take office. He was extremely loth to comply. He disapproved of the policy of the court party. He was for great reforms. He disliked Charles's obstinacy and insincerity. So distasteful, indeed, were they to him, that even after he had taken office it was difficult to him,—to him, the sweetest-mannered of men,—to maintain towards Charles the same amenity which he showed towards every one else. Compliant as he was to others, yet towards the king, says Clarendon, "he did not practise that condescension, but contradicted him with more bluntness and by sharp sentences; and in some particulars (as of the Church) to which the

king was in conscience most devoted; and of this his majesty often complained." Falkland feared that, if he took office, the king would require a submission which he could not give. He feared, too, and to a man of his high spirit this thought was most galling, that his previous opposition to the court might be sup- 5
posed to have had for its aim to heighten his value and to insure his promotion. He had no fancy, moreover, for official business, and believed himself unfit for it. Hyde at last, by earnestly pleading the considerations which, he thought, made his friend's acceptance of office a duty, overcame his reluctance. At the be- 10
ginning of 1642 Falkland became a member of the King's Council, and Secretary of State.

We approach the end. Falkland "filled his place," says Clarendon, "with great sufficiency, being well versed in languages, to understand any that are used in business and to make himself 15
understood." But in August 1642 the Civil War broke out. With that departure of the public peace fled for ever Falkland's own. He exposed himself at Edge-hill with even more than his ordinary carelessness of danger. As the war continued, his unhappiness grew upon him more and more. But let us quote Clarendon, 20
who is here admirable:—

"From his entrance into this unnatural war, his natural cheerfulness and vivacity grew clouded, and a kind of sadness and dejection of spirit stole upon him which he had never been used to. Yet being one of those who believed that one battle would end all differences, 25
and that there would be so great a victory on one side that the other would be compelled to submit to any conditions from the victor (which supposition and conclusion generally sank into the minds of most men, and prevented the looking after many advantages that might then have been laid hold of), he resisted those indispositions, 30
et in luctu, bellum inter remedia erat. But after the king's return from Brentford, and the furious resolution of the two Houses not to admit any treaty for peace, those indispositions, which had before touched him, grew into a perfect habit of uncheerfulness. And he who had been so exactly easy and affable to all men that his face 35
and countenance was always present and vacant to his company, and held any cloudiness and less pleasantness of the visage a kind of rudeness or incivility, became on a sudden less communicable, and thence very sad, pale, and exceedingly affected with the spleen. In

his clothes and habit, which he had minded before always with
more industry and neatness and expense than is usual to so great a
soul, he was now not only incurious, but too negligent."

   In this mood he came to Newbury. Before the battle he told
5 one of his friends that "he was weary of the times and foresaw
much misery to his country, and did believe he should be out
of it ere night." But now, as always, the close contact with danger reanimated him:—

   "In the morning before the battle, as always upon action, he was
10 very cheerful, and put himself into the first rank of the Lord Byron's regiment, then advancing upon the enemy, who had lined the
hedges on both sides with musketeers; from whence he was shot
with a musket in the lower part of the belly, and in the instant falling from his horse, his body was not found till the next morning; till
15 when there was some hope he might have been a prisoner, though
his nearest friends, who knew his temper, received small comfort
from that imagination. Thus fell that incomparable young man in
the four-and-thirtieth year of his age, having so much despatched
the true business of life that the eldest rarely attain to that immense
20 knowledge, and the youngest enter not into the world with more
innocency. Whosoever leads such a life, needs be the less anxious
upon how short warning it is taken from him."

   Falkland fell on the 20th of September 1643. His body was
carried to Great Tew and buried in the churchyard there. But
25 his grave is unmarked and unknown. The house too, in which
he lived, is gone and replaced by a new one. The stables and
dovecot, it is thought, existed in his time; and in the park are
oaks and limes on which his eyes must have rested. He left his
estates, and the control of his three children, all of them sons,
30 to his wife, with whom he had lived happily and in great affection. But the lands of Tew and Burford have long passed away
from his family.

   And now, after this review of Falkland's life, let us ask
whence arose that exalted esteem of him whereof Lord Carnar-
35 von speaks, and whether it was deserved. In the first place, then,
he had certainly, except personal beauty, everything to qualify
him for a hero to the imagination of mankind in general. He

had rank, accomplishment, sweet temper, exquisite courtesy, liberality, magnanimity, superb courage, melancholy, misfortune, early death. Of his accomplishment we have spoken. And he was accomplished, nay learned, "with the most dexterity and address," says Clarendon, "and the least pedantry and affectation, that ever man who knew so much was possessed with, of what quality soever." Of his amenity we have spoken also; of "his disposition so gentle and obliging, so much delighting in courtesy, that all mankind could not but admire and love him;" of "his gentleness and affability so transcendent and obliging, that it drew reverence, and some kind of compliance, from the roughest and most unpolished and stubborn constitutions, and made them of another temper of debate, in his presence, than they were in other places." Equally charming was his generosity and delicacy to all who stood in need of help, but especially to those "whose fortunes required, and whose spirits made them superior to, ordinary obligations." Such is Clarendon's euphemistical phrase for poor and proud men of letters. His highmindedness is well shown in his offer, which we have already mentioned, to resign his fortune to his father. Let me quote another fine instance of it. He never would consent, while he was Secretary of State, to two practices which he found established in his office,—the employment of spies and the opening of letters:—

"For the first, he would say, such instruments must be void of all ingenuousness and common honesty before they could be of use, and afterwards they could never be fit to be credited; and no single preservation could be worth so general a wound and corruption of human society, as the cherishing such persons would carry with it. The last he thought such a violation of the law of nature that no qualification by office could justify him in the trespass."

His courage, again, had just the characters which charm the imagination:—

"Upon any occasion of action, he always engaged his person in those troops which he thought, by the forwardness of the commanders, to be most like to be farthest engaged. And in all such encounters he had about him an extraordinary cheerfulness, without

at all affecting the execution that usually attended them, in which he took no delight, but took pains to prevent it where it was not by resistance made necessary. Insomuch that at Edge-hill, when the enemy was routed, he was like to have incurred great peril by in-
5 terposing to save those who had thrown away their arms, and against whom, it may be, others were more fierce for their having thrown them away. So that a man might think, he came into the field chiefly out of curiosity to see the face of danger, and charity to prevent the shedding of blood."

10 At the siege of Gloucester, when Hyde

"passionately reprehended him for exposing his person unnecessar-ily to danger, as being so much beside the duty of his place (of Secretary of State) that it might be understood rather to be against it, he would say merrily that his office could not take away the
15 privilege of his age, and that a *secretary*, in war, might be present at the greatest *secret* of danger; but withal alleged seriously, that it concerned him to be more active in enterprises of hazard than other men, that all might see that his impatiency for peace proceeded not from pusillanimity or fear to adventure his own person."

20 To crown all, Falkland has for the imagination the indefin-able, the irresistible charm of one who is and must be, in spite of the choicest gifts and graces, unfortunate,—of a man in the grasp of fatality. Like the Master of Ravenswood, that most in-teresting by far of all Scott's heroes, he is surely and visibly
25 touched by the finger of doom. And he knows it himself; yet he knits his forehead, and holds on his way. His course must be what it must, and he cannot flinch from it; yet he loves it not, hopes nothing from it, foresees how it will end.

"He had not the court in great reverence, and had a presaging
30 spirit that the king would fall into great misfortune; and often said to his friend that he chose to serve the king because honesty obliged him to it, but that he foresaw his own ruin by doing it."

Yes, for the imagination Falkland cannot but be a figure of ideal, pathetic beauty. But for the judgment, for sober reason?
35 Here opinions differ.

Lord Carnarvon insisted on the salutary example of Falkland's moderation. The Dean of Westminster, who could not go to the Newbury meeting, wrote to say that in his opinion Falkland "is one of the few examples of political eminence unconnected with party, or rather equally connected with both parties; and he is the founder, or nearly the founder, of the best and most enlightening tendencies of the Church of England." And Principal Tulloch, whose chapter on Falkland is perhaps the most delightful chapter of his delightful book,[1] calls him "the inspiring chief of a circle of rational and moderate thinkers amidst the excesses of a violent and dogmatic age."

On the other hand, the *Spectator* pronounces Falkland to have been capricious and unstable, rather than truly moderate. It thinks that "he was vacillating, and did not count the cost of what he undertook." It judges his life to have been wasted. It says that "the heart of moderation is strength," and that "it seems to us easier to maintain that either Cromwell, or Pym, or Hampden, or Fairfax, presented the true type of moderation, than Falkland." Falkland recoiled, and changed sides; the others recognised the duty for a man "to take strong measures, if none less strong will secure an end which he deems of supreme importance."

Severe, too, upon Falkland, as might be expected, is the *Nonconformist*. It talks of his "amiable and hesitating inconsistency." It says that he was moved by "intellectual perception and spiritual sentiment" rather than by "moral impulse," while the Puritan leaders were "moved mainly by moral impulse." It adds that "the greatest reformers have always been those who have been swayed by moral feeling rather than by intellectual conceptions, and the greatest reforming movements have been those accomplished not by the enlightened knowledge of a few, but by the moral enthusiasm of the many." The Puritan leaders had faith. "They drew no complete picture of the ideal to be arrived at. But they were firmly and fixedly resolved, that, come what might, the wrongs of which they were conscious should not be endured." They followed, then, the voice of conscience and of duty; "and, broadly speaking, the voice of conscience is the voice of God." And therefore, while Falkland's death "has

[1] *Rational Theology in England in the Seventeenth Century.*

a special sadness as the end of an inconsistent and in a certain
sense of a wasted life, on the other hand the death of Hampden
was a martyr's seal to truths assured of ultimate triumph."

Truths assured of ultimate triumph! Let us pause upon those
words. The Puritans were victors in the Civil War, and fash-
ioned things to their own liking. How far was their system at
home an embodiment of "truth?" Let us consult a great writer,
too little read. *Who now reads Bolingbroke?* asked Burke scorn-
fully. And the right answer is, so far as regards, at any rate, the
historical writings of Bolingbroke: "Far too few of us; the
more's the pity!" But let us hear Bolingbroke on the success of
Puritanism at home:—

"Cavaliers and Roundheads had divided the nation, like Yorkists
and Lancastrians. To reconcile these disputes by treaty became impracticable, when neither side would trust the other. To terminate
them by the sword was to fight, not for preserving the constitution,
but for the manner of destroying it. The constitution might have
been destroyed under pretence of prerogative. It was destroyed under pretence of liberty. We might have fallen under absolute monarchy. We fell into absolute anarchy."

And to escape from that anarchy, the nation, as every one
knows, swung back into the very hands from which Puritanism
had wrested it, to the bad and false system of government of the
Stuarts.

But the Puritan government, though it broke down at home,
was a wise and grand government abroad. No praise is more
commonly heard than this. But it will not stand. The Puritan
government, Cromwell's government, was a *strong* government
abroad; a wise and true-sighted government abroad it was not.
Again let us hear Bolingbroke:—

"Our Charles the First was no great politician, and yet he seemed
to discern that the balance of power was turning in favour of
France, some years before the treaties of Westphalia. He refused to
be neuter, and threatened to take part with Spain. Cromwell either
did not discern this turn of the balance of power, long afterward
when it was much more visible; or, discerning it, he was induced by
reasons of private interest to act against the general interest of Europe. Cromwell joined with France against Spain; and though he

got Jamaica and Dunkirk, he drove the Spaniards into a necessity of making a peace with France, that has disturbed the peace of the world almost fourscore years, and the consequences of which have well-nigh beggared in our times the nation he enslaved in his."

Bolingbroke deals in strong language, but there can be no doubt that the real imminent danger for Europe, in Cromwell's time, was French ambition and French aggrandisement. There can be no doubt that Cromwell either did not discern this, or acted as if he did not discern it; and that Europe had to bear, in consequence, the infliction of the Grand Monarch and of all he brought with him.

But is it meant that the Puritan triumph was the triumph of religion,—of conduct and righteousness? Alas! it was its defeat. So grossly imperfect, so false, was the Puritan conception and presentation of righteousness, so at war with the ancient and inbred integrity, piety, good nature, and good humour of the English people, that it led straight to moral anarchy, the profligacy of the Restoration. It led to the court, the manners, the stage, the literature, which we know. It led to the long discredit of serious things, to the dryness of the eighteenth century, to the "irreligion" which vexed Butler's righteous soul, to the aversion and incapacity for all deep inquiries concerning religion and its sanctions, to the belief so frequently found now among the followers of natural science that such inquiries are unprofitable. It led, amongst that middle class where religion still lived on, to a narrowness, an intellectual poverty, almost incredible. They "entered the prison of Puritanism, and had the key turned upon their spirit there for two hundred years." It led to that character of their steady and respectable life which makes one shiver: its hideousness, its immense ennui.

But is it meant, finally, that, after all, political liberty re-emerged in England, seriousness re-emerged; that they re-emerged and prevail, and that herein, and in the England of to-day, is the triumph of Puritanism? Yes, this is what is really meant. It is very commonly believed and asserted. But let us imitate the society of Great Tew, and make it our business "to examine and refine those grosser propositions which laziness and consent make current in vulgar conversation." Undoubtedly

there has been a result from the long travail which England has
passed through between the times of the Renascence and our
own. *Something* has come of it all; and that something is the
England of to-day, with its seriousness, such as it is, with its un-
5   deniable political liberty. Let us be thankful for what we have,
and to the Puritans for their share in producing it. But, in the
first place, is it certain that the England of to-day is the best
imaginable and possible result from the elements with which
we started at the Renascence? Because, if not, then by some
10 other shaping of events, and without the Puritan triumph, we
might conceivably have stood even yet better than we stand
now. In the second place, is it certain that of the good which
we admittedly have in the England of to-day,—the seriousness
and the political liberty,—the Puritans and the Puritan triumph
15 are the authors? The assumption that they are so is plausible,—
it is current; it pervades, let me observe in passing, Mr. Green's
fascinating History. But is the assumption sound? When one
considers the strength, the boldness, the self-assertion, the instincts of resistance and independence in the English nature, it
20 is surely hazardous to affirm that only by the particular means
of the Puritan struggle and the Puritan triumph could we have
become free in our persons and property. When we consider
the character shown, the signal given, in the thinking of Thomas
More and Shakspeare, of Bacon and Harvey, how shall we say
25 that only at the price of Puritanism could England have had
free thought? When we consider the seriousness of Spenser,
that ideal Puritan before the fanatical Puritans and without their
faults, when we consider Spenser's seriousness and pureness, in
their revolt against the moral disorder of the Renascence, and
30 remember the allies which they had in the native integrity and
piety of the English race, shall we even venture to say that only
at the price of Puritanism could we have had seriousness? Puritanism has been one element in our seriousness; but it is not the
whole of our seriousness, nor the best in it.

35   Falkland himself was profoundly serious. He was "in his nature so severe a lover of justice and so precise a lover of truth,
that he was superior to all possible temptations for the violation
of either." Far from being a man flighty and unstable, he was a

man, says Clarendon, *constant and pertinacious;* "constant and pertinacious, and not to be wearied with any pains." And he was, as I have said, a born constitutionalist, a hater of "exorbitances" of all kinds, governmental or popular. He "thought no mischief so intolerable as the presumption of ministers of state to break positive rules for reasons of state, or judges to transgress known laws upon the title of conveniency or necessity; which made him so severe against the Earl of Strafford and the Lord Finch, contrary to his natural gentleness and temper." He had the historic sense in politics; an aversion to root-and-branch work, to what he called "great mutations." He was for using compromise and adjustment, for keeping what had long served and what was ready to hand, but amending it and turning it to better account. "I do not believe bishops to be *jure divino*," he would say; "nay, I believe them not to be *jure divino*." Still, he was not disposed to "root up this ancient tree." He had no superstition about it. "He had in his own judgment," says Clarendon, "such a latitude in opinion that he did not believe any part of the order or government of it to be so essentially necessary to religion, but that it might be parted with and altered for a notable public benefit or convenience." On the other hand, "he was never in the least degree swayed or moved by the objections which were made against that government (episcopacy) in the Church, holding them most ridiculous; or affected to the other which those men (the Puritans) fancied to themselves." There Episcopacy and the Church of England had been for ages, and it was the part of a statesman, Falkland thought, rather to use them than to destroy them. All this is in the very spirit of English political liberty, as we now conceive it, and as, by the Revolution of 1688, it triumphed. But it is not in the spirit of the Puritans. The *truths assured of ultimate triumph* were, then, so far as political liberty is concerned, rather with Falkland than with the Puritans.

It was his historic sense, again, which made him, when compromise was plainly impossible, side with the king. Things had come, and by no fault of Falkland, to that pass, when the contention, as Bolingbroke truly says, was "not for preserving the constitution but for the manner of destroying it." In such a

juncture Falkland looked for the best *power* or *purchase*, to use
Burke's excellent expression, that he could find. He thought he
found it in the Crown. He thought the Parliament a less available *power* or *purchase* than the Crown. He thought renovation
more possible by means of the triumph of the Crown than by
means of the triumph of the Parliament. He thought the triumph of the Parliament the greater leap into chaos. He may
have been wrong. Whether a better result might have been got
out of the Parliament's defeat than was got out of its triumph
we can never know. What is certain is that the Parliament's triumph did bring things to a dead-lock, that the nation reverted
to the monarchy, and that the final victory was neither for Stuarts nor Puritans. And it could not be for either of them, for the
cause of neither was sound. Falkland had lucidity enough to see
it. He gave himself to the cause which seemed to him least unsound, and to which "honesty," he thought, bound him; but he
felt that the truth was not there, any more than with the Puritans,—neither the truth nor the future. This is what makes his
figure and situation so truly tragic. For a sound cause he could
not fight, because there was none; he could only fight for the
least bad of two unsound ones. "Publicans and sinners on the
one side," as Chillingworth said; "Scribes and Pharisees on the
other." And Falkland had, I say, the lucidity of mind and
the largeness of temper to see it.

Shall we blame him for his lucidity of mind and largeness of
temper? Shall we even pity him? By no means. They are his
great title to our veneration. They are what make him ours;
what link him with the nineteenth century. He and his friends,
by their heroic and hopeless stand against the inadequate ideals
dominant in their time, kept open their communications with
the future, lived with the future. Their battle is ours too; and
that we pursue it with fairer hopes of success than they did, we
owe to their having waged it and fallen. To our English race,
with its insularity, its profound faith in action, its contempt for
dreamers and failers, inadequate ideals in life, manners, government, thought, religion, will always be a source of danger. Energetic action makes up, we think, for imperfect knowledge.
We think that all is well, that a man is following "a moral im-

pulse," if he pursues an end which he "deems of supreme importance." We impose neither on him nor on ourselves the duty of discerning whether he is *right* in deeming it so.

Hence our causes are often as small as our noise about them is great. To see people busy themselves about Ritualism, that question of not the most strong-minded portion of the clergy and laity, or to see them busy themselves about that "burning question" of the fierce and acrimonious political Dissenters, the Burials Bill, leading up to the other "burning question" of Disestablishment—to see people so eager about these things, one might sometimes fancy that the whole English nation, as in Chillingworth's time it was divided into two great hosts of publicans and sinners on the one side, Scribes and Pharisees on the other, so in ours it was going to divide itself into two vast camps of Simpletons here, under the command, suppose, of Mr. Beresford Hope, and of Savages there, under the command of Mr. Henry Richard. And it is so notorious that great movements are always led by aliens to the sort of people who make the mass of the movement—by gifted outsiders—that I shall not, I hope, be suspected of implying that Mr. Beresford Hope is a simpleton or Mr. Henry Richard a savage. But what we have to do is to raise and multiply in this country a third host, with the conviction that the ideals both of Simpletons and Savages are profoundly inadequate and profoundly unedifying, and with the resolve to win victory for a better ideal than that of either of them.

Falkland and his friends had in their day a like task. On the one hand was the Royalist party, with its vices, its incurable delusions; on the other, the Puritans, with their temper, their false, old-Jewish mixture of politics with an ill-understood religion. I should have been glad to say not one word against Hampden in his honourable grave. But the lovers of Hampden cannot forbear to extol him at Falkland's expense. Alas! yet with what benign disdain might not Jesus have whispered to that exemplary but somewhat Philistine Buckinghamshire squire, *seeking the Lord* about militia or ship-money: "Man, who made me a judge or a divider over you?"

No, the true martyr was not Hampden. If we are to find a

martyr in the history of the Great Civil War, let it be Falkland.
He was the martyr of lucidity of mind and largeness of temper,
in a strife of imperfect intelligences and tempers illiberal. Like
his friend Hales of Eton, who in our century will again, he too,
5   emerge, after having been long obscured by the Lauds and the
Sheldons, by the Owens and the Baxters,—like Hales, Falkland
in that age of harsh and rancorous tempers was "of a nature so
kind, so sweet, that it was near as easy a task for any one to become so knowing as so obliging." Like Hales, too, Falkland
10   could say: "The pursuit of truth hath been my only care ever
since I fully understood the meaning of the word. For this I
have forsaken all hopes, all friends, all desires which might bias
me, and hinder me from driving right at what I aimed." Like
Hales, and unlike our nation in general, Falkland concerned
15   himself with the *why* of things as well as the *what*. "I comprise
it all," says Hales, "in two words: *what* and *wherefore*. That
part of your burden which contains *what*, you willingly take
up. But that other, which comprehends *why*, that is either too
hot or too heavy; you dare not meddle with it. But I must add
20   that also to your burden, or else I must leave you for idle persons; for without the knowledge of why, of the grounds or reasons of things, there is no possibility of not being deceived."
How countless are the deceived and deceiving from this cause!
Nay, and the fanatics of the *what*, the neglecters of the *why*, are
25   not unfrequently men of genius; they have the temperament
which influences, which prevails, which acts magnetically upon
men. So we have the Philistine of genius in religion,—Luther;
the Philistine of genius in politics,—Cromwell; the Philistine of
genius in literature,—Bunyan. All three of them, let us remark,
30   are Germanic, and two of them are English. Mr. Freeman must
be enchanted.

But let us return to Falkland,—to our martyr of sweetness
and light, of lucidity of mind and largeness of temper. Let us
bid him farewell, not with compassion for him, and not with
35   excuses, but in confidence and pride. Slowly, very slowly, his
ideal of lucidity of mind and largeness of temper conquers; but
it conquers. In the end it will prevail; only we must have pa-

tience. The day will come when this nation shall be renewed by it. But, O lime-trees of Tew, and quiet Oxfordshire field-banks where the first violets are even now raising their heads!—how often, ere that day arrive for Englishmen, shall your renewal be seen!

5

German Letters on English Education*

Twenty-six years ago—in 1850—Dr. Wiese, then at the head
of one of the great public schools of Berlin, came over here to
see our English public schools. On his return home he published
a first series of letters on English education. The book was favourably received and was translated into English. Last year
Dr. Wiese again visited England, and a second series of letters
on English education is the result. Of this second series, too,
there is, we believe, or immediately will be, an English translation.

In Germany Dr. Wiese's first book was accused of exhibiting
the English schools by their bright side only. In the preface to
his present book our author explains how he came to lay himself open to this charge. He was at the head of the largest board-
ing-school in Berlin; he had experienced the bad influence upon
schoolboys of a great city in a disturbed, revolutionary time,
and he had just read the Life of Dr. Arnold. Full of that book,
he came to England. He saw the English public schoolboy "in
his happy liberty, growing up healthy and strong;" and attracted by "the poetry of this youthful life," he regarded mainly
what was enviable in it, and gave little heed to its imperfections.
In 1876 Dr. Wiese's point of view was no longer the same as in
1850. For many years he had been one of the chief permanent
officers in the Education Department at Berlin, the secretary
charged with the affairs of Prussian secondary schools. His
point of view was now, therefore, that of an administrator, not
of a teacher. For England herself the question of a national organization of schools may be said to have emerged since Dr.

* "Deutsche Briefe über Englische Erziehung." Von Dr. L. Wiese.
(Berlin. 1877.)

208

Wiese's visit in 1850, and to have become a question, at present, of the most pressing concern for us. An administrator's view of our school system is the view, therefore, which at this actual moment most interests us.

Dr. Wiese likes and admires England, and to the good points of our schools, schoolmasters, and scholars, he still does justice. But the total result of his observations is far more unfavourable to us than in 1850. It could not but be so. Instead of fixing his eyes upon the work and influence of a single gifted English schoolmaster, Dr. Wiese now surveys English education as a whole. As a whole it is chaotic. It shows that defect which so much of what is done in England shows—defect in power to co-order things in view of a general result. Good bits and strokes of work one sees in abundance; work well and intelligently co-ordered in view of a large general result distinctly conceived, one hardly ever sees. Our architecture—indeed all our art—bears tokens of this weak side in English performance. But nowhere are they more displayed than in our school organization.

The State has been the great bugbear. Englishmen do not want, they say, to have a paternal Government meddling with their schools and directing them. Or, at any rate, if the poor require it, the middle and upper classes do not. These classes will manage their schools for themselves. At last, however, Englishmen open their eyes to see that in this way they have got a few good schools and a multitude of very bad ones. Some norm-giving agency, some common standard for testing the work of schools, some guarantee of their efficiency, are absolutely needed. The State is not to be thought of. So recourse is had to the universities as a norm-giving power, and to examinations as a test and guarantee of school instruction. But in the universities we have chosen, says Dr. Wiese, an agency by its very nature not well fitted for the task assigned to it; and in our examination test, an influence which, instead of promoting good school instruction, impedes it. And at the same time, inadequate as is our procedure to bring forth good educational results, it has an arbitrariness, a meddlesomeness, and an exuberance of routine not to be matched in bureaucratic Prussia.

But we will let Dr. Wiese, as far as possible, speak for himself on these points. What English education wants is above all, says Dr. Wiese, "unity of plan, and a firm guiding hand—'Einheit des Plans und eine feste leitende Hand.' " There are great re-
5   sources, innumerable experiments; there is no clearly marked aim, well chosen, steadily and consistently followed. German schools have their faults; but in arranging the system of German schools and in laying out their instruction, an aim, chosen after the best consideration and the most capable advice, is kept
10 clear in view and is steadily followed. Much has still to be done; but Germany has, at any rate, the great advantage of having its schools co-ordered according to a regular, well-devised system, and their instruction laid out according to a regular, well-devised plan.

15   This we owe to the State, to the Government; we are fully conscious what it is that we get from it. It is above all this unity of procedure, free from arbitrariness, and in general conducted, both at the centre of government and in the provinces, by men who have come to their administrative posts after long practical acquaintance
20 with schools. In all important questions the counsel of experts throughout the country is taken. In the schools themselves the regulations fixed by law are of a nature not to deprive either the headmaster or his assistants of free play in the work of teaching.

In England, on the other hand, we find in the same sphere "the
25 direct opposite of an organization. All clear distribution, all assignment of limits to the different sorts of schools, all fixedly given aims, are utterly wanting." There is absolute freedom, with occasionally a vain complaint of the too evident waste of power, of the reign of caprice and chaos. What the English
30 schools need is "a man in whom a clear perception of requirements and needs is united with practical executive capacity and with energetic will. But if such a man were found, how is he to attain, in England, to the position of a guiding authority? The English jealousy of interference, of dictation, would make it
35 impossible." And therefore "the sensitive and tenacious self-assertion of the English involves weakness of organization." For the English schools "the very ground lines of an organization

have yet to be drawn—'Die Grundlinien einer Organisation müssen erst noch gezogen werden.' "

In their terror of bureaucracy and authoritative State-guidance, the English have had recourse to the universities and to examinations for the purpose of keeping or of bringing their schools up to the mark. "The question arises: Is it the proper function of a university, as such, to employ itself in visiting and examining schools? In Germany, we think not." But even could the university, without departing from its proper sphere, undertake the inspection and examination of schools, the university has no power to give the schools what they most want—*unity of plan and a firm guiding hand.* Everything is voluntary. The university is free to inspect or not as it likes, the schools are free to submit to inspection or to repel it, the public is free to attach weight to its results or to treat them with indifference. "We cannot," says Dr. Wiese, "look upon such an arrangement as supplying any effectual substitute for the official objectivity *(die amtliche Objectivität)* which attends the proceedings of a real independent school authority."

Yet our English arrangements, ineffective as they are, show less regard to the due claims of schools and teachers than such an authority would show.

It is intelligible that the schools should prefer a supervision of this nature to a supervision by a State-authority. What is surprising is that so much mistrust in one direction should be accompanied by so much readiness in another to renounce all exercise of independence and co-operation. What could be of more importance to head-masters than to unite together and request the universities to begin by settling, *in conjunction with them, the head-masters,* the objects for instruction and the requirements for examination? Nothing of the kind has been done. The university rules, with all their detailed directions and provisoes, are accepted without further question as regulative, and are spoken of as the edicts of a superior authority. For example: "*We are now allowed* the same latitude in modern languages that we are in classics, and that is an important concession." Those are the words of a head-master.

Dr. Wiese continually notices how the absence of all general direction is accompanied, in the case of the English schools, by a bondage in points of detail such as strikes a foreigner with wonder.

That he should submit to bureaucracy is an intolerable thought to an Englishman. And yet their schools submit to another and far more oppressive dependence in the system of examinations now prevalent. From complaints I have heard, I think it possible that what the English have of bureaucracy and centralization already, and can see at work upon their elementary schools, heightens their dislike to it. For the endowed schools, also, many of the regulations issued are too bureaucratic for our German notions. The Act of 1869 directs, for instance, as regards the teachers: "In every scheme the Commissioners shall provide for the dismissal at pleasure of every teacher and officer, including the principal teacher, with or without a power of appeal, as to the Commissioners may seem expedient." With us, again, the governing body of an institution not in receipt of State-aid would be at liberty to part with a piece of land belonging to it, if their so doing were likely to benefit the institution. In England the governors must first get the consent of the Court of Chancery.

But it is our mania for examinations, and our reliance upon them, which most excite Dr. Wiese's astonishment. He points out how they interfere with good school-work, and thus continues: —

The method of operating through examinations and prizes is looked upon in England as the most effective; the English have, or venture to apply, no other. German school-administrations regard much more the object of assuring the right way to the goal, and providing that it shall be rightly followed. The number of candidates at a German leaving examination who have been privately prepared is a very small proportion of the whole. In England hardly anything is heeded but the demonstrable final result. Like a bell, the sound goes out at intervals through the land: Come and be examined! And they come, boys and girls, the young and the adult, and have scraped together what knowledge they could. How they have come by it, nobody asks; what is the best way, nobody shows them; and yet what work could be more worthy of a university? Results, results! It is characteristic of England, and best explains the present high value set on examinations in school and university.

The apparent grandiosity, the wide sweep of the examination-system by which the same set of printed questions is given out in England and sent all over the world, to Canada, the Mauritius, and so on, has no imposingness for us. Where is the great difference between that and the mechanical French centralization, where the Minister in Paris could look at his watch and tell the foreigner what chapter of Caesar was at that moment being read in every *lycée* in France? We rather consider it a great and unnecessary piece of circumlocution, to have simple elementary questions, such as many of them must be, in grammar, geography, Bible history, &c., printed and sent all over the world. The English have transplanted their examination system to India. A young Hindoo from Calcutta, who was my travelling companion for some time, spoke very unfavourably of the result. The English teachers in their schools simply urged them, he said, to get ready for examination, and they were thus made to cram their memory with unconnected and often but half-comprehended facts, without acquiring any power of thinking independently. It is singular that the English, who attach so much value to the free development of a man's individuality, do not see that this overdoing of examinations is all against it.

The exaggerated prize-system of our schools seems to Dr. Wiese as false and un-English as their exaggerated examination system.

This brings me to the *prizes*. Of all the contrasts which the English fashion of thought and life contains within itself, none has, to my mind, more of inner contradiction than that a nation, which accounts the idea of duty so high and sacred, should make no use whatever of that idea in educating the young, but should have adopted the principle, or rather the negation of principle, to employ the lure of reward and distinction as the grand motive to exertion. Even those who are not so severe as to exclude this motive in schools altogether must be displeased with the stress laid upon it in schools in England. In every stage of instruction, from the university down to the elementary school, rewards and prizes are made in England the chief incentives to industry; even in the Sunday school, the English cannot, incredible as it may seem, do without this motive. And not merely for good work are there prizes and medals; there are prizes and medals for good behaviour too. So universal is the habit that every one follows it without scruple; they can conceive no other way of proceeding. The Monthyon Prize for virtue in France is justly considered by English people to be a thing eminently and characteristically French; but in the premium system of the schools of the two countries, England and France are absolutely alike. Even the College of Preceptors offers prizes, although it stands in no connection with the schools; but it employs the means of prizes in order to induce the schools and scholars to let themselves be examined by it. At a railway-station, when the English schools were breaking up, I heard a father greet his son with the inquiry, How many prizes? and when the boy answered, Three, the father's face seemed to say, Not more? Even girls are urged to the same sort of competition, and are brought forward at the field-days when prizes are distributed.

After all this we shall not be surprised to hear that what distinguishes, in Dr. Wiese's opinion, the German from the English pupil is that the former carries away from his school a sense of the connection of things in what he has studied, the latter a quantity of isolated, unrelated fragments of knowledge —*einzelne, notizen-artige Kenntnisse.*

Our elementary schools are connected with the State, but in their management Dr. Wiese finds just the same faults as in that of our higher schools which are exempt from State control: an absence of well-chosen aims pursued by well-conceived methods. He describes our Education Department as "an extraordinarily complicated machinery, with a vast deal of bureaucratic deskwork and very little free play for personal initiative." It has plenty of routine, he says, plenty of centralization, more than the Prussian department; but this is not the same thing as guidance and furtherance of popular instruction. The famous panacea of "payment by results" finds no favour in his eyes. "The main hindrance to a sound development of the elementary schools lies in the connection now regnant there between schoolwork and money. *Payment by results* is a spur for teachers and scholars: but the impulse comes from without, not from within. It is impossible that a real organization—a formation, that is, which carries within itself the living law of its own growth—should be created on such a system."

Dr. Wiese deserves our gratitude, in spite of the severe things he says of us, for calling attention to what is, indeed, the great want of English public instruction: careful, intelligent design, with a firm guiding hand. Some day, perhaps, we may have a statesman of genius who will recognize the want and do something to remove it. But he will have to begin by convincing the great English middle class of an unpalatable truth: that what they achieve by their boasted repudiation of State interference 5 is simply, as has been said, to maintain the aristocratic class in its preponderance, and the middle class, their own class, in its vulgarity.

George Sand

The months go round, and anniversaries return; on the ninth of June[1] George Sand will have been dead just one year. She was born in 1804; she was almost seventy-two years old when she died. She came to Paris after the revolution of 1830, with her *Indiana* written, and began her life of independence, her life of authorship, her life as *George Sand*. She continued at work till she died. For forty-five years she was writing and publishing, and filled Europe with her name.

It seems to me but the other day that I saw her, yet it was in the August of 1846, more than thirty years ago. I saw her in her own Berry, at Nohant, where her childhood and youth were passed, where she returned to live after she became famous, where she died and has now her grave. There must be many who, after reading her books, have felt the same desire which in those days of my youth, in 1846, took me to Nohant,—the desire to see the country and the places of which the books that so charmed us were full. Those old provinces of the centre of France, primitive and slumbering,—Berry, La Marche, Bourbonnais; those sites and streams in them, of name once so indifferent to us, but to which George Sand gave such a music for our ear,—La Châtre, Ste. Sévère, the *Vallée Noire*, the Indre, the Creuse; how many a reader of George Sand must have desired, as I did, after frequenting them so much in thought, fairly to set eyes upon them!

I had been reading *Jeanne*. I made up my mind to go and see Toulx Ste. Croix and Boussac, and the Druidical stones on Mont Barlot, the *Pierres Jaumâtres*. I remember looking out Toulx

[1] 1877.

in Cassini's great map at the Bodleian Library. The railway through the centre of France went in those days no farther than Vierzon. From Vierzon to Châteauroux one travelled by an ordinary diligence, from Châteauroux to La Châtre by a humbler diligence, from La Châtre to Boussac by the humblest diligence of all. At Boussac diligence ended, and *patache* began. Between Châteauroux and La Châtre, a mile or two before reaching the latter place, the road passes by the village of Nohant. The Château of Nohant, in which Madame Sand lived, is a plain house by the roadside, with a walled garden. Down in the meadows, not far off, flows the Indre, bordered by trees. I passed Nohant without stopping, at La Châtre I dined and changed diligence, and went on by night up the valley of the Indre, the *Vallée Noire*, past Ste. Sévère to Boussac. At Ste. Sévère the Indre is quite a small stream. In the darkness we quitted its valley, and when day broke we were in the wilder and barer country of La Marche, with Boussac before us, and its high castle on a precipitous rock over the Little Creuse.

That day and the next I wandered through a silent country of heathy and ferny *landes*, a region of granite boulders, holly, and broom, of copsewood and great chestnut trees; a region of broad light, and fresh breezes, and wide horizons. I visited the *Pierres Jaumâtres*. I stood at sunset on the platform of Toulx Ste. Croix, by the scrawled and almost effaced stone lions,—a relic, it is said, of the English rule,—and gazed on the blue mountains of Auvergne filling the distance, and, south-eastward of them, in a still farther and fainter distance, on what seemed to be the mountains over Le Puy and the high valley of the Loire.

From Boussac I addressed to Madame Sand the sort of letter of which she must in her lifetime have had scores, a letter conveying to her, in bad French, the homage of a youthful and enthusiastic foreigner who had read her works with delight. She received the infliction good-naturedly, for on my return to La Châtre I found a message left at the inn by a servant from Nohant that Madame Sand would be glad to see me if I called. The mid-day breakfast at Nohant was not yet over when I reached the house, and I found a large party assembled. I en-

tered with some trepidation, as well I might, considering how
I had got there; but the simplicity of Madame Sand's manner
put me at ease in a moment. She named some of those present;
amongst them were her son and daughter, the Maurice and
Solange so familiar to us from her books, and Chopin with his
wonderful eyes. There was at that time nothing astonishing in
Madame Sand's appearance. She was not in man's clothes, she
wore a sort of costume not impossible, I should think (although
on these matters I speak with hesitation), to members of the fair
sex at this hour amongst ourselves, as an out-door dress for the
country or for Scotland. She made me sit by her and poured out
for me the insipid and depressing beverage, *boisson fade et mé-
lancolique*, as Balzac called it, for which English people are
thought abroad to be always thirsting,—tea. She conversed of
the country through which I had been wandering, of the Berry
peasants and their mode of life, of Switzerland whither I was
going; she touched politely, by a few questions and remarks,
upon England and things and persons English,—upon Oxford
and Cambridge, Byron, Bulwer. As she spoke, her eyes, head,
bearing, were all of them striking; but the main impression she
made was an impression of what I have already mentioned,—of
simplicity, frank, cordial simplicity. After breakfast she led the
way into the garden, asked me a few kind questions about myself and my plans, gathered a flower or two and gave them to
me, shook hands heartily at the gate, and I saw her no more. In
1859 M. Michelet gave me a letter to her, which would have
enabled me to present myself in more regular fashion. Madame
Sand was then in Paris. But a day or two passed before I could
call, and when I called, Madame Sand had left Paris and had
gone back to Nohant. The impression of 1846 has remained my
single impression of her.

Of her gaze, form, and speech, that one impression is enough;
better perhaps than a mixed impression from seeing her at sun-
dry times and after successive changes. But as the first anniversary of her death draws near, there arises again a desire which I
felt when she died, the desire, not indeed to take a critical survey of her,—very far from it. I feel no inclination at all to go
regularly through her productions, to classify and value them

one by one, to pick out from them what the English public may most like, or to present to that public, for the most part ignorant of George Sand and for the most part indifferent to her, a full history and a judicial estimate of the woman and of her writings. But I desire to recall to my own mind, before the occasion offered by her death passes quite away,—to recall and collect the elements of that powerful total-impression which, as a writer, she made upon me; to recall and collect them, to bring them distinctly into view, to feel them in all their depth and power once more. What I here attempt is not for the benefit of the indifferent; it is for my own satisfaction, it is for myself. But perhaps those for whom George Sand has been a friend and a power will find an interest in following me.

Le sentiment de la vie idéale, qui n'est autre que la vie normale telle que nous sommes appelés à la connaître;—"the sentiment of the ideal life, which is none other than man's normal life as we shall some day know it,"—those words from one of her last publications give the ruling thought of George Sand, the ground-*motive*, as they say in music, of all her strain. It is as a personage inspired by this motive that she interests us.

The English public conceives of her as of a novel-writer who wrote stories more or less interesting; the earlier ones objectionable and dangerous, the later ones, some of them, unexceptionable and fit to be put into the hands of the youth of both sexes. With such a conception of George Sand, a story of hers like *Consuelo* comes to be elevated in England into quite an undue relative importance, and to pass with very many people for her typical work, displaying all that is really valuable and significant in the author. *Consuelo* is a charming story. But George Sand is something more than a maker of charming stories, and only a portion of her is shown in *Consuelo*. She is more, likewise, than a creator of characters. She has created, with admirable truth to nature, characters most attractive and attaching, such as Edmée, Geneviève, Germain. But she is not adequately expressed by them. We do not know her unless we feel the spirit which goes through her work as a whole.

In order to feel this spirit it is not, indeed, necessary to read all that she ever produced. Even three or four only out of her many books might suffice to show her to us, if they were well chosen; let us say, the *Lettres d'un Voyageur, Mauprat, Fran-*
5   *çois le Champi*, and a story which I was glad to see Mr. Myers, in his appreciative notice of Madame Sand, single out for praise, —*Valvèdre*. In these may be found all the principal elements of their author's strain: the cry of agony and revolt, the trust in nature and beauty, the aspiration towards a purged and renewed
10 human society.

Of George Sand's strain, during forty years, these are the grand elements. Now it is one of them which appears most prominently, now it is another. The cry of agony and revolt is in her earlier work only, and passes away in her later. But in the
15 evolution of these three elements,—the passion of agony and revolt, the consolation from nature and from beauty, the ideas of social renewal,—in the evolution of these is George Sand and George Sand's life and power. Through their evolution her constant motive declares and unfolds itself, that motive which we
20 have set forth above: "the sentiment of the ideal life, which is none other than man's normal life as we shall one day know it." This is the motive, and through these elements is its evolution; an evolution pursued, moreover, with the most unfailing resolve, the most absolute sincerity.

25 The hour of agony and revolt passed away for George Sand, as it passed away for Goethe, as it passes away for their readers likewise. It passes away and does not return; yet those who, amid the agitations, more or less stormy, of their youth, betook themselves to the early works of George Sand, may in later life
30 cease to read them, indeed, but they can no more forget them than they can forget *Werther*. George Sand speaks somewhere of her "days of *Corinne*." Days of *Valentine*, many of us may in like manner say,—days of *Valentine*, days of *Lélia*, days never to return! They are gone, we shall read the books no more, and
35 yet how ineffaceable is their impression! How the sentences from George Sand's works of that period still linger in our memory and haunt the ear with their cadences! Grandiose and moving, they come, those cadences, like the sighing of the wind

through the forest, like the breaking of the waves on the sea-shore. Lélia in her cell on the mountain of the Camaldoli—

"Sibyl, Sibyl forsaken; spirit of the days of old, joined to a brain which rebels against the divine inspiration; broken lyre, mute instrument, whose tones the world of to-day, if it heard them, could not 5 understand, but yet in whose depth the eternal harmony murmurs imprisoned; priestess of death, I, I who feel and know that before now I have been Pythia, have wept before now, before now have spoken, but who cannot recollect, alas, cannot utter the word of healing! Yes, yes! I remember the cavern of truth and the access of 10 revelation; but the word of human destiny, I have forgotten it; but the talisman of deliverance, it is lost from my hand. And yet, indeed, much, much have I seen! and when suffering presses me sore, when indignation takes hold of me, when I feel Prometheus wake up in my heart and beat his puissant wings against the stone which 15 confines him,—oh! then, in prey to a frenzy without a name, to a despair without bounds, I invoke the unknown master and friend who might illumine my spirit and set free my tongue; but I grope in darkness, and my tired arms grasp nothing save delusive shadows. And for ten thousand years, as the sole answer to my cries, as the 20 sole comfort in my agony, I hear astir, over this earth accurst, the despairing sob of impotent agony. For ten thousand years I have cried in infinite space: *Truth! Truth!* For ten thousand years infinite space keeps answering me: *Desire, Desire.* O Sibyl forsaken! O mute Pythia! dash then thy head against the rocks of thy cavern, 25 and mingle thy raging blood with the foam of the sea; for thou deemest thyself to have possessed the almighty Word, and these ten thousand years thou art seeking him in vain."

Or Sylvia's cry over Jacques by his glacier in the Tyrol—

"When such a man as thou art is born into a world where he can 30 do no true service; when, with the soul of an apostle and the courage of a martyr, he has simply to push his way among the heartless and aimless crowds which vegetate without living; the atmosphere suffocates him and he dies. Hated by sinners, the mock of fools, disliked by the envious, abandoned by the weak, what can he do but 35 return to God, weary with having laboured in vain, in sorrow at having accomplished nothing? The world remains in all its vileness and in all its hatefulness; this is what men call, 'the triumph of good sense over enthusiasm.' "

Or Jacques himself, and his doctrine—

"Life is arid and terrible, repose is a dream, prudence is useless; mere reason alone serves simply to dry up the heart; there is but one virtue, the eternal sacrifice of oneself."

5   Or George Sand speaking in her own person, in the *Lettres d'un Voyageur*—

"Ah, no, I was not born to be a poet, I was born to love. It is the misfortune of my destiny, it is the enmity of others, which have made me a wanderer and an artist. What I wanted was to live a hu-
10   man life; I had a heart, it has been torn violently from my breast. All that has been left me is a head, a head full of noise and pain, of horrible memories, of images of woe, of scenes of outrage. And because in writing stories to earn my bread I could not help remembering my sorrows, because I had the audacity to say that in mar-
15   ried life there were to be found miserable beings, by reason of the weakness which is enjoined upon the woman, by reason of the brutality which is permitted to the man, by reason of the turpitudes which society covers and protects with a veil, I am pronounced immoral, I am treated as if I were the enemy of the human race."

20   If only, alas, together with her honesty and her courage, she could feel within herself that she had also light and hope and power; that she was able to lead those whom she loved, and who looked to her for guidance! But no; her very own children, witnesses of her suffering, her uncertainty, her struggles,
25   her evil report, may come to doubt her:—

"My poor children, my own flesh and blood, will perhaps turn upon me and say: 'You are leading us wrong, you mean to ruin us as well as yourself. Are you not unhappy, reprobated, evil spoken of? What have you gained by these unequal struggles, by these
30   much trumpeted duels of yours with custom and belief? Let us do as others do; let us get what is to be got out of this easy and tolerant world.'

"This is what they will say to me. Or at best, if, out of tenderness for me, or from their own natural disposition, they give ear to my
35   words and believe me, whither shall I guide them? Into what abysses shall we go and plunge ourselves, we three?—for we shall be our own three upon earth, and not one soul with us. What shall I reply to them if they come and say to me: 'Yes, life is unbearable in a

world like this. Let us die together. Show us the path of Bernica, or the lake of Sténio, or the glaciers of Jacques.' "

Nevertheless the failure of the impassioned seekers of a new and better world proves nothing, George Sand maintains, for the world as it is. Ineffectual they may be, but the world is still more ineffectual, and it is the world's course which is doomed to ruin, not theirs. "What has it done," exclaims George Sand in her preface to Guérin's *Centaure*, "what has it done for our moral education, and what is it doing for our children, this society shielded with such care?" Nothing. Those whom it calls vain complainers and rebels and madmen, may reply:—

"Suffer us to bewail our martyrs, poets without a country that we are, forlorn singers, well versed in the causes of their misery and of our own. You do not comprehend the malady which killed them; they themselves did not comprehend it. If one or two of us at the present day open our eyes to a new light, is it not by a strange and unaccountable good Providence; and have we not to seek our grain of faith in storm and darkness, combated by doubt, irony, the absence of all sympathy, all example, all brotherly aid, all protection and countenance in high places? Try yourselves to speak to your brethren heart to heart, conscience to conscience! Try it!—but you cannot, busied as you are with watching and patching up in all directions your dykes which the flood is invading. The material existence of this society of yours absorbs all your care, and requires more than all your efforts. Meanwhile the powers of human thought are growing into strength, and rise on all sides around you. Amongst these threatening apparitions, there are some which fade away and re-enter the darkness, because the hour of life has not yet struck, and the fiery spirit which quickened them could strive no longer with the horrors of this present chaos; but there are others that can wait, and you will find them confronting you, up and alive, to say: 'You have allowed the death of our brethren, and we, we do not mean to die.' "

She did not, indeed. How should she faint and fail before her time, because of a world out of joint, because of the reign of stupidity, because of the passions of youth, because of the difficulties and disgusts of married life in the native seats of the *homme sensuel moyen*, the average sensual man, she who could feel so well the power of those eternal consolers, nature and beauty? From the very first they introduce a note of suavity in her strain of grief and passion. Who can forget the lanes and meadows of *Valentine?*

5   George Sand is one of the few French writers who keep us closely and truly intimate with rural nature. She gives us the wild-flowers by their actual names,—snowdrop, primrose, columbine, iris, scabious. Nowhere has she touched her native Berry and its little-known landscape, its *campagnes ignorées,*

10   with a lovelier charm than in *Valentine.* The winding and deep lanes running out of the high road on either side, the fresh and calm spots they take us to, "meadows of a tender green, plaintive brooks, clumps of alder and mountain ash, a whole world of suave and pastoral nature,"—how delicious it all is! The

15   grave and silent peasant whose very dog will hardly deign to bark at you, the great white ox, "the unfailing dean of these pastures," staring solemnly at you from the thicket; the farmhouse "with its avenue of maples, and the Indre, here hardly more than a bright rivulet, stealing along through rushes and

20   yellow iris, in the field below,"—who, I say, can forget them? And that one lane in especial, the lane where Athénaïs puts her arm out of the side window of the rustic carriage and gathers May from the over-arching hedge,—that lane with its startled blackbirds, and humming insects, and limpid water, and sway-

25   ing water-plants, and shelving gravel, and yellow wagtails hopping half-pert, half-frightened, on the sand,—that lane with its rushes, cresses, and mint below, its honeysuckle and traveller's-joy above,—how gladly might one give all that strangely English picture in English, if the charm of Madame Sand's lan-

30   guage did not here defy translation! Let us try something less difficult, and yet something where we may still have her in this her beloved world of "simplicity, and sky, and fields and trees, and peasant life,—peasant life looked at, by preference, on its good and sound side." *Voyez donc la simplicité, vous autres,*

35   *voyez le ciel et les champs, et les arbres, et les paysans, surtout dans ce qu'ils ont de bon et de vrai.*

The introduction to *La Mare au Diable* will give us what we want. George Sand has been looking at an engraving of Hol-

bein's *Labourer*. An old thick-set peasant, in rags, is driving his
plough in the midst of a field. All around spreads a wild landscape, dotted with a few poor huts. The sun is setting behind a
hill; the day of toil is nearly over. It has been a hard one; the
ground is rugged and stony, the labourer's horses are but skin   5
and bone, weak and exhausted. There is but one alert figure, the
skeleton Death, who with a whip skips nimbly along at the
horses' side and urges the team. Under the picture is a quotation in old French, to the effect that after the labourer's life of
travail and service, in which he has to gain his bread by the   10
sweat of his brow, here comes Death to fetch him away. And
from so rude a life does Death take him, says George Sand, that
Death is hardly unwelcome; and in another composition by
Holbein, where men of almost every condition,—popes, sovereigns, lovers, gamblers, monks, soldiers,—are taunted with   15
their fear of Death and do indeed see his approach with terror,
Lazarus alone is easy and composed, and sitting on his dunghill
at the rich man's door, tells Death that he does not dread him.
     With her thoughts full of Holbein's mournful picture,
George Sand goes out into the fields of her own Berry:—   20

"My walk was by the border of a field which some peasants were
getting ready for being sown presently. The space to be ploughed
was wide, as in Holbein's picture. The landscape was vast also; the
great lines of green which it contained were just touched with rus-
set by the approach of autumn; on the rich brown soil recent rain   25
had left, in a good many furrows, lines of water, which shone in the
sun like silver threads. The day was clear and soft, and the earth
gave out a light smoke where it had been freshly laid open by the
plough-share. At the top of the field an old man, whose broad back
and severe face were like those of the old peasant of Holbein, but   30
whose clothes told no tale of poverty, was gravely driving his
plough of an antique shape, drawn by two tranquil oxen, with coats
of a pale buff, real patriarchs of the fallow, tall of make, somewhat
thin, with long and backward-sloping horns, the kind of old workmen who by habit have got to be *brothers* to one another, as   35
throughout our country-side they are called, and who, if one loses
the other, refuse to work with a new comrade, and fret themselves
to death. People unacquainted with the country will not believe in
this affection of the ox for his yoke-fellow. They should come and

see one of the poor beasts in a corner of his stable, thin, wasted, lash-
ing with his restless tail his lean flanks, blowing uneasily and fastidi-
ously on the provender offered to him, his eyes for ever turned
towards the stable door, scratching with his foot the empty place
5 left at his side, sniffing the yokes and bands which his companion has
worn, and incessantly calling for him with piteous lowings. The ox-
herd will tell you: There is a pair of oxen done for! his *brother* is
dead, and this one will work no more. He ought to be fattened for
killing; but we cannot get him to eat, and in a short time he will
10 have starved himself to death."

How faithful and close it is, this contact of George Sand with
country things, with the life of nature in its vast plenitude and
pathos! And always in the end the human interest, as is right,
emerges and predominates. What is the central figure in the
15 fresh and calm rural world of George Sand? It is the peasant.
And what is the peasant? He is France, life, the future. And
this is the strength of George Sand, and of her second movement, after the first movement of energy and revolt was over,
towards nature and beauty, towards the country, towards prim-
20 itive life, the peasant. She regarded nature and beauty, not with
the selfish and solitary joy of the artist who but seeks to appropriate them for his own purposes, she regarded them as a treasure of immense and hitherto unknown application, as a vast
power of healing and delight for all, and for the peasant first
25 and foremost. Yes, she cries, the simple life is the true one! but
the peasant, the great organ of that life, "the minister in that
vast temple which only the sky is vast enough to embrace," the
peasant is not doomed to toil and moil in it for ever, overdone
and unawakened, like Holbein's labourer, and to have for his
30 best comfort the thought that death will set him free. *Non, nous
n'avons plus affaire à la mort, mais à la vie.* "Our business henceforth is not with death, but with life."

Joy is the great lifter of men, the great unfolder. *Il faut que
la vie soit bonne afin qu'elle soit féconde.* "For life to be fruitful,
35 life must be felt as a blessing":—

"Nature is eternally young, beautiful, bountiful. She pours out
beauty and poetry for all that live, she pours it out on all plants, and
the plants are permitted to expand in it freely. She possesses the se-

cret of happiness, and no man has been able to take it away from
her. The happiest of men would be he who possessing the science of
his labour and working with his hands, earning his comfort and his
freedom by the exercise of his intelligent force, found time to live
by the heart and by the brain, to understand his own work and to 5
love the work of God. The artist has satisfactions of this kind in the
contemplation and reproduction of nature's beauty; but when he
sees the affliction of those who people this paradise of earth, the upright and human-hearted artist feels a trouble in the midst of his enjoyment. The happy day will be when mind, heart, and hands shall 10
be alive together, shall work in concert; when there shall be a harmony between God's munificence and man's delight in it. Then, instead of the piteous and frightful figure of Death, skipping along
whip in hand by the peasant's side in the field, the allegorical painter
will place there a radiant angel, sowing with full hands the blessed 15
grain in the smoking furrow.

"And the dream of a kindly, free, poetic, laborious, simple existence for the tiller of the field is not so hard to realise that it must
be banished into the world of chimæras. Virgil's sweet and sad cry:
'O happy peasants, if they but knew their own blessings!' is a regret; 20
but like all regrets, it is at the same time a prediction. The day will
come when the labourer may be also an artist;—not in the sense of
rendering nature's beauty, a matter which will be then of much less
importance, but in the sense of feeling it. Does not this mysterious
intuition of poetic beauty exist in him already in the form of instinct 25
and of vague reverie?"

It exists in him, too, adds Madame Sand, in the form of that
nostalgia, that home-sickness, which for ever pursues the genuine French peasant if you transplant him. The peasant has here,
then, the elements of the poetic sense, and of its high and pure 30
satisfactions.

"But one part of the enjoyment which we possess is wanting to
him, a pure and lofty pleasure which is surely his due, minister that
he is in that vast temple which only the sky is vast enough to embrace. He has not the conscious knowledge of his sentiment. Those 35
who have sentenced him to servitude from his mother's womb, not
being able to debar him from reverie, have debarred him from reflection.

"Well, for all that, taking the peasant as he is, incomplete and
seemingly condemned to an eternal childhood, I yet find him a 40

more beautiful object than the man in whom his acquisition of knowledge has stifled sentiment. Do not rate yourselves so high above him, many of you who imagine that you have an imprescriptible right to his obedience; for you yourselves are the most incom-
5 plete and the least seeing of men. That simplicity of his soul is more to be loved than the false lights of yours."

In all this we are passing from the second element in George Sand to the third,—her aspiration for a social new-birth, a *renaissance sociale*. It is eminently the ideal of France; it was hers.
10 Her religion connected itself with this ideal. In the convent where she was brought up, she had in youth had an awakening of fervent mystical piety in the Catholic form. That form she could not keep. Popular religion of all kinds, with its deep internal impossibilities, its "heaven and hell serving to cover the
15 illogical manifestations of the Divinity's apparent designs respecting us," its "God made in our image, silly and malicious, vain and puerile, irritable or tender, after our fashion," lost all sort of hold upon her:—

"Communion with such a God is impossible to me; I confess it.
20 He is wiped out from my memory: there is no corner where I can find him any more. Nor do I find such a God out of doors either; he is not in the fields and waters, he is not in the starry sky. No, nor yet in the churches where men bow themselves; it is an extinct message, a dead letter, a thought that has done its day. Nothing of this belief,
25 nothing of this God, subsists in me any longer."

She refused to lament over the loss, to esteem it other than a benefit:—

"It is an addition to our stock of light, this detachment from the idolatrous conception of religion. It is no loss of the religious sense,
30 as the persisters in idolatry maintain. It is quite the contrary, it is a restitution of allegiance to the true Divinity. It is a step made in the direction of this Divinity, it is an abjuration of the dogmas which did him dishonour."

She does not attempt to give of this Divinity an account much
35 more precise than that which we have in Wordsworth,—"*a presence that disturbs me with the joy of animating thoughts.*"

"Everything is divine (she says), even matter; everything is superhuman, even man. God is everywhere; he is in me in a measure proportioned to the little that I am. My present life separates me from him just in the degree determined by the actual state of childhood of our race. Let me content myself, in all my seeking, to feel after him, and to possess of him as much as this imperfect soul can take in with the intellectual sense I have."

And she concludes:—

"The day will come when we will no longer talk about God idly, nay, when we shall talk about him as little as possible. We shall cease to set him forth dogmatically, to dispute about his nature. We shall put compulsion on no one to pray to him, we shall leave the whole business of worship within the sanctuary of each man's conscience. And this will happen when we are really religious."

Meanwhile the sense of this spirit or presence which animates us, the sense of the divine, is our stronghold and our consolation. A man may say of it: "It comes not by my desert, but the atom of divine sense given to me nothing can rob me of." *Divine sense,*—the phrase is a vague one; but it stands to Madame Sand for that to which are to be referred "all the best thoughts and the best actions of life, suffering endured, duty achieved, whatever purifies our existence, whatever vivifies our love."

Madame Sand is a Frenchwoman, and her religion is therefore, as we might expect, with peculiar fervency social. Always she has before her mind "the natural law which *will have it* (the italics are her own) that the species *man* cannot subsist and prosper but by *association.*" Whatever else we may be in creation, we are, first and foremost, "at the head of the species which are called by instinct, and led by necessity, to the life of *association.*" The word *love*—the great word, as she justly says, of the New Testament—acquires from her social enthusiasm a peculiar significance to her:—

"The word is a great one, because it involves infinite consequences. To love means to help one another, to have joint aspirations, to act in concert, to labour for the same end, to develop to its ideal consummation the fraternal instinct, thanks to which mankind

have brought the earth under their dominion. Every time that he
has been false to this instinct which is his law of life, his natural destiny, man has seen his temples crumble, his societies dissolve, his intellectual sense go wrong, his moral sense die out. The future is
founded on love."

So long as love is thus spoken of in the general, the ordinary
serious Englishman will have no difficulty in inclining himself
with respect while Madame Sand speaks of it. But when he finds
that love implies, with her, social equality, he will begin to be
staggered. And in truth for almost every Englishman Madame
Sand's strong language about equality, and about France as the
chosen vessel for exhibiting it, will sound exaggerated. "The
human ideal," she says, "as well as the social ideal, is to achieve
equality." France, which has made equality its rallying cry, is
therefore "the nation which loves and is loved," *la nation qui
aime et qu'on aime*. The republic of equality is in her eyes "an
ideal, a philosophy, a religion." She invokes the "holy doctrine
of social liberty and fraternal equality, ever reappearing as a ray
of love and truth amidst the storm." She calls it "the goal of
man and the law of the future." She thinks it the secret of the
civilisation of France, the most civilised of nations. Amid the
disasters of the late war she cannot forbear a cry of astonishment at the neutral nations, *insensibles à l'égorgement d'une
civilisation comme la nôtre*, "looking on with insensibility while
a civilisation such as ours has its throat cut." Germany, with its
stupid ideal of corporalism and *Kruppism*, is contrasted with
France, full of social dreams, too civilised for war, incapable of
planning and preparing war for twenty years, she is so incapable of hatred;—*nous sommes si incapables de haïr!* We seem to
be listening, not to George Sand, but to M. Victor Hugo, half
genius, half charlatan; to M. Victor Hugo, or even to one of
those French declaimers in whom we come down to no genius
and all charlatan.

The form of such outbursts as we have quoted will always
be distasteful to an Englishman. It is to be remembered that they
came from Madame Sand under the pressure and anguish of the
terrible calamities of 1870. But what we are most concerned

with, and what Englishmen in general regard too little, is the degree of truth contained in these allegations that France is the most civilised of nations, and that she is so, above all, by her "holy doctrine of equality." How comes the idea to be so current; and to be passionately believed in, as we have seen, by such a woman as George Sand? It was so passionately believed in by her, that when one seeks, as I am now seeking, to recall her image, the image is incomplete if the passionate belief is kept from appearing.

I will not, with my scanty space, now discuss the belief; but I will seek to indicate how it must have commended itself, I think, to George Sand. I have somewhere called France the "country of Europe where *the people* is most alive." *The people* is what interested George Sand. And in France *the people* is, above all, the peasant. The workman in Paris or in other great towns of France may afford material for such pictures as those which M. Zola has lately given us in *L'Assommoir*—pictures of a kind long ago labelled by Madame Sand as "the *literature of mysteries of iniquity*, which men of talent and imagination try to bring into fashion." But the real *people* in France, the foundation of things there, both in George Sand's eyes and in reality, is the peasant. The peasant was the object of Madame Sand's fondest predilections in the present, and happiest hopes in the future. The Revolution and its doctrine of equality had made the French peasant. What wonder, then, if she saluted the doctrine as a holy and paramount one?

And the French peasant is really, so far as I can see, the largest and strongest element of soundness which the body social of any European nation possesses. To him is due that astonishing recovery which France has made since her defeat, and which George Sand predicted in the very hour of ruin. Yes, in 1870 she predicted *ce réveil général qui va suivre, à la grande surprise des autres nations, l'espèce d'agonie où elles nous voient tombés,* "the general re-arising which, to the astonishment of other nations, is about to follow the sort of agony in which they now see us lying." To the condition, character, and qualities of the French peasant this recovery is in the main due. His material

well-being is known to all of us. M. de Laveleye, the well-known economist, a Belgian and a Protestant, says that France, being the country of Europe where the soil is more divided than anywhere except in Switzerland and Norway, is at the
5   same time the country where well-being is most widely spread, where wealth has of late years increased most, and where population is least outrunning the limits which, for the comfort and progress of the working classes themselves, seem necessary. George Sand could see, of course, the well-being of the French
10 peasant, for we can all see it.

But there is more. George Sand was a woman, with a woman's ideal of gentleness, of "the charm of good manners," as essential to civilisation. She has somewhere spoken admirably of the variety and balance of forces which go to make up true
15 civilisation; "certain forces of weakness, docility, attractiveness, suavity, are here just as real forces as forces of vigour, encroachment, violence, or brutality." Yes, as real *forces*, although Prince Bismarck cannot see it; because human nature requires them, and, often as they may be baffled, and slow as may be the
20 process of their asserting themselves, mankind is not satisfied with its own civilisation, and keeps fidgeting at it and altering it again and again, until room is made for them. George Sand thought the French people,—meaning principally, again, by the French people the *people* properly so called, the peasant,—
25 she thought it "the most kindly, the most amiable, of all peoples." Nothing is more touching than to read in her *Journal*, written in 1870, whilst she was witnessing what seemed to be "the agony of the Latin races," and undergoing what seemed to be the process of "dying in a general death of one's family,
30 one's country, and one's nation," how constant is her defence of the people, the peasant, against her Republican friends. Her Republican friends were furious with the peasant; accused him of stolidity, cowardice, want of patriotism; accused him of having given them the Empire, with all its vileness; wanted to take
35 away from him the suffrage. Again and again does George Sand take up his defence, and warn her friends of the folly and danger of their false estimate of him. "The contempt of the masses, there," she cries, "is the misfortune and crime of the present

moment!" "To execrate the people," she exclaims again, "is real blasphemy; the people is worth more than we are."

If the peasant gave us the Empire, says Madame Sand, it was because he saw the parties of liberals disputing, gesticulating, and threatening to tear one another asunder and France too; he was told *the Empire is peace*, and he accepted the Empire. The peasant was deceived, he is uninstructed, he moves slowly; but he moves, he has admirable virtues, and in him, says George Sand, is our life:—

"Poor Jacques Bonhomme! accuse thee and despise thee who will; for my part I pity thee, and in spite of thy faults I shall always love thee. Never will I forget how, a child, I was carried asleep on thy shoulders, how I was given over to thy care and followed thee everywhere, to the field, the stall, the cottage. They are all dead, those good old people who have borne me in their arms; but I remember them well, and I appreciate at this hour, to the minutest detail, the pureness, the kindness, the patience, the good humour, the poetry, which presided over that rustic education amidst disasters of like kind with those which we are undergoing now. Why should I quarrel with the peasant because on certain points he feels and thinks differently from what I do? There are other essential points on which we may feel eternally at one with him,—probity and charity."

Another generation of peasants had grown up since that first revolutionary generation of her youth, and equality, as its reign proceeded, had not deteriorated but improved them.

"They have advanced greatly in self-respect and well-being, these peasants from twenty years old to forty; they never ask for anything. When one meets them they no longer take off their hat. If they know you they come up to you and hold out their hand. All foreigners who stay with us are struck with their good bearing, with their amenity, and the simple, friendly, and polite ease of their behaviour. In presence of people whom they esteem they are, like their fathers, models of tact and politeness; but they have more than that mere *sentiment* of equality which was all that their fathers had, —they have the *idea* of equality, and the determination to maintain it. This step upwards they owe to their having the franchise. Those who would fain treat them as creatures of a lower order dare not now show this disposition to their face; it would not be pleasant."

Mr. Hamerton's interesting book about French life has much, I think, to confirm this account of the French peasant. What I have seen of France myself (and I have seen something) is fully in agreement with it. Of a civilisation and an equality which
5 makes the peasant thus *human*, gives to the bulk of the people well-being, probity, charity, self-respect, tact, and good manners, let us pardon Madame Sand if she feels and speaks enthusiastically. Some little variation on our own eternal trio of Barbarians, Philistines, Populace, or on the eternal solo of Philistinism
10 among our brethren of the United States and the Colonies, is surely permissible.

Where one is more inclined to differ from Madame Sand is in her estimate of her Republican friends of the educated classes. They may stand, she says, for the genius and the soul of France;
15 they represent its "exalted imagination and profound sensibility," while the peasant represents its humble, sound, indispensable body. Her *protégé*, the peasant, is much ruder with those eloquent gentlemen, and has his own name for one and all of them, *l'avocat*, by which he means to convey his belief that
20 words are more to be looked for from that quarter than seriousness and profit. It seems to me by no means certain but that the peasant is in the right.

George Sand herself has said admirable things of these friends of hers; of their want of patience, temper, wisdom; of their
25 "vague and violent way of talking;" of their interminable flow of "stimulating phrases, cold as death." Her own place is of course with the party and propaganda of organic change. But George Sand felt the poetry of the past; she had no hatreds; the furies, the follies, the self-deceptions of secularist and revolu-
30 tionist fanatics filled her with dismay. They are indeed the great danger of France, and it is amongst the educated and articulate classes of France that they prevail. If the educated and articulate classes in France were as sound in their way as the inarticulate peasant is in his, France would present a different spectacle.
35 Not "imagination and sensibility" are so much required from the educated classes of France, as simpler, more serious views of life; a knowledge how great a part *conduct* (if M. Challemel-Lacour will allow me to say so) fills in it; a better example. The

few who say this, such as Madame Sand among the dead, and M. Renan among the living, perhaps awaken, on that account, amongst quiet observers at a distance, all the more sympathy; but in France they are isolated.

All the later work of George Sand, however, all her hope of genuine social renovation, take the simple and serious ground so necessary. "The cure for us is far more simple than we will believe. All the better natures amongst us see it and feel it. It is a good direction given by ourselves to our hearts and consciences;—*une bonne direction donnée par nous-mêmes à nos cœurs et à nos consciences.*" These are among the last words of her *Journal* of 1870.

Whether or not the number of George Sand's works,—always fresh, always attractive, but poured out too lavishly and rapidly,—is likely to prove a hindrance to her fame, I do not care to consider. Posterity, alarmed at the way in which its literary baggage grows upon it, always seeks to leave behind it as much as it can, as much as it dares,—everything but masterpieces. But the immense vibration of George Sand's voice upon the ear of Europe will not soon die away. Her passions and her errors have been abundantly talked of. She left them behind her, and men's memory of her will leave them behind also. There will remain of her to mankind the sense of benefit and stimulus from the passage upon earth of that large and frank nature, of that large and pure utterance—the *large utterance of the early gods.* There will remain an admiring and ever widening report of that great and ingenuous soul, simple, affectionate, without vanity, without pedantry, human, equitable, patient, kind. She believed herself, she said, "to be in sympathy, across time and space, with a multitude of honest wills which interrogate their conscience and try to put themselves in accord with it." This chain of sympathy will extend more and more.

It is silent, that eloquent voice! it is sunk, that noble, that speaking head! we sum up, as we best can, what she said to us, and we bid her adieu. From many hearts in many lands a troop of tender and grateful regrets converge towards her humble churchyard in Berry. Let them be joined by these words of sad

homage from one of a nation which she esteemed, and which knew her very little and very ill. Her guiding thought, the guiding thought which she did her best to make ours too, "the sentiment of the ideal life, which is none other than man's normal
5   life as we shall one day know it," is in harmony with words and promises familiar to that sacred place where she lies. *Exspectat resurrectionem mortuorum, et vitam venturi sæculi.*

A Guide to English Literature

People repeat, till one is almost tired of hearing it, the story of
the French Minister of Instruction who took out his watch and
said complacently to a foreigner, that at that moment, in all the
public grammar-schools of France, all boys of the same class
were saying the same lesson. In England the story has been   5
eagerly used to disparage State-meddling with schools. I have
never been able to see that it was in itself so very lamentable a
thing that all these French boys should be saying the same lesson at the same time. Everything, surely, depends upon what
the lesson was. Once secure what is excellent to be taught, and   10
you can hardly teach it with too much insistence, punctuality,
universality. The more one sees of the young, the more one is
struck with two things: how limited is the amount which they
can really learn, how worthless is much of what goes to make
up this amount now. Mr. Grant Duff, misled by his own accom-   15
plishments and intelligence, is, I am convinced, far too encyclo-
pædic in his requirements from young learners. But the heart-
breaking thing is, that what they *can* be taught and *do* learn is
often so ill-chosen. "An apple has a stalk, peel, pulp, core, pips,
and juice; it is odorous and opaque, and is used for making a   20
pleasant drink called cider." There is the pedant's fashion of
using the brief lesson-time, the soon-tired attention, of little
children. How much, how far too much, of all our course of
tuition, early and late, is of like value!

For myself, I lament nothing more in our actual instruction   25
than its multiformity,—a multiformity, too often, of false direction and useless labour. I desire nothing so much for it as
greater uniformity,—but uniformity in good. Nothing is taught
well except what is known familiarly and taught often. The

Greeks used to say: Δὶς ἢ τρὶς τὰ καλά,—Give us a fine thing two
and three times over! And they were right.

   In literature we have present, and waiting ready to form us,
the best which has been thought and said in the world. Our
business is to get at this best and to know it well. But even to
understand the thing we are dealing with, and to choose the
best in it, we need a guide, a clue. The literature most accessible
to all of us, touching us most nearly, is our own literature, English literature. To get at the best in English literature and to
know that best well, nothing can be more helpful to us than a
guide who will show us, in clear view, the growth of our literature, its series of productions, and their relative value. If such a
guide is good and trustworthy, his instructions cannot be too
widely brought into use, too diligently studied, too thoroughly
fixed in the mind.

   But to deserve such universal acceptance and such heedful
attention our guide ought to have special qualifications. He
ought to be clear. He ought to be brief,—as brief as is consistent
with not being dry. For dry he must not be; but we should be
made to feel, in listening to him, as much as possible of the
power and charm of the literature to which he introduces us.
His discourse, finally, ought to observe strict proportion and to
observe strict sobriety. He should have one scale and should
keep to it. And he should severely eschew all violence and exaggeration; he should avoid, in his judgments, even the least appearance of what is arbitrary, personal, fantastic.

   Mr. Stopford Brooke has published a little book entitled *A
Primer of English Literature*. I have read it with the most lively
interest and pleasure. I have just been saying how very desirable
is a good guide to English literature, and what are a good guide's
qualifications. Mr. Stopford Brooke seems to me to possess them
all. True, he has some of them in a higher degree than others.
He is never dry, never violent; but occasionally he might, I
think, be clearer, shorter, in more perfect proportion, more
thoroughly true of judgment. To say this is merely to say that
in a most difficult task, that of producing a book to serve as a
guide to English literature, a man does not reach perfection all
at once. The great thing was to produce a primer so good as

Mr. Stopford Brooke's. It is easy to criticise it when it has once been produced, easy to see how in some points it might have been made better. To produce it at all, so good as it is, was not easy. On the whole, and compared with other workmen in the same field, Mr. Stopford Brooke has been clear, short, interest- 5 ing, observant of proportion, free from exaggeration and free from arbitrariness. Yet with the book lying before one as a whole, one can see, I think, that with respect to some of these merits the work might be brought to a point of excellence higher than that at which it now stands. Mr. Stopford Brooke 10 will not, I am sure, take it amiss if an attentive and gratified reader of his book, convinced of the great importance of what it attempts, convinced of its merits, desirous to see it in every one's hands,—he will not take it ill, I say, if such a reader asks his leave to go rapidly through the book with him, to point 15 out what seem imperfections, to suggest what might bring his book yet nearer towards the ideal of what such a book should be.

I will begin at the beginning, and will suggest that Mr. Stop- ford Brooke should leave out his first two pages, the pages in 20 which he lays down what literature is, and what its two main divisions (as he calls them), prose and poetry, are. His primer is somewhat long, longer than most primers. It is a gain to shorten it by expunging anything superfluous. And the reader does not require to be told what literature is, and what prose 25 and poetry are. For all practical purposes he knows this suffi- ciently well already. Or even if he were in doubt about it, Mr. Stopford Brooke's two pages would not make the matter much clearer to him; they are a little embarrassed themselves, and tend to embarrass the attentive reader. And a primer, at any 30 rate, should be above all things quite plain and clear; it should contain nothing to embarrass its reader, nothing not perfectly thought out and lucidly laid down. So I wish Mr. Stopford Brooke would begin his primer with what is now the fourth section: "The history of English literature is the story of what 35 English men and women thought and felt, and then wrote down in good prose or beautiful poetry in the English language. The

story is a long one. It begins about the year 670 and it is still
going on in the year 1875. Into this little book, then, is to be put
the story of 1200 years." Nothing can be better.

The sentence which follows is questionable:—

5   "No people that have ever been in the world can look back so far
as we English can to the beginnings of our literature; no people can
point to so long and splendid a train of poets and prose-writers, no
nation has on the whole written so much and so well."

The first part of this sentence makes an assertion of very doubt-
10   ful truth; the second part is too much to the tune of *Rule Bri-
tannia*. Both parts offend against sobriety. The four cardinal
virtues which are, as I have said, to be required in the writer of
a primer of English literature are these: clearness, brevity, proportion, sobriety. Sobriety needs to be insisted upon, perhaps,
15   the most, because in things meant, and rightly meant, to be popular, there is such danger of sinning against it. Anything of
questionable and disputed truth, even though we may fairly
hold it and in a longer performance might fairly lay it down
and defend it, is out of place in a primer. It is an offence against
20   sobriety to insert it there. And let Mr. Stopford Brooke ask
himself what foreigner, or who except an Englishman, would
admit that "no people can point to so long and splendid a train
of poets and prose-writers as the English people, no nation has
on the whole written so much and so well?" Nay, it is not every
25   Englishman who, with Greece before his eyes, would admit it.
What follows is in a truer strain, in the right strain for a guide
to take:—

"Every English man and woman has good reason to be proud of
the work done by their forefathers in prose and poetry. Every one
30   who can write a good book or a good song may say to himself: 'I
belong to a great company which has been teaching and delighting
men for more than a thousand years.' And that is a fact in which
those who write and those who read ought to feel a noble pride."

This is unquestionable, and it is sufficient.

35   Nothing, in a task like Mr. Stopford Brooke's, is more difficult than the start, and it was natural, therefore, that his first
page or two should be peculiarly open to criticism. Once

started, Mr. Stopford Brooke proceeds safely and smoothly, and page after page is read with nothing but acquiescence. His first chapter is excellent, and has that great merit for which his primer is, as I have said, conspicuous: the merit of so touching men and works of which the young reader, and the general reader, knows and can be expected to know very little, as to make them cease to be mere names;—as to give a real sense of their power and charm. His manner of dealing with Cædmon and Bede is a signal instance of this. I shall not quote the passage, because I wish to quote presently another passage with the like merit, in which Mr. Stopford Brooke is even happier: the passage where he treats of Chaucer.

In the second chapter there is in several places a want of clearness, due to a manner of writing which leaves something to be filled out and completed by the reader himself. This task should not be thrown upon readers of a primer. "The last memoranda of the *Peterborough Chronicle* are of the year 1154, the last English Charter can scarcely be earlier than 1155." Mr. Stopford Brooke gives these words as a quotation, but it is not fully clear how they relate themselves to the context, or exactly what is to be deduced from them. In another instance, the want of clearness arises from an attempt to give a piece of information by the way, and because the piece of information seems to be a part of the argument, but is not. "The first friars were foreigners, and they necessarily used many French words in their English teaching, and Normans as well as English now began to write religious works in English." The point to be made out is that English came into greater use because even foreigners had for certain purposes to adopt it. Mr. Stopford Brooke wishes to inform by the way his young reader, that the foreigners in doing so used many French words. But the manner in which he throws this in must cause puzzle; for the young reader imagines it to lead up somehow to the main point that English came into more general use, and it does not. Or the want of clearness arises from something being put forward, about which Mr. Stopford Brooke, after he has put it forward, feels hesitation. "The poem marks the close of the religious influence of the friars. They had been attacked before in a poem of 1320; but in this poem

there is not a word said against them. It is true, the author living
far in the country may not have been thrown much with them."
Mr. Stopford Brooke means here, so far as I understand him, to
imply that there not being a word said against the friars in the
poem in question marks the close of their religious influence.
That is rather a subtle inference for a young reader to follow.
Mr. Stopford Brooke, however, seems to feel (for I am really
not quite sure that I understand him) that he may have been
too subtle; and he adds: "It is true, the author living far in the
country may not have been thrown much with them." That is
to say: "If you consider the thing more subtly, perhaps you had
better not make the inference I have suggested." A subtlety requiring immediately to be relieved by another subtlety, is rather
too much for a young reader. The writer of a primer should
attempt to convey nothing but what can be conveyed in a quite
plain and straightforward fashion.

But presently we come to Layamon's *Brut*, and here we see
how admirably Mr. Stopford Brooke understands his business.
It is not difficult to be dull in speaking of Layamon's *Brut*, or
even in quoting from it. But what Mr. Stopford Brooke says of
Layamon and his work is just what every one will feel interested in hearing of them; and what he quotes is exactly what
will complete and enhance this feeling of interest:—

" 'There was a priest in the land,' Layamon writes of himself,
'whose name was Layamon; he was son of Leovenath; may the Lord
be gracious unto him! He dwelt at Earnley, a noble church on the
bank of Severn, near Radstone, where he read books. It came in
mind to him and in his chiefest thought that he would tell the noble
deeds of England, what the men were named, and whence they
came, who first had English land.' "

Freshness of touch, a treatment always the very opposite of
the pedant's treatment of things, make the great charm of Mr.
Stopford Brooke's work. He owes them, no doubt, to his genuine love for nature and poetry:—

"In 1300 we meet with a few lyric poems, full of charm. They
sing of spring-time with its blossoms, of the woods ringing with the
thrush and nightingale, of the flowers and the seemly sun, of coun-

try work, of the woes and joy of love, and many other delightful things."

No such secret of freshness as delight in all these "delightful things" and in the poetry which tells of them!

This second chapter, giving the history of English literature 5 from the Conquest to Chaucer, is admirably proportioned. The personages come in due order, the humblest not without his due word of introduction; the chief figures pause awhile and stand clear before us, each in his due degree of prominence. To do justice to the charm of Mr. Stopford Brooke's primer, let the 10 reader turn to the pages on Chaucer. Something I must quote from them; I wish I could quote all!

"Chaucer's first and great delight was in human nature, and he makes us love the noble characters in his poems, and feel with kindliness towards the baser and ruder sort. He never sneers, for he had 15 a wide charity, and we can always smile in his pages at the follies and forgive the sins of men. He had a true and chivalrous regard for women, and his wife and he must have been very happy if they fulfilled the ideal he had of marriage. He lived in aristocratic society, and yet he thought him the greatest gentleman who was 'most ver- 20 tuous alway, Privé and pert (open), and most entendeth aye To do the gentil dedes that he can.' He lived frankly among men, and, as we have seen, saw many different types of men, and in his own time filled many parts as a man of the world and of business. Yet with all this active and observant life, he was commonly very quiet and kept 25 much to himself. The Host in the Tales japes at him for his lonely abstracted air. 'Thou lookest as thou wouldest find a hare, And ever on the ground I see thee stare.' Being a good scholar, he read morning and night alone, and he says that after his office-work he would go home and sit at another book as dumb as a stone, till his look was 30 dazed. While at study and when he was making of songs and ditties, 'nothing else that God had made' had any interest for him. There was but one thing that roused him then, and that too he liked to enjoy alone. It was the beauty of the morning and the fields, the woods, the streams, the flowers, and the singing of the little birds. 35 This made his heart full of revel and solace, and when spring came after winter, he rose with the lark and cried, 'Farewell my book and my devotion.' He was the first who made the love of nature a distinct element in our poetry. He was the first who, in spending the

whole day gazing alone on the daisy, set going that lonely delight in natural scenery which is so special a mark of our later poets. He lived thus a double life, in and out of the world, but never a gloomy one. For he was fond of mirth and good-living, and when he grew
5   towards age was portly of waist, 'no poppet to embrace.' But he kept to the end his elfish countenance, the shy, delicate, half-mischievous face which looked on men from its gray hair and forked beard, and was set off by his light gray-coloured dress and hood. A knife and inkhorn hung on his dress, we see a rosary in his hand, and
10   when he was alone he walked swiftly."

I could not bring myself to make the quotation shorter, although Mr. Stopford Brooke may ask me, indeed, why I do not observe in a review the proportion which I demand in a primer.

15   The third and fourth chapters bring us to the Renascence and the Elizabethan age. Spenser is touched by Mr. Stopford Brooke almost as charmingly as Chaucer. The pages on Shakspeare are full of interest, and the great poet gains by the mode in which we are led up to him. Mr. Stopford Brooke has re-
20   membered that Shakspeare is, as Goethe said, not truly seen when he is regarded as a great single mountain rising straight out of the plain; he is truly seen when seen among the hills of his *Riesen-Heimath*, his giant home,—among them, though towering high above them. Only one or two sentences I could
25   wish otherwise. Mr. Stopford Brooke says of Shakspeare's last plays:—

"All these belong to and praise forgiveness, and it seems, if we may conjecture, that looking back on all the wrong he had suffered and on all that he had done, Shakspeare could say in the forgiveness
30   he gave to men and in the forgiveness he sought of heaven the words he had written in earlier days: *The quality of mercy is not strained.*"

Perhaps that might not be out of place in a volume of lectures on Shakspeare. But it is certainly somewhat far-fetched and fanciful; too fanciful for our primer. Nor is it quite sound and
35   sober criticism, again, to say of Shakspeare: "He was altogether, from end to end, an artist, and the greatest artist the modern world has known." Or again: "In the unchangeableness of pure art-power Shakspeare stands entirely alone." There is a pecu-

liarity in Mr. Stopford Brooke's use of the words *art, artist*. He means by an artist one whose aim in writing is not to reveal himself, but to give pleasure; he says most truly that Shakspeare's aim was to please, that Shakspeare "made men and women whose dramatic action on each other and towards a catastrophe was intended to please the public, not to reveal himself." This is indeed the true temper of the artist. But when we call a man emphatically *artist*, a *great artist*, we mean something more than this temper in which he works; we mean by art, not merely an aim to please, but also, and more, a law of pure and flawless workmanship. As living always under the sway of *this* law, and as, therefore, a perfect artist, we do not conceive of Shakspeare. His workmanship is often far from being pure and flawless.

> "Till that Bellona's bridegroom, lapp'd in proof,
> Confronted him with self-comparisons—"

There is but one name for such writing as that, if Shakspeare had signed it a thousand times,—it is detestable. And it is too frequent in Shakspeare. In a book, therefore, where every sentence should be sure, simple, and solid, not requiring mental reservations nor raising questions, we ought not to speak of Shakspeare as "altogether, from end to end, an artist;" as "standing entirely alone in the unchangeableness of pure art-power." He is the richest, the most wonderful, the most powerful, the most delightful of poets; he is not altogether, nor even eminently, an artist.

In the fifth chapter we reach Milton. Mr. Stopford Brooke characterises Milton's poems well, when he speaks of "their majestic movement, their grand style, and their grave poetry." But I wonder at his designating Milton *our greatest poet.* Nor does the criticism of *Paradise Lost* quite satisfy me. I do not think that "as we read the great epic, we feel that the lightness and grace of Milton's youthful time are gone." True, the poet of *Paradise Lost* differs from the poet of *L'Allegro* and *Il Penseroso;* but the feeling raised by *Paradise Lost* is not a feeling that lightness and grace are gone. That would be a negative feeling, a feeling of disappointment; and the feeling raised by *Paradise Lost* is far other. Yet neither is it a feeling which justifies Mr. Stopford Brooke in saying that "at last all thought and emotion centre round Adam and Eve, until the closing lines leave us with their lonely image in our minds." The personages have no growing, absorbing interest of this kind; when we finish the poem, it is not with our minds agitated by them and full of them. The power of *Paradise Lost* is to be sought elsewhere. Nor is it true to say that Milton "summed up in himself all the higher influences of the Renascence." The disinterested curiosity, the *humanism* of the Renascence, are not characteristics of Milton,—of Milton, that is to say, when he is fully formed and has taken his ply. Nor again can it rightly be said that Milton "began that pure poetry of natural description which has no higher examples to show in Wordsworth, or Scott, or Keats, than his *L'Allegro* and *Il Penseroso*." *L'Allegro* and *Il Penseroso* are charming, but they are not pure poetry of natural description in the sense in which the *Highland Reaper* is, or the *Ode to Autumn*. The poems do not touch the same chords or belong to the same order. Scott is altogether out of place in the comparison. His natural description in verse has the merits of his natural description in prose, which are very considerable. But it never has the grace and felicity of Milton, or the natural magic of Wordsworth and Keats. As poetical work, it is not to be even named with theirs.

Shakspeare and Milton are such prominent objects in a primer of English literature that one dwells on them, strives to have them presented quite aright. After Milton we come to a century whose literature has no figures of this grandeur. The literary importance of the eighteenth century lies mainly in its having wrought out a revolution begun in the seventeenth,—no less a revolution than the establishment of what Mr. Stopford Brooke well calls "the second period of English prose, in which the style is easy, unaffected, moulded to the subject, and the proper words are put in their proper places." With his strong love of poetry, Mr. Stopford Brooke could not, perhaps, feel the same sympathy and delight in dealing with this prose century as in dealing with the times of Chaucer or Elizabeth. Still his account of its writers does not fail in interest, and is in general just. But his arrangement is here not quite satisfactory. The periods of time covered by his chapters should be literary periods, not merely periods in political history. His sixth chapter has for its title: *From the Restoration to George III.* The period from the Restoration to George the Third is a period in political history only. George the Third has nothing to do with literature; his accession marks no epoch in our civilisation or in our literature, such as is marked by the Conquest or by the reign of Elizabeth. I wish that Mr. Stopford Brooke would change the title of this chapter, and make it: *From the Restoration to the Death of Pope and Swift.* Pope died in 1744, Swift in 1745. The following chapter should be: *From 1745 to the French Revolution.* The next and last: *From the French Revolution to the Death of Scott.*

These are real periods in our literature. Mr. Stopford Brooke enumerates, at the beginning of his seventh chapter, causes which from the early part of the eighteenth century were at work to influence literature.

"The long peace after the accession of the House of Hanover had left England at rest and given it wealth. The reclaiming of waste tracts, the increased wealth and trade, made better communication necessary; and the country was soon covered with a network of highways. The leisure gave time to men to think and write; the quicker interchange between the capital and the country spread over England the literature of the capital, and stirred men everywhere to write. The coaching services and the post carried the new book and the literary criticism to the villages. Communication with the Continent had increased during the peaceable times of Walpole."

By the middle of the century, by a time well marked by the death of Pope and Swift, these influences had been in operation long enough to form a second period in the eighteenth century, sufficiently distinguishable from the period of Addison and Pope, and lasting down to a period of far more decisive change, the period of the French Revolution.

Prose and poetry, within these periods, should not have each their separate chapter; it is unnecessary, and leads to some confusion. Sir Walter Scott is at present noticed in one of Mr. Stopford Brooke's chapters as a poet, in another as a prose writer.

And the limits of each period should be observed; authors and
works should not be mentioned out of their order of date. At
present Mr. Stopford Brooke mentions the *Rivals* and *School
for Scandal* of Sheridan in his sixth chapter, a chapter which
5   professes to go from the Restoration to the accession of George
the Third. At the very beginning of the following chapter,
which goes from 1760 to 1837, he introduces his mention of the
Morning Chronicle, the *Post,* the *Herald,* and the *Times,* of
the *Edinburgh* and the *Quarterly Reviews,* and of *Black-*
10 *wood's Magazine.* By being freed from all such defects in
lucid and orderly arrangement, the primer would gain in
clearness.

It would gain in brevity and proportion by ending with the
death of Scott in 1832. I wish I might prevail upon Mr. Stop-
15 ford Brooke to bring his primer to an end with Scott's death in
that year. I wish he would leave out every word about his contemporaries, and about publications which have appeared since
1832. The death of Sir Walter Scott is a real epoch; it marks the
end of one period and the beginning of another,—of the period
20 in which we are ourselves now living. No man can trust himself to speak of his own time and his own contemporaries with
the same sureness of judgment and the same proportion as of
times and men gone by; and in a primer of literature we should
avoid, so far as we can, all hindrances to sureness of judgment
25 and to proportion. The readers of the primer, also, are not likely
to hear too little of contemporary literature, if its praises are
unrehearsed in their primer; they are certain, under all circumstances, to hear quite enough of it, probably too much.

"Charlotte Brontë revived in *Jane Eyre* the novel of Passion, and
30 Miss Yonge set on foot the Religious novel in support of a special
school of theology. Miss Martineau and Mr. Disraeli carried on the
novel of Political opinion and economy, and Charles Kingsley applied the novel to the social and theological problems of our own
day."

35 Let Mr. Stopford Brooke make a clean sweep of all this, I en-
treat him. And if his date of 1832 compels him to include Rogers
and his poetry, let him give to them, not a third part of a page,

but one line. I reckon that these reductions would shorten the last part of the primer by five pages. A little condensation in the judgments on Wordsworth, Byron, and Shelley would abridge it by another page; the omission of the first pages of the volume by two more. Our primer shortened by eight pages! no small gain in a work of this character.

The last three chapters of the book, therefore, I could wish recast, and one or two phrases in his criticism Mr. Stopford Brooke might perhaps revise at the same time. He says most truly of Addison that his *Spectator* "gave a better tone to manners and a gentler one to political and literary criticism." He says truly, too, of Addison's best papers: "No humour is more fine and tender; and, like Chaucer's, it is never bitter." He has a right to the conclusion, therefore, that "Addison's work was a great one, lightly done." But to say of Addison's style, that "in its varied cadence and subtle ease it has never been surpassed," seems to me to be going a little too far. One could not say more of Plato's. Whatever his services to his time, Addison is for us now a writer whose range and force of thought are not considerable enough to make him interesting; and his style cannot equal in varied cadence and subtle ease the style of a man like Plato, because without range and force of thought all the resources of style, whether in cadence or in subtlety, are not and cannot be brought out.

Is it an entirely accurate judgment, again, on the poems of Gray and Collins, to call them "exquisite examples of perfectly English work wrought in the spirit of classic art?" I confess, this language seems to me to be too strong. Much as I admire Gray, one feels, I think, in reading his poetry, never quite secure against the false poetical style of the eighteenth century. It is always near at hand, sometimes it breaks in; and the sense of this prevents the security one enjoys with truly classic work, the fulness of pleasure, the cordial satisfaction.

> "Thy joys no glittering female meets"—

or even things in the *Elegy:*

> "He gave to misery all he had—a tear;
> He gained from Heaven ('twas all he wish'd) a friend"—

are instances of the sort of drawback I mean. And the false style, which here comes to the surface, we are never very far from in Gray. Therefore, to call his poems "exquisite examples of perfectly English work wrought in the spirit of classic art" seems
5 to me an exaggeration.

    Mr. Stopford Brooke's Cowper is excellent, but again there seems to me to be some want of sobriety in the praise given. Philanthropy, no doubt, animated Cowper's heart and shows itself in his poetry. But it is too much to say of the apparition of
10 Cowper and of his philanthropy in English poetry: "It is a wonderful change, a change so wonderful that it is like a new world. It is, in fact, the concentration into one retired poet's work of all the new thought upon the subject of mankind which was soon to take so fierce a form in Paris." Cowper, with his morbid
15 religion and lumbering movement, was no precursor, as Mr. Stopford Brooke would thus make him, of Byron and Shelley. His true praise is, that by his simple affections and genuine love of nature he was a precursor of Wordsworth.

    Of Wordsworth's philosophy of Nature Mr. Stopford
20 Brooke draws out, I think, a more elaborate account than we require in a primer. No one will be much helped by Wordsworth's philosophy of Nature, as a scheme in itself and disjoined from his poems. Nor shall we be led to enjoy the poems the more by having a philosophy of Nature abstracted from them
25 and presented to us in its nakedness. Of the page and a quarter which Mr. Stopford Brooke has given to Wordsworth's philosophy of Nature, all might with advantage, perhaps, be dropped but this:—

    "Nature was a person to Wordsworth, distinct from himself, and
30 capable of being loved. He could brood on her character, her ways, her words, her life. Hence arose his minute and loving observation of her, and his passionate description of all her forms."

    There might be some condensation, too, in the criticism of Byron as the poet of *Don Juan* and as the poet of Nature. But
35 some touches in the criticism of Byron are admirable. "We feel naturally great interest in this strong personality, put before us with such obstinate power; but it wearies at last. *Finally it*

wearied himself." Or again: "It is his colossal power and the ease which comes from it, in which he resembles Dryden, that marks him specially." Nothing could be better.

On Shelley, also, Mr. Stopford Brooke has an excellent sentence. He says of his lyrics: "They form together the most sensitive, the most imaginative, and the most musical, but the least tangible lyrical poetry we possess." But in the pages on Shelley, yet more than in those on Byron, condensation is desirable. Shelley is a most interesting and attractive personage; but in a work of the dimensions of this primer, neither his *Queen Mab*, nor his *Alastor*, nor his *Revolt of Islam*, nor his *Prometheus Unbound*, deserve the space which Mr. Stopford Brooke gives to them. And finally, as the sentence which I have last quoted is just a sentence of the right stamp for a primer, so a passage such as the following is just of the sort which is unsuitable:—

"Shelley wants the closeness of grasp of nature which Words-worth and Keats had, but he had the power in a far greater degree than they of describing a vast landscape melting into indefinite distance. In this he stands first among English poets, and is in poetry what Turner was in landscape painting. Along with this special quality of vastness his colour is as true as Scott's, but truer in this, that it is full of half tones, while Scott's is laid out in broad yellow, crimson, and blue, in black and white."

Very clever, but also very fantastic; and at all events quite out of place in a primer!

Mr. Stopford Brooke will forgive me for my plain-speaking. It comes from my hearty esteem and admiration for his primer, and my desire to clear it of every speck and flaw, so that it may win its way into every one's hands. I hope he will revise it, and then I shall read it again with a fresh pleasure. But indeed, whether he revises it or no, I shall read it again: δὶς ἢ τρὶς τὰ καλά.

A French Critic on Goethe

It takes a long time to ascertain the true rank of a famous writer.
A young friend of Joseph de Maistre, a M. de Syon, writing in
praise of the literature of the nineteenth century as compared
with that of the eighteenth, said of Chateaubriand, that "the
5 Eternal created Chateaubriand to be a guide to the universe."
Upon which judgment Joseph de Maistre comments thus:
"Clear it is, my good young man, that you are only eighteen;
let us hear what you have to say at forty." "*On voit bien, excellent jeune homme, que vous avez dix-huit ans; je vous attends à
10 quarante.*"

The same Joseph de Maistre has given an amusing history of
the rise of our own Milton's reputation:—

"No one had any suspicion of Milton's merits, when one day Addison took the speaking-trumpet of Great Britain (the instrument
15 of loudest sound in the universe), and called from the top of the
Tower of London: 'Roman and Greek authors, give place!'

"He did well to take this tone. If he had spoken modestly, if he
had simply said that there were great beauties in *Paradise Lost*, he
would not have produced the slightest impression. But this tren-
20 chant sentence, dethroning Homer and Virgil, struck the English
exceedingly. They said one to the other: 'What, we possessed the
finest epic poem in the world, and no one suspected it! What a
thing is inattention! But now, at any rate, we have had our eyes
opened.' In fact, the reputation of Milton has become a national
25 property, a portion of the Establishment, a Fortieth Article; and the
English would as soon think of giving up Jamaica as of giving up
the pre-eminence of their great poet."

Joseph de Maistre goes on to quote a passage from a then recent English commentator on Milton,—Bishop Newton. Bishop

Newton, it seems, declared that "every man of taste and genius must admit *Paradise Lost* to be the most excellent of modern productions, as the Bible is the most perfect of the productions of antiquity." In a note M. de Maistre adds: "This judgment of the good bishop appears unspeakably ridiculous." 5

Ridiculous, indeed! but a page or two later we shall find the clear-sighted critic himself almost as far astray as his "good bishop" or as his "good young man":—

"The strange thing is that the English, who are thorough Greek scholars, are willing enough to admit the superiority of the Greek 10 tragedians over Shakspeare; but when they come to Racine, *who is in reality simply a Greek speaking French*, their standard of beauty all of a sudden changes, and Racine, who is at least the equal of the Greeks, has to take rank far below Shakspeare, who is inferior to them. This theorem in *trigonometry* presents no difficulties to the 15 people of soundest understanding in Europe."

So dense is the cloud of error here that the lover of truth and daylight will hardly even essay to dissipate it: he does not know where to begin. It is as when M. Victor Hugo gives his list of the sovereigns on the world's roll of creators and poets: "Ho- 20 mer, Æschylus, Sophocles, Lucretius, Virgil, Horace, Dante, Shakspeare, *Rabelais, Molière, Corneille, Voltaire*." His French audience rise and cry enthusiastically: "*And Victor Hugo!*" And really that is perhaps the best criticism on what he has been saying to them. 25

Goethe, the great poet of Germany, has been placed by his own countrymen now low, now high; and his right poetical rank they have certainly not yet succeeded in finding. Tieck, in his introduction to the collected writings of Lenz, noticing Goethe's remark on Byron's *Manfred*,—that Byron had "assimi- 30 lated *Faust*, and sucked out of it the strangest nutriment to his hypochondria,"—says tartly that Byron, when he himself talked about his obligations to Goethe, was merely using the language of compliment, and would have been highly offended if any one else had professed to discover them. And Tieck proceeds:— 35

"Everything which in the Englishman's poems might remind one of *Faust*, is in my opinion far above *Faust;* and the Englishman's feeling, and his incomparably more beautiful diction, are so entirely his own, that I cannot possibly believe him to have had *Faust* for his model."

But then there comes a scion of the excellent stock of the Grimms, a Professor Herman Grimm, and lectures on Goethe at Berlin, now that the Germans have conquered the French, and are the first military power in the world, and have become a great nation, and require a national poet to match; and Professor Grimm says of *Faust*, of which Tieck had spoken so coldly: "The career of this, the greatest work of the greatest poet of all times and of all peoples, has but just begun, and we have been making only the first attempts at drawing forth its contents."

If this is but the first letting out of the waters, the coming times may, indeed, expect a deluge.

Many and diverse must be the judgments passed upon every great poet, upon every considerable writer. There is the judgment of enthusiasm and admiration, which proceeds from ardent youth, easily fired, eager to find a hero and to worship him. There is the judgment of gratitude and sympathy, which proceeds from those who find in an author what helps them, what they want, and who rate him at a very high value accordingly. There is the judgment of ignorance, the judgment of incompatibility, the judgment of envy and jealousy. Finally, there is the systematic judgment, and this judgment is the most worthless of all. The sharp scrutiny of envy and jealousy may bring real faults to light. The judgments of incompatibility and ignorance are instructive, whether they reveal necessary clefts of separation between the experiences of different sorts of people, or reveal simply the narrowness and bounded view of those who judge. But the systematic judgment is altogether unprofitable. Its author has not really his eye upon the professed object of his criticism at all, but upon something else which he wants to prove by means of that object. He neither really tells us, therefore, anything about the object, nor anything about his own ignorance of the object. He never fairly looks at it, he is looking at something else. Perhaps if he looked at it straight and

full, looked at it simply, he might be able to pass a good judgment on it. As it is, all he tells us is that he is no genuine critic,
but a man with a system, an advocate.

Here is the fault of Professor Herman Grimm, and of his
Berlin lectures on Goethe. The professor is a man with a sys- 5
tem; the lectures are a piece of advocacy. Professor Grimm is
not looking straight at "the greatest poet of all times and of all
peoples;" he is looking at the necessities, as to literary glory, of
the new German empire.

But the definitive judgment on this great Goethe, the judg- 10
ment of mature reason, the judgment which shall come "at
forty years of age," who may give it to us? Yet how desirable
to have it! It is a mistake to think that the judgment of mature
reason on our favourite author, even if it abates considerably
our high-raised estimate of him, is not a gain to us. Admiration 15
is positive, say some people, disparagement is negative; from
what is negative we can get nothing. But is it no advantage,
then, to the youthful enthusiast for Chateaubriand, to come to
know that "the Eternal did *not* create Chateaubriand to be a
guide to the universe"? It is a very great advantage, because 20
these over-charged admirations are always exclusive, and prevent us from giving heed to other things which deserve admiration. Admiration is salutary and formative, true; but things admirable are sown wide, and are to be gathered here and gathered
there, not all in one place; and until we have gathered them 25
wherever they are to be found, we have not known the true
salutariness and formativeness of admiration. The quest is large;
and occupation with the unsound or half sound, delight in the
not good or less good, is a sore let and hindrance to us. Release
from such occupation and delight sets us free for ranging far- 30
ther, and for perfecting our sense of beauty. He is the happy
man, who, encumbering himself with the love of nothing which
is not beautiful, is able to embrace the greatest number of things
beautiful in his love.

I have already spoken of the judgment of a French critic, 35
M. Scherer, upon Milton. I propose now to draw attention to
the judgment of the same critic upon Goethe. To set to work
to discuss Goethe thoroughly, so as to arrive at the true defini-

tive judgment respecting him, seems to me a most formidable
enterprise. Certainly one should not think of attempting it
within the limits of a single review-article. M. Scherer has devoted to Goethe not one article, but a series of articles. I do not
5 say that the adequate, definitive judgment on Goethe is to be
found in these articles of M. Scherer. But I think they afford a
valuable contribution towards it. M. Scherer is well-informed,
clear-sighted, impartial. He is not warped by injustice and ill-
will towards Germany, although the war has undoubtedly left
10 him with a feeling of soreness. He is candid and cool, perhaps a
little cold. Certainly he will not tell us that "the Eternal created
Goethe to be a guide to the universe." He is free from all heat
of youthful enthusiasm, from the absorption of a discoverer in
his new discovery, from the subjugation of a disciple by the
15 master who has helped and guided him. He is not a man with a
system. And his point of view is in many respects that of an
Englishman. We mean that he has the same instinctive sense re-
belling against what is verbose, ponderous, roundabout, inane,
—in one word, *niais* or silly,—in German literature, just as a
20 plain Englishman has.

    This ground of sympathy between Englishmen and French-
men has not been enough remarked, but it is a very real one.
They owe it to their having alike had a long-continued national
life, a long-continued literary activity, such as no other mod-
25 ern nation has had. This course of practical experience does of
itself beget a turn for directness and clearness of speech, a dislike for futility and fumbling, such as without it we shall rarely
find general. Dr. Wiese, in his recent useful work on English
schools, expresses surprise that the French language and litera-
30 ture should find more favour in Teutonic England than the
German. But community of practice is more telling than community of origin. While English and French are printed alike,
and while an English and a French sentence each of them says
what it has to say in the same plain fashion, a German newspaper
35 is still printed in black letter, and a German sentence is framed
in the style of this which we quote from Dr. Wiese himself:
"Die Engländer einer grossen, in allen Erdtheilen eine Achtung
gebietende Stellung einnehmenden Nation angehören!" The

Italians are a Latin race, with a clear-cut language; but much of
their modern prose has all the circuitousness and slowness of
the German, and from the same cause: the want of the pressure
of a great national life, with its practical discipline, its ever-
active traditions; its literature, for centuries past, powerful and
incessant. England has these in common with France.

M. Scherer's point of view, then, in judging the productions
of German literature, will naturally, I repeat, coincide in several important respects with that of an Englishman. His mind
will make many of the same instinctive demands as ours, will
feel many of the same instinctive repugnances. We shall gladly
follow him, therefore, through his criticism of Goethe's works.
As far as possible he shall be allowed to speak for himself, as he
was when we were dealing with his criticism on Milton. But as
then, too, I shall occasionally compare M. Scherer's criticism on
his author with the criticism of others. And I shall by no means
attempt, on the present opportunity, a substantive criticism of
my own, although I may from time to time allow myself to
comment, in passing, upon the judgments of M. Scherer.

We need not follow M. Scherer in his sketch of Goethe's life.
It is enough to remember that the main dates in Goethe's life
are, his birth in 1749; his going to Weimar with the Grand
Duke, Carl-August, in 1775; his stay in Italy from September
1786 to June 1788; his return in 1788 to Weimar; a severe and
nearly fatal illness in 1801; the loss of Schiller in 1805, of Carl-
August in 1828; his own death in 1832. With these dates fixed
in our minds, we may come at once to the consideration of
Goethe's works.

The long list begins, as we all know, with *Götz von Berlichingen* and *Werther*. We all remember how Mr. Carlyle,
"the old man eloquent," who in his younger days, fifty years
ago, betook himself to Goethe for light and help, and found
what he sought, and declared his gratitude so powerfully and
well, and did so much to make Goethe's name a name of might
for other Englishmen also, a strong tower into which the
doubter and the despairer might run and be safe,—we all remember how Mr. Carlyle has taught us to see in *Götz* and in

Werther the double source from which have flowed those two mighty streams,—the literature of feudalism and romance, represented for us by Scott, and the literature of emotion and passion, represented for us by Byron.

5   M. Scherer's tone throughout is, we have said, not that of the ardent and grateful admirer, but of the cool, somewhat cold critic. He by no manner of means resembles Mr. Carlyle. Already the cold tone appears in M. Scherer's way of dealing with Goethe's earliest productions. M. Scherer seems to me to rate
10   the force and interest of *Götz* too low. But his remarks on the derivedness of this supposed *source* are just. The Germans, he says, were bent, in their "Sturm und Drang" period, on throwing off literary conventions, imitation of all sorts, and on being original. What they really did, was to fall from one sort of imi-
15   tation, the imitation of the so-called classical French literature of the seventeenth century, into another.

"*Götz von Berlichingen* is a study composed after the dramatised chronicles of Shakspeare, and *Werther* is a product yet more direct of the sensibility and declamation brought into fashion by Jean
20   Jacques Rousseau. All in these works is infantine, both the aim at being original, and the way of setting about it. It is exactly as it was with us about 1830. One imagines one is conducting an insurrection, making oneself independent; what one really does is to cook up out of season an old thing. Shakspeare had put the history of his nation upon the stage; Goethe goes for a subject to German history. Shak-
25   speare, who was not fettered by the scenic conditions of the modern theatre, changed the place at every scene; *Götz* is cut up in the same fashion. I say nothing of the substance of the piece, of the absence of characters, of the nullity of the hero, of the commonplace of Weislingen 'the inevitable traitor,' of the melodramatic machinery
30   of the secret tribunal. The style is no better. The astonishment is not that Goethe at twenty-five should have been equal to writing this piece; the astonishment is that after so poor a start he should have subsequently gone so far."

35   M. Scherer seems to me quite unjust, I repeat, to this first dramatic work of Goethe. Mr. Hutton pronounces it "far the most noble as well as the most powerful of Goethe's dramas." And the merit which Mr. Hutton finds in *Götz* is a real one; it is the

work where Goethe, young and ardent, has most forgotten
himself in his characters. "There was something," says Mr. Hutton (and here he and M. Scherer are entirely in accord), "which
prevented Goethe, we think, from ever becoming a great dram-
atist. He could never lose himself sufficiently in his creations."   5
It is in *Götz* that he loses himself in them the most. *Götz* is full
of faults, but there is a life and a power in it, and it is not dull.
This is what distinguishes it from Schiller's *Robbers*. The *Robbers* is at once violent and tiresome. *Götz* is violent, but it is not
tiresome.   10
Werther, which appeared a year later than *Götz*, finds more
favour at M. Scherer's hands. *Werther* is superior to *Götz*, he
says, "inasmuch as it is more modern, and is consequently alive,
or, at any rate, has been alive lately. It has sincerity, passion,
eloquence. One can still read it, and with emotion." But then   15
come the objections:—

"Nevertheless, and just by reason of its truth at one particular
moment, *Werther* is gone by. It is with the book as with the blue
coat and yellow breeches of the hero; the reader finds it hard to
admit the pathetic in such accoutrement. There is too much enthu-   20
siasm for Ossian, too much absorption in nature, too many exclama-
tions and apostrophes to beings animate and inanimate, too many
torrents of tears. Who can forbear smiling as he reads the scene of
the storm, where Charlotte first casts her eyes on the fields, then on
the sky, and finally, laying her hand on her lover's, utters this one   25
word: *Klopstock!* And then the cabbage-passage! . . . *Werther* is
the poem of the German middle-class sentimentality of that day. It
must be said that our sentimentality, even at the height of the *Héloïse* season, never reached the extravagance of that of our neighbours
. . . Mdlle. Flachsland, who married Herder, writes to her betrothed   30
that one night in the depth of the woods she fell on her knees as she
looked at the moon, and that having found some glowworms she
put them into her hair, being careful to arrange them in couples that
she might not disturb their loves."

One can imagine the pleasure of a victim of "Kruppism and   35
corporalism" in relating that story of Mdlle. Flachsland. There
is an even better story of the return of a Dr. Zimmermann to his
home in Hanover, after being treated for hernia at Berlin; but

for this story I must send the reader to M. Scherer's own pages.

After the publication of *Werther* began Goethe's life at Weimar. For ten years he brought out nothing except occasional
pieces for the Court theatre, and occasional poems. True, he
5   carried the project of his *Faust* in his mind, he planned *Wilhelm
Meister*, he made the first draft of *Egmont*, he wrote *Iphigeneia*
and *Tasso* in prose. But he could not make the progress he
wished. He felt the need, for his work, of some influence which
Weimar could not give. He became dissatisfied with the place,
10 with himself, with the people about him. In the autumn of 1786
he disappeared from Weimar, almost by a secret flight, and
crossed the Alps into Italy. M. Scherer says truly that this was
the great event of his life.

Italy, Rome above all, satisfied Goethe, filled him with a sense
15 of strength and joy. "At Rome," he writes from that city, "he
who has eyes to see, and who uses them seriously, becomes solid.
The spirit receives a stamp of vigour; it attains to a gravity in
which there is nothing dry or harsh,—to calm, to joy. For my
own part, at any rate, I feel that I have never before had the
20 power to judge things so justly, and I congratulate myself on
the happy result for my whole future life." So he wrote while
he was in Rome. And he told the Chancellor von Müller,
twenty-five years later, that from the hour when he crossed the
Ponte Molle on his return to Germany, he had never known a
25 day's happiness. "While he spoke thus," adds the Chancellor,
"his features betrayed his deep emotion."

The Italy, from which Goethe thus drew satisfaction and
strength, was Græco-Roman Italy, pagan Italy. For mediæval
and Christian Italy he had no heed, no sympathy. He would not
30 even look at the famous church of St. Francis at Assisi. "I passed
it by," he says, "in disgust." And he told a young Italian who
asked him his opinion of Dante's great poem, that he thought
the *Inferno* abominable, the *Purgatorio* dubious, and the *Para-
diso* tiresome.

35 I have not space to quote what M. Scherer says of the influence on Goethe's genius of his stay in Rome. We are more especially concerned with the judgments of M. Scherer on the principal works of Goethe as these works succeed one another. At

Rome, or under the influence of Rome, *Iphigeneia* and *Tasso* were recast in verse, *Egmont* was resumed and finished, the chief portion of the first part of *Faust* was written. Of the larger works of Goethe in poetry, these are the chief. Let us see what M. Scherer has to say of them.

Tasso and *Iphigeneia*, says M. Scherer very truly, mark a new phase in the literary career of Goethe:—

"They are works of finished style and profound composition. There is no need to inquire whether the *Iphigeneia* keeps to the traditional data of the subject; Goethe desired to make it Greek only by its sententious elevation and grave beauty. What he imitates are the conditions of art as the ancients understood them, but he does not scruple to introduce new thoughts into these mythological *motives*. He has given up the aim of rendering by poetry what is characteristic or individual; his concern is henceforth with the ideal, that is to say, with the transformation of things through beauty. If I were to employ the terms in use amongst ourselves, I should say that from romantic Goethe had changed to being classic; but, let me say again, he is classic only by the adoption of the elevated style, he imitates the ancients merely by borrowing their peculiar sentiment as to art, and within these bounds he moves with freedom and power. The two elements, that of immediate or passionate feeling, and that of well-considered combination of means, balance one another, and give birth to finished works. *Tasso* and *Iphigeneia* mark the apogee of Goethe's talent."

It is curiously interesting to turn from this praise of *Tasso* and *Iphigeneia* to that by the late Mr. Lewes, whose *Life of Goethe*, a work in many respects of brilliant cleverness, will be in the memory of many of us. "A marvellous dramatic poem!" Mr. Lewes calls *Iphigeneia*. "Beautiful as the separate passages are, admirers seldom think of passages, they think of the wondrous whole." Of *Tasso*, Mr. Lewes says: "There is a calm, broad effulgence of light in it, very different from the concentrated lights of *effect* which we are accustomed to find in modern works. It has the clearness, unity, and matchless grace of a Raphael, not the lustrous warmth of a Titian, or the crowded gorgeousness of a Paul Veronese."

Every one will remark the difference of tone between this

criticism and M. Scherer's. Yet M. Scherer's criticism conveyed
praise, and, for him, warm praise. *Tasso* and *Iphigeneia* mark,
in his eyes, the period, the too short period, during which the
forces of inspiration and of reflection, the poet in Goethe and
5 the critic in him, the thinker and the artist, in whose conflict
M. Scherer sees the history of our author's literary development, were in equilibrium.

Faust also, the first part of *Faust*, the only one which counts,
belongs by its composition to this *Tasso* period. By common
10 consent it is the best of Goethe's works. For while it had the
benefit of his matured powers of thought, of his command over
his materials, of his mastery in planning and expressing, it possesses by the nature of its subject an intrinsic richness, colour,
and warmth. Moreover, from Goethe's long and early occupa-
15 tion with the subject, *Faust* has preserved many a stroke and
flash out of the days of its author's fervid youth. To M. Scherer,
therefore, as to the world in general, the first part of *Faust* seems
Goethe's masterpiece. M. Scherer does not call *Faust* the greatest work of the greatest poet of all times and all peoples, but
20 thus he speaks of it:—

"Goethe had the good fortune early to come across a subject,
which, while it did not lend itself to his faults, could not but call
forth all the powers of his genius. I speak of *Faust*. Goethe had begun to occupy himself with it as early as 1774, the year in which
25 *Werther* was published. Considerable portions of the First Part appeared in 1790; it was completed in 1808. We may congratulate ourselves that the work was already, at the time of his travels in Italy,
so far advanced as it was; else there might have been danger of the
author's turning away from it as from a Gothic, perhaps unhealthy,
30 production. What is certain is, that he could not put into *Faust* his
preoccupation with the antique, or, at any rate, he was obliged to
keep this for the Second Part. The first *Faust* remained, whether
Goethe would or no, an old story made young again, to serve as the
poem of thought, the poem of modern life. This kind of adaptation
35 had evidently great difficulties. It was impossible to give the story a
satisfactory ending; the compact between the Doctor and the Devil
could not be made good, consequently the original condition of the
story was gone, and the drama was left without an issue. We must,
therefore, take *Faust* as a work which is not finished, and which

could not be finished. But, in compensation, the choice of this subject had all sorts of advantages for Goethe. In place of the somewhat
cold symbolism for which his mind had a turn, the subject of *Faust*
compelled him to deal with popular beliefs. Instead of obliging him
to produce a drama with beginning, middle, and end, it allowed him   5
to proceed by episodes and detached scenes. Finally, in a subject
fantastic and diabolic there could hardly be found room for the imitation of models. Let me add, that in bringing face to face human
aspiration represented by Faust and pitiless irony represented by
Mephistopheles, Goethe found the natural scope for his keen ob-   10
servations on all things. It is unquestionable that *Faust* stands as one
of the great works of poetry; and, perhaps, the most wonderful
work of poetry in our century. The story, the subject, do not exist
as a whole, but each episode by itself is perfect, and the execution is
nowhere defective. *Faust* is a treasure of poetry, of pathos, of the   15
highest wisdom, of a spirit inexhaustible and keen as steel. There is
not, from the first verse to the last, a false tone or a weak line."

This praise is discriminating, and yet earnest, almost cordial.
"*Faust* stands as one of the great works of poetry; and, perhaps,
the most wonderful work of poetry in our century." The *per-*   20
haps might be away. But the praise is otherwise not coldly
stinted, not limited ungraciously and unduly.

Goethe returned to "the formless Germany," to the Germanic north with its "cold wet summers," of which he so
mournfully complained. He returned to Weimar with its petty   25
Court and petty town, its society which Carl-August himself,
writing to Knebel, calls "the most tiresome on the face of the
earth," and of which the ennui drove Goethe sometimes to "a
sort of internal despair." He had his animating friendship with
Schiller. He had also his connection with Christiana Vulpius,   30
whom he afterwards married. That connection both the moralist and the man of the world may unite in condemning. M. Scherer calls it "a degrading connection with a girl of no education,
whom Goethe established in his house to the great embarrassment of all his friends, whom he either could not or would not   35
marry until eighteen years later, and who punished him as he
deserved by taking a turn for drink,—a turn which their unfortunate son inherited." In these circumstances was passed the
second half of Goethe's life, after his return from Italy. The

man of reflection, always present in him, but balanced for a while by the man of inspiration, became now, M. Scherer thinks, predominant. There was a *refroidissement graduel,* a gradual cooling down, of the poet and artist.

5   The most famous works of Goethe which remain yet to be mentioned are *Egmont, Hermann and Dorothea, Wilhelm Meister,* the *Second Part of Faust,* and the *Gedichte,* or short poems. Of *Egmont* M. Scherer says:—

"This piece also belongs, by the date of its publication, to the
10 period which followed Goethe's stay in Rome. But in vain did Goethe try to transform it, he could not succeed. The subject stood in his way. We need not be surprised, therefore, if *Egmont* remains a mediocre performance, Goethe having always been deficient in dramatic faculty, and not in this case redeeming his defect by qual-
15 ities of execution, as in *Iphigeneia.* He is too much of a generaliser to create a character, too meditative to create an action. *Egmont* must be ranked by the side of *Götz;* it is a product of the same order. The hero is not a living being; one does not know what he wants; the object of the conspiracy is not brought out. The unfortunate Count
20 does certainly exclaim, as he goes to the scaffold, that he is dying for liberty, but nobody had suspected it until that moment. It is the same with the popular movement; it is insufficiently rendered, without breadth, without power. I say nothing of Machiavel, who preaches toleration to the Princess Regent and tries to make her un-
25 derstand the uselessness of persecution; nor of Claire, a girl sprung from the people, who talks like an epigram of the Anthology: 'Neither soldiers nor lovers should have their arms tied.' *Egmont* is one of the weakest among Goethe's weak pieces for the stage."

But now, on the other hand, let us hear Mr. Lewes: "When
30 all is said, the reader thinks of Egmont and Clärchen, and flings criticism to the winds. These are the figures which remain in the memory; bright, genial, glorious creations, comparable to any to be found in the long galleries of art!" What a different tone!

35   Aristotle says, with admirable common-sense, that the determination of how a thing really is, is ὡς ἂν ὁ φρόνιμος ὁρίσειεν, "as the judicious would determine." And would the judicious, after reading *Egmont,* determine with Mr. Lewes, or determine with M. Scherer? Let us for the present leave the judicious to try,

and let us pass to M. Scherer's criticism of *Hermann and Dorothea*. "Goethe's epic poem," writes Schiller, "you have read; you will admit that it is the pinnacle of his and all our modern art." In Professor Grimm's eyes, perhaps, this is but scant praise, but how much too strong is it for M. Scherer!   5

"Criticism is considerably embarrassed in presence of a poem in many respects so highly finished as the antico-modern and heroico-middle-class idyll of Goethe. The ability which the author has spent upon it is beyond conception; and, the kind of poem being once allowed, the indispensable concessions having been once made, it is   10 certain that the pleasure is doubled by seeing, at each step, difficulty so marvellously overcome. But all this cannot make the effort to be effort well spent, nor the kind of poem a true, sound and worthy kind. *Hermann and Dorothea* remains a piece of elegant cleverness, a wager laid and won, but for all that, a feat of ingenuity and noth-   15 ing more. It is not quite certain that our modern society will continue to have a poetry at all; but most undoubtedly, if it does have one, it will be on condition that this poetry belongs to its time by its language, as well as by its subject. Has any critic remarked how Goethe's manner of proceeding is at bottom that of parody, and   20 how the turn of a straw would set the reader laughing at these farm-horses transformed into coursers, these village innkeepers and apothecaries who speak with the magniloquence of a Ulysses or a Nestor? Criticism should have the courage to declare that all this is not sincere poetry at all, but solely the product of an exquisite dilettantism,   25 and,—to speak the definitive judgment upon it,—a factitious work."

Once again we will turn to Mr. Lewes for contrast:—

"Do not let us discuss whether *Hermann and Dorothea* is or is not an epic. It is a poem. Let us accept it for what it is,—a poem full of life, character, and beauty; of all idylls it is the most truly idyllic, of   30 all poems describing country life and country people it is the most truthful. Shakspeare himself is not more dramatic in the presentation of character."

It is an excellent and wholesome discipline for a student of Goethe to be brought face to face with such opposite judg-   35 ments concerning his chief productions. It compels us to rouse ourselves out of the passiveness with which we in general read a celebrated work, to open our eyes wide, to ask ourselves frankly how, according to our genuine feeling, the truth stands. We all recollect Mr. Carlyle on *Wilhelm Meister*, "the mature product of the first genius of our times":—

"Anarchy has now become peace; the once gloomy and perturbed
5 spirit is now serene, cheerfully vigorous, and rich in good fruits. . . . The ideal has been built on the actual; no longer floats vaguely in darkness and regions of dreams, but rests in light, on the firm ground of human interest and business, as in its true scene, and on its true basis."

10 Schiller, too, said of *Wilhelm Meister*, that he "accounted it the most fortunate incident in his existence to have lived to see the completion of this work." And again: "I cannot describe to you how deeply the truth, the beautiful vitality, the simple fulness of this work has affected me. The excitement into which it has
15 thrown my mind will subside when I shall have thoroughly mastered it, and that will be an important crisis in my being."

Now for the cold-water douche of our French critic:—

"Goethe is extremely great, but he is extremely unequal. He is a genius of the first order, but with thicknesses, with spots, so to
20 speak, which remain opaque and where the light does not pass. Goethe, to go farther, has not only genius, he has what we in France call *esprit*, he has it to any extent, and yet there are in him sides of commonplace and silliness. One cannot read his works without continually falling in with trivial admirations, solemn pieces of simplic-
25 ity, reflections which bear upon nothing. There are moments when Goethe turns upon society and upon art a ken of astonishing penetration; and there are other moments when he gravely beats in an open door, or a door which leads nowhere. In addition, he has all manner of hidden intentions, he loves byways of effect, seeks to in-
30 sinuate lessons, and so becomes heavy and fatiguing. There are works of his which one cannot read without effort. I shall never forget the repeated acts of self-sacrifice which it cost me to finish *Wilhelm Meister* and the *Elective Affinities*. As Paul de Saint-Victor has put it: 'When Goethe goes in for being tiresome he succeeds with
35 an astonishing perfection, he is the *Jupiter Pluvius* of ennui. The very height from which he pours it down, does but make its weight greater.' What an insipid invention is the pedagogic city! What a trivial world is that in which the Wilhelms and the Philinas, the Eduards and the Ottilias, have their being! Mignon has been ele-

vated into a poetic creation; but Mignon has neither charm, nor mystery, nor veritable existence; nor any other poetry belonging to her,—let us say it right out,—except the half-dozen immortal stanzas put into her mouth."

And, as we brought Schiller to corroborate the praise of *Wilhelm Meister,* let us bring Niebuhr to corroborate the blame. Niebuhr calls *Wilhelm Meister* "a menagerie of tame animals."

After this the reader can perhaps imagine, without any specimens of it, the sort of tone in which M. Scherer passes judgment upon *Dichtung und Wahrheit,* and upon Goethe's prose in general. Even Mr. Lewes declares of Goethe's prose: "He has written with a perfection no German ever achieved before, and he has also written with a feebleness which it would be gratifying to think no German would ever emulate again."

Let us return, then, to Goethe's poetry. There is the continuation of *Faust* still to be mentioned. First we will hear Mr. Carlyle. In *Helena* "the design is," says Mr. Carlyle, "that the story of *Faust* may fade away at its termination into a phantasmagoric region, where symbol and thing signified are no longer clearly distinguished," and that thus "the final result may be curiously and significantly indicated rather than directly exhibited." *Helena* is "not a type of one thing, but a vague, fluctuating, fitful adumbration of many." It is, properly speaking, "what the Germans call a *Mährchen,* a species of fiction they have particularly excelled in." As to its composition, "we cannot but perceive it to be deeply studied, appropriate and successful."

The "adumbrative" style here praised, in which "the final result is curiously and significantly indicated rather than directly exhibited," is what M. Scherer calls Goethe's "last manner."

"It was to be feared that, as Goethe grew older and colder, the balance between those two elements of art, science and temperament, would not be preserved. This is just what happened, and hence arose Goethe's last manner. He had passed from representing characters to representing the ideal, he is now to pass from the ideal to the symbol. And this is quite intelligible; reflection, as it develops, leads to abstraction, and from the moment when the artist begins to prefer ideas to sensation he falls inevitably into allegory, since allegory is his only means for directly expressing ideas. Goethe's third epoch is characterised by three things: an ever-increasing devotion to the antique as to the supreme revelation of the beautiful, a disposition to take delight in æsthetic theories, and, finally, an irresistible desire for giving didactic intentions to art. This last tendency is evident in the continuation of *Wilhelm Meister,* and in the second *Faust.* We may say that these two works are dead of a hypertrophy of reflection. They are a mere mass of symbols, hieroglyphics, sometimes even mystifications. There is something extraordinarily painful in seeing a genius so vigorous and a science so consummate thus mistaking the elementary conditions of poetry. The fault, we may add, is the fault of German art in general. The Germans have more ideas than their plasticity of temperament, evidently below par, knows how to deal with. They are wanting in the vigorous sensuousness, the concrete and immediate impression of things, which makes the artist, and which distinguishes him from the thinker."

So much for Goethe's "last manner" in general, and to serve as introduction to what M. Scherer has to say of the second *Faust* more particularly:—

"The two parts of *Faust* are disparate. They do not proceed from one and the same conception. Goethe was like Defoe, like Milton, like so many others, who after producing a masterpiece have been bent on giving it a successor. Unhappily, while the first *Faust* is of Goethe's fairest time, of his most vigorous manhood, the second is the last fruit of his old age. Science, in the one, has not chilled poetic genius; in the other, reflection bears sway and produces all kind of symbols and abstractions. The beauty of the first comes in some sort from its very imperfection; I mean, from the incessant tendency of the sentiment of reality, the creative power, the poetry of passion and nature, to prevail over the philosophic intention and to make us forget it. Where is the student of poetry who, as he reads the monologues of Faust or the sarcasms of Mephistopheles, as he witnesses the fall and the remorse of Margaret, the most poignant history ever traced by pen, any longer thinks of the *Prologue in Heaven* or of the terms of the compact struck between Faust and the Tempter? In the second part it is just the contrary. The idea is everything. Allegory reigns there. The poetry is devoid of that simple and natural realism without which art cannot exist. One feels oneself in a sheer region of didactics. And this is true even of the finest parts,—of the third act, for example,—as well as of the weakest. What can be more burlesque than this Euphorion, son of Faust and Helen, who is found at the critical moment under a cabbage-leaf!—no, I am wrong, who descends from the sky 'for all the world like a Phœbus,' with a little cloak and a little harp, and ends by breaking his neck as he falls at the feet of his parents? And all this to represent Lord Byron, and, in his person, modern poetry, which is the offspring of romantic art! What decadence, good heavens! and what a melancholy thing is old age, since it can make the most plastic of modern poets sink down to these fantasticalities worthy of Alexandria!"

In spite of the high praise which he has accorded to *Tasso* and *Iphigeneia*, M. Scherer concludes, then, his review of Goethe's productions thus:—

"Goethe is truly original and thoroughly superior only in his lyrical poems (the *Gedichte*), and in the first part of *Faust*. They are immortal works, and why? Because they issue from a personal feeling, and the spirit of system has not petrified them. And yet even his lyrical poems Goethe has tried to spoil. He went on correcting them incessantly; and, in bringing them to that degree of perfection in which we now find them, he has taken out of them their warmth."

The worshipper of Goethe will ask with wrath and bitterness of soul whether M. Scherer has yet done. Not quite. We have still to hear some acute remarks on the pomposity of diction in our poet's stage pieces. The English reader will best understand, perhaps, the kind of fault meant, if we quote from the *Natural Daughter* a couple of lines not quoted, as it happens, by M. Scherer. The heroine has a fall from her horse, and the Court physician comes to attend her. The Court physician is addressed thus:—

> "Erfahrner Mann, dem unseres König's Leben,
> Das unschätzbare Gut, vertraut ist ..."

"Experienced man, to whom the life of our sovereign, that inestimable treasure, is given in charge." Shakspeare would have said *Doctor*. The German drama is full of this sort of roundabout, pompous language. "Every one has laughed," says M. Scherer, "at the pomposity and periphrasis of French tragedy." The heroic King of Pontus, in French tragedy, gives up the ghost with these words:—

"Dans cet embrassement dont la douceur me flatte,
Venez, et recevez l'âme de Mithridate."

"What has not been said," continues M. Scherer, "and justly
said, against the artificial character of French tragedy?" Nevertheless, "people do not enough remember that, convention being universally admitted in the seventeenth century, sincerity
and even a relative simplicity remained possible" with an artificial diction; whereas Goethe did not find his artificial diction
imposed upon him by conditions from without,—he made it
himself, and of set purpose.

"It is a curious thing; this style of Goethe's has its cause just in that
very same study which has been made such a matter of reproach
against our tragedy-writers,—the study to maintain a pitch of general nobleness in all the language uttered. Everything with Goethe
must be grave, solemn, sculptural. We see the influence of Winckel-
mann, and of his views on Greek art."

Of Goethe's character, too, as well as of his talent, M. Scherer
has something to say. English readers will be familiar enough
with complaints of Goethe's "artistic egotism," of his tendency
to set up his own intellectual culture as the rule of his life. The
freshness of M. Scherer's repetition of these old complaints consists in his connecting them, as we have seen, with the criticism
of Goethe's literary development. But M. Scherer has some direct blame of defects in his author's character which is worth
quoting:—

"It must fairly be confessed, the respect of Goethe for the mighty
of this earth was carried to excesses which make one uncomfortable
for him. One is confounded by these earnestnesses of servility. The
King of Bavaria pays him a visit; the dear poet feels his head go
round. The story should be read in the journal of the Chancellor
von Müller:—Goethe after dinner became more and more animated
and cordial. 'It was no light matter,' he said, 'to work out the powerful impression produced by the King's presence, to assimilate it
internally. It is difficult, in such circumstances, to keep one's balance
and not to lose one's head. And yet the important matter is to extract from this apparition its real significance, to obtain a clear and
distinct image of it.'

"Another time he got a letter from the same sovereign; he talks of it to Eckermann with the same devout emotion—he 'thanks Heaven for it as for a quite special favour.' And when one thinks that the king in question was no other than that poor Louis of Bavaria, the ridiculous dilettante of whom Heine has made such fun! Evidently 5
Goethe had a strong dose of what the English call 'snobbishness.' The blemish is the more startling in him, because Goethe is, in other respects, a simple and manly character. Neither in his person nor in his manner of writing was he at all affected; he has no self-conceit; he does not pose. There is in this particular all the difference in the 10
world between him and the majority of our own French authors, who seem always busy arranging their draperies, and asking themselves how they appear to the world and what the gallery thinks of them."

Goethe himself had in like manner called the French "the 15
women of Europe." But let us remark that it was not "snobbishness" in Goethe, which made him take so seriously the potentate who loved Lola Montes; it was simply his German "corporalism." A disciplinable and much-disciplined people, with little humour, and without the experience of a great national 20
life, regards its official authorities in this devout and awe-struck way. To a German it seems profane and licentious to smile at his Dogberry. He takes Dogberry seriously and solemnly, takes him at his own valuation.

We are all familiar with the general style of the critic who, 25
as the phrase is, "cuts up" his author. Such a critic finds very few merits and a great many faults, and he ends either with a phrase of condemnation, or with a phrase of compassion, or with a sneer. We saw, however, in the case of Milton, that one must not reckon on M. Scherer's ending in this fashion. After a 30
course of severe criticism he wound up with earnest, almost reverential, praise. The same thing happens again in his treatment of Goethe. No admirer of Goethe will be satisfied with the treatment which hitherto we have seen Goethe receive at M. Scherer's hands. And the summing-up begins in a strain 35
which will not please the admirer much better:—

"To sum up, Goethe is a poet full of ideas and of observation, full of sense and taste, full even of feeling no less than of acumen, and

all this united with an incomparable gift of versification. But Goethe
has no artlessness, no fire, no invention; he is wanting in the dramatic fibre and cannot create; reflection, in Goethe, has been too
much for emotion, the *savant* in him for poetry, the philosophy of
5   art for the artist."

And yet the final conclusion is this:—

"Nevertheless, Goethe remains one of the exceeding great among
the sons of men. 'After all,' said he to one of his friends, 'there are
honest people up and down the world who have got light from my
10   books; and whoever reads them, and gives himself the trouble to
understand me, will acknowledge that he has acquired thence a certain inward freedom.' I should like to inscribe these words upon the
pedestal of Goethe's statue. No juster praise could be found for him,
and in very truth there cannot possibly be for any man a praise
15   higher or more enviable."

And in an article on Shakspeare, after a prophecy that the hour
will come for Goethe, as in Germany it has of late come for
Shakspeare, when criticism will take the place of adoration,
M. Scherer, after insisting on those defects in Goethe of which
20   we have been hearing so fully, protests that there are yet few
writers for whom he feels a greater admiration than for Goethe,
few to whom he is indebted for enjoyments more deep and
more durable; and declares that Goethe, although he has not
Shakspeare's power, is a genius more vast, more universal, than
25   Shakspeare. He adds, to be sure, that Shakspeare had an advantage over Goethe in not outliving himself.

After all, then, M. Scherer is not far from being willing to
allow, if any youthful devotee wishes to urge it, that "the Eternal created Goethe to be a guide to the universe." Yet he deals
30   with the literary production of Goethe as we have seen. He is
very far indeed from thinking it the performance "of the greatest poet of all times and of all peoples." And this is why I have
thought M. Scherer's criticisms worthy of so much attention:
—because a double judgment, somewhat of this kind, is the
35   judgment about Goethe to which mature experience, the experience got "by the time one is forty years old," does really, I
think, bring us.

I do not agree with all M. Scherer's criticisms on Goethe's literary work. I do not myself feel, in reading the *Gedichte*, the truth of what M. Scherer says,—that Goethe has corrected and retouched them till he has taken all the warmth out of them. I do not myself feel the irritation in reading Goethe's Memoirs, and his prose generally, which they provoke in M. Scherer. True, the prose has none of those positive qualities of style which give pleasure, it is not the prose of Voltaire or Swift; it is loose, ill-knit, diffuse; it bears the marks of having been, as it mostly was, dictated,—and dictating is a detestable habit. But it is absolutely free from affectation; it lets the real Goethe reach us.

In other respects I agree in the main with the judgments passed by M. Scherer upon Goethe's works. Nay, some of them, such as *Tasso* and *Iphigeneia*, I should hesitate to extol so highly as he does. In that peculiar world of thought and feeling, wherein *Tasso* and *Iphigeneia* have their existence, and into which the reader too must enter in order to understand them, there is something factitious; something devised and determined by the thinker, not given by the necessity of Nature herself; something too artificial, therefore, too deliberately studied,—as the French say, *trop voulu*. They cannot have the power of works where we are in a world of thought and feeling not invented but natural,—of works like the *Agamemnon* or *Lear*. *Faust*, too, suffers by comparison with works like the *Agamemnon* or *Lear*. M. Scherer says, with perfect truth, that the first part of *Faust* has not a single false tone or weak line. But it is a work, as he himself observes, "of episodes and detached scenes," not a work where the whole material together has been fused in the author's mind by strong and deep feeling, and then poured out in a single jet. It can never produce the single, powerful total-impression of works which have thus arisen.

The first part of *Faust* is, however, undoubtedly Goethe's best work. And it is so for the plain reason that, except his *Gedichte*, it is his most straightforward work in poetry. Mr. Hayward's is the best of the translations of *Faust* for the same reason,—because it is the most straightforward. To be simple and straightforward is, as Milton saw and said, of the essence of first-rate poetry. All that M. Scherer says of the ruinousness, to a poet, of "symbols, hieroglyphics, mystifications," is just. When Mr. Carlyle praises the *Helena* for being "not a type of one thing, but a vague, fluctuating, fitful adumbration of many," he praises it for what is in truth its fatal defect. The *Mährchen*, again, on which Mr. Carlyle heaps such praise, calling it "one of the notablest performances produced for the last thousand years," a performance "in such a style of grandeur and celestial brilliancy and life as the Western imagination has not elsewhere reached;" the *Mährchen*, woven throughout of "symbol, hieroglyphic, mystification," is by that very reason a piece of solemn inanity, on which a man of Goethe's powers could never have wasted his time, but for his lot having been cast in a nation which has never lived.

Mr. Carlyle has a sentence on Goethe which we may turn to excellent account for the criticism of such works as the *Mährchen* and *Helena:*—

"We should ask," he says, "what the poet's aim really and truly was, and how far this aim accorded, not with us and our individual crotchets and the crotchets of our little senate where we give or take the law, but with human nature and the nature of things at large; with the universal principles of poetic beauty, not as they stand written in our text-books, but in the hearts and imaginations of all men."

To us it seems lost labour to inquire what a poet's *aim* may have been; but for aim let us read *work*, and we have here a sound and admirable rule of criticism. Let us ask how a poet's work accords, not with any one's fancies and crotchets, but "with human nature and the nature of things at large, with the universal principles of poetic beauty as they stand written in the hearts and imaginations of all men," and we shall have the surest rejection of symbol, hieroglyphic, and mystification in poetry. We shall have the surest condemnation of works like the *Mährchen* and the second part of *Faust*.

It is by no means as the greatest of poets that Goethe deserves the pride and praise of his German countrymen. It is as the clearest, the largest, the most helpful thinker of modern times. It is not principally in his published works, it is in the immense Goethe-literature of letter, journal, and conversation, in the volumes of Riemer, Falk, Eckermann, the Chancellor von Müller, in the letters to Merck and Madame von Stein and many others, in the correspondence with Schiller, the correspondence with Zelter, that the elements for an impression of the truly great, the truly significant Goethe are to be found. Goethe is the greatest poet of modern times, not because he is one of the half-dozen human beings who in the history of our race have shown the most signal gift for poetry, but because, having a very considerable gift for poetry, he was at the same time, in the width, depth, and richness of his criticism of life, by far our greatest modern man. He may be precious and important to us on this account above men of other and more alien times, who as poets rank higher. Nay, his preciousness and importance as a clear and profound modern spirit, as a master-critic of modern life, must communicate a worth of their own to his poetry, and may well make it erroneously seem to have a positive value and perfectness as poetry, more than it has. It is most pardonable for a student of Goethe, and may even for a time be serviceable, to fall into this error. Nevertheless, poetical defects, where they are present, subsist, and are what they are. And the same with defects of character. Time and attention bring them to light; and when they are brought to light, it is not good for us, it is obstructing and retarding, to refuse to see them. Goethe himself would have warned us against doing so. We can imagine, indeed, that great and supreme critic reading Professor Grimm's laudation of his poetical work with lifted eyebrows, and M. Scherer's criticisms with acquiescence.

Shall we say, however, that M. Scherer's tone in no way jars upon us, or that his presentation of Goethe, just and acute as is the view of faults both in Goethe's poetry and in Goethe's character, satisfies us entirely? By no means. One could not say so of M. Scherer's presentation of Milton; of the presentation of Goethe one can say so still less. Goethe's faults are shown by M. Scherer, and they exist. Praise is given, and the right praise. But there is yet some defect in the portraiture as a whole. Tone and perspective are somehow a little wrong; the distribution of colour, the proportions of light and shade, are not managed quite as they should be. One would like the picture to be painted over again by the same artist with the same talent, but a little 5 differently. And meanwhile we instinctively, after M. Scherer's presentation, feel a desire for some last words of Goethe's own, something which may give a happier and more cordial turn to our thoughts, after they have been held so long to a frigid and censorious strain. And there rises to the mind this sentence: 10 *"Die Gestalt dieser Welt vergeht;* und ich möchte mich nur mit dem beschäftigen, was bleibende Verhältnisse sind." *"The fashion of this world passeth away;* and I would fain occupy myself only with the abiding." There is the true Goethe, and with that Goethe we would end!

15   But let us be thankful for what M. Scherer brings, and let us acknowledge with gratitude his presentation of Goethe to be, not indeed the definitive picture of Goethe, but a contribution, and a very able contribution, to that definitive picture. We are told that since the war of 1870 Frenchmen are abandoning lit- 20 erature for science. Why do they not rather learn of this accomplished senator of theirs, with his Geneva training, to extend their old narrow literary range a little, and to know foreign literatures as M. Scherer knows them?

Equality[1]

There is a maxim which we all know, which occurs in our copy-books, which occurs in that solemn and beautiful formulary against which the Nonconformist genius is just now so angrily chafing,—the Burial Service. The maxim is this: "Evil communications corrupt good manners." It is taken from a chapter of the First Epistle to the Corinthians; but originally it is a line of poetry, of Greek poetry. *Quid Athenis et Hierosolymis?* asks a Father; what have Athens and Jerusalem to do with one another? Well, at any rate, the Jerusalemite Paul, exhorting his converts, enforces what he is saying by a verse of Athenian comedy,—a verse, probably, from the great master of that comedy, a man unsurpassed for fine and just observation of human life, Menander: Φθείρουσιν ἤθη χρήσθ' ὁμιλίαι κακαί—"Evil communications corrupt good manners."

In that collection of single, sententious lines, printed at the end of Menander's fragments, where we now find the maxim quoted by St. Paul, there is another striking maxim, not alien certainly to the language of the Christian religion, but which has not passed into our copy-books: "Choose equality and flee greed." The same profound observer, who laid down the maxim so universally accepted by us that it has become commonplace, the maxim that evil communications corrupt good manners, laid down also, as a no less sure result of the accurate study of human life, this other maxim as well: "Choose equality and flee greed"—'Ισότητα δ' αἱροῦ καὶ πλεονεξίαν φύγε.

Pleonexia, or greed, the wishing and trying for the bigger share, we know under the name of covetousness. We under-

---

[1] Address delivered at the Royal Institution.

stand by covetousness something different from what *pleonexia*
really means: we understand by it the longing for other people's
goods: and covetousness, so understood, it is a commonplace of
morals and of religion with us that we should shun. As to the
duty of pursuing equality, there is no such consent amongst us.
Indeed, the consent is the other way, the consent is against equality. Equality before the law we all take as a matter of course;
that is not the equality which we mean when we talk of equality. When we talk of equality, we understand social equality;
and for equality in this Frenchified sense of the term almost
everybody in England has a hard word. About four years ago
Lord Beaconsfield held it up to reprobation in a speech to the
students at Glasgow;—a speech so interesting, that being asked
soon afterwards to hold a discourse at Glasgow, I said that if
one spoke there at all at that time it would be impossible to
speak on any other subject but equality. However, it is a great
way to Glasgow, and I never yet have been able to go and
speak there.

But the testimonies against equality have been steadily accu-
mulating from the date of Lord Beaconsfield's Glasgow speech
down to the present hour. Sir Erskine May winds up his new
and important *History of Democracy* by saying: "France has
aimed at social equality. The fearful troubles through which
she has passed have checked her prosperity, demoralised her
society, and arrested the intellectual growth of her people." Mr.
Froude, again, who is more his own master than I am, has been
able to go to Edinburgh and to speak there upon equality. Mr.
Froude told his hearers that equality splits a nation into a "multitude of disconnected units," that "the masses require leaders
whom they can trust," and that "the natural leaders in a healthy
country are the gentry." And only just before the *History of
Democracy* came out, we had that exciting passage of arms between Mr. Lowe and Mr. Gladstone, where equality, poor
thing, received blows from them both. Mr. Lowe declared that
"no concession should be made to the cry for equality, unless it
appears that the State is menaced with more danger by its refusal than by its admission. No such case exists now or ever has
existed in this country." And Mr. Gladstone replied that equal-

ity was so utterly unattractive to the people of this country, inequality was so dear to their hearts, that to talk of concessions being made to the cry for equality was absurd. "There is no broad political idea," says Mr. Gladstone quite truly, "which has entered less into the formation of the political system of this country than the love of equality." And he adds: "It is not the love of equality which has carried into every corner of the country the distinct undeniable popular preference, wherever other things are equal, for a man who is a lord over a man who is not. The love of freedom itself is hardly stronger in England than the love of aristocracy." Mr. Gladstone goes on to quote a saying of Sir William Molesworth, that with our people the love of aristocracy "is a religion." And he concludes in his copious and eloquent way: "Call this love of inequality by what name you please,—the complement of the love of freedom, or its negative pole, or the shadow which the love of freedom casts, or the reverberation of its voice in the halls of the constitution, —it is an active, living, and life-giving power, which forms an inseparable essential element in our political habits of mind, and asserts itself at every step in the processes of our system."

And yet, on the other side, we have a consummate critic of life like Menander, delivering, as if there were no doubt at all about the matter, the maxim: "Choose equality!" An Englishman with any curiosity must surely be inclined to ask himself how such a maxim can ever have got established, and taken rank along with "Evil communications corrupt good manners." Moreover, we see that among the French, who have suffered so grievously, as we hear, from choosing equality, the most gifted spirits continue to believe passionately in it nevertheless. "The human ideal, as well as the social ideal, is," says George Sand, "to achieve equality." She calls equality "the goal of man and the law of the future." She asserts that France is the most civilised of nations, and that its pre-eminence in civilisation it owes to equality.

But Menander lived a long while ago, and George Sand was an enthusiast. Perhaps their differing from us about equality need not trouble us much. France, too, counts for but one nation, as England counts for one also. Equality may be a religion

with the people of France, as inequality, we are told, is a religion
with the people of England. But what do other nations seem to
think about the matter?

Now, my discourse to-night is most certainly not meant to
be a disquisition on law, and on the rules of bequest. But it is
evident that in the societies of Europe, with a constitution of
property such as that which the feudal Middle Age left them
with,—a constitution of property full of inequality,—the state
of the law of bequest shows us how far each society wishes the
inequality to continue. The families in possession of great estates will not break them up if they can help it. Such owners
will do all they can, by entail and settlement, to prevent their
successors from breaking them up. They will preserve inequality. Freedom of bequest, then, the power of making entails and
settlements, is sure, in an old European country like ours, to
maintain inequality. And with us, who have the religion of inequality, the power of entailing and settling, and of willing
property as one likes, exists, as is well known, in singular fulness,
—greater fulness than in any country of the Continent. The
proposal of a measure such as the Real Estates Intestacy Bill is,
in a country like ours, perfectly puerile. A European country
like ours, wishing not to preserve inequality but to abate it, can
only do so by interfering with the freedom of bequest. This is
what Turgot, the wisest of French statesmen, pronounced before the Revolution to be necessary, and what was done in
France at the great Revolution. The *Code Napoléon*, the actual
law of France, forbids entails altogether, and leaves a man free
to dispose of but one-fourth of his property, of whatever kind,
if he have three children or more, of one-third if he have two
children, of one-half if he have but one child. Only in the rare
case, therefore, of a man's having but one child, can that child
take the whole of his father's property. If there are two children, two-thirds of the property must be equally divided between them; if there are more than two, three-fourths. In this
way has France, desiring equality, sought to bring equality
about.

Now the interesting point for us is, I say, to know how far
other European communities, left in the same situation with us

and with France, having immense inequalities of class and property created for them by the Middle Age, have dealt with these inequalities by means of the law of bequest. Do they leave bequest free, as we do? then, like us, they are for inequality. Do they interfere with the freedom of bequest, as France does? then, like France, they are for equality. And we shall be most interested, surely, by what the most civilised European communities do in this matter,—communities such as those of Germany, Italy, Belgium, Holland, Switzerland. And among those communities we are most concerned, I think, with such as, in the conditions of freedom and of self-government which they demand for their life, are most like ourselves. Germany, for instance, we shall less regard, because the conditions which the Germans seem to accept for their life are so unlike what we demand for ours; there is so much personal government there, so much *junkerism*, militarism, officialism; the community is so much more trained to submission than we could bear, so much more used to be, as the popular phrase is, sat upon. Countries where the community has more a will of its own, or can more show it, are the most important for our present purpose,—such countries as Belgium, Holland, Italy, Switzerland. Well, Belgium adopts purely and simply, as to bequest and inheritance, the provisions of the *Code Napoléon*. Holland adopts them purely and simply. Italy has adopted them substantially. Switzerland is a republic, where the general feeling against inequality is strong, and where it might seem less necessary, therefore, to guard against inequality by interfering with the power of bequest. Each Swiss canton has its own law of bequest. In Geneva, Vaud, and Zurich,—perhaps the three most distinguished cantons,—the law is identical with that of France. In Berne, one-third is the fixed proportion which a man is free to dispose of by will; the rest of his property must go among his children equally. In all the other cantons there are regulations of a like kind. Germany, I was saying, will interest us less than these freer countries. In Germany,—though there is not the English freedom of bequest, but the rule of the Roman law prevails, the rule obliging the parent to assign a certain portion to each child, —in Germany entails and settlements in favour of an eldest son are generally permitted. But there is a remarkable exception. The Rhine countries, which in the early part of this century were under French rule, and which then received the *Code Napoléon*, these countries refused to part with it when they were restored to Germany; and to this day Rhenish Prussia, Rhenish Hesse, and Baden, have the French law of bequest, forbidding entails, and dividing property in the way we have seen.

The United States of America have the English liberty of bequest. But the United States are, like Switzerland, a republic, with the republican sentiment for equality. Theirs is, besides, a new society; it did not inherit the system of classes and of property which feudalism established in Europe. The class by which the United States were settled was not a class with feudal habits and ideas. It is notorious that to acquire great landed estates and to entail them upon an eldest son, is neither the practice nor the desire of any class in America. I remember hearing it said to an American in England: "But, after all, you have the same freedom of bequest and inheritance as we have, and if a man tomorrow chose in your country to entail a great landed estate rigorously, what could you do?" The American answered: "Set aside the will on the ground of insanity."

You see we are in a manner taking the votes for and against equality. We ought not to leave out our own colonies. In general they are, of course, like the United States of America, new societies. They have the English liberty of bequest. But they have no feudal past, and were not settled by a class with feudal habits and ideas. Nevertheless it happens that there have arisen, in Australia, exceedingly large estates, and that the proprietors seek to keep them together. And what have we seen happen lately? An Act has been passed which in effect inflicts a fine upon every proprietor who holds a landed estate of more than a certain value. The measure has been severely blamed in England; to Mr. Lowe such a "concession to the cry for equality" appears, as we might expect, pregnant with warnings. At present I neither praise it nor blame it; I simply count it as one of the votes for equality. And is it not a singular thing, I ask you, that while we have the religion of inequality, and can hardly bear to hear equality spoken of, there should be, among the

nations of Europe which have politically most in common with
us, and in the United States of America, and in our own colonies, this diseased appetite, as we must think it, for equality?
Perhaps Lord Beaconsfield may not have turned your minds to
this subject as he turned mine, and what Menander or George
Sand happens to have said may not interest you much; yet
surely, when you think of it, when you see what a practical revolt against inequality there is amongst so many people not so
very unlike to ourselves, you must feel some curiosity to sift
the matter a little further, and may be not ill-disposed to follow
me while I try to do so.

I have received a letter from Clerkenwell, in which the writer
reproaches me for lecturing about equality at this which he
calls "the most aristocratic and exclusive place out." I am here
because your secretary invited me. But I am glad to treat the
subject of equality before such an audience as this. Some of you
may remember that I have roughly divided our English society
into Barbarians, Philistines, Populace, each of them with their
prepossessions, and loving to hear what gratifies them. But I remarked at the same time, that scattered throughout all these
classes were a certain number of generous and humane souls,
lovers of man's perfection, detached from the prepossessions of
the class to which they might naturally belong, and desirous
that he who speaks to them should, as Plato says, not try to
please his fellow-servants, but his true and legitimate masters—
the heavenly Gods. I feel sure that among the members and fre-
quenters of an institution like this, such humane souls are apt to
congregate in numbers. Even from the reproach which my
Clerkenwell friend brings against you of being too aristocratic,
I derive some comfort. Only I give to the term *aristocratic*
a rather wide extension. An accomplished American, much
known and much esteemed in this country, the late Mr. Charles
Sumner, says that what particularly struck him in England was
the large class of gentlemen as distinct from the nobility, and
the abundance amongst them of serious knowledge, high accomplishment, and refined taste,—taste fastidious perhaps, says
Mr. Sumner, to excess, but erring on virtue's side. And he goes
on: "I do not know that there is much difference between the

manners and social observances of the highest classes of England and those of the corresponding classes of France and
Germany; but in the rank immediately below the highest,—as
among the professions, or military men, or literary men,—there
5 you will find that the Englishmen have the advantage. They are
better educated and better bred, more careful in their personal
habits and in social conventions, more refined." Mr. Sumner's
remark is just and important; this large class of gentlemen in
the professions, the services, literature, politics,—and a good
10 contingent is now added from business also,—this large class,
not of the nobility, but with the accomplishments and taste of
an upper class, is something peculiar to England. Of this class
I may probably assume that my present audience is in large measure composed. It is aristocratic in this sense, that it has the tastes
15 of a cultivated class, a certain high standard of civilisation. Well,
it is in its effects upon *civilisation* that equality interests me.
And I speak to an audience with a high standard of civilisation.
If I say that certain things in certain classes do not come up to
a high standard of civilisation, I need not prove how and why
20 they do not; you will feel instinctively whether they do or no.
If they do not, I need not prove that this is a bad thing, that a
high standard of civilisation is desirable; you will instinctively
feel that it is. Instead of calling this "the most aristocratic and
exclusive place out," I conceive of it as a *civilised* place; and in
25 speaking about civilisation half one's labour is saved when one
speaks about it among those who are civilised.

Politics are forbidden here; but equality is not a question of
English politics. The abstract right to equality may, indeed, be
a question of speculative politics. French equality appeals to this
30 abstract natural right as its support. It goes back to a state of
nature where all were equal, and supposes that "the poor con-
sented," as Rousseau says, "to the existence of rich people," reserving always a natural right to return to the state of nature.
It supposes that a child has a natural right to his equal share in
35 his father's goods. The principle of abstract right, says Mr.
Lowe, has never been admitted in England, and is false. I so
entirely agree with him, that I run no risk of offending by discussing equality upon the basis of this principle. So far as I can

sound human consciousness, I cannot, as I have often said, perceive that man is really conscious of any abstract natural rights at all. The natural right to have work found for one to do, the natural right to have food found for one to eat—rights sometimes so confidently and so indignantly asserted—seem to me quite baseless. It cannot be too often repeated: peasants and workmen have no natural rights, not one. Only we ought instantly to add, that kings and nobles have none either. If it is the sound English doctrine that all rights are created by law and are based on expediency, and are alterable as the public advantage may require, certainly that orthodox doctrine is mine. Property is created and maintained by law. It would disappear in that state of private war and scramble which legal society supersedes. Legal society creates, for the common good, the right of property; and for the common good that right is by legal society limitable. That property should exist, and that it should be held with a sense of security and with a power of disposal, may be taken, by us here at any rate, as a settled matter of expediency. With these conditions a good deal of inequality is inevitable. But that the power of disposal should be practically *unlimited*, that the inequality should be *enormous*, or that the degree of inequality admitted at one time should be admitted *always*,—this is by no means so certain. The right of bequest in early times, as Sir Henry Maine and Mr. Mill have pointed out, seldom recognised. In later times it has been limited in many countries in the way that we have seen; even in England itself it is not formally quite unlimited. The question is one of expediency. It is assumed, I grant, with great unanimity amongst us, that our signal inequality of classes and property is expedient for our civilisation and welfare. But this assumption, of which the distinguished personages who adopt it seem so sure that they think it needless to produce grounds for it, is just what we have to examine.

Now, there is a sentence of Sir Erskine May, whom I have already quoted, which will bring us straight to the very point that I wish to raise. Sir Erskine May, after saying, as you have heard, that France has pursued social equality, and has come to

fearful troubles, demoralisation, and intellectual stoppage by
doing so, continues thus: "Yet is she high, if not the first, in the
scale of civilised nations." Why, here is a curious thing, surely!
A nation pursues social equality, supposed to be an utterly false
5 and baneful ideal; it arrives, as might have been expected, at
fearful misery and deterioration by doing so; and yet, at the
same time, it is high, if not the first, in the scale of civilised nations. What do we mean by *civilised?* Sir Erskine May does not
seem to have asked himself the question, so we will try to an-
10 swer it for ourselves. Civilisation is the humanisation of man in
society. To be humanised is to comply with the true law of our
human nature: *servare modum, finemque tenere, Naturamque
sequi,* says Lucan; "to keep our measure, and to hold fast our
end, and to follow Nature." To be humanised is to make prog-
15 ress towards this, our true and full humanity. And to be civilised
is to make progress towards this in civil society; in that civil society "without which," says Burke, "man could not by any possibility arrive at the perfection of which his nature is capable,
nor even make a remote and faint approach to it." To be the
20 most civilised of nations, therefore, is to be the nation which
comes nearest to human perfection, in the state which that perfection essentially demands. And a nation which has been
brought by the pursuit of social equality to moral deterioration,
intellectual stoppage, and fearful troubles, is perhaps the nation
25 which has come nearest to human perfection in that state which
such perfection essentially demands! Michelet himself, who
would deny the demoralisation and the stoppage, and call the
fearful troubles a sublime expiation for the sins of the whole
world, could hardly say more for France than this. Certainly
30 Sir Erskine May never intended to say so much. But into what
a difficulty has he somehow run himself, and what a good action
would it be to extricate him from it! Let us see whether the
performance of that good action may not also be a way of clearing our minds as to the uses of equality.
35   When we talk of man's advance towards his full humanity,
we think of an advance, not along one line only, but several.
Certain races and nations, as we know, are on certain lines pre-
eminent and representative. The Hebrew nation was pre-emi-

nent on one great line. "What nation," it was justly asked by
their lawgiver, "hath statutes and judgments so righteous as the
law which I set before you this day? Keep therefore and do
them; for this is your wisdom and your understanding in the
sight of the nations which shall hear all these statutes and say:
Surely this great nation is a wise and understanding people!"
The Hellenic race was pre-eminent on other lines. Isocrates
could say of Athens: "Our city has left the rest of the world so
far behind in philosophy and eloquence, that those educated by
Athens have become the teachers of the rest of mankind; and
so well has she done her part, that the name of Greeks seems no
longer to stand for a race but to stand for intelligence itself, and
they who share in our culture are called Greeks even before
those who are merely of our own blood." The power of intellect and science, the power of beauty, the power of social life
and manners,—these are what Greece so felt, and fixed, and may
stand for. They are great elements in our humanisation. The
power of conduct is another great element; and this was so felt
and fixed by Israel that we can never with justice refuse to permit Israel, in spite of all his shortcomings, to stand for it.

So you see that in being humanised we have to move along
several lines, and that on certain lines certain nations find their
strength and take a lead. We may elucidate the thing yet further. Nations now existing may be said to feel or to have felt
the power of this or that element in our humanisation so signally that they are characterised by it. No one who knows this
country would deny that it is characterised, in a remarkable degree, by a sense of the power of conduct. Our feeling for religion is one part of this; our industry is another. What foreigners
so much remark in us,—our public spirit, our love, amidst all
our liberty, for public order and for stability,—are parts of it
too. Then the power of beauty was so felt by the Italians that
their art revived, as we know, the almost lost idea of beauty,
and the serious and successful pursuit of it. Cardinal Antonelli,
speaking to me about the education of the common people in
Rome, said that they were illiterate indeed, but whoever mingled with them at any public show, and heard them pass judgment on the beauty or ugliness of what came before them,—

"*è brutto*," "*è bello*,"—would find that their judgment agreed admirably, in general, with just what the most cultivated people would say. Even at the present time, then, the Italians are pre-eminent in feeling the power of beauty. The power of knowl-
5   edge, in the same way, is eminently an influence with the Ger-mans. This by no means implies, as is sometimes supposed, a high and fine general culture. What it implies is a strong sense of the necessity of knowing *scientifically*, as the expression is, the things which have to be known by us; of knowing them
10 systematically, by the regular and right process, and in the only real way. And this sense the Germans especially have. Finally, there is the power of social life and manners. And even the Athenians themselves, perhaps, have hardly felt this power so much as the French.
15   Voltaire, in a famous passage where he extols the age of Louis the Fourteenth and ranks it with the chief epochs in the civilisa-tion of our race, has to specify the gift bestowed on us by the age of Louis the Fourteenth, as the age of Pericles, for instance, bestowed on us its art and literature, and the Italian Renascence
20 its revival of art and literature. And Voltaire shows all his acute-ness in fixing on the gift to name. It is not the sort of gift which we expect to see named. The great gift of the age of Louis the Fourteenth to the world, says Voltaire, was this: *l'esprit de so-ciété*, the spirit of society, the social spirit. And another French
25 writer, looking for the good points in the old French nobility, remarks that this at any rate is to be said in their favour: they established a high and charming ideal of social intercourse and manners, for a nation formed to profit by such an ideal, and which has profited by it ever since. And in America, perhaps,
30 we see the disadvantages of having social equality before there has been any such high standard of social life and manners formed.
        We are not disposed in England, most of us, to attach all this importance to social intercourse and manners. Yet Burke says:
35 "There ought to be a system of manners in every nation which a well-formed mind would be disposed to relish." And the power of social life and manners is truly, as we have seen, one of the great elements in our humanisation. Unless we have cul-

tivated it, we are incomplete. The impulse for cultivating it is not, indeed, a moral impulse. It is by no means identical with the moral impulse to help our neighbour and to do him good. Yet in many ways it works to a like end. It brings men together, makes them feel the need of one another, be considerate of one another, understand one another. But, above all things, it is a promoter of equality. It is by the humanity of their manners that men are made equal. "A man thinks to show himself my equal," says Goethe, "by being *grob*,—that is to say, coarse and rude; he does not show himself my equal, he shows himself *grob*." But a community having humane manners is a community of equals, and in such a community great social inequalities have really no meaning, while they are at the same time a menace and an embarrassment to perfect ease of social intercourse. A community with the spirit of society is eminently, therefore, a community with the spirit of equality. A nation with a genius for society, like the French or the Athenians, is irresistibly drawn towards equality. From the first moment when the French people, with its congenital sense for the power of social intercourse and manners, came into existence, it was on the road to equality. When it had once got a high standard of social manners abundantly established, and at the same time the natural, material necessity for the feudal inequality of classes and property pressed upon it no longer, the French people introduced equality and made the French Revolution. It was not the spirit of philanthropy which mainly impelled the French to that Revolution, neither was it the spirit of envy, neither was it the love of abstract ideas, though all these did something towards it; but what did most was the spirit of society.

The well-being of the many comes out more and more distinctly, in proportion as time goes on, as the object we must pursue. An individual or a class, concentrating their efforts upon their own well-being exclusively, do but beget troubles both for others and for themselves also. No individual life can be truly prosperous, passed, as Obermann says, in the midst of men who suffer; *passée au milieu des générations qui souffrent*. To the noble soul, it cannot be happy; to the ignoble, it cannot be secure. Socialistic and communistic schemes have generally, how-

ever, a fatal defect; they are content with too low and material
a standard of well-being. That instinct of perfection, which is
the master-power in humanity, always rebels at this, and frus-
trates the work. Many are to be made partakers of well-being,
5   true; but the ideal of well-being is not to be, on that account,
lowered and coarsened. M. de Laveleye, the political economist,
who is a Belgian and a Protestant, and whose testimony therefore we may the more readily take about France, says that
France, being the country of Europe where the soil is more
10 divided than anywhere except in Switzerland and Norway, is
at the same time the country where material well-being is most
widely spread, where wealth has of late years increased most,
and where population is least outrunning the limits which, for
the comfort and progress of the working classes themselves,
15 seem necessary. This may go for a good deal. It supplies an answer to what Sir Erskine May says about the bad effects of
equality upon French prosperity. But I will quote to you from
Mr. Hamerton what goes, I think, for yet more. Mr. Hamerton
is an excellent observer and reporter, and has lived for many
20 years in France. He says of the French peasantry that they are
exceedingly ignorant. So they are. But he adds: "They are at
the same time full of intelligence; their manners are excellent,
they have delicate perceptions, they have tact, they have a certain refinement which a brutalised peasantry could not possibly
25 have. If you talk to one of them at his own home, or in his field,
he will enter into conversation with you quite easily, and sustain his part in a perfectly becoming way, with a pleasant combination of dignity and quiet humour. The interval between
him and a Kentish labourer is enormous."
30   This is indeed worth your attention. Of course all mankind
are, as Mr. Gladstone says, of our own flesh and blood. But you
know how often it happens in England that a cultivated person,
a person of the sort that Mr. Charles Sumner describes, talking
to one of the lower class, or even of the middle class, feels, and
35 cannot but feel, that there is somehow a wall of partition between himself and the other, that they seem to belong to two
different worlds. Thoughts, feelings, perceptions, susceptibilities, language, manners,—everything is different. Whereas, with

a French peasant, the most cultivated man may find himself in sympathy, may feel that he is talking to an equal. This is an experience which has been made a thousand times, and which may be made again any day. And it may be carried beyond the range of mere conversation, it may be extended to things like pleasures, recreations, eating and drinking, and so on. In general the pleasures, recreations, eating and drinking of English people, when once you get below that class which Mr. Charles Sumner calls the class of gentlemen, are to one of that class unpalatable and impossible. In France there is not this incompatibility. Whether he mix with high or low, the gentleman feels himself in a world not alien or repulsive, but a world where people make the same sort of demands upon life, in things of this sort, which he himself does. In all these respects France is the country where the people, as distinguished from a wealthy refined class, most lives what we call a humane life, the life of civilised man.

Of course, fastidious persons can and do pick holes in it. There is just now, in France, a *noblesse* newly revived, full of pretension, full of airs and graces and disdains; but its sphere is narrow, and out of its own sphere no one cares very much for it. There is a general equality in a humane kind of life. This is the secret of the passionate attachment with which France inspires all Frenchmen, in spite of her fearful troubles, her checked prosperity, her disconnected units, and the rest of it. There is so much of the goodness and agreeableness of life there, and for so many. It is the secret of her having been able to attach so ardently to her the German and Protestant people of Alsace, while we have been so little able to attach the Celtic and Catholic people of Ireland. France brings the Alsatians into a social system so full of the goodness and agreeableness of life; we offer to the Irish no such attraction. It is the secret, finally, of the prevalence which we have remarked in other continental countries of a legislation tending, like that of France, to social equality. The social system which equality creates in France is, in the eyes of others, such a giver of the goodness and agreeableness of life, that they seek to get the goodness by getting the equality.

Yet France has had her fearful troubles, as Sir Erskine May justly says. She suffers too, he adds, from demoralisation and intellectual stoppage. Let us admit, if he likes, this to be true also. His error is that he attributes all this to equality. Equality, as we have seen, has brought France to a really admirable and enviable pitch of humanisation in one important line. And this, the work of equality, is so much a good in Sir Erskine May's eyes, that he has mistaken it for the whole of which it is a part, frankly identifies it with civilisation, and is inclined to pronounce France the most civilised of nations.

But we have seen how much goes to full humanisation, to true civilisation, besides the power of social life and manners. There is the power of conduct, the power of intellect and knowledge, the power of beauty. The power of conduct is the greatest of all. And without in the least wishing to preach, I must observe, as a mere matter of natural fact and experience, that for the power of conduct France has never had anything like the same sense which she has had for the power of social life and manners. Michelet, himself a Frenchman, gives us the reason why the Reformation did not succeed in France. It did not succeed, he says, because *la France ne voulait pas de réforme morale*—moral reform France would not have; and the Reformation was above all a moral movement. The sense in France for the power of conduct has not greatly deepened, I think, since. The sense for the power of intellect and knowledge has not been adequate either. The sense for beauty has not been adequate. Intelligence and beauty have been, in general, but so far reached as they can be and are reached by men who, of the elements of perfect humanisation, lay thorough hold upon one only,—the power of social intercourse and manners. I speak of France in general; she has had, and she has, individuals who stand out and who form exceptions. Well then, if a nation laying no sufficient hold upon the powers of beauty and knowledge, and a most failing and feeble hold upon the power of conduct, comes to demoralisation and intellectual stoppage and fearful troubles, we need not be inordinately surprised. What we should rather marvel at is the healing and bountiful operation of Nature, whereby the laying firm hold on one real ele-

ment in our humanisation has had for France results so beneficent.

And thus, when Sir Erskine May gets bewildered between
France's equality and fearful troubles on the one hand, and the
civilisation of France on the other, let us suggest to him that
perhaps he is bewildered by his data because he combines them
ill. France has not exemplary disaster and ruin as the fruits of
equality, and at the same time, and independently of this, an
exemplary civilisation. She has a large measure of happiness and
success as the fruits of equality, and she has a very large measure of dangers and troubles as the fruits of something else.

We have more to do, however, than to help Sir Erskine May
out of his scrape about France. We have to see whether the
considerations which we have been employing may not be of
use to us about England.

We shall not have much difficulty in admitting whatever
good is to be said of ourselves, and we will try not to be unfair
by excluding all that is not so favourable. Indeed, our less favourable side is the one which we should be the most anxious
to note, in order that we may mend it. But we will begin with
the good. Our people has energy and honesty as its good characteristics. We have a strong sense for the chief power in the
life and progress of man,—the power of conduct. So far we
speak of the English people as a whole. Then we have a rich,
refined, and splendid aristocracy. And we have, according to
Mr. Charles Sumner's acute and true remark, a class of gentlemen, not of the nobility, but well-bred, cultivated, and refined,
larger than is to be found in any other country. For these last
we have Mr. Sumner's testimony. As to the splendour of our
aristocracy, all the world is agreed. Then we have a middle class
and a lower class; and they, after all, are the immense bulk of
the nation.

Let us see how the civilisation of these classes appears to a
Frenchman, who has witnessed, in his own country, the considerable humanisation of these classes by equality. To such an
observer our middle class divides itself into a serious portion and
a gay or rowdy portion; both are a marvel to him. With the

gay or rowdy portion we need not much concern ourselves; we shall figure it to our minds sufficiently if we conceive it as the source of that war-song produced in these recent days of excitement:

5   "We don't want to fight, but by jingo, if we do,
         We've got the ships, we've got the men, and we've got the money too."

We may also partly judge its standard of life, and the needs of its nature, by the modern English theatre, perhaps the most con-
10 temptible in Europe. But the real strength of the English middle class is in its serious portion. And of this a Frenchman, who was here some little time ago as the correspondent, I think, of the *Siècle* newspaper, and whose letters were afterwards published in a volume, writes as follows. He had been attending some of
15 the Moody and Sankey meetings, and he says: "To understand the success of Messrs. Moody and Sankey, one must be familiar with English manners, one must know the mind-deadening in-fluence of a narrow Biblism, one must have experienced the sense of acute ennui, which the aspect and the frequentation of
20 this great division of English society produce in others, the want of elasticity and the chronic ennui which characterise this class itself, petrified in a narrow Protestantism and in a perpet-ual reading of the Bible."

       You know the French;—a little more Biblism, one may take
25 leave to say, would do them no harm. But an audience like this, —and here, as I said, is the advantage of an audience like this,— will have no difficulty in admitting the amount of truth which there is in the Frenchman's picture. It is the picture of a class which, driven by its sense for the power of conduct, in the be-
30 ginning of the seventeenth century entered,—as I have more than once said, and as I may more than once have occasion in future to say,—*entered the prison of Puritanism, and had the key turned upon its spirit there for two hundred years.* They did not know, good and earnest people as they were, that to the
35 building up of human life there belong all those other powers also,—the power of intellect and knowledge, the power of beauty, the power of social life and manners. And something,

by what they became, they gained, and the whole nation with
them; they deepened and fixed for this nation the sense of conduct. But they created a type of life and manners, of which they
themselves indeed are slow to recognise the faults, but which is
fatally condemned by its hideousness, its immense ennui, and   5
against which the instinct of self-preservation in humanity
rebels.

Partisans fight against facts in vain. Mr. Goldwin Smith, a
writer of eloquence and power, although too prone to acerbity,
is a partisan of the Puritans, and of the Nonconformists who are   10
the special inheritors of the Puritan tradition. He angrily resents
the imputation upon that Puritan type of life, by which the life
of our serious middle class has been formed, that it was doomed
to hideousness, to immense ennui. He protests that it had beauty,
amenity, accomplishment. Let us go to facts. Charles the First,   15
who, with all his faults, had the just idea that art and letters are
great civilisers, made, as you know, a famous collection of pictures,—our first National Gallery. It was, I suppose, the best
collection at that time north of the Alps. It contained nine
Raphaels, eleven Correggios, twenty-eight Titians. What be-   20
came of that collection? The journals of the House of Commons will tell you. There you may see the Puritan Parliament
disposing of this Whitehall or York House collection as follows: "Ordered, that all such pictures and statues there as are
without any superstition, shall be forthwith sold. . . . Ordered,   25
that all such pictures there as have the representation of the
Second Person in Trinity upon them, shall be forthwith burnt.
Ordered, that all such pictures there as have the representation of the Virgin Mary upon them, shall be forthwith burnt."
There we have the weak side of our parliamentary government   30
and our serious middle class. We are incapable of sending Mr.
Gladstone to be tried at the Old Bailey because he proclaims his
antipathy to Lord Beaconsfield. A majority in our House of
Commons is incapable of hailing, with frantic laughter and ap-
plause, a string of indecent jests against Christianity and its   35
Founder. But we are not, or were not, incapable of producing
a Parliament which burns or sells the masterpieces of Italian art.
And one may surely say of such a Puritan Parliament, and of

those who determine its line for it, that they had not the spirit of beauty.

What shall we say of amenity? Milton was born a humanist, but the Puritan temper, as we know, mastered him. There is nothing more unlovely and unamiable than Milton the Puritan disputant. Some one answers his *Doctrine and Discipline of Divorce.* "I mean not," rejoins Milton, "to dispute philosophy with this pork, who never read any." However, he does reply to him, and throughout the reply Milton's great joke is, that his adversary, who was anonymous, is a serving-man. "Finally, he winds up his text with much doubt and trepidation; for it may be his trenchers were not scraped, and that which never yet afforded corn of savour to his noddle,—the salt-cellar,—was not rubbed; and therefore, in this haste, easily granting that his answers fall foul upon each other, and praying you would not think he writes as a prophet, but as a man, he runs to the black jack, fills his flagon, spreads the table, and serves up dinner." There you have the same spirit of urbanity and amenity, as much of it, and as little, as generally informs the religious controversies of our Puritan middle class to this day.

But Mr. Goldwin Smith insists, and picks out his own exemplar of the Puritan type of life and manners; and even here let us follow him. He picks out the most favourable specimen he can find,—Colonel Hutchinson, whose well-known memoirs, written by his widow, we have all read with interest. "Lucy Hutchinson," says Mr. Goldwin Smith, "is painting what she thought a perfect Puritan would be; and her picture presents to us not a coarse, crop-eared, and snuffling fanatic, but a highly accomplished, refined, gallant, and most amiable, though religious and seriously minded, gentleman." Let us, I say, in this example of Mr. Goldwin Smith's own choosing, lay our finger upon the points where this type deflects from the truly humane ideal.

Mrs. Hutchinson relates a story which gives us a good notion of what the amiable and accomplished social intercourse, even of a picked Puritan family, was. Her husband was governor of Nottingham. He had occasion, she says, "to go and break up a private meeting in the cannoneer's chamber"; and in the can-

noneer's chamber "were found some notes concerning pædobaptism, which, being brought into the governor's lodgings, his
wife having perused them and compared them with the Scriptures, found not what to say against the truths they asserted
concerning the misapplication of that ordinance to infants." 5
Soon afterwards she expects her confinement, and communi-
cates the cannoneer's doubts about pædobaptism to her husband.
The fatal cannoneer makes a breach in him too. "Then he
bought and read all the eminent treatises on both sides, which
at that time came thick from the presses, and still was cleared 10
in the error of the pædobaptists." Finally, Mrs. Hutchinson is
confined. Then the governor "invited all the ministers to dinner, and propounded his doubt and the ground thereof to them.
None of them could defend their practice with any satisfactory
reason, but the tradition of the Church from the primitive times, 15
and their main buckler of federal holiness, which Tombs and
Denne had excellently overthrown. He and his wife then, professing themselves unsatisfied, desired their opinions." With the
opinions I will not trouble you, but hasten to the result:
"Whereupon that infant was not baptized." 20

No doubt to a large division of English society at this very
day, that sort of dinner and discussion, and, indeed, the whole
manner of life and conversation here suggested by Mrs. Hutchinson's narrative, will seem both natural and amiable, and such
as to meet the needs of man as a religious and social creature. 25
You know the conversation which reigns in thousands of middle-class families at this hour, about nunneries, teetotalism, the
confessional, eternal punishment, ritualism, disestablishment. It
goes wherever the class goes which is moulded on the Puritan
type of life. In the long winter evenings of Toronto Mr. Gold- 30
win Smith has had, probably, abundant experience of it. What
is its enemy? The instinct of self-preservation in humanity. Men
make crude types and try to impose them, but to no purpose.
"*L'homme s'agite, Dieu le mène,*" says Bossuet. "There are
many devices in a man's heart; nevertheless the counsel of the 35
Eternal, that shall stand." Those who offer us the Puritan type
of life offer us a religion not true, the claims of intellect and
knowledge not satisfied, the claim of beauty not satisfied, the

claim of manners not satisfied. In its strong sense for conduct
that life touches truth; but its other imperfections hinder it
from employing even this sense aright. The type mastered our
nation for a time. Then came the reaction. The nation said:
5 "This type, at any rate, is amiss; we are not going to be all like
that!" The type retired into our middle class, and fortified itself
there. It seeks to endure, to emerge, to deny its own imperfections, to impose itself again;—impossible! If we continue to live,
we must outgrow it. The very class in which it is rooted, our
10 middle class, will have to acknowledge the type's inadequacy,
will have to acknowledge the hideousness, the immense ennui
of the life which this type has created, will have to transform
itself thoroughly. It will have to admit the large part of truth
which there is in the criticisms of our Frenchman, whom we
15 have too long forgotten.

After our middle class he turns his attention to our lower
class. And of the lower and larger portion of this, the portion
not bordering on the middle class and sharing its faults, he says:
"I consider this multitude to be absolutely devoid, not only of
20 political principles, but even of the most simple notions of good
and evil. Certainly it does not appeal, this mob, to the principles
of '89, which you English make game of; it does not insist on
the rights of man; what it wants is beer, gin, and *fun*."[1]

That is a description of what Mr. Bright would call the re-
25 siduum, only our author seems to think the residuum a very
large body. And its condition strikes him with amazement and
horror. And surely well it may. Let us recall Mr. Hamerton's
account of the most illiterate class in France; what an amount
of civilisation they have notwithstanding! And this is always to
30 be understood, in hearing or reading a Frenchman's praise of
England. He envies our liberty, our public spirit, our trade, our
stability. But there is always a reserve in his mind. He never
means for a moment that he would like to change with us. Life
seems to him so much better a thing in France for so many more
35 people, that, in spite of the fearful troubles of France, it is best
to be a Frenchman. A Frenchman might agree with Mr. Cob-

[1] So in the original.

den, that life is good in England for those people who have at
least £5000 a year. But the civilisation of that immense majority who have not £5000 a year, or £500, or even £100,—of
our middle and lower class,—seems to him too deplorable.

And now what has this condition of our middle and lower
classes to tell us about equality? How is it, must we not ask, how
is it that, being without fearful troubles, having so many
achievements to show and so much success, having as a nation
a deep sense for conduct, having signal energy and honesty,
having a splendid aristocracy, having an exceptionally large
class of gentlemen, we are yet so little civilised? How is it that
our middle and lower classes, in spite of the individuals among
them who are raised by happy gifts of nature to a more humane
life, in spite of the seriousness of the middle class, in spite of the
honesty and power of true work, the *virtus verusque labor,*
which are to be found in abundance throughout the lower, do
yet present, as a whole, the characters which we have seen?

And really it seems as if the current of our discourse carried
us of itself to but one conclusion. It seems as if we could not
avoid concluding, that just as France owes her fearful troubles
to other things and her civilisedness to equality, so we owe our
immunity from fearful troubles to other things, and our uncivilisedness to inequality. "Knowledge is easy," says the wise man,
"to him that understandeth;" easy, he means, to him who will
use his mind simply and rationally, and not to make him think
he can know what he cannot, or to maintain, *per fas et nefas,* a
false thesis with which he fancies his interests to be bound up.
And to him who will use his mind as the wise man recom-
mends, surely it is easy to see that our shortcomings in civilisation are due to our inequality; or in other words, that the great
inequality of classes and property, which came to us from the
Middle Age and which we maintain because we have the religion of inequality, that this constitution of things, I say, has the
natural and necessary effect, under present circumstances, of
materialising our upper class, vulgarising our middle class, and
brutalising our lower class. And this is to fail in civilisation.

For only just look how the facts combine themselves. I have
said little as yet about our aristocratic class, except that it is

splendid. Yet these, "our often very unhappy brethren," as Burke calls them, are by no means matter for nothing but ecstasy. Our charity ought certainly, Burke says, to "extend a due and anxious sensation of pity to the distresses of the miserable great." Burke's extremely strong language about their miseries and defects I will not quote. For my part, I am always disposed to marvel that human beings, in a position so false, should be so good as these are. Their reason for existing was to serve as a number of centres in a world disintegrated after the ruin of the Roman Empire, and slowly re-constituting itself. Numerous centres of material force were needed, and these a feudal aristocracy supplied. Their large and hereditary estates served this public end. The owners had a positive function, for which their estates were essential. In our modern world the function is gone; and the great estates, with an infinitely multiplied power of ministering to mere pleasure and indulgence, remain. The energy and honesty of our race does not leave itself without witness in this class, and nowhere are there more conspicuous examples of individuals raised by happy gifts of nature far above their fellows and their circumstances. For distinction of all kinds this class has an esteem. Everything which succeeds they tend to welcome, to win over, to put on their side; genius may generally make, if it will, not bad terms for itself with them. But the total result of the class, its effect on society at large and on national progress, are what we must regard. And on the whole, with no necessary function to fulfil, never conversant with life as it really is, tempted, flattered, and spoiled from childhood to old age, our aristocratic class is inevitably materialised, and the more so the more the development of industry and ingenuity augments the means of luxury. Every one can see how bad is the action of such an aristocracy upon the class of newly enriched people, whose great danger is a materialistic ideal, just because it is the ideal they can easiest comprehend. Nor is the mischief of this action now compensated by signal services of a public kind. Turn even to that sphere which aristocracies think specially their own, and where they have under other circumstances been really effective,—the sphere of politics. When there is need, as now, for any large forecast of the course of human affairs, for an acquaintance with the ideas which in the end sway mankind, and for an estimate of their power, aristocracies are out of their element, and materialised aristocracies most of all. In the immense spiritual movement of our day, the English aristocracy, as I have elsewhere said, always reminds me of Pilate confronting the phenomenon of Christianity. Nor can a materialised class have any serious and fruitful sense for the power of beauty. They may imagine themselves to be in pursuit of beauty; but how often, alas, does the pursuit come to little more than dabbling a little in what they are pleased to call art, and making a great deal of what they are pleased to call love!

Let us return to their merits. For the power of manners an aristocratic class, whether materialised or not, will always, from its circumstances, have a strong sense. And although for this power of social life and manners, so important to civilisation, our English race has no special natural turn, in our aristocracy this power emerges and marks them. When the day of general humanisation comes, they will have fixed the standard of manners. The English simplicity, too, makes the best of the English aristocracy more frank and natural than the best of the like class anywhere else, and even the worst of them it makes free from the incredible fatuities and absurdities of the worst. Then the sense of conduct they share with their countrymen at large. In no class has it such trials to undergo; in none is it more often and more grievously overborne. But really the right comment on this is the comment of Pepys upon the evil courses of Charles the Second and the Duke of York and the court of that day: "At all which I am sorry; but it is the effect of idleness, and having nothing else to employ their great spirits upon."

Heaven forbid that I should speak in dispraise of that unique and most English class which Mr. Charles Sumner extols—the large class of gentlemen, not of the landed class or of the nobility, but cultivated and refined. They are a seemly product of the energy and of the power to rise in our race. Without, in general, rank and splendour and wealth and luxury to polish them, they have made their own the high standard of life and manners of an aristocratic and refined class. Not having all the

dissipations and distractions of this class, they are much more
seriously alive to the power of intellect and knowledge, to the
power of beauty. The sense of conduct, too, meets with fewer
trials in this class. To some extent, however, their contiguous-
5 ness to the aristocratic class has now the effect of materialising
them, as it does the class of newly enriched people. The most
palpable action is on the young amongst them, and on their
standard of life and enjoyment. But in general, for this whole
class, established facts, the materialism which they see regnant,
10 too much block their mental horizon, and limit the possibilities
of things to them. They are deficient in openness and flexibility
of mind, in free play of ideas, in faith and ardour. Civilised they
are, but they are not much of a civilising force; they are somehow bounded and ineffective.

15   So on the middle class they produce singularly little effect.
What the middle class sees is that splendid piece of materialism,
the aristocratic class, with a wealth and luxury utterly out of
their reach, with a standard of social life and manners, the offspring of that wealth and luxury, seeming utterly out of their
20 reach also. And thus they are thrown back upon themselves—
upon a defective type of religion, a narrow range of intellect
and knowledge, a stunted sense of beauty, a low standard of
manners. And the lower class see before them the aristocratic
class, and its civilisation, such as it is, even infinitely more out
25 of *their* reach than out of that of the middle class; while the life
of the middle class, with its unlovely types of religion, thought,
beauty, and manners, has naturally, in general, no great attrac-
tions for them either. And so they too are thrown back upon
themselves; upon their beer, their gin, and their *fun*. Now, then,
30 you will understand what I meant by saying that our inequality
materialises our upper class, vulgarises our middle class, brutalises our lower.

And the greater the inequality the more marked is its bad action upon the middle and lower classes. In Scotland the landed
35 aristocracy fills the scene, as is well known, still more than in
England; the other classes are more squeezed back and effaced.
And the social civilisation of the lower middle class and of the
poorest class, in Scotland, is an example of the consequences.

Compared with the same class even in England, the Scottish
lower middle class is most visibly, to vary Mr. Charles Sumner's
phrase, *less* well-bred, *less* careful in personal habits and in social conventions, *less* refined. Let any one who doubts it go,
after issuing from the aristocratic solitudes which possess Loch   5
Lomond, let him go and observe the shopkeepers and the middle class in Dumbarton, and Greenock, and Gourock, and the
places along the mouth of the Clyde. And for the poorest class,
who that has seen it can ever forget the hardly human horror,
the abjection and uncivilisedness of Glasgow?   10
    What a strange religion, then, is our religion of inequality!
Romance often helps a religion to hold its ground, and romance
is good in its way; but ours is not even a romantic religion. No
doubt our aristocracy is an object of very strong public interest.
The *Times* itself bestows a leading article by way of epithala-   15
mium on the Duke of Norfolk's marriage. And those journals
of a new type, full of talent, and which interest me particularly
because they seem as if they were written by the young lion of
our youth,—the young lion grown mellow and, as the French
say, *viveur*, arrived at his full and ripe knowledge of the world,   20
and minded to enjoy the smooth evening of his days,—those
journals, in the main a sort of social gazette of the aristocracy,
are apparently not read by that class only which they most concern, but are read with great avidity by other classes also. And
the common people too have undoubtedly, as Mr. Gladstone   25
says, a wonderful preference for a lord. Yet our aristocracy,
from the action upon it of the Wars of the Roses, the Tudors,
and the political necessities of George the Third, is for the
imagination a singularly modern and uninteresting one. Its
splendour of station, its wealth, show, and luxury, is then what   30
the other classes really admire in it; and this is not an elevating
admiration. Such an admiration will never lift us out of our vulgarity and brutality, if we chance to be vulgar and brutal to
start with; it will rather feed them and be fed by them. So that
when Mr. Gladstone invites us to call our love of inequality "the   35
complement of the love of freedom or its negative pole, or the
shadow which the love of freedom casts, or the reverberation
of its voice in the halls of the constitution," we must surely an-

swer that all this mystical eloquence is not in the least necessary
to explain so simple a matter; that our love of inequality is really
the vulgarity in us, and the brutality, admiring and worshipping
the splendid materiality.

5   Our present social organisation, however, will and must endure until our middle class is provided with some better ideal of
life than it has now. Our present organisation has been an appointed stage in our growth; it has been of good use, and has
enabled us to do great things. But the use is at an end, and the
10   stage is over. Ask yourselves if you do not sometimes feel in
yourselves a sense, that in spite of the strenuous efforts for good
of so many excellent persons amongst us, we begin somehow to
flounder and to beat the air; that we seem to be finding ourselves stopped on this line of advance and on that, and to be
15   threatened with a sort of standstill. It is that we are trying to
live on with a social organisation of which the day is over. Certainly equality will never of itself alone give us a perfect civilisation. But, with such inequality as ours, a perfect civilisation is
impossible.

20   To that conclusion, facts, and the stream itself of this discourse, do seem, I think, to carry us irresistibly. We arrive at it
because they so choose, not because we so choose. Our tendencies are all the other way. We are all of us politicians, and in
one of two camps, the Liberal or the Conservative. Liberals
25   tend to accept the middle class as it is, and to praise the nonconformists; while Conservatives tend to accept the upper class as
it is, and to praise the aristocracy. And yet here we are at the
conclusion, that whereas one of the great obstacles to our civilisation is, as I have often said, British nonconformity, another
30   main obstacle to our civilisation is British aristocracy! And this
while we are yet forced to recognise excellent special qualities
as well as the general English energy and honesty, and a number of emergent humane individuals, in both nonconformists
and aristocracy. Clearly such a conclusion can be none of our
35   own seeking.

Then again, to remedy our inequality, there must be a change
in the law of bequest, as there has been in France; and the faults
and inconveniences of the present French law of bequest are

obvious. It tends to over-divide property; it is unequal in operation, and can be eluded by people limiting their families; it makes the children, however ill they may behave, independent of the parent. To be sure, Mr. Mill and others have shown that a law of bequest fixing the maximum, whether of land or money, which any one individual may take by bequest or inheritance, but in other respects leaving the testator quite free, has none of the inconveniences of the French law, and is in every way preferable. But evidently these are not questions of practical politics. Just imagine Lord Hartington going down to Glasgow, and meeting his Scotch Liberals there, and saying to them: "You are ill at ease, and you are calling for change, and very justly. But the cause of your being ill at ease is not what you suppose. The cause of your being ill at ease is the profound imperfectness of your social civilisation. Your social civilisation is indeed such as I forbear to characterise. But the remedy is not disestablishment. The remedy is social equality. Let me direct your attention to a reform in the law of bequest and entail." One can hardly speak of such a thing without laughing. No, the matter is at present one for the thoughts of those who think. It is a thing to be turned over in the minds of those who, on the one hand, have the spirit of scientific inquirers, bent on seeing things as they really are; and, on the other hand, the spirit of friends of the humane life, lovers of perfection. To your thoughts I commit it. And perhaps, the more you think of it, the more you will be persuaded that Menander showed his wisdom quite as much when he said *Choose equality*, as when he assured us that *Evil communications corrupt good manners*.

Johnson's *Lives of the Poets*

Preface

Da mihi, Domine, scire quod sciendum est—"Grant that the knowledge I get may be the knowledge which is worth having!"—the spirit of that prayer ought to rule our education. How little it does rule it, every discerning man will acknowl-
5 edge. Life is short, and our faculties of attention and of recollection are limited; in education we proceed as if our life were endless, and our powers of attention and recollection inexhaustible. We have not time or strength to deal with half of the matters which are thrown upon our minds, they prove a useless
10 load to us. When some one talked to Themistocles of an art of memory, he answered: "Teach me rather to forget!" The sarcasm well criticises the fatal want of proportion between what we put into our minds and their real needs and powers.

From the time when first I was led to think about education,
15 this want of proportion is what has most struck me. It is the great obstacle to progress, yet it is by no means remarked and contended against as it should be. It hardly begins to present itself until we pass beyond the strict elements of education,—beyond the acquisition, I mean, of reading, of writing, and of
20 calculating so far as the operations of common life require. But the moment we pass beyond these, it begins to appear. Languages, grammar, literature, history, geography, mathematics, the knowledge of nature,—what of these is to be taught, how much, and how? There is no clear, well-grounded consent. The
25 same with religion. Religion is surely to be taught, but what of it is to be taught, and how? A clear, well-grounded consent is again wanting. And taught in such fashion as things are now, how often must a candid and sensible man, if he were offered an art of memory to secure all that he has learned of them, be

inclined, as to a very great deal of it, to say with Themistocles: "Teach me rather to forget!"

In England the common notion seems to be that education is advanced in two ways principally: by for ever adding fresh matters of instruction, and by preventing uniformity. I should be inclined to prescribe just the opposite course; to prescribe a severe limitation of the number of matters taught, a severe uniformity in the line of study followed. Wide ranging, and the multiplication of matters to be investigated, belong to private study,—to the development of special aptitudes in the individual learner, and to the demands which they raise in him. But separate from all this should be kept the broad plain lines of study for almost universal use. I say *almost* universal, because they must of necessity vary a little with the varying conditions of men. Whatever the pupil finds set out for him upon these lines, he should learn; therefore it ought not to be too much in quantity. The essential thing is that it should be well chosen. If once we can get it well chosen, the more uniformly it can be kept to, the better. The teacher will be more at home; and besides, when we have once got what is good and suitable, there is small hope of gain, and great certainty of risk, in departing from it.

No such lines are laid out, and perhaps no one could be trusted to lay them out authoritatively. But to amuse oneself with laying them out in fancy is a good exercise for one's thoughts. One may lay them out for this or that description of pupil, in this or that branch of study. The wider the interest of the branch of study taken, and the more extensive the class of pupils concerned, the better for our purpose. Suppose we take the department of letters. It is interesting to lay out in one's mind the ideal line of study to be followed by all who have to learn Latin and Greek. But it is still more interesting to lay out the ideal line of study to be followed by all who are concerned with that body of literature which exists in English, because they are so much more numerous amongst us. The thing would be, one imagines, to begin with a very brief introductory sketch of our subject; then to fix a certain series of works to serve as what the French, taking an expression from the builder's busi-

ness, call *points de repère,*—points which stand as so many natural centres, and by returning to which we can always find our
way again, if we are embarrassed; finally, to mark out a number of illustrative and representative works, connecting them-
5 selves with each of these *points de repère.* In the introductory
sketch we are amongst generalities, in the group of illustrative
works we are amongst details; generalities and details have, both
of them, their perils for the learner. It is evident that, for purposes of education, the most important parts by far in our
10 scheme are what we call the *points de repère.* To get these
rightly chosen and thoroughly known is the great matter. For
my part, in thinking of this or that line of study which human
minds follow, I feel always prompted to seek, first and foremost, the leading *points de repère* in it.
15   In editing for the use of the young the group of chapters
which are now commonly distinguished as those of the Baby-
lonian Isaiah, I drew attention to their remarkable fitness for
serving as a point of this kind to the student of universal history.
But a work which by many is regarded as simply and solely a
20 document of religion, there is difficulty, perhaps, in employing
for historical and literary purposes. With works of a secular
character one is on safer ground. And for years past, whenever
I have had occasion to use Johnson's Lives of the Poets, the
thought has struck me how admirable a *point de repère,* or fixed
25 centre of the sort described above, these lives might be made to
furnish for the student of English literature. If we could but
take, I have said to myself, the most important of the lives in
Johnson's volumes, and leave out all the rest, what a text-book
we should have! The volumes at present are a work to stand in
30 a library, "a work which no gentleman's library should be without." But we want to get from them a text-book to be in the
hands of every one who desires even so much as a general acquaintance with English literature;—and so much acquaintance
as this who does not desire? The work as Johnson published it
35 is not fitted to serve as such a text-book; it is too extensive, and
contains the lives of many poets quite insignificant. Johnson
supplied lives of all whom the booksellers proposed to include
in their collection of British Poets; he did not choose the poets

himself, although he added two or three to those chosen by the booksellers. Whatever Johnson did in the department of literary biography and criticism possesses interest and deserves our attention. But in his Lives of the Poets there are six of pre-eminent interest, because they are the lives of men who, while the other names in the collection are of inferior rank, stand out as names of the first class in English literature: Milton, Dryden, Swift, Addison, Pope, Gray. These six writers differ among themselves, of course, in power and importance, and every one can see that if we were following certain modes of literary classification, Milton would have to be placed on a solitary eminence far above any of them. But if, without seeking a close view of individual differences, we form a large and liberal first class among English writers, all these six personages,—Milton, Dryden, Swift, Addison, Pope, Gray,—must, I think, be placed in it. Their lives cover a space of more than a century and a half, from 1608, the year of Milton's birth, down to 1771, the date of the death of Gray. Through this space of more than a century and a half the six lives conduct us. We follow the course of what Warburton well calls "the most agreeable subject in the world, which is literary history," and follow it in the lives of men of letters of the first class. And the writer of their lives is himself, too, a man of letters of the first class. Malone calls Johnson "the brightest ornament of the eighteenth century." He is justly to be called, at any rate, a man of letters of the first class, and the greatest power in English letters during the eighteenth century. And in his Lives of the Poets, in this mature and most characteristic work, not finished until 1781, and "which I wrote," as he himself tells us, "in my usual way, dilatorily and hastily, unwilling to work and working with vigour and haste," we have Johnson mellowed by years, Johnson in his ripeness and plenitude, treating the subject which he loved best and knew best. Much of it he could treat with the knowledge and sure tact of a contemporary; even from Milton and Dryden he was scarcely further separated than our generation is from Burns and Scott. Having all these recommendations, his Lives of the Poets do indeed truly stand for what Boswell calls them, "the work which of all Dr. Johnson's writings will perhaps be

read most generally and with most pleasure." And in the lives of
the six chief personages of the work, the lives of Milton, Dryden, Swift, Addison, Pope, and Gray, we have its very kernel
and quintessence. True, Johnson is not at his best in all of these
5 six lives equally; one might have wished, in particular, for a
better life of Gray from him. Still these six lives contain very
much of his best work, and it is not amiss, perhaps, to have specimens of a great man's less excellent work by the side of his best.
By their subjects, at any rate, the six lives are of pre-eminent
10 interest. In these we have Johnson's series of critical biographies
relieved of whatever is less significant, retaining nothing which
is not highly significant, brought within easy and convenient
compass, and admirably fitted to serve as a *point de repère*, a
fixed and thoroughly known centre of departure and return, to
15 the student of English literature.

I know of no such first-rate piece of literature, for supplying
in this way the wants of the literary student, existing at all in
any other language; or existing in our own language for any
period except the period which Johnson's six lives cover. A stu-
20 dent cannot read them without gaining from them, consciously
or unconsciously, an insight into the history of English literature and life. He would find great benefit, let me add, from
reading in connexion with each biography something of the
author with whom it deals; the first two books, say, of Para-
25 dise Lost, in connexion with the Life of Milton; Absalom and
Achitophel, and the Dedication of the Æneid, in connexion
with the Life of Dryden; in connexion with Swift's life, the
Battle of the Books; with Addison's, the Coverley Papers; with
Pope's, the Imitations of the Satires and Epistles of Horace. The
30 Elegy in a Country Churchyard everybody knows, and will
have it present to his mind when he reads the life of Gray. But
of the other works which I have mentioned how little can this
be said; to how many of us are Pope and Addison and Dryden
and Swift, and even Milton himself, mere names, about whose
35 date and history and supposed characteristics of style we may
have learnt by rote something from a handbook, but of the real
men and of the power of their works we know nothing! From
Johnson's biographies the student will get a sense of what the

real men were, and with this sense fresh in his mind he will find the occasion propitious for acquiring also, in the way pointed out, a sense of the power of their works.

This will seem to most people a very unambitious discipline. But the fault of most of the disciplines proposed in education is that they are by far too ambitious. Our improvers of education are almost always for proceeding by way of augmentation and complication; reduction and simplification, I say, is what is rather required. We give the learner too much to do, and we are over-zealous to tell him what he ought to think. Johnson, himself, has admirably marked the real line of our education through letters. He says in his life of Pope: "Judgment is forced upon us by experience. He that reads many books must compare one opinion or one style with another; and when he compares, must necessarily distinguish, reject, and prefer." Nothing could be better. The aim and end of education through letters is to get this experience. Our being told by another what its results will properly be found to be, is not, even if we are told aright, at all the same thing as getting the experience for ourselves. The discipline, therefore, which puts us in the way of getting it, cannot be called an inconsiderable or inefficacious one. We should take care not to imperil its acquisition by refusing to trust to it in its simplicity, by being eager to add, set right, and annotate. It is much to secure the reading, by young English people, of the lives of the six chief poets of our nation between the years 1650 and 1750, related by our foremost man of letters of the eighteenth century. It is much to secure their reading, under the stimulus of Johnson's interesting recital and forcible judgments, famous specimens of the authors whose lives are before them. Do not let us insist on also reviewing in detail and supplementing Johnson's work for them, on telling them what they ought really and definitively to think about the six authors and about the exact place of each in English literature. Perhaps our pupils are not ripe for it; perhaps, too, we have not Johnson's interest and Johnson's force; we are not the power in letters for our century which he was for his. We may be pedantic, obscure, dull,—everything that bores, rather than everything that stimulates; and so Johnson and his Lives will repel, and will not be received, because we insist on being received along with them.

And again, as we bar a learner's approach to Homer and Virgil by our *chevaux de frise* of elaborate grammar, so we are apt to stop his way to a piece of English literature by imbedding it in a mass of notes and additional matter. Mr. Croker's edition of Boswell's Life of Johnson is a good example of the labour and ingenuity which may be spent upon a masterpiece, with the result, after all, really of rather encumbering than illustrating it. All knowledge may be in itself good, but this kind of editing seems to proceed upon the notion that we have only one book to read in the course of our life, or else that we have eternity to read in. What can it matter to our generation whether it was Molly Aston or Miss Boothby whose preference for Lord Lyttelton made Johnson jealous, and produced in his Life of Lyttelton a certain tone of disparagement? With the young reader, at all events, our great endeavour should be to bring him face to face with masterpieces and to hold him there, not distracting or rebutting him with needless excursions or trifling details.

I should like to think that a number of young people might be brought to know an important period of our literary and intellectual history, through means of the lives of six of its leading and representative authors, told by a great man. I should like to think that they would go on, under the stimulus of the lives, to acquaint themselves with some leading and representative work of each author. In the six lives they would at least have secured, I think, a most valuable *point de repère* in the history of our English life and literature, a point from which afterwards to find their way; whether they might desire to ascend upwards to our anterior literature, or to come downwards to the literature of yesterday and of the present.

The six lives cover a period of literary and intellectual movement in which we are all profoundly interested. It is the passage of our nation to prose and reason; the passage to a type of thought and expression modern, European, and which on the whole is ours at the present day, from a type antiquated, peculiar, and which is ours no longer. The period begins with a prose like this of Milton: "They who to states and governors of the commonwealth direct their speech, high court of parliament! or wanting such access in a private condition, write that which they foresee may advance the public good; I suppose them, as at the beginning of no mean endeavour, not a little altered and moved inwardly in their minds." It ends with a prose like this of Smollett: "My spirit began to accommodate itself to my beggarly fate, and I became so mean as to go down towards Wapping, with an intention to inquire for an old schoolfellow, who, I understood, had got the command of a small coasting vessel then in the river, and implore his assistance." These are extreme instances; but they give us no unfaithful notion of the change in our prose between the reigns of Charles the First, and of George the Third. Johnson has recorded his own impression of the extent of the change and of its salutariness. Boswell gave him a book to read, written in 1702 by the English chaplain of a regiment stationed in Scotland. "It is sad stuff, sir," said Johnson, after reading it; "miserably written, as books in general then were. There is now an elegance of style universally diffused. No man now writes so ill as Martin's account of the Hebrides is written. A man could not write so ill if he should try. Set a merchant's clerk now to write, and he'll do better."

It seems as if a simple and natural prose were a thing which we might expect to come easy to communities of men, and to come early to them; but we know from experience that it is not so. Poetry and the poetic form of expression naturally precede prose. We see this in ancient Greece. We see prose forming itself there gradually and with labour; we see it passing through more than one stage before it attains to thorough propriety and lucidity, long after forms of consummate adequacy have already been reached and used in poetry. It is a people's growth in practical life, and its native turn for developing this life and for making progress in it, which awaken the desire for a good prose —a prose plain, direct, intelligible, serviceable. A dead language, the Latin, for a long time furnished the nations of Europe with an instrument of the kind, superior to any which they had yet discovered in their own tongue. But nations such as England and France, called to a great historic life, and with powerful interests and gifts either social or practical, were sure to feel the need of having a sound prose of their own, and to bring such a prose forth. They brought it forth in the seventeenth century; France first, afterwards England.

The Restoration marks the real moment of birth of our modern English prose. Men of lucid and direct mental habit there were, such as Chillingworth, in whom before the Restoration the desire and the commencement of a modern prose show themselves. There were men like Barrow, weighty and powerful, whose mental habit the old prose suited, who continued its forms and locutions after the Restoration. But the hour was come for the new prose, and it grew and prevailed. In Johnson's time its victory had long been assured, and the old style seemed barbarous. Johnson himself wrote a prose decidedly modern. The reproach conveyed in the phrase "Johnsonian English" must not mislead us. It is aimed at his words, not at his structure. In Johnson's prose the words are often pompous and long, but the structure is always plain and modern. The prose writers of the eighteenth century have indeed their mannerisms and phrases which are no longer ours. Johnson says of Milton's blame of the Universities for permitting young men designed for orders in the Church to act in plays: "This is sufficiently peevish in a man, who, when he mentions his exile from college, relates, with great luxuriance, the compensation which the pleasures of the theatre afford him. Plays were therefore only criminal when they were acted by academics." We should nowadays not say *peevish* here, nor *luxuriance*, nor *academics*. Yet the style is ours by its organism, if not by its phrasing. It is by its organism,—an organism opposed to length and involvement, and enabling us to be clear, plain, and short,—that English style after the Restoration breaks with the style of the times preceding it, finds the true law of prose, and becomes modern; becomes, in spite of superficial differences, the style of our own day.

Burnet has pointed out how we are under obligations in this matter to Charles the Second, whom Johnson described as "the last king of England who was a man of parts." A king of England by no means fulfils his whole duty by being a man of parts, or by loving and encouraging art, science, and literature.

Yet the artist and the student of the natural sciences will always
feel a kindness towards the two Charleses for their interest in
art and science; and modern letters, too, have their debt to
Charles the Second, although it may be quite true that that
prince, as Burnet says, "had little or no literature." "The King
had little or no literature, but," continues Burnet, "true and
good sense, and had got a right notion of style; for he was in
France at the time when they were much set on reforming their
language. It soon appeared that he had a true taste. So this
helped to raise the value of these men (Tillotson and others),
when the king approved of the style their discourses generally
ran in, which was clear, plain, and short."

It is the victory of this prose style, "clear, plain, and short,"
over what Burnet calls "the old style, long and heavy," which
is the distinguishing achievement, in the history of English letters, of the century following the Restoration. From the first it
proceeded rapidly and was never checked. Burnet says of the
Chancellor Finch, Earl of Nottingham: "He was long much
admired for his eloquence, but it was laboured and affected, and
he saw it much despised before he died." A like revolution of
taste brought about a general condemnation of our old prose
style, imperfectly disengaged from the style of poetry. By
Johnson's time the new style, the style of prose, was altogether
paramount in its own proper domain, and in its pride of victorious strength had invaded also the domain of poetry.

That invasion is now visited by us with a condemnation not
less strong and general than the condemnation which the eighteenth century passed upon the unwieldy prose of its predecessors. But let us be careful to do justice while we condemn. A
thing good in its own place may be bad out of it. Prose requires
a different style from poetry.

Poetry, no doubt, is more excellent in itself than prose. In
poetry man finds the highest and most beautiful expression of
that which is in him. We had far better poetry than the poetry
of the eighteenth century before that century arrived, we have
had better since it departed. Like the Greeks, and unlike the
French, we can point to an age of poetry anterior to our age of
prose, eclipsing our age of prose in glory, and fixing the future

character and conditions of our literature. We do well to place
our pride in the Elizabethan age and Shakespeare, as the Greeks
placed theirs in Homer. We did well to return in the present
century to the poetry of that older age for illumination and inspiration, and to put aside, in a great measure, the poetry and
poets intervening between Milton and Wordsworth. Milton, in
whom our great poetic age expired, was the last of the immor-
tals. Of the five poets whose lives follow his in our present volume, three, Dryden, Addison, and Swift, are eminent prose-
writers as well as poets; two of the three, Swift and Addison,
are far more distinguished as prose-writers than as poets. The
glory of English literature is in poetry, and in poetry the
strength of the eighteenth century does not lie.

Nevertheless, the eighteenth century accomplished for us an
immense literary progress, and its very shortcomings in poetry
were an instrument to that progress, and served it. The example of Germany may show us what a nation loses from having
no prose style. The practical genius of our people could not but
urge irresistibly to the production of a real prose style, because
for the purposes of modern life the old English prose, the prose
of Milton and Taylor, is cumbersome, unavailable, impossible.
A style of regularity, uniformity, precision, balance, was
wanted. These are the qualities of a serviceable prose style. Poetry has a different *logic,* as Coleridge said, from prose; poetical
style follows another law of evolution than the style of prose.
But there is no doubt that a style of regularity, uniformity, precision, balance, will acquire a yet stronger hold upon the mind
of a nation, if it is adopted in poetry as well as in prose, and so
comes to govern both. This is what happened in France. To the
practical, modern, and social genius of the French a true prose
was indispensable. They produced one of conspicuous excellence, supremely powerful and influential in the last century,
the first to come and standing at first alone, a modern prose.
French prose is marked in the highest degree by the qualities of
regularity, uniformity, precision, balance. With little opposition from any deep-seated and imperious poetic instincts, the
French made their poetry also conform to the law which was
moulding their prose. French poetry became marked with the

qualities of regularity, uniformity, precision, balance. This may have been bad for French poetry, but it was good for French prose. It heightened the perfection with which those qualities, the true qualities of prose, were impressed upon it. When England, at the Restoration, desired a modern prose, and began 5 to create it, our writers turned naturally to French literature, which had just accomplished the very process which engaged them. The King's acuteness and taste, as we have seen, helped. Indeed, to the admission of French influence of all kinds, Charles the Second's character and that of his court were but too fa- 10 vourable. But the influence of the French writers was at that moment on the whole fortunate, and seconded what was a vital and necessary effort in our literature. Our literature required a prose which conformed to the true law of prose; and that it might acquire this the more surely, it compelled poetry, as in 15 France, to conform itself to the law of prose likewise. The classic verse of French poetry was the Alexandrine, a measure favourable to the qualities of regularity, uniformity, precision, balance. Gradually a measure favourable to those very same qualities,—the ten-syllable couplet,—established itself as the 20 classic verse of England, until in the eighteenth century it had become the ruling form of our poetry. Poetry, or rather the use of verse, entered in a remarkable degree, during that century, into the whole of the daily life of the civilised classes; and the poetry of the century was a perpetual school of the qualities 25 requisite for a good prose, the qualities of regularity, uniformity, precision, balance. This may have been of no great service to English poetry, although to say that it has been of no service at all, to say that the eighteenth century has in no respect changed the conditions for English poetical style, or that it has 30 changed them for the worse, would be untrue. But it was undeniably of signal service to that which was the great want and work of the hour, English prose.

Do not let us, therefore, hastily despise Johnson and his century for their defective poetry and criticism of poetry. True, 35 Johnson is capable of saying: "Surely no man could have fancied that he read Lycidas with pleasure had he not known the author!" True, he is capable of maintaining "that the descrip-

tion of the temple in Congreve's 'Mourning Bride' was the finest poetical passage he had ever read—he recollected none in Shakespeare equal to it." But we are to conceive of Johnson and of his century as having a special task committed to them—the
5   establishment of English prose; and as capable of being warped and narrowed in their judgments of poetry by this exclusive task. Such is the common course and law of progress; one thing is done at a time, and other things are sacrificed to it. We must be thankful for the thing done, if it is valuable, and we must put
10 up with the temporary sacrifice of other things to this one. The other things will have their turn sooner or later. Above all, a nation with profound poetical instincts, like the English nation, may be trusted to work itself right again in poetry after periods of mistaken poetical practice. Even in the midst of an age of
15 such practice, and with his style frequently showing the bad influence of it, Gray was saved, we may say, and remains a poet whose work has high and pure worth, simply by his knowing the Greeks thoroughly, more thoroughly than any English poet had known them since Milton. Milton was a survivor from the
20 great age of poetry; Dryden, Addison, Pope, and Swift were mighty workers for the age of prose. Gray, a poet in the midst of the age of prose, a poet, moreover, of by no means the highest force and of scanty productiveness, nevertheless claims a place among the six chief personages of Johnson's Lives, be-
25 cause it was impossible for an English poet, even in that age, who knew the great Greek masters intimately, not to respond to their good influence, and to be rescued from the false poetical practice of his contemporaries. Of such avail to a nation are deep poetical instincts even in an age of prose. How much more
30 may they be trusted to assert themselves after the age of prose has ended, and to remedy any poetical mischief done by it! And meanwhile the work of the hour, the necessary and appointed work, has been done, and we have got our prose.

Let us always bear in mind, therefore, that the century so
35 well represented by Dryden, Addison, Pope, and Swift, and of which the literary history is so powerfully written by Johnson in his Lives, is a century of prose—a century of which the great work in literature was the formation of English prose. Johnson

was himself a labourer in this great and needful work, and was
ruled by its influences. His blame of genuine poets like Milton
and Gray, his over-praise of artificial poets like Pope, are to be
taken as the utterances of a man who worked for an age of
prose, who was ruled by its influences, and could not but be   5
ruled by them. Of poetry he speaks as a man whose sense for
that with which he is dealing is in some degree imperfect.

Yet even on poetry Johnson's utterances are valuable, because
they are the utterances of a great and original man. That indeed he was; and to be conducted by such a man through an im-   10
portant century cannot but do us good, even though our guide
may in some places be less competent than in others. Johnson
was the man of an age of prose. Furthermore, Johnson was a
strong force of conservatism and concentration, in an epoch
which by its natural tendencies seemed to be moving towards   15
expansion and freedom. But he was a great man, and great men
are always instructive. The more we study him, the higher will
be our esteem for the power of his mind, the width of his interests, the largeness of his knowledge, the freshness, fearlessness,
and strength of his judgments. The higher, too, will be our es-   20
teem for his character. His well-known lines on Levett's death,
beautiful and touching lines, are still more beautiful and touching because they recall a whole history of Johnson's goodness,
tenderness, and charity. Human dignity, on the other hand, he
maintained, we all know how well, through the whole long and   25
arduous struggle of his life, from his undergraduate days at Oxford, down to the *Jam moriturus* of his closing hour. His faults
and strangenesses are on the surface, and catch every eye. But
on the whole we have in him a fine and admirable type, worthy
to be kept in view for ever, of "the ancient and inbred integrity,   30
piety, good-nature and good-humour of the English people."

It was right that a Life of Johnson himself should stand as an
introduction to the present volume, and I long ago conceived
the wish that it should be the Life contributed by Lord Macaulay to the Encyclopædia Britannica. That Life is a work which   35
shows Macaulay at his very best; a work written when his style
was matured, and when his resources were in all their fulness.
The subject, too, was one which he knew thoroughly, and for

which he felt cordial sympathy; indeed by his mental habit Macaulay himself belonged, in many respects, to the eighteenth century rather than to our own. But the permission to use in this manner a choice work of Lord Macaulay's was no light fa-
5   vour to ask. However, in my zeal for the present volume I boldly asked it; and by the proprietors of the Encyclopædia Britannica, the Messrs. Black, it has been most kindly and generously accorded. I cannot sufficiently express my sense of obligation to them for their consent, and to Mr. Trevelyan for his
10 acquiescence in it. They have enabled me to fulfil a long-cherished desire, to tell the story of a whole important age of English literature in one compendious volume—itself, at the same time, a piece of English literature of the very first class. Such a work the reader has in his hands in the present volume; its editor
15 may well be fearful of injuring it by a single superfluous line, a single unacceptable word.

Advertisement
[1886]

I was asked to make a school-edition of these Lives by striking out a few things in them which might be thought objectionable reading for girls and young people, and by adding some
20 short notes. I have done both the one and the other, and I have also sought to relieve the young reader, for whose use this edition is designed, by omitting here and there a Latin extract, and still further by abridging certain details which Johnson himself treats as meriting little notice, and which have now almost en-
25 tirely lost their interest. Some abridgment has thus been applied to Johnson's copious quotations from the criticisms of Settle and Milbourne upon Dryden. My notes I have strictly limited to what seemed required for making the Lives intelligible and interesting to that class of readers which I have here in view.
30 These notes of mine are placed at the end of the volume, and are marked by an asterisk in the text; the notes marked by numbers, and placed at the foot of the text, are Johnson's own.

Irish Catholicism and British Liberalism

All roads, says the proverb, lead to Rome; and one finds in like manner that all questions raise the question of religion. We say to ourselves that religion is a subject where one is prone to be too copious and too pertinacious, where it is easy to do harm, easy to be misunderstood; that what we felt ourselves bound to say on it we have said, and that we will discuss it no longer. And one may keep one's word faithfully so far as the direct discussion of religion goes; but then the irrepressible subject manages to present itself for discussion indirectly. Questions of good government, social harmony, education, civilisation, come forth and ask to be considered; and very soon it appears that we cannot possibly treat them without returning to treat of religion. Ireland raises a crowd of questions thus complicated.

Our nation is not deficient in self-esteem, and certainly there is much in our achievements and prospects to give us satisfaction. But even to the most self-satisfied Englishman, Ireland must be an occasion, one would think, from time to time of mortifying thoughts. We may be conscious of nothing but the best intentions towards Ireland, the justest dealings with her. But how little she seems to appreciate them! We may talk, with the *Daily Telegraph*, of our "great and genial policy of conciliation" towards Ireland; we may say, with Mr. Lowe, that by their Irish policy in 1868 the Liberal Ministry, of whom he was one, "resolved to knit the hearts of the empire into one harmonious concord, and knitted they were accordingly." Only, unfortunately, the Irish themselves do not see the matter as we do. All that by our genial policy we seem to have succeeded in inspiring in the Irish themselves is an aversion to us so violent, that for England to incline one way is a sufficient reason to make Ireland incline another; and the obstruction offered by the Irish members in Parliament is really an expression, above all, of this uncontrollable antipathy. Nothing is more honourable to French civilisation than its success in attaching strongly to France,—France, Catholic and Celtic,—the German and Protestant Alsace. What a contrast to the humiliating failure of British civilisation to attach to Germanic and Protestant Great Britain the Celtic and Catholic Ireland!

For my part, I have never affected to be either surprised or indignant at the antipathy of the Irish to us. What they have had to suffer from us in past times, all the world knows. And now, when we profess to practise "a great and genial policy of conciliation" towards them, they are really governed by us in deference to the opinion and sentiment of the British middle class, and of the strongest part of this class, the Puritan community. I have pointed out this before, but in a book about schools, and which only those who are concerned with schools are likely to have read. Let me be suffered, therefore, to repeat it here. The opinion and sentiment of our middle class controls the policy of our statesmen towards Ireland. That policy does not represent the real mind of our leading statesmen, but the mind of the British middle class controlling the action of statesmen. The ability of our popular journalists and successful statesmen goes to putting the best colour they can upon the action so controlled. But a disinterested observer will see an action so controlled to be what it is, and will call it what it is. Now the great failure in our actual national life is the imperfect civilisation of our middle class. The great need of our time is the transformation of the British Puritan. Our Puritan middle class presents a defective type of religion, a narrow range of intellect and knowledge, a stunted sense of beauty, a low standard of manners. And yet it is in deference to the opinion and sentiment of such a class that we shape our policy towards Ireland. And we wonder at Ireland's antipathy to us! Nay, we expect Ireland to lend herself to the make-believe of our own journalists and statesmen, and to call our policy "genial."

The Irish Catholics, who are the immense majority in Ireland, want a Catholic university. Elsewhere both Catholics and

Protestants have universities where their sons may be taught by persons of their own form of religion. Catholic France allowed the Protestants of Alsace to have the Protestant university of Strasburg. Protestant Prussia allows the Catholics of the Rhine Province to have the Catholic university of Bonn. True, at 5 Strasburg, men of any religious persuasion might be appointed to teach anatomy or chemistry; true, at Bonn there is a Protestant faculty of theology as well as a Catholic. But I call Strasburg a Protestant and Bonn a Catholic university in this sense: that religion and the matters mixed up with religion are taught 10 in the one by Protestants, and in the other by Catholics. This is the guarantee which ordinary parents desire, and this at Bonn and at Strasburg they get. The Protestants of Ireland have in Trinity College, Dublin, a university where the teachers in all those matters which afford debatable ground between Catholic 15 and Protestant are Protestant. The Protestants of Scotland have universities of a like character. In England the members of the English Church have in Oxford and Cambridge universities where the teachers are almost wholly Anglican. Well, the Irish Catholics ask to be allowed the same thing. 20

There is extraordinary difficulty in getting this demand of theirs directly and frankly met. They are told that they want secondary schools even more than a university. That may be very true, but they do also want a university; and to ask for one institution is a simpler affair than to ask for a great many. They 25 are told they have the Queen's Colleges, invented expressly for Ireland. But they do not want colleges invented expressly for Ireland; they want colleges such as those which the English and Scotch have in Scotland and England. They are told that they may have a university of the London type, an examining board, 30 and perhaps a system of prizes. But all the world is not, like Mr. Lowe, enamoured of examining boards and prizes. The world in general much prefers to universities of the London type universities of the type of Strasburg, Bonn, Oxford; and the Irish are of the same mind as the world in general. They are told that 35 Mr. Gladstone's government offered them a university without theology, philosophy, or history, and that they refused it. But the world in general does not desire universities with theology, philosophy, and history left out; no more did Ireland. They are told that Trinity College, Dublin, is now an unsectarian university no more Protestant than Catholic, and that they may use Trinity College. But the teaching in Trinity College is, and long 5 will be (and very naturally), for the most part in the hands of Protestants; the whole character, tradition, and atmosphere of the place are Protestant. The Irish Catholics want to have on their side, too, a place where the university teaching is mainly in the hands of Catholics, and of which the character and atmo- 10 sphere shall be Catholic. But then they are asked whether they propose to do away with all the manifold and deep-rooted results of Protestant ascendency in Ireland, and they are warned that this would be a hard, nay, impossible matter. But they are not proposing anything so enormous and chimerical as to do 15 away with all the results of Protestant ascendency; they propose merely to put an end to one particular and very cruel result of it:—the result that they, the immense majority of the Irish people, have no university, while the Protestants in Ireland, the small minority, have one. For this plain hardship they 20 propose a plain remedy, and to their proposal they want a plain and straightforward answer.

And at last they get it. It is the papal answer: *Non possumus.* The English Ministry and Parliament may wish to give them what they demand, may think their claim just, but they *cannot* 25 give it them. In the mind and temper of the English people there is an unconquerable obstacle. "The claims of the Irish Roman Catholics," says the *Times,* "are inconsistent with the practical conditions of politics. It is necessary to repeat the simple fact that the temper of the people of Great Britain will not admit of 30 any endowment of Roman Catholic institutions. We should recognise the futility of contending against the most rooted of popular prejudices." "The demand for the State endowment of a Roman Catholic university, or of a Roman Catholic college," says the *Saturday Review,* "may be perfectly just, but it is at 35 the same time perfectly impracticable. The determination not to grant it may be quite illogical, but it is very firmly rooted." A radical and almost miraculous change in the mind and temper of the objectors is required, the *Saturday Review* adds, be-

fore such a thing can be granted. And in the House of Commons
Mr. Lowe said: "He would not argue whether it would be good
or bad to found out of public funds a Catholic university in Ireland; all he said was that it was not in the power of that House
to do so. Every one who knew the state of feeling in England,   5
Scotland, and a part of Ireland, must know that if the Government were to attempt such a thing, it would be running its head
against a wall, running upon its own destruction. It would be
perfectly impossible to carry any such measure through the
House." So that in our "genial policy of conciliation" towards   10
Ireland we are fettered by a *non possumus*. And the *non possumus* has provided itself with a short formula which is everywhere current among us, and which is this: "The Liberal party
has emphatically condemned religious endowment: the Protestants of Great Britain are emphatically hostile to the endow-   15
ment of Catholicism in any shape or form."

Let us leave for a moment the Protestants of Great Britain,
and let us think of the Liberal party only. Mr. Lowe has in the
Fortnightly Review, not many months ago, admirably set forth
the ideal of the Liberal party. "The ideal of the Liberal party,"   20
says Mr. Lowe, "consists in a view of things undisturbed and
undistorted by the promptings of interest or prejudice, in a
complete independence of all class interests, and in relying for
its success on the better feelings and higher intelligence of mankind." Happier words could not well be found; such is indeed   25
the true ideal of the Liberal party. Well, then, if the demand of
the Irish for a Catholic university is perfectly just, if the refusal
of it is perfectly illogical, how bitter it must be for a true Liberal to refuse it on the score of "the futility of contending
against the most rooted of popular prejudices"! To be undis-   30
turbed by the promptings of prejudice, and to rely for success
on the better feelings and higher intelligence of mankind, is the
very ideal which a true Liberal has to follow. And to the best
and most reflecting Liberals, accordingly, it seems to have been
given to see that, whether religious endowment be in itself good   35
or bad, Great Britain cannot justly refuse Ireland's claim for a
university of that kind which we ourselves, in England and
Scotland, prefer and adopt, and that to withhold it in deference

to popular prejudice is wrong. Mr. John Morley has recorded
Mr. Mill's opinion, declared in the last conversation which Mr.
Mill ever had with him. "He seemed disposed to think that the
most feasible solution of the Irish University question is a Catholic university, the restrictive and obscurantist tendencies of
which you may expect to have checked by the active competition of life with men trained in more enlightened systems."

Mr. Morley, who thus records Mr. Mill's opinion, has avowed
that he himself shares it. But of still more importance was the
practical adhesion given the other day in the House of Commons to Mr. Mill's opinion, by a certain number of English
Liberals, on the occasion of the O'Conor Don's resolution affirming the claims of Ireland to a Catholic university. A certain
number of English Liberal members, and amongst them men so
prominent and so ardently Liberal as Mr. Chamberlain and Sir
Charles Dilke, voted in favour of the O'Conor Don's resolution.
True, there was after all a great majority against the resolution.
The mass of Liberals, as well as the mass of Conservatives, were,
like the *Times*, for "recognising the futility of contending
against the most rooted of popular prejudices." The claims, the
just claims, of Ireland were sacrificed, as they have been sacrificed so often, to the opinion and sentiment of the British middle
class, of the British Puritan, who cries that if the State endows
a Roman Catholic university, the State is, "by force of the tax-
gatherer, compelling us to teach as truth that which we before
God assert without the slightest misgiving to be dismal error,
and making us parties to a lie." They were sacrificed to the prejudices of people whose narrowness and whose imperfect civilisation every cultivated man amongst us perceives and deplores.
And the continued rule of these prejudices is presented as a
fatality from which there can be no escape without a miracle.
But perhaps when Liberals of such mark as Sir Charles Dilke
and Mr. Chamberlain have the courage to set them at nought,
and have the courage to set at nought also, at least for this one
occasion, the formula that "the Liberal party has emphatically
condemned religious endowment," the miracle has begun.

At all events, few things in politics have ever given me more
pleasure than to see the aid courageously afforded to Irish Cath-

olics by this little band of advanced English Liberals. I do not profess to be a politician, but simply one of a disinterested class of observers, who, with no organised and embodied set of supporters to please, set themselves to observe honestly and to report faithfully the state and prospects of our civilisation. But the ideal of the Liberal party, as we have seen it declared by Mr. Lowe, is certainly also the ideal of such a class of observers. However, the practice of Liberals has seemed to me to fall a good deal short of this ideal, and, instead of relying for its success on the better feelings and higher intelligence of mankind, to lend itself very often to the wishes of narrow and prejudiced people, in the hope of finding its account by so doing. And I have again and again, for a good many years past, being a humble follower of the true Liberal ideal, remarked that by their actual practice our Liberals, however prosperous they might seem, could not really succeed;—that their doings wanted more of simple and sincere thought to direct them, that their performance was far less valuable than they supposed, and that it and they were more and more losing their charm for the nation. This I said in their prosperity. But in their present adversity I prefer to remember only that their cause is in a general way, at any rate, mine also; that I serve and would fain follow the Liberal ideal.

And as we are told that, in the depressed days of Israel, "they that feared the Eternal spake often one to another," to confirm one another in a belief of the final triumph of their cause, so, in the present evil days, Liberals ought to speak often one to another of relying upon the better feelings and higher intelligence of mankind, that we may keep up our faith and spirits. Or if, in addressing advanced Liberals, it should seem out of place to cite the example of a set of antiquated Jewish religionists, let me quote the comfortable words of a blameless Liberal, Condorcet, who assures us that "the natural order of things tends to bring general opinion more and more into conformity with truth." *L'ordre naturel tend à rendre l'opinion générale de plus en plus conforme à la vérité.* And the politician who would be of real service must manage, Condorcet says, to get at this *vérité*, this truth. *Connaître la vérité pour y conformer l'ordre de la société,*

telle est l'unique source du bonheur public. Therefore, when
Mr. Chamberlain and Sir Charles Dilke and other Liberal politicians have just given a signal proof of their faith in justice and
reason, and of their willingness to contend for them "against
5 the most rooted of popular prejudices," let us seize the opportunity of fortifying them and ourselves in the conviction that
"the natural order of things tends to bring general opinion more
and more into conformity with truth," and that it is an excellent
principle in government to believe that to what is reasonable
10 one may always hope to make the majority of men at last come
in. Let us see if this may not even lead us to recast entirely the
programme of our practical Liberalism, and to use our present
dull times for bringing it more into correspondence with the
true Liberal ideal. Perhaps the weakness of Liberalism will be
15 found to lie in its having followed hitherto with a too eager
solicitude the wishes of a class narrow-minded and imperfectly
civilised; its strength in the future must lie more in complying
with the order which for our progress appears the true one, and
in co-operating with nature to bring general opinion into har-
20 mony with it.

For take the formula which is supposed to govern the action
of British Liberalism towards Irish Catholicism, and which long
has governed it, but which a small band of Liberal heroes the
other day set at nought: "The Liberal party has emphatically
25 condemned religious endowment; the Protestants of Great Britain are implacably hostile to the endowment of Catholicism in
any shape or form."

This may seem a convenient formula for Liberals to adopt,
because it enables us to act in concert with English Noncon-
30 formity and Scotch Puritanism. But evidently it tends to divide
British Liberals from Irish Liberals. It costs British Liberals the
support of Liberalism in Ireland, which they can ill afford to do
without. Therefore it extremely behoves them to examine the
formula well, and to ascertain how far it corresponds with the
35 natural truth of things; for this is always and surely tending, as
we have seen, to prevail. And if the formula has natural truth
on its side, then there is good reason for hoping that the Irish
Catholics, however ignorant, may at last come into it and be

reconciled to its operation. But if it has not natural truth on its side, then the irritation and estrangement which its operation must produce in Ireland will be perpetual. On the other hand, British Puritanism, however prejudiced, may be trusted to resign itself at some distant day to the abandonment of the formula if it is false, because time and nature will beneficently help towards such abandonment.

"The Liberal party has emphatically condemned religious endowment." This maxim is not even now quite true in fact, for many members of the Liberal party favour religious endowment. And if that view of things out of which the maxim arises turns out to be erroneous, there is no reason why even those Liberals who have adopted the maxim should not drop it; their cause, and their work, and their reason for existing are in no wise bound up with it. But it is not denied that "the Protestants," or at any rate the Puritans, "of Great Britain, are implacably hostile to the endowment of Catholicism in any shape or form." And however that view out of which their hostility arises may be shown to be erroneous, there is every reason why they should long and obstinately shut their minds to the thought of abandoning that view and that hostility, because their cause, and their work, and their reason for existing are in great measure bound up with it. Still, if there appears to be no rational ground for objecting to the endowment of Catholicism in particular, any more than to religious endowment in general, but, on the contrary, rational ground for allowing both the one and the other, Liberals ought not to set themselves stubbornly against even the endowment of Catholicism.

As to the Church of England there are special errors of their own into which our Liberals are apt to fall, but as to Catholicism their usual and grand error is one which they have in common with Continental Liberals. This error consists in always regarding what is prodigious, mischievous, impossible in Catholicism, rather than what is natural, amiable, likely to endure. It is by this natural and better side that we should accustom ourselves to consider Catholicism, and we cannot conceive this side too simply. We should begin with Catholicism at that elementary stage when it is not yet even in conscious conflict with Protestantism. Let us take a Protestant example of the power of religion, since with Protestant examples we ourselves are naturally most familiar, and let us see on what it hinges, and we shall be satisfied that the true power of religion in all forms of Christianity hinges at bottom on the same thing. Here is a letter written the other day by a common soldier in Walmer barracks to a lady whom he had met at a Methodist prayer-meeting, and who had interested herself in him:—

"A few weeks ago I was thoroughly tired of Deal, but since I found my Saviour I thank God most heartily that ever I enlisted. I had been going on loosely for years. From the death of a sister I left off for a time, but soon relapsed, and went from bad to worse until I came here, when one day walking by the chapel in a most miserable state of mind, I heard singing and was induced to go in. There I was powerfully wrought upon, resolved at once to give up sin, and am now happy in the enjoyment of God's love. God bless you, madam, and may God spare your useful life many years!"

Here, then, to what Epictetus calls "the madness and the misery of one who has been using as his measure of things that which *seems* to the senses and appetites, and misusing it," the influence of the religion of Jesus Christ has been applied, and has operated as a cure. Cases of exactly the same sort of emotion and conversion may be witnessed among the Breton mariners, hanging on the lips of an impassioned Jesuit preacher in one of the crowded churches of Brittany. And no wonder. Men conscious of a bent for being modest, temperate, kindly, affectionate, find themselves shameless, dissolute, living in malice and envy, hateful and hating one another. The experience is as old as the world, and the misery of it. And it is no cure whatever to be told that the Pope is not infallible, or that miracles do not happen; but a cure, a divine cure, for the bondage and the misery, has been found for nearly two thousand years to lie in the word, the character, the influence of Jesus. In this cure resides the power and the permanence of the Christian religion.

Liberals who have no conception of the Christian religion as of a real need of the community, which the community has to satisfy, should learn to fix their view upon this simple source, common to Catholics and Protestants alike, of Christianity's power and permanence. The power and permanence come from Christianity's being a real source of cure for a real bondage and misery. Men have adapted the source to their use according to their lights, often very imperfect;—have piled fantastic build- 5 ings around it, carried its healing waters by strange and intricate conduits, done their best to make it no longer recognisable. But, in their fashion, they have used and they do still use it; and whenever their religion is treated, often because of their mis- handling and disfigurement of it, as an obsolete nuisance to be 10 discouraged and helped to die out, a profound sentiment in them rebels against such an outrage, because they are conscious not of their vain disfigurements of the Christian religion, but of its genuine curativeness.

Catholicism is that form of Christianity which is fullest of 15 human accretions and superstitions, because it is the oldest, the largest, the most popular. It is the religion which has most reached the people. It has been the great popular religion of Christendom, with all the accretions and superstitions insepara- ble from such a character. The bulk of its superstitions come 20 from its having really plunged so far down into the multitude, and spread so wide among them. If this is a cause of error, it is also a cause of attachment. Who has seen the poor in other churches as they are seen in Catholic churches? Catholicism, besides, enveloped human life, and Catholics in general feel 25 themselves to have drawn not only their religion from the Church, they feel themselves to have drawn from her, too, their art and poetry and culture. Her hierarchy, again, originally stamped in their imaginations with the character of a beneficent and orderly authority springing up amidst anarchy, appeared 30 next as offering a career where birth was disregarded and merit regarded, and the things of the mind and the soul were hon- oured, in the midst of the iron feudal age which worshipped solely birth and force. So thus Catholicism acquired on the imagination a second hold. And if there is a thing specially alien 35 to religion, it is divisions; if there is a thing specially native to religion, it is peace and union. Hence the original attraction towards unity in Rome, and hence the great charm and power

for men's minds of that unity when once attained. All these spells for the heart and imagination has Catholicism to Catholics, in addition to the spell for the conscience of a divine cure for vice and misery. And whoever treats Catholicism as a nuisance,
5 to be helped to die out as soon as possible, has the heart, the imagination, and the conscience of Catholics, in just revolt against him.

True, the accretions and superstitions, gathered round the curative religious germ, are dense; true, the system of the Rom-
10 ish hierarchy carried with it the seeds of a thousand temptations and dangers, which have abundantly struck root; true, as the individuality of the European nations has ripened, and unity in one's nation has become a dominant habit and idea, the collisions between this unity and the unity in Rome have become a mat-
15 ter for just disquietude. Here are hindrances to be combated by us undoubtedly, and if possible to be removed; nevertheless, even in combating and removing them we should always re-member that to the mass of Catholics they present themselves by a good side, not by their bad one. However, they are hin-
20 drances to civilisation, and we ought to regard them as such. But in a modern community they meet with natural counterac-tions of great power. And the power of those counteractions is greater, the more the community has education, good govern-ment, happiness; it is least when the community is misgoverned,
25 sunk in ignorance and misery. The national sense, in a free and high-spirited modern nation, may be trusted to assert itself, as time goes on, against that dependence on a government of for-eigners, that meddling and intrigue by a government of foreign-ers, which is what the Ultramontane system, judged by prac-
30 tice, not theory, is seen really to bring with it. The family spirit, in a nation prosperous, educated, and of sound morals, may be trusted to assert itself against the excessive intervention of the priest. Finally and above all, religion, like human society itself, follows a law of progress and growth; and this law may be
35 trusted, in a well-governed, sound, and progressive community, advancing in intelligence and culture, to clear away the accre-tions and the superstitions which have gathered round religion. In short, to the retention and aggravation of the mischiefs of

the Catholic system—its Ultramontanism, sacerdotalism, superstition—the great auxiliaries are ill-government, vice, ignorance.
Ultramontanism, sacerdotalism, and superstition a good statesman must desire and hope to be rid of, but he cannot extirpate
them off-hand, he must let their natural counteractors have   5
play. And their natural counteractors are freedom, good government, sound morals, intelligence. With the help of these they
may be got rid of, but not without.

But when Ultramontanism, sacerdotalism, and superstition
are gone, Catholicism is not, as some may suppose, gone too.   10
Neither is it left with nothing further but what it possesses in
common with all the forms of Christianity,—the curative power
of the word, character, and influence of Jesus. It is, indeed, left
with this, which is the root of the matter, but it is left with a
mighty power besides. It is left with the beauty, the richness,   15
the poetry, the infinite charm for the imagination, of its own
age-long growth, a growth such as we have described,—unconscious, popular, profoundly rooted, all-enveloping.

It is the sure sign of a shallow mind, to suppose that the
strength of the Catholic Church is really in its tone of absolute 20
certainty concerning its dogmas, in its airs of omniscience. On
the contrary, as experience widens, as the scientific and dogmatic pretensions of the Church become more manifestly illusory, its tone of certitude respecting them, so unguarded, so
reiterated, and so grossly calculated for immediate and vulgar   25
effect, will be an embarrassment to it. The gain to-day, the effect upon a certain class of minds, will be found to be more
than counterbalanced by the embarrassment to-morrow. No
doubt there are pious souls to-day which are edified and fortified at being told by Cardinal Manning that "whoever does not   30
in his heart receive and believe the doctrine of the Immaculate
Conception, as defined by the supreme authority of the Church,
does by that very fact cease to be a Catholic;" and that "in the
Encyclical *Ineffabilis Deus,* of the 8th of December 1854, the
Sovereign Pontiff, the supreme authority of the Church, de-   35
fined that the most blessed Virgin Mary was, by a singular grace
and privilege of Almighty God, and by reason of the merits of
Jesus Christ, the Saviour of mankind, preserved in the first mo-

ment of her conception free from all stain of original sin." But
even in Catholics the irrepressible question will arise: "How
can he possibly know?" Then the solemnity of the assurance
will turn out to be a weakness, not a strength. Monsignor Capel
5 may elate his auditory to-day by telling them that Protestants
are more and more discovering that their Bible, which they
used to oppose to the Catholic's Church, is not infallible. How
delightful, think his devout hearers, to have an infallible Church,
since the Bible is not infallible! But sooner or later will come the
10 irrepressible question: "Is there, can there be, either an infallible
Bible or an infallible Church?" What a ridiculous argument will
the argument, *Because there exists no infallible Bible, there must
exist an infallible Church*, be then perceived to be! It is like arguing: Because there are no fairies, therefore there must be
15 gnomes. There are neither fairies nor gnomes, but nature and
the course of nature.

Its dogma and its confident assertion of its dogma are no more
a real source of strength and permanence to the Catholic
Church than its Ultramontanism. Its real superiority is in its
20 charm for the imagination,—its poetry. I persist in thinking that
Catholicism has, from this superiority, a great future before it;
that it will endure while all the Protestant sects (in which I do
not include the Church of England) dissolve and perish. I persist in thinking that the prevailing form for the Christianity of
25 the future will be the form of Catholicism; but a Catholicism
purged, opening itself to the light and air, having the consciousness of its own poetry, freed from its sacerdotal despotism and
freed from its pseudo-scientific apparatus of superannuated
dogma. Its forms will be retained, as symbolising with the force
30 and charm of poetry a few cardinal facts and ideas, simple indeed, but indispensable and inexhaustible, and on which our
race could lay hold only by materialising them.

From this ideal future of Catholicism, truly, few countries
can be farther removed than the Ireland of the present day. All
35 the mischiefs of Catholicism are rampant there. Irish Catholicism is Ultramontane, priest-governed, superstitious, self-confi-
dent. It could hardly be otherwise. The Irish Catholic has no
public education beyond the elementary school. His priests are

educated in the closest of seminaries. The national sense has been so managed in him by us, with our oppression and ill-government, that national sense as a member of our nation and empire he has none. His national sense is that of a conquered people, held down by a superior force of aliens, and glad to conspire against them with Rome or with any one else. If we want the Irish to be less superstitious, less priest-governed, less Ultramontane, let us do what is likely to serve this end. The Irish will use Catholic schools and no other. Let us give them secondary and higher Catholic schools with a public character. They have at present no secondary schools with a public character. As public higher schools the Queen's Colleges have been offered to them; but they will not use the Queen's Colleges, any more than we, either, are disposed to use colleges of that type. The Catholic layman has, therefore, neither secondary nor higher school; the priest has for a higher school Maynooth, a close seminary. What an admirable and likely cure is this for Irish ignorance, sacerdotalism, Ultramontanism, and disaffection!

Let us try, at any rate, a more hopeful treatment. Let us make no needless difficulties for ourselves by pulling to pieces what is established and what is working well. The distinguished past and the honourable present of Trinity College, Dublin, as well as the large proportion of the wealth and property of Ireland which belongs to Protestants, amply justify its continuance. The endowed secondary schools of Ireland are Protestant. It is alleged that the endowments are wasted, and that a share in some of them, at any rate, belongs by right to Catholics. Let waste and abuse be put an end to, and let Catholics have that share in the endowments which belongs to them; but here, too, let us be unwilling to disturb what is established, what is consonant with the terms of the endowment, and what is working well. Their legal share in the actual endowed schools of Ireland is not likely to afford to Catholics the supply of education needed; while schools of the type of those old endowed schools are, besides, not so desirable for them as schools of a more directly public institution and character. Let us give them public schools.

A clearing and enlarging spirit is in the air; all the influences

of the time help it. Wherever the pressure of the time and of collective human life can make itself felt, and therefore in all public and national institutions for education, the spirit works. The one way to prevent or adjourn its working is to keep edu-
5 cation what is called a hole-and-corner affair, cut off from the public life of the nation and the main current of its thoughts, in the hands of a clique who have been narrowly educated them-selves. Irish Catholicism has been entirely dissociated from the public life of the country, has been left to be an entirely private
10 concern of the persons attached to it. Its education has been kept a hole-and-corner thing, with its teachers neither of public appointment nor designated by public opinion as eminent men. We have prevented all access of the enlarging influences of the time to either teacher or taught. Well, but what has been the
15 consequence? Has Irish Catholicism died out because of this wholesome neglect by the State? Among no people is their religion so vigorous and pervasive. Has it fewer faults and dis-advantages than Catholicism in countries where Catholic educa-tion is publicly instituted? In no country, probably, is Catholi-
20 cism so crude, blind, and unreasoning as in Ireland. The public institution of Catholic education in Ireland is not only, there-fore, what the Irish themselves want; it is also just the very thing to do them good.

The public institution of Catholic education with the proper
25 and necessary guarantees. Our newspapers always assume that Catholic education must be "under complete clerical control." We are reminded that the Irish bishops claimed from Lord Mayo the entire government of their Irish university, the right of veto on the appointment of professors, the right of dismissing
30 professors. This would make the university simply a religious seminary with a State payment. But the State has no right, even if it had the wish, to abandon its duties towards a national uni-versity in this manner. The State, in such a university, is proctor for the nation. The appointment and dismissal of the professors
35 belong to no corporation less large and public than the nation itself; and it is best in the hands of the nation, and not made over to any smaller and closer corporation like the clergy, however respectable. The professors should be nominated and removed,

not by the bishops, but by a responsible minister of State acting for the Irish nation itself. They should be Catholics, but he should choose them; exercising his choice as a judicious Catholic would be disposed to exercise it, who had to act in the name and for the benefit of the whole community. While the bishops, if they have the appointment of professors in a Catholic university, will be prone to ask: "Who will suit the bishops?" the community, or the minister representing it, is interested in asking solely: "Who is the best and most distinguished Catholic for the chair?"

In the interest of the Irish themselves, therefore, the professors in a publicly instituted Catholic university ought to be nominated by a minister of State, acting under a public responsibility, and proctor for the Irish nation. Would Ireland reject a Catholic university offered with such a condition? I do not believe it. At any rate, if we offered it, and if Ireland refused it, our conscience would be clear; for only with such a condition can the State fairly and rightly bestow a university. At present the Roman Catholic hierarchy perceive that the Government cannot seriously negotiate with them, because it is controlled by popular prejudice and unreason. In any parleyings, therefore, they feel themselves free to play at a mere game of brag, and to advance confidently pretensions the most exorbitant, because they are sure that nothing reasonable can be done. But once break resolutely with the prejudice and unreason; let it be clear that the Government can and will treat with the Irish Catholics for the public institution of a Catholic university such as they demand, such as they have a right to, such as in other Protestant countries Catholics enjoy. Would the Irish bishops prove impracticable *then*, or would Ireland allow them to be so, even if they were so inclined? I do not believe it. I believe that a wholesome national feeling, thus reasonably appealed to, would be found to spring up and respond; and that here we should have the first instalment of the many ameliorations which the public establishment of Catholic education is calculated to produce in Ireland.

This is so evident, that no one in Great Britain with clear and calm political judgment, or with fine perception, or with high

cultivation, or with large knowledge of the world, doubts it.
Statesmen see it, the aristocracy see it, the important class which
we have to thank Mr. Charles Sumner for noting,—the large
class of gentlemen, not of the squirearchy or nobility, but cul-
5 tivated and refined,—they see it too. The populace know and
care nothing about the matter. And yet there is in one quarter,
—in the British middle class,—a force of prejudice on this subject so strong and so rooted, that we are bidden to recognise the
futility of contending with it, and to treat the claims of the Irish
10 Catholics for a Catholic university as inconsistent with the practical conditions of politics.

   This it is which is, indeed, calculated to drive the Irish to rage
and despair. If the English race may be said, by one speaking
favourably of it but not extravagantly, to be characterised by
15 energy and honesty, the Irish race may be described, in like
manner, as being characterised by sentiment and perception.
And they find themselves sacrificed to the prejudices of a class
which they see, as the rest of the world sees it, to be, in its present state, imperfectly civilised and impossible; a class ill-edu-
20 cated as the Irish middle class itself, knowing how to make
money, but not knowing how to live when they have made it;
and in short, of the powers which, as we saw when we were
discussing Equality, go to constitute civilisation,—the powers
of conduct, intellect, beauty, manners,—laying hold upon one
25 only, the power of conduct. But for this factor in civilisation
the Irish, in the first place, have by nature not sufficient sympathy, and it comes up in our middle class so strangely mis-
grown and disguised that strangers may easily fail to recognise
it; and then besides, of the sense for conduct in our middle class,
30 though the sense is there, the Irish have really had no experience
at all, but have had a long experience of this class as unjust, hard,
and cruel. And they see that our government and upper class
quite share their opinions about this class, but that we have a
system which requires that the upper class should be cultivated
35 and attractive and should govern, and that the middle class
should be, as it is, impossible, but that it should be flattered and
humoured; and therefore to the deep-rooted prejudices of the
middle class against Catholicism Ireland must be sacrificed. But

the Irish are quite out of this singular game, which our notorious passion for inequality makes us play with such zest in England; they cannot appreciate its ways and laws. All they feel is that they are kept from having what they want, and what is fair, and what we have ourselves, because the British middle class, being such as we have described it, pronounces their religion to be *a lie* and *heathenish superstition*.

Now I am here pouring out my heart to advanced Liberals, in my joy at their sound and hopeful vote on the O'Conor Don's resolution. I am sure that Sir Charles Dilke does not suppose that Mr. Arthur or Mr. Spurgeon is in possession of *the truth* in some eminent way, compared with which the tenets of Lacordaire, for instance, were *a lie* and *heathenish superstition*. Each, Sir Charles Dilke would probably say, can at most but be pronounced free from some bondage still confining the mind of the other; Mr. Arthur and Mr. Spurgeon from the delusion of an infallible church, and Lacordaire from the jungle of the justification theology. But then I, on my part, must ask leave to say that they all, nevertheless, possess as their foundation, however overlaid, a germ of inestimable power for lifting human life out of misery and servitude, and for assuring its felicity. And Sir Charles Dilke, again, is thereupon likely to rejoin that this may possibly be so, but that the whole natural history of that germ, the whole philosophy of the thing, as they and theirs have constructed it for themselves, is, with all of them alike, a construction utterly fantastic and hollow; the *Quicunque vult* like the Westminster Confession, and the Tridentine Decrees like the Thirty-nine Articles. Bits, he will say, the Protestant may have more right than the Catholic, and in other bits, again, the Catholic may have the advantage; and the being right on some points may happen to contribute more help towards making progress on the line of liberty, let us say, or industry, than the being right on others. But the whole philosophy of the thing is fantastic in both. And if Sir Charles Dilke chooses to say this, I shall not contend with him; for I hate contention, and besides, I do not know that I much disagree with him.

So I shall acquiesce and say: Well, then, let us be agreed. Both Catholic and Protestant have the germ, both Catholic and Prot-

estant have a false philosophy of the germ. But Catholicism has
the germ invested in an immense poetry, the gradual work of
time and nature, and of that great impersonal artist, Catholic
Christendom. And here it has the superiority over Protestantism. So that when the British Puritan prevents our doing justice
to the Irish Catholic because his religion is, says the Puritan, *a
lie* and *heathenish superstition,* the Irish Catholic is conscious
that he has the germ like the Puritan; that the philosophy of the
germ those who prate of such things would allow neither that
he nor that the Puritan has, but he has it, they would allow,
quite as much as the Puritan; while in the beauty and poetry of
his clothing of the germ he has an immeasurable superiority.
And he is not to have a Catholic university because, though this
is so, and though all the world except the British middle class
see it to be so, this class must be humoured and flattered by the
governing class in England, and its mail of prejudice is impene-
trable! Let Sir Charles Dilke ask himself with what feelings this
state of things would fill him, if he were an Irishman affected by
it. But he *has* asked himself, and hence his vote. It would be
likely to fill him, he saw, with rage and despair; and when his
mind dwelt on it he might even be inclined, instead of marvelling at the extravagance of Mr. Biggar and Mr. Parnell and the
other obstructionists, rather to chafe at their moderation.

But then, if Sir Charles Dilke and his friends wish to have
truth and nature on their side in their political labours, and to
bring them to a happy end, they ought to proceed boldly and
unwaveringly in the excellent course which by their vote on
the O'Conor Don's resolution they have begun. The present
government leans naturally for its support upon the feeling of
the upper class, and to the just claims of Ireland in the matter
of education the feeling of this class is not opposed. If the present government, therefore, should show a disposition to do justice to Ireland in this matter, let the advanced Liberals, who
have so well begun, steadily support the government in such a
disposition, and steadily refuse, in this question, for the sake of
snatching a party advantage, to trade upon the baneful fund of
middle-class prejudice, which is so easy and so tempting to use
even while one despises it. There will be plenty of other occa-

sions on which the pursuit of the true Liberal ideal must inevitably bring Liberals into conflict with the present government, and with the feeling of the upper class. But on this particular question for a Liberal to thwart the government, if the government were inclined to do what Ireland justly desires, would be to put himself into conflict with truth and nature, and, therefore, with the Liberal ideal itself.

And how can I forbear adding,—though the space which remains to me is short, and though on this subject Mr. Chamberlain will be hard to persuade, and he may still be under the spell, besides, of that recent article by Mr. Jenkins in the *Fortnightly Review*,—yet how can I forbear adding that the same considerations of the sure loss and defeat at last, from coming into conflict with truth and nature, ought to govern the action of Liberals as to the disestablishment of the Church of England, and to make this action other than what it now is? For if to the building up of human life and civilisation there go these four powers, the power of conduct, the power of intellect and knowledge, the power of beauty, and the power of social life and manners, and if to the disengagement and strengthening and final harmony of these powers we are pushed by the instinct of self-preservation in humanity, then to go against any one of them is to go against truth and nature. And the case for the Church of England is really, in respect of its Puritan reproachers and attackers, just like that of the Church of Rome, and has the same sort of natural strength. The Church of England has the germ of Christianity like its attackers; the philosophy of the germ (so we understood Sir Charles Dilke to say) neither the Church nor its attackers have; in the beauty and poetry of its clothing of the germ, the Church has an immeasurable superiority. Joseph de Maistre, that ardent Catholic, remarked that the Church of England was the only one of the Reformation Churches which still showed promise and vitality; and he attributed this superiority to its retention of bishops. Sir Charles Dilke will probably say that this is one of those explanations which explain nothing. But suppose we fill out the term bishops a little, and understand the retention of bishops to mean that the

Church of England, while getting rid of Ultramontanism, and
of many other things plainly perceived to be false or irksome,
yet kept in great measure the traditional form of Catholicism,
and thus preserved its link with the past, its share in the beauty
5 and the poetry and the charm for the imagination of Catholicism,—its inheritance in all that work of ages, and of nature,
and of popular instinct, and of the great impersonal artist whom
we can only name Catholic Christendom. Then in the retention
of bishops, thus explained, we arrive at a real superiority,—a
10 superiority in beauty.

And if one man's notion of beauty were as good as another's,
and there were not an instinct of self-preservation in humanity
working upwards towards a real beauty, then this superiority
would be of no avail. But now Nature herself fights against the
15 Puritan, with his services of religion such as they visibly are,—
free from all touch or suspicion of the great impersonal artist,
but just what the British middle class, left to itself, might be
expected to make them; while his intellectual conception of
religion is no more adequate than the conception current in the
20 Church, or indeed is even less adequate, since a great public
body is more open to the enlarging influences of the time. And
so the Church of England is likely to grow stronger rather than
weaker. The desire to keep it a public institution will grow
stronger rather than weaker. The more its superiority to the
25 sects is perceived, and the source of this superiority, the
stronger will be the desire to continue that public institution of
it which gives more weight, solemnity, and grandeur to religion, which makes religion less like a thing of private fancy or
invention. The community will wish religion to be a thing
30 which may grow according to their needs, and be administered
according to their needs; and also to be a thing of public institution, removed from the freaks of private caprice, ignorance,
and vulgarity.

People, therefore, will use the germ of curative power which
35 lies in Christianity, because they cannot do without it; and the
intellectual conception they will shape for themselves as they
can; and for beauty and poetry of religious service they will go
to the Church. There have been a few Liberals, such as Sir John

Lubbock, in whom the scientific spirit was so strong that they wanted fairly to know how things stood and how many adherents the Church numbered even now, and to get a religious census taken. But in general it fared with the religious census as it fared with the Catholic university for Ireland; Liberals recognised the futility of contending against rooted Puritan prejudice. However, if the present government remain in office, a religious census will, one may hope, be taken; and that is one good reason, at any rate, for wishing stability to the present government. It is dangerous to prophesy; yet I will venture to prophesy, and to say that if a religious census is taken, the majority in England ranging themselves with the Church will be found to be overwhelming, and the Dissenters will be found much less numerous than they give themselves out to be.

But I must end. Out of gratitude for the pleasure given to me by the Liberal votes for the O'Conor Don's resolution, I have been endeavouring to caution my benefactors against the common Liberal error of supposing that all the influences of truth and nature are against Catholicism, whether on the Continent or in Ireland, and against the Established Church in England. On the contrary, they are, many of them, in their favour. They are, many of them, against the Puritan and Nonconformist cause, which, in this country, Liberals are always tempted to think themselves safe in supporting. The need for beauty is a real and now rapidly growing need in man; Puritanism cannot satisfy it, Catholicism and the English Church can. The need for intellect and knowledge in him, indeed, neither Puritanism, nor Catholicism, nor the English Church can at present satisfy. That need has to seek satisfaction nowadays elsewhere,— through the modern spirit, science, literature. But, as one drops the false science of the Churches, one perceives that what they had to deal with was so simple that it did not require science. Their beauty remains, investing certain elementary truths of inestimable depth and value, yet of extreme simplicity. But the Puritan Churches have no beauty. This makes the difficulty of maintaining the Established Church of Scotland. Once drop the false science on which successive generations of Scotchmen have so vainly valued themselves, once convince oneself that

the Westminster Confession, whatever Principal Tulloch may
think, is a document absolutely antiquated, sterile, and worthless, and what remains to the Church of Scotland? Besides the
simple elementary truths present in all forms of Christianity,
there remains to the Church of Scotland merely that which remains to the Free Church, to the United Presbyterians, to Puritanism in general,—a religious service which is perhaps the most
dismal performance ever invented by man. It is here that Catholicism and the Church of England have such a real superiority; and nothing can destroy it, and the present march of
things is even favourable to it. Let Liberals do their best to open
Catholicism and the Church of England to all the enlarging influences of the time, to make tyranny and vexatiousness on the
part of their clergy impossible; but do not let them think they
are to be destroyed, nor treat them as their natural enemies.

Perhaps Lord Granville has come a little late in life to the
consideration of these matters, and assumes over-hastily that
because the alliance with the Dissenters persecuted was valuable
for the Liberal party, the alliance with the Dissenters aggressive
must be valuable for them too. Let him bring his acute mind to
see the thing as it really is. He is for admitting, in a public rite,
the services of Dissent on the same footing as the services of the
Church of England. But let him accustom himself to attend
both, and he will perceive what the difference between the services is. The difference is really very much the difference between a reading from Milton and a reading from Eliza Cook,—
a poetess, I hasten to add, of wide popularity, full of excellent
sentiments, of appeals to the love of liberty, country, home.
And for a long while the English Church, with the State to
back her, committed the fatal mistake of trying to compel
everybody to forsake the reading of Eliza Cook and come to
the reading of Milton; nay, to declare that they utterly abjured
Eliza Cook, and that they preferred Milton. And sometimes,
when it would have suited a man to come to the reading of Milton, they would not let him, if he and his family had ever preferred Eliza Cook. This was the time of the strong and fruitful
alliance of the Whigs with Dissent. It may be said to have closed
with the death of a man whom we all admired, Lord Russell. He

established the right of the Dissenters to be not cross-questioned and persecuted about the preferability of Milton to Eliza Cook; they were to be free to prefer which they pleased. Yet Milton remains Milton, and Eliza Cook remains Eliza Cook. And a public rite, with a reading of Milton attached to it, is another thing from a public rite with a reading from Eliza Cook. The general sentiment has gone heartily with Lord Russell in leaving the Dissenters perfectly free to prefer and use Eliza Cook as much as they please; but is it certain that it will be found equally to go with Lord Granville in letting them import her into a public rite?

Not in this direction, I think, shall we do well to seek to extend the conquests of Liberalism. They are to be extended on other lines, some of them hardly entered upon at present. It is a long time since last February, and things are easily forgotten; let me, therefore, recall to my Liberal benefactors what I said at the Royal Institution last February, that the excesses to which our love of inequality has carried us have ended in materialising our upper class, vulgarising our middle class, and brutalising our lower class; and that they do this, if we will look at the thing simply, by a kind of necessary and fatal operation, throwing the middle class,—to speak now of that one class only,—in upon itself, and giving it over to the narrownesses, and prejudices, and hideousnesses, which many people regard as incurable, but which are not. And therefore, for the good of the whole community, and by no means from any enmity to the upper class, —who are indeed better than one could have thought their circumstances would allow them to be, and who are much more pricked by an uneasy consciousness of being materialised, than the middle class are of being vulgarised, or the lower of being brutalised,—Liberals would do well to set seriously about the reform of our law of bequest and inheritance. Another object for them is the establishment of a system of public schools for the middle class, such as in all other civilised countries it enjoys, but which alike in England and in Ireland is wanting. The *Times* itself, though too prone to "recognise the futility of contending against rooted prejudices," is yet "convinced that one of the best guarantees for the stability and progress of society is the

influence of an educated middle class." The *Times* is indeed
here speaking of Ireland, but this influence is just what in England, no less than in Ireland, is so sadly wanting; and the Irish,
if they are to be ruled by our middle class, have at least a right
5   to supplicate us, in Mr. Lowe's words, to "educate their masters." And the real obstacle to the establishment of public
schools for the middle class is, that both the upper and the middle class have a lurking sense that by such schools the middle
class would be transformed; and the upper class do not care to
10   be disturbed in their preponderance, or the middle class in their
vulgarity. To convince the one resistance of its selfishness, and
the other of its folly, should be the aim of all true Liberals.
Finally, Liberals should remember that the country districts
throughout England have their municipal organisation still to
15   get; that they have at present only the feudal and ecclesiastical
organisation of the Middle Ages. Nothing struck me more than
this, on my return to England after seeing the Continental
schools for the people, and the communal basis on which everything there rested. Our agricultural labourer will doubtless have
20   the franchise, and that is well; but how much more constant and
sure a training for him than that of the franchise is the public
life in common of a true municipal system universally diffused!
To this, rather than to the institution in our country churchyards of readings from Eliza Cook, Liberals might with much
25   advantage turn their thoughts. Still the great work to be done
in this country, and at this hour, is not with the lower class, but
with the middle; a work of raising its whole level of civilisation,
and, in order to do this, of transforming the British Puritan.

Hume relates that the well-known Praise God Barebones had
30   a brother less famous than himself, but with a yet more singular
name. He was called: "If Christ had not died for thee thou wert
damned Barebones." But to go through all this was a terribly
long business, and so the poor man came to be called simply:
Damned Barebones. And the misfortune of this poor owner of
35   an edifying name comes to one's mind when one thinks of what
is happening now to the Puritan middle class. After all its sermons, all its victories, all its virtues, all its care for conduct, all
its zeal for righteousness, to be told that it must transform itself,

that the body of which it is the nerve and sinew is at a low level
of civilisation! But so great and wide a thing is human progress;
tentatives, approximations, hold good only for a certain time,
and bring us only a certain way on our road; then they have to
be changed. Happy the workers whose way and work have to   5
be changed only, not abolished! The Puritan middle class, with
all its faults, is still the best stuff in this nation. Some have hated
and persecuted it, many have flattered and derided it,—flattered
it that while they deride it they may use it; I have believed in it.
It is the best stuff in this nation, and in its success is our best   10
hope for the future. But to succeed it must be transformed.

"Porro Unum Est Necessarium"

An acute French critic says that a wise man's best happiness is to be found, perhaps, in his having the sense *de ne pas être dupe*, of not being taken in. At any rate, we may allow that such happiness is better than none at all, and sometimes it is the only
5 happiness within our reach. Certainly it is the only happiness to which the would-be reformer of secondary instruction in England can at present pretend.

There has just appeared in the French *Journal Officiel* a report by M. Bardoux, the Minister of Public Instruction, on the
10 present state of the secondary schools in France, and on their movement since 1865, the date of a like decennial report on them by M. Duruy. With an interest not unmixed with the sense of defeat and weakness, I have studied this picture of the schools of that immense class of society, which in France has
15 even more greatness and extent than with us,—the middle class. Yes, the schools for this class are indeed, as the French themselves say, the keystone of a country's whole system of public instruction: they are what fixes and maintains the intellectual level of a people. And in our country they have been left to
20 come forth as they could and to form themselves at haphazard, and are now, as a whole, in the most serious degree inadequate and unsatisfactory. For some twenty years I have been full of this thought, and have striven to make the British public share it with me; but quite vainly. At this hour, in Mr. Gladstone's
25 programme of the twenty-two engagements of the Liberal party, there is not a word of middle-class education. Twenty-two Liberal engagements, and the reform of middle-class education not one of them! What a blow for the declining age of a sincere but ineffectual Liberal, who so long ago as 1859

wrote with faith and ardour the words following,—buried in a blue-book, and now disinterred to show the vanity of human wishes:—

"Let me be permitted to call the attention of Englishmen to the advantage which France possesses in its vast system of public secondary instruction; in its 63 lyceums and 244 communal colleges, inspected by the State, aided by the State; drawing from this connection with the State both efficiency and dignity; and to which, in concert with the State, the departments and the communes and private benevolence all co-operate to provide free admission for poor and deserving scholars. M. de Talleyrand said that the education of the great English public schools was the best in the world. He added, to be sure, that even this was detestable. But allowing it all its merits, how small a portion of the population does it embrace! It embraces the aristocratic class, it embraces the higher professional class, it embraces a certain number from the richer families of the commercial class; from the great body of the commercial class and of the immense middle class of this country, it embraces hardly one. They are left to an education which, though among its professors are many excellent and honourable men, is deplorable. Our middle classes are among the worst educated in the world. But it is not this only; although, when I consider this, all the French commonplaces about the duty of the State to protect children from the charlatanism and cupidity of individual speculation seem to me to be justified. It is far more that a great opportunity is missed of fusing all the upper and middle classes into one powerful whole, elevating and refining the middle classes by the contact and stimulating the upper. In France this is what the system of public secondary education effects; it effaces between the middle and upper classes the sense of social alienation; it gives to the boy of the middle class the studies, the superior teaching, the sense of belonging to a great school, which the Eton or Harrow boy has with us; it tends to give to the middle classes precisely what they most want, and their want of which makes the great gulf between them and the upper,—it tends to give them personal dignity. The power of such an education is seen in what it has done for the professional classes in England. The clergy, and barristers, and officers of both services, who have commonly passed through the great public schools, are nearly identified in thought, feeling, and manners with the aristocratic class. They have not been unmixed gainers by this identification; it has too much isolated them from a class to which by income and social position they, after all, naturally belong; while towards the highest class it has made them, not vulgarly servile, certainly, but intellectually too deferential, too little apt to maintain entire mental independence on questions where the prepossessions of that class are concerned. Nevertheless they have, as a class, acquired the unspeakable benefit of that elevation of the mind and feelings which it is the best office of superior education to confer. But they have bought this elevation at an immense money-price,—at a price which they can no better than the commercial classes afford to pay; which they who have paid it long, and who know what it has bought for them, will continue to pay while they must, but which the mass of the middle classes will never even begin to pay. Either the education of this mass must remain what it is, vulgar and unsound; or the State must create by its legislation, its aid, its inspection, institutions honourable because of their public character, and cheap because nationally frequented, in which they may receive a better. The French middle classes may well be taxed for the education of the poor, since public provision has already been made for their own education. But already there are complaints among the lower middle classes of this country that the Committee of Council is providing the poor with better schools than those to which they themselves have access. The Education Commissioners would excite, I am convinced, in thousands of hearts, a gratitude of which they little dream, if in presenting the result of their labours on primary instruction they were at the same time to say to the government: 'Regard the necessities of a not distant future, and *organise your secondary instruction.*' "

The emotions of gratitude here promised were suffered to slumber on unawakened. This was in 1859. In 1865, having again been sent to visit the schools of the Continent, I struck the same note once more:—

"Neither is the secondary and superior instruction given in England so good on the whole, if we regard the whole number of those to whom it is due, as that given in Germany or France, nor is it given in schools of so good a standing. Of course, what good instruction there is, and what schools of good standing there are to get it in, fall chiefly to the lot of the upper class. It is on the middle class that the injury, such as it is, of getting inferior instruction, and of getting it in schools of inferior standing, mainly comes. This injury, as it strikes one after seeing attentively the schools of the Continent, has two aspects. It has a social aspect, and it has an intellectual aspect.

"The social injury is this. On the Continent the upper and middle class are brought up on one and the same plane. In England the middle class, as a rule, *is brought up on the second plane.* One hears many discussions as to the limits between the middle and the upper class in England. From a social and educational point of view these limits are perfectly clear. Ten or a dozen famous schools, Oxford or Cambridge, the church or the bar, the army or navy, and those posts in the public service supposed to be posts for gentlemen,— these are the lines of training, all or any of which give a cast of ideas, a stamp or habit, which make a sort of association of all those who share them; and this association is the upper class. Except by one of these modes of access, an Englishman does not, unless by some special play of aptitude or of circumstances, become a vital part of this association, for he does not bring with him the cast of ideas in which its bond of union lies. This cast of ideas is naturally in the main that of the most powerful and prominent part of the association,—the aristocracy. The professions furnish the more numerous but the less prominent part; in no country, accordingly, do the professions so naturally and generally share the cast of ideas of the aristocracy as in England. Judged from its bad side, this cast of ideas is characterised by over-reverence for things established, by an estrangement from the powers of reason and science. Judged from its good side, it is characterised by a high spirit, by dignity, by a just sense of the greatness of great affairs,—all of them governing qualities; and the professions have accordingly long recruited the governing force of the aristocracy, and assisted it to rule. But they are separate, to a degree unknown on the Continent, from the commercial and industrial classes with which in social standing they are naturally on a level. So we have amongst us the spectacle of a middle class cut in two in a way unexampled anywhere else; of a professional class brought up on the first plane, with fine and governing qualities, but disinclined to rely on reason and science; while that immense business class, which is becoming so important a power in all countries, on which the future so much depends, and which in the great public schools of other countries fills so large a place, is in England brought up on the second plane, cut off from the aristocracy and the professions, and without governing qualities.

"If only, in compensation, it had science, systematic knowledge, reason! But here comes in the intellectual mischief of the bad con-

dition of the mass of our secondary schools. In England the business
class is not only inferior to the professions and aristocracy in the
social stamp of its places of training; it is actually inferior to them,
maimed and incomplete as their development of reason is, in its de-
5 velopment of reason. Short as the offspring of our public schools
and universities come of the idea of science and systematic knowledge, the offspring of our middle-class academies probably come, if
that be possible, even shorter. What these academies fail to give in
social and governing qualities, they do not make up for in intellec-
10 tual power. Their intellectual result is as faulty as their social result.

"If this be true, then that our middle class does not yet itself see
the defects of its own education, is not conscious of the injury to itself from them, and is satisfied with things as they are, is no reason
for regarding this state of things without disquietude."

15 Alas, in 1865, it was hardly permissible even to be disquieted
at the state of middle-class education! "We must confess to a
feeling of shame," cried one newspaper, "at the nonsense which
is being uttered on this subject. It might be thought from what
is said, that this section of the community, which has done
20 everything else so well, which has astonished the world by its
energy, enterprise, and self-reliance, which is continually striking out new paths of industry and subduing the forces of nature, cannot, from some mysterious reason, get their children
properly educated!" "All the world knows," cried another,
25 "that the great middle class of this country supplies the mind,
the will, and the power, for all the great and good things that
have to be done, and it is not likely that that class should surrender its powers and privileges in the one case of the training
of its own children. How the idea of such a scheme can have
30 occurred to anybody, how it can have been imagined that parents and schoolmasters in the most independent and active and
enlightened class of English society, how it can have been supposed that the class which has done all the great things that have
been done in all departments, will beg the government to send
35 inspectors through its schools, when it can itself command
whatever advantages exist, seems almost unintelligible."

This dithyrambic style about the middle class and its schools
has, it is true, been dropped for the last few years. It seems even

a little grotesque as one surveys it now; not "unintelligible" perhaps, but somewhat ridiculous. In this respect there is progress; but still middle-class education remains just as it was. The commercial travellers or the licensed victuallers have the happy thought of making a school entirely for children of commercial travellers or of licensed victuallers, and royal dukes and ministerial earls are still found to go down and bless the young institution, and to glorify the energy and self-reliance of the commercial travellers and the licensed victuallers. A satisfactory system of public secondary schools nobody calls for. It finds, as we have seen, no place among the twenty-two engagements of the Liberal party. The newspapers never touch the subject. Both upper and middle class appear content that their schools should stay as they are. And the enthusiast who has had a vision of better things is left to console himself with what is alleged, certainly, to be the wise man's true satisfaction—the sense *de ne pas être dupe,* of not being taken in. He has the pleasure, such as it is, of knowing that our body of secondary schools is suffered to remain the most imperfect and unserviceable in civilised Europe, because our upper class does not care to be disturbed in its preponderance, or our middle class in its vulgarity.

A report like that of M. Bardoux is calculated, however, to make the poor enthusiast restless and impatient, to set him asking himself whether the middle class in England is really always to be ruled by the fatal desire not to be disturbed in its vulgarity, whether that class is always to be taken in by grandees extolling this desire as energy and self-reliance, and whether his own only comfort for ever is to consist in not being taken in too. The impulse is irresistible to seek to communicate his impatience to others, and for this end nothing can be more useful, one would think, than simply to retrace the main lines of the picture drawn by M. Bardoux.

The public secondary schools of France are of two kinds,— *lycées,* or lyceums, and communal colleges. The *lycées* are maintained by the State. The communal colleges are maintained by the municipalities, but may be aided by the State. The instruction in both is of the same type, as to its general features,

with the instruction given in the great grammar-schools of this country. It is classical, with a side or department, called by us modern, by the French special, by the Germans real, intended to suit the requirements of practical life in the present day, by
5   teaching the natural sciences and the modern languages in place of Greek and Latin. Alike in the *lycées* and in the communal colleges, all the teaching staff have to furnish guarantees of their capacity to teach the matters of instruction confided to them. The guarantee takes generally the form of a university degree,
10 varying in kind and in rank according to the post to be filled by the holder.

At the end of 1865, the date to which the report of M. Duruy, —the last report previous to M. Bardoux's,—goes down, France had at work 77 *lycées* and 251 communal colleges. Three of the
15 77 *lycées* (those of Strasburg, Metz, and Colmar), and 15 of the 251 communal colleges, have been lost to France in consequence of the war of 1870. But new ones have in the meanwhile been added, so that on the 31st of December, 1876, the date to which M. Bardoux's report comes down, France had 81 *lycées*
20 at work, with five others building, and 252 communal colleges. If we deduct Strasburg, Metz, and Colmar, which are not now part of the territory of France, the French *lycées*, in 1865, had 31,321 pupils. At the end of 1876 they had, for the same extent of territory, 40,995 pupils,—an average of 506 pupils to each
25 *lycée*, about half of whom are boarders and half day-boys. The communal colleges had in 1865 a total number of 32,881 pupils, with an average of 139 pupils to each college; at the end of 1876 they had 38,236 pupils, with an average of 152 for each college.

Eighty-one great secondary schools of the first class, two
30 hundred and fifty-two of the second, all of them with a public character, all of them under inspection, all of them offering guarantees of the capacity of their teaching staff! and in these schools a total of 79,231 scholars!

Let us note, in passing, that the modern or special instruction
35 in these schools is constantly growing. The *lycées* are the stronghold of the classics; yet in the *lycées* the number of boys on the modern side had risen from 5002 at the end of 1865 to 8628 at the end of 1876, and the average number of such schol-

ars for each *lycée* from 71 to 107. The teaching of the natural
sciences, of the living languages, of geography, modern history,
and literature, is being continually strengthened. The class of
pupils receiving special preparation in the *lycées* for schools
such as the Polytechnic, Saint Cyr, the Naval, Central, and For-   5
est Schools, steadily increases. In the communal colleges the development of the modern side is much greater still, and is extremely remarkable. Of the 38,236 pupils in these colleges at the
end of 1876, 9232 are little boys not yet going beyond primary
instruction; of the remainder, 14,992 are on the classical side,   10
and very nearly as many, 14,012, are on the modern. The number of teacherships for the modern languages has more than
doubled in these colleges since 1865.

But I am not here writing for schoolmasters and specialists,
for whose benefit, indeed, I have formerly given a full account   15
of the French secondary schools, of their organisation and
teaching. I am writing now for that great public which is interested in the provision of secondary schools for its children;
the broad plain lines of the subject are all that they will care for,
and are what I shall keep to. I repeat, then: 81 *lycées*, 252 com-   20
munal colleges, with a total of nearly 80,000 scholars; a modern
side established, and constantly growing; all the schools under
inspection, and of all their teachers guarantees of capacity
required.

As to the quality of the instruction, it is at the same general   25
level as the instruction in our great secondary schools which are
called public. In Greek it is not so strong. In Latin it is much
on a par with ours, though with a nearer sense of the Latin
language, because of its affinity with the French. In modern
languages it is, again, much on a par with our instruction. In   30
arithmetic and mathematics, in the natural sciences, in modern
history, and above all in knowledge of the mother-tongue and
its literature, it is stronger. The boarders are fed and lodged in
a different mode from the boarders of our public schools, but,
in my opinion, quite as well. They are, however, more confined   35
and harder worked, and have less freedom, air, and exercise.
This is a disadvantage. But it comes from the dangers of confinement and study for boys being less apprehended, the good

of play for them less valued, in the whole body of Continental schools, whether public or private, than they are by us all in England.

I pass from the public secondary schools to the private,—the *écoles libres*, as the French call them. This part of the subject has a peculiar interest for us in England, because our secondary instruction is in so large a measure supplied by private adventure schools. In France the private secondary schools are of two kinds, lay and ecclesiastical. There were 803 of them at the end of 1876. But in these schools, as a whole, we do not find the progressive advance in numbers which we find in the public schools; we find, on the contrary, a progressive diminution. In 1854 the private secondary schools in France numbered 1081; in 1865 they numbered 935; in 1876 their number had fallen to 803. And it is in the lay establishments that the diminution has taken place; the ecclesiastical establishments are more in number than formerly. But whereas the lay establishments in 1854 were as many as 825,—more than the whole number of private secondary schools at the present day,—in 1865 they had fallen to 657, in 1876 to 494. The ecclesiastical establishments in 1854 numbered 256; in 1865, 278; in 1876, 309. From 1806, when the University of France was instituted, down to 1850, private establishments for secondary instruction could not exist. All the secondary schools belonged to the University, a State-institution, and all the teachers in them were its functionaries. The law of March the 15th, 1850, the organic law which at present governs public instruction in France, was conceived in a spirit of dissatisfaction with this exclusive rule of the University, and permitted the opening, upon certain conditions, of private schools. The result has been, as we have seen, favourable especially to the growth of ecclesiastical establishments, and it disquiets French Liberals exceedingly. It deserves investigation and discussion, but I must abstain from everything of that kind here. The lay private schools had in 1865, eleven years after the passing of the new law, 43,009 scholars to the 34,897 of their ecclesiastical rivals. The proportion is now reversed, and the ecclesiastical private schools have 46,816 pupils, while the lay private schools have but 31,249.

The ecclesiastical schools are either under episcopal control, or they belong to one of the teaching orders, amongst whom the Jesuits have the chief place. Both the episcopal schools and the *congreganist* schools, as they are called, have increased in number, but the congreganist schools are by far the more numerous and important division. They have nearly 20,000 pupils. The episcopal schools have 12,300. A third class of establishments under ecclesiastical direction is formed by schools under the secular Catholic clergy or under ministers of other religious denominations. Of these schools the non-Catholic form a quite insignificant proportion; they are but 13 out of 165. But this whole class of schools has decreased in number since 1865, while the episcopal and congreganist schools keep increasing. And this, again, is a matter of disquietude to French Liberals, who consider the influence of the secular clergy as less unfavourable to independence of thought than episcopal influence or the influence of the teaching orders. And strong discontent is expressed with the law of March 1850, which has rendered such a development of episcopal and congreganist schools possible.

For the present, however, let us not be diverted by this contest between liberalism and clericalism from what is the central point of interest for us,—the actual supply in France of a sound secondary instruction, apart from all question of the religious bias given. In these private establishments for instruction of which we have been speaking, no less than in the public, guarantees are taken for its soundness. A private or free school in France is not free in the sense that any man may keep one who likes. The head of such a school must be at least twenty-five years old, must have had five years' practice in school-keeping, and must hold either the University degree of bachelor, or a certificate which is given after an examination of the same nature as the examination required for the degree of bachelor. His school is, moreover, under government inspection as regards its state of commodiousness, healthiness, and repair. These are serious guarantees. And, in fact, by them and by other causes which co-operate with them, the soundness of the secular instruction in the *écoles libres* is sufficiently secured. The secular instruction, having the degree of bachelor or the admission to govern-

ment schools, such as the Polytechnic, in view, cannot but follow in general the same line as that of the public secondary
schools. Some of the schools of the religious, such as the Jesuits'
school at Vaugirard, and the school in the Rue des Postes, are
in direct competition with the Paris *lycées*, and in very successful competition. They employ, along with their own teachers,
the best lay instructors accessible, often the very same whom
the *lycées* employ. Whatever clerical influence may be super-
added to it, the secular instruction in the schools of the teaching
orders, and in the *écoles libres* in general, does not fall below
the ordinary level of this instruction in the public schools.

It is true that, owing to a recent law permitting the formation of free Catholic universities and recognising their degrees,
the degree required for those who conduct free secondary
schools can now be obtained from bodies not of public appointment or public responsibility. Undoubtedly, new and denominational universities, in which the professors are not of public
appointment, ought not to be entrusted with power to confer
degrees. The law in question is said to have been obtained by
accident; an overwhelming majority of the Legislative Assembly are for its repeal, and after the next elections to the Senate
it will certainly, people say, be repealed. But whatever the de-
merits of that law may be, it has not been in operation long
enough to affect injuriously the standard of secular instruction.
Secular instruction in the private schools remains in general, as
I have said already, at the same level as in the public schools.
Before the level can have been lowered by the inferior standard
for degrees (if it is inferior) of the free Catholic universities,
those universities will have lost the power of granting them.

But I grudge every word which is here given to these questions of religious politics, so attractive to the middle-class Englishman, so fatally apt to divert his mind from what is the point
of cardinal importance for him, the one thing needful. For him
the point to be seized and set in clear light, and again and again
to be insisted upon until seized and set in clear light it is, is this:
that while we have not more than 20,000 boys in Great Britain
and Ireland receiving a secondary instruction which can in any
possible sense be said to offer guarantees for its efficiency,

France has 79,231 boys receiving secondary instruction in inspected public schools, and 78,065 more who are receiving it in
schools giving public guarantees for their efficiency. It is this:
that whereas in England the middle class is brought up on the
second plane, in France the middle class is brought up on the
first plane.

In 1865 there was published a statement by which it appeared
that we had in England, counting not only the nine great public schools which formed the subject of an inquiry by a Royal
Commission, but counting also all the important endowed
schools of the country, and all the important schools of recent
foundation, such as Cheltenham and Marlborough,—that we
had in all these taken together a total number of scholars
amounting, in round figures, to 16,000. Let us consider all these
schools as being sufficiently in the public eye to afford, through
that very publicity, guarantees for their efficiency. Let us add
4000 scholars more. We remember the picture which was the
other day officially drawn for us of the secondary schools of
Ireland. In Scotland, deservedly celebrated for its elementary
schools, the secondary schools of high standing and character
are few in number. But both Ireland and Scotland make considerable use of the English secondary schools. If we add 4000 for
increase in England since 1865, and for Scotland and Ireland,
and put at 20,000 our total number of boys under secondary
instruction which may be called guaranteed, we make a liberal
estimate. In France they have 157,296.

The middle class in France has, in consequence, a homogene-
ity, an extent, and an importance, which it has nowhere else. "It
is our middle class in France," says M. Bardoux, "which makes
the *grandeur et originalité,* the greatness and originality, of the
nation." Above the peasant and artisan, the class who live by
the labour of their hands and who are the subjects for elementary instruction, the rest of the nation consists, for all intents
and purposes, of one immense class who are subjects for secondary instruction, and who receive it of one equal quality and in
schools of one equal standing. The professions and that whole
class which Mr. Charles Sumner distinguishes as the class of
gentlemen are in England separated from the great bulk of the

middle class, and are brought up along with the aristocracy in a superior order of schools. In France the professions and the great bulk of the middle class are brought up in schools of one equal standing. This creates a middle class larger, more homo-
5 geneous, and better educated than ours. The French aristocracy are chiefly brought up at Vaugirard and at schools under ecclesiastics. I have no prejudice against schools under ecclesiastics, and Vaugirard is an excellent school. But Vaugirard is not a school with better instruction and of higher standing than the
10 great public schools used by the middle class. It stands to them not as with us Eton and Harrow stand to a middle-class academy, but rather as Stonyhurst stands to Eton and Harrow. The aristocracy in France, therefore, is not a class which, in addition to its advantages of birth and wealth over the middle class, has
15 received a higher training than the middle class, in schools of a superior standing. Aristocracy and middle class are brought up in schools of one equal standing. The French aristocracy has, it is true, the spirit of caste; it strives to separate itself, to assert its superiority, to give effect to its prepossessions. But the im-
20 mense homogeneous middle class in France is too strong for it. The mind and imagination of this class is not subjugated by aristocracy like the mind and imagination of the middle class in our country. The mere comparison of the governments of the two countries at the present moment is evidence enough of the
25 truth of what I say. In England the government is composed of a string of aristocratical personages, with one or two men from the professional class who are engaged with them, and a man of genius of whom it is not easy to say whether he is engaged with them or they with him. In France the government is composed
30 entirely of men from the professional and middle class. True, the difference between the two aristocracies in property and standing, since the French Revolution, accounts for much of the difference in political influence. But the training of the middle class in France counts for more. Its great mass has not, as
35 with us, the sense of an inferior training. It is not cut in two, as with us; it is homogeneous. And this immense homogeneous class is brought up in schools of as good standing as those of

the aristocracy; it is brought up on the first plane. It is possible
and producible.

The Exhibition has this year drawn English people over to
Paris in great numbers. They have had the astonishing beauty
of Paris, and the civilisation and prosperity of the French peo-   5
ple, brought close before their eyes, and they have been struck
by it. Prince Bismarck says, we know, that the French nation
has a social solidity such as no other nation of Europe enjoys.
This can only come from the broad basis of well-being, and of
cause for satisfaction with life, which in France, more than in   10
other European countries, exists. We have the testimony of the
Belgian economist, M. de Laveleye, to the superior well-being
of the French peasant, and we ought not to be tired of repeating
it to ourselves over and over again, that we may get it well fixed
in our minds. "France is the country of Europe," says M. de   15
Laveleye, "where the soil is more divided than anywhere else
except in Switzerland and Norway, and it is at the same time
the country where material well-being is most widely spread,
where wealth has of late years increased most, and where population is least outrunning the limits which, for the comfort and   20
progress of the working classes themselves, seem necessary."
And Mr. Hamerton, an acute observer, and an Englishman to
boot, has remarked on "the enormous interval," as he calls it, by
which the French peasant is raised above the Kentish labourer.
Thus much for the lower class in France, and for its causes of   25
satisfaction with life. And if we consider the beauty and the
ever-advancing perfection of Paris,—nay, and the same holds
good, in its degree, of all the other great French cities also,—if
we consider the theatre there; if we consider the pleasures, recreations, even the eating and drinking; if we consider the whole   30
range of resources for instruction, and for delight, and for the
conveniences of a humane life generally; and if we then think
of London, and Liverpool, and Glasgow, and of the life of English towns generally, we shall find that the advantage of France
arises from its immense middle class making the same sort of   35
demands upon life which only a small upper class makes elsewhere.

Delicate and gifted single natures are sown in all countries. The French aristocracy will not bear a moment's comparison for splendour and importance with ours, neither have the French our exceptional class, registered by Mr. Charles Sumner, 5 of gentlemen. But these are, after all, only two relatively small divisions broken off from the top of that whole great class which does not live by the labour of its hands. These small divisions make upon life the demands of humane and civilised men. But they are too small and too weak to create a civilisation, to make 10 a Paris. The great bulk of the class from which they are broken off makes, as is well known, no such demands upon life. London, Liverpool, and Glasgow, with their kind of building, physiognomy, and effects; with their theatres, pleasures, recreations, and resources in general of delight and convenience for a hu-15 mane life, are the result. But in France the whole middle class makes, I say, upon life the demands of civilised men, and this immense demand creates the civilisation we see. And the joy of this civilisation creates the passionate delight and pride in France which we find in Frenchmen. Life is so good and agreeable a 20 thing there, and for so many.

French society has, in my opinion, whatever Prince Bismarck may say, sources of great danger as well as of great strength. English society has its sources of great strength as well as its sources of danger. But I am calling attention now to one single 25 point in the social condition of the two nations,—to the demand which the middle class, in each of them, makes upon life, and to the results which flow from it. It is surely impossible to deny that the whole immense middle class in France makes upon life the demands which are elsewhere those of a limited upper class 30 only, and that French civilisation gains enormously in both volume and quality by this being so. It is not difficult, of course, in England, for one of the aristocratic class, or for one of the class of gentlemen, to see that our middle class rests satisfied with a defective type of religion, a narrow range of intellect and 35 knowledge, a stunted sense of beauty, a low standard of manners. But an ordinary Frenchman of the middle class sees it just as clearly as any great lord or refined gentleman sees it with us, because his standard of civilisation is so comparatively high. It is not the French aristocracy and professions, it is the whole French middle class, which is astonished at the pleasures of the gay and pleasure-seeking portion of our middle class. It is not the French aristocracy and professions, it is the whole French middle class, which is astonished at the hideousness and immense ennui of the life of the graver portion. "The sense of acute ennui which the aspect and frequentation of this great division of English society produce in others, the want of elasticity and the chronic ennui which characterise this class itself"—that is not an expression of the feeling merely of a fastidious upper class or of a superfine individual, it is the genuine sentiment of the mass of middle-class France.

The French middle class is called Voltairian, as the French University and its schools, in which the middle class is educated, are called Voltairian too. Voltairian the French middle class in the main is. A great deal may be said in dispraise of Voltaire. But this is his centenary year; it is a hundred years ago this year since he died. *Il avait beaucoup travaillé dans ce monde*, as Michelet says of our own Henry the Fifth:—"he had done a big spell of work in this world;" and of the indefatigable worker let us on this occasion speak good rather than evil. He looked at things straight, and he had a marvellous logic and lucidity. The *Morning Star*, I remember, which has passed away from amongst us, used to say that what characterises Englishmen, and above all, Englishmen of the middle class, is "clear, manly intelligence, which penetrates through sophisms, ignores commonplaces, and gives to conventional illusions their true value." And the French, in like manner, the French middle class above all, pique themselves on their logic and lucidity. The French mind craves it, the French language almost compels it; Voltaire, the French Luther of the eighteenth century, was a splendid professor and propagator of it. And to a middle-class Frenchman it seems a matter of the plainest reasoning in the world, that the civilisation of the middle class must suffer in England and thrive in France. "Equality," he thinks with M. Gambetta, "is in France the source of all our strength in the present, of all our good hope for the future." England has, in Mr. Gladstone's famous words, the religion of inequality. "With your enormous

inequality of conditions and property," our Frenchman would
say, "a middle class is naturally thrown back upon itself and
upon an inferior type of social life and of civilisation. Add to
this your want of public schools for this class, and that it is
5 brought up anyhow, brought up in hugger-mugger, brought
up on the second plane;—its being thrown back upon an inferior type of social life and of civilisation is an irresistible necessity. In France we have got equality, and we bring up our middle class on the first plane; hence French civilisation." And the
10 *Morning Star*, which should have answered this man of logic
and lucidity, and should have shown why it is the part of the
clear, manly intelligence of Englishmen which penetrates
through sophisms, ignores commonplaces, and gives to conventional illusions their true value, rather to insist on introducing
15 readings from Eliza Cook into our public churchyards, or on
legalising marriage with a deceased wife's sister, than to abate
our enormous inequality of conditions and property, or to provide schools for bringing up our middle class on the first plane
instead of the second,—the *Morning Star*, I say, is unhappily
20 defunct.

And if, in the regretted absence of that powerful disputant,
our man of logic and lucidity were to be told by some ingenuous person that after all we were not all of us in England satisfied
with the state of our secondary instruction, although our aristo-
25 cratic class and our middle class itself apparently were, but that
there was a project on foot for bettering it, and if our Frenchman were then to ask what it was,—what should we say? We
should say that a generous and humane soul, a lover of light and
perfection, detached from the prepossessions both of the aristo-
30 cratic and of the middle class, and not willing that our middle
class should continue to be the worst schooled in civilised Europe, had adopted a bill which he found waiting for some one
to take charge of it and to put it forward, and which he hoped
might improve matters if it could become law; that his name
35 was Playfair, and that he was member for the University of
Edinburgh. And Dr. Playfair's bill proposes, we should say, to
form a Council of Public Instruction such as exists in France,
and to give power to this council to send its inspectors into en-

dowed schools, and to offer to send its inspectors into schools which are not endowed, if the schools like to receive them. For not even a generous and humane soul, we should have to say, such as Dr. Playfair, thinks it possible to attempt in England, for the rescue of the middle class from its state of inferior schooling, more than this. And our man of logic and lucidity would certainly reply, that this was like attempting to cure our enormous inequality of conditions and property by the Real Estates Intestacy Bill; that the real *objective* for us, as the military phrase is, was the bringing up of the middle class on the first plane, not the second, and that this is not to be done by inspecting a certain number of schools whether they will or no, and offering to inspect others if they like it, but by creating a system of public secondary schools.

And certainly, as a matter of fact, a plan of annual examination of secondary schools by inspectors, such as that which we have in elementary schools, does not seem likely in itself to work well and smoothly, while at the same time it fails, as the Frenchman says, to bring us to what is our real objective. The examination of secondary schools by inspectors is a matter of far greater difficulty and delicacy than the examination of elementary schools, is far more likely to produce impatience and opposition among the schoolmasters subjected to it, and is really far less necessary. All our good secondary schools have at present some examination proceeding from the universities; and if this kind of examination, customary and admitted already, were generalised and regularised, it would be sufficient for the purpose. What is really needed is to follow the precedent of the Elementary Education Act, by requiring the provision throughout the country of a proper supply of secondary schools, with proper buildings and accommodations, at a proper fee, and with proper guarantees given by the teachers in the shape either of a university degree or of a special certificate for secondary instruction. An inquiry, as under that Act, would have to be made as to the fulfilment of the necessary conditions by the actual schools now professing to meet the demand for secondary instruction, and as to the correspondence of the supply of schools fulfilling those conditions with the supply fixed after

due calculation as requisite. The existing resources for secondary instruction, if judiciously co-ordered and utilised, would
prove to be immense; but undoubtedly gaps would have to be
filled, an annual State grant and municipal grants would be nec-
5 essary. That is to say, the nation would perform, as a corporate
and co-operative work, a work which is now never conceived
and laid out as a whole, but is done sporadically, precariously,
and insufficiently. We have had experience how elementary instruction gains by being thus conceived and laid out, instead of
10 being left to individual adventure or individual benevolence.
The middle class who contribute so immense a share of the cost
incurred for the public institution of elementary schools, while
their own school supply is so miserable, would be repaid twenty
times over for their share in the additional cost of publicly in-
15 stituting secondary instruction by the direct benefit which they
and theirs would get from its system of schools. The upper
class, which has bought out the middle class at so many of the
great foundation schools designed for its benefit, and which has
monopolised what good secondary instruction we have, owes
20 to the middle class the reparation of contributing to a public
system of secondary schools. Perhaps *secondary* is a bad word
to use, because it is equivocal. Intermediate is a better. A system of public intermediate schools we require to have throughout the country, of two grades, the classical side predominating
25 in the schools of one grade, the modern side in the other; where
for a fee of from £30 to £50 a year for boarders, and from
£10 to £20 a year for day boys, the middle class might obtain
education. All existing schools which give, under proper guarantees, secondary instruction, should be classed as public inter-
30 mediate schools. Nor should their scale of fees be interfered
with. But it should be calculated for what proportion of the
class requiring secondary instruction schools with such fees can
be considered to make provision. For the proportion remaining,
—for the great bulk, that is, of the middle class,—provision
35 ought to be found or made at the lower rates.

The intervention and inspection of government should be
limited to the following points mainly:—First, to inquiring and
announcing what is the provision requisite, to taking care that

within a certain time it is supplied, and that when supplied it is maintained. Secondly, to ascertaining that the teaching staff is provided with the degrees or certificates prescribed as a public guarantee of efficiency, that some examination of the schools by other teachers than their own, an examination proceeding 5 either from the universities or from some recognised scholastic authority, takes place in them every year, and that the school premises are sufficient, suitably fitted and kept, and wholesome. Inspection of this kind is the function of a ministerial department rather than of a council, and it is not of a nature to irritate 10 schoolmasters' susceptibilities.

The function of a council is consultative: to consider and advise as to methods and studies. The function is a very important one. But a Council of Public Instruction is generally a body framed so as to represent several great interests. It is so in 15 France, at any rate. And the consequence is, I believe, that instead of there being much consideration of school methods and studies, the interests generally break out and begin a war, religious, professional, or administrative, amongst themselves; and the minister finds it expedient to convoke and consult his coun- 20 cil as little as possible.

It is not always quite easy to follow our French friends, men of logic and lucidity though they may be, when they are singing the glories of the ideas of 1789. But the French system of public secondary instruction is one of the real, one of the best 25 conquests of 1789 and of the Revolution. Decreed and begun by the Convention, organised by Fourcroy's law in 1802, secured by the establishment of the University in 1806, this system provides effective schooling, and on one common plane, for the whole class requiring an instruction more than elementary; 30 while with the elementary schools it connects itself in an unbroken order, offering a second stage by which the new social strata, as M. Gambetta calls them, may move onward, if they are worthy, and may rise. And our want of any such system in England is like the want of any municipal system for our coun- 35 try parishes, where the mode of government by vestry answers to that in use formerly in the rural districts of France, and described by Turgot: a kind of mass-meeting of the parishioners

held by the curé in the churchyard after service. Both wants are
due to what Thiers was never weary of pointing out as matter
for remark and reflection: the purely political character of our
revolutions; the absence from them,—the unavoidable and irre-
5 proachable absence it may be, but still the absence,—of all aim
at social renovation.

Schools for the licensed victuallers, schools for the commercial travellers, schools for the Wesleyans, schools for the Quak-
ers,—to educate a middle class in this way is to doom it to grow
10 up on an inferior plane, with the claims of intellect and knowledge not satisfied, the claim of beauty not satisfied, the claim of
manners not satisfied. At a very great money-price the upper
class has got possession of what public secondary schools of
good standing there are, and does not feel bound to lend its en-
15 deavours towards stripping itself of the advantage which this
higher training gives to it. That an upper class should not care
to be disturbed in its preponderance is perhaps natural; that a
middle class should acquiesce in a state of things which dooms
it to inferiority does at first sight seem astonishing. Yet we ought
20 not to be too much astonished at it, for human nature resists instinctively any change in its habits. And an English middle class
brought up in public schools and on the first plane, an English
middle class homogeneous, intelligent, civilised, would undergo
more than some slight and partial change of habits. It would un-
25 dergo transformation. A transformation devoutly to be wished,
indeed, yet so vast a one that the wise man may be inclined to
shrink from the toil of trying single-handed to bring it to pass,
—may content himself with not being made a dupe of, not being taken in, when he is told that it is undesirable and impossible.
30 And yet if all those generous and humane souls, free from the
prepossessions of class, who are scattered about in every society,
were to turn their thoughts this way, and to see what is the
truth, that perhaps our chief and gravest want in this country
at present, our *unum necessarium*, is a middle class, homogene-
35 ous, intelligent, civilised, brought up in good public schools and
on the first plane, something surely might be done!

Mr. Lowe says that "an English government should be guided
simply by the consideration how to produce for the country

the greatest amount of happiness of which the condition of its
existence admits." Mr. Gladstone says that "with the true Liberal statesman, England's first care is held to be the care of her
own children within her own shores, the redress of wrongs, the
supply of needs, the improvement of laws and institutions." If   5
there is one thing more certain than another, it is this: that the
middle class is in France *happier* than with us. If there is one
need more crying than another, it is the need of the English
middle class to be rescued from a defective type of religion, a
narrow range of intellect and knowledge, a stunted sense of   10
beauty, a low standard of manners. And what could do so much
to deliver them and to render them happier, as to give them
proper education, public education, to bring them up on the
first plane; to make them a class homogeneous, intelligent, civilised? Nay, and our upper class itself, though it may be sup-   15
posed to be not naturally inclined to lend a hand to deprive itself of preponderance, has far too much public spirit not to be
concerned and disquieted if it really comes to see that our civilisation is maimed by our middle class being left as it is, and that
the whole country, the whole English nation, suffers by it.   20
Where is there in the world an upper class which has in it so
many who know well that it will not do for a man simply to
think of himself,—to aggrandise himself; that a man must be *in
commune bonus*, good with a goodness serviceable to the common cause? And this is just what is required of every worthier   25
soul amongst our upper classes; that in the matter of middle
class education he should be *in commune bonus*, good with a
goodness serviceable to the common cause:—

> "Nec sibi, sed toti genitum se credere mundo . . .
> Justitiæ cultor, rigidi servator honesti,   30
> *In commune bonus*."

Preface
[to *Mixed Essays*]

The first essay in this volume was published nearly twenty years ago, as preface to a work on Continental Schools, which has probably been read by specialists only. The other essays have appeared in well-known reviews.

5 The present volume touches a variety of subjects, and yet it has a unity of tendency—a unity which has more interest for an author himself, no doubt, than for other people; but which my friendly readers, whose attention has long been my best encouragement and reward, will not unwillingly suffer me, per-
10 haps, to point out to them.

Whoever seriously occupies himself with literature will soon perceive its vital connection with other agencies. Suppose a man to be ever so much convinced that literature is, as indisputably it is, a powerful agency for benefiting the world and for civilis-
15 ing it, such a man cannot but see that there are many obstacles preventing what is salutary in literature from gaining general admission, and from producing due effect. Undoubtedly, literature can of itself do something towards removing those obstacles, and towards making straight its own way. But it cannot do
20 all. In other words, literature is a part of civilisation; it is not the whole. What then is civilisation, which some people seem to conceive of as if it meant railroads and the penny post, and little more, but which is really so complex and vast a matter that a great spiritual power, like literature, is a part of it, and a part
25 only? Civilisation is the humanisation of man in society. Man is civilised when the whole body of society comes to live with a life worthy to be called *human*, and corresponding to man's true aspirations and powers.

The means by which man is brought towards this goal of his

endeavour are various. It is of great importance to us to attain
an adequate notion of them, and to keep it present before our
minds. They may be conceived quite plainly, and enounced
without any parade of hard and abstruse expression.

First and foremost of the necessary means towards man's civi-   5
lisation we must name *expansion.* The need of expansion is as
genuine an instinct in man as the need in plants for the light, or
the need in man himself for going upright. All the conveniences
of life by which man has enlarged and secured his existence—
railroads and the penny post among the number—are due to the   10
working in man of this force or instinct of expansion. But the
manifestation of it which we English know best, and prize most,
is the love of liberty.

The love of liberty is simply the instinct in man for expansion. Not only to find oneself tyrannised over and outraged is   15
a defeat to this instinct, but in general, to feel oneself over-
tutored, over-governed, *sate upon* (as the popular phrase is) by
authority, is a defeat to it. Prince Bismarck says: "After all, a
benevolent rational absolutism is the best form of government."
Plenty of arguments may be adduced in support of such a thesis.   20
The one fatal objection to it is that it is against nature, that it
contradicts a vital instinct in man—the instinct of expansion.
And man is not to be civilised or humanised, call it which you
will, by thwarting his vital instincts. In fact, the benevolent rational absolutism always breaks down. It is found that the ruler   25
cannot in the long run be trusted; it is found that the ruled de-
teriorate. Why? Because the proceeding is against nature.

The other great manifestation of the instinct of expansion is
the love of equality. Of the love of equality we English have
little; but, undoubtedly, it is no more a false tendency than the   30
love of liberty. Undoubtedly, immense inequality of conditions
and property is a defeat to the instinct of expansion; it depresses
and degrades the inferior masses. The common people is and
must be, as Tocqueville said, more uncivilised in aristocratic
countries than in any others. A thousand arguments may be   35
discovered in favour of inequality, just as a thousand arguments may be discovered in favour of absolutism. And the one
insuperable objection to inequality is the same as the one in-

superable objection to absolutism: namely, that inequality, like absolutism, thwarts a vital instinct, and being thus against nature, is against our humanisation. On the one side, in fact, inequality harms by pampering; on the other, by vulgarising and
5 depressing. A system founded on it is against nature, and in the long run breaks down.

    I put first among the elements in human civilisation the instinct of expansion, because it is the basis which man's whole effort to civilise himself presupposes. General civilisation pre-
10 supposes this instinct, which is inseparable from human nature; presupposes its being satisfied, not defeated. The basis being given, we may rapidly enumerate the powers which, upon this basis, contribute to build up human civilisation. They are the power of conduct, the power of intellect and knowledge, the
15 power of beauty, the power of social life and manners. Expansion, conduct, science, beauty, manners,—here are the conditions of civilisation, the claimants which man must satisfy before he can be humanised.

    That the aim for all of us is to make civilisation pervasive and
20 general; that the requisites for civilisation are substantially what have been here enumerated; that they all of them hang together, that they must all have their development, that the development of one does not compensate for the failure of others; that one nation suffers by failing in this requisite, and another by failing
25 in that: such is the line of thought which the essays in the present volume follow and represent. They represent it in their variety of subject, their so frequent insistence on defects in the present actual life of our nation, their unity of final aim. Undoubtedly, that aim is not given by the life which we now see
30 around us. Undoubtedly, it is given by "a sentiment of the ideal life." But then the ideal life is, in sober and practical truth, "none other than man's normal life, as we shall one day know it."

Appendix I

Three Public Speeches of Arnold's, 1873–1877

At a banquet to commemorate the Oxford Union Society's fiftieth anniversary, held in the Corn Exchange, Oxford, on the evening of October 22, 1873, Arnold, a former president of the society, responded to the toast to "Literature, Science, and Art." Since the hour was past midnight, he said only a few 5 words which the newspapers did not report.

On Saturday evening, May 1, 1875, the anniversary banquet of the Royal Academy was held in the Academy's rooms in Burlington House, to signal the opening of the Academy's annual exhibition. There, surrounded by the paintings, were as- 10 sembled a very distinguished company of members and guests. After the toasts to the Queen, the Royal family, the Army and the Navy, the President of the Academy proposed "Prosperity to the Interests of Science and Literature," Sir John Lubbock responding for the former. "With literature," said the President, 15 "I beg to couple the name of Mr. Matthew Arnold, a graceful writer, scholar, and poet, and son of the distinguished Dr. Arnold, of Rugby (cheers), a name that will ever be held in honour in this country. (Cheers.)"

Mr. Matthew Arnold, in returning thanks for Literature, 20 said,—Sir Francis Grant, your Royal Highness, my Lords, and gentlemen,—Literature, no doubt, is a great and splendid art, allied to that great and splendid art of which we see around us

373

the handiwork. But, Sir, you do me an undeserved honour
when, as President of the Royal Academy, you desire me to
speak in the name of Literature. Whatever I may have once
wished or intended, my life is not that of a man of letters, but
5 of an Inspector of Schools (a laugh), and it is with embarrassment that I now stand up in the dreaded presence of my own
official chiefs (a laugh), who have lately been turning upon their
Inspectors an eye of some suspicion. (A laugh.) Therefore, Sir,
I cannot quite with propriety speak here as a literary man and
10 a brother artist; but, since you have called upon me, let me at
least quote to you, and apply for my own benefit and that of
others, something from an historian of literature. Fauriel, the
French literary historian, tells us of a colony of Greeks settled
somewhere in Southern Italy, who retained for an extraordi-
15 nary length of time their Greek language and civilization. However, time and circumstance were at last too strong for them;
they began to lose, they felt themselves losing their distinctive
Greek character; they grew like all the other people about
them. Only, once every year they assembled themselves to-
20 gether at a public festival of their community, and there, in
language which the inroads of barbarism were every year more
and more debasing, they reminded one another that they were
once Greeks. (Cheers and a laugh.) How many of your guests
to-night, Sir, may remind one another of the same thing. (Hear,
25 hear.) The brilliant statesman at the head of Her Majesty's Government, to whom we shall listen with so much admiration by-
and-by, may even boast that he was born in Arcadia. (Cheers
and a laugh.) To no people, probably, does it so often happen
to have to break in great measure with their vocation and with
30 the Muses, as to the men of letters for whom you have sum-
moned me to speak. (Cheers.) But perhaps there is no one man
here, however positive and prosaic, who has not at some time
or other of his life, and in some form or other, felt something of
that desire for the truth and beauty of things which makes the
35 Greek, the artist. (Hear, hear.) The year goes round for us
amid other pre-occupations; then, with the Spring, arrives your
hour. You collect us at this festival; you surround us with en-
chantment, and call upon us to remember, and in our stam-

mering and imperfect language to confess that we were once
Greeks. (Cheers.) If we have not forgotten it, the reminder is
delightful; if we have forgotten it, it is salutary. (Hear, hear.)
In the common and practical life of this country, in its government, politics, commerce, law, medicine—even in its religion—   5
some compliance with men's conventionality, vulgarity, folly,
and ignobleness, a certain dose of claptrap (a laugh) passes almost for a thing of necessity. But in that world to which we
have sometimes aspired, in your world of art, Sir, in the Greek
world—for so I will call it after the wonderful people who in-   10
troduced mankind to it—in the Greek world of art and science,
claptrap and compliance with the conventional are simply fatal.
(Hear, hear.) Let us be grateful to you for recalling it to us; for
reminding us that strength and success are possible to find by
taking one's law, not from the form and pressure of the passing   15
day, but from the living forces of our genuine nature;—
        "Vivitur ingenio; cetera mortis erunt."
(Cheers.)

At a banquet to commemorate the opening of the New Hall
of Balliol College on Tuesday, January 16, 1877, at which the   20
first speaker was A. C. Tait, archbishop of Canterbury, Arnold
responded to a toast proposed by T. H. Green to the Balliol men
who had gained reputations in literature and science. He "returned thanks in a speech in which he contrasted his position as
regards preferment and emoluments with that of the Arch-   25
bishop of Canterbury, and declared that whatever might be
thought of literature, he knew no path half so dusty and stony
as his."—*Oxford University Herald*, Saturday, January 20,
1877, pp. 8–9; *Oxford Chronicle*, same date, p. 5, col. 3.

ask wilbur to expand
questions

Appendix II

Arnold's Notes to Johnson's *Lives of the Poets*

For his school text edition of Johnson's *Six Lives* Arnold provided seven pages of notes, "strictly limited," he said, "to what
seemed required for making the Lives intelligible and interesting to that class of readers which I have here in view." These
5 notes are for the most part simply factual information—identification of people named, explanation of classical allusions, etc.
One note, which Arnold supplied not only in the school text
edition but in the earlier editions and which he mentioned in his
Preface, is here reproduced, and so also are two notes from the
10 school edition which may continue to have some interest:

[On Addison's alleged public contempt for Steele in *The
Old Whig*, after their years of friendship; "Life of Addison,"
two-fifths through:]

Macaulay has conclusively shown that Johnson was wrong in
15 supposing that by 'little Dicky' Addison meant Steele. In an
article in the Edinburgh Review (July 1843), on Miss Aikin's
Life and Writings of Addison, Macaulay says:—"It is asserted
in the Biographia Britannica that Addison designated Steele as
'little Dicky.' This assertion was repeated by Johnson, who had
20 never seen The Old Whig, and was therefore excusable. It is
true that the words 'little Dicky' occur in The Old Whig, and
that Steele's name was Richard. It is equally true that the words
'little Isaac' occur in The Duenna, and that Newton's name was
Isaac. But we confidently affirm that Addison's 'little Dicky'
25 had no more to do with Steele than Sheridan's 'little Isaac' with
Newton. If we apply the words 'little Dicky' to Steele, we de-

prive a very lively and ingenious passage not only of all its wit
but of all its meaning. 'Little Dicky' was evidently the nickname
of some comic actor who played the usurer Gomez, then a most
popular part, in Dryden's Spanish Friar."

Shortly afterwards, in a letter to Mr. Napier, the editor of the   5
Edinburgh Review, Macaulay writes as follows:—"I am much
pleased with one thing. You may remember how confidently I
asserted that 'little Dicky,' in The Old Whig, was the nickname
of some comic actor. Several people thought that I risked too
much in assuming this so strongly on mere internal evidence. I   10
have now, by an odd accident, found out who the actor was.
An old prompter of Drury Lane theatre, named Chetwood,
published, in 1749, a small volume containing an account of all
the famous performers he remembered, arranged in alphabeti-
cal order. This little volume I picked up yesterday, for sixpence,   15
at a bookstall in Holborn; and the first name on which I opened
was that of Henry Norris, a favourite comedian, who was nick-
named 'Dicky' because he first obtained celebrity by acting the
part of Dicky in the Trip to the Jubilee. It is added that his
figure was very diminutive. He was, it seems, in the height of   20
his popularity at the very time when The Old Whig was written. You will, I think, agree with me that this is decisive. I am
a little vain of my sagacity, which I really think would have
dubbed me a *vir clarissimus*, if it had been shewn on a point of
Greek or Latin learning; but I am still more pleased that the   25
vindication of Addison from an unjust charge, which has been
universally believed since the publication of the Lives of the
Poets, should thus be complete. Should you have any objection
to inserting a short note at the end of the next Number?"

[On Johnson's discussion of the Alexandrine, in "Life of   30
Dryden," six-sevenths through:]

By this in English poetry is meant merely a twelve-syllable line.
By the Alexandrine metre is meant a poem in couplets of such
lines, rhyming together. It is the celebrated metre of French
tragedy, and takes its name from the *Alexandreis,* a popular ro-   35

mance poem in French on Alexander the Great, published in 1184.

[On Johnson's attack upon Gray's "Progress of Poesy" and "The Bard":]

5 Johnson is seen at his worst in his criticism of "the two Sister Odes"; but it is instructive to read him on Gray, and to weigh for oneself the value of what he says. Gray's Progress of Poesy gives, with admirable skill, a poetical history of Poetry; his Bard gives, with like skill, a poetical history of England.

Critical and Explanatory Notes

References to Arnold's diary-notebooks are drawn from H. F. Lowry, K. Young, and W. H. Dunn, eds., *The Note-Books of Matthew Arnold* (London: Oxford University Press, 1952), supplemented by W. B. Guthrie, ed., *Matthew Arnold's Diaries: the Unpublished Items* (Ann Arbor: University Microfilms, 1959). Arnold's correspondence with his publishers is quoted from W. E. Buckler, ed., *Matthew Arnold's Books* (Geneva: Droz, 1958). Most quotations from his other letters are taken from the collected edition by G. W. E. Russell, where they can be found under their dates; the collection has been published in so many editions that page references are not helpful. A very few quotations are from unpublished letters; most of these can be traced through Arthur Kyle Davis's *Matthew Arnold's Letters: a Descriptive Checklist* (Charlottesville: The University Press of Virginia, 1968). Notes to canceled passages are placed in the same sequence as the notes to the final text; when the parenthetical word "(variant)" appears, the note is in explanation of a passage that will be found only in the Textual Notes.

[A DEPTFORD POET]

The unsigned review of Charles P. O'Conor's *Songs of a Life* in *The Pall Mall Gazette* for June 25, 1875, was first identified as Arnold's by Dean Roger L. Brooks, "'A Deptford Poet': an Addition and a Correction to the Matthew Arnold Bibliography," *Philological Quarterly* XLI, 515–17 (April, 1962), on the strength of entries in Arnold's diary for 1875, which on June 20–22 noted "write on O'Conor" or "work at O'Conor," on June 23, "send O'Conor," and on June 24, "correct proof." The diary also indicated that Arnold carried on some correspondence with O'Conor, but this is not now known to survive. He received three guineas in payment for the

article. The identification of this review as Arnold's serves at the
same time to deny his authorship of the anonymous review of *The
Autobiography of Mrs. Fletcher,* published in *The Pall Mall Gazette*
on June 10, 1875, and reprinted as Arnold's on admittedly inconclusive evidence by Fraser Neiman, *Essays, Letters, and Reviews by
Matthew Arnold* (Cambridge: Harvard University Press, 1960), pp.
201–4.

Arnold continued his support for O'Conor by seconding with
vigor the attempts made to gain a pension for him. "I want you to
keep poor O'Conor in mind, and to induce Tennyson, if possible, to
sign the memorial for a pension to the poor creature," he wrote to
Frederick Locker, and when Gladstone was back in power he wrote
directly to him, on July 6, 1881, to "put in a word for . . . a poor
Irishman called O'Conor. He has a small vein, but it is a genuine one;
among scores of books of verse that are sent to me, I felt the presence, in his, of this vein which is so rare, and so, I know, did Mr.
Tennyson and Archbishop Trench. The writer has really lived by
the work of his hands and educated himself as he could; his character is trustworthy, but he is in dreadful health and has a family depending on him. A very small pension would be to him a very great
boon, and I honestly think him a deserving object for it." The pension was procured, and Arnold thanked Gladstone on September 26:
"He will now be relieved by your kindness from his great present
danger, which is that he is tempted to work [his] vein much too fast
and too hard in order to get a living by contributing verses to the
newspapers."—W. H. G. Armytage, "Arnold and Gladstone: Some
New Letters," *University of Toronto Quarterly* XVIII, 225 (April,
1949).

2:14. Gladstone's collection of art, of which the china and porce-
lain formed the most valuable and extensive portion, was sold by
auction at Christie's on June 23–26, 1875.

6:20. Preface to *Die Braut von Messina*, in *Sämmtliche Werke*
(Stuttgart, 1862), V, 344; quoted by Arnold in his Preface to *Poems*
(1853), *Prose Works*, ed. Super, I, 2.

6:21–25. Deptford is a metropolitan borough south of the Thames,
a dock area between Bermondsey and Greenwich. A School Board
Visitor was an investigating officer of the Board who looked into
matters such as non-compliance with the regulation that children
were obliged to attend school until the age of thirteen. On May 1,
1875, a young woman named Elizabeth Marks appeared before a
magistrate in the Guildhall to ask his help: her husband had been

confined to a lunatic asylum six months before, leaving her with five children and the necessity of working away from home from 8 a.m. to 8 p.m. to earn a living. She kept her oldest girl, an eleven-year-old, at home to care for the two youngest, while a nine-year-old and a five-year-old went to school. A School Board Visitor, responding to a neighbor's complaint, made a remark to the oldest child which was construed as threatening to send the family to a workhouse unless some means were found for sending her to school. *The Times* published two indignant leading articles and the vice president of the Committee of Council was questioned in the Commons. "A woman who is struggling in this way, and teaching her children by example and practice the lesson of independence, is giving them an education of far greater value than mere reading and writing, and, instead of being hindered, she ought to be encouraged in every possible way," wrote *The Times* on May 4, p. 9, col. 6. Sympathetic readers forwarded to the magistrate contributions sufficient to provide Mrs. Marks with a mangle and other amenities, a more comfortable home, and a savings account. See *The Times* also for May 3, p. 13, col. 5; May 5, p. 7, col. 6; May 7, p. 6, col. 1; p. 9, col. 4, and p. 10, col. 6; May 10, p. 13, col. 4.

[EDOARDO FUSCO]

When Arnold reached Naples on his official journey to investigate secondary and higher education on the Continent at the end of May, 1865, he found as inspector-general for education there a man he had actually entertained at dinner at 2, Chester Square, Edoardo Fusco. His letters from Naples are full of Fusco's attentions, and when Fusco visited London in the summer of 1866 he was given the privileges of the Athenaeum Club "as distinguished foreigner" at Arnold's behest. After his death, Fusco's widow in 1876 began to publish in *Macmillan's Magazine* a series of at least four lectures Fusco had delivered in English during his earlier exile, when he held the chair of Italian language and literature at Queen's College, London. Two installments of "Italian Art and Literature Before Giotto and Dante: A.D. 1000–1300" appeared in January and July, with an indication that more would follow, but none did. The papers were more striking for their rhetoric and their patriotism than for their information. Arnold's "breve, ma nobilissimo" introductory sketch of Fusco's career was prefixed to the first installment. His pocket diary shows that he wrote it on November 24–25, 1875, and sent it off on the latter day. He does not record any payment for it. See Grecca Ida Fusco, *Della Vita e delle opere di Edoardo Fusco* (Naples, 1880), I, 40 and II, 149–50.

8:7. "Den einzelnen Verkehrtheiten des Tags sollte man immer nur grosse weltgeschichtliche Massen engegensetzen."—"Maximen und Reflexionen," *Werke* (Stuttgart, 1833), XLIX, 100, jotted in Arnold's pocket diary at the beginning of 1878.—*Note-Books*, ed. Lowry, p. 291.

8:11–12. "Art and literature are the two landmarks by which we can assign to nations their place in the history of human intellect," wrote Fusco in the tenth paragraph of his first essay.

8:14–16. Arnold repeats Dante's definition as Fusco gives it early in his essay. It may be derived from Dante's discussion of the function of the state ("civilitas") at the beginning of his *Monarchia*.

8:16–18. *Goethes Unterhaltungen mit dem Kanzler Friedrich von Müller*, ed. C. A. H. Burkhardt (3rd ed.; Stuttgart, 1904), pp. 150–51 (August 23, 1827); jotted in Arnold's pocket diary for the beginning of 1875.—*Note-Books*, ed. Lowry, p. 224.

8:23–24. Vergil *Aeneid* XII, 435; quoted also by Arnold in "Equality" (1878), p. 299, and in the review of Renan's *La Réforme intellectuelle* (1872), *Prose Works*, ed. Super, VII, 48.

[LAST ESSAYS ON CHURCH AND RELIGION]

Arnold emphasized the word "Last" when late in November, 1876, he prepared to republish in a volume the four essays on church and religious questions that had appeared in the magazines that year. Their order was not that of their original appearance (which is the order adopted for the present edition): "A Psychological Parallel," "Bishop Butler and the Zeit-Geist," "The Church of England," and "A Last Word on the Burials Bill" were preceded by the long and carefully worked "Preface." The book was advertised at 7 s. in *The Athenaeum* for March 24, 1877. Sales were even more disappointing than those of *God and the Bible;* the essays were included in the edition of Arnold's works prepared for the American market in 1883, but no second edition appeared in England in Arnold's lifetime.

Epigraph: "Entrez, qu'on fonde ici la foi profonde" ("Enter: let us found here a faith profound") is a line from the long inscription above the portal of Gargantua's Abbey of Thélème in the 54th chapter of Rabelais' book. Arnold found the line quoted in Edmond Scherer's essay on Rabelais, *Études critiques de littérature* (Paris, 1876), p. 83, and jotted it in his pocket diary for October 18, 1876. —*Note-Books*, ed. Lowry, p. 259.

[BISHOP BUTLER AND THE ZEIT-GEIST]

Nowhere in his writings on religion had Arnold found opportunity to do justice to the English theologians he most admired, and especially to Joseph Butler, the strenuous opponent of the deists in the age of reason. Butler, like Aristotle, had been required reading when Arnold was an undergraduate at Oxford, as indeed he had been when Arnold's father was there, and for Dr. Arnold, Butler was "never to be named without respect." Matthew Arnold's earliest allusion to Butler was the ambiguous but presumably satirical sonnet, "Written in Butler's Sermons," that appeared in his first volume of poetry. Once he began to turn his attention to religious questions, however, with the Preface to *Culture and Anarchy* (1869), he began to cite Butler with increasing frequency for the strength of his good sense. If from Spinoza Arnold learned to apply the methods of historical criticism to Scripture, by Butler he was trained even earlier in the application of a central intellectual position to religion and in the criticism of dogma through the hardheaded observation of the operation of the human mind. Butler's *Analogy* is unreadable for its formlessness and repetitiveness; it has been simply left behind by the altered preconceptions of modern thought. Nevertheless *Literature and Dogma* could hardly have been written without it. And so Arnold looked for, and found, the opportunity to make clear both what Butler's achievement was and how the currents of thought in an era may control even the strongest mind. A somewhat older Oxford man than Arnold, W. E. Gladstone, wrote voluminously on Butler and at the close of his life published an edition of Butler's works, with commentary.

An invitation to lecture at the Edinburgh Philosophical Institution gave Arnold the opportunity he wanted. Whether his subject would have been Butler at the time he first agreed to lecture, January 7 and 10, 1873, is uncertain; these lectures, however, he found himself unable to give. By the latter part of 1874 he had accepted an engagement for November, 1875, and promised James T. Knowles, editor of the *Contemporary Review*, that he might publish the lectures. As the date drew near he found himself unable to prepare in time and deferred the engagement until January 4 and 7, 1876. He wrote the lectures in mid-December, as he approached his fifty-third birthday. There is indeed about them the tone of a man who conceives that he is beginning to grow old and that his major critical and scholarly efforts have been made. The Philosophical, founded in 1846, had its club rooms and meeting hall at No. 4, Queen Street, and there Arnold spoke to a crowded room.

"The Scotch made an admirable audience and let me say what I liked without a sign of disapproval," Arnold told Mark Pattison on January 20, "though the Free Church organ says that 'a thrill of awe' ran through the assembly when I said, in the second lecture, that the Bible contained 'plenty of truth and plenty of legend.' . . . The second will interest you, perhaps, as showing the effect really produced by Butler's arguments upon one who went to him with a sincere conviction of his being a great man, and a sincere disposition to use anything given by Butler which he found to be useable." "The first [lecture] is mainly biographical," Arnold told Knowles—and very largely a condensation of Bishop Steere's brief account of Butler's life, he might have added; "the second [lecture] is, I think, important." When it came to publication, Knowles asked Arnold to change the form of the papers from that of lectures to that of reviews, "because the *Contemporary* had a rule, said he, not to print lectures or speeches," but "having . . . read the first proof, with the lecture form remaining unchanged," he wrote "to beg me," Arnold said, "to leave it as it is, he is so well pleased with it. That is because of the rhythm. . . . It confirms what you [Pattison] say about my writing to the ear." Knowles paid Arnold £18 10s. for the first article (in February), £21 for the second (in March).

The first article won commendation, Arnold told his sister, from George Eliot, Carlyle, and Gladstone. The last conveyed his message—and an invitation to breakfast which Arnold was obliged to decline—through Knowles, to whom Arnold replied: "Pray [tell] Mr. Gladstone . . . how much pleasure it gives me that he should have liked what I have said of Butler. I knew that he was an admirer of Butler, and Butler is one of those men that one does not admire by halves." It has been suggested that Gladstone had not read Arnold's essay very carefully; at any rate, the greater part of one of his late articles on "Bishop Butler and His Censors" is devoted to

Arnold.—*Nineteenth Century* XXXVIII, 1056–74 (December, 1895).

Arnold had some thought of adding the Butler papers to a new edition of *St. Paul and Protestantism* as a means of increasing his profits from that work, but the new edition actually appeared before he expected it and so these lectures became the weightiest portion of *Last Essays*. Arnold's use of the term "Zeit-Geist," always a favorite of his, is the subject of an essay by Fraser Neiman, "The Zeitgeist of Matthew Arnold," *PMLA* LXXII, 977–96 (December, 1957). For an account of the Edinburgh Philosophical Institution see W. Addis Miller, *The "Philosophical."* Edinburgh, 1949.

12:22–24. Sermon XV, "Upon the Ignorance of Man," ¶11, and "Charge to the Clergy of Durham, 1751," ¶11.—*The Works of Joseph Butler*, ed. W. E. Gladstone (Oxford, 1896), II, 268, 404. The former is quoted in one of Arnold's "General Note-Books."—*Note-Books*, ed. Lowry, p. 518. And see p. 59:24–25.

12:25–28. *The Analogy of Religion, Natural and Revealed, to the Constitution and Course of Nature*, II, iii, 3.—ed. Gladstone, I, 222. See Arnold, *Literature and Dogma, Prose Works*, ed. Super, VI, 376.

12:30–32. Sermon VII, "Upon the Character of Balaam," ¶16.— ed. Gladstone, II, 134. Arnold quoted this passage also in "The Church of England," p. 80:32–34, in "A Psychological Parallel," p. 146:11–13, and in "Numbers," *Prose Works*, ed. Super, vol. X.

12:37–13:4. Edward Steere, "A Memoir of Bishop Butler," in his edition of *The Sermons and Remains of . . . Joseph Butler* (London, 1862), p. xviii. This Memoir is the source of most of Arnold's account of Butler's life; Steere in his turn drew largely upon Thomas Bartlett, *Memoirs of the Life, Character, and Writings of Joseph Butler*. London, 1839.

13:4–9. Bishop Halifax, in his Preface to an edition of Butler, says: "This way of arguing from what is acknowledged to what is disputed, from things known to other things that resemble them, . . . is on all hands confessed to be just. By this method Sir Isaac Newton has unfolded the system of nature; by the same method Bishop Butler has explained the system of grace; and thus, to use the words of a writer, whom I quote with pleasure, 'has formed and concluded a happy alliance between faith and philosophy.' "—ed. Gladstone, I, xxv. Halifax quotes from the Dissertation prefixed to John Mainwaring's *Sermons*.

13:12–22. Mackintosh, *A General View of the Progress of Ethical Philosophy* (Philadelphia, 1832), p. 115 (near the beginning of sect.

vi). Arnold may have found the greater part of these comments in Bartlett, *Memoirs*, pp. 27, 62.

13:28–36. Morley, "Diderot: IV. *The Encyclopaedia*," *Fortnightly Review* XXIV, 391–93 (September, 1875).

14:8–17. Sermon X, "Upon Self-Deceit," ¶19, 5, 9.—ed. Gladstone, II, 184, 172, 175.

14:23. Arnold's longest discussion of "Hebraism" is in chapter iv (1868) of *Culture and Anarchy, Prose Works*, ed. Super, V, 163–75. "The governing idea of . . . Hebraism [is] *strictness of conscience*."

14:34–36. Steere, "Memoir," p. xi.

14:36–15:19. *Ibid.*, pp. xii–xiii, xvi–xvii. Clarke (1675–1729), whose mode of reasoning was in the tradition of Descartes, was regarded as the principal English metaphysician in the quarter of a century following the death of Locke; see *God and the Bible, Prose Works*, ed. Super, VII, 179. Butler's remark, "I design the search after truth as the business of my life," was made in his fourth letter to Clarke, December 16, 1713.—*Works*, ed. Gladstone, I, 430. Arnold takes his title for Butler's "Charge to the Clergy of Durham" not from Butler but from Steere, who took it from a pamphlet in reply to the charge. William Talbot (1659?–1730), a kinsman of the Duke of Shrewsbury, was successively bishop of Oxford, of Salisbury, and (after 1721) of Durham. To his memory and to his son Charles, Lord Talbot (1685–1737), lord chancellor under Robert Walpole from 1734, Butler dedicated his *Analogy*. Edward Talbot, fellow of Oriel College, Oxford, died in 1720.

15:19–33. "Memoir," pp. xx, xxii–xxiii, xxvii–xxviii.

15:33–35. *Ibid.*, pp. xxix–xxx.

15:35–16:3. *Ibid.*, pp. xxxii–xxxiii.

16:6–12. *Ibid.*, p. xix, drawing on Bartlett, *Memoirs*, pp. 76–77 (letter from Bishop Philpotts dated January 25, 1835).

16:16–28. *Sermons and Remains*, ed. Steere, pp. xxxvi–xxxvii, drawing on Bartlett, *Memoirs*, pp. 73–74.

16:31–33. Thomas Ken (1637–1711), bishop of Bath and Wells under James II and a man of great sanctity, was author of the well-known hymn, "Awake, my soul, and with the sun." Robert Leighton (1611–84), born a Scottish Presbyterian but at the Restoration a bishop in the new Scottish Episcopal establishment, was described by his friend Bishop Burnet as having "the greatest elevation of soul, the largest compass of knowledge, the most mortified and heavenly disposition that I ever yet saw in mortal." Coleridge's *Aids to Re-*

flection draws heavily upon him. Thomas Wilson (1663–1755), bishop of Sodor and Man, wrote the *Maxims of Piety and of Christianity* Arnold was so fond of quoting in *Culture and Anarchy* and in his religious writings. In *St. Paul and Protestantism* (1870) Arnold linked Wilson and Ken with George Herbert as types of righteousness at its best, pre-eminent over the worthies of Puritanism; in the Preface to *Higher Schools and Universities in Germany* (1874) he linked Wilson and Ken with Fénelon as types of modern sainthood. —*Prose Works,* ed. Super, VI, 104; VII, 104.

16:36. "If therefore thine eye be single, thy whole body shall be full of light."—Matthew 6:22 (Luke 11:34).

17:3–15. "Memoir," pp. xxx–xxxi, drawing on Bartlett, *Memoirs,* pp. 277, 196–97.

17:15–22. *Sermons and Remains,* ed. Steere, pp. xl–xli; Bartlett, p. 115. Butler wrote "in the close of it" and "with respect to."

17:26–18:6. *Ibid.,* p. xli; Bartlett, p. 116. Butler wrote "entirely depends on."

18:14–19. *Ibid.,* p. xlvi; Bartlett, pp. 275–76.

18:22–30. "Memoir," pp. xxv, ix, xxxii; Bartlett, pp. 93, 201.

18:34–19:22. *Sermons and Remains,* ed. Steere, pp. xlii–xliii. Auckland Castle, at Bishop Auckland, eleven miles from Durham, has been a seat of the Bishops of Durham since the twelfth century.

19:24–35. Steere, "Memoir," pp. xxiii–xxv. Steere draws from the manuscripts in the British Museum written by the antiquary William Cole, who visited Bristol in 1746. The Bristol Reform riots took place on October 29–31, 1831.

19:39–20:22. Bartlett, *Memoirs,* pp. 152–56. The pamphlet war was not opened until 1767. Thomas Secker (1693–1768), archbishop of Canterbury from 1758, was a friend of Butler's from their school days in Gloucester and Tewkesbury.

20:24–21:7. "A Charge Delivered to the Clergy at the Primary Visitation of the Diocese of Durham, in the Year MDCCLI," ¶2, 12, 20, 24–26.—ed. Gladstone, II, 398, 405, 410, 413–16. And for "that immoral thoughtlessness, which far the greatest part of [men] are fallen into," see *Analogy* I, viii, 12.—ed. Gladstone, I, 183.

21:9–16. Steere, "Memoir," p. xxvi. Wesley's account of the meeting is given in Appendix III to vol. II (434–36) of Gladstone's edition of Butler; Arnold seems not to have known it.

21:19–32. "Memoir," pp. xxxi–xxxii, or Bartlett, *Memoirs,* p. 231, quoting Robert Surtees, *History of Durham* (London, 1816), I, cxxii (with omissions) and William Hutchinson, *The History and Antiquities of the County Palatine of Durham* (Newcastle, 1785), I, 578.

22:7–16. ¶5.—ed. Gladstone, II, 4–5.

22:21–24. Preface to Sermons, ¶29.—ed. Gladstone, II, 21. Butler wrote "one continued exercise."

22:35–23:11. Mark Pattison, "Tendencies of Religious Thought in England, 1688–1750," *Essays and Reviews* (9th ed.; London, 1861), pp. 286–87, 288. Pattison speaks of "the Deistical notions," not "the deistical writers." "If you look at this first lecture on Butler you will find what appreciative use I have made of your article in Essays & Reviews," Arnold wrote to Pattison.

23:18–19. *Ibid.*, p. 313. Edward Dowden has pointed out that Pattison misled Arnold: "The first edition of the *Analogy* bears a date previous to Butler's appointment as Clerk of the Closet."—Review of *Last Essays, Academy* XI, 430 (May 19, 1877).

23:20–22, 27–24:2. "Charge to the Clergy of Durham," ¶7–8.—ed. Gladstone, II, 401.

24:7. The satirist Juvenal proclaimed of his work, "Facit indignatio versum"—"Indignation produces my verse" (I, 79). Swift adapted the concept in his own epitaph: "Hic depositum est corpus Jonathan Swift . . . ubi saeva indignatio ulterius cor lacerare nequit" —"Here is laid the body of Jonathan Swift, where savage indignation can no longer tear his heart."

24:9–24. *Analogy* II, ix, 5.—ed. Gladstone, I, 373.

24:27–29. *Six Sermons Preached upon Public Occasions.* II. "Before the Corporation of London," ¶20.—ed. Gladstone, II, 315.

24:32–25:2. ¶1; ed. Gladstone, II, 397.

25:21–24. Jules Michelet, *Histoire de France* (nouv. éd.; Paris, 1876), XIX, 190, 200. Anne-Robert-Jacques Turgot (1727–81) was a vigorously reforming comptroller-general of France from August, 1774, to May, 1776.

25:26. See p. 20:32–33.

25:29–31. Butler, Sermon IV, "Upon the Government of the Tongue," ¶12.—ed. Gladstone, II, 86.

26:3–4. Michelet, *Histoire,* XIX, 190.

26:12–14. Philippians 4:8. Arnold's "nobly serious" translates the Greek σεμνά; in the Authorized Version it is rendered "honest." See *God and the Bible, Prose Works,* ed. Super, VII, 385:31.

26:26–27:3, 18–19. *Essays and Reviews,* p. 313. Pattison reads "laugh themselves," not "hug themselves," but the sense is clearer as Arnold gives it.

27:21–26, 31–32. *Ibid.*, pp. 281, 284–85, 281. "[The religious writer] appeared at the bar of criticism, and must gain the wits and the town."

27:31. Milton in *Paradise Lost* (I, 24–26) invokes the Holy Spirit to the end

> That to the highth of this great Argument
> I may assert Eternal Providence,
> And justifie the wayes of God to men."

Robert Southey's memorial inscription for the monument to Butler in Bristol cathedral (1834) speaks of Butler's "laying his strong foundations in the depth of that great argument."

27:35–36. See p. 23:31–32.

28:7–8. Arnold discussed this term in *St. Paul and Protestantism* and *Literature and Dogma, Prose Works*, ed. Super, VI, 115, 219, 299–301.

29:1–15. *Analogy* II, viii, 21–22.—ed. Gladstone, I, 365–66.

29:37–30:6. See p. 13:13–20, 5–9. The affirmation with respect to the superiority of Butler's position in the Sermons over those of Hobbes, Shaftesbury, Bolingbroke, and Hume, is made by Bartlett, *Memoirs*, pp. 283–84. Southey's inscription for Butler's monument declares that Butler constructed "another and irrefragable proof" of the truth of the Christian religion.

30:28–31:32. Preface to the *Sermons*, ¶15–18, 8,—ed. Gladstone, II, 12–14, 6 (abridged). The italics are Arnold's, and Butler reads "to his constitution of nature" in line 20.

31:38–32:4. Sermon III, "Upon Human Nature," ¶4.—ed. Gladstone, II, 70.

32:6–12. *Analogy*, Introduction, ¶13 ("the voice of God speaking in us"); Sermon V, "Upon Compassion," note to ¶1; Sermon II, "Upon Human Nature," ¶19.—ed. Gladstone, I, 15; II, 96, 64. The italics are Arnold's.

32:17–23. Preface to the *Sermons*, note to ¶29, with a reference to "the Epicureans of old," Hobbes, and others.—ed. Gladstone, II, 21. For a longer confutation of Hobbes, see Butler's note to Sermon I, ¶4. Thomas Hobbes' *Leviathan* (1651) set forth a doctrine of political absolutism that was in its own day condemned as atheistic.

32:25–30. Preface to the *Sermons*, ¶20, with a reference to Shaftesbury's *Characteristics*, vol. ii, p. 69 [i.e., "An Inquiry Concerning Virtue," Book I, sect. iii, "Atheism"].—ed. Gladstone, II, 14–15.

32:30–35. Sermon VI, "Upon Compassion," ¶10.—ed. Gladstone, II, 116.

33:1–5. Sermon III, "Upon Human Nature," ¶6.—ed. Gladstone, II, 70–71.

33:12–16. For a much earlier commentary upon Butler's array of the aspects of the human mind, see Arnold's sonnet, "Written in Butler's Sermons," published in his first volume of poetry (1849). And for a gloss on that sonnet see Butler's Preface to his *Sermons,* ¶11–13.—ed. Gladstone, II, 8–10.

33:18–19. "In the six hundredth year of Noah's life, in the second month, the seventeenth day of the month, the same day were all the fountains of the great deep broken up, and the windows of heaven were opened."—Genesis 7:11. Arnold makes the same substitution of "foundations" for "fountains" on p. 37:10–11.

33:32–35. See p. 13:3–12.

33:36–34:7. Preface to the *Sermons,* ¶15, and Sermon VIII, "Upon Resentment," ¶4, 1.—ed. Gladstone, II, 12, 138, 136.

34:8–18. Sermon V, "Upon Compassion," ¶4.—ed. Gladstone, II, 98.

34:21–34. Sermon IX, "Upon Forgiveness of Injuries," ¶1.—ed. Gladstone, II, 150–51.

35:2–3. "Hypotheses non fingo. Quicquid enim ex phaenomenis non deducitur, *Hypothesis* vocanda est; & hypotheses, seu Metaphysicae, seu Physicae, seu Qualitatum Occultarum, seu Mechanicae, in *Philosophiâ Experimentali* locum non habent. In hâc Philosophiâ Propositiones deducuntur ex phaenomenis, & redduntur generales per inductionem."—*Philosophiae Naturalis Principia Mathematica,* conclusion of Book III. Arnold quoted the same sentence in *Literature and Dogma* (1873), *Prose Works,* ed. Super, VI, 275.

35:9–11. See p. 13:12–18.

35:20–22. See p. 34:26–29, 23–24.

35:33–36:8. Sermon V, "Upon Compassion," ¶3.—ed. Gladstone, II, 97. The italics are Arnold's.

36:14–15. "*Hobbes's* Definition of Benevolence, that 'tis the Love of Power is *base* and false," wrote Butler in a manuscript fragment first published by Edward Steere, *Some Remains . . . of Joseph Butler* (London, 1853), pp. 9–10, and again in Gladstone's edition, II, 423. The confutation of Hobbes is the aim of Butler's Sermon V, "Upon Compassion."

36:16–37:5. Sermon VIII, "Upon Resentment," ¶7–9 (with omissions, some rearrangement and summary), 11, 16.—ed. Gladstone, II, 140–43, 146–47. For the place of conscience or reflection, see Sermon II, "Upon Human Nature," ¶17–19.—ed. Gladstone, II, 62–65.

37:10–11. See p. 33:18–19n.

38:5–15, 20–21, 25–27. Sermon V, "Upon Compassion," ¶10, 16.—ed. Gladstone, II, 103, 106–7. The italics are Arnold's.

38:34–36, 39:5–8. Sermon VI, "Upon Compassion," ¶6.—ed. Gladstone, II, 113.

39:13–15. Sermon V, "Upon Compassion," ¶15.—ed. Gladstone, II, 106.

39:21–27. This is the thesis of Sermons I–III, "Upon Human Nature."

40:1–9, 11–13. Sermon VI, "Upon Compassion," ¶11.—ed. Gladstone II, 116–17.

40:21–23. Senancour, *Oberman,* ed. A. Monglond (Paris, 1947), I, 160 (end of letter xxxviii).

40:24–26. Psalm 97:12; I Thessalonians 5:16.

40:29–30. Sermon VI, "Upon Compassion," ¶11.—ed. Gladstone, II, 117. This sentence comes between the two passages quoted at lines 1–13.

40:36. Arnold was 53 on December 24, 1875, fourteen days before he delivered this lecture.

41:5, 8–15. Sermon XI, "Upon the Love of Our Neighbour," ¶3 or 4; *Analogy* I, v, 38; Sermon XI, ¶4, 7, 9 or 5.—ed. Gladstone, II, 187 or 188; I, 134; II, 188, 190, 193 or 189. Sermons XI and XII are filled with such expressions as "the pursuit of private interest" (XI, 2), "the cool principle of self-love, or general desire of our own happiness" (XI, 4), "a regard to our own private good" (XI, 9), "the general pursuit of our own interest" (XI, 17), "cool reflection upon what is for our interest" (XII, 10). Indeed, the word "cool," for "calculating," is, like the word "disinterested," a favorite of Butler's; see *Analogy* I, viii, 12 ("cool expectations of pleasure and interest") and Preface to *Sermons,* ¶29 ("cool or settled selfishness").—ed. Gladstone, I, 183; II, 22. Butler wrote (l. 12) "private and contracted."

41:33–34. *Confessions of an Inquiring Spirit,* end of Letter I and beginning of Letter II: "In the Bible there is more that *finds* me than I have experienced in all other books put together." Arnold quoted this expression also in "The Function of Criticism at the Present Time" (1864), *Prose Works,* ed. Super, III, 279.

42:14. Sermon I, "Upon Human Nature," ¶7.—ed. Gladstone, II, 41.

43:32–35. See p. 32:25–30.

44:18. See p. 41:14–15.

44:36–45:4. Matthew 16:24–26 (Mark 8:34–36, Luke 9:23–25), John 10:10, 5:40.

45:20–23, 46:1–4. Dissertation II, "Of the Nature of Virtue," ¶13, 15 (with omissions and slight modification).—ed. Gladstone, I, 408, 410.

46:30–31. Sophocles *Oedipus Tyrannos* 869–70. The passage from which these two lines are taken was for Arnold the epitome of religious expression; he quoted it in "Pagan and Mediaeval Religious Sentiment" (1864) and *Literature and Dogma* (1871).—*Prose Works*, ed. Super, III, 231 and VI, 178.

47:24–25. See p. 62:19–30 and note.

47:37–48:6. See pp. 29:37, 13:21–22, 9–12.

48:32–34. See pp. 27–29.

49:6–9. A summary of Butler's summary of the first part of his *Analogy*, I, iii, 38.—ed. Gladstone, I, 92–94.

50:1–6. *Analogy* I, i, 3.—ed. Gladstone, I, 22.

50:18–22. *Ibid.* I, i, 6.—ed. Gladstone, I, 25, condensed.

50:28–30. *Ibid.* I, i, 10.—ed. Gladstone, I, 27.

51:1–3. *Ibid.* I, i, 12.—ed. Gladstone, I, 30.

51:11. E.g., *Ibid.* I, v, 21.—ed. Gladstone, I, 119.

51:15–16. *Ibid.* I, iii, 28.—ed. Gladstone, I, 86.

51:16–19. *Ibid.* Introduction, ¶14–15.—ed. Gladstone, I, 15–16, summarized.

51:23–27. *Ibid.* I, ii, 9.—ed. Gladstone, I, 55. Arnold's "the moral and intelligent Author of all things" is inferrable from such expressions of Butler's as "an intelligent Author and Governor of nature, . . . a moral Governor of it."—*Ibid.* I, viii (Conclusion), ¶2.—ed. Gladstone, I, 177.

51:37. For the "restitution of all things" (i.e., the Day of Judgment), see Acts 3:21.

52:22–23. See p. 13:10–11.

52:32–33. *Confessions* I, xii. The passage was quoted by Isaac Barrow, "The Profitableness of Godliness," *Theological Works*, ed. A. Napier (Cambridge, 1859), I, 218, and perhaps through Barrow in Arnold's pocket diary for August 20, 1870.—*Note-Books*, ed. Lowry, p. 133.

53:13–16. See *God and the Bible, Prose Works*, ed. Super, VII, 177–82.

53:33–54:4. *Analogy* I, iv, 12; I, i, 22; II, v, 11n.—ed. Gladstone, I, 104, 38, 262–63n.

54:20–26. *Ibid.* I, v, 34–35.—ed. Gladstone, I, 131. Butler wrote "absolutely destroyed."

54:34–55:2. *Ibid.* I, viii, 2; II, vii, 2.—ed. Gladstone, I, 177, 302.

55:11–13. Arnold deals with the impact of the spirit of the time upon men's view of miracles in *Literature and Dogma* and *God and the Bible, Prose Works*, ed. Super, VI, 256–57, VII, 164–66.

55:16–27. *Analogy* II, v, 13.—ed. Gladstone, I, 265. The author of Hebrews 10:5 quotes the Septuagint (Greek) version of Psalm 40:6. In the Authorized Version (which, like the Vulgate, bases its translation of the Old Testament on the Hebrew, not the Greek), the distinction Arnold makes is plain.

55:28–32. *Analogy* II, vii, 6, 45.—ed. Gladstone, I, 306, 340.

55:35–37. Matthew 2:13–15, Luke 2:22, 39–40.

56:5–6. See p. 12:30–32.

56:10–12, 14–20. *Analogy* II, vii, 11–12.—ed. Gladstone, I, 313.

56:30–31. "If we were to suppose the evidence, which some have of religion, to amount to little more than seeing that it may be true; but that they remain in great doubts and uncertainties about both its evidence and its nature, and great perplexities concerning the rule of life: . . . the evidence so blended . . . as to leave the mind in the utmost doubtfulness and uncertainty about the whole."—*Analogy*, II, vi, 5; ed. Gladstone, I, 280–81.

56:32–36, 57:1–3. *Analogy* II, ix, 20; II, vi, 24; "Charge to the Clergy of Durham," ¶6.—ed. Gladstone, I, 382, 301; II, 400.

57:17. "Thou shalt go before the face of the Lord to prepare his ways; . . . To give light to them that sit in darkness and in the shadow of death, to guide our feet into the way of peace."—Luke 1:76, 79 (of John the Baptist).

57:22–26. Psalm 27:1; II Timothy 2:19; John 8:46 and 5:40, 24.

58:22–23. See p. 56:30–31.

58:24–26. *Analogy* II, viii, 17.—ed. Gladstone, I, 362–63.

58:28–35. Sermon XV, "Upon the Ignorance of Man," ¶1.—ed. Gladstone, II, 259–60.

59:6–8. Ecclesiastes 12:13. For the inclusion of Ecclesiastes in the canon, see *God and the Bible, Prose Works*, ed. Super, VII, 251.

59:14–18. *Analogy* II, ix, 3; II, vi, 20.—ed. Gladstone, I, 372, 297.

59:24–25. "Now the evidence of religion may be laid before men without any air of controversy. The proof of the being of God, from final causes, or the design and wisdom which appears in every part of nature; together with the law of virtue written upon our hearts."—"Charge to the Clergy of Durham," ¶11; ed. Gladstone, II,

404. For "the law written in their hearts," see Romans 2:15, as well as Jeremiah 31:33 and Hebrews 8:10.

59:31–60:3. Sermon XV, "Upon the Ignorance of Man," ¶11; *Analogy* I, ii, 20; Sermon VII, "Upon the Character of Balaam," ¶16 (conclusion); *Analogy* II, iii, 3.—ed. Gladstone, II, 268; I, 62; II, 134; I, 222.

60:6–13. *Analogy* I, vii, 18; Sermon XV, "Upon the Ignorance of Man," ¶3, 11 or Sermon I, "Upon Human Nature," ¶2.—ed. Gladstone, I, 170; II, 260–61, 268 or 33. See p. 12:23–24. Butler in the first passage speaks of "the natural government of the world."

60:20–31. *Analogy* I, iii, 31, 34, 28, 22.—ed. Gladstone, I, 89, 90, 86, 80.

60:32–61:13. *Analogy* II, iv, 8; I, iii, 25; I, ii, 12–17 (summarized); I, viii, 6; I, iii, 29; I, iii, 26 (summarized).—ed. Gladstone, I, 251, 84, 56–60, 180, 86, 84–85.

61:23–30. Mark 1:15; Luke 9:11, 60; Acts 8:12 (20:25, 28:31), 19:8.

62:3–6. Romans 6:10–11; II Timothy 1:10.

62:19–30. *Works*, ed. Gladstone, II, 423, drawing from Edward Steere, ed. *Some Remains, Hitherto Unpublished, of Joseph Butler* (London, 1853), pp. 10–11. The Scriptural passage is Psalm 123:2 (Vulgate 122:2), but Butler's Latin is not the Vulgate and Arnold's English is his own modification of the Prayer-Book version. This memorandum of Butler's is in fact dated Sunday, June 13, 1742, not (as Arnold suggests) ten years later and three days before his death.

[THE CHURCH OF ENGLAND]

Even more significantly than the lectures on Bishop Butler, Arnold's lecture on "The Church of England," which he delivered on Tuesday, February 22, 1876, was a necessary sequel to *Literature and Dogma*, answering the question so many of his readers raised, how it was that a critic so apparently destructive of Christian dogma could be so warm a supporter of the Church establishment. His answer was very much the same as the Coleridgean one his father gave nearly forty-five years earlier. At the time of the debate on the first Reform Bill, Dr. Arnold wrote: "My conviction of the benefits of a Church Establishment arises from this: that thus, and thus only, can we ensure the dispersion of a number of well-educated men over the whole kingdom, whose sole business is, *to do good of the highest kind.*"—*Miscellaneous Works*, ed. A. P. Stanley (London, 1874), p. 219. Arnold gave a rather full account of the lecture and the debate that followed it in a letter to his sister two days after he delivered it: "My address went off very well, though it gave me some horrid days in the preparing. But I took great pains, as it was of no use speaking at Sion College unless I could in some degree carry my audience with me, and I did carry them, in so much that Bishop Piers Claughton [formerly bishop of Colombo, Ceylon], and [R. F.] Littledale, and Malcolm MacColl, who had all come to curse, remained to bless, and the comic thing was that clergyman after clergyman got up and turned upon Claughton (who is a weak man), who had thought he must caution people against something in my address, and, as I had insisted on *the kingdom of God upon earth* having been the original gospel, and pointed out how no church could be in harmony with the popular classes and their ideal without reverting to this original gospel, thought he would caution them against this, and said it behoved them to remember that the real kingdom of God was not what I had said it was. Clergyman on clergyman, I say, turned upon Claughton and said they agreed with me far more than they did with him. The President said, that to some one who had expressed his astonishment at my being invited to speak at Sion College, he had answered that it would be found, he was certain, that Mr. Arnold would not speak ten minutes without managing to establish a *rapport* between himself and the clergy, and so it had turned out. Altogether I was much pleased, and in my little speech at the end I spoke of my being a clergyman's son, of its being against my nature to be estranged from the clergy, and of the pleasure it gave me to be in sympathy with them. The address will do good by directing attention to substantials. [James] Martineau and [Henry] Allon spoke on the Dissenting side. Of course, they did not like my treating it as clear that on the question of a national Establishment the Church was all right and they were all wrong, but Martineau's speech was pleasing and touching."—*Letters,* ed. Russell.

James Knowles, when he heard of the lecture, asked to have it for the *Contemporary,* but Arnold had already promised it to George Grove, editor of *Macmillan's,* at whose behest the President of Sion College had earnestly entreated his audience not to report the lecture for the press to anticipate this publication. Arnold finished writing it too late for the March number; it was set in type before March

10, however, and appeared in April. Arnold was paid £25 for the article.

63n. Sion College is a charitable foundation, a library and a meeting place for the London clergy, founded in 1626 and when Arnold spoke still in its original situation in London Wall. Arnold delivered his address at the invitation of the president, the Reverend William Henry Milman, eldest son of the former dean of St. Paul's, whom Arnold had named to his hypothetical British Academy in the Preface to *Culture and Anarchy.—Prose Works*, ed. Super, V, 234. For an account of Sion College, see E. H. Pearce, *Sion College and Library* (Cambridge, 1913). Arnold was pressed to speak at Sion College in the winter of 1871–72 and very nearly accepted at that time, when only two parts of *Literature and Dogma* had appeared. Even then he planned to talk on "The Church of England." —*Letters*, ed. Russell (November 28, 1871).

63:8–11. On the occasion of the earlier invitation from Sion College Arnold had said that he preferred a non-Church audience such as an audience of working men. He thought of Huxley's South London College for working men, but Huxley told him the rooms were too small to accommodate a suitable assembly and Arnold himself, going to have a look, found it a wretched place into which scarcely eighty people could crowd. When he did address a working men's audience on January 8, 1879, his subject was far more general: "Ecce, Convertimur ad Gentes."—*Prose Works*, ed. Super, vol. IX.

63:19–24. "Rules and Advices to the Clergy," xliv–xlv, *Whole Works*, ed. R. Heber and C. P. Eden (London, 1859), I, 107–8. Arnold jotted these and other passages from Taylor in his pocket diary for January, 1872.—*Note-Books*, ed. Lowry, p. 171. Taylor wrote "preach to his parish, and urge"; Arnold in his diary copied it "preach to his hearers, and urge."

65:8–16. Sermon XV, "Upon the Ignorance of Man," ¶15; *Works*, ed. Gladstone (1896), II, 272–73, with the omission of three sentences after "astonishing." Arnold's "business" with Butler was, of course, his preparation of the lectures on "Bishop Butler and the Zeit-Geist," delivered a month earlier than this lecture.

65:17–18. *De Imitatione Christi* IV, i, 10, jotted in Arnold's pocket diaries for 1871, 1873, 1875, 1876, 1885, and 1887.—*Note-Books*, ed. Lowry, pp. 154, 190, 229, 247, 418, 428.

65:27–37. Sermon XV, ¶14, 13; ed. Gladstone, II, 271, 270–71. For the opinion of Moses Butler cites Deuteronomy 29:29.

66:2–5. *Ibid.*, ¶13; ed. Gladstone, II, 270.

67:8–9. "The children of this world are in their generation wiser than the children of light. And I say unto you, Make to yourselves friends of the mammon of unrighteousness; that, when ye fail, they may receive you into everlasting habitations."—Luke 16:8–9.

67:33–35. Sermon XII, ¶22; ed. Gladstone, II, 227.

68:35–38. "Six Sermons: I. Before the Society for the Propagation of the Gospel," ¶15; ed. Gladstone, II, 288.

69:1–8. *Analogy*, II, i, 10; ed. Gladstone, I, 192–93.

69:8–18. ¶13, 15; ed. Gladstone, II, 405, 407. There is a sizable break between "to the lowest" and "and without."

69:26–71:11. "Home and Foreign Affairs," *Fortnightly Review* XXV, 150–51, 153 (January, 1876). The editor of the *Fortnightly* was John Morley, a friend and reader of Arnold's who concluded this article (p. 156) with a phrase from *Culture and Anarchy* and *Friendship's Garland*, "Thyestean banquet of clap-trap."—*Prose Works*, ed. Super, V, 227, 355. He describes his program (p. 154) as "the line of passage from sentimental radicalism to scientific liberalism," but in the passage Arnold quotes on p. 71:3 his word is "liberals," not "Radicals." Taper and Tadpole were political wire-pullers in Disraeli's novels *Sibyl* and *Coningsby*. For Arnold on the Spirit of the Time (*Zeit-Geist*), see Fraser Neiman, "The Zeitgeist of Matthew Arnold," *PMLA* LXXII, 977–96 (December, 1957), revised for his *Matthew Arnold* (New York: Twayne, 1968), pp. 113–35; and consult the indexes to *Prose Works*, ed. Super, *s.v.* "Zeit-Geist." The general sense of reviewers was that the Zeit-Geist was Matthew Arnold in disguise.

71:27–28. "There's a good time coming" was the opening line of a poem by Charles Mackay, published as "Wait a Little Longer" in his *Voices from the Crowd* (1846); later the title was changed to "The Good Time Coming." Arnold used the expression in the Introduction to his version of Isaiah XL–LXVI.—*Prose Works*, ed. Super, VII, 71.

71:28–29. First in "A Recantation and Apology" (August, 1869), a newspaper letter Arnold never reprinted, then in "Modern Dissent," written in April, 1870, as Preface to *St. Paul and Protestantism.* —*Prose Works*, ed. Super, V, 322; VI, 121.

72:3–4. For the communist revolt in Paris, see p. 77:32n.

72:14. Arnold's apothegm has something of the flavor of Emerson's "An institution is the lengthened shadow of one man" ("Self-

Reliance") and of Carlyle's "The history of the world was the biography of great men" (*Heroes and Hero Worship:* "The Hero as Divinity").

72:25–27. *Pensées*, sect. v, no. 295; ed. L. Brunschvicg (Paris, 1908–21), XIII, 222.

72:27–73:13. "Trois discours sur la condition des grands," *ibid.*, IX, 366, 368–69, with omission. The editor discredits the notion that these essays were addressed to the duc de Rouannez.

73:28–32. Goldwin Smith, speaking before the Trades Union Congress at Sheffield on January 14, 1874; reported by *The Times* on January 15, p. 12, col. 4 and jotted in Arnold's pocket diary for January 6–7.—*Note-Books*, ed. Lowry, p. 206.

73:32–35. *The Struggle for National Education* (London, 1873), p. 3, jotted in Arnold's pocket diary for January 8, 1874, and used in his "Speech at Westminster" (December 6, 1873).—*Note-Books*, ed. Lowry, p. 207, and *Prose Works*, ed. Super, VII, 82–83.

73:36–74:4. Jotted in Arnold's pocket diary for February 7, 1874. —*Note-Books*, ed. Lowry, p. 209. *The Beehive*, The People's Paper and Organ of Industry (London) was founded by George Potter in 1861 and was still edited by him in 1874 as a weekly organ of the labor movement.

74:17–75:2. Barrow, "The Duty and Reward of Bounty to the Poor," *Theological Works*, ed. A. Napier (Cambridge, 1859), I, 54, 51–53, omitting sixty words after "primitive design." Barrow wrote "by-blows of our fall," "to continue, and enjoins us a contented submission to them: but we mistake," and "among some few."

76:16–32. Mark 1:14–15; Matthew 9:35 (Luke 8:1); Luke 9:11, 9:60 (Matthew 10:7); Luke 10:8–9; Matthew 6:10 (Luke 11:2); Matthew 6:33, 24:14; Luke 11:2.

76:34–77:1. Acts 8:12, 19:8, 28:23, 28:31; I Corinthians 1:17.

77:8–13. Acts 8:12, 8:35, 9:20, 9:22.

77:16–19. See, for example, II Thessalonians 1:5–10, II Timothy 4:1, and Revelation 20:4.

77:28–29. Matthew 6:33, which in the Authorized Version reads: "Seek ye first the kingdom of God, and his righteousness." The Sinaitic MS reads "his kingdom and righteousness," the Vatican MS reads "his righteousness and kingdom."

77:31–33. Fifth Monarchy Men (see Daniel 2:44), a sect of English Puritans, for a time supported Cromwell in the supposition that the Commonwealth was a preparation for the thousand-year reign of Christ and His saints (Revelation 20:4). After the Restoration they attempted to seize London violently on January 6, 1661, but were defeated, and their leaders were executed. The Anabaptists, extremist reformers who were disclaimed by Luther, attempted to use the Peasants' War to set up an ideal Christian commonwealth with absolute equality and community of goods, but were quickly defeated in May, 1525, and their leaders executed. Another group, under Johann Buckholdt, "John of Leiden," held Münster, in Westphalia, for over a year, but were destroyed in 1535. In the wake of the surrender of Paris to the Germans in January, 1871, large numbers of the citizens and troops revolted against their government and from mid-March to the latter part of May the "commune" ruled Paris, executing whatever leaders of the government fell into their hands and setting fire to a number of government buildings. They were defeated on May 28, only a few months before Arnold visited Paris en route to a holiday in Switzerland.

78:27–29. "A Letter to a Noble Lord" (1796), three-fifths through. Arnold jotted this phrase in his pocket diaries eight times between 1869 and 1879 (most recently on February 6, 1876) and once in his "General Note-Books," and he used it in the Dedicatory Letter to *Friendship's Garland* (1871) and the Preface to *Higher Schools and Universities in Germany* (1874).—*Note-Books*, ed. Lowry, p. 105, etc.; *Prose Works*, ed. Super, V, 353; VII, 123.

78:31–32. Arnold is no doubt alluding, on his own account, to John Morley, editor of the *Fortnightly Review* and (in 1881) biographer of Cobden; perhaps also to Fitzjames Stephen.

78:36. Jeremy Bentham (1748–1832) was the founder of Utilitarianism or "philosophical radicalism"; Richard Cobden (1804–65) was the chief apostle of free trade in England and an occasional correspondent of Arnold's. Arnold explained in the Preface to *Higher Schools and Universities in Germany* that he was adopting the term "secularist radicalism" for what he had formerly designated "Millism."—*Prose Works*, ed. Super, VII, 99–100.

79:14–29. "Six Sermons: I. Before the Society for the Propagation of the Gospel," ¶18; ed. Gladstone, II, 292–93. Butler wrote "deceive themselves, and so liable to be deceived by others, as."

80:2–3. *Maximes*, no. 151; *Oeuvres complètes*, ed. L. Martin-Chauffier (Paris, 1964), p. 423. Arnold jotted fourteen passages from La Rochefoucauld (but not this one) in his pocket diaries between February 23 and July 22, 1876.—*Note-Books*, ed. Lowry, pp. 247–53.

80:27. "Six Sermons: III. Before the House of Lords [on the anniversary of the martyrdom of King Charles I]," ¶11 ("so mild and reasonable an establishment"); "V. Before the House of Lords [on the anniversary of the accession of George II]," ¶7 ("a reasonable establishment"); ed. Gladstone, II, 326, 366. See p. 82:22.

80:32. A reversal of Horace's "splendide mendax," *Carmina* III, xi, 35.

80:32–34. See p. 12:30–32.

81:11–13. *Analogy*, II, vii, 61; ed. Gladstone, I, 351.

81:22–24. *Analogy*, II, i, 32; ed. Gladstone, I, 206.

82:1–7. *St. Paul and Protestantism* was devoted largely to a refutation of these positions.

82:17–18. "Ye are the light of the world. A city that is set on an hill cannot be hid."—Matthew 5:14. "This gospel of the kingdom shall be preached in all the world for a witness unto all nations."—Matthew 24:14. See p. 69:1–8.

82:22–28. "Six Sermons," V, ¶7; ed. Gladstone, II, 366.

82:30–83:5. "Six Sermons," I, ¶19, 17; ed. Gladstone, II, 293, 291–92.

83:9–12. Gilbert Burnet, *Life of Sir Matthew Hale*, in his *Lives, Characters, and an Address to Posterity*, ed. John Jebb (London, 1833), p. 51 (two-fifths through the work).

83:12–15. Richard Ward, *The Life of . . . Henry More* (London, 1710), p. 360 (letter XIII); jotted in Arnold's pocket diary for August 27, 1871.—*Note-Books*, ed. Lowry, p. 157.

84:21–24. Sermon "Of a Peaceable Temper and Carriage," *Theological Works*, ed. A. Napier, II, 402–3.

84:29–31. For Collings and Chamberlain, see p. 109:15–17n. R. W. Dale, Congregationalist minister in Birmingham, was an influential and scholarly theologian and co-worker with Chamberlain in municipal reform and educational policy.

84:34–36. *The Times*, commenting upon the campaign waged by Dale and James Guinness Rogers on behalf of disestablishment, remarked: "The leading Nonconformist ministers are now, at all events, not inferior in ability, and not much inferior in influence among their class of the community, to those of the Church."—February 16, 1876, p. 9, col. 2.

85:16–18. "For the tyranny of our own lawless passions is the nearest and most dangerous of all tyrannies," he continued.—"Six Sermons," V, ¶15; ed. Gladstone, II, 373.

85:26. See p. 87:15n.

85:33–34. I Corinthians 1:17; see p. 76:38–77:1.

86:8–9. I.e., from his inspecting of the Dissenters' schools.

86:14. Arnold was now 53. He made a similar reference to his age in "Bishop Butler and the Zeit-Geist," pp. 40:36, 47:16–17.

[A LAST WORD ON THE BURIALS BILL]

Arnold in his lecture at Sion College deliberately started a subject on which he meant to write more—"a shorter paper which grows out of it"—the proper relation of the parish churchyards to the population at large, whether Anglican or not. From medieval times, the customary place of burial in England, as in most European countries, was the churchyard. As the urban population grew, new provision was made in the form of public cemeteries and many of the churchyards were closed, but in the country districts there was still no alternative to burial in the churchyard. Burial there was the statutory right of every Englishman except the unbaptized, the excommunicate, and the suicide, but the service was prescribed by the Book of Common Prayer and the conduct of it was the prerogative of the Church of England clergyman. Some egregious instances of the clergyman's excluding a Nonconformist on the ground of defective baptism (or a Baptist child who in keeping with the doctrines of that sect had not yet been baptized) were cited in the debates upon burials, but the principal issue was the form of service and the person who conducted it.

Despite his eagerness to write the paper, its composition was subject to the usual delays. The editor of *Macmillan's Magazine* claimed the right of publishing it as sequel to "The Church of England" and Arnold promised it for the May number, 1876. His diary after April 26 shows repeated attempts to begin work on it, but he did not make the start until May 4. Progress was slow; the article went off on June 25 and he read proofs next day, for publication in the July number. He received £25 in payment.

The entire debate seems today to share something of the absurdity of that kindred issue Arnold found such lively source of amusement, marriage with a deceased wife's sister, and Arnold's article does not escape, if not absurdity, at least triviality. But Arnold conceived it to have a certain solidity: "[It] will do good, and is in many quarters much liked. It is a seed sown in the thoughts of the young and fair-minded, the effect of which will be gradual but persistent. In all I write, this is the sort of effect I aim at," he told his sister. "Of course the Liberals will not like what I have said, but I think I have put the thing in a way to satisfy reasonable people who wish to decide the disputed matters fairly; and perhaps these reasonable people are not so few as is supposed. [Lord] Coleridge told me he thought the Dissenters had a right not only to have their services in the parish churchyard, but also to have them in the parish church. For my part, I do not think that anybody has, or can have, any rights except such as are given him by the law; and I do not think the law will ever, in England, confer such rights as these. I met Gladstone in the street yesterday, who began to talk to me about my article. He said that undoubtedly, as soon as you got beyond abstract resolutions and had to legislate practically, the necessity of insuring a *proper* service in the churchyard would have to be provided for; and the difficulty of doing this while the Dissenters make the pretensions they do now was almost insuperable. He said he was extremely glad I had dealt with the question," and he invited Arnold to take tea with him that afternoon. "I could not, . . . but his asking me shows his friendly feeling. I think at one time he positively disliked me." —*Letters*, ed. Russell.

The Saturday Review (July 15, 1876, pp. 69–70) was much amused at Arnold's view of the burial service as performing an educative function upon the taste of the lower classes, just as some of Arnold's contemporaries, who did not share his view of the aesthetic aspects of religious ceremonial, found either quaintness or hypocrisy in his facing the altar and bowing his head at the proper places during the recitation of a creed he had described as merely "the *popular science* of Christianity." But that beautiful civic surroundings influence moral character is a doctrine as old as Plato and it persists wherever public buildings are designed or public money is used to support, for instance, the composition or performance of music.

87:1–13. See pp. 85:25–86:6.

87:14–18. George Osborne Morgan (1826–97), M.P. for Denbighshire, himself a member of the Church of England, for ten successive years introduced bills or resolutions in Parliament to reform the burials statutes; his bill finally succeeded in 1880. He moved the resolution Arnold described on March 3, 1876; it was defeated by a vote of 279–248, and Arnold's brother-in-law, W. E. Forster, like most of the Liberals, voted in its favor. The debate was reported in *The Times* on March 4, pp. 6–8.

87:20–88:5. *Times*, January 17, 1876, p. 9, col. 3, with omissions. The passage begins, "But the Legislature will have to put . . ."

88:6–7. Lord Granville's resolution, much to the same effect as Osborne Morgan's, was moved in the House of Lords on May 15, 1876, and defeated there by a vote of 148 to 92. Every bishop was opposed except Arnold's friend Frederick Temple (Exeter).

88:11–21. Lord Selborne's speech in the House of Lords is reported in *The Times*, May 16, 1876, pp. 7–8. Roundell Palmer (1812–95), lord chancellor under Gladstone in 1872–74 and 1880–85, was created Baron Selborne in 1872. He was a high churchman and editor of a popular collection of English hymns, *The Book of Praise*, on which Arnold commented in the lectures *On the Study of Celtic Literature* (1866).—*Prose Works*, ed. Super, III, 368.

88:22–27. The memorial of the clergy to Disraeli included the signatures of at least two close friends of Arnold's, Dean Stanley and F. W. Farrar. One of its prime movers was J. Llewelyn Davies. —*Times*, February 29, 1876, pp. 10–11.

88:29–89:3. *Times*, February 29, 1876, p. 9, col. 5.

89:4–7. "Death is an absolute natural necessity. . . . Burial is not only a natural necessity, but is necessary in the interest of the community and the State."—Lord Selborne, reported in *The Times*, May 16, 1876, p. 8, col. 1. A leading article next day supported Selborne's view, without repeating the words.—p. 11, cols. 3–4.

90:11. Goethe, "Epilog zu Schillers Glocke," line 32; quoted by Arnold in "The Literary Influence of Academies" (1864) and the Preface to *Essays in Criticism* (1865).—*Prose Works*, ed. Super, III, 235, 290.

92:22–24. Sir Wilfrid Lawson, Liberal M.P. for Carlisle, addressed his constituents there on January 24, 1876, and his speech was reported in *The Times* next day, p. 6, col. 5. Sir Wilfrid was of opinion that "there was less to be said for the Church Establishment in England than there was to be said for Church Establishment in Ireland. As to the Burials Bill, the scandal involved in the present system must be removed at all hazards."

93:5–6. "I think the time has arrived when it is right to teach a small minority of the clergy a lesson which they much need to learn," said Arnold's friend Lord Coleridge, speaking in support of Lord Granville's resolution in the House of Lords.—*Times*, May 16, 1876, p. 7, col. 4.

93:34. The words are part of Morgan's resolution.

93:34–36. Lord Granville's resolution affirmed the right of rela-

tives or friends of the deceased to conduct the funeral in the churchyard "with such Christian and orderly religious observances as to
them may seem fit."

94:7. Arnold in *Culture and Anarchy* (1868) quoted "Martinus
Scriblerus *Peri Bathous:* or the Art of Sinking in Poetry" (a joint
work of Pope, Arbuthnot, and Swift), beginning of Chapter II, on
"the taste of the bathos . . . implanted by nature itself in the soul of
man."—*Prose Works,* ed. Super, V, 147.

96:16. Presumably the Presbyterians, Congregationalists, and
Baptists, since Arnold places the Methodists in a somewhat different
category on p. 108:30.

96:23–24. A phrase from Burke's speech *On Conciliation with the
Colonies,* one-fourth through, "the dissidence of dissent and the
protestantism of the Protestant religion," was used as motto for the
chief weekly newspaper of the Congregationalists, *The Nonconformist.* Arnold first criticized the ideal it represented in his final
Oxford lecture on poetry (1867), which became the opening chapter of *Culture and Anarchy.*—*Prose Works,* ed. Super, V, 101.

96:30–31. The Primitive Methodists, a sect founded about
1807–10, were called Ranters. The Peculiar People, or Plumstead
Peculiars, were a religious sect founded in 1838 and most numerous
about London. "They have no preachers, creeds, ordinances, or
church organization, and they rely wholly on prayer for the cure of
disease, rejecting medical aid."—*O.E.D.*

98:7–15. In presenting his resolution, Lord Granville cited the
examples of France, Germany, and very many other countries.

100:25–28. After pointing out that dissenters were often obliged,
by the absence of other places of burial, to use the churchyards and
(hence) the offices of the Church of England clergymen, Lord
Granville asked his hearers to imagine how they would feel if, as
Churchmen, they were obliged to see their children or other rela-
tives "buried by a Roman Catholic priest with the Roman Catholic
service, or by a Dissenting minister with a Dissenting service." The
Wesleyans, he asserted, had no objection to the service of the
Church of England, but they did object "that the funeral service
over members of their congregation is not said by their own clergyman, but by one who does not sympathize with their religious opinions."—*Times,* May 16, 1876, p. 6, col. 2. Lord Granville, leader of
the Liberal opposition in the House of Lords during this debate, had
been lord president of the Privy Council when the Revised Code for

school inspection and grants was promulgated in 1862, and was (with Robert Lowe) its responsible author; Arnold's remark about Lord Granville's scruples may stem from Arnold's hostility to that code.

100:34–37. Arnold quotes the first rubric prefixed to the Order for the Burial of the Dead in the Book of Common Prayer.

101:20–21. Man, proud man,
    Drest in a little brief authority,
    . . . like an angry ape,
    Plays such fantastic tricks before high heaven
    As make the angels weep.
                    —*Measure for Measure*, II, ii, 117–22.

102:3–5. *The Life of Edward, Earl of Clarendon*, written by himself (Oxford, 1857), I, 61 (Part I, ¶69), jotted in Arnold's pocket diary for August 31, 1873.—*Note-Books*, ed. Lowry, p. 199.

103:3–4, 12. John 3:5; I Peter 3:21.

103:38–104:2, 7. Arnold quotes from the words of committal in the burial service, then from the final collect before the benediction: "We meekly beseech thee, O Father, to raise us from the death of sin unto the life of righteousness; that, when we shall depart this life, we may rest in him, as our hope is this our *brother* doth."

104:27. See "Eugénie de Guérin" (1863), *On the Study of Celtic Literature* (1866), *Culture and Anarchy* (1868), and *Literature and Dogma* (1871).—*Prose Works*, ed. Super, III, 98, 368–70; V, 184; VI, 191.

105:28–29. The Lesson for the burial service is I Corinthians 15:20–58.

106:26–28. "Protestants did practically in this way use the Bible more irrationally than Rome practically ever used it; for Rome had her hypothesis of the Church Catholic endued with talismanic virtues, and did not want a talismanic Bible too."—*Literature and Dogma, Prose Works*, ed. Super, VI, 161.

107:18–20. John 5:25.

109:9. Philippians 4:8.

109:12. "Those who, like ourselves, hope to see the Church of England disestablished, may rejoice at the kind of opposition offered by such men as Lord Salisbury to the resolution of Lord Granville, . . . a speech . . . remarkable for political blindness and prejudice and irritating heat of expression."—[John Morley], "Home and Foreign Affairs," *Fortnightly Review* XXV, 930 (June, 1876).

109:15–17. "King Agrippa, [believest thou the prophets?] I know that thou believest."—Paul, in Acts 26:27. When Paul was imprisoned at Caesarea, charges against him were heard by Felix, Roman procurator of Judea, who was accompanied by his wife Drusilla, great granddaughter of Herod the Great. After Felix was succeeded by Porcius Festus, Agrippa, king of Judea and Drusilla's brother, heard Paul's defence, but Paul was sent to Rome by Festus instead of being acquitted, since he had appealed as a Roman citizen to Caesar. Joseph Chamberlain (1836–1914), later a well-known politician and cabinet minister, mayor of Birmingham in 1873–75, was devoted to the cause of municipal sanitation and services and to national education, but was opposed to the Elementary Education Act of 1870; a Unitarian and Utilitarian, he was outspoken in his hostility to Church Establishment and all other remnants of medievalism in England. Jesse Collings (1831–1920), also from Birmingham, was his principal collaborator in the National Education League that advocated free, compulsory, non-sectarian elementary education. Arnold ridiculed both in *God and the Bible, Prose Works*, ed. Super, VII, 145.

110:16–17. See p. 78:27–29n.

[A PSYCHOLOGICAL PARALLEL]

"I regard the belief in miracles as on a par, in respect of its inevitable disappearance from the minds of reasonable men, with the belief in witches and hobgoblins. This is really no bravado, but the simple truth, and therefore I see with regret, and almost impatience, attempts on the part of a man whom I like and esteem to defend them," wrote Arnold with considerable frankness to acknowledge on October 19, 1874, his friend F. W. Farrar's *Life of Christ*. About the same time he wrote in his diary the title "A Psychological Parallel" among the essays he would write in 1875. In 1875, however, he got no further than a brief statement of his principle in the Conclusion of *God and the Bible*. Meanwhile his reading in 1876 of John Tulloch's excellent collection of essays on *Rational Theology and Christian Philosophy in England in the Seventeenth Century* aroused a latent enthusiasm for the Cambridge Platonists and gave greater substance to Arnold's reflections. As early as March 10, 1876, he promised his essay to Knowles—"my last theological paper, I hope"

—for the June or July number of the *Contemporary*. His diary shows that he did not begin work on it until Wednesday, September 20; that it occupied him daily until October 15, and that he read proofs of it on October 21. It appeared in the November number and Arnold was paid £27 for it, though not without some delay occasioned by the change in management of the *Contemporary*. The essay was so explicitly conceived as Arnold's last word upon the whole large subject of religion and ecclesiastical affairs that it has, for so short a piece, uncommon comprehensiveness; it was given the first place in his new volume, *Last Essays on Church and Religion*, and bears much the same relation to Arnold's religious writings that the essay on "The Function of Criticism at the Present Time" has to the *Essays in Criticism*.

Growing out of this essay was a scheme Arnold broached to Macmillan in January, 1877, for the publication of "the best of Hales and Whichcote, and Cudworth's two sermons," a volume to be called *Broad Church in the Seventeenth Century* for which he would write a twenty-page introduction. He regarded it as a pressing commitment in mid-March, and Macmillan was enthusiastic, but Arnold never actually came to the task and by the time he lent his aid to W. M. Metcalfe's selections from John Smith in 1882 he had abandoned it.

112:12–17. See *St. Paul and Protestantism* (1869), *Prose Works*, ed. Super, VI, 50–56.

113:10. St. Paul was converted to Christianity by a vision of a great light from heaven, and by hearing the voice of Jesus saying, "Saul, Saul, why persecutest thou me?"—Acts 9:3–18, 26:12–20.

113:21–22. See I Thessalonians 4:13–17.

114:2. See p. 78:27–29n.

114:8–13. *Spectator*, no. 110 (Friday, July 6, 1711), on Ghosts; no. 117 (Saturday, July 14, 1711), on Witchcraft.

114:13–16. Arnold's principal source for his discussion of witchcraft is the volume he mentions in his footnote to p. 116—a curious collection of six tracts of 1619–82, separately reprinted in type facsimile in 1837–38 and then gathered with a common title-page and frontispiece over the imprint of John Russell Smith, 4 Old Compton Street, Soho, in 1838. Two of the reprints were made at the press of Henry S. Richardson, Stockwell Street, Greenwich, and two at the private press of Charles Clark, Great Totham, Essex; indeed Clark seems to be the moving force behind the collection. Twice, on September 24 and 29, 1876, Arnold jotted in his diary a memorandum to read "in Witch book." His statement about the events of 1716–36 is drawn from Clark's Appendix to his 1838 reprint of *A Trial of Witches . . . at Bury St. Edmonds* (1682), p. 28.

115:1–2. These and others are named in the 1837 reprint of [Matthew Hopkins,] *The Discovery of Witches* (1647), pp. 2–3. Hopkins, a notorious profiteer in the exposing of witches, portrays these "familiars" in the frontispiece to the original edition of this pamphlet.

115:7–8. Clark's Appendix to his reprint of *A Trial of Witches*, p. 22.

115:11–14. Reprint of *The Wonderful Discoverie of the Witchcrafts of Margaret and Phillip Flower* (1619), p. 7.

115:16–17. Exodus 22:18, quoted in the 1837 reprint of *A Prodigious & Tragicall History of the Arraignment . . . of Six Witches at Maidstone* (1652), p. 8.

115:23–25. Reprint of *The Wonderful Discoverie*, p. 11. For "persons of great knowledge," see p. 118:21.

115:34–35. Bishop Burnet, who did not know Sir Matthew Hale personally, nevertheless saw him regularly at services in the Rolls Chapel, where Burnet preached. "In my life, I never saw so much gravity, tempered with that sweetness, and set off with so much vivacity, as appeared in his looks and behaviour," Burnet remarked in the Preface to his *Life and Death of Sir Matthew Hale.*—Gilbert Burnet, *Lives, Characters, and an Address to Posterity*, ed. John Jebb (London, 1833), p. 7.

116:7–17. The 1838 reprint of *A Trial of Witches* (1682), p. 3.

116:29–118:6. *Ibid.*, pp. 8–12. The stocks were invoked eighteen days, not ten days, after the original seizure of the child. And the pamphlet reads (192:27) "enforced to use," not "obliged to use."

118:19–34. *Ibid.*, p. 16.

119:1–120:6. *Ibid.*, pp. 16–18. For "then in court" the pamphlet reads "there in court," for "Sir Edward," "Sir Edmund."

120:7–121:3. *Ibid.*, pp. 20–21.

121:20–23. Simon Patrick's sermon is printed at the end of Smith's *Select Discourses*, ed. H. G. Williams (Cambridge, 1859); Arnold quotes from p. 512 a description he had jotted in his pocket diary for September 11, 1869.—*Note-Books*, ed. Lowry, p. 109.

121:23–28. The biographical data may come from Williams' prefatory memoir in the same edition. The phrase "after a long and tedious illness" occurs on p. xi; the funeral sermon uses the expression "under a lingering and tedious disease" (p. 511). Arnold follows the funeral sermon (p. 506) as regards Smith's age.

121:25. Here and elsewhere Arnold spells the name of Queens' College, Cambridge, like an Oxford man.

121:30–33. Gilbert Burnet, *History of His Own Time* (Oxford, 1823), I, 322; (Oxford, 1833), I, 340: *anno* 1661, not quite two-fifths through Book II. Burnet wrote "and a fierceness." Jotted in Arnold's pocket diary for October 2, 1876.—*Note-Books*, ed. Lowry, p. 258.

121:33. John Tulloch (1823–86), principal of St. Mary's College, University of St. Andrews, devoted the second volume of his work on *Rational Theology* to the Cambridge Platonists—Benjamin Whichcote, John Smith, Ralph Cudworth, Henry More, and others (including Joseph Glanvill, in whose *Vanity of Dogmatizing* Arnold read the story of the Scholar-Gipsy).

122:9. The Laudian clergy were followers of the high-church doctrines of William Laud (1573–1645), archbishop of Canterbury.

122:27–28. Tulloch devotes more than sixty pages to analysis of Cudworth's reply to Hobbes' *Leviathan* in *The True Intellectual System of the Universe* and his treatise on *Eternal and Immutable Morality*. The former appears on one of Arnold's early reading lists (October, 1845), along with Glanvill's *Vanity of Dogmatizing*. "Owen" is the theological controversialist John Owen (1616–83), who became a Congregationalist at the beginning of the civil wars and remained a Dissenter at the Restoration. See p. 206:6n.

122:34–35. Tulloch's chapter on Hales (vol. I, chapt. iv) begins: "John Hales—often dignified as the 'ever-memorable Mr. John Hales of Eton'—. . ."

123:8–9. A consequence of this remark appears in Arnold's letter to G. W. Boyle on March 11, 1877: "I have promised Macmillan to make a volume out of the best of Hales and Whichcote, and Cudworth's two sermons. I shall write twenty pages of introduction, and call the volume *Broad Church in the Seventeenth Century*. I think it will do good."—*Letters*, ed. Russell. The project was never accomplished, but Arnold permitted a few paragraphs from the present essay on Smith (pp. 121:23–122:1, 122:9–23, 122:31–123:6, 123:8–124:11) to be used as Introduction to W. M. Metcalfe's *The Natural Truth of Christianity: Selections from the "Select Discourses" of John Smith* (Paisley, 1882), a volume Arnold sent with a letter of recommendation to Ernest Fontanès on September 22— and notice that Metcalfe used a phrase of Arnold's as his title (p. 123:35). The discussion with Macmillan over the Broad Church volume (January–March, 1877) is reproduced in Buckler, *Matthew Arnold's Books*, pp. 158–59.

123:16. Jacques-Bénigne Bossuet (1627–1704), Blaise Pascal

(1623–62), Jeremy Taylor (1613–67) and Isaac Barrow (1630–77) are frequently quoted in Arnold's pocket diaries and his published works.

124:5–6. Arnold alludes to Smith's Discourse IX, pp. 387–459 of the *Select Discourses* (1859).

124:6–7. Édouard Reuss was a Protestant theologian at the University of Strasbourg whose *Histoire de la théologie chrétienne au siècle apostolique* (Strasbourg and Paris, 1852, 1860) seemed to Arnold to contain the most perceptive analysis of St. Paul's doctrine. Arnold and Reuss corresponded occasionally. See *Prose Works*, ed. Super, VI, 418 and the Indexes to vols. VI–VII.

124:16–27. Smith, *Select Discourses* (1859), pp. 461–87. The text is from James 4:7. Lady Day is March 25 (then regarded as the beginning of the new year). The account of the annual sermon is given in John Worthington's prefatory address "To the Reader," p. xxxii.

124:28–125:26. *Ibid.*, pp. 463–64, 467, 486–87.

126:1–3, 9–19. *Ibid.*, pp. 470, 471–72.

126:23–127:11. *Ibid.*, pp. 472–74, with omissions. Smith speaks of "the notion or name of God" at p. 126:32–33.

127:15–24. *Ibid.*, pp. 483–84, with omissions. Smith wrote "forcibly enter and penetrate."

127:27. Phillimore was the highest ecclesiastical judge in England from 1867 to 1875, years when matters of ritual and doctrine were especially troublesome. In the case of Jenkins v. Cook, Sir Robert as Dean of Arches asserted on July 16, 1875, that "as to the existence and personality of the devil—the spiritual enemy who slandered God to man—we must receive that doctrine unless we impute error and deceit to the writers of the New Testament," and therefore he gave judgment that "the avowed and persistent denial of the existence and personality of the devil" constituted the promoter an "evil liver" in such sense as to warrant his vicar to deny him Holy Communion until he disavowed or withdrew his heretical opinion. The judgment naturally achieved a certain notoriety. See *The Times*, July 17, p. 13, cols. 2–3 and July 19, p. 9, cols. 2–3 (leading article). "Sir Robert Phillimore seeks to tie up the Church of England to a belief in the personality of Satan, and he might as well seek to tie it up to a belief in the personality of Tisiphone," wrote Arnold in the Preface to *God and the Bible* (1875).—*Prose Works*, ed. Super, VII, 384.

128:10–11. Matthew 14:2 (Mark 6:14, 16; Luke 9:7).

128:11–13. Mark 6:15 (Luke 9:8).

128:15–16. Matthew 27:52–53.

128:16–21. See Luke 24:6–7.

128:31–34. The translation is presumably Arnold's own. He jotted the Greek text in his pocket diary for June 10, 1874, and again on June 13, 1874, and at the end of 1875.—*Note-Books,* ed. Lowry, pp. 213, 240.

130:1–5. Arnold's correspondent was, of course, alluding to the lecture on "The Church of England"; see p. 65:2–3.

130:19–25. The content of these oaths comes from the Act of Uniformity of 1662. Arnold describes also the change in form effected by the Clerical Subscription Act of 1865.

130:27. The Three Creeds are "*Nicene* Creed, *Athanasius's* Creed, and that which is commonly called the *Apostles'* Creed." "They may be proved by most certain warrants of Holy Scripture," the Eighth Article continues.

131:12–13. The question of marriage with a deceased wife's sister was a recurrent subject of ridicule for Arnold, most explicitly in the conclusion of *Culture and Anarchy* (August, 1868) and in Letter VIII of *Friendship's Garland* (June 8, 1869).—*Prose Works,* ed. Super, V, 205–8, 313–18.

131:18–20. Arnold probably alludes to Newman's ironic account of an imaginary Russian's tirade against the British for ascribing to the Queen, "to their crowned and sceptered idol, to their doll, . . . this puppet whom they have dressed up with a lion and a unicorn, the attribute of ABSOLUTE PERFECTION."—*Lectures on the Present Position of Catholics in England* (Dublin, 1857), pp. 27–28. The Russian mob ended by burning in effigy a John Bull, a lion and unicorn, and a Queen Victoria.

131:22–23. A new and elaborate form of the Oath of the Queen's Supremacy was introduced in 1858. But by the Clerical Subscription Act of 1865, oaths were not to be administered during the services of Ordination. Every person about to be ordained Priest or Deacon was required before ordination to subscribe the new declaration of assent and the oath of allegiance.

131:24–26. The deacon, at his ordination, was obliged to respond affirmatively to the question: "Do you unfeignedly believe all the Canonical Scriptures of the Old and New Testament?"

131:33–36. The priest, at his ordination, was required to reply affirmatively to the question: "Are you persuaded that the holy Scriptures contain sufficiently all Doctrine required of necessity for eternal salvation through faith in Jesus Christ? and are you determined out of the said Scriptures to instruct the people committed to your charge, and to teach nothing, as required of necessity to eternal salvation, but that which you shall be persuaded may be concluded and proved by the Scripture?"

132:4–5. *Works*, ed. Gladstone (1896), II, 424, from Steere, *Some Remains*, pp. 10–11. For date (1742, not 1752), see p. 62:19n.

132:15–16. Philippians 3:13.

132:22–27. An echo of *Literature and Dogma, Prose Works*, ed. Super, VI, 170–71 *et passim*.

133:34–35. Nicholas Brady and Nahum Tate published their *New Version of the Psalms* in 1696, which by an Order in Council of William III was authorized for use in churches; it was so used almost universally down to the early 19th century. The Prayer Book Version of the Psalms is that of Coverdale's translation of 1539.

134:9–14. Frederic Harrison, "The Religious and Conservative Aspects of Positivism," *Contemporary Review* XXVI, 1010–11 (November, 1875), jotted at the beginning of Arnold's pocket diary for 1876.—*Note-Books*, ed. Lowry, p. 243. Harrison wrote "of our common race," and so Arnold copied it in his diary. Harrison's article took cognizance of Arnold's theology when it remarked: "These Unseens, Unquestionables, Unknowables, Streams of Tendency, will take us a very short way either in creed, worship, or government." (p. 1006)

134:25. The prophet Daniel is told that his people are "to make an end of sins, and to make reconciliation for iniquity, and to bring in everlasting righteousness."—Daniel 9:24.

134:34. "Mane nobiscum, quoniam advesperascit, et inclinata est iam dies.—Abide with us: for it is toward evening, and the day is far spent."—Luke 24:29, the disciples at Emmaus speaking to the risen Christ, whom they do not yet recognize. Arnold introduces the word "Domine"—"Lord"—from the context. He jotted the Latin passage, with "Domine," in his pocket diary for New Year's Day of 1888, the year of his death.—*Note-Books*, ed. Lowry, p. 437.

136:1–3. In *Literature and Dogma, Prose Works*, ed. Super, VI, 340–44.

136:11–12. "God hath not appointed us to wrath, but to obtain salvation by our Lord Jesus Christ."—I Thessalonians 5:9.

137:18–21. Matthew 25:31–46.

137:28–30. Luke 22:30; Matthew 26:29.

137:38. Matthew 24:30, 26:64 (Mark 13:26, 14:62).

138:7–9. See Matthew 24:2–51 (Mark 13:2–37), especially "This generation shall not pass, till all these things be fulfilled."

138:11. "Behold, the kingdom of God is within you."—Luke 17:21.

138:14–15. Matthew 13:31–33 (Mark 4:30–32; Luke 13:18–21).

138:15–18. Arnold uses almost the same version, presumably his own, when he quotes this passage in "A Speech at Westminster," *Prose Works*, ed. Super, VII, 89.

138:18–19. Matthew 24:14 (Mark 13:10, 14:9). Also, "Go ye into all the world, and preach the gospel to every creature."—Mark 16:15.

138:27–28. "Can ye not discern the signs of the times?"—Matthew 16:3.

139:30. The Authorized Version of the Gospels uses "new testament in my blood," not "new covenant."—Luke 22:20 (Matthew 26:28, Mark 14:24).

140:5–6. Arnold earlier dealt with the Book of Enoch in *Literature and Dogma, Prose Works*, ed. Super, VI, 283–84.

140:22–31. The Book of Enoch, which was written originally partly in Hebrew, partly in Aramaic, probably dates from the second century B.C. The English traveler James Bruce, who lived some time in Abyssinia as he searched for the source of the Nile, brought out with him in 1771 the Ethiopic version of the book in an eighteenth-century manuscript which he deposited in the Bodleian Library, Oxford. It was translated into English by Richard Laurence, archbishop of Cashel (Oxford, 1821) and into German by August Dillmann (Leipzig, 1853). Arnold's compliment to Bishop Ellicott of Gloucester and Bristol, whose name had been coupled in ridicule so frequently with that of Bishop Wilberforce of Winchester in *Literature and Dogma*, is in keeping with the closer personal acquaintance with him that Arnold indicated in *God and the Bible*.—*Prose Works*, ed. Super, VII, 519.

141:7. "Children of light" occurs in Luke 16:8, John 12:36, Ephesians 5:8, and I Thessalonians 5:5. See Enoch 108:11.

141:13. Socrates gives a long description of Tartarus and its rivers in his discourse with his friends just before his death.—Plato *Phaedo* 111C–114C.

141:16–22. Matthew 26:24 (Mark 14:21); Luke 10:20; Matthew 18:10, 10:21, 13:43. See Enoch 38:2, 108:7, 60:2, 100:1–2, 58:3. R. H. Charles, in his English version of *The Book of Enoch* (Oxford, 1912), remarks "The influence of I Enoch on the New Testament has been greater than that of all the other apocryphal and pseudepigraphal books taken together."—p. xcv.

141:23–26. Matthew 18:17, 16:18.

141:33. See Enoch 38:1.

143:16–23. Mark 1:15; John 3:15, 5:24–25. In many of the following passages, Arnold has slightly modified the language of the Authorized Version, just as he did with his version of Isaiah. He jotted a number of them in his pocket diary early in 1877.

143:24–29. John 6:38–39, 6:44, 8:47, 7–16, 13:20 (Luke 9:48).

143:30–36. Luke 6:46; John 13:17; Matthew 23:26, 15:18, 7:3 (Luke 6:41); Matthew 16:6 and Luke 12:1; Luke 16:15; Matthew 5:8.

143:37–144:3. Matthew 11:28–30.

144:4–12. John 6:35, 6:51, 6:57, 6:63, 8:51, 10:27–28.

144:13–24. John 12:26; Luke 14:27, 9:23; Mark 8:35–36; John 10:17, 13:34; Matthew 20:28 (Mark 10:45).

144:25–37. John 11:25–26, 10:10; Luke 13:32; John 14:19, 15:10, 14:21, 14:23.

144:38–145:4. John 10:11, 10:16; Luke 12:32.

145:5–17. John 18:36; Luke 17:20–21, 13:19–21; Mark 4:26–27; Matthew 24:14.

145:26. The Scribes were the expounders of Jewish law, the Pharisees a severe sect of Jewish religionists who in the New Testament become the type of literal observance of religious duty without spiritual or moral commitment. "I say unto you, That except your righteousness shall exceed the righteousness of the scribes and Pharisees, ye shall in no case enter into the kingdom of heaven."—Matthew 5:20.

145:31–37. J. B. Mozley, *Sermons Preached before the University of Oxford and on Various Occasions* (London, 1876), pp. 332–33 (Sermon XVIII: "The Influence of Dogmatic Teaching on Education").

146:5. Arnold devotes two chapters of *God and the Bible* to "The God of Miracles" and "The God of Metaphysics."

146:11–13. Joseph Butler; see p. 12:30–32.

146:32. Psalms 2:4.

146:34–37. John 4:13; Luke 21:36.

147:1. Hebrews 11:10.

[PREFACE TO *LAST ESSAYS*]

Arnold's Preface to *Last Essays on Church and Religion* is often taken as his best and most concise statement of his position. It was certainly carefully worked out; his pocket diary for the latter part of 1876 has memoranda of the heads he wished to discuss and drafts of key passages. He had already determined upon collecting these *Last Essays* when three Continental reviews of the French translation of *Literature and Dogma* reached him (one published October 21, the second November 14, the third in December); they formed an instructive contrast to what the English reviewers had said. He was still at work on the Preface on January 25, 1877, along with his official general report as school inspector and the essay on "Falkland." The book was published about March 24.

148:26–149:2. "The Courses of Religious Thought," *Contemporary Review* XXVIII, 1–26 (June, 1876). "A religious system is only then truly tested, when it is set to reform and to train, on a territory of its own, great masses of mankind."—p. 18.

150:8, 11–16. Review of *La Crise religieuse,* the French translation of *Literature and Dogma,* signed "A.P.C.," *La République française,* November 14, 1876, pp. 3–4. Paul-Armand Challemel-Lacour (1827–96) had been professor at Pau, but was exiled during the decade of the fifties for opposition to Napoleon III. A friend of Gambetta's, he founded and edited, at Gambetta's instance, *La République française* in November, 1871, held various elective and appointive offices under the Third Republic, and was to become, in 1880, ambassador to England. For the articles on Humboldt, which were in the *Revue germanique,* not the *Revue des Deux Mondes,* see *On the Study of Celtic Literature, Prose Works,* ed. Super, III, 301 and n.

150:22–151:9. Angelo de Gubernatis, "Rassegna delle letterature straniere," *Nuova Antologia,* 2 ser., III, 880–81 (December, 1876). The reviewer describes the Bible as being no inspiration for "modern life," not "daily life." The sentence "And how . . . their object!" is not quoted from, but represents the tone of, the review. De Gubernatis (1840–1913) was at the time professor of Sanskrit at Florence, after a disillusioning career as a revolutionary. Arnold jotted these passages (in Italian, and correctly) in his pocket diary for December 24–28, 1876.—*Note-Books,* ed. Lowry, p. 262. See Textual Notes.

151:18. I.e., the war against revolutionary and Napoleonic France.

152:5. An expression of Bishop Butler's; see p. 12:30.

152:37–38. Arnold used this expression when he spoke of Burke in "The Function of Criticism at the Present Time" (1864), *Prose Works,* ed. Super, III, 267; thereafter the phrase crops up from time to time in his writings.

153:9. See p. 123:35.

153:37. In *Literature and Dogma* and elsewhere; *Prose Works*, ed. Super, VI, 172–79.

154:2–4. *Analogy* II.i.32.—ed. Gladstone (1896), I, 206.

154:24–25. For example, by Plato in his myth of the soul as a charioteer drawn by two horses working at odds.—*Phaedrus*, 246A etc.

154:36–38. John 8:31–32.

155:1–4. Fragment 16 (or 78), jotted at the beginning of Arnold's pocket diary for 1876, and again on May 30, 1885, and at the end of 1887, the last headed "Again and again!"—*Note-Books*, ed. Lowry, pp. 242, 418, 434.

156:1–2. A remark of Jesus' reported again and again in the Gospels: Matthew 10:39, 16:25; Mark 8:35; Luke 9:24, 17:33; John 12:25.

156:16–18. Arnold first quoted Émile Littré to this effect in *Literature and Dogma* (1871), *Prose Works*, ed. Super, VI, 174.

156:23–24. For example, Romans 7:22–23, 8:6.

156:27–30. John 12:25, 13:34; Matthew 5:8.

157:3. Littré in his *Dictionnaire de la langue française* (1872) defines "solidarité" as, "dans le langage ordinaire, responsabilité mutuelle qui s'établit entre deux ou plusieurs personnes. La solidarité qui nous lie." In *St. Paul and Protestantism* (1869) Arnold spoke of "the *solidarity* (to use the modern phrase) of mankind" and "what we have called, using an expressive modern term, the *solidarity* of men."—*Prose Works*, ed. Super, VI, 26, 43; and see Index *s.v.* "solidarity."

157:13–158:8. Arnold developed this idea at greater length in *God and the Bible, Prose Works*, ed. Super, VII, 225–29.

157:25–26. "Il y a peu d'honnêtes femmes qui ne soient lasses de leur métier."—*Réflexions morales*, no. 367.

157:26–29. Ninon to St.-Évremond, 1699, quoted by Ste.-Beuve, *Causeries du lundi* (3rd. ed.; Paris, 1859), IV, 186. Ninon de Lenclos (1620–1705) was famous for her beauty, her wit, and her lovers.

157:37–158:1. F. W. Riemer, *Mittheilungen über Goethe* (Berlin, 1841), II, 95, jotted in Arnold's pocket diary for March 26, 1871, at the beginning of 1872, at the beginning of 1875, and in one of his "General Note-Books."—*Note-Books*, ed. Lowry, pp. 152, 169, 224, 522.

158:26. For a longer discussion of the "sweet reason," or "epiei-keia," of Jesus, see *Literature and Dogma, Prose Works*, ed. Super, VI, 299–301.

159:1. "And the Word was made flesh, and dwelt among us, . . . full of grace and truth. . . . The law was given by Moses, but grace and truth came by Jesus Christ."—John 1:14, 17.

159:21–22. *Apologeticus adversus Gentes pro Christianis,* cap. xxiv; in Migne, *Patrologia Latina,* I, 481; jotted in Arnold's pocket diary for July 1, 1876.—*Note-Books,* ed. Lowry, p. 252.

160:5. John 17:13.

160:11–16. Quoted in P. Challemel-Lacour, "Un Bouddhiste contemporain en Allemagne," *Revue des Deux Mondes,* 2d. pér., LXXXVI, 326, 329 (March 15, 1870), jotted in Arnold's pocket diary for August 17 and 19, 1876.—*Note-Books,* ed. Lowry, p. 254.

160:21. Psalm 97:1, Prayer Book Version, but reading "the Eternal" for "the Lord."

160:23–26. John 4:14; Acts 20:35.

160:29–161:8. Maurice Vernes, "La Philosophie religieuse en Angleterre: Une nouvelle forme du christianisme" (review of the French translation of *Literature and Dogma*), *Revue scientifique de la France et de l'étranger,* 2nd ser., XI, 390, 392 (October 21, 1876); reprinted as "Le Christianisme renouvelé d'après Arnold" in Vernes, *Mélanges de critique religieuse* (Paris, 1880), pp. 288–89, 295–96. The essay is a very lucid and sympathetic discussion of Arnold's book, very flattering to the author. It begins by comparing the English qualities of *Literature and Dogma* with the German character of Eduard von Hartmann's *Die Selbstzersetzung des Christenthums und die Religion der Zukunft* (1874); see Arnold's amused allusion to the latter in *God and the Bible* (1874), *Prose Works,* ed. Super, VII, 200. Arnold is justified in alluding to Vernes's preconceptions, since Vernes in his discussion of Arnold's handling of messianic ideas refers to his own *Histoire des idées messianiques* (Paris, 1874), pp. 178–244.

160:30–31. Proverbs 11:19, 10:25.

161:22–25. *Revue scientifique,* pp. 390–91; *Mélanges,* pp. 290–94.

162:33–38. *The Dialogues of Plato,* tr. Benjamin Jowett (3rd ed., Oxford, 1892), I, 127.

[MIXED ESSAYS]

When Arnold in mid-August, 1878, proposed to his publisher George Smith a collection of the essays he had published since the beginning of the preceding year, he was confronted with a statement of the failure in sales of *God and the Bible* and *Last Essays*. "I shall have to turn to ballad-singing and to leave the base mechanical art of prose. But seriously I had hoped that the Last Essays, at any rate, would have done better," he wrote to Smith on August 25. "I think we will try this one volume more; it has a good deal of literature mixed up with it, and that may help it along." He agreed to accept £50 for an edition of 1000 copies. At the end of October he asked permission of John Murray, proprietor of the *Quarterly Review*, to republish the two essays on Scherer that had appeared in that journal. The collection was assembled at the end of the year; the latest article in it had appeared in November, 1878. Arnold first proposed the title "Literature and Civilisation—Mixed Essays."— Buckler, *Matthew Arnold's Books*, pp. 159–60. *Mixed Essays* was advertised as "nearly ready" in the *Athenaeum* of January 11, 1879, but was not published until the last week of February, at the price of 9 s. The *Athenaeum's* review of the book on March 8 so pleased Arnold as to impel him to write to the editor, Norman MacColl, a week later: "It is worth while to have passed all one's youth 'out in the cold,' so far as the public is concerned, to be so kindly brought in and treated in one's old age. Nothing too could be more serviceable to the book than the line followed in the article. Accept my cordial thanks for yourself and for the writer."—W. H. G. Armytage, "Matthew Arnold and a Reviewer," *Review of English Studies*, n.s. VI, 297 (July, 1955). The sale of the volume somewhat justified Arnold's hopes; an identical "second edition" was advertised at the same price on June 26, 1880.

The order of the essays in the book, after the short Preface, was: "Democracy," "Equality," "Irish Catholicism and British Liberalism," " 'Porro Unum Est Necessarium,' " "A Guide to English Literature," "Falkland," "A French Critic on Milton," "A French Critic on Goethe," and "George Sand." The first of these has already appeared in the present edition, vol. II, 3–29.

Mixed Essays is the latest collection from which selections were drawn for *Passages from the Prose Writings of Matthew Arnold*, conceived by Smith and published at 7 s. 6 d. on June 28, 1880.

[A FRENCH CRITIC ON MILTON]

"M. Scherer is a solid embodiment of Mr. Matthew Arnold's ideal critic," Henry James the elder remarked as early as 1865 in an interesting essay in *The Nation* in which he claimed a higher place as critic for Scherer than for Ste.-Beuve.—October 12, p. 469. Only a few months earlier, when Arnold was in Paris on his official mission of 1865, he was invited to dine with the Edmond Scherers at Versailles on April 28. "He is one of the most interesting men in France," Arnold told his mother. "He called his youngest boy *Arnold* after Papa—and a very nice boy, of about 9, he is. Scherer has made a pilgrimage to Fox How, and saw some of the family but not you. He interests me from his connection with Vinet, who has been occupying me a good deal lately: but he belongs now to the most advanced school among the French Protestants, and is a good deal troubled, I imagine, both from without and from within. At his house I met several of the writers in the Journal des Débats."—*Letters*, ed. Russell. The project of writing on Vinet Arnold continued to cling to but never carried out. His reading of the fourth and fifth series of Scherer's literary essays in 1876 led him to plan an article on that critic, however—"Review of Scherer," then "A French Critic on Milton &c.," as he mapped out his plans progressively in his diary, and finally, of course, the pair of essays he actually did write. He told Scherer his plan, apparently, in a letter of October 13, 1876. His diary then shows him reading in Scherer strenuously in mid-October and early November, writing his article on December 5–13, and reading proof on December 27. Arnold at this time seems to have come into frequent contact with Dr. William Smith, editor of the *Quarterly Review*, who gave him precisely the opportunity he wanted—that of writing anonymously but extensively upon a contemporary. The article appeared in the January number for 1877, and Arnold received £21 in payment. It has been reprinted with notes in J. D. Jump, ed., *A Matthew Arnold Prose Selection* (London: Macmillan, 1965), pp. 130–53. In the *Quarterly* the essay purported to be a review of Macaulay's Essay on Milton, Addison's Essays on *Paradise Lost*, Johnson's Life of Milton, and Scherer's "Milton et le *Paradis Perdu*." As an essay on critical method, it stands in much the same relation to Arnold's later critical essays as "The Function of Criticism" to the earlier.

165:8–23. George Otto Trevelyan, *The Life and Letters of Lord Macaulay* (New York, 1876), I, 116–17. The essay on Milton appeared in the *Edinburgh Review* for August, 1825, when Macaulay was twenty-four. Byron, upon the publication of the first two cantos of *Childe Harold's Pilgrimage* in 1812, "woke one morning and found himself famous." Robert Hall (1764–1831), a Baptist divine much admired for the eloquence of his sermons, was a minister in

Leicester when Macaulay's essay appeared. "This long disease, my life," is from Pope's "Epistle to Dr. Arbuthnot," line 132. Francis Jeffrey (1773–1850) was one of the founders of the *Edinburgh Review* and its editor from 1803 to 1829.

166:4–5. "No attempt has been made to remodel any of the pieces which are contained in these volumes. Even the criticism on Milton, which was written when the author was fresh from college, and which contains scarcely a paragraph such as his matured judgment approves, still remains overloaded with gaudy and ungraceful ornament."—Macaulay's Preface to *Critical and Historical Essays* (1843), paragraph 3. See Trevelyan, *Macaulay*, I, 116–17.

166:8. In "The Function of Criticism at the Present Time" (1864), Arnold quoted his own words from the second lecture *On Translating Homer* (1860): The critical effort is "the endeavour, in all branches of knowledge, . . . to see the object as in itself it really is." —*Prose Works*, ed. Super, III, 258 and I, 140.

166:21–167:5. Macaulay, *Complete Works* (Whitehall ed.; New York, 1898), XI, 32, 67, 21, 26; *Literary Essays* (Oxford, 1913), pp. 24, 50, 15, 19–20. The passages were jotted in Arnold's pocket diary for September 15, 22–23, and 6–11, 1876.—*Note-Books*, ed. Lowry, pp. 257, 258, 256. In Philip Massinger's *The Virgin-Martyr*, Act V, a basket of fruits and flowers was sent from heaven by Dorothea to Theophilus, the Roman persecutor who had caused her martyrdom, and brought about his conversion.

167:10–11. When Hezekiah, king of Judea, was sick unto death, he prayed for deliverance, and the Lord instructed the prophet Isaiah, "Go, and say to Hezekiah, Thus saith the Lord, the God of David thy father, I have heard thy prayer, I have seen thy tears: behold, I will add unto thy days fifteen years."—Isaiah 38:5.

167:29–31. In "Joubert" (1864) Arnold called Macaulay "the great apostle of the Philistines, . . . a born rhetorician; a splendid rhetorician doubtless . . . ; still, beyond the apparent rhetorical truth of things he never could penetrate. . . . Rhetoric so good as his excites and gives pleasure; but by pleasure alone you cannot permanently bind men's spirits to you." In "The Literary Influence of Academies" (1864) he added: "Lord Macaulay's style has in its turn suffered by his failure in ideas, and this cannot be said of Addison's." In *Friendship's Garland*, Letter VIII (1869), he attributed to Macaulay's style "the external characteristic [of] a hard metallic movement with nothing of the soft play of life, and the internal characteristic [of] a perpetual semblance of hitting the right nail on the head without the reality."—*Prose Works*, ed. Super, III, 210, 247; V, 317. Trevelyan's life of his uncle was reviewed by Gladstone in the *Quarterly* in what Arnold thought "the best article of his I have ever seen, full of good judgment and sense, and charming in tone and temper," but, he told his sister in July, 1876, "Macaulay is to me uninteresting, mainly, I think, from a dash of intellectual vulgarity which I find in all his performance."—*Letters*, ed. Russell. Yet he was pleased to reprint Macaulay's *Encyclopaedia Britannica* account of Johnson in his edition of Johnson's *Six Chief Lives of the Poets* (1879).

167:37–168:18. *Works* (Whitehall ed.), XI, 33, 65–67, 30, 31; *Literary Essays* (Oxford), pp. 25, 48, 50, 22–23, 23; jotted in Arnold's pocket diary for September 1, 20–21, and 12–14, 1876.—*Note-Books*, ed. Lowry, pp. 255–57. Oromasdes and Arimanes were the opposing powers of good and evil in the Zoroastrian religion.

168:26–28. See p. 204:21–23.

168:35–38. *Works* (Whitehall ed.), XI, 60; *Literary Essays* (Oxford), p. 45; jotted in Arnold's pocket diary for August 26, 1876, and in one of his "General Note-Books."—*Note-Books*, ed. Lowry, pp. 255, 504.

169:15–17. *Works* (Whitehall ed.), XI, 65; *Literary Essays* (Oxford), p. 48, jotted in Arnold's pocket diary for September 18, 1876. —*Note-Books*, ed. Lowry, p. 257.

169:19–26. "Colasterion: a Reply to a Nameless Answer against The Doctrine and Discipline of Divorce," half-way through, and sixth paragraph from the end; jotted in Arnold's pocket diary for September 24–25, 1876.—*Note-Books*, ed. Lowry, p. 258. Milton wrote "and by function."

170:1–4. John Morley, "Macaulay," *Fortnightly Review* XXV, 494–95 (April, 1876); reprinted in his *Critical Miscellanies*, Second Series (London, 1877), p. 373.

170:23–24. The critical power, Arnold remarked in "The Function of Criticism at the Present Time" (1864), "tends to establish an order of ideas, if not absolutely true, yet true by comparison with that which it displaces; to make the best ideas prevail. Presently these new ideas reach society, the touch of truth is the touch of life, and there is a stir and growth everywhere; out of this stir and growth come the creative epochs of literature."—*Prose Works*, ed. Super, III, 261.

171:4–33. In the *Spectator* of December 31, 1711, Addison announced that he would thereafter devote his Saturday numbers to "a regular Criticism upon . . . *Paradise lost,* . . . till I have given my Thoughts upon that Poem" (i.e., until May 3, 1712).—*Spectator,* ed. Donald F. Bond (Oxford: Clarendon Press, 1965), II, 520. Arnold altogether quotes passages from the numbers for January 5, 12, 26; March 1, 8; April 5, 19; May 3; here, III, 391, 169, 391–92.

171:36. "Positivism" is generally any philosophy that confines itself to the data of experience and declines metaphysical or *a priori* speculations. It is essentially the scientific spirit.

172:8–29. *Spectator,* ed. Bond, III, 284, 333, 11; II, 539.

173:5–26. *Ibid.,* II, 565; III, 141–42.

173:34–38. Trevelyan, *Macaulay,* I, 117.

174:3–7. Johnson's "Life of Milton," two-thirds through.

174:16–17. *Ibid.,* a few pages after the preceding.

174:28–31. Edmond Scherer (1815–89), Paris-born but of Protestant Swiss family, was editor of *Le Temps* from its founding in 1861. It remained one of the foremost French newspapers until it ceased during World War II; after the war it was succeeded by *Le Monde.* Scherer contributed literary essays under the general title of "Variétés," not unlike Sainte-Beuve's *Causeries,* which had appeared in *Le Constitutionnel, Le Moniteur,* and finally in *Le Temps* itself in 1869, the year of his death. Scherer's essay on "Milton et le Paradis Perdu" appeared in *Le Temps* on November 10, 17, and 24, 1868; it was reprinted in the collected *Études critiques de littérature* (Paris, 1876), pp. 151–94.

174:32–33. Alexandre Vinet (1797–1847) held chairs of both theology and French literature in his native Lausanne. As early as 1864 Arnold planned to write an essay on Vinet, as Sainte-Beuve had done, but never accomplished the task.—*Note-Books,* ed. Lowry, p. 577. See R. L. Brooks, "Some Unaccomplished Projects of Matthew Arnold," *Studies in Bibliography* (Charlottesville), XVI, 215 (1963).

175:1. Arnold and Scherer dined as guests of Sainte-Beuve at the Café de Chartres, by the Palais Royal, on May 11, 1866, "in a little room on the garden where we can converse."—Sainte-Beuve to Scherer, May 9, 1866.

175:13–32. Scherer, *Études critiques,* pp. 151–54; the quoted passages are on p. 154. Scherer began his essay by quoting at length the judgment on Milton of Count Pococurante in chapt. xxv of Voltaire's *Candide;* his allusions to Addison and Macaulay were briefer but pointed.

175:25. Arnold found the word *milieu* in Scherer; both critics doubtless alluded to the work of Taine, though both had reservations about it. Arnold sent a copy of *Mixed Essays* to Taine, with an admiring letter dated March 9, 1880.—F. C. Roe, *Taine et l'Angleterre* (Paris, 1923), p. 176. In "The Function of Criticism at the Present Time" (1864), Arnold had said: "For the creation of a master-work of literature two powers must concur, the power of the man and the power of the moment, and the man is not enough without the moment; the creative power has, for its happy exercise, appointed elements, and those elements are not in its own control."— *Prose Works*, ed. Super, III, 261.

176:9. "Ars longa, vita brevis est," an aphorism of the Greek doctor Hippocrates which in its Latin version has become proverbial.

176:19-33. *Études*, pp. 176-77.

177:7-20. *Ibid.*, p. 175.

177:21-178:7. *Ibid.*, p. 178. The Schoolmen were the medieval Scholastics, philosophers and theologians whose work dominated the intellectual life of western Europe from the ninth to the fifteenth centuries.

178:12-16. *Études*, p. 160.

178:21-25. *Ibid.*, p. 169.

178:28-179:3. *Ibid.*, pp. 179 ("alla s'assombrissant avec l'âge et les événements"), 180-81.

179:7-19. *Ibid.*, p. 182.

179:25-30. *Ibid.*, p. 184.

179:34-37. *Ibid.*, p. 189.

180:6-181:2. *Ibid.*, pp. 187-89.

181:3-24. *Ibid.*, pp. 189-90.

181:25-27. *Ibid.*, p. 191.

181:32-182:4. *Ibid.*, p. 192.

182:8-13. *Ibid.*, pp. 192-93.

182:14-28. *Ibid.*, pp. 193-94.

182:31-35. Nearly half-way through.

183:10, 12. *Paradise Lost*, III, 36; XII, 644.

183:19. *Prelude*, III, 17. Arnold's judgment of this line, which has become axiomatic, does Wordsworth a serious disservice. The passage humorously describes the first approach to Cambridge of a wide-eyed provincial freshman, for whom the student in cap and gown was an object of wonder, the Cam was a legendary stream, and the Hoop was indeed a "famous Inn." The inflation is not Wordsworth's attempt to give false dignity to his commonplace statement, but the mature man's tolerant smile at the boyish wonder of the lad. See *On Translating Homer, Prose Works*, ed. Super, I, 187.

184:31-32. II Corinthians 6:6.

185:10–35. "An Apology for Smectymnuus," one-fourth through. Scherer translates this passage, with more of its context, in *Études*, pp.163–65.

186:24–26. *Études*, p. 185.

186:28–31. In the same volume with the essay on Milton, Scherer published essays on Shakespeare and on Goethe, one on "Le Cabaret du Mouton Blanc" in which Racine is discussed, and one on Taine's *Histoire de la littérature anglaise* in which Byron receives half a dozen pages. Elsewhere he has essays on Lamartine's death, his *Mémoires*, and his *Correspondence*. When he discussed Arnold by way of reviewing his selections from Wordsworth in 1881, Scherer remarked: "Il n'est pas d'écrivain étranger qui connaisse mieux la littérature de notre pays et qui ait en général autant de sympathie, j'allais dire de faiblesse pour notre tour d'esprit, nos moeurs, nos institutions. . . . Il a fait connaître à ses compatriotes Senancour, Joubert, Maurice de Guérin et sa soeur. Il est vrai que, sur l'article de notre poésie, je le crois moins orthodoxe; il y a quelque part, dans un de ses articles, une phrase malsonnante au sujet de Lamartine. Je ne serais pas étonné que Racine le laissât indifférent. Mais je n'ai garde de lui en vouloir. Il y a longtemps que je me suis fait une raison là-dessus, et que je vois sans déplaisir les étrangers rester indifférents à des beautés qui, pour ne pas être senties de tous, n'en sont que plus chères et plus sacrées aux vrais adorateurs."—"Wordsworth," *Nouvelles études sur la littérature contemporaine* (Paris, 1886), VII (or II), 5–6.

187:3–7. *Spectator*, February 2, 1712.—ed. Bond, III, 36.

[FALKLAND]

After writing "A Psychological Parallel," Arnold told James Knowles, "I mean to return to literature proper and to my old place the *Cornhill*. But I shall always be grateful to you for the valuable stage you have given me, to strut and fret my little theological hour upon." An unexpected event modified this plan somewhat: the *Contemporary Review*, which under Knowles's editorship from 1870 had broadened from spokesman for the Church of England to a journal that represented a wide spectrum of theological and philosophical opinion, was now bought by a more narrowly evangelical group of proprietors and Knowles resigned, with the resolution to establish a new journal that would give the best writers in England a free forum in the widest range of subjects. Tennyson and Arnold were among those named as contributors to the *Nineteenth Century* in the announcement of its establishment in February, 1877. At the time Arnold promised Knowles a contribution, he was full of his plan for a book of selections from the Latitudinarians of the seventeenth century and still fresh from reading Tulloch's *Rational Theology and Christian Philosophy in England in the Seventeenth Century*. And therefore the new essay represented less of a break from theology than Arnold foresaw.

At least from the date of the posthumous publication of Clarendon's *History of the Rebellion* in 1702–4, Lucius Cary, Viscount Falkland, had been something of a sentimental hero to the English, especially those of anti-Cromwellian sympathies. Pope in the *Essay on Man* called him "the virtuous and the just" and linked his name with Sidney's. Dr. Thomas Arnold praised him in his sixth lecture from the chair of Modern History at Oxford. The proposal to place a monument to Falkland near the scene of his death gave timeliness to the essay.

To some, however, the issues of Cavalier *versus* Roundhead still seemed vital, and Goldwin Smith eloquently replied in the *Contemporary Review* in April, 1877, to what he regarded as one more instance of Arnold's wantonly seeking occasion to belabor the Nonconformists. The two men were acquaintances of long standing; Arnold had provided Smith with a letter of introduction to Emerson in 1864 and in 1884 he was to be Smith's guest in Toronto. But Smith was savagely personal in his attack: he not only revived the old image of Arnold as Hotspur's courtier "by the battle field, pouncet-box in hand," sniffing and sneering, and renewed the fourteen-year-old accusation that Arnold had one standard of truth for the elite and another for the common man, but he accused Arnold of encouraging, even persuading, the clergy by the thousands to preach from the pulpit doctrines they derided in the company of cultivated men. Arnold mildly characterized Smith as "a writer of eloquence and power, although too prone to acerbity" and—perhaps not pointedly—cited some passages of Milton at his worst as a pamphleteer by way of illustrating the Puritan conception of urbanity and amenity (see pp. 295–97). Smith's tone and Arnold's in polemics are an instructive contrast. (Contrary to a statement by E. K. Brown, no alteration in Arnold's later version of his essay is attributable to

Smith's attack, except perhaps three words on p. 198:35: "Here opinions differ.")

The essay impresses one as on the whole rather half-hearted, a gesture for Knowles and a dutiful appeal "in aid of the Falkland Memorial," as Smith called it. It is very dependent on Tulloch, who (with more space at his disposal) gives more attention to Falkland's intellectual milieu. Nevertheless it has been interestingly treated as the type of Arnold's conception of the essence of tragedy in life by John P. Farrell, "Matthew Arnold's Tragic Vision," *PMLA* LXXXV, 107–17 (January, 1970). Arnold sent the manuscript to the printer on February 20 and read the proofs two days later; the article appeared in the first number of the *Nineteenth Century* in March, 1877; for it Arnold received the rather small sum of £15. It has recently been reprinted with notes in J. D. Jump, ed., *A Matthew Arnold Prose Selection* (London: Macmillan, 1965), pp. 109–29.

188:1. Eugène Goblet, comte d'Alviella, "La Mission de l'Angleterre dans l'Inde," *Revue des Deux Mondes*, 3d. pér., XVI, 620 (August 1, 1876). The English expression, "not kind," is given by Goblet himself. A Belgian journalist, he accompanied the Prince of Wales on his visit to India in 1875–76.

188:15–18. See p. 189:21n.

188:25–189:4. Edward Hyde, Earl of Clarendon, *The History of the Rebellion and Civil Wars in England*, Book VII, ¶217. (Arnold must have used the edition of 1826.) The Latin is from Lucan *Civil Wars* IX, 108: "It would be shameful to die after you from any other cause than grief alone." Arnold, in "The Literary Influence of Academies" (1864) described the Asiatic style as, in the definition of the ancients, "prose somewhat barbarously rich and overloaded."—*Prose Works*, ed. Super, III, 247 and note. John Tulloch remarks: "It is true that Clarendon's portrait is warmly coloured." —*Rational Theology and Christian Philosophy in England in the Seventeenth Century* (Edinburgh, 1872), I, 76.

189:10–15. *History*, Book VII, ¶233; quoted by Tulloch, I, 150.

189:21–27. The account of the meeting at Newbury on January 9, 1877, to launch the campaign for the Falkland monument appears in *The Times* next day, p. 10, cols. 3–4. Henry Herbert, fourth Earl of Carnarvon, was colonial secretary in Disraeli's administration; his speech occupies the great part of the report. An Earl of Carnarvon of a previous creation fell at the battle along with Falkland and the fourth Earl had his residence near Newbury. He spoke also at the unveiling of the monument on September 9, 1878.

189:35–36. Walpole, *A Catalogue of the Royal and Noble Authors of England* (2nd ed.; London, 1759), II, 216–21. Arnold drew the allusion from Tulloch, *Rational Theology*, I, 77.

190:1–18. Arnold's summary of Falkland's career is very like Tulloch's. Great Tew is a village five miles east of Chipping Norton in Oxfordshire, Burford a market town about ten miles south of Chipping Norton. Both are some fifteen or twenty miles from Oxford.

190:3–7, 10–191:3. *The Life of Edward Earl of Clarendon,* written by himself (Oxford, 1857), I, 35–37 (Book I, ¶35–37). The university alluded to was Dublin. Clarendon wrote "two very excellent houses excellently well furnished" and "above £2000"; Arnold follows Tulloch (I, 81n) in the first misquotation, not in the second. Clarendon also wrote: "no man was less beholden" and "carried another kind of lustre and admiration in it." Tulloch quotes part of Clarendon's sketch of Falkland, I, 154.

191:4–16. Tulloch discusses these friendships in *Rational Theology*, I, 95–118. He prints the strophe of Jonson's "To the Immortal Memory and Friendship of that Noble Pair, Sir Lucius Cary and Sir Henry Morison" (a strophe included by Palgrave in his *Golden Treasury*) on p. 85. The "Apollo" was the large room in the Devil Tavern, near Temple Bar, where Jonson presided over his "tribe." Sir John Suckling, Thomas Carew, Sir William Davenant, Edmund Waller, George Sandys, and Digby were poets and men of letters; John Selden was a lawyer; Thomas Hobbes of Malmesbury was a philosopher; John Hales and William Chillingworth were Anglican divines. Clarendon remarks in his *Life* (Book I, ¶55–56): "[Mr. Hales] was one of the least [i.e., smallest] men in the kingdom; and one of the greatest scholars in Europe. Mr. Chillingworth was of a stature little superior to Mr. Hales, (and it was an age in which there were many great and wonderful men of that size)." Tulloch points out the parallel (I, 153).

191:25–37. Clarendon, *Life*, I, 37–38 (Book I, ¶38), partially quoted by Tulloch, I, 90.

192:1–15. Clarendon, *Life*, I, 38–39 (Book I, ¶39–41), including the expressions *convivium philosophicum* and *convivium theologicum*. Falkland's mother was a Roman Catholic convert; his younger brothers Patrick and Placid took orders in the Catholic church.

192:19–39. Clarendon, *Life*, I, 39–40 (Book I, ¶41), partly quoted by Tulloch, I, 120–21, 128–29. Gilbert Sheldon, George Morley, Henry Hammond, and John Earle were all royalist clergymen; three of them became bishops after the Restoration.

193:1–3. *Ibid.*, I, 40 (Book I, ¶42), and *History*, Book VII, ¶230.

193:6. The Short Parliament sat only from April 13 to May 5, 1640.

193:9–14. Clarendon, *History*, Book VII, ¶222, quoted by Tulloch, I, 131–32. Clarendon wrote "gravity and sobriety."

193:17–21. Ship money was a royal tax to provide ships for the navy; it was imposed more and more widely as Charles I sank further into debt. It was challenged in the courts by John Hampden and was upheld in 1638 by the narrowest of margins. One of the earliest acts of the Long Parliament of 1640 was to declare the tax contrary to law. Thomas Wentworth, Earl of Strafford, lord lieutenant of Ireland and one of Charles's principal advisers, was impeached by the House of Commons at the very beginning of the Long Parliament. His trial before the Lords lasted three weeks, without a verdict being returned; but the impatient Commons, without waiting, passed a bill of attainder under which he was executed on May 12, 1641. For Falkland's part in these matters, see Tulloch, I, 132–46.

193:32–194:2. Falkland's speech of February 8, 1641, quoted by Tulloch, I, 138–39. The speech is given entire in J. A. R. Marriott, *The Life and Times of Lucius Cary, Viscount Falkland* (London, 1907), pp. 181–90; see pp. 182, 183–84, 186. Falkland said "no little Complement to those, and no little Apology for those to whom . . . "

194:18–25. Clarendon, *History*, Book IV, ¶94, canceled passage; partially quoted by Tulloch, I, 144. Arnold has copied correctly a muddled passage Clarendon's most recent editor emends to: "as well to things as to persons." Falkland was a Scottish, not an English, peer, and hence before the Union might sit in the House of Commons (where he represented Newport, Isle of Wight).

194:35–195:2. Clarendon, *Life*, I, 86 (Book II, ¶9).

195:2–12. Clarendon, *History*, Book IV, ¶123–24. "Hyde" was (subsequently) Clarendon.

195:13–16. *Ibid.*, Book VII, ¶227. Clarendon wrote "make himself again understood."

195:22–196:3. *Ibid.*, Book VII, ¶231, partially quoted by Tulloch, I, 149–50. Clarendon wrote "from the entrance," "generally sunk into," and "was not now only." The Latin is from Tacitus *Agricola* xxix: "And in his grief, war was one of the remedies."

196:4–22. Tulloch, I, 152, quoting Bulstrode Whitelocke, *Memorials of the English Affairs* (Oxford, 1853), I, 73; Clarendon, *History*, Book VII, ¶234. Sir John Byron was one of King Charles's cavalry commanders who was created Baron Byron in recognition of his services at the battle of Newbury. The poet Byron was his collateral descendant.

196:28–30. Clarendon, *Life*, I, 176 (Book III, ¶35).

197:4–17. *Ibid.*, I, 41, 37, 41, 38–39 (Book I, ¶42, 37, 43, 40).

197:25–31. Clarendon, *History*, Book VII, ¶226. Clarendon wrote "of all ingenuity."

197:34–198:9. *Ibid.*, ¶230.

198:10–19. *Ibid.*, ¶233. Tulloch mentions the incident, I, 152.

198:23. The hero of *The Bride of Lammermoor*. Arnold's reading list for 1873 contained eight of Scott's novels.—*Note-Books*, ed. Lowry, p. 588.

198:29–32. Clarendon, *Life*, I, 85 (Book II, ¶8).

198:36–37. "The distinguishing note of Lord Falkland's character [is] the spirit of singular moderation which pervaded it. . . . He gave us the great lesson that moderation is consistent with strength, and also as we plainly see with honour."—*Times*, January 10, 1877, p. 10, cols. 3–4.

198:37–199:5. Dean Stanley's letter is quoted near the beginning of the same article.

199:5–9. I, 77.

199:10–20. "Lord Carnarvon on Moderation," *Spectator* L, 43 (January 13, 1877).

199:21–200:3. "The Falkland Memorial," *The Nonconformist*, January 17, 1877, p. 62. Though Arnold calls the article "severe," it is generally respectful and good-tempered, even to opposing *The Spectator*'s strong views. When Arnold's article was published, *The Nonconformist* spoke admiringly of it, but did continue the debate Arnold began over its earlier article on Falkland.—March 14, p. 261.

200:8. Burke, attacking the "atheistic and infidel" philosophic writers of France, says of those of England at the beginning of the eighteenth century: "At present they repose in lasting oblivion. Who, born within the last forty years, has read one word of Collins, and Toland, . . . and that whole race who called themselves Free-thinkers? Who now reads Bolingbroke? Who ever read him through?"—*Reflections on the Revolution in France*, one-third through.

200:13–20. Henry St. John, Viscount Bolingbroke, *Remarks on the History of England* (1730), Letter XIX, ¶4.

200:31–201:4. *Letters on the Study and Use of History* (1735), Letter VII, ¶3.

201:10. I.e., Louis XIV.

201:15–17. See p. 78:27–29n.

201:21. See p. 24.

201:27–28. See p. 294:32–33n.

201:36–38. Clarendon, *History*, Book VII, ¶220.

202:16–17. John Richard Green (1837–83) in 1874 published his *Short History of the English People*, which aimed at combining all aspects of history—constitutional, social, economic, political, etc.—into a single picture of the progress of the nation and its people.

202:24. Francis Bacon (1561–1626) and the physician William Harvey (1578–1657), who in 1628 published his epoch-making discovery of the circulation of the blood, represent freedom of scientific thought.

202:35–203:9. Clarendon, *Life*, I, 41 (Book I, ¶43); *History*, Book VII, ¶219, 222, the last quoted by Tulloch, I, 136. John, Lord Finch, Lord Privy Seal, one of the judges who supported the king's prerogative in the ship money trial, fled to Holland rather than face the articles of impeachment brought against him by the Long Parliament at the end of 1640.

203:10. A bill introduced into the House of Commons in May, 1641, proposed to abolish bishops, deans, and chapters, "root and branch."

203:11–16. Tulloch, I, 141, quoting Falkland's speech of February 8, 1641. See Marriott, *Falkland*, p. 189.

203:17–26. Clarendon, *Life*, I, 85 (Book II, ¶8); *History*, Book VII, ¶229.

203:31. See p. 200:3.

204:1. "A politician, to do great things, looks for a *power*, what our workmen call a *purchase;* and if he finds that power, in politics as in mechanics, he cannot be at a loss to apply it."—*Reflections on the Revolution in France*, three-fifths through.

204:21–23. First sermon at Oxford, ¶16, *Works* (Oxford, 1838), III, 14; quoted by Tulloch, I, 294.

205:5–10. Ritualism, the introduction of Roman Catholic ceremonial practices into the services of the Church of England, kept the ecclesiastical courts and the privy council busy in the mid nineteenth century. It was the subject of an article by Gladstone, *Contemporary Review* XXIV, 663–81 (October, 1874). For the burials bill, see p. 87.

205:15–17. A. J. Beresford Hope (1820–87), a high churchman and independent conservative in Parliament, was "the unswerving defender of the rights of the church in its relation to the state."— *D.N.B.* He firmly opposed bills to legalize marriage to a deceased wife's sister and moved the rejection of Osborne Morgan's Burials Bill in 1873. He was partner with the editor John Douglas Cook in founding the *Saturday Review* in 1855. Henry Richard (1812–88), Welsh Congregationalist minister, was a member of Parliament from 1868 and a strenuous advocate of church disestablishment.

205:36–37. Luke 12:14.

206:6. John Owen (1616–83) and Richard Baxter (1615–91), both Puritan divines of great moderation, took part in the Savoy Conference of 1661 that attempted in vain to reconcile the Episcopalian and the Presbyterian interests. In the first version of this passage Arnold wrote "Owen the dreariest of theologians and Baxter the king of bores."

206:7–9. Bishop John Pearson on Hales, prefatory note "To the Reader," *Golden Remains of the Ever Memorable Mr. John Hales* (London, 1688), p. [vi]; quoted by Tulloch, I, 218.

206:10–13. Letter from Hales to Archbishop Laud, quoted by Tulloch, I, 213. Hales wrote "since I first understood."

206:15–22. Hales, *Works* (Glasgow, 1765), III, 150, 152, or *Sermons Preach'd at Eton* (2nd ed.; London, 1673), pp. 39, 40–41 (Sermon "Of Enquiry and Private Judgment in Religion," on Galatians 6:7, not quite halfway through); quoted by Tulloch, I, 245. Hales wrote: "I see you will willingly take up" and "of the true grounds or reasons"; Tulloch misquotes the former as Arnold does.

206:27–29. Arnold called Luther, like Bunyan, "a Philistine of genius" in *On the Study of Celtic Literature* (1866), *Prose Works*, ed. Super, III, 364.

206:30. The historian Edward Augustus Freeman (1823–92), a prolific contributor to the *Saturday Review*, was ridiculed (though not by name) in Arnold's essays on "Marcus Aurelius" (1863) and "The Literary Influence of Academies" (1864) for his warm support of the Germans and his hatred of Napoleon III.—*Prose Works*, ed. Super, III, 140, 250. "Freeman is an ardent, learned, and honest man, but he is a ferocious pedant," Arnold told Ernest Fontanès on December 15, 1878.—*Letters,* ed. Russell.

[GERMAN LETTERS ON ENGLISH EDUCATION]

When Arnold visited Berlin on his tour of enquiry into Continental educational systems in late June, 1865, his principal official host in the Ministry of Public Worship and Education there was Ludwig Wiese (1806–1900), whose statistical and descriptive book about Prussian education was the chief written source of Arnold's information about the German schools and universities. Wiese, while still head of the Joachimsthal School in Berlin, had visited England in 1850 to look at secondary schools and had published on his return a volume of *Deutsche Briefe über englische Erziehung* (1851), which Arnold's younger brother William Delafield Arnold translated into English in 1854. Their father, Dr. Thomas Arnold, was highly praised in the book for his impact upon English education. After serving in the Prussian education ministry from 1852 to 1875, Wiese retired and traveled once more in England, looking at schools and writing long accounts of them for friends and former colleagues back home. These he revised and published on his return as a supplement to a third edition (1877) of his earlier book. Among those to whom he made special acknowledgment for help were Matthew Arnold, his brother-in-law W. E. Forster, and his father's biographer Dean Stanley. The new letters were published in English translation by Leonhard Schmitz, a German who was classical examiner in the University of London (*German Letters on English Education.* London: William Collins, Sons, and Company, 1877); but Arnold began reading the book in German late in March or early in April, and without waiting for the translation, published an anonymous review of it in *The Pall Mall Gazette* for May 3, 1877. "Wiese will like my having given an account of his book, and that was why I wrote it; then at the end I had a little fling on my own account," he told his wife two days later. The editor of *The Pall Mall Gazette,* Frederick Greenwood, told Arnold he "was very grateful for the article, and said, what was true, that it is invaluable to have such criticism as Wiese's put resolutely before the British public." Indeed, when the English translation appeared, Greenwood found space for another notice on September 22, p. 12. "It gave me a great deal of trouble to write the thing," said Arnold, and his diary shows that he worked on the composition from about April 16 to April 22, but he had the satisfaction of hearing the Master of Trinity College, Cambridge, W. H. Thompson, say he thought Wiese's view was perfectly just and that his great predecessor as Master of Trinity, William Whewell, would have thought so too.—*Letters,* ed. Russell. Arnold received 4½ gns. in payment for the article. It has been reprinted by Fraser Neiman, *Essays, Letters, and Reviews by Matthew Arnold* (Cambridge: Harvard University Press, 1960), pp. 205–10.

208:11–20. Wiese, *Deutsche Briefe über englische Erziehung* (Berlin, 1877), II, v. The "revolutionary time" was that of the liberal uprisings in 1848.

209:29–31. Wiese describes the Oxford and Cambridge "Middle Class" or "Local" Examinations, instituted in 1858, and their newer school certificate examinations, instituted in 1874. The "meddlesomeness" Arnold alludes to springs from the fact that the examinations (and hence the course of study) were set entirely by the universities, who gave the schoolmasters no voice.

210:2–4. *Deutsche Briefe,* II, 112; tr. Schmitz, p. 90.

210:15–23. *Ibid.,* II, 110; tr. Schmitz, p. 88.

210:24–27. *Ibid.,* II, 111; tr. Schmitz, p. 89.

210:29–36. *Ibid.,* II, 113; tr. Schmitz, p. 90. Wiese wrote: "What is needful in such times is a man of the character of Thomas Arnold, in whom . . ."

210:37–211:2. *Deutsche Briefe,* II, 332–33; tr. Schmitz, p. 270.

211:6–8. *Ibid.,* II, 149; tr. Schmitz, p. 121.

211:15–19. *Ibid.,* II, 151; tr. Schmitz, p. 122.

211:23–36. *Ibid.,* II, 152–53; tr. Schmitz, p. 124.

212:3–19. *Ibid.,* II, 138–39; tr. Schmitz, pp. 112–13. The Act of 1869 is the Endowed Schools Act.

212:24–213:19. *Deutsche Briefe,* II, 185–87; tr. Schmitz, pp. 150–52. For the story of the French minister and his watch, see p. 237:1–5.

213:23–214:11. *Deutsche Briefe,* II, 230–33, with omissions; tr. Schmitz, pp. 188–90. Jean-Baptiste-Antoine Auget, baron de Montyon (1733–1820), in 1783 endowed an annual prize, which he reestablished after the Restoration, for a member of the French poorer class who should in the judgment of the French Academy have that year performed the most virtuous act.

214:17. *Deutsche Briefe,* II, 229; tr. Schmitz, p. 186.

214:22–24. *Ibid.,* II, 324; tr. Schmitz, p. 263. The paragraph goes on: "It could not but appear strange to me that the services of a man like Matthew Arnold . . . should be employed for hours in a Wesleyan training college, where I saw him superintending about sixty pupil teachers writing out their tasks, which he himself had not set for them; with us any teacher would be sufficient for such a function."

214:29–35. *Deutsche Briefe*, II, 325; tr. Schmitz, p. 263.

[GEORGE SAND]

The death of Sainte-Beuve on October 13, 1869, led Arnold to remark to his mother that he was obliged to write an article on him, and that "when George Sand and Newman go, there will be no writers left from whom I have received a strong influence: they will all have departed." Newman outlived Arnold, but the death of George Sand on June 8, 1876, set Arnold to re-reading her that summer; since he was talking to John Morley about her he may have contracted soon after her death for the article he did not in fact get to until the following May. "Her death has been much in my mind," he told his sister in June, 1876; "she was the greatest spirit in our European world from the time that Goethe departed. With all her faults and Frenchism, she was this. I must write a few pages about her." But to his wife he confessed, on May 5, 1877, "G. Sand is beginning to weigh upon me greatly, though she also interests me very much; the old feeling of liking for her and of refreshment from her, in spite of her faults, comes back."—*Letters*, ed. Russell. He did not finish the article until May 25; it appeared in the June number of Morley's *Fortnightly Review* and Arnold was paid £25 for it. On August 12, 1884, he published in *The Pall Mall Gazette* a short commemorative article on her, and only a few months before his death he was reading the latter volumes of her correspondence, and finding them "so interesting that I shall write an article on 'the old age of George Sand,' " he told his daughter Lucy. Her impact upon him is treated in Iris E. Sells, *Matthew Arnold and France: the Poet* (Cambridge: at the University Press, 1935) and F. J. W. Harding, *Matthew Arnold, the Critic, and France* (Geneva: Droz, 1964).

216:25. *Jeanne* was first published serially in *Le Constitutionnel* in 1844 and in book form in 1845. The places Arnold mentions are well illustrated by photographs in Georges Lubin, *George Sand en*

Berry (Paris: Hachette, 1967). George Sand spells the name of the druidical stones "Jomâtres" (in *Jeanne*) or "Jaumâtres" (in *Journal d'un Voyageur pendant la guerre*).

217:1. The maps of France by César and Jacques Cassini de Thury appeared in 1744–93. Arnold alluded to them in his essay on "Ordnance Maps" (1862), *Prose Works*, ed. Super, II, 256.

217:1–29. Arnold's itinerary for this holiday tour is recorded in his pocket diary for 1846. He left Oxford on Wednesday, June 24, reached Paris on the 26th, traveled to Orléans on the 28th, and on the 30th went through Châteauroux to La Châtre and reached Boussac on July 1. After spending some days in the region of the Mont-Dore, he was back in La Châtre on July 13; on the 14th he records: "Nohant—saw G.S." On July 15 he returned to Paris through Châteauroux and Blois, left there on the 17th and was in London on the 19th, in time to see Rachel perform two of the next three nights. He did not go to Switzerland this year or the next, but there can be little doubt that George Sand stimulated his interest in Senancour, whose memory guided his pilgrimage to Switzerland in 1848. George Sand later told Renan, who told John Morley, that Arnold's appearance at her door reminded her of "a young Milton on his travels." —*Letters*, ed. Russell.

217:24–25. George Sand describes "les trois lions de granit, monuments de la conquête anglaise au temps de Charles VI, renversés par les paysans au temps de la Pucelle, brisés, mutilés et devenus informes, qui gisent le nez dans la fange, au beau milieu de la place de Toulx."—*Jeanne*, Chapt. i.

218:26. Arnold, who had been introduced to Michelet by Philarète Chasles in 1847 because of Michelet's interest in Dr. Arnold's *History of Rome*, wrote to him from his Paris hotel on April 10, 1859, a few weeks after his arrival on a tour of inquiry into French elementary education.—J.-M. Carré, *Michelet et son temps* (Paris, 1926), p. 181. Arnold planned to call on G. Sand in Paris on May 9. Having failed to see her, he wrote to his sister from Geneva on July 9 that he would return to Paris through Châteauroux about the 25th, "as I have a visit to pay to George Sand (Michelet has given me a letter to her)." But his plans changed when he discovered that the schools he proposed to visit in the interval were closed for the long vacation. Her recent novel *La Daniella* was a companion of his travels. Later he thought of going from Paris to Berri on August 21 to see her, but again gave up the plan because he needed the time for work on his official mission. Sainte-Beuve took him to dinner on the

19th *chez le Restaurant du Quartier,* "the only good one, he says, and we dined in the cabinet where G. Sand, when she is in Paris, comes and dines every day." But Sainte-Beuve's gossip about her both fascinated Arnold and repelled him. "Sainte-Beuve rather advised me to go and see [her], but I am still disinclined 'to take so long a journey to see such a fat old Muse,' as M. de Circourt says in his funny English. All Sainte-Beuve told me of her present proceedings made me less care about seeing her; however, if Berri was nearer, the weather less hot, and French travelling less of a bore, I should go—as it is I shall not."—*Letters,* ed. Russell.

219:14–15. From the opening paragraphs, dated September 15, 1870, of *Journal d'un Voyageur pendant la guerre* (4th ed.; Paris, 1871), p. 2; jotted in Arnold's pocket diary for May 21, 1877.—*Note-Books,* ed. Lowry, p. 277.

219:27. *Consuelo* was a novel published in 1842–43.

219:34–35. Edmée is the heroine of *Mauprat,* Geneviève the heroine of *André* (1835); the widower Germain is the principal character of *La Mare au Diable.*

220:4–7. *Lettres d'un Voyageur* (1837) is a semi-autobiographical miscellaneous discussion of many matters; *Mauprat* (1837), *François le Champi* (1848) and *Valvèdre* (1861) are novels.

220:5. F. W. H. Myers, "George Sand," *Nineteenth Century* I, 221–41 (April, 1877). See p. 236. Myers was like Arnold an inspector of schools. Near the close of his essay he defined the fundamental controversy of his day as that between Spiritualism and Materialism, "between those who base their life upon God and immortality, and those who deny or are indifferent to both. And the spiritual cause has the more need of champions now that a distinct *moral* superiority can no longer be claimed on either side. Perhaps the loftiest and most impressive strain of ethical teaching which is to be heard in England now, comes from one who invokes no celestial assistance, and offers to virtue no ultimate recompense of reward. The Stoics are again among us; the stern disinterestedness of their 'counsels of perfection' is enchaining some of our noblest souls."—p. 240. That this last sentence glances at Arnold is perfectly clear from Myers' affectionate article on Arnold a few days after his death.—"Matthew Arnold," *Fortnightly Review* XLIX, 719–28 (May, 1888).

220:32–33. *Valentine* was published in 1832, *Lélia* in 1833. *Corinne* (1807) is a novel by Mme. de Staël.

221:3–28. *Lélia* (Paris: Calmann-Lévy, n.d.), II, 159–61 (final chapter), with omissions. These are the last words of Lélia before her death.

221:29–222:4. *Jacques* (1834) (Paris: Calmann-Lévy, n.d.), pp. 346–47, 132.

222:5–19, 26–223:2. *Lettres d'un Voyageur* (nouv. éd.; Paris, 1869), pp. 267, 113. Sténio and Jacques were suicides in George Sand's novels *Lélia* and *Jacques*.

223:7–10, 12–33. Sand, "Poètes et romanciers modernes de la France: George de Guérin," *Revue des Deux Mondes*, 4th ser., XXII, 581–83 (May 15, 1840), with omissions. She reprinted this essay at the end of the volume that contains her novel *La Dernière Aldini* (Paris: Calmann-Lévy, n.d.), pp. 269–96; the quoted passages are on pp. 282–84. Arnold began his essay on Guérin (1862) with a reference to her essay.—*Prose Works*, ed. Super, III, 12.

223:35. "The time is out of joint."—*Hamlet* I, v, 188.

223:38. "The sensuousness of the Latinised Frenchman makes Paris; . . . [he is] sensuous and sociable, . . . with the talent to make this bent of his serve to a practical embellishment of his mode of living."—*On the Study of Celtic Literature* (1866). "France is *l'homme sensuel moyen*, the average sensual man; Paris is the city of *l'homme sensuel moyen*. . . . France . . . develops him confidently and harmoniously. She makes the most of him, because she knows what she is about and keeps in a mean, as her climate is in a mean, and her situation. . . . [Hers is] the ideal of *l'homme sensuel moyen*."—*Literature and Dogma* (1873), *Prose Works*, ed. Super, III, 346; VI, 390. Othon Guerlac, *Les Citations françaises* (Paris, 1931), p. 236, credits Arnold with originating the expression, and Harry Levin says that the expression "is never used in the sensual land of France," but "seems to have been invented by Matthew Arnold, who, to be sure, was writing about George Sand" (but not, be it noted, when he first used it).—"The Unbanning of Books," *Refractions: Essays in Comparative Literature* (New York, 1966), p. 297. Without being able to disprove Levin, I have my doubts. There is some suggestion of the idea in Montesquieu's *Lettres persanes*, no. 106: "Paris est peut-être la ville du Monde la plus sensuelle, et où l'on rafine le plus sur les plaisirs." The expression "homme sensuel" occurs in Rousseau's *La nouvelle Héloïse*, Part II, letter xv, and no doubt in many other places. Whether or not Arnold invented the phrase, his use of it must have been responsible for its being taken as the criterion of decency in the courts of the United States (Judge Woolsey's decision removing the ban on *Ulysses*).

224:8–28. *Valentine* (nouv. éd.; Paris, 1864), pp. 3–5, 17–18.

224:32–36. *La Mare au Diable*, ed. P. Salomon et J. Mallion (Paris: Garnier, 1956), p. 5: prefatory "Notice" (1851).

224:37–225:18. *La Mare au Diable* was published in 1846. In her prefatory "L'Auteur au lecteur," George Sand describes Holbein's engraving of "The Plowman" (the French call it "Le Laboureur") from the "Dance of Death" series. Arnold summarizes her first three paragraphs.

225:21–226:10. *La Mare au Diable*, ed. Salomon and Mallion, pp. 16–18.

226:25–227:26, 32–228:6. *Ibid.*, pp. 24, 8, 14–16, 23–24. The quotation from Vergil is *Georgics* II, 458–59.

228:8–9. "Nous sommes dans la situation la plus périlleuse et la plus tourmentée qui fût peut-être jamais; et cependant cette situation est très-favorable à une renaissance sociale si nous voulons la comprendre."—"Réponse à une amie" (1871), *Impressions et souvenirs* (Paris, 1896), pp. 122–23.

228:13–33. Chapter viii (October 28, 1871), *Impressions et souvenirs*, pp. 135–36, 137.

228:35–36. "Tintern Abbey," lines 94–95. Wordsworth wrote "of elevated thoughts."

229:1–14. *Impressions et souvenirs*, pp. 136, 138, 139.

229:17–18, 20–22. *Ibid.*, pp. 141, 143. Arnold might better have written: "A man may say in his moments of great distress, 'I did not deserve this, and the atom . . .' "

229:25–30, 33–230:5. "L' Homme et la femme" (1872), *Impressions et souvenirs*, pp. 266, 264, 269.

230:12–14. "La Révolution pour l'idéal" (1872), *Impressions et souvenirs*, p. 252. See "Equality," p. 279:30–31.

230:15–25. *Journal d'un Voyageur pendant la guerre*, pp. 299, 162, 20.

230:26. "Mais quel réveil vous attend, si vous poursuivez l'idéal stupide et grossier du caporalisme, disons mieux, du *krupisme!* Pauvre Allemagne des savants, des philosophes et des artistes, Allemagne de Goëthe et de Beethoven! Quelle chute, quelle honte."—*Ibid.*, pp. 119–20. The firm of Krupp, in Essen, was Prussia's principal manufacturer of armament.

230:28–29. *Ibid.*, p. 117. See Arnold's "Renan" (1872), *Prose Works*, ed. Super, VII, 44.

231:12–13. In "The Function of Criticism at the Present Time" (1864), *Prose Works*, ed. Super, III, 265.

231:17. *L'Assommoir* (1877), one of Zola's masterpieces, gives a vivid account of the lives of the vulgar in Paris. It created a great sensation in England as well as France.

231:31–36. *Journal d'un Voyageur*, p. 305 (February 10, 1871).

232:1–8. See p. 290:6–15n.

232:12–13. "La civilisation, qui est l'ouvrage des nations intelli-gentes, n'est pas responsable de l'abus qu'on fait d'elle. La moralité y puise tout ce dont elle a besoin; la science, l'art, les grandes indus-tries, l'élégance et le charme des bonnes moeurs ne peuvent se passer d'elle. Soyons donc fiers d'être le plus civilisé des peuples."—*Journal d'un Voyageur*, p. 114; jotted in one of Arnold's "General Note-Books."—*Note-Books*, ed. Lowry, p. 499.

232:13–17. "La Révolution pour l'idéal," *Impressions et souvenirs*, p. 254; jotted in Arnold's pocket diary at the beginning of 1882.— *Note-Books*, ed. Lowry, p. 367.

232:17–18. "France is a nation of nonentities—a flock of sheep without any individuality. . . . They are 30,000,000 of obedient Caf-fres, . . . utterly destitute of distinctive attributes. . . . The French are gregarious, easily led and governed," said Bismarck, reported in an account of Moritz Busch, *Graf Bismarck und seine Leute* in *The Times*, November 19, 1878, p. 3, col. 1.

232:25–26. "Je crois à un immense avenir pour le peuple française. . . . C'est le meilleur et le plus aimable peuple de la terre."—*Impres-sions et souvenirs*, p. 26.

232:26–30. *Journal d'un Voyageur*, pp. 28, 96.

232:37–233:2. *Ibid.*, pp. 203, 219.

233:6, 10–23. *Ibid.*, pp. 165, 220–21.

234:1–2. See p. 290:20–29n.

234:19, 25. "M. Gambetta a une manière vague et violente de dire les choses qui ne porte pas la persuasion dans les esprits équitables." —*Journal d'un Voyageur*, p. 143. For "l'avocat," see *ibid.*, p. 173.

234:37–38. See p. 153:38.

235:7–11. *Journal d'un Voyageur*, p. 309 (February 10, 1871).

235:25–26. Keats, *Hyperion*, I, 51.

236:3–5. See p. 219:14–17.

236:6–7. "She looks for the Resurrection of the dead, And the life of the world to come." Arnold has adapted the closing words of the Nicene Creed ("I look for . . ."). Myers ends his essay on the same note with a long quotation from George Sand on the true meaning of a trust in an eternal life, but Arnold may also have had in mind a briefer statement of hers: "Je crois que nous vivons éternellement, que le soin que nous prenons d'élever notre âme vers le vrai et le bien nous fera acquérir des forces toujours plus pures et plus intenses pour le développement de nos existences futures."— *Journal d'un Voyageur*, p. 16; or the even briefer sentence he jotted in his pocket diary for October 8, 1882: "Mon âme est pleine d'espérance en l'avenir éternel."—*Note-Books*, ed. Lowry, p. 381, quoting *Spiridion* (Paris, 1867), p. 395.

[A GUIDE TO ENGLISH LITERATURE]

The series of "primers" on various subjects, prepared by distinguished scholars for the use of school children and brought out by Arnold's publisher Macmillan, interested Arnold very much: those on the sciences appeared on his reading lists for 1876 and 1877 and his diary shows him busy with the one on English literature in mid-May and again in mid-July, 1876. He promised its author, Stopford Brooke, that he would review it for *The Pall Mall Gazette* (where he could publish anonymously), but moved so slowly that he was anticipated by another reviewer in that paper. He then asked Knowles (in August) if he would accept an eight or ten page notice of it for the January or February (1877) number of the *Contemporary*. Knowles promptly agreed to the review, but then Arnold withdrew: "I shall push in somewhere without my name my review of him. Already I am bothered by people asking me to review their books—and if I print a review of this kind with my name it will be hard for me to say, as I do at present, that I never review books." Knowles's resignation from the *Contemporary* and his founding of the *Nineteenth Century* altered the picture: Arnold's discussion of the book was published as a signed article, not a review, in the December, 1877, number of the new journal. Arnold received £40 in payment—by a substantial amount the highest sum he had ever received for an article.

Stopford Brooke in 1865 published a biography of the preacher Frederick W. Robertson that so much impressed Arnold as to make him think of lecturing upon Robertson from the chair of poetry at Oxford; the intention to write an essay on Robertson was a recurring one as late as 1875, but was never carried out.—*Letters*, ed. Russell (November 18, 1865; June 18, 1869); *Note-Books*, ed. Lowry, p. 589. Arnold is said to have gone to St. James's Chapel, York Street,

Piccadilly, to hear Brooke preach, and after the service to have walked "thoughtfully down the staircase [from the gallery], detached and analytical." He wrote to Brooke about this *Primer:* "You have made a delightful book, and one which may have a wide action—the thing which one ought to desire for a good product almost as much as its production."—L. P. Jacks, *Life and Letters of Stopford Brooke* (London, 1917), I, 288, 286. The two men were not personally congenial, however; when Brooke withdrew from the Church of England in 1880 Arnold wrote to a clerical friend: "I read the 'Guardian' report of what Stopford Brooke said. I read it with regret but without any very great surprise, as I have not a high esteem for his judgment though he is full of talent and feeling." Brooke undertook to lecture on Arnold in the latter part of 1901, among other things "picturing how very much distressed [he] would have been if he had been really put back into the Athens he was so fond of. I sketched him criticizing Aeschylus and Euripides, and only living with Sophocles, calling Alcibiades his typical 'Barbarian,' and hating Cleon and his lot as much as he hated the Nonconformists. How uncomfortable he would have been, how he would have wished himself back in the Athenaeum Club."—Jacks, *Stopford Brooke*, II, 541. Brooke was less flippant in *Four Poets: a Study of Clough, Arnold, Rossetti and Morris* (London, 1908).

A distinguished contemporary of Arnold's remarked of the article when it first appeared "that Mr. Brooke had been told he had written a most charming book, only unfortunately he had said nothing in it which he ought to say, and put in everything he ought to have left out."—*Athenaeum*, March 8, 1879, p. 303. Brooke wrote to tell Arnold that he was gratefully following Arnold's suggestions. "It is worth while reviewing a man when you produce so much positive result," Arnold wrote to his sister. "However, the *Primer* will be much improved by his following my advice. It is a good little book, and my great desire in education is to get a few good books universally taught and read."—*Letters*, ed. Russell. As for the *Primer*, it was successful enough—25,000 copies were sold in the first ten months, nearly half a million by 1916. It was much praised. Yet Brooke's willingness to reverse his critical judgments on the basis of Arnold's review does indeed call into question the real strength of his intellect and may equally call into question the value of any such capsule criticism of literature.

The essay is by no means one of Arnold's best, for its intent constrained his freedom; but it serves as a reminder that the essays on

Johnson, Gray, Wordsworth, Byron, and Keats were all to come forth within the next two or three years.

237:1–5. Arnold himself first used the story in his inspectoral report for 1874.—*Reports on Elementary Schools,* ed. F. Sandford (London, 1889), p. 183; ed. F. S. Marvin (London, 1908), p. 163. The story was alluded to even earlier by John Stuart Mill. See also p. 213:3–7.

237:15–17. "A Plea for a Rational Education," *Fortnightly Review* XXVIII, 170–94 (August, 1877), reprinted in his *Miscellanies, Political and Literary* (London, 1878), pp. 164–213. The child of fourteen, Grant Duff believed, should read and write his own language well, know arithmetic, geography, astronomy, geology, history, natural science, and the great masterpieces of English literature; he should speak and write French with ease and easily translate an ordinary French or German book; he should have some knowledge of drawing and music. Latin and Greek were entirely unnecessary, unless the child were to proceed further in his schooling.

237:19–21. In his Inspectoral Report for 1878, Arnold makes the point that any pedagogic doctrine depends for its success on the talent of the teachers who practice it: the unimaginative and old-fashioned teacher will do the same old thing even while he fancies that he is following the new principles. Thus the Pestalozzian doctrine that we are to teach things "in the concrete instead of in the abstract" "may be excellent, and no one can say that it has not found ardent friends to accept it and employ it; and the result is that one sees a teacher holding up an apple to a gallery of little children, and saying: 'An apple has a stalk, peel, pulp, core, pips, and juice; it is odorous and opaque, and is used for making a pleasant drink called cider.' "—Arnold, *Reports on Elementary Schools,* ed. Sandford, pp. 212–13; ed. Marvin, p. 189. Arnold jotted this definition of an apple at the end of his pocket diary for 1877.

238:1–2. Plato *Philebus* 60A: "Well says the proverb that we ought to repeat twice and even thrice that which is good." *Gorgias* 498E: "It is good to repeat and review what is good twice and thrice over, as they say." (Jowett's translation.) Arnold jotted the proverb in his pocket diary for June 10, 1877.—*Note-Books,* ed. Lowry, p. 278.

238:4. Arnold is using the phrase he made current in "The Function of Criticism at the Present Time" (1864): Criticism is "a disinterested endeavour to learn and propagate the best that is known and thought in the world, and thus to establish a current of fresh and true ideas."—*Prose Works,* ed. Super, III, 282.

238:27–28. A series of primers in science, history, and literature (the two latter groups edited by the historian J. R. Green) was published by Arnold's publisher Macmillan in London, by D. Appleton & Co. in New York. Their object was "to convey information in such a manner as to make it both intelligible and interesting to very young pupils, and so to discipline their minds as to incline them to more systematic after-studies. They are not only an aid to the pupil, but to the teacher, lightening the task of each by an agreeable, easy, and natural method of instruction." The literature primers were devoted to comprehensive subjects or (in three instances) to individual authors—Homer, Shakespeare, and William Cullen Bryant. Stopford Brooke's *English Literature* (London, 1876) ran to 167 pages. As he drew to a close with his own generation, Brooke remarked: "Some of its best writers are Robert Browning and his wife, Matthew Arnold, and A. H. Clough. One of them, ALFRED TENNYSON, has for forty years remained the first."—p. 166. When Macmillan republished the book in larger and more attractive format in 1880, Brooke revised his text to remedy nearly all the passages Arnold faulted.

239:35–240:3. Brooke, p. 7. He wrote "what great English men and women . . ." The edition of 1880 followed Arnold's suggestion and began with this sentence. Arnold repeats his "Nothing can be better" on p. 251:3 and 311:15–16.

240:5–8. *Ibid*. The edition of 1880 omitted this sentence.

240:28–33. Pp. 7–8. Brooke wrote "teaching and delighting the world."

241:16–18. P. 20. Brooke wrote "last extant English charter." He placed the sentence in quotation marks without explanation; he may have been quoting Professor John Earle, but neither Earle's name nor any other indication of a source appears and Arnold's complaint was entirely justified. Brooke omitted the sentence in 1880.

241:24–27. P. 22. Brooke in 1880 cleared up this statement.

241:36–242:2. P. 23. Again, Brooke in 1880 cleared up this passage —which turned out to be a good deal less subtle than Arnold was willing to suppose.

242:24–30, 35–243:2. Pp. 25, 27.

243:13–244:10. Pp. 37–38. Brooke wrote "woods, and streams, and flowers, and . . ."

244:15. Arnold uses the spelling "renascence" which he deliberately adopted in 1868.—*Prose Works*, ed. Super, V, 172:6 and note. Brooke spelled it "Renaissance," but generally avoided the word in favor of "revival."

244:20–24. J. P. Eckermann, *Gespräche mit Goethe*, ed. E. Castle (Berlin, 1916), II, 27–28 (January 2, 1824). Goethe's expression was "in seiner riesigen Heimat."

244:27–31. P. 87. Brooke wrote "sought from God." He dropped the passage in 1880.

244:35–38. P. 88. Brooke in 1880 modified both statements.

245:4–6. *Ibid.*

245:14–15. *Macbeth* I, ii, 54–55.

245:27–28. P. 104. Brooke wrote "their grave beauty."

245:29. "We may perhaps regret that our greatest poet was shut away from his art for twenty years during which no verse was written but the sonnets."—pp. 103–4. In 1880 this sentence became simply: "We may regret that Milton was shut away from his art during twenty years of controversy."

245:31–32. P. 104. Brooke wrote "is gone." In 1880 he modified his statement and corrected his syntax.

246:1–3. Pp. 104–5. Brooke wrote "on our minds." He did not change this sentence in 1880.

246:7–8. P. 106. Brooke altered the passage in 1880. For Arnold's use of "curiosity" and "disinterestedness," see "The Function of Criticism at the Present Time" (1864), *Prose Works*, ed. Super, III, 268.

246:11–14. Pp. 106–7. In 1880 Brooke reduced this sentence to merely: "He began the poetry of pure natural description."

246:21–22. Arnold dealt with "natural magic" in "Maurice de Guérin" (1862) and *On the Study of Celtic Literature* (1866).— *Prose Works*, ed. Super, III, 13–14, 33, 374–80. Arnold commonly miscalled Wordsworth's "The Solitary Reaper" "The Highland Reaper."

246:31–33. Pp. 117–18.

247:8–13. Brooke in 1880 accepted these suggestions and somewhat rearranged his material to conform to them.

247:18–28. Pp. 126–27. Arnold omits a long passage between "to the villages" and "Communication." In 1880 Brooke curiously altered one sentence to read: "and stirred men everywhere to express his thoughts."

248:3–10. Pp. 125–26, 127. Brooke did not alter his arrangement here as regards Sheridan, but he did in 1880 introduce a new subheading, "The Drama from the Restoration to 1780." He transposed his list of newspapers and journals to a later page.

248:29–34. P. 131. In 1880, Brooke did "make a clean sweep of all this," and of all poetry after the death of Scott except for that of Browning and Tennyson.

248:36–249:1. Brooke did reduce the passage on Rogers (p. 158), but not quite so drastically as Arnold suggested.

249:9–17. P. 124. In 1880 Brooke qualified the last sentence. Arnold made clear his estimate of Addison in "The Literary Influence of Academies" (1864), *Prose Works*, ed. Super, III, 247–48. See also p. 167:29–31n.

249:26–27. P. 140. In 1880, this sentence became: "Their best poems . . . are exquisite examples of English work wrought in the spirit of the imaginative scholar and the moralist. The affectation of the age touches them now and again, but . . ."

249:34, 36–37. "Ode on the Spring," line 45; "Elegy Written in a Country Churchyard," lines 123–24.

250:10–14. P. 149. Brooke omitted the second sentence in 1880.

250:29–32. Pp. 154–55. Arnold condenses even here. Brooke in 1880 made his discussion of Wordsworth and Nature somewhat briefer. Arnold reiterated his view of "Wordsworth's philosophy of Nature, as a scheme in itself" in his essay on Wordsworth (1879).— *Prose Works*, ed. Super, vol. IX.

250:35–251:3. P. 160. Brooke changed his account of Byron very little in 1880.

251:5–7. P. 163.

251:16–23. P. 164. Brooke toned this passage down drastically in 1880, but otherwise modified very little what he said about Shelley.

251:31. See p. 238:1.

[A FRENCH CRITIC ON GOETHE]

"After breakfast . . . I must work at my Goethe, which I have begun, but am not yet thoroughly into," Arnold wrote to his sister on a Saturday in December, 1877. "I have promised it by this day week. Considering how much I have read of Goethe, I have said in my life very little about him; to write an article in general about him would be an alarming task; I am very glad to be limited by having only to speak of my Frenchman's talk of him. . . . On looking back at Carlyle, one sees how much of *engouement* there was in his criticism of Goethe, and how little of it will stand. That is the thing—to write what will *stand*. Johnson, with all his limitations, will be found to *stand* a great deal better than Carlyle."—*Letters,* ed. Russell. The essay on Edmond Scherer's critique of Goethe is a sequel to Arnold's essay on his critique of Milton; like its predecessor it was published anonymously in the *Quarterly Review,* where it appeared in January, 1878; Arnold was paid £31 10s. for it. Arnold saw Scherer in Paris the following September, when he escorted his daughter to the Exposition there. Scherer returned the compliment of Arnold's review with an article on Arnold's selections from Wordsworth in *Le Temps* on June 17, 24 and July 1, 1881, "Wordsworth et la poésie moderne de l'Angleterre," *Nouvelles études sur la littérature contemporaine* (Paris, 1886), II, 1–59. He wrote the obituary on Arnold for *Le Temps* on April 18, 1888, p. 3.

Arnold's essay rather disappointed his readers, yet it contains one of his best statements of his critical principles illustrated by a comprehensive representation of a critique that seemed to him in many ways a model. His translations of Scherer's French are patterns of style for translators.

252:2–10. De Maistre, *Lettres et opuscules inédits* (3rd ed.; Paris, 1853), II, 399.

252:11–253:16. *Ibid.,* II, 208–9, 211, in "Cinquième paradoxe: La réputation des livres ne dépend point de leur mérite" (1795). De Maistre adds to this last passage, however: "Il me semble même que le défaut général du théâtre français est d'être grec. . . . Qu'est-ce qu'une tragédie française, où rien n'est français que le langage?" Thomas Newton (1704–82), bishop of Bristol after 1761, published his edition of *Paradise Lost* in 1749. It went through nine editions by 1790.

253:28–254:3. J. M. R. Lenz, *Gesammelte Schriften,* ed. Ludwig Tieck (Berlin, 1828), I, cxxxix. Goethe made his statement about *Manfred* at the beginning of his review of the drama in *Über Kunst und Alterthum, Werke* (Weimar, 1902), XLI (1), 189.

254:10–13. "Die Laufbahn dieses grössten Werkes des grössten Dichters aller Völker und Zeiten hat erst begonnen und es sind für die Ausnutzung seines Inhalts nur die ersten Schritte gethan worden."—Grimm, *Goethe: Vorlesungen gehalten an der Kgl. Universität zu Berlin* (Berlin, 1877), II, 296 (Lecture 25). Herman Grimm (1828–1901), professor in Berlin from 1873, was the eldest son of Wilhelm and nephew of Jacob, the brothers Grimm.

256:3–4. The articles on Goethe appeared in *Le Temps* on May 21 and 28 and June 7, 1872; one on "Dante et Goethe" appeared on October 30, 1866. All were collected in *Études critiques de littéra-*

ture (Paris, 1876). The series of 1872 took the form of a review of A. Mézières, *W. Goethe: les oeuvres expliquées par la vie* (Paris, 1872) and A. Bossert, *Goethe: ses précurseurs et ses contemporains* (Paris, 1872). The first article begins with some rather bitter reflections on Germany's recent conquest of France, which will at least, Scherer hopes, enable the French to judge Germany's intellectual achievements without infatuation.

256:17–19. "Goethe, enfin, n'a pas seulement le génie, . . . il y a, chez lui, des côtés de banalité et de niaiserie. On ne peut lire ses oeuvres sans y rencontrer à chaque pas des admirations triviales, des ingénuités solonnelles, des réflexions sans portée."—*Études critiques*, pp. 331–32. (See Arnold's translation of this passage on p. 266:21–25.) "Son Werther est niais," says Scherer again (p. 299).

256:28–31. Ludwig Wiese, *German Letters on English Education*, tr. Leonhard Schmitz (London, 1877), p. 168. Arnold reviewed this book in *The Pall Mall Gazette;* see pp. 208–15.

256:37–38. Letter II; in the English version, p. 11.

257:30–258:4. Carlyle, "Goethe" (1828), *Critical and Miscellaneous Essays, Works* (Centenary ed.; New York, 1899), XXVI, 211–12, 217–18. Milton alluded to the Greek orator Isocrates as "that old man eloquent" (Sonnet X: "To the Lady Margaret Ley," line 8); G. H. Lewes applied the expression to Goethe himself.—*The Life and Works of Goethe* (London, 1855) II, 417 (Book VII, chapter v).

258:17–34. *Études critiques*, pp. 335–36.

258:36–259:5. R. H. Hutton, "Goethe and His Influence," *Essays in Literary Criticism* (Philadelphia, 1876), pp. 40, 7.

259:12–34. *Études critiques*, pp. 336–38.

259:35–36. See p. 230:26n.

259:36–38. "Il y a un docteur Zimmermann qui avait été à Berlin se faire opérer d'une hernie, et qui revient chez lui, à Hanovre: 'C'est avec des milliers de larmes de joie, dit'il, que je fus reçu par mon fils, mes amis et mes amies. Les uns avaient perdu la parole de bonheur, les autres s'évanouissaient, d'autres tombaient en convulsions.' "—*Études critiques*, pp. 337–38.

260:12–13. *Études critiques*, p. 313.

260:15–21. Mézières, *Goethe*, I, 320–21, quoted by Scherer, p. 317.

260:22–26. *Goethes Unterhaltungen mit dem Kanzler Friedrich von Müller*, ed. C. A. H. Burkhardt (Stuttgart, 1904), p. 8 (May 30, 1814), quoted by Scherer, p. 320.

260:29–34. Mézières, *Goethe*, I, 310–11, quoted by Scherer, p. 318.

261:1–3. *Études critiques*, p. 320.

261:6–25. *Ibid.*, pp. 339–40.

261:27–37. Lewes, *Goethe*, II, 13, 100 (Book V, chapters ii, ix). Lewes died on November 28, 1878, eleven months after Arnold's essay was first published.

262:18–19. See p. 254:10–11.

262:21–263:17. *Études critiques*, pp. 347–49. The phrase Arnold picks up for repetition is: "Tant il y a que *Faust* est resté l'une des grandes oeuvres de la poésie, et peut-être la plus étonnante de notre siècle."

263:23–264:4. *Études critiques*, pp. 314, 321, 313, 319 ("refroidissement graduel"). And see F. W. Riemer, *Mittheilungen über Goethe* (Berlin, 1841), II, 311: "Aus Italien, dem formreichen, war ich in das *gestaltlose* Deutschland zurückgewiesen, heitern Himmel mit einem düstern zu vertauschen."

264:9–28. *Ibid.*, p. 344.

264:29–34. Lewes, *Goethe*, II, 65 (Book V, chapter vi). Lewes wrote: "flings criticism to the dogs."

264:35–37. This is Aristotle's way of determining the "mean" which is virtue.—*Nicomachean Ethics* 1107a.

265:2–4. Schiller to Johann Heinrich Meyer, quoted by Lewes, *Goethe*, II, 237 (Book VI, chapter iv).

265:6–26. *Études critiques*, pp. 340–41.

265:28–33. Lewes, *Goethe*, II, 234–35 (Book VI, chapter iv), partially paraphrased and with omissions.

266:2–9. "Goethe" (1828), *Works* (Centenary ed.), XXVI, 229, 224–25. Carlyle has no "and" before the last phrase.

266:10–16. Letter to Goethe, quoted by Lewes, *Goethe*, II, 213–14 (Book VI, chapter ii).

266:18–267:4. *Études critiques*, pp. 331–32. *The Elective Affinities* (*Die Wahlverwandtschaften*) is a novel of Goethe's. Paul de St. Victor (1825–81) was a French critic and man of letters, highly regarded in his day. Jupiter Pluvius is the Roman god of rain.

267:6–7. Quoted by Scherer, p. 299. Barthold Georg Niebuhr (1776–1831) was the historian of Rome.

267:9–11. See Scherer, pp. 299–301, 332–33. He is especially severe upon *Dichtung und Wahrheit* for its posing. As for the prose, "La prose allemande n'existe pas. . . . Faut-il accuser le seul manque de goût de nos voisins? Resterait à expliquer comment le même écrivain peut être exquis en vers et balourd en prose. Quoi qu'il en soit, tel est le fait."

267:11–14. *Goethe*, II, 342 (Book VI, chapter viii).

267:16–26. "Goethe's Helena" (1828), *Works* (Centenary ed.), XXVI, 195–96. When Carlyle wrote this, the second part of *Faust* had not yet been published as a whole.

267:30–268:15. *Études critiques*, pp. 344–46.

268:19–269:9. "Dante et Goethe," *Études critiques*, pp. 91–92. For the cabbage leaf allusion, see p. 259:26.

269:13–19. *Études critiques*, p. 346.

269:29–30. *Die natürliche Tochter*, lines 199–200 (I, iv, 2–3). Scherer chooses another passage of this drama for ridicule.

269:34–270:16. *Études critiques*, pp. 341–42. Scherer repeats a criticism of Taine's upon the close of Racine's *Mithridate*.

270:18–19. See, for example, Lewes' expression, "the egoism of genius," *Goethe*, II, 50 (Book V, chapter iv).

270:26–271:14. *Études critiques*, pp. 330–31. Scherer draws upon *Goethes Unterhaltungen mit . . . Müller*, ed. Burkhardt (Stuttgart, 1904), pp. 153–54 (August 30, 1827), and Johann Peter Eckermann, *Gespräche mit Goethe*, ed. Eduard Castle (Berlin, 1916), II, 165 (February 14, 1830).

271:15–16. Riemer, *Mittheilungen über Goethe*, II, 707n, where the remark was attributed to J. D. Falk. The edition of Riemer's *Mittheilungen* by Arthur Pollmer (Leipzig, 1921), p. 308, shows the remark to have been Goethe's.

271:17–18. Ludwig I (1786–1868), king of Bavaria from 1825, was exceedingly popular for his anti-French sentiments during the Napoleonic wars; he was a warm patron of the arts, who was largely responsible for Munich's fine buildings and collections. Not until fourteen years after Goethe's death did Ludwig meet and become infatuated with the "Spanish" dancer "Lola Montez" (an Irish girl named Marie Gilbert), whose influence over him was one of the causes that forced his abdication in 1848.

271:37–272:15. *Études critiques*, p. 351. Arnold quoted Goethe to much the same effect, as "liberator," in his essay on "Heinrich Heine" (1863), *Prose Works*, ed. Super, III, 109.

272:16–26. "Shakspeare et la critique" (1869, a review of Émile Montégut's translation and Gustav Rümelin's *Shakespeare-studien*), *Études critiques*, pp. 149–50.

273:26–31. See p. 263.

273:35–37. Abraham Hayward's prose translation of *Faust*, Part I, which was admired also by Lewes, first appeared in 1833. Arnold praised Hayward's translation in the third lecture *On Translating Homer* (1861).—*Prose Works*, ed. Super, I, 167–68.

273:37–274:1. Scherer concluded his essay on Milton by saying:

"Milton a donné lui-même la règle de la poésie. Selon lui, 'it ought to be simple, sensuous, and impassioned,' ce qui revient à ces trois conditions: la simplicité, l'image et le mouvement."—*Études critiques*, p. 194. See Milton, "Of Education," two-thirds through.

274:1–5. See pp. 268:7–8, 267:22–23.

274:6–10. Carlyle's Introduction to his translation (1832) of Goethe's *Das Märchen* ("The Tale"), *Works* (Centenary ed.) XXVII, 448–49.

274:18–24. "Goethe" (1828), *ibid.*, XXVI, 253. The "little senate" is an allusion to a line from Pope's description of Atticus in the "Epistle to Dr. Arbuthnot" (line 209): "Like Cato, give his little Senate laws."

275:1. In the Preface to his *Poems* (1853), Arnold described Goethe as the man of strongest head whom the age had produced. —*Prose Works*, ed. Super, I, 14 and Textual Note.

275:4–7. F. W. Riemer, *Mittheilungen über Goethe*. Berlin, 1841. J. D. Falk, *Goethe aus näherm persönlichen Umgange dargestellt*. Leipzig, 1832. J. P. Eckermann, *Gespräche mit Goethe*. Leipzig, 1836. Friedrich von Müller, *Goethes Unterhaltungen mit dem Kanzler F. von Müller*, ed. C. A. H. Burkhardt. Stuttgart, 1870. *Briefe an J. H. Merck, von Goethe, Herder, Wieland* [&c.], ed. Karl Wagner. Darmstadt, 1835. Other collections were published by the same editor in 1838, 1847. *Goethe's Briefe an Frau von Stein aus den Jahren 1776 bis 1826*, ed. A. Schöll. 3 vols.; Weimar, 1848–51. *Briefwechsel zwischen Schiller und Goethe in den Jahren 1794 bis 1805*, ed. J. W. von Goethe. Stuttgart and Tübingen, 1828–29. *Briefwechsel zwischen Goethe und* [C. F.] *Zelter, in den Jahren 1796 bis 1832*, ed. F. W. Riemer. Berlin, 1833–34.

275:22–23. An echo of an expression of Bishop Butler's that Arnold much admired; see p. 12:30–32.

276:10–13. Riemer, *Mittheilungen über Goethe*, II, 281, jotted in Arnold's pocket diary for January 28, 1871.—*Note-Books*, ed. Lowry, p. 150. Arnold quoted the same remark at the end of his essay on Renan.—*Prose Works*, ed. Super, VII, 50.

276:21–22 (variant). Scherer, though of Genevese family, was born in Paris.

[EQUALITY]

Arnold's essay on "Equality" is one of the most perceptive statements of his social doctrine, touching upon ideas that will continue to occur in his writings, and most appropriately paired with "Democracy" (1861) at the beginning of *Mixed Essays* both to set the tone for that volume and to testify for how many years he had held these doctrines. It is a remarkable corrective for those who fancy that *Culture and Anarchy* savors too much of the élite. Stimulated, no doubt, in part by Goldwin Smith's attack on "Falkland," it serves above all to show the inadequacy of nineteenth-century liberal ideology to cope with the modern world.

The "Royal Institution of Great Britain for the Promotion, Diffusion, and Extension of Science and of Useful Knowledge" was founded by Count Rumford in 1799 and chartered by George III the next year. It provides laboratories for scientific research—Davy and Faraday worked there—sponsors courses of lectures on a variety of subjects, and holds weekly meetings in the winter to hear papers in the arts and literature as well as science. Arnold read his paper at the Institution's buildings in Albemarle Street at the weekly meeting at nine in the evening on Friday, February 8, 1878, with his friend Lord Arthur Russell in the chair. The week before he spoke, the subject of the paper had been Alexander Graham Bell's new invention. "Equality" was published in the *Fortnightly Review* for March, and brought Arnold £40 from that journal. It has recently been reprinted in J. D. Jump, ed., *A Matthew Arnold Prose Selection* (London: Macmillan, 1965), pp. 78–108.

277:1–4. The Lesson read in the Church of England Burial Service was I Corinthians 15:20–58. For the Nonconformist revolt against the Burial Service and Arnold's suggested modification of the Lesson, see pp. 85–110.

277:4–7. "Be not deceived: evil communications corrupt good manners."—I Corinthians 15:33. The verse is attributed to Menander by St. Jerome, to Euripides by Socrates the church historian. The latest editor of Menander supposes it to have been written by Euripides, then incorporated by Menander in his *Thais.*—*Menandri quae supersunt,* ed. A. Koerte and A. Thierfelder (Leipzig: B. G. Teubner, 1959), II, 74, fragment 187. Arnold's source was presumably *Menandri et Philemonis Reliquiae,* ed. A. Meineke (Berlin, 1823), p. 75.

277:7. "Quid Academiae et Ecclesiae? Quid haereticis et Christianis?" Tertullian continued.—*De praescriptionibus adversus haereticos,* cap. 7; Migne, *Patrologia Latina,* II, 23. Jotted in Arnold's pocket diary for June 26, 1875, and January 6, 1878.—*Note-Books,* ed. Lowry, pp. 230, 294.

277:19–20. Ed. A. Meineke, p. 336 ("Gnomai Monostichoi," supplement, no. 35); jotted in Arnold's pocket diary for August 23, 1868.—*Note-Books*, ed. Lowry, p. 81.

277:26–27. In nearly every instance, the word which our Bible translates "covetousness" in the New Testament is represented by "pleonexia" in the Greek.

278:11–13. Benjamin Disraeli, *Inaugural Address . . . as Lord Rector of the University of Glasgow* (Glasgow, 1873), pp. 15–23. The address was reported in *The Times*, November 20, 1873, p. 10, cols. 1–3 and was the subject of a leading article, p. 7, cols. 2–3. A memorandum in Arnold's diary for June 13–15, 1875, suggests that his invitation to lecture in Glasgow may have been about that time. Only about two months before delivering this lecture on "Equality," Arnold declined an invitation to stand for election as Lord Rector of St. Andrews University.

278:21–25. Thomas Erskine May, *Democracy in Europe: a History* (New York, 1878), II, 348 (end of chapter xvii). May speaks of "the intellectual growth of her gifted people." The French Revolution of 1789 was dedicated to "Liberty, Equality, Fraternity."

278:26–31. J. A. Froude, "On the Uses of a Landed Gentry," *Short Studies on Great Subjects*, 3rd ser. (New York, 1877), p. 299. The paper was first delivered at the Philosophical Institution at Edinburgh on November 6, 1876, ten months after Arnold delivered there his lectures on "Bishop Butler and the Zeit-Geist."

278:32–33. The debate between Lowe and Gladstone was carried on in the journals: Lowe, "A New Reform Bill," *Fortnightly Review* XXVIII, 437–52 (October, 1877); Gladstone, "The County Franchise and Mr. Lowe Thereon," *Nineteenth Century* II, 537–60 (November, 1877); Lowe, "Mr. Gladstone on Manhood Suffrage," *Fortnightly Review* XXVIII, 733–46 (December, 1877); Gladstone, "Last Words on the County Franchise," *Nineteenth Century* III, 196–208 (January, 1878). Arnold's essay on "Equality" appeared in the *Fortnightly* for March.

278:34–38. *Fortnightly Review* XXVIII, 451 (October, 1877).

278:38–279:20. *Nineteenth Century* II, 547–48 (November, 1877). Gladstone wrote "whenever other things are exactly equal" and "acting, living, and life-giving power." Sir William Molesworth (1810–55), whose remark was made in conversation with Gladstone, was a radical politician who only three months before his death became colonial secretary in the Palmerston government.

279:30–31. *Impressions et souvenirs* (Paris, 1896), pp. 252, 256–57 (chapter xv, "La Révolution pour l'idéal"). See p. 230:12–14.

279:31–34. *Journal d'un Voyageur pendant la guerre* (Paris, 1871), pp. 162 (November 4, 1870, end), 114–15. See p. 230:19–21.

280:20–23. The most recent Real Estate Intestacy Bill had its first reading in the House of Commons on January 18, 1878. It was defeated at the second reading on July 10. Arnold had ridiculed an earlier bill to the same effect in the final chapter of *Culture and Anarchy* (1868), *Prose Works*, ed. Super, V, 200–205. Since such bills proposed to control the distribution of estates of men who died intestate, but exercised no limitation upon the power of making a will, they were in Arnold's view aiming at a trifle.

280:24–25. Turgot believed that all a man's property should be divided equally among his children and that charitable endowments should not be controlled indefinitely by the testator but should be under the jurisdiction of the state.—A. N. de Condorcet, *Vie de M. Turgot, Oeuvres* (Paris, 1847), V, 187–88.

282:8–9. The laws of inheritance in the United States are in the province of the several states, not the federal government. Mill made the point that the American freedom of bequest had led not to accumulation of landed estates but to munificence of bequests and gifts to public purposes on an exceedingly large scale.—*Principles of Political Economy*, Book II, chapter ii, section 4; *Collected Works* (Toronto, 1965), II, 226.

282:30–34. Lowe alluded to "the proposal of the Parliament of the colony of Victoria to punish by a heavy fine the possessor of 2,500 acres of land."—*Fortnightly Review* XXVIII, 448 (October, 1877). For "concession to the cry for equality," see p. 278:35.

283:12–14. Clerkenwell is a part of the London borough of Finsbury, lying north of St. Paul's cathedral and Smithfield market. It has something of a history of radicalism in the nineteenth century. Arnold's lecture was, of course, announced in advance in the newspapers (e.g., *Athenaeum*, February 2, p. 162).

283:15. The secretary was the mathematician and physicist William Spottiswoode (1825–83), who a few months later was elected president of the Royal Society. He was a contemporary of Arnold's at Balliol.

283:16–23. See *Culture and Anarchy, Prose Works*, ed. Super, VI, 143–46.

283:24–26. *Phaedrus* 274A.

283:31–284:7. Edward L. Pierce, *Memoir and Letters of Charles Sumner, 1811–1845* (Boston, 1877), II, 215 (letter of July 8, 1842). Arnold probably found this passage in the review of the book in the

Spectator LI, 57 (January 12, 1878). Sumner has one more category in his list: "literary men" is followed by "politicians."

284:35–36. "A New Reform Bill," *Fortnightly Review* XXVIII, 451 (October, 1877).

285:1–3. "Now does anyone, if he simply and naturally reads his consciousness, discover that he has any rights at all? For my part, the deeper I go in my own consciousness, and the more simply I abandon myself to it, the more it seems to tell me that I have no rights at all, only duties."—*Culture and Anarchy, Prose Works*, ed. Super, V, 201. And see "Endowments" (1870), *Literature and Dogma* (1871), and *God and the Bible* (1874), *ibid.*, VI, 134, 188; VII, 145.

285:23–25. "In all indigenous societies, a condition of jurisprudence in which Testamentary privileges are *not* allowed, or rather not contemplated, has preceded that later stage of legal development in which the mere will of the proprietor [has overriding authority]."—Maine, *Ancient Law* (6th ed.; London, 1876), p. 177 (chapter vi). "Bequest, in a primitive state of society, was seldom recognised."—Mill, *Principles of Political Economy*, Book II, chapter ii, section 3; *Collected Works* (Toronto), II, 219.

286:2–3. *Democracy in Europe*, II, 348.

286:12–13. Lucan *Civil War* II, 381–82, jotted in Arnold's pocket diary for February 10, 1878.—*Note-Books*, ed. Lowry, p. 295.

286:16–19. *Reflections on the Revolution in France*, nearly two-fifths through.

287:1–6. Moses, in Deuteronomy 4:8, 6; jotted in Arnold's pocket diary for December 27 and 31, 1877.—*Note-Books*, ed. Lowry, pp. 287–88.

287:8–14. *Panegyricus* 50, quoted (in Sainte-Beuve's French) in Arnold's pocket diary for August 9, 1877.—*Note-Books*, ed. Lowry, p. 281.

287:14–16. Arnold discusses these powers more fully in "Literature and Science" (1882), *Prose Works*, ed. Super, vol. X.

287:34. Arnold was presented to Cardinal Antonelli, the papal secretary of state, by the British representative Odo Russell on June 6, 1865, during his tour of the Continent to gather data on higher education. He mentions the conversation with Antonelli in *Schools and Universities on the Continent* (1868), *Prose Works*, ed. Super, IV, 304 and note.

288:8. In "Literature and Science," Arnold cites Friedrich Wolf's definition of "science": "I call all teaching *scientific* which is systematically laid out and followed up to its original sources."

288:15–24. "L'Europe a dû sa politesse et l'esprit de société à la cour de Louis XIV."—*Siècle de Louis XIV*, chapter i; *Oeuvres complètes* (Paris, 1878), XIV, 156.

288:35–36. *Reflections on the Revolution in France*, nearly one-third through; jotted in Arnold's pocket diary for February 17, 1878. —*Note-Books*, ed. Lowry, p. 296.

289:35–36. E. P. de Senancour, *Oberman*, letter vii; ed. A. Monglond (Paris, 1947), I, 50. Senancour wrote "passée au milieu des peuples souffrans."

290:6–15. Émile de Laveleye, "Le Socialisme contemporain en Allemagne," *Revue des Deux Mondes*, 3rd pér., XVIII, 882 (December 15, 1876); jotted at the end of Arnold's pocket diary for 1877.— *Note-Books*, ed. Lowry, pp. 289–90. Arnold cited this statement also in the essay on "George Sand," p. 232.

290:20–29. Philip Gilbert Hamerton, *Round My House: Notes of Rural Life in France in Peace and War* (3rd ed.; London, 1876), pp. 229–30. Hamerton (1834–94) was an English artist and art critic who married a French wife and settled near Autun.

290:30–31. Gladstone, during the Reform Bill debate of 1866, responded obliquely to Lowe's accusation against the venality, ignorance, drunkenness and violence of the working class by asserting that these were "our fellow-subjects, our fellow-Christians, our own flesh and blood."—March 23.

290:32–38. "Mr. Matthew Arnold, lamenting the profound chasm which divides the different ranks in English society, confesses that the conversation of those in a station inferior to his own is utterly unpalatable to him. This is the true Whig spirit."—[W. J. Courthope,] "The Crown and the Constitution," *Quarterly Review*, American ed., CXLV, 156 (April, 1878).

291:14–17. Arnold's admiration of the French common man was expressed as early as 1859 in *England and the Italian Question*, and in "The Function of Criticism at the Present Time" (1864), *Prose Works*, ed. Super, I, 78–79; III, 265. See "George Sand," p. 231:12–13.

291:18–21. The *noblesse*, abolished during the first two French republics, was revived by the imperial government that succeeded each; Arnold alludes to the new nobility under Napoleon III.

291:27–30. Arnold repeats what he said in his review (1872) of Renan's *La Réforme intellectuelle et morale de la France*, *Prose*

Works, ed. Super, VII, 47. France lost Alsace to Germany in the war of 1870–71.

292:20–22. Arnold quoted this remark of Michelet's in "A French Elijah," in his review of Renan's *La Réforme,* and in "Numbers" (1883).—*Prose Works,* ed. Super, VII, 11, 44 and vol. X.

293:21–22. Arnold attributed this quality to the English in "The Literary Influence of Academies" (1864), *On the Study of Celtic Literature* (1866), and "My Countrymen" (1866).—*Prose Works,* ed. Super, III, 237, 341; V, 13.

293:29–30. See the quotation from *The Times* on p. 303:15n.

294:3–7. This song by G. W. Hunt was made popular in the London music halls by "the great Macdermott" when in 1878 the British government was threatening to intervene on behalf of Turkey in the Russo-Turkish war.

294:30–33. In "Heinrich Heine" (1863), *Literature and Dogma* (1873) and "Falkland" (1877).—*Prose Works,* ed. Super, III, 121; VI, 390; VIII, 201. And see a passage from Renan which Arnold jotted in one of his "General Note-Books": "Des dogmes étroits, secs, n'ayant rien de plastique ni de traditionnel, ne prêtant à aucune interprétation, sont pour l'esprit humain une bien plus étroite prison que la mythologie populaire."—"De l'Avenir religieux des sociétés modernes," *Revue des Deux Mondes,* 2 ser. XXIX, 791 (October 15, 1860); Arnold, *Note-Books,* ed. Lowry, p. 470.

295:8–15. See Goldwin Smith, "Falkland and the Puritans: In Reply to Mr. Matthew Arnold," *Contemporary Review* XXIX, 938–43 (April, 1877).

295:24–29. Cited by Horace Walpole, *Anecdotes of Painting in England* (2nd ed.; Strawberry Hill, 1765), II, 68.

295:33–36. In the violent debate on clericalism in the French Chamber of Deputies on May 4, 1877, a young Catholic deputy indignantly "quoted passages of an article in which the grossest insults [were] addressed to the Founder of the Christian Church," whereupon "the Left, by roars of laughter, associated itself with these indecent attacks."—*Times,* May 5, p. 7, col. 5. Cardinal Manning picked up the phrase and referred to the French National Assembly as the "gentlemen who receive the name of the Redeemer of the world with roars of laughter."—"The True Story of the Vatican Council," *Nineteenth Century* I, 805 (July, 1877).

296:6–17. "Colasterion: a Reply to a Nameless Answer against The Doctrine and Discipline of Divorce," half-way through and two-thirds through. See p. 169:18–26.

296:25–30. *Contemporary Review* XXIX, 933.

296:34–297:20. *Memoirs of the Life of Colonel* [*John*] *Hutchinson*, written by his widow Lucy (Everyman's Library; London: J. M. Dent), pp. 238–39 (*anno* 1646). Both John Tombes (1603–76) and Henry Denne (died *c*. 1660) were in Anglican orders, but conceived doubts about infant baptism, became Baptists, and were vigorous polemicists for their views in writing and in oral debate.

297:30–31. Goldwin Smith, after a little more than two years as professor in Ezra Cornell's new university, moved to Toronto in 1871 and lived there until his death in 1910, though with frequent visits to England. He was a personal acquaintance of Arnold's.

297:34. This expression, often attributed to Bossuet, is in fact from de La Mothe-Fénelon, "Sermon pour la fête de l'Épiphanie (1685): Sur la vocation des gentils," ¶11.

297:34–36. Proverbs 19:21.

297:37–298:1. Arnold jotted this sentence in his pocket diary for March 15, 1879, and in one of his "General Note-Books."—*Note-Books*, ed. Lowry, pp. 316, 542.

298:24–25. John Bright, in the Reform Bill debate of March 26, 1867, confessed that there was "a small class which it would be much better . . . that they should be excluded [from the franchise]. I call this class the residuum, which there is in almost every constituency, of almost hopeless poverty and dependence."—*Times*, March 27, p. 7, col. 4. Arnold picked up the term "residuum" in both *Culture and Anarchy* (1868) and *Friendship's Garland* (1870).—*Prose Works*, ed. Super, V, 143, 329.

298:36–299:2. Richard Cobden did not set a precise figure, but in urging extension of the franchise at the end of a speech to his constituency at Rochdale on November 24, 1863, he said: "England may perhaps compare very favourably with most other countries, if you draw the line in society tolerably high. . . . I don't think a rich man —barring the climate, which is not very good—could be very much happier anywhere else than in England." But the masses he finds far worse off than elsewhere because so many more of them are propertyless.—*Speeches on Questions of Public Policy*, ed. John Bright and J. E. Thorold Rogers (London, 1880), p. 367.

299:15. Vergil *Aeneid* XII, 435.

299:23–24. Proverbs 14:6.

299:26. Livy describes the impact of the demagogue Marcus Manlius upon the populace of Rome: "Their spirits were so inflamed that they would clearly follow this champion of their liberty in everything, right or wrong [*per omne fas ac nefas*]."—VI, xiv, 10.

300:1–6. *Reflections on the Revolution in France*, two-fifths through.

300:20–23. Arnold jotted this sentence at the end of his pocket diary for 1878.—*Note-Books*, ed. Lowry, p. 307.

301:5–7. "Even the Roman governor has his close parallel in our celebrated aristocracy, with its superficial good sense and good nature, its complete inaptitude for ideas, its profound helplessness in presence of all great spiritual movements."—*Literature and Dogma* (1873), *Prose Works*, ed. Super, VI, 399.

301:27–30. Diary for November 3, 1662, jotted in Arnold's pocket diary for July 3, 1877.—*Note-Books*, ed. Lowry, p. 279.

302:21–23. See pp. 322:29–32 and n., 362:34–36, 369:9–11.

303:15–16. On November 21, 1877, the Duke of Norfolk and Lady Flora Hastings were married at the Brompton Oratory. The fourth leading article of *The Times* next day might have been written by Mr. Podsnap: "Perhaps there is no man in the world who can maintain so exalted a position with so little self-assertion [as the Duke of Norfolk]. He has only to keep his place in society and to be respectable, and he is that which kings and emperors may envy. . . . There is no other country in the world where the like of [this ceremony] could occur. Nowhere else are there the wealth, the hereditary rank and power, and the position far above the people, all but encroaching, indeed, on the dignity of the throne and the province of the legislature, combined with absolute liberty of conscience, whether in civil or religious matters. In every other country, whether of the Old or the New World, there would at least be one drawback."— P. 9, cols. 4–5.

303:16–24. A rash of weekly "journals of society" followed the founding of *Vanity Fair* on November 7, 1868. Two of the most successful were *The World*, founded by Edmund Yates on July 8, 1874, and *Truth*, founded on January 4, 1877, by Henry Labouchere, who had been on the staff of *The World* from its beginning. A decade earlier Arnold ridiculed the popularity of the first of the penny daily newspapers as "the magnificent roaring of the young lions of the *Daily Telegraph*" (Preface to *Essays in Criticism*, 1865) and continued the joke in *Friendship's Garland* (1869, 1871).—*Prose Works*, ed. Super, III, 287; V, 66, 313, 350–56. *Truth*, especially, devoted most of its pages to short paragraphs of personal and political gossip.

303:35–38. See p. 279:15–17.

304:32. See p. 293:21–22n.

305:4–9. *Principles of Political Economy*, Book II, chapt. ii, sect. 4; *Collected Works* (Toronto), II, 224–25. Arnold's essay is, among other things, a reply to this section.

305:10. Spencer Cavendish, Marquis of Hartington and (after 1891) Duke of Devonshire, leader of the Liberal party, was given the freedom of the city of Glasgow on November 5, 1877.

[JOHNSON'S *LIVES OF THE POETS*]

When Arnold told his sister that his great wish in education was to get a few good books universally taught and read, he went on (December, 1877): "I think twenty is about all I would have, in the direct teaching of the young and to be learnt as text-books. Young people may read for themselves, collaterally, as much as they like." Later in the same month he remarked that the great thing is "to write what will *stand*. Johnson, with all his limitations, will be found to *stand* a great deal better than Carlyle."—*Letters*, ed. Russell. He was by then beginning to turn seriously to a project he had proposed to Macmillan more than a year earlier, and which Macmillan encouraged on November 23, 1876: "Select Lives from Johnson's *Lives of the Poets*, with a short Preface." From the first Macmillan thought it would be more used in schools "if some notes could be added of an illustrative & explanatory kind such as the lapse of time since they were written might make needful, or at least useful," and offered to find someone who would perform this chore under Arnold's supervision if he should be disinclined to do it himself. But Arnold's first response to the suggestion was negative: "I am against having many notes. Let us not aim at a *school-book*, but rather at a literary book which schools can and will use." Macmillan was obliged to jog Arnold into activity; not until mid-March of 1878 did he actually face up to planning the contents of the book, and then his list of lives was far too great to be manageable. "My notion is that the book should be read by all young students of literature, who want a good history of the poetical literature of England from Waller to Gray, without the surplusage that Johnson was obliged to put with it. But not a library book, nor yet a cheap book for the general public (there is already, I believe, a cheap Johnson's Lives at 1s/6d), is what I design; I design a book to hit the needs of the young student of English literature."—Buckler, *Matthew Arnold's Books*, p. 126. Arnold planned no notes except the one about Macaulay's correction to the "Life of Addison"; he hoped to be able to use Macaulay's article on Johnson from the *Encyclopaedia Britannica* but feared the proprietors would not allow it, and he hoped for publication by Whitsuntide. The number of lives had to be pruned even further than Arnold envisioned, but he made the best of it: "I am . . . not sorry to have been obliged to limit the volume to what may be called *first class matters* of Johnson's collection." Permission was obtained to reprint the Macaulay. In order to increase Arnold's income from the work Macmillan published the prefatory essay in the June, 1878, number of *Macmillan's Magazine* and paid £20 for the article. The book did not come out until about September 14, priced at 6 *s.*

For once Arnold's optimism proved truer than his publisher's skepticism: new editions, from stereotypes, were published in 1879 and 1881. An offer from Roberts Brothers of Boston to buy the stereotypes for publication in America fell through when Macmillan honorably insisted upon a royalty on sales for Arnold, and so the American market was supplied by Macmillan's branch in New York. A competing edition was also published there by Holt. Late in December, 1882, Arnold proposed what Macmillan gladly accepted, "a school edition . . . compressed by the elimination of matter unsuited to the juvenile & feminine mind & moderately *annotated*." Again he suggested that Arnold might want to pay someone for helping with the notes. The execution of the plan was deferred until Arnold's return from his American lecture tour in March, 1884; then, with some help and advice from his brother Tom, he began to work. The book appeared about February 20, 1886, at 4 *s.* 6 *d.* and reached a second edition in 1889. It remained in print at Macmillans and continued to serve students as a textbook until nearly the middle of the present century (1948).

306:1. *De Imitatione Christi* III, l, 7, jotted in Arnold's pocket diary at the end of 1866, for September 28, 1869, and at the beginning of 1871.—*Note-Books*, ed. Lowry, pp. 39, 110, 147.

306:10–11. An Athenian professor who developed a system of mnemonics offered to teach it to Themistocles, and promised that it would enable him to remember everything. Themistocles replied that he would be more grateful to the man if he could teach him to *forget* what he wished, rather than to remember.—Cicero *de Oratore* II, lxxiv, 299 and lxxxvi, 351. "Vain was the prayer of Themistocles for a talent of Forgetting," wrote Teufelsdröckh in Carlyle's *Sartor Resartus,* Book I, chapter vii. Arnold alluded to the story also in *The Popular Education of France* (1861) and *God and the Bible* (1875).—*Prose Works,* ed. Super, II, 136; VII, 244–45.

308:1. In his pocket diary for October 6, 1877, Arnold jotted Littré's definition of *point de repère:* "point qui sert à se retrouver." —*Note-Books,* ed. Lowry, p. 284.

308:15–18. See *Prose Works,* ed. Super, VII, 71.

308:36–309:2. A group of London booksellers having embarked on a joint venture of publishing the works of the English poets starting with Cowley (died 1667) and ending with Gray (died 1771) and George Lord Lyttelton (died 1773), the arrangement being in general by date of death, commissioned Dr. Johnson to provide for them a series of "Prefaces, biographical and critical." He seems to have suggested the inclusion in the collection of Thomson, Blackmore, Pomfret, Yalden, and Watts. Though the booksellers later also published the Prefaces separately as *Lives of the English Poets,* they had never been intended to perform the function that title suggests. There were fifty-two in all, and Johnson himself thought the life of Cowley the best, for its critical discussion of the metaphysical poets.

309:20–21. Quoted by Boswell, *Life of Johnson,* sixth paragraph.

309:23–24. In the Preface (1790) to his edition of Shakespeare; *The Plays and Poems of William Shakespeare,* ed. Edmond Malone [and James Boswell the Younger] (London, 1821), I, 244.

309:28–30. Johnson, *Prayers and Meditations,* quoted by Boswell, *Life of Johnson,* beginning of 1781 (*aet.* 72).

309:34–36. Johnson was born 35 years after the death of Milton, nine after the death of Dryden. Arnold was born 26 years after the death of Burns, ten before the death of Scott.

309:37–310:1. *Life of Johnson,* beginning of 1781.

311:12–15. "Pope," paragraph 32, jotted in Arnold's pocket diary at the end of 1878.—*Note-Books,* ed. Lowry, p. 308.

312:4. Chevaux-de-frise are rails with transverse spikes placed atop walls to prevent persons from climbing over them.

312:6–16. John Wilson Croker's five-volume edition of Boswell's *Johnson,* "with numerous additions and notes" (1831), was savagely attacked by Macaulay in the *Edinburgh Review* of September, 1831, as "ill compiled, ill arranged, ill written, and ill printed." The incompetence of the editor is pilloried with gusto for pages. In his discussion of the *Lives of the Poets* Boswell says that "Johnson seems to have been not favourably disposed towards [Lord Lyttelton]. Mrs. Thrale suggests that he was offended by Molly Aston's preference of his Lordship to him." Croker was not the first to point out that Mrs. Thrale in fact attributed the animosity to Johnson's and Lyttelton's emulation for the preference of Mistress Hill Boothby.

312:10. "We regard all knowledge as beautiful and valuable, but one kind more so than another, either in virtue of its accuracy, or because it relates to higher and more wonderful things."—Aristotle *de Anima* 402a (the opening words), tr. W. S. Hett (Loeb Classical Library). "Scire aliquid laus est."—Dionysius Cato *Disticha de Moribus* IV, 29.

312:19 (variant). Presumably the edition of 1783, though those of 1790–91, 1793, or 1794 would answer the description.

312:19 (variant). For Arnold's note, see Appendix II, pp. 376–77. Arnold drew the substance of it from G. O. Trevelyan, *The Life and Letters of Lord Macaulay*, chapter ix, letter of July 22, 1843, and note.

312:37–313:5. The opening words of *Areopagitica*.

313:6–10. *Roderick Random* (1748), beginning of chapter xxiv.

313:16–21. Boswell, *Life of Johnson, anno* 1778, about one-sixth through.

314:6, 8. William Chillingworth (1602–44) and Isaac Barrow (1630–77) were Anglican divines.

314:14–17. Arnold jotted this remark at the end of his pocket diary for 1878.—*Note-Books*, ed. Lowry, p. 307.

314:21–25. "Milton," paragraph 16.

314:35–36. Boswell, *Life of Johnson, anno* 1763, two-thirds through.

315:5–12. Gilbert Burnet, *History of His Own Time* (Oxford, 1823), I, 330 (end of the year 1661, in a discussion of Tillotson, Stillingfleet, and others).

315:17–20. *Ibid.*, II, 37 (*anno* 1674, paragraph 2).

316:16–18. A common theme of Arnold's; see "A French Critic on Goethe" (1878), p. 256:35–38 and *On the Study of Celtic Literature* (1866), *Prose Works*, ed. Super, III, 351.

316:21. Arnold criticized Jeremy Taylor's prose style in "The Literary Influence of Academies" (1864), *Prose Works*, ed. Super, III, 245–46. Taylor (1613–67) was an Anglican divine, contemporary with Chillingworth and Barrow.

316:24. In the third paragraph of *Biographia Literaria* Coleridge said: "I learnt . . . that Poetry, even that of the loftiest and, seem-

ingly, that of the wildest odes, had a logic of its own, as severe as
that of science; and more difficult, because more subtle, more complex, and dependent on more, and more fugitive causes."

316:32 (variant). Gibbon said of a history of Switzerland which
he began but discarded, "My ancient habits . . . encouraged me to
write in French for the continent of Europe; but I was conscious
myself that my style, above prose and below poetry, degenerated
into a verbose and turgid declamation. . . . Perhaps I may suspect
that the language itself is ill adapted to sustain the vigour and dignity of an important narrative. But if France, so rich in literary
merit, had produced a great original historian, his genius would have
formed and fixed the idiom to the proper tone, the peculiar mode
of historical eloquence."—*Memoirs of the Life of Edward Gibbon*,
by Himself (the *Autobiography*), ed. G. B. Hill (London, 1900),
pp. 172–73. Clearly Arnold did not have this passage fresh in his
mind; he may have had a slightly inaccurate recollection of the beginning of Sainte-Beuve's first *Causerie* on Gibbon.—*Causeries du
lundi* (2nd ed.; Paris, 1855), VIII, 347.

317:17. Arnold discussed the Alexandrine—which he found inadequate as a vehicle for high poetry—in his essay on Maurice de
Guérin (1862) and quoted as "deeply unsatisfying" an Alexandrine
couplet of Guérin's sister Eugénie in the essay on Heinrich Heine
(1863).—*Prose Works*, ed. Super, III, 14, 124. In one of his "General Note-Books" he twice copied a footnote from chapt. iii of
Stendhal's *Racine et Shakespeare*, which he headed "The Alexandrine": "Les vers italiens et anglais permettent de tout dire; le vers
alexandrin seul, fait pour une cour dédaigneuse, en a tous les ridi-
cules."—*Note-Books*, ed. Lowry, pp. 520, 531. See Appendix II, pp.
377–78.

317:36–38. "Life of Milton," five-sevenths through.

317:38–318:3. Boswell, *Life of Johnson, anno* 1769, not quite half-
way through. Johnson quoted the passage from *The Mourning
Bride* in his "Life of Congreve," with the remark: "If I were required to select from the whole mass of English poetry the most
poetical paragraph, I know not what I could prefer to [it]." The
passage is in blank verse.

319:27. "At six in the morning [of the day of his death], he inquired the hour, and, on being informed, said that all went on regularly, and he felt he had but a few hours to live."—Boswell, *Life of
Johnson, anno* 1784.

319:30–31. This quotation, one of Arnold's favorites, is from

Burke's "Letter to a Noble Lord," three-fifths through. Arnold jotted it nine times in his note-books, the latest at the beginning of his
pocket diary for 1879.—*Note-Books*, ed. Lowry, p. 313. See pp.
78:27–29, 110:16–17, 114:1–2.

320:6–10. The Edinburgh publishing firm of Adam and Charles
Black acquired the copyright of the *Encyclopaedia Britannica* in
1827. Macaulay wrote his article on Johnson for the eighth edition
in December, 1856; Arnold was later to contribute an article on
Sainte-Beuve for the ninth edition in 1886. George Otto Trevelyan,
Macaulay's nephew and biographer, added a note to the later editions of *The Life and Letters of Lord Macaulay:* "Matthew Arnold
paid [the Johnson essay] as sincere a compliment as ever was paid
by a great critic, for he asked leave to reprint it at length as an introduction to his own [selection from Johnson's *Lives*], in front of
which it now stands. . . . When Mr. Arnold applied for permission
to use Macaulay's article,—a permission which, as far as in me lay,
was gladly given,—he told me that he esteemed the piece to be the
most admirable example of literary biography in our language."—
chapter iv, end.

[IRISH CATHOLICISM AND BRITISH LIBERALISM]

"One of the many blessings, my dear Fan, which we owe to Puritanism is this impracticable condition of Ireland," Arnold wrote to
his sister in December, 1877. He had been at a small dinner party
with Huxley, Gladstone, and half a dozen others, and was sorry to
report that Gladstone "seemed full of the deep opposition in Ireland
to England and English policy—for the present at any rate—that to
go contrary was the main impulse there."—*Letters*, ed. Russell. The
disappointing sale of the new edition (1874) of *Higher Schools and
Universities in Germany* must have made clear to him that his Preface to that book, devoted as it was to the Irish university question,
had reached few readers; who, in any case, would look in a book on
Germany for a discussion of Irish affairs? And so when the O'Conor
Don presented a resolution on the question, Arnold wrote upon it
once more, repeating *verbatim* some passages from the earlier Preface, and published it in the journal of a man whom he cited in its
pages as sympathetic to the government endowment of a Catholic
university in Ireland. It appeared in the July, 1878, number of John
Morley's *Fortnightly Review*. For it Arnold was paid £25.

Arnold's public concern with the Irish question was evident as early as *Culture and Anarchy* (1868), but the present essay is the first of a series that extended over the next three years and led him to call his next volume of collected essays *Irish Essays* (though this essay was one of the latest to be included in *Mixed Essays*, where its importance was stressed by its being placed third, immediately after the two general discussions of social theory, "Democracy" and "Equality"). His principle, in all Irish matters, is that a national, a racial, a religious minority must decide for itself what it wants; it cannot be told what is good for it by a dominant but alien majority, it need not even convince that majority that what it wants is in the long run best and most reasonable.

Arnold sent a copy of his article to Ernest Fontanès in France; Fontanès had been looking for subjects on which to write and Arnold suggested that there was an abundance of interesting matters concerning Ireland. "I think this article will interest you; your Huguenot feeling will no doubt be revolted a little, however, by my weakness for the historic religions." Fontanès corrected somewhat what he said in the article about the University of Strasbourg, and Arnold took cognizance of the correction when he republished the article in *Mixed Essays*. When Disraeli's government brought in its University Education (Ireland) Bill in the spring of 1879, Arnold told his sister: "I think about the Irish University Question I have effected some real good. You saw Lowe's speech [May 21], and Sir Louis Mallet told me that Bright was dining with him the other night and said there was not a word of my argument for the Catholics which did not carry him thoroughly along with it." In view of Bright's previous association with the anti-Roman attitude of the Nonconformists, this must have seemed a triumph indeed. Disraeli's bill passed; it was hardly nearer to what Arnold believed than Gladstone's unsuccessful bill had been in 1873.

321:1. The proverb is at least as old as Chaucer, who uses a version of it in the Prologue to his *Astrolabe*.

321:5–6. See p. 148:1–15.

321:21–25. Arnold quoted *The Daily Telegraph* and Lowe thus in his Preface to *Higher Schools and Universities in Germany* (1874). —*Prose Works*, ed. Super, VII, 129. Lowe's remark was made at Sheffield on September 4, 1873, reported next day in *The Times*, p. 3, col. 3, and jotted in Arnold's pocket diary for August 10, 1873.— *Note-Books*, ed. Lowry, p. 199.

322:1–2. See p. 340:22–23n.

322:3–6. See p. 291:27–28 and note.

322:16–18. Most recently in the Preface (1874) to *Higher Schools
. . . in Germany;* earlier in *Culture and Anarchy* (1868) and "A Recantation and Apology" (1869).—*Prose Works,* ed. Super, VII, 129;
V, 193–99, 321–24.

322:26–28. See p. 299:36.

322:29–32. A repetition of p. 302:21–23 and pp. 362:34–36,
369:9–11. Arnold jotted the sentence in his pocket diary for March
22, 1879, and used it again in "The Future of Liberalism" (1880).—
Prose Works, ed. Super, vol. IX. He also wrote it down in one of
his "General Note-Books."—*Note-Books,* ed. Lowry, pp. 317, 542.

323:2–11. Arnold's alteration of this passage (see Textual Notes)
is presumably due to the comment upon it of Ernest Fontanès, to
whom he wrote on October 5, 1878: "Je vous remercie de la rectifi-
cation au sujet de l'université de Strasbourg, et j'en profiterai. Peu
emporte, cependant, que l'université soit mixte à quelques égards, si
pour les chaires de théologie, de philosophie et d'histoire, chaires où
il est parlé de la religion, il y a séparation."—*Letters,* ed. Russell.

323:21–32. On May 31, 1878, Charles Owen O'Conor, the
O'Conor Don, moved a resolution "That in the opinion of this
House [of Commons], the present condition of University Education in Ireland is most unsatisfactory, and demands the immediate
attention of Parliament with the view of extending more generally
and equally the benefits of such education." Lowe, in reply, asserted
that the first step, however, should be the foundation of good and
sound secondary schools. He also proposed an examining board to
offer prizes to secondary school students and scholarships to whatever university they might choose. In the debate on Irish University
Education in 1873 he had made the distinction between the teaching
function of a "college" and the additional examining and degree-
giving function of a "university." The University of London, which
Lowe represented in Parliament, had become very much the latter.
"It did not assume that simple character of an Examining Board,
which has charmed Mr. Lowe, until 1858," when "the senate were
empowered to make regulations for admitting to all degrees, other
than medical, persons not educated in any University or College, or
authorised institution."—"The Ministry and University Education
in Ireland," *Quarterly Review,* American ed., CXXXIV, 145 (January, 1873).

323:25–27. The Queen's University, with colleges in Cork, Gal-
way, and Belfast, was established by an act of 1845 to provide non-

sectarian education to all faiths, but it left the Roman Catholics entirely unsatisfied; over a ten-year span, on the evidence of the O'Conor Don, only 218 Roman Catholic students had taken degrees at these colleges—an average of about seven per year in each college.

323:35–37. For a description of Gladstone's Irish University Education Bill of 1873, see Arnold's Preface (1874) to *Higher Schools . . . in Germany* and "Roman Catholics and the State" (1875).— *Prose Works*, ed. Super, VII, 90–137 and notes.

324:1–4. Tests were abolished at Trinity College in 1873, except for lecturers and professors of divinity, so that *The Times* was able to say that "the two existing Irish Universities are now nonsectarian."—June 4, 1878, p. 9, col. 3.

324:12. Burke described the coinage of the new word "ascendency" near the beginning of his "Letter to Richard Burke, Esq." (179–): "This protestant ascendency means nothing [like] an influence obtained by virtue, by love, or even by artifice and seduction. . . . New *ascendency* is the old mastership. It is neither more nor less than the resolution of one set of people in Ireland to consider themselves as the sole citizens in the commonwealth; and to keep a dominion over the rest by reducing them to absolute slavery under a military power; and thus fortified in their power, to divide the publick estate, which is the result of general contribution, as a military booty solely amongst themselves."

324:22–25. Arnold picks up the language of George Errington, one of the Irish members, who in the debate of June 3 challenged those who took refuge in the proposition that no ministry could pass a measure providing funds for a Catholic university "to tell us plainly and openly whether they themselves share those prejudices, or whether they are merely taking refuge behind the prejudices of others, and using this as a convenient if not very creditable *non possumus*."

324:26–32. Leading article, June 4, 1878, p. 9, cols. 3–4.

324:32–36. "Irish University Education," *Saturday Review* XLV, 714 (June 8, 1878). The article is sympathetic to the Irish demands and, following Arnold's terminology in the Preface to *Higher Schools . . . in Germany*, blames the failure of Gladstone's Irish University Education Bill of 1873 partly on "the dislike felt to it by the Secularist Liberals." See *Prose Works*, ed. Super, VII, 100.

325:1–10. In the debate on May 31, 1878, reported in *The Times* next day, p. 9, col. 3, and rearranged by Arnold.

325:13–16. Arnold repeats the formula he quoted in his Preface of 1874.—*Prose Works,* ed. Super, VI, 121–22. It is based on such a declaration as Gladstone's in introducing his Irish University Education Bill on February 13, 1873: "Denominational endowment [i.e., by the government], whether applied to a University or to a College in Ireland, would be in opposition to the uniform and explicit declarations which have been made, ever since this question assumed a new position six or seven years ago, by, I believe, every Member of the Government, and, as I can safely assert, by myself."

325:18–25. Lowe, "A New Reform Bill," *Fortnightly Review* XXVIII, 441 (October, 1877). Lowe wrote "ideal of a Liberal party."

326:1–7. Morley, "The Death of Mr. Mill," *Fortnightly Review* XIX, 675 (June, 1873); reprinted in his *Critical Miscellanies,* second ser. (London, 1877), p. 249. Jotted in Arnold's pocket diary for November 28, 1877.—*Note-Books,* ed. Lowry, p. 285.

326:9–16. The O'Conor Don's resolution was lost by a vote of 200 to 67 on June 3; most of the English Liberals did not vote, but Sir Charles Dilke (representing Chelsea) and Joseph Chamberlain (representing Birmingham) cast their votes with the minority. Both were prominent radicals who were soon to take office in the Liberal government that came in in 1880, Chamberlain as president of the Board of Trade, Dilke as under-secretary for foreign affairs.

326:24–27. "The actual consciences of three-fifths of the population of the United Kingdom . . . rise up and cry—'You, the State, are being generous with our money. By force of the tax-gatherer you are compelling us to teach as truth that which we before God assert without the slightest misgiving to be dismal error. You make us parties to a lie. . . . [You force] us to pay money in support of heathenish superstitions. . . . Secular elementary education is the porch to religious and all other knowledge, and . . . the teaching of religion, so far as it is capable of being taught by man, is the work of the loving heart and pure example of father, pastor, or friend—not of the State schoolmaster.'"—"National Education.—The 'Parental Conscience' Difficulty," letter signed "E. B.," *The Nonconformist,* January 29, 1873, p. 113; quoted by Arnold in his Preface of 1874.—*Prose Works,* ed. Super, VII, 106.

327:8–19. Writing to M. E. Grant Duff, one of his Liberal friends, on Christmas day, 1872, Arnold remarked: "As to the Liberals, I believe that the wish and intention of the best and most intelligent of them is as you say; but what they actually manage to get done is very often not 'as reason would,' but as violent and ignorant influences in the mass of their party will; and I cannot look upon it as a triumph of reason, though it passes as one of the triumphs of the Liberal party."—*Letters*, ed. Russell.

327:20. The Liberal government was defeated over the Irish University Education Bill of 1873, lost the general election of 1874, and was out of power until 1880.

327:24–26. Malachi 3:16.

327:32–328:1. A.-N. de Condorcet, *Vie de M. Turgot, Oeuvres* (Paris, 1847), V, 211, 203; jotted in Arnold's pocket diary for February 24 and 20, 1878, with the comment: "And therefore the politician who would really serve his country must get at this natural truth of things."—*Note-Books*, ed. Lowry, p. 296.

330:9–17. Arnold copied this letter (dated December 31, 1877) and another from Walmer barracks into the back pages of his pocket diary for 1878.—*Note-Books*, ed. Lowry, pp. 307–8. Walmer, with cavalry, infantry and marine barracks, adjoins Deal, Kent, on the southeastern coast of England.

330:18–20. An expansion of Epictetus *Discourses* II, xi, 18. Arnold jotted passages from this chapter in his pocket diary for July 6 and 13, 1878.—*Note-Books*, ed. Lowry, p. 301.

334:4. Thomas John Capel (1836–1911), of a devout Irish Catholic family, after a number of years at a mission for English-speaking Catholics in the South of France, returned to London in 1868 and proved an effective preacher and proselytizer; he figures as Monsignor Catesby in Disraeli's *Lothair* (1870). He founded a Catholic public school in Kensington in 1873 and became rector of what was intended to become a Catholic university there; both went bankrupt not long after Arnold wrote. He published a pamphlet *Reply to Gladstone's 'Vaticanism'* (1874).

335:16. The seminary for the education of the Roman Catholic clergy at Maynooth, some fifteen miles from Dublin, was founded in 1795. From 1844 to 1869 it received an annual grant from the British government, but the grant was withdrawn as part of Gladstone's Irish Church Act of 1869.

335:25–37. Irish secondary schools are the subject of Arnold's essay, "An Unregarded Irish Grievance," first published in August, 1881, and reprinted in *Irish Essays.—Prose Works*, ed. Super, vol. IX. Lord Randolph Churchill spoke of the poor management of the Irish educational endowments in the House of Commons on June 4, 1878.

336:11. "While a national establishment of religion favours totality, *hole-and-corner* forms of religion (to use an expressive popular

word) inevitably favour provincialism," said Arnold of Nonconformity in the Preface to *Culture and Anarchy* (1869).—*Prose
Works*, ed. Super, V, 240. The passage at 335:38–336:12 is quoted
nearly *verbatim* from the Preface of 1874, *Prose Works*, VII, 114.

336:25–26. Leading article in *The Times*, June 4, 1878, p. 9, col. 4.

336:27–30. The Irish bishops on March 31, 1868, submitted a
memorandum to Lord Mayo, chief secretary for Ireland, respecting
their notion of the constitution and government appropriate to a
Catholic university in Ireland; their views were so far from what
the Government was prepared to offer that the matter was dropped.
—House of Commons, *Sessional Papers*, 1867–68, LIII, 779–94. See
Arnold's Preface to *Higher Schools . . . in Germany* (1874), *Prose
Works*, ed. Super, VII, 97–98 and note. Again Arnold is quoting his
earlier work almost *verbatim*.

338:3. See p. 283:32 and note.

338:14–15. See p. 293:21–22n.

338:22–24. See p. 287:14–18.

339:7. So called by the correspondent in *The Nonconformist*
whom Arnold quoted on p. 326:24–27.

339:16. William Arthur (1819–1901), an Irish Methodist
preacher, president of the Wesleyan Conference in 1866, entered
the controversy over the Vatican council and papal infallibility with
a two-volume work on the papacy from 1864 to 1870, *The Pope, the
Kings and the People* (1877). Charles Haddon Spurgeon, a very
popular London Baptist preacher of strong Calvinist doctrine, was
criticized sharply for his intolerance of Irish Catholicism in *Culture
and Anarchy* (1868).—*Prose Works*, ed. Super, V, 194–99.

339:17. Jean-Baptiste-Henri Lacordaire (1802–61), a French Do-
minican, was visited by Arnold at his school at Sorèze in 1859 and
is subject of an admiring portrait in *A French Eton* (1863).—*Prose
Works*, ed. Super, II, 271–78.

339:26–28. The *Quicunque vult* is the Athanasian creed, which
denies the possibility of salvation to those who do not confess the
doctrines of the Trinity and the Incarnation; it was still used in the
Book of Common Prayer. The Westminster Confession is the Calvinist (Presbyterian) creed drawn up by the Westminster Assembly
of Divines in 1646. The Tridentine Decrees, or "Creed of Pius IV"
(1564) summarize the specific doctrines of the Roman Catholic
Church; they were the product of the Council of Trent and continue to be essential articles of the Catholic faith. The Thirty-nine
Articles (1563) define the dogmatic position of the Church of
England.

340:22–23. Charles Stewart Parnell, M.P. for Meath, and Joseph G. Biggar, M.P. for Cavan, the latter a Fenian, took advantage of the parliamentary rules governing freedom of debate to draw attention to the political wishes of Ireland by obstructing the business of the House of Commons and at least twice in July, 1877, kept the Commons sitting all night.

341:11–12. Edward Jenkins, "Liberalism and Disestablishment," *Fortnightly Review* XXIX, 889–908 (June, 1878), an attack on Church Establishment in England and Scotland, and especially on the arguments used in support of the respective establishments by two Liberals, W. E. Forster and the Duke of Argyll. "According to Mr. Matthew Arnold, everyone is legally a member of the Church of England," said Jenkins (p. 896).

341:31–34. "L'Église anglicane . . . a conservé une dignité et une force absolument étrangères à toutes les autres Églises réformées, uniquement parce que le bon sens anglais a conservé la hiérarchie." —*Lettres et opuscules inédits* (3rd ed.; Paris, 1853), II, 268. Arnold himself put the matter a little more comprehensively in a letter to his sister in June, 1876: "I . . . believe that [Catholicism] will transform itself; I see no other possible solution. Not to break one's connexion with the past in one's religion is one of the strongest instincts in human nature. Protestantism is breaking up everywhere where it has severed this connexion; only in England has it any hold upon the educated class, and that is because the Church of England is the one Protestant Church which maintained its connexion with the past."—*Letters*, ed. Russell.

342:38–343:4. Sir John Lubbock (1834–1913), well-known anthropologist and student of animal behavior, was M.P. for Maidstone from 1870. In the debate on the Census Bill of 1870, his scientific spirit led him on July 26 to move the inclusion of a question, not on religious adherence, but on whether one was married to a first cousin, in order that data might be available for a study of the effects of consanguinity on the physical and mental health of the offspring. The Conservatives were defeated by the Liberals in 1880 and the Census Bill of that year passed without the inclusion of the religious question.

343:35–344:3. "The old question of the relation of the Churches to the Westminster Confession of Faith has come once more to the front," wrote John Tulloch in a discussion of the "Progress of Religious Thought in Scotland." He quoted a severe condemnation of the Confession by a Scottish Presbyterian and commented: "It is beyond our province to inquire whether Mr. [David] Macrae's rep-

resentations of the doctrines of the Westminster Confession are to
be accepted as correct. They are highly coloured beyond doubt, and
drawn out into rhetorical flourishes from which no document in
the world is more free than the production of the Westminster Divines. If Mr. Macrae were more of an historical student of Christian
dogma, he would have laid on his colour less strongly, and been
more careful of exaggeration." Tulloch believed that the Scottish
churches would keep the Confession but change the formula of subscription to a general declaration of assent.—*Contemporary Review*
XXIX, 548–50 (March, 1877).

344:5–7. The Established Church of Scotland is Presbyterian. The
Disruption of 1843, a secession of more than a third of its ministers,
produced the Free Church of Scotland. The United Presbyterian
Church was formed in 1847 by the union of two earlier secessionist
groups.

344:16–23. See pp. 88:6 and 100:3–28, with notes.

344:26. Eliza Cook (1818–89), an almost entirely self-educated
poetess who published her first volume when she was seventeen,
celebrated for the most part domestic affections in a way that appealed strongly to the middle class. She received a civil list pension
in 1863. Arnold's use of Milton and Eliza Cook is meant to be merely
illustrative of the difference between the dignity of the Anglican
burial service and that of the Dissenters; Milton is not read in the
former and there was no specific claim on the part of the Nonconformists to read the latter.

344:38. John, Lord Russell died on May 28, 1878, about a month
before Arnold's essay was published.

345:17–20. "Equality," pp. 299:34–36, 301–2.

345:32–35. This is one of Arnold's chief aims in *A French Eton*
(1863–64) and in the recommendations that accompany both his
reports on foreign schools.

345:35–346:1. Leading article, June 4, 1878, p. 9, col. 3. See p. 324:
31–32.

346:5–6. In reference to the new Reform Bill, Lowe remarked in
the House of Commons on July 15, 1867: "I believe it will be absolutely necessary that you should prevail on our future masters to
learn their letters"—a remark popularized into "We must educate
our masters."

346:13–16. This sentence comes almost *verbatim* from the concluding chapter of *Schools and Universities on the Continent* (1868),
Prose Works, ed. Super, IV, 306:23–26.

346:19–20. The agricultural laborer received the franchise by the Reform Act of 1884.

346:29–34. David Hume, *History of England* (Boston, 1856), V, 443n (Chapter lxi, ¶10n).

["PORRO UNUM EST NECESSARIUM"]

The publication of a new statistical report on French schools in 1878 gave Arnold the excuse for pointing out to the British public that though the Elementary Education Act of 1870 had been a landmark in the provision of elementary schools for all, nothing significant had been done for secondary education. In his inspectoral report for 1878 he used the French statistics to show that the cost of elementary education in England was far above what it should have been in terms of the results; but more significant for his purpose were the statistics on secondary education, which he moulded into an article that was a brief reiteration of his three earlier books on Continental education. The article was published in the *Fortnightly Review* for November, 1878, and brought him £30.

348, Title: "But one thing is needful: [and Mary hath chosen that good part, which shall not be taken away from her.]"—Luke 10:42. Arnold also used these words of Jesus to Martha, in the Vulgate version, as title of a chapter of *Culture and Anarchy* in the 1875 edition and subsequently.

348:1–3. The expression is a favorite of Amiel's, but he was still living and his diary was still unpublished when Arnold wrote this.

348:9. Agénor Bardoux (1829–97), lawyer and man of letters, entered politics at the fall of France in 1871; he was a member of the National Assembly until its dissolution in 1875, then of the Chamber of Deputies until, failing of re-election in 1881, he was named senator for life. He was a very energetic and fair-minded minister of public instruction from December, 1877, to February, 1879. The statistical report to which Arnold refers was the *Statistique de l'enseignement secondaire en 1876* (Paris, 1878). A convenient summary of this and four other volumes of statistics published about the same time (three on elementary education, one on superior education) was prepared by John Eaton, U.S. Commissioner of Education: *Circulars of Information of the Bureau of Education*. No. 4—1881. *Education in France* (Washington, D.C.: Government Printing Office, 1881). Arnold's friend Jean-Jacques Rapet was a member of the statistical commission which prepared the report on elementary education.

348:12. Victor Duruy (1811–94), historian and career inspector of schools, held the post of minister of public instruction from 1863 to 1869, a term distinguished by the intelligence of his reforms. Arnold met him during his visit to France in 1865 to study the French schools. See *Schools and Universities on the Continent, Prose Works,* ed. Super, IV, Index. Duruy's report on secondary education for the year 1865 was published in 1868 and hence not available when Arnold in 1867 completed his account of his tour of inquiry. The only full statistical report on secondary education in France before Duruy's was published by Villemain in 1843.

348:24–26. In an article on "England's Mission," Gladstone complains of the increasing difficulty in carrying on the nation's business in Parliament (most recently because of Irish obstruction) and adds "a slight sketch of some of our unredeemed engagements," twenty-two in number.—*Nineteenth Century* IV, 582 (September, 1878). Arnold jotted fourteen of them in his pocket diary for November 9.

349:4–350:27. *The Popular Education of France,* chapter viii; *Prose Works,* ed. Super, II, 87–90, with omissions and slight alterations. Arnold based his report on a journey to the Continent in March–August, 1859, but he did not write it until 1860. It appeared both in its official form (as a "blue-book") and separately as a book published on Arnold's own account in 1861. The latter form was still available from the publisher when Arnold wrote this essay. Its Preface he reprinted in *Mixed Essays* with the title "Democracy."

350:32–352:14. *Schools and Universities on the Continent,* chapter xxiii; *Prose Works,* ed. Super, IV, 308–10, with omissions and a few changes, the most striking of which are the substitution of "injury" for "inconvenience" at pp. 350:38, 40; 351:3, and 352:12, and increasing the number of acceptable secondary schools from "half-a-dozen" to "ten or a dozen." Arnold kept all the changes when he published the paragraphs in *Passages from the Prose Writings of Matthew Arnold* in 1880. As with the preceding quotation, Arnold gives the date of his tour rather than of the publication of his report (1868).

352:16–36. Leading articles in *The Nonconformist* XXIV, 966 (November 30, 1864) and *The Daily News,* December 7, 1864, p. 4, cols. 3–4, quoted by Arnold in "My Countrymen" (1866), *Prose Works,* ed. Super, V, 5.

353:3–9. Arnold alludes to what he said at greater length on this subject in *Culture and Anarchy*, chapter iii (1868), *Prose Works*, ed. Super, V, 154-55.

354:15. Metz is in Lorraine, Strasbourg and Colmar in Alsace, provinces lost by France to Germany after the war of 1870-71.

355:5. St.-Cyr is the military academy; the Central school is the École Centrale des Arts et Manufactures.

356:25-30. See *Schools and Universities on the Continent, Prose Works*, ed. Super, IV, 56.

357:3. The Liberals were soon to prevail: the Jesuit order was suppressed in France and her colonies on March 29, 1880. Their exile lasted only two years, however.

358:3-4. Arnold described these in *Schools and Universities on the Continent, Prose Works*, ed. Super, IV, 107-10.

358:12-22. By authorization of the law of July 26, 1875, the bishops established private Catholic degree-granting universities at Angers, Lille, Lyons, Paris, and Toulouse. Jules Ferry, successor to Bardoux as minister of public instruction, in 1880 procured a law repealing the privileges granted to the private universities and the "Catholic universities" became "Catholic institutes."

358:33. "The one thing needful" is the "unum necessarium" of the title. See p. 368:34-36.

359:7-14. Arnold repeats the figures he took from the *Public Schools Calendar* in *Schools and Universities on the Continent, Prose Works*, ed. Super, IV, 105-6, 28:12 and note. The "nine great public schools" were Eton, Winchester, Westminster, Charterhouse, St. Paul's, Merchant Taylors', Harrow, Rugby, and Shrewsbury.

359:17-19. Arnold presumably refers to the debates on the Government's Intermediate Education (Ireland) Bill, which had its second reading in the Commons on July 15 and its third on August 12, 1878.

359:36-360:1. See pp. 283:31-284:7.

360:12. The Jesuit College at Stonyhurst, in Lancashire, was founded in France in 1593 and moved to England in 1794. When Arnold wrote it had about 300 boys.

360:17-19. Arnold is agreeing with what is said on the subject by P. E. Hamerton, *Round My House* (3rd ed.; London, 1876), pp. 82-95.

360:25-29. The "man of genius" was Disraeli, the prime minister. His cabinet included the Duke of Northumberland, the Duke of Richmond, the Marquess of Salisbury, Sir Stafford Northcote, bart., Lord John Manners, Viscount Sandon, Sir Michael Hicks Beach, bart., F. A. Stanley (later 16th Earl of Derby), the lawyers Lord Cairns and G. Gathorne Hardy (Viscount Cranbrook), the banker Richard Assheton Cross, and the newsagent and bookseller W. H. Smith.

361:3. The Universal Exhibition of Paris in the summer of 1878 attracted some 16,000,000 visitors, of whom Arnold himself was one. For it was built the old Trocadéro Palace, opposite the Eiffel tower, a landmark until it was replaced by the Palais de Chaillot for the Exhibition of 1937.

361:7–8. "A surprising transformation has occurred in public opinion since 1872, when M. Gambetta delivered at Grenoble the famous speech in which he announced the advent of new social strata. . . . Now, after the lapse of only six years Prince Bismarck acknowledges that France possesses an internal security lacking to other countries, and M. Gambetta can recall that speech while affirming his adhesion to the principle of a second chamber."—*Times*, October 12, 1878, p. 5, col. 3.

361:11–21. See pp. 290:6–15.

361:22–24. See p. 290:20–29.

362:33–36. See pp. 302:21–23, 322:29–32, 369:8–11.

363:6–9. See p. 294:19–22.

363:18–20. *Histoire de France* (nouv. éd.; Paris, 1876), VI, 117 (Book IX, chapt. iii).

363:23–27. Leading article, December 2, 1864, p. 4, col. 3; quoted in "My Countrymen" (1866), *Prose Works*, ed. Super, V, 5–6. *The Morning Star*, a newspaper of the Manchester school of radicals, began publication on March 17, 1856, and was absorbed by *The Daily News* on October 13, 1869.

363:35–37. Perhaps a summary of the part of Gambetta's speech at Grenoble on October 10, 1878, reported in *The Times*, October 14, p. 5, col. 5. See J. Reinach, ed., *Discours et plaidoyers politiques de M. Gambetta* (Paris, 1883), VIII, 277–78.

363:37–38. See p. 279:11–13.

364:15–16. For the readings from Eliza Cook, see p. 344:26 and note. Bills to legalize marriage with a deceased wife's sister were a perennial subject of ridicule with Arnold; see *Culture and Anarchy* (1868) and *Friendship's Garland*, Letter VIII (1869), *Prose Works*, ed. Super, V, 205–8, 313–18.

364:36. Arnold mentioned Playfair's proposal in a letter of October 26, 1878, but the bill was not introduced in 1878 or 1879.

365:8–9. See p. 280:20.

365:29. The Elementary Education Act of 1870, sponsored in

Parliament by Arnold's brother-in-law W. E. Forster, set up machinery to provide schools where none existed.

367:32–34. "We wish that, under the shield of the Republic, the capacities of all citizens may freely develope; and it is certainly not at Grenoble, where I testified to the accession of a new social stratum, that I could say our task is completed. It never will be. After the first stratum will come a second; then others; for the effort of peoples now consists in drawing those who are below and constantly making them ascend towards light, well-being, and morality."—Gambetta at Grenoble, October 10, 1878, reported in *The Times*, October 17, p. 5, col. 4; see Gambetta, *Discours*, VIII, 273.

367:36–368:1. Turgot, as intendant of the province of Limoges (1761–74), in order to carry out reforms that would increase the prosperity of that impoverished rural district, attempted to persuade a mistrustful people of his intent through letters addressed to the *curés* or parish priests; as John Morley put it, he "had his plans laid before [the people in the country] in their parish meetings held after mass on Sundays."—"Turgot in Limousin," *Fortnightly Review* XXVII, 728 (May, 1877); reprinted in his *Critical Miscellanies*, Second Series (London, 1877), p. 205. In the latter, augmented version, Morley concluded by quoting Arnold's tribute to Turgot in "Bishop Butler and the Zeit-Geist" (1876), p. 25:25–29.

368:10–12. See p. 287:14–16.

368:25. "A consummation | Devoutly to be wished."—*Hamlet* III, i, 63–64.

368:37–369:2. Robert Lowe, "Imperialism," *Fortnightly Review* XXX, 454 (October, 1878), paraphrased.

369:2–5. "England's Mission," *Nineteenth Century* IV, 570 (September, 1878).

369:29–31. Lucan *Civil Wars* II, 383, 389–90, jotted in Arnold's pocket diary for February 10, 1878. He quoted from the same passage in "Equality," p. 286:12–13.

[PREFACE TO *MIXED ESSAYS*]

Brief as it is, the Preface to *Mixed Essays* is an excellent statement of the thesis that unites Arnold's essays on literature and society in the last decade of his life.

370:1–3. The essay entitled "Democracy," which appears in vol. II, 3–29 of this edition of Arnold's *Prose Works*.

371:18–19. Quoted from Moritz Busch's *Graf Bismarck und seine*

Leute in *The Times*, November 21, 1878, p. 4, col. 1; jotted in Arnold's pocket diary for November 3, 1878.—*Note-Books*, ed. Lowry, p. 304.

371:33–35. "Le peuple est plus grossier dans les pays aristocratiques que partout ailleurs."—*De la Démocratie en Amérique* (Paris, 1836), I, 40–41 (two-thirds through chapter i). Arnold quoted this passage in his essay on "Democracy," reprinted in *Mixed Essays* from *The Popular Education of France* (1861).

372:13–15. See p. 287:14–18.

372:30–32. See p. 219:14–17.

[SPEECH AT THE ROYAL ACADEMY]

Arnold's pocket diary attests that he wrote this speech on April 7. It is reported in *The Times* for May 3, 1875, p. 9, col. 2, and has been reprinted by Fraser Neiman, *Essays, Letters, and Reviews by Matthew Arnold* (Cambridge: Harvard University Press, 1960), pp. 199–200.

Seven years later, *The World*, in anticipation of Arnold's visit to America, addressed him: "You have been the vogue in fashionable circles; but you have never failed to let the fine gentlemen and ladies with whom you have consorted clearly understand that you considered yourself their superior, and that your presence amongst them was an act of condescension on your part. There is, perhaps, no other man of letters now alive who would have had the intrepidity to make such a speech as you did a couple years ago in returning thanks for the toast of literature at the Academy dinner. The citizens of a Republic may well admire the attributes in you to which that speech testified."—September 13, 1882, pp. 5–7.

373:21. Sir Francis Grant (1803–78), the most fashionable portrait painter of his day, was president of the Royal Academy from 1866. There were two English "royal highnesses" present, as well as several from the Continent; Arnold alludes to the Prince of Wales (later Edward VII).

374:7. Arnold's "official chiefs" in the Education Department— both present at the banquet—were the Duke of Richmond, lord president of the Privy Council, and Viscount Sandon, vice president of the Committee of Council for Education.

374:12–23. "Des Grecs établis dans les parties montagneuses de la

Basse-Italie avaient perdu, dans cette situation isolée, la culture et les moeurs de la patrie. Tout ce qu'ils en avaient gardé, c'était un souvenir vague et confus; et ils se réunissaient, dit-on, une fois par an, pour se lamenter ensemble de n'être plus Grecs."—Claude Fauriel, *Histoire de la poésie provençale* (Paris, 1846), I, 66. Arnold listed this in his pocket diary for 1858 among the books to be read "for March lecture" (i.e., the unpublished lecture on "Dante, the Troubadours, and the Early Drama," delivered from the chair of poetry at Oxford on March 12, 1859).—*Note-Books*, ed. Lowry, p. 564.

374:25–27. Disraeli, prime minister since early in 1874, was the son of a literary man and was himself a novelist and man of letters before he became a politician. He followed Arnold on the program, with a response to a toast to "The Health of Her Majesty's Ministers."

375:17. The anonymous Elegy I *In Maecenatam*, line 38.— A. Baehrens, ed. *Poetae Latinae Minores* (Leipzig, 1879), I, 127. The poem has sometimes been attributed to Vergil and may, therefore, also be found in editions of the *Appendix Vergiliana*.

[SPEECH AT BALLIOL COLLEGE]

Though Arnold's speech was not reported in the London papers, the memory of it was still fresh among his friends of *The Pall Mall Gazette* when nearly seven years later they commented upon his statement to the New York reporters, "After all I think there is no place to live in like dear smoky old London": "To be of London and yet not in it is a fate to which few people would object [Arnold did not live in London, but in a country town some nineteen miles away], and the humorous stoicism with which he puts up with his good fortune is eminently characteristic of Mr. Arnold. 'My path in life,' he once told an Oxford audience, with the most engaging smile, 'has been rough and thorny,' and the audience smiled back in complete sympathy with the good humour with which the speaker has always borne his hard lot as one of the most admired of writers and most popular of men."—October 25, 1883, p. 2. Browning was among the guests at the banquet.

Textual Notes

[A DEPTFORD POET]

PMG   "A Deptford Poet," *Pall Mall Gazette*, June 25, 1875, p. 12. Anonymous.

[EDOARDO FUSCO]

Macm. Edoardo Fusco, "Italian Art and Literature before Giotto and Dante," *Macmillan's Magazine* XXXIII, 228–40 (January, 1876). Signed prefatory note by Arnold, p. 228.
Title: *supplied by ed.*

[LAST ESSAYS ON CHURCH AND RELIGION]

77.*   Last Essays | on | Church and Religion | By | Matthew Arnold | Formerly Professor of Poetry in the University of Oxford | and Fellow of Oriel College | London | Smith, Elder, & Co., 15 Waterloo Place | 1877 | *All rights reserved*

80.   Passages from | the Prose Writings | of | Matthew Arnold | London | Smith, Elder, & Co., 15 Waterloo Place | 1880 | [*All rights reserved*]

83s. St. Paul & Protestantism | with an Essay on | Puritanism & the Church of England | and | Last Essays | on Church & Religion | By Matthew Arnold | New York | Macmillan and Co. | 1883

03l.   Last Essays | on | Church and Religion | By | Matthew

---

* For 77 read 1877, etc.

Arnold | *Popular Edition* | London | Smith, Elder, & Co.,
15 Waterloo Place | 1903 | [*All rights reserved*]
This edition has no textual authority and is not collated.

[BISHOP BUTLER AND THE ZEIT-GEIST]

Cont. "Bishop Butler and the Zeit-Geist," *Contemporary Review*
XXVII, 377–95, 571–92 (February, March, 1876); in this
edition, pp. 11–35, 35–62.

Lit. "Bishop Butler and the Zeit-Geist," *Littell's Living Age*
CXXIX, 67–78 (April 8, 1876). Part I only. Not collated.
Reprinted 77, 83s, o3l (not collated).

The following passages appear in 80: 25:16–26:25 (pp.
307–9, headed "Turgot and Butler"); 41:35–42:25 (pp.
309–11, headed "Butler's Psychology"); 49:3–50:16 (pp.
311–13, headed "Butler's Argument from Analogy"); 53:35–
54:14 (pp. 313–14, headed "Butler's Appeal to Our Ignorance"); 56:27–57:28 (pp. 314–15, headed "Result of the
'Analogy'"); 57:29–58:2 (pp. 315–16, headed "The 'Analogy' To-day"); 59:9–60:5 (pp. 316–17, headed "Greatness
of Butler").

11:26. *The following discourse, and a second which will succeed
it, were two lectures given at the   *Cont.*

13:5. words of one of his   *Cont.*

13:9–10. which all then   *mispr.* 77

13:12. experiment." Sir   *Cont.*

13:13. the "Sermons:" "In   *Cont.*

13:29. which he is publishing in   *Cont.*

13:31–32. purposes, intents,   *Cont.*, 77, 83s; *corrected from Morley*

14:22. Scotland, that country   *Cont.*

14:26. these important matters   *Cont.*

14:30–31. it is solid.   *Cont.*

14:32. *section not numbered*, Cont.

14:36–15:1. school. Before   *Cont.*

15:5. him; he   *Cont.*

15:10. of his life.   *Cont.*

15:19. noise, and it was   *Cont.*

15:20. required. But he had   *Cont.*

15:25. The Queen, however, had, before   *Cont.*

15:29. he was appointed   *Cont.*

15:35. His health   *Cont.*

16:1. on June 16th,   *Cont.*

16:7. followed him in   *Cont.*

16:9. predecessor; all   *Cont.*

16:20. measure,   *Cont. and Butler;* measures,   77, 83s

16:20–21. accident.   *Cont.,* 77, 83s; *corrected from Butler*

16:22. circumstances, nor,   *Cont.,* 77, 83s; *corrected from Butler*

16:27. please let   *Cont.,* 77, 83s; *corrected from Butler*

16:36. single; austerely   *Cont.*

17:5–6. a person coming . . . with the plan for   *Cont.*

17:7. asked how much   *Cont.*

17:12. were his rule at Durham; he   *Cont.*

17:19.   the station of itself   *Cont.,* 77, 83s; *corrected from Butler*

17:23. *no* ¶   *Cont.,* 77

18:10. these to his   *Cont.;* this to his   77, 83s

18:24. reader; it   *Cont.*

19:8. completely wooded,   *Cont.,* 77, 83s; *corrected from Butler*

19:36–37. Charge, on the use and importance of external religion, [*rom.*]   *Cont.*

20:1. style we   *Cont.*

20:4. put up; and   *Cont.*

20:10–11. and the charge   *Cont.*

20:11–13. amounted . . . Rome,   *not in quotes, Cont.*

21:10. is, that when   *Cont.*

21:37. off; but   *Cont.*

22:18. in following him,   *Cont.*

22:19–20. Nearly . . . conflict.   *not in Cont.*

22:37. unreasoned   *Cont.,* 77, 83s; *corrected from Pattison*

23:5. the determining   *Cont.*

23:7–8. (the deistical objections)   *not in Cont.*

23:11. unite all into . . . it ought to be.' "   *Cont.,* 77, 83s; *corrected from Pattison and Butler*

23:12. *no* ¶ That connection of   *Cont.*

23:14. These parties   *Cont.*

23:28. preparatory and   *Cont.,* 77, 83s; *corrected from Butler*

24:25. *no* ¶   *Cont.*

24:28. prospects   *Cont.,* 77, 83s; *corrected from Butler*

25:12–13. something; yet,   *Cont.*

25:19. ever had—Turgot.   *Cont.*

25:23–24. his *ferocity*—   *Cont.*

26:2. in France it then   *Cont.*

26:33. then it goes on:— *Cont.*

27:1. *the panic ... sex,* [*ital.*] *Cont.*

27:12–13. has, it is almost certain, something of exaggeration in it. *Cont.*

27:15–16. were the circumstances ... especially trying *Cont.*

27:22. criticism! "If *Cont.*

28:7–9. that which is sweetly reasonable, or sweet reasonableness. But the more original meaning of *epieikes, epieikeia,* is *Cont.*

28:10–12. likelihood, the prepossessingness of that which has this air; and *epieikeia* is to be rendered "sweet *Cont.*

28:16. Jesus Christ; *epieikeia Cont.*

28:17. And this Christianity *Cont.*

28:21. yield. But *Cont.*

28:22. that tends *Cont.*

28:23. way that he *Cont.*

28:24–25. of it; and he does lay *Cont.*

28:27–28. be Christianity's characteristic way *Cont.*

29:16. *no* ¶ *Cont.*

29:21–22. after all, if religion is your object, and to change people's behaviour, what is the use *Cont.*

29:23. what they *are, Cont.*

29:24. *ought to behave?* [*ital.*] *Cont.*

29:31. triumphs over *mispr.* 83s

29:35. too; and *Cont.*

29:37. affirmed that *Cont.*

30:2. asserted that *Cont.*

30:8–9. respect; achievement *Cont.*

30:13. so deeply? *Cont.*

30:14–15. he turns out *Cont.*

30:17. is it; and *Cont.,* 77

30:19. *section not numbered, Cont.*

30:27. own in his *Cont.*

31:24. as learning in *Cont.,* 77, 83s; *corrected from Butler*

32:1. wrong? is *Cont.*

32:7. us," when *Cont.*

32:10. mankind," when *Cont.*

32:23–25. knowledge;"—these delineators of human nature represent it fantastically. *Cont.*

32:29. remedy, this *Cont.*

33:23. is worth, they *Cont.*

33:25–26. to the scheme; they *Cont.*

33:32. work; it is a   *Cont.*

33:36–37. *no quotes, Cont.*

34:6–7. of the moral   *Cont., 77, 83s; corrected from Butler*

34:7. passions and possessions seem   *Cont.*

34:9–10. stock of natural affections, because   *Cont.*

34:20. he says—   *Cont.*

34:34. occasion of.   *Cont., 77, 83s; corrected from Butler*

35:3. And a man,   *Cont.*

35:5. acceptance, looking   *Cont.*

35:7. stay, and coming to   *Cont.*

35:11. acquainted," such   *Cont.*

35:12–15. think, cannot but be disconcerted and impatient to find
that . . . affections.   *Cont.*

35:19. he tells us how   *Cont.*

35:30. ¶He notices   *Cont.*

36:9. ¶That explanation why   *Cont.*

36:10–11. was necessitated, no doubt, by Butler's   *Cont.*

36:17. sudden anger and there   *Cont.*

36:19. and the end   *Cont., 77, 83s; corrected from Butler;* end,"
says Butler, "for   *Cont.*

37:18. us; he   *Cont.*

37:23. principle of reflexion or conscience is   *Cont.*

37:28. And his theory   *Cont.*

38:7–8. *as a guard* and *further security,* [*ital.*]   *Cont.*

38:22. find him marvelling   *Cont.*

38:33. And . . . more:—   *not in Cont.*

38:38. all at sea about the rule of conduct,   *Cont.*

39:19. and that to   *Cont.*

39:24. than the other?   *Cont.*

39:25. God, but   *Cont.*

39:27. when he has   *Cont.*

39:35. hungry; it   *Cont.*

39:37–38. enjoyment. And how does it prove this? It proves it as
follows:—   *Cont.*

40:2. that provision   *Cont., 77, 83s; corrected from Butler*

40:12. business, to be   *Cont., 77, 83s; corrected from Butler*

40:13. appetite;" and   *Cont.*

40:23. misery." Butler   *Cont.*

40:27. getting free from   *Cont.*

40:29. the consideration of   *Cont., 77, 83s; corrected from Butler*

40:31. nature, to serve   *Cont.*

40:38–41:1. own definition   *Cont.*

41:5–10. happiness." But he explains always that he means, by this, the pursuit of our *temporal* good,   *Cont.*

41:24. manner, as   *Cont.*

41:25. to man   *Cont.*

41:26. when hungry,   *Cont.*

41:32. this mechanical psychology   *Cont.*

42:6. His error   *Cont.*

42:8, 12. further   *Cont.*

42:26. to live, [*rom.*]   *Cont.*

43:5–6. But it has the right to get the better of it, because of its superiority in   *Cont.*

43:12–13. question between a regard   *Cont.*

43:14–15. experience having established it, that, from   *Cont.*

43:16. in such a conflict to   *Cont.*

43:25–26. neighbour—that they have, in   *Cont.*

43:28. race; nor does   *Cont.*

43:31. our desire   *Cont.*; or desire   *mispr.* 77, 83s

43:36. if he does not,   *Cont.*

44:2. be what we must   *Cont.*

44:3–4. nature, because he was afraid of the contracted   *Cont.*

44:8. Bible-word—the difficulty   *Cont.*

44:11–12. contracted self; of two selves,   *Cont.*

44:14. following the first and   *Cont.*

44:15. the two do not   *Cont.*

44:22. God; and   *Cont.*

44:24–25. lesson the experience involves,   *Cont.*

44:25. blow; but   *Cont.*

44:28. *no* ¶   *Cont.*

44:37. a man advantaged,   *Cont.*

45:2. *will* [*ital.*]   *Cont.*

45:3. yet he said: *Cont.*

45:25–26. theory of the independence of virtue and conscience of all   *Cont.*

45:30. virtue; he   *Cont.*

45:38. But it did   *Cont.*

46:5. this; this is not *experience,*   *Cont.*

46:7. their apparent happiness,   *Cont.*

46:9–10. itself felt, but . . . of obedience to those common rules of *Cont.*

46:10–11. virtue, which rules, however,   *Cont.*

46:14. *no* ¶   *Cont.*

46:16. happiness; to which experience   *Cont.*

46:17. adapted, to which he may   *Cont.*

46:18. conform himself than to   *Cont.*

46:19. judgment upon "appearances," and which has, if he   *Cont.*

46:24. with that which   *Cont.*

46:26–27. results of this experience . . . constitute happiness.   *Cont.*

46:28–30. of its obligation must rather be: *Cont.*

46:31–32. But it had its origin in   *Cont.*

46:33. *section not numbered, Cont.*

46:34. contain that is   *Cont.*

47:2. comes to them.   *Cont.*

47:5. of Butler's age   *Cont.*

47:9. *does* [ital.]   *Cont.*

47:9–10. satisfactory; he is hardly   *Cont.*

47:13. It appeared in   *Cont.*

47:26. *no* ¶   *Cont.*

48:3–4. *metaphysics, . . . support them*   *Cont.*

48:12. does the "Analogy" afford them?   *Cont.*

48:26. clearly that they   *Cont.*

48:29. he establishes this   *Cont.*

48:36–37. against Butler; no wish at all   *Cont.*

48:38. angered him; still   *Cont.*

49:3. ¶I do not   80

49:4. which a cool inquirer must,   80

49:9. is used to prove, really, not   *Cont.*

49:24. *experience;* and   *Cont.*

49:36–37. It goes through   *Cont.*

49:38. For example:—   *not in Cont.*

50:7. experience [*rom.*]   *Cont.*

50:20. capacity for   *Cont.*, 77, 83s; *corrected from Butler*

51:3. of their bodies,   *Cont.*, 77, 83s; *corrected from Butler*

51:6. *experience;* [*ital.*]   *Cont.*

51:18–19. religion." "Yes," is the answer, "but we   *Cont.*

51:28–29. matter? What is matter of experience is, that   *Cont.*

51:31. *outward* [*ital.*]   *Cont.*

51:36. suggested the notion   *Cont.*

52:2. of Nature, moral and   *Cont.*

52:6. operation, nature, this world as we see it, necessarily   *Cont.*

52:9. agent, an intelligent   *Cont.*

52:10–12. character, being all-wise . . . and governing the world,

. . . punishments, exercising *moral* government   *Cont.*

52:14. government,—must be   *Cont.*

52:21. common to   *Cont.*

52:24. of observation. The   *Cont.*

52:33. That proposition produces,   *Cont.*

53:5. *no* ¶   *Cont.*

53:11–12. Therefore, to get rid of the foundation of   *Cont.*

53:20. experimental; it   *Cont.*

53:25, 27. the house . . . the tree   *Cont.*

53:35. ¶Butler appeals,   80

53:37. Difficulties alleged against the truth of religion, he says,   80

54:15. *no* ¶   *Cont.*

54:16–20. It . . . effect.   *not in Cont.*

54:20. Butler urges   *Cont.*

54:21. *intended* [*ital.*]   *Cont.*

54:22. generality do not   *Cont.*

55:4. even from an   *Cont.*

55:6–8. that Butler's handling of these . . . is not able in proportion   *Cont.*

55:10. not well have then   *Cont.*

55:15. than Butler could.   *Cont.*

55:19. of the prophecy, "Sacrifice   *Cont.*

56:13–14. know what men's observation, under   *Cont.*

56:21–22. of *informing themselves* . . . of *doubting* [*ital.*]   *Cont.*

56:27. ¶The wonderful   80

57:4. Such is the "happy   *Cont.*

57:16. motive for following   *Cont.*

57:18. ¶How utterly unlike is   80

57:22. "The Lord is the   *Cont.*

57:29. *section not numbered, Cont.*

57:34–35. upon one, as one contemplates   *Cont.*

58:8–9. authority, on the part of free-living   *Cont.*

58:23. perplexity." He   *Cont.*

58:26. what he had   *Cont.*

59:1. a right description of the tone and   *Cont.*

59:5–6. the true tradition of   *Cont.*

59:7–8. for that is   *Cont.*, 77, 83s; *corrected from A.V.*

59:9. ¶And yet,   80

59:13. does help   *Cont.*

59:21. gains upon us   80

59:22. of his day   *Cont.*

59:27–28. the clearness, certainty,   *Cont.*

59:30. law, and it was   *Cont.*

59:38. And ... reason.   *not in Cont.*

60:3. even religion itself."   *mispr.* 77, 80, 83s

60:25. overborne; but   *Cont.*

60:34. time; for the   *Cont. and Butler;* time; the   77, 83s

61:4. which are in   *Cont.,* 77, 83s; *corrected from Butler*

61:7. grow to prevail,   *Cont.*

61:9. cannot unite   *Cont.*

61:15. it may now be   *Cont.*

61:25–26. He talked to ... of God; he told   *Cont.*

61:33. are surely though   *Cont.*

62:1–2. that impersonal life of which I have spoken, and of thus no
    Cont.

62:19. before Death brushed   *Cont.*

62:24. in this place   *Cont.*

62:28. maiden unto the   *Cont.*

[THE CHURCH OF ENGLAND]

Macm.   "The Church of England: an Address Delivered at Sion
         College," *Macmillan's Magazine* XXXIII, 481–94 (April,
         1876).

             Reprinted 77, 83s, o3l (not collated).

             The following passages appear in 80: 64:29–65:17, 66:7–23
         (pp. 201–3, headed "What Is the Church?"); 71:24–72:27
         (pp. 203–4, headed "The Church and Social Progress");
         76:10–27, 77:35–78:9 (pp. 205–6, headed "The Kingdom of
         God"); 78:30–79:10, 80:4–5, 9–13 (pp. 218–19, headed
         "Philosophical Radicals"); 84:9–85:13 (pp. 197–98, headed
         "Pugilistic Dissent"); 86:17–26 (p. 206, headed "True
         Strength of the Church of England").

63:28–29. *not in Macm.*

64:4. are parties   *Macm.*

64:10. no ¶ But this   *Macm.*

64:21. reasons, to set   *Macm.*

64:29. deal that is   *Macm.*

65:8–10. 'Our province,' says Butler, 'our province is   80

65:37. as entertainment and   *Macm.,* 77, 83s; *corrected from Butler*

66:2. I will not quarrel; and when he   *Macm.*

66:10. do really interest   *Macm.*

66:11. things much more   *Macm.*

66:16. far rather   *Macm.*

66:21. such tasks   *Macm.*

66:24. *no* ¶   *Macm.*

67:10. *no* ¶   *Macm.*

67:17. *section not numbered, Macm.*

67:33–35. *not in Macm.*

68:10. *no* ¶   *Macm.*

68:21. exists formed,   *Macm.*

68:33. quoted, and whom I have, as I said, just now a special disposition to quote, but whose practical view of things is, besides, in
itself almost always   *Macm.*

69:5,7. to remind . . . to propagate   *Macm., 77, 83s; corrected from
Butler*

69:23. public character and a   *not in Macm.*

69:38. *not in Macm.*

70:1. fictitious   *mispr. Macm.*

70:19. that the laity   *Macm. and Fortn.;* that a laity   77, 83s

71:5. Liberals, he says, the real   *Macm.*

71:18. belongs—its sentiment   *Macm.*

71:23. settled, and the   *Macm.*

71:24. ¶Now, the ideal of this class is   *Macm.*

71:37. the devoted   *Macm.*

71:38–72:1. religion; the   *Macm.*

72:3. that Communists   *Macm.*

72:4. spirit of Christianity.   80

73:3. produced   *Macm., 77;* produces   *mispr.* 83s

73:5. which renders you   *Macm.*

73:16. magnificent; they   *Macm.*

73:19. cruelly and overwhelmingly; but   *Macm.*

73:35. leaders; and the   *Macm.*

74:5. observe, and it   *Macm.*

74:9. both: the   *Macm.*

74:14, 16. survive; they . . . down; they   *Macm.*

74:26. those ingrossings and   *Macm.;* those ingrossing and   77, 83s;
corrected from Barrow

75:14, 31, 32. with it; and . . . clergy; they . . . upon; but in   *Macm.*

76:2, 7. ideals; and . . . true; and   *Macm.*

76:10. ¶It is really   80

76:19. He went   *Macm.*

76:20, 22. Him, and He ... His   *Macm.*

76:24–25. told them to pray for it: "Thy   *Macm.;* told his disciples
to pray for it. 'Thy   80

76:27–28. that it should be proclaimed throughout   *Macm.*

76:31. unseen; it   *Macm.*

76:36. of God;" at Rome   *Macm.*

77:4. inevitable; the kingdom   *Macm.*

77:5. without Jesus, and   *Macm.*

77:9. *Jesus Christ;*" we   *Macm.*

77:13. His death and   *Macm.*

77:14. *no* ¶   *Macm.*

77:19–20. His saints. They conceived   *Macm.*

77:35. *no* ¶   *Macm.;* ¶It is a   80

78:5. of any class or classes,—however   80

78:6. which are perfectly   80

78:22–23. classes, and it   *Macm.*

78:24. head; but if   *Macm.*

78:29. in their piety.   *Macm.*

78:32. Radicals   *Macm.*

79:2–3. For the ... may perhaps take   *Macm.*

79:5. over; but for   *Macm.*

79:15. power of   *Macm.,* 77, 83s; *corrected from Butler*

79:28. lengths   *Macm.,* 77, 83s; *corrected from Butler*

79:30–33. And one does see ... of things.   *Macm.*

80:2. that no one   *Macm.*

80:6. beliefs that   *Macm.*

80:9. Undoubtedly, there are   *Macm.,* 80

80:11. Church, or national   *Macm.*

80:12. country; and   *Macm.*

80:18–19. disorder and need   *Macm.*

80:28. sense; I know   *Macm.*

80:34. take in such   *Macm.*

81:1. *no* ¶   *Macm.*

81:10–11. to us: "To be influenced by this   *Macm.*

81:14. could no further   *Macm.*

81:15. *no* ¶   *Macm.*

81:18–19. real truth; so little false   *Macm.*

81:27. Burke—their piety,   *Macm.*

81:32–33. those constituents, and the way of thinking that naturally
Macm.

81:35–36. largeness and easiness of mind,   *Macm.*

82:3. Scriptural   *Macm.*

82:5. or that *the gospel*   *Macm.*
82:14. *no* ¶   *Macm.*
82:19. comes in in favour   *Macm.*
82:22. Establishment   *Macm.*
82:24. nation"—that seems   *Macm.*
82:29. *no* ¶   *Macm.*
82:36. objection,   *Macm.*, 77, 83s; *corrected from Butler*
83:12. beautiful soul, is   *Macm.*
83:18–19. prevail: that the Church is   *Macm.*
83:31–32. these are   *Macm.*
83:34. preferred; and   *Macm.*
84:1. is that it will be   *Macm.*
84:2–3. perceived that they are,   *Macm.*
84:5. *no* ¶   *Macm.*
84:9. ¶The more   80
84:14. not get hold   *Macm.*
84:18. peace; but   *Macm.*
84:24–25. have not this excuse for   *Macm.*
84:25–26. peace; and   *Macm.*
84:27. *no* ¶   *Macm.*
84:36. equals of the chief of the clergy.   *Macm.*
84:37. thing to brace a man's   *Macm.*
85:2. peace; and   *Macm.*
85:12. Dissenters, the less has   *Macm.*
85:23–24. good; what . . . action having the appearances of . . . in the individual.   *Macm.*
85:34. deliver the good news." But if   *Macm.*
85:37. advantage (for I put   *Macm.*
86:2–3. country, to do; as much as it will finally be found necessary to do; and as much as is required in order to end,   *Macm.*
86:16. people on their waste of power, but to   *Macm.*
86:17. ¶This is the   80
86:18. Church: to make   80
86:26. nothing; it may last, such a Church may last, as long as   80

[A LAST WORD ON THE BURIALS BILL]

Macm.   "A Last Word on the Burials Bill," *Macmillan's Magazine*
XXXIV, 276–88 (July, 1876).
Reprinted 77, 83s, o3l (not collated)

The following passages appear in 80: 90:1–26 (pp. 189–90, headed "Rationale of Public Ceremonial"); 92:18–38 (p. 191, headed "Burials Bill"); 101:3–102:9 (pp. 192–93, headed "Burials Rubric"); 104:25–105:3 (pp. 49–50, headed "Hymns Again"); 109:20–110:17 (pp. 199–200, headed "Dissidence of Dissent").

88:6. *no* ¶ And Lord Selborne, in *Macm.*

89:1. nature"; for, *Macm.*

89:2–3. must be optional, *mispr. Macm.*, 77, 83s

89:11. Dissenters; and here, again, is *Macm.*

89:25. disinterested; who have no *Macm.*

89:27–31. Dissenters, who do not . . . answer it; who on the other hand have no . . . clergy, and who are without . . . bias; but who simply *Macm.*

89:34. and for my own, *Macm.*

89:38. strongly engaged. *Macm.*

90:1. *no section division, Macm.*

90:4. for it; gets credit *Macm.*

90:11–12. in the performance *Macm.*

90:21. elevated; on *Macm.*

90:29. occasions, and our character *Macm.*

91:5. he was speaking *Macm.*

91:22. *no* ¶ *Macm.*

91:25. places. He enjoys *Macm.*

92:18. ¶The hearty 80

92:26. wishing to do a thing 80

92:28–29. he can urge *Macm.*

92:31. *no* ¶ *Macm.*

93:10. what they ask for in the *Macm.*

93:12. from the desire to *Macm.*

93:32. force; and Mr. *Macm.*

93:34. decency;" and Lord *Macm.*

94:8. character; but *Macm.*

94:9–10. And the very politicians who advocate the Dissenters' cause admit that they ought. *Macm.*

94:13–14. Christians—to suit *Macm.*

94:14. Some object *Macm.*

94:18–19. rubric of that service *Macm.*

94:21. things, and it *Macm.*

94:26. *no section division, Macm.*

94:31–32. yet the forms *Macm.*

95:9. and be accepted   *Macm.*
95:15–16. with this design.   *Macm.*
95:16–17. on the same ground   *Macm.*
95:22. truth expressly so presented as to suit   *Macm.*
95:27. are, and the Church   *Macm.*
95:33. than the Church in   *Macm.*
96:4. in silence; in a   *Macm.*
96:5. Offices for the Dead   *Macm.*
96:13. burial question   *Macm.*
96:18–19. and the Dissenters   *Macm.*
96:20–21. or one of two or   *Macm.*
96:22. *no* ¶   *Macm.*
96:26. but in one hundred and   *Macm.*
96:34. forms; that   *Macm.*
97:13–14. much, or they think that   *Macm.*
97:15. be as good as   *Macm.*
97:17. *no* ¶   *Macm.*
97:17, 22. a great difference   *Macm.*
97:24. England; but   *Macm.*
97:27. affords, the other   *Macm.*
97:31–32. where these are.   *Macm.*, 77, 83s; *corrected by ed.*
98:1. thing!" The   *Macm.*
98:15. what [*rom.*]   *Macm.*
98:35. taking security   *Macm.*
99:9. community, and   *Macm.*
99:24. further   *Macm.*
99:25. own; and   *Macm.*
100:8. that its orders must   *Macm.*
100:25. approvable; but   *Macm.*
100:38–101:1. perhaps in the abstract consonant   *Macm.*
101:5. *no* ¶   *Macm.*
101:26. *no* ¶   *Macm.*
102:8. enjoy; and   *Macm.*
102:20. have already spoken.   *Macm.*
102:22. It excludes   *Macm.*
103:3. because Christ said: *Macm.*
103:7. of Christ's   *Macm.*
103:8. Him . . . He   *Macm.*
103:10. He meant   *Macm.*
103:16. to condemn reliance on   *mispr. Macm.*
103:24. upon them; and in   *Macm.*

103:30. against [*rom.*]   *Macm.*
104:6. service; and the   *Macm.*
104:16. churchyard,   *Macm.*
104:23. grave; we   *Macm.*
104:30. purposes he may   *Macm.*
104:31. are mischievous and   *Macm.*
104:32. him; somewhere   *Macm.*
105:1. of our hymns and   *Macm.*
105:3. suddenly; we   *Macm.*
105:5–6. They meet   *Macm.*
105:19. mourners would   *Macm.*
105:21. it should be   *Macm.*
105:30. and, admirable as it is, it is as a   *Macm.*
105:33. embarrassed; and I   *Macm.*
106:2. and should   *Macm.*
106:3. lesson read at   *Macm.*
106:20. together; and   *Macm.*
106:29. *no* ¶   *Macm.*
107:8. *no* ¶   *Macm.*
107:15. have, from our   *Macm.*
107:16. Just that short   *Macm.*
108:5. *section not numbered, Macm.*
108:25–26. question of burials, would seem   *Macm.*
109:32. *no* ¶   *Macm.*
110:7. Future; but   *Macm.*
110:8–9. powers, effect,   *Macm.*
110:10. untransformed [*rom.*]   *Macm.*

[A PSYCHOLOGICAL PARALLEL]

Cont.   "A Psychological Parallel," *Contemporary Review* XXVIII, 892–919 (November, 1876).
Reprinted 77, 83s, o3l (not collated)
    The following passages appear in 80: 132:4–31 (pp. 236–37, headed " 'Offendiculum' of Scrupulousness"); 137:4–138:34 (pp. 237–40, headed "Jesus Christ Used Popular Language"); 142:6–36 (pp. 240–41, headed "Avoid Violent Revolution"); 145:27–146:22 (pp. 228–30, headed "Weak Side of Popular Christianity").

113:9–10. His own vision   *Cont.*

113:27. *no section division, Cont.;* mentioned in this Rᴇᴠɪᴇᴡ Sir *Cont.*

113:35. *not in Cont.*

115:2. Greezel Greedigut,   *Cont.*

115:25–26. is sufficiently clear   *Cont.*

115:32–33. were abundantly possessed by   *Cont.*

117:17. interval   *Cont.*, 77, 83s; *corrected from pamphlet*

119:38. was accepted.   *Cont.*

120:33. This seems   *Cont.*

121:16. *no section division, Cont.;* ¶He is very   *Cont.*

121:17. have the opportunity   *Cont.*

121:28. the college chapel.   *Cont.*, 77

121:34. a good work   *Cont.*

122:1–2. His ... value.   *not in Cont.*

122:2–3. But in his recent account of them he has   *Cont.*

122:4. far too much   *Cont.*

122:8. extraordinarily   *Cont.;* extraordinary 77, 83s

122:9–11. Laudian clergy and the ... Puritans, they saw   *Cont.*

122:11–13. —saw that stand ... could not,   *not in Cont.*

122:20. used them; Bishop   *Cont.*

122:23. already given,   *Cont.*

122:25–26. have said, has given too   *Cont.*

122:32. of them which   *Cont.*

122:34–36. Their ... with them.   *not in Cont.*

122:37–38. *not in Cont.*

123:3. with the sermon printed   *Cont.*

123:6. what the Cambridge Platonists have   *Cont.*

123:7–8. would himself extract it and give it to us;   *Cont.*

123:10. ¶For the Cambridge   *Cont.*

123:13. not take   *Cont.*

123:16–20. Barrow. These are, indeed, religious writers, yet it is in ... that they are mainly eminent. What counts in the history of religion, is to give   *Cont.*

123:24. of our time,   *Cont.*

123:25–27. shall look for in vain in the soul . . . in the sense . . . in the superb . . . or in the passion-filled   *Cont.*

123:30. opinion, much the   *Cont.*

123:32. history. The neglect to republish them is even on that ground inexcusable. Yet the   *Cont.*

123:33. is religious, not   *Cont.*

124:4. simply to read   *Cont.*

124:8–9. hope of getting,   *Cont.*

125:21. manner   *Cont.,* 77, 83s; *corrected from Smith*

125:28. Smith accepted   *Cont.*

125:30–32. But . . . took it.   *not in Cont.*

125:32. But it was   *Cont.*

125:38. makes a fresh   *Cont.*

126:20. ¶This was   *Cont.*

126:33. apprehensions   *Cont.,* 77, 83s; *corrected from Smith*

126:37. can but comply   *Cont.,* 77, 83s; *corrected from Smith*

127:12. ¶O fortunate . . . Phillimore! Finally   *Cont.* (*see* 127:25–27)

127:13–14. preacher confutes even his own   *Cont.*

127:25–27. *placed before 127:12 in Cont.*

127:38. here is   *Cont.*

128:11. *dead;* the Jewish   *Cont.*

128:16. himself had   *Cont.*

128:18. were a part   *Cont.*

128:37 *footnotes not in Cont.*

129:1. upon the very   *Cont.*

129:3. the same moment   *Cont.*

129:3–5. that popular belief . . . bodily resurrection by which our   *Cont.*

129:6. he seizes also this other idea   *Cont.*

129:12. be an imbecile or credulous   *Cont.*

129:13. untruthful and unprofitable?   *Cont.*

129:15. nothing against   *Cont.*

129:22. *section not numbered,*   *Cont.*

129:25. by their opponents. The partisans   *Cont.*

129:28. have admitted it. And they themselves are   *Cont.*

130:4. things that every   *Cont.*

130:6. *no* ¶   *Cont.*

130:7. because he asserted   *Cont.*

130:17. at ordination   *Cont.*

130:26. Articles, and the   *Cont.*

130:29–31. to this Article, or merely . . . to it, one certainly   *Cont.*

130:37–38. general consent to the Eighth Article, or can   *Cont.*

131:4. once employed   *Cont.*

131:5. vigorously, and was meant   *Cont.*

131:6–9. yoke. But it has a great power of   *Cont.*

131:15–17. engagement. There are things in the Ordination Service which one might wish otherwise. Some of them are matters of taste. The introduction   *Cont.*

131:17. is a part, *Cont.*

131:21–23. ridiculousness. If the Oath of Supremacy is to be taken at all, it should be taken before the civil magistrate. But apart from such *Cont.*

131:24. there is the requirement, *Cont.*

131:28. and seems to *Cont.*

132:2. matter; and probably in the present *Cont.*

132:8. am the last *Cont.*

132:9. Those who *Cont.*

132:11. do very ill *Cont.*

132:16. to those *Cont.*, 77, 80, 83s; *corrected from Bible*

132:18. goodness; for *Cont.*

132:32–33. They aim . . . document. *not in Cont.*

133:2. day, many a *Cont.*

133:3–4. cannot, then, profess to accept it; cannot, consequently, take *Cont.*

133:6. between him and *Cont.*; It is not *Cont.*

133:10. exist; it *Cont.*

133:21. are a good deal *Cont.*

133:22. could it manage *Cont.*

133:24. In the very effort to benefit by them it has *Cont.*

133:33. poetry is literal truth. But *Cont.*

133:37. use it as if *Cont.*

134:1. But will a *Cont.*

134:15. wonderful power of habit tells, *Cont.*

134:20–21. Comtists is mistaken; that the power *Cont.*

134:26–27. and they were to be got elsewhere, *Cont.*

134:35. ¶Nay, so *Cont.*

134:36–37. that it unsettles *Cont.*

134:37. chaos; and when it *Cont.*

135:8. and that the world *Cont.*

135:11. were wrong. *Cont.*

135:12. men had to *Cont.*

135:19. improbability of our *Cont.*

135:25. see and measure. *Cont.*

135:29. who still take *Cont.*

135:30. will still use *Cont.*; who no *Cont.*

136:1. have called *Cont.*

136:7. The one exalts *Cont.*

136:8–9. ideas. They are the august amplifications and high *Cont.*

136:11. upon this inexhaustible *Cont.*

136:15. on our own ever since   *Cont.*

136:22. *no* ¶   *Cont.;* foundations of the   *Cont.*

136:28–29. memories, we need not   *Cont.*

136:31. the Prayer-Book services as time   *Cont.*

136:31–32. drop away, other things   *Cont.*

136:37. felt ... to be   *not in Cont.*

137:1. ¶After all, our great confirmation in believing   *Cont.*

137:4. ¶The great reason   80

137:5–6. around us, as poetry and as approximative language, al-though   *Cont.*

137:7. was the   *Cont.;* was, likewise, the   80

137:9. him and of his   *Cont.*

137:10. practice. If he used   *Cont.*

137:13. one. It   *Cont.*

137:14. all the old images,   *Cont.*

137:21–22. literally, and did he mean that   *Cont.*

137:23. But very   *Cont.*

137:24. that he was   *Cont.*

137:32. Yet his thus   *Cont.*

137:34. and Christendom after   *Cont.*

137:35. ¶But   80

138:3–4. that he did not really share their beliefs, or   *Cont.*

138:9. lifetime. And they themselves   *Cont.*

138:14. He compares it to a   *Cont.*

138:15. and a handful of leaven; he says: *Cont.*

138:18. He told his disciples that   *Cont.*

138:21. but of centuries; and then,   *Cont.*

138:22. last day, the grand   *Cont.*

138:23. their heads   *Cont.*

138:24. True, they also make him speak   *Cont.*

138:25–26. that he spoke   *Cont.*

138:30. he saw   *Cont.*

138:32. imagery, it cannot   *Cont.*

138:33–34. And yet he uses it.   *Cont.*

138:35. the language of   *Cont.*

138:38. *not in Cont.*, 80

139:1–2. deeply the speakers' minds are inoculated with the contents   *Cont.*

139:9. to that time.   *Cont.*, 77, 83s; *corrected from Bible*

139:16. governs the language   *Cont.*

139:17. literally; Jesus ... poetry; but   *Cont.*

139:19–20. ¶The texts from Daniel every one knows.   *Cont.*
139:20. has a very close   *Cont.*
139:24. on which he and   *Cont.*
139:25. adopted by him, and   *Cont.*
139:31–32. prophecy of the   *Cont.*
139:35. himself and his   *Cont.*
139:37–38. *footnotes not in Cont.*
140:10. Testament. If   *Cont.*
140:12. exhibits the further   *Cont.*
140:16. And this further growth   *Cont.*
140:18. he had to   *Cont.*
140:19–20. though the book be—for   *Cont.*
140:37. *not in Cont.*
141:2. did not get   *Cont.*
141:8. when Jesus came,   *Cont.*
141:9. not make them,   *Cont.*
141:28. of Enoch. In   *Cont.*
141:34. Just One, his company or   *Cont.*
141:35. Jesus said: *Cont.*
141:36–37. *not in Cont.*
142:6. ¶But the practical   *Cont.;* ¶We   80
142:16. see. Yet what   *Cont.*
142:26. his real   *Cont.*
142:32–33. make his true meaning, in using it, emerge and   *Cont.*
142:37. *no* ¶   *Cont.*
142:38. poetry to him,   *Cont.*
143:6. [in]   *added by ed.*
143:8. and connecting   *Cont.*
143:9. what he himself   *Cont.*
145:18. ¶With this construction   *Cont.*
146:32. believe, whatever   *Cont.*
146:34. sparkling, that "whosoever   *Cont.*
146:38–147:1. belief are fellow-citizens   *Cont.*
147:2–3. He who shares it not, is a wanderer, as St.   *Cont.*
147:3. says, in "the   *Cont.*

[PREFACE TO *LAST ESSAYS*]

Printed in 77, 83s, 03l (not collated)
The following passages appear in 80: 148:19–25 (p. 114,

headed "Letters and the Masses"); 151:14–153:9 (pp. 208–
11, headed "The Religious Situation"); 161:36–162:29 (pp.
221–22, headed "Christianity Will Survive").

150:31. obscurities and   77, 83s; *corrected from Gubernatis*
151:14. ¶When we   80
151:16. to all change,   80
151:28. which at present   80
156:2. do love his life   *mispr.* 77
161:26. Is it,   77; It is,   *mispr.* 83s
161:36. ¶Christianity will   80

[MIXED ESSAYS]

79.*   Mixed Essays | By | Matthew Arnold | London | Smith,
          Elder, & Co., 15 Waterloo Place | 1879 | [*All rights
          reserved*]
              Also issued with the imprint: New York | Macmillan and
          Co., | 1879.
80m   Mixed Essays | By | Matthew Arnold | *Second Edition* |
          London | Smith, Elder, & Co., 15 Waterloo Place | 1880 |
          [*All rights reserved*]
              From the same setting of type as 79.
80.   Passages from | the Prose Writings | of | Matthew Arnold |
          London | Smith, Elder, & Co., 15 Waterloo Place | 1880 |
          [*All rights reserved*]
              Also issued with the imprint: New York | Macmillan and
          Co., | 1880
83m.   Mixed Essays | Irish Essays | and Others | By | Matthew
          Arnold | New York | Macmillan and Co. | 1883
03m.   Mixed Essays | By | Matthew Arnold | *Popular Edition* |
          London | Smith, Elder, & Co., 15 Waterloo Place | 1903 |
          [*All rights reserved*]
              From the same setting of type as 79, 80m; not collated.

[A FRENCH CRITIC ON MILTON]

Quart.   "A French Critic on Milton," *Quarterly Review* CXLIII,
           186–204 (January, 1877). Anonymous.
Lit.   "A French Critic on Milton," *Littell's Living Age* CXXXII,

* For 79 read 1879, etc.

579–89 (March 10, 1877). Anonymous. Not collated.
Reprinted 79, 83m, 03m (not collated)

    The following passages appear in 80: 169:28–170:38 (pp. 66-68, headed "Macaulay's Place in Civilisation"); 182:37–184:17 (pp. 34-37, headed "Milton's Power of Style").

165:2-3. With that Essay began   *Quart.*

165:6. The 'Essay on Milton' appeared   *Quart.*

165:7-8. 1825:—'The effect . . . reputation,' says Mr. Trevelyan, and we believe truly, 'was   *Quart.*

165:28-29. wrapping its object in a robe of rhetoric; not,   *Quart.*

166:1. rendering its object's very form and   *Quart.*

166:2. rendering his object in this   *Quart.*

166:28. of other souls   *Quart.*, 79, 83m; *corrected from Macaulay*

167:27. but it is   *Quart.*

167:29. is, no doubt, a multitude of readers for   *Quart.*

167:37. will satisfy them.   *Quart.*

168:19. could most   *Quart.*

168:38-169:1. more 'kindly affectioned' such   *Quart.*

170:24. in which their mind   *Quart.*

170:25. to their judgments   *Quart.*

170:28. treatment of it, is at   *Quart.*

170:34-35. have never known it. So that   *Quart.*

171:28. imagination   *Quart.*, 79, 83m; *corrected from Addison*

171:36. upon conventions,   *Quart.*

172:27-28. *quotation marks added by ed.*

172:32-33. criticism goes on certain conventions: the conventions, that incidents   *Quart.*

174:24. to the other an offence.   *Quart.*

174:29. before us,   *Quart.*

174:30-31. he comes originally from Geneva, that   *Quart.*

174:34-35. think quite as Vinet thought or not.   *Quart.*

176:4-5. because his mind   *Quart.*

176:9. life being long and art short and   *Quart.*

176:16-17. their reversions and redundancies   *mispr.* 83m

177:20. farther.   *Quart.*, 79

178:15. all this at the same time, without   *Quart.*

178:26. ¶Milton arrived at the   *Quart.*

178:27. life in which its outward   *mispr. Quart.*

179:1. Renaissance.'   *Quart.*

179:27. subject is a story,   *Quart.*

179:32. for us comes from our   *Quart.*

181:30. which our readers will   *Quart.*

182:37. ¶Milton's true . . . is undoubtedly his   80

183:6. Milton's style has   *Quart.*

183:28. being counted to them.   *Quart.*

184:7–9. in form. For the English artist in any branch, if he   *Quart.*

184:12. which English literature, in general, seems too much bent on   *Quart.*

184:25–27. Certain . . . power.   *not in Quart.*

184:28. *no* ¶ Some moral qualities are certainly connected   *Quart.*

184:30. elevation; [*rom.*]   *Quart.*

185:22. tell ye   *Quart. and Milton;* tell you   79, 83m

186:4–6. we did not . . . of our own . . . We proposed . . . we have been tempted,   *Quart.*

186:10. hardly, we think, draws out   *Quart.*

186:17. *no* ¶   *Quart.*

186:27. seems to us to be just, and to be supported by   *Quart.*

186:31. seem to us   *Quart.*

186:35. we think   *Quart.*

186:37–38. Our readers, we hope, have been interested   *Quart.*

187:2. with what we have given them may   *Quart.*

[FALKLAND]

Ninet.   "Falkland," *Nineteenth Century* I, 141–55 (March, 1877).

Lit.   "Falkland," *Littell's Living Age* CXXXIII, 34–43 (April 7, 1877). Not collated.

Reprinted 79, 83m, 03m (not collated)

The following passages appear in 80: 201:12–30 (pp. 179–80, headed "The Puritans and Religion"); 202:12–34 (pp. 97–98, headed "Puritanism and Liberty"); 204:33–205:26 (pp. 213–14, headed "Simpletons and Savages").

188:4. It conveys,   *Ninet.*

188:16. meeting has been held   *Ninet.*

188:22. to our memory.   *Ninet.*

188:25–26. At the battle of Newbury (says Clarendon) was   *Ninet.*

188:28. so glowing and   *Ninet.,* 79, 83m; *corrected from Clarendon*

189:5. is here a little Asiatic.   *Ninet.*

189:16–17. touch in the *Life* is simpler   *Ninet.*

189:24. said Lord   *Ninet.*

189:29. he hardly counts. *Ninet.*

189:30. soldiers were in his day not *Ninet.*

190:11. who passed over *Ninet.*

191:4. or two he mixed in the *Ninet.*

191:17. ¶Falkland *Ninet.*

192:2. of his life ... a great thoroughness *Ninet.*

192:6. was then keen. *Ninet.*

192:13–14. death soon after, from an accident, forced *Ninet.*

193:7. that was violent *Ninet.*

194:12–13. removal of bishops from . . . all that they *Ninet.*

194:35. everybody else. *Ninet.*

196:1. clothes and habits, *Ninet.*, 79, 83m; *corrected from Clarendon*

196:23. ¶He fell *Ninet.*

196:28. eyes may have rested. Falkland left *Ninet.*

198:14. say merely that *Ninet.*, 79, 83m; *corrected from Clarendon*

198:34–36. sober reason? Lord Carnarvon *Ninet.*

201:5. ¶Bolingbroke *Ninet.*

201:12. ¶Is it contended that the Puritan triumph in the Civil War was the 80

202:12. ¶Is it certain 80

202:13. in our England of 80

202:35. ¶Falkland was profoundly *Ninet.*

203:14–15. he said; "nay, *Ninet.*

203:26. And there Episcopacy *Ninet.*

204:19. situation truly *Ninet.*

204:20. because ... none *not in Ninet.*

204:27. *the nineteenth century.* [*ital.*] *Ninet.*

205:4. *no* ¶ *Ninet.*

205:9. the burials, leading up to the 'burning *Ninet.*

205:10–11. disestablishment—one might *Ninet.*

205:19. not be *Ninet.*

205:36. *me* [*ital.*] *Ninet.*

205:38. ¶No; if we are *Ninet.*

206:6. by Owen the dreariest of theologians and Baxter the king of bores—like *Ninet.*

206:16. it all in two *Ninet.*

206:32. ¶Let us *Ninet.*

[GERMAN LETTERS ON ENGLISH EDUCATION]

PMG   "German Letters on English Education," *Pall Mall Gazette*,
         May 3, 1877, pp. 11-12. Reprinted in *The Pall Mall Budget*,
         May 5, 1877. Anonymous.

[GEORGE SAND]

Fortn.   "George Sand," *Fortnightly Review* XXVII (n.s. XXI),
           767-81 (June, 1877).
Lit.   "George Sand," *Littell's Living Age* CXXXIV, 195-204
           (July 28, 1877). Not collated.
Ecl.   "George Sand," *Eclectic Magazine* XXVI n.s., 225-35
           (August, 1877). Not collated.
           Reprinted 79, 83m, 03m (not collated)
               The following passages appear in 80: 220:2-24 (pp. 68-69,
           headed "George Sand's Novels"); 235:13-236:7 (pp. 69-70,
           headed "George Sand").

216:25. no ¶   *Fortn.*
216:27, 217:23. Jaunâtres   *mispr. Fortn.*, 79, 83m
216:28. *not in Fortn.*
217:19. no ¶   *Fortn.*
217:20. of granite-stones, holly,   *Fortn.*
217:27. further   *Fortn.*, 79
218:21. mentioned—an impression of   *Fortn.*
218:29-30. and gone back   *Fortn.*
219:13. following me. ¶Yes; and it is *here* that one should speak of
         her, in this Review, not dominated by the past, not devoted to
         things established, not over-occupied with theology, but in search
         of some more free and wide conceptions of human life, and turned
         towards the future and the unrealised. George Sand felt the poetry
         of the past, she had no hatreds; the furies, the follies, the self-
         deceptions of secularist and revolutionist fanatics filled her in her
         latter years with pity, sometimes with dismay; but still her place is
         with the party and propaganda of organic change. For any party
         tied to the past, for any party, even, tied to the present, she is too
         new, too bold, too uncompromisingly sincere. *Fortn. (see
         234:26-30)*
219:17. shall one day   *Fortn.*
219:22. no ¶   *Fortn.*

220:1. *no* ¶ *Fortn.*

220:2. out of George Sand's 80

220:11. *no* ¶ *Fortn.*

220:14. earlier work, and *Fortn.*

220:19–20. itself, that motive which we set forth above: *Fortn.*, itself, and that motive is this: 80

221:4. that rebels *Fortn.*

222:20. ¶And if only, *Fortn.*

222:21. could feel that she *Fortn.*

222:30. Custom and Belief? *Fortn.*

222:31. got from this *Fortn.*

223:3. ¶But the failure *Fortn.*

223:4. proves nothing for *Fortn.*

223:23. invading; the *Fortn.*

224:1–2. Nature and Beauty? *Fortn.*

224:5. *no* ¶ *Fortn.*

224:6. closely, truly, intimate *Fortn.*

224:16. "the inevitable dean *Fortn.*

225:18. not mind him. *Fortn.*

225:34. long and blunt horns, *Fortn.*

225:35–36. as in our *Fortn.*

226:2–3. flanks, sniffing with uneasiness and disdain at the provender *Fortn.*

226:5. smelling the yokes and *Fortn.*

226:7. of oxen gone! *Fortn.*

226:9. but one cannot *Fortn.*

226:19–20. country, primitive life, the peasant. She regarded not with [*sic*] *Fortn.*

226:33. *no* ¶And joy is *Fortn.*

226:36. pours but *mispr.* 83m

227:13–14. skipping whip in hand *Fortn.*

227:19. be sent away into *Fortn.*

228:21. find him out of *Fortn.*

229:9. when we shall *Fortn.*, 79

229:24. therefore, as I have said, with *Fortn.*

230:8. respect at what Madame Sand says of it. *Fortn.*

230:34. ¶The forms of *Fortn.*

231:8–9. is kept hidden. *Fortn.*

231:20. people [*rom.*] *Fortn.*

231:34. general arising *Fortn.*

232:1. is generally known. M. de *Fortn.*

232:17–18. real *forces;* because human   *Fortn.*

232:27. while she   *Fortn.,* 79

233:1. ¶"To   *Fortn.*

233:3. *no* ¶   *Fortn.*

233:8–9. in him is our   *Fortn.*

233:34. of tact; but they   *Fortn.*

233:35. sentiment [*rom.*]   *Fortn.*

233:37. having the suffrage.   *Fortn.*

234:4–5. which make the   *Fortn.*

234:23. *no* ¶   *Fortn.*

234:26–32. Her own ... prevail.   *not in Fortn. (see 219:13, variant)*

234:32–33. educated and speaking classes   *Fortn.*

234:33–34. as the peasant   *Fortn.*

234:37. conduct [*rom.*]   *Fortn.*

235:1. who see this,   *Fortn.,* 79

235:5. *no* ¶   *Fortn.*

235:16. at the rate at which   80

235:17. seeks to throw away as much   80

235:23. of her the sense   *Fortn.*

235:27. great soul, simple,   *Fortn.*

235:33–34. voice; ... head;   *Fortn.*

235:34. as we can,   80

[A GUIDE TO ENGLISH LITERATURE]

Ninet.   "A Guide to English Literature," *Nineteenth Century* II, 843–53 (December, 1877).

Ecl.   "A Guide to English Literature," *Eclectic Magazine* XXVII n.s., 142–49 (February, 1878). Not collated.

Reprinted 79, 83m, 03m (not collated)

The following passage appears in 80: 244:34–245:25 (pp. 33–34, entitled "Shakspeare").

237, *footnote to title:* [1]*Primer of English Literature;* by the Rev. Stopford Brooke. Macmillan & Co.   *Ninet.*

237:1. tired of it,   *Ninet.*

237:15. this limited amount   *Ninet.*

237:18–19. thing is, when what they *can* be taught and *do* learn is ill-chosen.   *Ninet.*

238:2. And ... right.   *not in Ninet.*

238:3. *no* ¶In ... and prepared to form   *Ninet.*

238:27. Brooke published last year a   *Ninet.*

239:1. Brooke's; it is   *Ninet.*

239:14. it ill, if such   *Ninet.*

239:19. and suggest   *Ninet.*

239:23. primers; and it is   *Ninet.*

239:26. are; for all   *Ninet.*

240:18. in a longer writing might   *Ninet.*

240:25. Englishman who would   *Ninet.*

241:21. them. Or the want   *Ninet.*

243:29. after his (office) work   *Ninet.*

244:34. ¶It is not quite   80

244:35. criticism to say, as Mr. Stopford Brooke does of Shakspeare:
80

244:37. known;' or again: *Ninet.*

245:3. but to please; he   *Ninet.*

245:16. there is   80

245:17–18. it abounds in   *Ninet.*

245:18–20. In ... questions,   *not in* 80

245:20. We ought not, therefore, to   80

246:26–27. century when literature has   *Ninet.*

247:14. *no* ¶   *Ninet.*

248:9. *Reviews, Ninet.; Review,* 79, 83m

248:13. *no* ¶   *Ninet.*

248:22. same sureness and proportion as   *Ninet.*

248:24–25. to sureness of speech and to   *Ninet.*

248:25. primer, too, are not   *Ninet.*

249:23–24. are not brought out.   *Ninet.*

249:29–30. quite safe against the poetical   *Ninet.*

250:3. Gray; and therefore to   *Ninet.*

250:12. into our retired   *Ninet.,* 79, 83m; *corrected from Brooke*

250:16. would make him,   *Ninet.*

251:24. clever, but rather fantastic, and utterly out   *Ninet.*

[A FRENCH CRITIC ON GOETHE]

Quart.   "A French Critic on Goethe," *Quarterly Review* CXLV,
143–63 (January, 1878). Anonymous.

Lit.   "A French Critic on Goethe," *Littell's Living Age*

CXXXVI, 451–62 (February 23, 1878). Attributed to
Arnold on Contents page. Not collated.
   Reprinted 79, 83m, 03m (not collated)
      The following passages appear in 80: 254:16–255:9 (pp.
   12–13, headed "Systematic Judgments"); 256:17–257:6 (pp.
   51–52, headed "German Style"); 271: 16–24 (pp. 46–47,
   headed "Goethe's Corporalism"); pp. 273:33–274:14 (pp.
   45–46, headed "Symbolism in Poetry"); 274: 35–275:27 (pp.
   39–40, headed "Goethe's Greatness").

252:7. my best of young men,   *Quart.*
252:8. let me hear   *Quart.*
252:14–15. (the loudest sounding instrument in the   *Quart.*
252:28. *no* ¶And Joseph   *Quart.*
253:8. his 'best of young men':—   *Quart.*
254:4. ¶But now there   *Quart.*
254:5, 255:4. Hermann   *Quart.*, 79, 80, 83m; *corrected by ed.*
254:11. and all peoples,   *Quart.*
254:12. have taken only the first steps towards drawing forth
   Quart.
254:27. judgment   *mispr. Quart.*
254:29. of different people,   *Quart.*
255:4. *no* ¶   *Quart.*
255:35. We spoke a year ago* of the [*footnote:* *See 'Quarterly
   Review,' vol. 143, p. 186, *seqq.*]   *Quart.*
255:36. We propose now to draw our readers' attention to   *Quart.*
256:1. seems to us a   *Quart.*
256:2. we should not   *Quart.*
256:3. of a review-article.   *Quart.*
256:4, 6. We do not . . . But we think   *Quart.*
256:11. Probably he will not   *Quart.*
256:17. ¶Englishmen and Frenchmen have alike the same instinctive
   80
256:19–20. literature, as a   *Quart.*; just . . . has.   *not in* 80
256:21. *no* ¶   *Quart.*
256:34. same direct fashion,   80
257:8. we repeat,   *Quart.*
257:12–15. works, letting him as far as possible speak for himself, as
   we did when we were dealing . . . Milton. As we did then, too, we
   shall occasionally   *Quart.*
257:16–18. others. We shall . . . attempt a substantive . . . of our own,
   although we may . . . allow ourselves   *Quart.*

257:21. enough to remind our reader that the   *Quart.*

258:7. He ... Carlyle.   *not in Quart.*

258:8. Already this tone   *Quart.*

258:9. seems to us   *Quart.*

258:10. and the interest of   *Quart.*

258:21. way of proceeding to be so.   *Quart.*

258:34. have ever gone   *Quart.*

258:35. seems to us ... we repeat,   *Quart.*

260:1. we must send   *Quart.*

260:7-8. But he ... wished.   *not in Quart.*

260:8. But he felt   *Quart.*

260:31. 'with disgust.'   *Quart.*

260:35. ¶We have not   *Quart.*

261:26. ¶It is interesting   *Quart.*

261:27. by Mr. Lewes,   *Quart.*

261:29. memory of many amongst our readers.   *Quart.*

261:34. *lights* of effect   *Quart.*, 79, 83m; *italicising corrected from Lewes*

262:2. praise. But 'Tasso' and   *Quart.*

262:8. *no* ¶   *Quart.*

262:9. to this period.   *Quart.*

262:10. while it has the   *Quart.*

262:36. satisfactory end;   *Quart.*

263:25. complained; to Weimar   *Quart.*

263:31. ¶That connection   *Quart.*

264:19. brought out; the   *Quart.*

264:33-34. What ... tone!   *not in Quart.*

264:36. of what a thing is, is   *Quart.*

265:16-17. our modern societies ... if they do have   *Quart.*

265:26. definite judgment   *mispr.* 83m

265:27. we turn to   *Quart.*

266:6. built of the   *mispr. Quart.*

266:17. our Genevese critic:—   *Quart.*

266:27. gravely forces an   *Quart.*

267:8-9. without our quoting it,   *Quart.*

267:31. those two   *Quart.*, 79; these two   83m

269:10. of the praise   *Quart.*

270:17-18. Of ... say.   *not in Quart.*

271:1. *no* ¶   *Quart.*

271:16. ¶Let us   80

271:17. Goethe, as M. Scherer harshly calls it, which   80

272:13. statue; no   *Quart.*

272:32, 36–37. we have ... we think,   *Quart.*

273:1. no ¶ We do not   *Quart.*

273:2, 4–5. We do not ourselves ... We do not ourselves   *Quart.*

273:13. no ¶ In other respects we agree   *Quart.*

273:15. we hesitate to   *Quart.*

273:33. is undoubtedly   80

273:34. best work in poetry.   80

274:3. praises 'Helena'   *Quart.*

274:6. he heaps   *Quart.*

274:35–36. greatest of all poets that Goethe may rightly call forth
the pride and   80

275:14. greatest man.   *Quart.*

275:17–18. profound spirit ... of life,   *Quart.*

275:21–22. of him, ... to make this   *Quart.*

275:34, 36. We could not ... we can   *Quart.*

275:36–37. The faults are shown, and they   *Quart.*

275:38. whole; tone   *Quart.*

276:9. to our minds   *Quart.*

276:21–22. accomplished Genevese, to whom they have given the
right of citizenship, to extend   *Quart.*

[EQUALITY]

Fortn.   "Equality," *Fortnightly Review* XXIX (n.s. XXIII), 313–34
(March, 1878).

Lit.   "Equality," *Littell's Living Age* CXXXVII, 67–80 (April 13,
1878). Not collated.

Reprinted 79, 83m, 03m (not collated)

The following passages appear in 80: 288:24–32 (p. 90,
headed "America and France"); 289:30–290:6 (p. 111,
headed "The Greatest Happiness of the Greatest Number"); 297:32 ["Men make ...] –298:13 (pp. 96–97, headed
"The Puritan Type"); 299:29–36 (p. 124, headed "Fruits of
Inequality"); 301:31–302:14 (pp. 90–91, headed "The
English Gentleman").

277:5–6. from one of the chapters of the Epistles to the Corinthians;
Fortn.

277:24. maxim also: *Fortn.*

278:19. no ¶   *Fortn.*

278:21. hour, when Sir *Fortn.*

278:26. Froude is more . . . I am, and he has *Fortn.*

280:4. *no* ¶ Now this is most certainly not a lecture on law and the rules *Fortn.*

280:11. The owners *Fortn.*

281:1. and France, *Fortn.*

281:28. Each canton *Fortn.*

281:30. it is identical *Fortn.*

282:12. feudalism formed in *Fortn.*

282:13. they were settled *Fortn.*

282:14. to hold great *Fortn.*

282:35. take it as *Fortn.*

283:6. happen *Fortn.*, 79

283:20–21. all these three classes *Fortn.*, 79

283:25. masters, *Fortn.*, 79; master— 83m

284:18. I say, certain things *Fortn.*

284:20. feel whether *Fortn.*

286:9. question. So *Fortn.*

286:26. M. Michelet *Fortn.*

287:1. justly said by *Fortn.*

287:19–20. to allow Israel, *Fortn.*

287:32. too. The power *Fortn.*

288:24. ¶A recent French 80

288:26. says that *Fortn.*

288:33. *no* ¶ *Fortn.*

289:20. on its road *Fortn.*

289:26–29. mainly caused that Revolution, neither was it the spirit of envy; it was the spirit of society. *Fortn.*

289:31. distinctly, as time *Fortn.*

290:30. *no* ¶ *Fortn.*

290:37. perception, *Fortn.*

290:38. manners—everything—are different. *Fortn.*

291:2. sympathy, feel that *Fortn.*

291:10–11. incompatibility. The gentleman feels *Fortn.*

291:18. *no* ¶ *Fortn.*

292:11. *no* ¶ *Fortn.*

292:33. no true hold *Fortn.*

294:24. *no* ¶ *Fortn.*

295:12. on which *Fortn.*

295:33. Beaconsfield; a *Fortn.*

295:36. founder; but *Fortn.*

296:13. corn of favour   *Fortn.*, 79, 83m; *corrected from Milton*
296:29. *amiable*, [*ital.*]   *Fortn.*
296:34. *no* ¶   *Fortn.*
297:25. both as a religious and as a social   *Fortn.*
298:35. is far best   *Fortn.*
299:6. class   *Fortn.*, 79, 83m; *corrected by ed.*
299:7-8. having so ... success,   *not in Fortn.*
299:12. and lower class,   *Fortn.*
299:14-15. the general honesty and   *Fortn.*
299:15-16. true work, *verus labor,* which prevail throughout the   *Fortn.*
299:29. ¶ Surely it . . . the shortcomings in our English civilisation   80
299:30-31. the inequality of   *Fortn.*
300:3. certainly, as he says,   *Fortn.*
300:17-18. without witness, and in no class are there   *Fortn.*
300:20-25. For ... regard.   *not in Fortn.*
300:25. But on the   *Fortn.*
300:33-35. comprehend. The effect on society at large, and on national progress, is what we must regard. Turn even   *Fortn. (see lines 24-25)*
300:38. need for any   *Fortn.*
301:3-4. materialist aristocracies   *mispr. Fortn.*
301:5. have said,   *Fortn.*
301:9. themselves in pursuit   *Fortn.*
301:13. Let . . . merits.   *not in Fortn.; no* ¶For . . . manners, on the other hand, an   *Fortn.*
301:17. our race   *Fortn.*
301:33. or the nobility,   *Fortn.*
302:3-4. with fewer temptations. To   *Fortn.*
302:5-6. class materialises them, as it does   *Fortn.*
302:7. on the young, and on   *Fortn.*
302:20. also; and thus   *Fortn.*
302:28. either; and   *Fortn.*
302:31. our middle, brutalises   *Fortn.*
302:33. *no* ¶   *Fortn.*
302:36-37. effaced, and   *Fortn.*
303:11-13. inequality! Romance is good in   *Fortn.*
303:14. of strong   *Fortn.*
303:32-34. Such ... by them.   *not in Fortn.*
304:7. That organisation has   *Fortn.*

304:10. do not often feel *Fortn.*
304:15. with a standstill. *Fortn.*
304:20. *no* ¶ *Fortn.*
304:23. are most of us *Fortn.*
304:24. Conservative; and Liberals tend *Fortn.*
304:28–30. conclusion, that one of the great obstacles to our civilisation is British nonconformity, and the other, British aristocracy!
—and this *Fortn.*
304:33–34. in both of them. *Fortn.*
304:36. *no* ¶ *Fortn.*
304:37. as in France; *Fortn.*
305:9–10. politics. Imagine *Fortn.*
305:20. is one for *Fortn.*

[JOHNSON'S *LIVES OF THE POETS*]

Macm.   "Johnson's Lives," *Macmillan's Magazine* XXXVIII, 153–60
(June, 1878).

Ecl.   "Johnson's Lives of the Poets," *Eclectic Magazine* XXVIII
n.s., 202–9 (August, 1878). Not collated.

78.   The | Six Chief Lives | from | Johnson's "Lives of the
Poets," | with | Macaulay's "Life of Johnson." | *Edited, with
a Preface,* | by | Matthew Arnold. | London: | Macmillan
and Co. | 1878. | *The Right of Translation and Reproduction
is Reserved.*
Reissued 1879, 1881.

78a.   The *Publishers' Weekly* for October 26, 1878, announced:
Johnson's chief lives of the poets; being those of Milton,
Dryden, Swift, Addison, Pope, Gray, and Macaulay's life of
Johnson; with a preface by Mat. Arnold, to which are ap-
pended Macaulay's and Carlyle's essays on Boswell's life of
Johnson. New York, Henry Holt & Co., 1878.
This edition has no textual authority and is not collated.

86.   The | Six Chief Lives | from | Johnson's "Lives of the
Poets," | with | Macaulay's "Life of Johnson." | *Edited, with
a Preface and Notes,* | by | Matthew Arnold. | London: |
Macmillan and Co. | 1886
Reissued 1889 and frequently thereafter. The first edition
with the "Advertisement."
The following passage appears in 80: 315:32–318:10 (pp.
54–57, headed "English Prose and Poetry").

306:9. minds, and they *Macm.*

306:27. if he could be offered *Macm.*, 78

306:29–307:1. them, as to a very great deal of it be inclined to say *Macm.*, 78

307:20. we have got *Macm.*

307:34–35. because this class is so *Macm.*, 78

309:5–6. interest; the lives of six men who, while the rest in the collection are *Macm.*; interest, because they are the lives of men who, while the rest in the collection are 78

309:27–28. century. And in those characteristic lives, not finished until *Macm.*

310:4–11. quintessence; we have the work relieved *Macm.*

310:5. might have hoped, 78

310:26. *Dedication of the Æneis,* *Macm.*

311:15–16. Nothing . . . better. *not in Macm.*

311:32. really and definitively to *Macm.;* really and definitely to 78, 86

311:38. that attracts; and so *Macm.*, 78

312:3. *no* ¶ Again, as *Macm.*

312:19. ¶I should like, therefore, to reprint Johnson's six chief lives, simply as they are given in the edition in four volumes octavo,— the edition which passes for being the first to have a correct and complete text,—and to leave the lives, in that natural form, to have their effect upon the reader. I should like *Macm.;* ¶In the present volume, therefore, I have reprinted Johnson's six chief Lives simply as they are given in the edition in four volumes octavo, the edition which passes for being the first to have a correct and complete text; and I have left the lives, in that natural form, to have their own effect upon the reader. I have added one single note myself, and one only,—a note on the mistake committed by Johnson in identifying Addison's "Little Dicky" with Sir Richard Steele. And this note I have added, not because of the importance of the correction in itself, but because it well exhibits, in one striking example, the acuteness and resource of that famous man of letters, Lord Macaulay, and is likely to rouse and enliven the reader's attention rather than to dull it. ¶I should like 78

312:19–20. might thus be *Macm.*, 78

312:21. by means of *Macm.*

313:3–4. if at the beginning *Macm.*, 78, 86; *corrected from Milton*

313:19. Martin's *Account of the Hebrides* *Macm.*

313:29. consummate adequacy *Macm.;* consummate accuracy 78, 86

313:36. in their own. But *Macm.*

314:13–17. Johnson . . . and modern. *not in Macm.*

315:6. literature, but true and *Macm.,* 78

315:15. distinguishing achievement, *Macm.;* distinguished achievement, 78, 86

315:32. *no* ¶ *Macm.*

316:8–11. Of the . . . as poets. *not in* 80

316:15. and even its shortcomings *Macm.*

316:32–34. excellence, one marked in the *Macm.;* excellence, so powerful and influential in the last century, having been the first to come and standing at first alone, that Gibbon, as is well known, hesitated whether he should not write his history in French. French prose is marked in the 78; excellence,—a prose marked in 15 the 80

316:36–37. instincts, they made their poetry conform to *Macm.;* instincts, the French made their poetry conform to 78

317:8. and taste helped. 80

318:17. simply by knowing *Macm.*

319:13. Furthermore, he was *Macm.*

319:14. conservation and concentration, *Macm.*

319:15. seemed moving *Macm.*

319:26. his servitor days *Macm.*

319:29. a good and admirable *Macm.*

319:30. in our view *Macm.*

319:32–320:16. ¶A volume giving us Johnson's Lives of Milton, Dryden, Swift, Addison, Pope, Gray, would give us, therefore, the compendious story of a whole important age in English literature, told by a great man, and in a performance which is itself a piece of 30 English literature of the first class. If such a volume could but be prefaced by Lord Macaulay's *Life of Johnson*, it would be perfect. *Macm.*

[IRISH CATHOLICISM AND BRITISH LIBERALISM]

Fortn.   "Irish Catholicism and British Liberalism," *Fortnightly Review* XXX (n.s. XXIV), 26–45 (July, 1878).
Reprinted 79, 83m, 03m (not collated)
The following passages appear in 80: 321:14–322:36 (pp.

132–35, headed "England and Ireland"); 330:35–331:14 (p. 181, headed "The Liberals and Christianity"); 331:15–332:7 (pp. 184–85, headed "Catholicism to Catholics"); 333:9–28, 334:17–32 (pp. 185–87, headed "True Strength of Catholicism"); 343:24–344:15 (pp. 187–88, headed "The Need for Beauty"); 344:21–345:11 (pp. 188–89, headed "Milton and Eliza Cook").

322:26. it is. The great *Fortn.*

322:27. failure of our 80

323:5–13. True, . . . they get. *not in Fortn.*

323:15. those great matters *Fortn.*

323:26. are are told *mispr. Fortn.*

323:28. as those the English *Fortn.*

324:8–9. is in the hands *Fortn.*

325:18–19. in this very Review, not *Fortn.*

325:22. interests *Fortn.*, 79, 83m; *corrected from Lowe*

326:1. The Editor of this Review has recorded *Fortn.*

326:8. no ¶ The Editor who thus *Fortn.*

326:29–30. man perceives and deplores. The *Fortn.*

327:6. exhibited by Mr. *Fortn.*

327:22. and would follow *Fortn.*

327:23. *no ¶ Fortn.*

327:29–30. Or if, in this Review, and addressing . . . it is out of *Fortn.*

327:33. assuring us that *Fortn.*

327:36. And, therefore the politician *Fortn.*

327:37. manage to get at *Fortn.*

328:1. *public*. And when *Fortn.*

328:11–12. not lead us to recast the programme . . . Liberalism altogether, and *Fortn.*

328:28. *no ¶* This . . . for Liberalism to *Fortn.*

329:6–7. beneficently work towards *Fortn.*

329:8. ¶The part of the formula which Liberals have to sift and examine is the first part. "The Liberal party *Fortn.*

329:23–28. Still, . . . Catholicism. *not in Fortn.*

329:36. consider it, and *Fortn.*

330:2. we are naturally *Fortn.*

330:5. thing. The following is a *Fortn.*

330:9. tired of drill, *mispr. Fortn.*

330:21. influence of Jesus has *Fortn.*

330:22. the same emotion *Fortn.*

330:25. And . . . wonder. *not in Fortn.*

330:31. a cure, a wonderful cure, *Fortn.*

330:37. upon the simple 80

331:8. fashion they use it; *Fortn.*

331:12. against the outrage, *Fortn.*

331:25. Catholics feel *Fortn.*

331:34. Thus it so acquired *Fortn.*

331:38. Rome, and the great *Fortn.*

332:2. spells for the imagination *Fortn.*

332:5-6. possible, has both the imagination and *Fortn.*

332:7. against him. *Fortn.,* 79, 80; against them. 83m

332:10. with it a thousand *Fortn.*

332:11. abundantly borne issue; *Fortn.*

333:5. them out of hand, he *Fortn.*

333:9. ¶When 80

333:10-11. are gone, is Catholicism left with *Fortn.*

333:13. of Jesus? *Fortn.*

333:15. besides; with the beauty, *Fortn.*

333:17-18. age-long growth, proceeding as we have seen—unconscious, *Fortn.*

334:2. will soon rise: *Fortn.;* will soon arise: 79

334:12-13. *no talismanic Bible, . . . a talismanic Church,* *Fortn.*

334:17. *no* ¶ 80

334:22. (amongst which I 80

334:36-37. superstitious. It could *Fortn.*

335:4. none; his *Fortn.*

335:8. They will use *Fortn.*

335:14. we, too, are *Fortn.*

335:36-37. Let . . . schools. *not in Fortn.*

336:1. it; wherever *Fortn.*

336:9. country, and been *Fortn.*

336:30-31. simply a seminary *Fortn.*

337:8. community is interested in asking *Fortn.*

338:12. *no* ¶ *Fortn.*

338:17. they see themselves *Fortn.*

338:19-20. ill educated as their own middle class, knowing *Fortn.*

338:35. and govern, *Fortn.*

339:1. are out of *Fortn.*

339:14-16. will probably say, was at most but free . . . bondage which still held the other; *Fortn.*

339:18. part, shall say *Fortn.*

339:19. they all possess   *Fortn.*

339:22. is likely   *Fortn.*

339:37. *no* ¶   *Fortn.*

340:23. to groan at   *Fortn.*

340:33. let the Liberals who have   *Fortn.*

341:2. bring them into   *Fortn.*

341:4. question to thwart the Government,   *Fortn.*

341:6. put themselves into   *Fortn.*

341:11–12. that long article . . . in the last number of this Review—
Fortn.

341:16. and make   *Fortn.*

341:28. germ (we supposed Sir   *Fortn.*

341:33. which had still promise and   *Fortn.*

342:5–6. imagination of all that work of   *Fortn.*

342:15–16. of religion free from   *Fortn.*

342:23–33. The desire . . . vulgarity.   *not in Fortn.*

342:34. *no* ¶ People will   *Fortn.*

343:6. rooted prejudice.   *Fortn.*

343:20. against the Church in England.   *Fortn.*

343:26–27. needs of intellect and   80

343:27–29. in him, neither Puritanism, Catholicism, nor . . . can
satisfy. It is satisfied nowadays   *Fortn.*

343:29. Those needs have to   80

343:32. to do with was   *Fortn.*

343:33–34. , investing . . . simplicity   *not in Fortn.*

344:3–5. Scotland? Merely that which   *Fortn.*

344:15. or treat   *Fortn.*

344:16. *no* ¶   *Fortn.*

344:21. ¶Lord Granville is for   80

344:32. nay, declare   *Fortn.*

345:9. as they like; . . . found finally to   *Fortn.*

345:15. since March, and   *Fortn.*

345:16–17. said in this Review in March, that   *Fortn.*

345:22. middle class in upon   *Fortn.*

345:25. of the community,   *Fortn.*

345:31. seriously to set   *Fortn.*

345:36–37. contending" with narrowness and prejudice, is "convinced   *Fortn.*

346:19. everything rested.   *Fortn.*

346:32–33. But all this was a long business to go through, and so
Fortn.

347:9. use it. I   *Fortn.*

["PORRO UNUM EST NECESSARIUM"]

Fortn.   *"Porro Unum Est Necessarium,"* Fortnightly Review **XXX**
(n.s. **XXIV**), 589–604 (November, 1878).
Reprinted 79, 83m, 03m (not collated)
      The following passages appear in 80: 350:32–352:14 (pp.
125–28, headed "Our Middle-Class Education"); 361:26–
362:20 (pp. 129–30, headed "Demands on Life").

348:1–2. is found, perhaps,   *Fortn.*

348:3–7. At ... pretend.   *not in Fortn.*

348:8. *no ¶   Fortn.*

348:21. are now a whole in   *mispr. Fortn.*

348:26. party, not a   *Fortn.*

350:20. lower middling classes   *Fortn. and 1861 report.*

350:28. here mentioned were   *Fortn.*

351:7. From an educational point   *Fortn.*

351:9. church and the   *Fortn.*

351:17. naturally for the most part that   *Fortn.*

351:30. in social   *Fortn.*, 79, 80; in a social   *mispr.* 83m

352:8. even much shorter.   *Fortn.*

352:11. this is true,   *Fortn.*

352:14. with disquietude."   *mispr. Fortn.*

352:35. through the schools,   *Fortn.*, 79, 83m; *corrected from vol.*
   V, 5:25.

353:16. alleged to be   *Fortn.*

353:17. sense of *ne ... dupe,* not   *Fortn.*

353:20. in Western Europe,   *Fortn.*

354:27. 131 pupils   *Fortn.*, 79, 83m; *corrected by ed.*

354:33. 79,241   *mispr. Fortn.*, 79, 83m

354:38. the average of   *Fortn.*

355:2. sciences, of geography,   *Fortn.*

355:3. literature, of the modern languages, is   *Fortn.*

355:16–17. and of their teaching.   *Fortn.*

356:10. schools we do not   *Fortn.*

356:24–25. to the State University, and all the   *Fortn.*

356:33. abstain from them here.   *Fortn.*

357:20. by the contest   *Fortn.*

357:24. establishments of which   *Fortn.*

358:7. accessible, the very   *Fortn.*

358:25. This in the private   *Fortn.*

358:30. which is given   *Fortn.*

359:4. that while in   *Fortn.*

359:13. all these together   *Fortn.*

359:20. of standing and   *Fortn.*

359:21. number. Both   *Fortn.*

359:24. our total of boys   *Fortn.*

360:22–23. in this country.   *Fortn.*

361:16–17. anywhere except   *Fortn.*

361:23. on the enormous interval, as [*no quotes*]   *Fortn.*

361:26. ¶If we   80

361:30–31. the range of   *Fortn.*

361:36–37. only a comparatively small upper class makes amongst ourselves.   80

362:17–18. the joy of civilisation   *Fortn.*

362:37. or any refined   *Fortn.*

363:16–17. Voltaire, but this   *Fortn.*

364:15. in the public   *Fortn.*

364:27. Frenchman   *Fortn.*, 79; Frenchmen   *mispr.* 83m

364:31. in Western Europe,   *Fortn.*

366:37. mainly. First,   *Fortn.*, 79

367:4–5. some examination by other teachers   *Fortn.*

367:12. *no* ¶   *Fortn.*

367:25. public secondary institutions is   *Fortn.*

367:33. move on, if   *Fortn.*

368:23–24. would involve more than   *Fortn.*

368:24–25. habits, it would be a transformation.   *Fortn.*

368:37. *no* ¶   *Fortn.*

369:18. if it comes to   *Fortn.*

[PREFACE TO *MIXED ESSAYS*]

Printed in 79, 83m, 03m (not collated)

The following passage appears in 80: 372:7–18 (p. 94, headed "Requisites for Civilisation").

372:12. may next enumerate   80

Index

A reference to a page of text should be taken to include the notes to that page.

522